The Evolving American Presidency

Series Editors
Michael A. Genovese
Loyola Marymount University
Los Angeles, CA, USA

Todd L. Belt
Graduate School of Political Management
George Washington University
Washington, DC, USA

This series is stimulated by the clash between the presidency as invented and the presidency as it has developed. Over time, the presidency has evolved and grown in power, expectations, responsibilities, and authority. Adding to the power of the presidency have been wars, crises, depressions, industrialization. The importance and power of the modern presidency makes understanding it so vital. How presidents resolve challenges and paradoxes of high expectations with limited constitutional resources is the central issue in modern governance and the central theme of this book series.

More information about this series at
http://www.palgrave.com/gp/series/14437

Stanley Renshon

The Real Psychology of the Trump Presidency

palgrave
macmillan

Stanley Renshon
Department of Political Science
City University of New York
New York City, NY, USA

The Evolving American Presidency
ISBN 978-3-030-45390-9   ISBN 978-3-030-45391-6   (eBook)
https://doi.org/10.1007/978-3-030-45391-6

© The Editor(s) (if applicable) and The Author(s), under exclusive license to Springer
Nature Switzerland AG 2020
This work is subject to copyright. All rights are solely and exclusively licensed by the
Publisher, whether the whole or part of the material is concerned, specifically the rights
of translation, reprinting, reuse of illustrations, recitation, broadcasting, reproduction on
microfilms or in any other physical way, and transmission or information storage and
retrieval, electronic adaptation, computer software, or by similar or dissimilar methodology
now known or hereafter developed.
The use of general descriptive names, registered names, trademarks, service marks, etc.
in this publication does not imply, even in the absence of a specific statement, that such
names are exempt from the relevant protective laws and regulations and therefore free for
general use.
The publisher, the authors and the editors are safe to assume that the advice and information in this book are believed to be true and accurate at the date of publication. Neither
the publisher nor the authors or the editors give a warranty, expressed or implied, with
respect to the material contained herein or for any errors or omissions that may have been
made. The publisher remains neutral with regard to jurisdictional claims in published maps
and institutional affiliations.

Cover credit: © Drop of Light/shutterstock.com

This Palgrave Macmillan imprint is published by the registered company Springer Nature
Switzerland AG
The registered company address is: Gewerbestrasse 11, 6330 Cham, Switzerland

EPIGRAPH

"I am large; I contain multitudes."
Walt Whitman, *Song of Myself*

For our wonderful new granddaughter Mira
May her life be filled with love, courage, strength, and accomplishment
And knowing her parents, we're sure it will be

Preface

The purpose of this book is to provide a more accurate analysis and understanding of an unusual and unprecedented president, Donald J. Trump, his real psychology, and his extremely controversial presidency.

When he first announced his candidacy, I thought he had little, if any chance of winning the nomination and said so in an interview.[1] However, as Trump's campaign took hold and he stumbled and lurched past one candidate and then another, I began to realize that not only might he have a chance, but that he was a truly unique candidate who seemed to be tapping into some very deep and powerful political currents that only he of all the candidates seemed to see and understand.

As a psychoanalyst who studies presidential leadership and a political scientist who specializes in the presidency, how could I not be interested? I was. Actually, I was much more than interested. I was genuinely curious and puzzled.

How could a presidential candidate with no political background—a bombastic, brazen, and incredibly confident man who violated every rule of political decorum and breached every assumption of how to win a presidential campaign, prevail? It was clear that people across the country responded to Trump as if they had found an oasis in a large desert of political contrivance, dishonesty, and ineffectiveness. In some respects, they had.

Others felt quite differently. Mr. Trump's surprising and wholly unexpected election to the presidency resulted in a vitriolic emotional and political reaction among his detractors that has not subsided. Indeed, it is remarkable both for the level of its intensity and its longevity.

I am well aware of those currents both personally and professionally. However, throughout this research, a deep interest and genuine puzzlement as to how Trump's nomination, general election campaign, and presidency would play out helped me to maintain a general state of emotional and political calm even as anti-Trump vitriol has exploded across almost all aspects of public debate about this unprecedented presidency, and Trump engaged in his latest provocation to establishment assumptions and power centers assumptions.

Standing apart from the emotional maelstrom, and obscured by the president's own theatrics and his opponents' excesses, one can notice that President Trump has built a substantial presidential record. It has, of course, been substantially effected but surprisingly not yet been wholly interrupted by the traumatic impact of the Coronavirus both domestically and abroad and the ferocious opposition he has faced since before he entered office. Whether, against enormous political and historical odds, including an unprecedent modern world-wide pandemic, and the traumatic impact of the tragic death of George Floyd and the peaceful demonstrations and riots that followed, it is possible for Mr. Trump to accomplish his presidential purposes, ambitions that I analyze in this book as the *Politics of American Restoration* is one basic question this analysis attempts to answer.

A second major question underlying this book is about Mr. Trump himself, and his leadership style. What real capacities and deficiencies does Mr. Trump actually bring to his presidential leadership? Enormous numbers of observations about his very real deficits abound. Yet, many of them are harsh, speculative, and devoid of evidence beyond critics' confident assertions. Fair minded, substantive, comprehensive, and accurate analyses of Mr. Trump and his presidency are extremely rare, and therefore much needed.

This book's third and final underlying question is this: Trump's *Politics of American Restoration* is an effort to become a "reconstructive" president in Stephen Skowronek's terms. That *restoration* is premised on Trump's effort to engage and reform (as he sees it) eight pillars of establishment assumptions, thinking, and policy: the courts; economic growth and opportunity (including jobs and energy development); de-regulation; health care; immigration; foreign policy; trade; and lifting the fear of discussing many political debate topics (aka "political correctness").

All of these areas contain a great many discrete policies within them. He is, at the same time, trying to change and reform several major institutions, both domestically (eg., FBI, CDC, DOJ) and abroad (eg., WTO, WHO, NATO). It would be difficult for any president, much less a president in Trump's political circumstances, to successfully accomplish these monumentally ambitious set of goals. Trump must answer the questions, and so must we: How do long—term entrenched policy narratives change, and is it possible for Trump to successfully do so?

Those three large questions frame this book. This is where a dual background with training both in psychology and psychoanalysis and being a political scientist whose field is the presidency is helpful. The clinical and psychoanalytic psychology that I'm trained in and has been the basis of my three other books[2] on sitting presidents and my other analysis that provides a model for the psychological assessment of presidential candidates[3] all seek a framework to establish core psychological patterns of the presidents they analyze and trace their development through their life-histories.

Finally, a word about the adjective "Real" in the book's title preceding its primary focus—the *Psychology of the Trump Presidency*. That word is meant to convey a comparison between the reductionist and highly partisan psychological and political caricatures that permeate what is presented as Trump analysis and an effort to consider and weigh a wide array of information in forming provisional theories of Trump's psychology and presidential leadership. Those are then checked again against additional unfolding data and their capacity to effectively explain and understand Mr. Trump and his presidency. This is nothing more or less than basic social science research procedure, even as my basic theoretical framework owes much to Freud and his innovative legatees like Horney, Erikson, Kohut, and my two mentors, colleagues, and friends in Political Science, Harold D. Lasswell and Alexander L. George.

I am aware that this stance, and the formulations and evidence developed herein as a result of it, will be controversial. It is hoped however, that this research strategy followed and the evidence produced and documented will provide a fair, accurate, and theoretical useful analysis of a controversial man and presidency.

My further hope is that this book will help deepen the way Trump is thought about and, as a result, we will be better able to understand this unique president and presidency.

New York City, USA   Stanley Renshon
2020

NOTES

1. Ben Smith. 2015. "I Asked a Psychoanalyst to Explain Donald Trump," *BuzzFeed*, December 3.
2. Stanley Renshon. 1996 [1998]. *High Hopes: The Clinton Presidency and the Politics of Ambition*. New York: New York University Press [Routledge Press]; Stanley Renshon. 2004. *In His Father's Shadow: The Transformations of George W. Bush*. Palgrave Macmillan; Stanley Renshon. 2012. *Barack Obama and the Politics of Redemption*. New York: Routledge Press.
3. Stanley Renshon. 1996. *The Psychological Assessment of Presidential Candidates*. New York: New York University Press.

Acknowledgments

I owe a debt of appreciation to those who have given their time and offered their views on the ideas contained in this book—agreeing with the author or not. Offered, with few exceptions, in the spirit of friendship, collegiality, and scholarship they have provided valuable observations to consider, and the book and I have substantially benefited as a result.

For very helpful conversations about portions of this book, I would like to thank: Colin Dueck, Richard C. Friedman, Fred I. Greenstein, Charles Lipson, Peter Lowenberg, Sue Matorin, Henry Nau, Harry Paul, Peter Suedfeld, and Alan I. Teger.

A special word of appreciation is due to my dear friends and social science colleagues Professors Robert Badden and Thomas Halper. Their acute editorial eye and extremely helpful observations were very valuable for my thinking and analysis.

At the beginning of this project I taught my Graduate Center seminar on the Modern Presidency. As has been the case with my other books, I benefited from the opportunity to begin to develop my thoughts on Mr. Trump and his presidency in the context of an able group of CUNY graduate students.

I would like to express my appreciation to Michelle Chen, North American Editor for US Politics, Public Policy, and Political Theory for very informative and effective help at many points in the publication process.

Rebecca Roberts, my go-to point of contact for all things having to do with production matters in all their diverse ramifications, has been an incredibly reliable source of information and help. This book and its author owe a great deal to her efforts.

Christine Ranft had the important job of editing this book. Her excellent eye, terrific skills, and easiness to work with are much appreciated. Shukkanthy Siva provided excellent guidance through the galley review process.

Palgrave Macmillan takes its scholarly vetting seriously, and I would like to thank the three anonymous reviewers who provided detailed commentary on my eighty-page book proposal. As expected, the reviewers did not necessarily agree with each other or with me on the ideas that form the basis of this analysis, but the analysis was strengthened by taking their observations seriously, even when I didn't agree with them.

I would also like to thank Michael A. Genovese and Todd Belt—editors for The Evolving American Presidency series at Palgrave Macmillan who also read the proposal and drafts of the book chapters. Additional thanks are due to the two external anonymous reviewers for their willingness to provide detailed commentary on drafts of each chapter of the book.

Through a strange quirk of fate, the proposal for this book reached the desk of Beth Farrow, UK Commissioning Editor for Psychology and Neuroscience. She read the proposal, was interested in it, and we talked—after which the proposal made a transatlantic trip to the desk of Michelle Chen—Palgrave Macmillan editor for North American Politics and Political Theory.

My wife Judith has supportively and lovingly been by my side as I researched and wrote this book, as she has been through our forty-three years of marriage.

Praise for *The Real Psychology of the Trump Presidency*

"Fascinating. Having interviewed six American presidents and known some of them very well, traveling with them for months on end and visiting with them alone for hours and days at a time, it is stunning to me to see how Stanley Renshon can capture so much from their public lives."

—Doug Wead, *Presidential Historian and* New York Times *bestselling author of* Inside Trump's White House *(2019)*

"Trump's leadership and the Trump phenomenon have needed serious, noncartoon-like analysis from a scholar who understands both the country and the personality of America's unusual 45th president. Dr. Renshon provided it, in readable, illuminating fashion."

—Holman W. Jenkins Jr., Columnist, *The Wall Street Journal*

"Stanley Renshon offers a systematic and pungent challenge to the wide range of critics of Donald Trump, the man and the President. He and the framework he offers see *capabilitie*s where others see close to madness, as Trump offers his own *reconstruction* of the American presidency designed toward the *restoration* of the nation to greatness. This is a most provocative book for the 2020 election year."

—Robert Y. Shapiro, Wallace S. Sayre *Professor of Government and International and Public Affairs, Columbia University, USA*

"This is a wide-ranging work that brings together several strands of political science, including party polarization, regime cycles, presidential character, and psycho-biography. Renshon shatters the often unreflective conventional wisdom surrounding this president, acknowledging his weaknesses while also taking seriously his political goals and the foundations of his popular support. Instead of one-dimensional caricatures of Trump and his followers, Renshon provides a rich intermix of character study, historical context, and political critique. In the end, Trump's rise is closely tied to the failures of the political class and its assumptions and orthodoxies, with Trump representing a concerted attempt to bring about the '*Politics of American Restoration*.' This book is essential reading for anyone desiring a more nuanced understanding of the Trump presidency and of the president himself."

—David Crockett, *Professor of Political Science, Trinity University, USA*

"This highly instructive and engaging new book presents an empirically grounded psychological assessment of Donald Trump's presidential leadership and governance. The argument that Trump seeks to achieve the politics of American restoration is developed with evidence-based analysis, which systematically discusses the leadership qualities needed to attain this goal as well as the challenges they pose. The careful research and clear writing make an enduring contribution to understanding the American presidency and American politics in the twenty-first century."

—Meena Bose, *Executive Dean for Public Policy and Public Service Programs, Hofstra University, USA*

"Donald John Trump may be the most anti-establishment, disruptive and perplexing president since Andrew Jackson. His critics pounce on his utterances and at rallies his supporters celebrate his actions and statements. In this book, Stanley Renshon critically reviews what has been written about his first term and provides a thought-provoking, compelling and fresh analysis of the man, his rhetoric, and policies. It is indeed a fascinating reading. For those readers who like to highlight sentences in provocative books, you will find much to underline and quote."

—Wilbur C. Rich, *William R. Kenan Jr. Professor Emeritus of Political Science, Wellesley College, USA*

PRAISE FOR *THE REAL PSYCHOLOGY OF THE TRUMP PRESIDENCY*   xvii

"In psychoanalyst Stanley Renshon's insightful new study of Donald Trump, he carefully sifts the evidence for clues as to whether the president will be a 'fading flash' or a successful reconstructive president. His persuasive nonpartisan conclusion: it would be unwise to place a large bet against President Trump."

—Bruce Buchanan, *Professor Emeritus of Government, University of Texas at Austin, USA*

THE REAL PSYCHOLOGY OF THE TRUMP PRESIDENCY: AN OVERVIEW

This psychological analysis of Mr. Trump and his presidency unfolds conceptually rather than in strictly historical order. It does not begin by focusing on the president's childhood and following his history and development into his presidency. Rather this book, like my three other psychologically framed analyses of a sitting president, develops a theoretical framework drawn from both Psychology and Political Science, to frame four interconnected questions: (1) what are the core psychological elements that define this president; (2) how did they develop over the course of his life; (3) what implications do they have for his presidential ambitions and leadership style; and (4) how do the country's expectations and its political circumstances shape how successful the president's leadership efforts will be?

With President Trump, as has been the case for my other presidential analyses, I have spent considerable time, beginning with the Republican Party primary battle, assembling and evaluating the evidence necessary to develop a set of psychological and political patterns for this unique American president. This analysis covers his life and development before the presidency, his presidential leadership, and what they mean both for his presidential purposes and the country.

My research began in earnest with the first Republican presidential debate on August 7, 2015. As a result of those efforts, I can write with some confidence, with the evidence to back that statement up, that there

xix

is much more to President Trump than meets the eye, and certainly more than the many and repeated caricatures of him.

The book is divided into five Parts and their associated chapters as it unfolds.

Part I: Preliminaries: The Real Psychology of the Trump Presidency sets out the basic foundation of the analysis that follows, both setting the stage for it, and beginning to set out some of its basic elements and considerations.

Chapter 1: "Building a Theory of Donald Trump and His Presidency" addresses the issues of what it takes, theoretically and evidentiarily, to develop a viable theory of the psychology of the Trump presidency. This book addresses the literature on presidents, presidential leadership, political time, and the motivations of Trump voters to name a few areas. However, the real literature for this book is derived from Trump himself— the man, his development, his thinking, and his actions. Is it possible to find patterns in Trump's kaleidoscopic presidency? Is it possible to do so while he is still in office—analyzing the essential dual nature of his presidency, discerning and analyzing the "real" Trump presidency beyond the many caricatures and setting out Trump's ultimate presidential ambitions—*The Politics of American Restoration?* We argue that it is and explain why.

Chapter 2: "In the Eye of the Hurricane: Strategies for Analyzing the Trump Presidency" discusses the issues associated with psychological analyses of a president "at a distance." It takes up the issues of narratives as major explanatory vehicles, including conspiracy theories, and how they differ from real efforts at theory building based on considering and weighing a range of evidence. The nature and range of that evidence, including "events data," is considered, as well as how they differ from the more ordinary varieties of anti-Trump analysis. Is making use of more comprehensive consideration of information tantamount to "defending Trump"? That is not its purpose. The chapter ends by laying out the book's strategy of analysis.

Part II: Donald Trump's Presidential Leadership and Governing Style sets out the basic foundation and operating style of the Trump presidency.

Chapter 3: "The Paradoxical Foundations of the Trump Presidency: Causes and Consequences" begins with the role of the presidency in

American political life and how that has developed. We then turn to an analysis of the 2016 presidential election from the perspective of two major opposing views, both of whom saw the election in starkly dire terms. In reality, that election brought to the fore a set of simmering political crises that had been brewing for decades, including the abortive rise of the "Tea Party" in 2008. That movement centered on profound issues of trust. We link those with Trump's election victory and his presidential ambitions, understood as the *Politics of American Restoration.* We close with a consideration of Trump's leadership style and demeanor, their relationship to presidential "guardrails," and the rise of vehement, determined, and irreconcilable opposition to the Trump Presidency.

Chapter 4: "Donald Trump's Fight Club Presidency" examines Mr. Trump's combativeness. That is an important element in his psychology and performs important functions in his presidential leadership and governing style. We examine its early origins in Trump's family life, its motivations and consequences including Trump's search for recognition and respect, and its surprising impact on Trump's sense of freedom and creativity. We also analyze Trump's first real adult political fight, centered around accusations about housing discrimination, as a template for his business and political career. We conclude with an analysis of Trump's fight club strategy for realizing his goal of the *Politics of American Restoration,* its utility and its limits, and how it is related to Trump's needed on the job training on how to be an effective president.

Chapter 5: "Leadership Style, Presidential Success, and Political Time" takes up the issue of Trump's presidential style and demeanor arguing that there are really two Trump presidencies. One is the bombastic tabloid presidency whose latest provocations and opposition to his presidency play out across American political media and institutional venues. That presidency receives the majority of sensational headlines and commentary. Yet there is another, equally, if not ultimately more important Trump presidency consisting of the deeply serious administration efforts to put into place Trump's signature presidential ambitions. We examine why Trump survives his ferocious opposition in spite of his own missteps, and examine several metrics of presidential "success." We assess Trump's slow but gathering momentum towards his *Restoration* goals, and ask if he will remain stuck in political time as a "Disjunctive" president or have a chance to become a "Reconstructive" one.

Part III: Psychiatry in the White House: Trump's Narcissism and "Fitness" for Office directly addresses two key political psychology questions about Mr. Trump and his presidency: What exactly, is the real psychology of this president? And, is he psychologically and political "fit" to be president?

Chapter 6: "President Trump's Narcissism Reconsidered" focuses on several key Trump psychological traits, all related to the dominant narrative and related memes of Trump's narcissism and its political consequences. We again take up issues concerned with psychological assessment in relation to diagnosis and the so-called Goldwater Rule. We argue that simplistically assigning a name to a behavior without an understanding of the term used or familiarity with, or making use of, the evidence needed to support claims associated with it is a recipe for poor evaluation and analysis. For those do so with some professional psychological training, it also reflects a lapse of professional ethics and personal integrity.

The chapter analyzes Trump's impatience, impulsiveness, and narcissism, and examines alternative patterns of understanding these elements in the context of Trump's psychology and leadership style. The chapter concludes with a detailed analysis of Trump's motivation to seek the presidency, including several that have never before been examined.

Chapter 7: "On President Trump's Psychological and Political Fitness for Office" directly takes up that central question. We examine the concept of psychological and political "unfitness," noting the diverse ways Trump critics have used it. We then examine efforts to bypass the Goldwater Rule prohibitions by focusing on Trump's supposed "dangerousness" rather than his "mental illness." In terms of conceptual reliability and validity that is no improvement. Analyzing the fiasco that gave rise to the Goldwater Rule makes clear the ethical and conceptual dangers of unanchored psychological characterizations and accusations. They are not made less so when Trump's supposed dangerousness crosses the line from his psychology to accusations that he is politically unfit because he has subverted the "Guardrails of Democracy."

Chapter 8: "The Unexpected Trump" takes the examination of Trump's real psychology into new territory. One of the drawbacks of the anti-Trump narratives about his psychology is their confirmation bias; only the worst will do. Their narrow focus on Trump's psychological and political pathologies make him the presidential equivalent of Marcuse's *One Dimensional Man*,[1] which is he not. In this chapter we analyze evidence concerning Mr. Trump that some will consider heretical, perhaps even politically blasphemous. These include his compassion, his charitable giving, his being there for others in their times of need, his vision and creativity in business and politics, his basic operational metric in life, business, and the presidency—Think Big, and his very surprising and unexpected capacity for reflectiveness.

Part IV: The Trump Presidency in Practice directly examines the basic elements of the Trump presidency as it has unfolded in both theory and practice.

Chapter 9: "Prelude to a Unique Presidency: Preparation, Expectations, and Judgment" begins with an examination of the relevance of Trump's CEO experience to his presidency. His was not a typical business career and that unorthodox experience helped shape an equally unorthodox presidency. Trump's success at building a business empire has proved instructive for building its political equivalent. There are similarities including Trump's ambition, vision, courage, determination, flexibility, an astute sense of timing, and discipline. There are also lessons to be carried into this presidency about resilience and successfully coming back from almost catastrophic failure. However, whatever help the nature of his unusual career has been, it did not provide him with the basic political grounding and understanding that more traditional paths to the White House have provided its other occupants.

First Trump has to learn how to be a possibly successful president and move on from the many sobering surprises about the office that he found on assuming it. We conclude by examining the large range of Trump's presidential interests, his presidential work patterns, and his approach to the core function of any presidency—his decision-making style and judgment.

Chapter 10: "Essentials of Leadership: The Core Sources of Trump's Presidency" examines several basic elements Trump of presidency and leadership. They include: The nature of the president's base supporters—real or imagined; including their supposed "racial resentment"; the powerful emotional connections of respect and standing linking Trump and his base supporters; *TrumpThink*—a magical mystery tour reflecting how Trump understands his world, full of unexpected associative detours, logical lane changing, and surprisingly clear reconnection to his original train of thought; *TrumpTalk*—often meandering, frequently exaggerated, regularly provocative, and honestly heartfelt if rarely fact-check level "correct"; Trump facts and tweets—the president's serially imprecise relationship with "the Truth," including "larger Truths"; and promise keeping as an essential truth.

Chapter 11: "Conservative American Nationalism: The Trump Doctrine in Theory and Practice" examines Trump's foreign policy thinking and initiatives. The most fitting conceptual name for the Trump Doctrine is Conservative American Nationalism. It is a framework that we argue is composed of six essential elements: (1) An America First premise in Trump policies; (2) An emphasis on American National Identity as a cornerstone of America's elemental and dual relationship with itself and the world; (3) Highly selective involvement, with a non-exclusive emphasis on its own terms and interests in defining America's role in the world; (4) An emphasis on American strength in all its forms, resilience, and resolve; (5) The use of maximum repeated pressure along a continuum of points in pursuit of key goals; and (6) Maximum tactical and strategic flexibility. That doctrine is at least as much a reflection of Trump's psychology as it is of his thinking and we explore its relationship with his impatience, emphasis on action, ambition, the use of force, and the future of the Trump Doctrine.

Part V: Political Transformation in the Balance takes up the varied possible futures of the Trump Presidency from fading flash to successful "Reconstruction" and *Restoration*.

Chapter 12: "The Future of the Trump Presidency" takes up two questions: Does the Trump presidency have a future and, if so, what kind? Much will depend on the 2020 election and whether Trump wins reelection, as well as the distribution of power in the House and Senate. In order to be successful, he will have to have deal with an unprecedent modern worldwide pandemic, but also the traumatic impact of the tragic death of George Floyd during a police encounter and the peaceful demonstrations and riots that followed.

Much will also depend on whether Trump can succeed in changing the dominant narratives with a focus on the eight policy pillars that define his *Politics of American Restoration.*

We examine how entrenched political paradigms and narratives change in less than dire circumstances and also how they change during catastrophic political or economic circumstances, like wars, economic depressions, and pandemics. Obviously, a very crucial element for Trump's reelection is how effectively he responds to the unprecedented modern economic, social, and political catastrophe of the Coronavirus, and how the public judges those efforts.

We then ask how likely it is that Trump can accomplish his presidential purposes in a second term given a mix of possible election outcomes and the divided nature of American political life? In examining Trump's post-election circumstances and possible strategies we ask: Is Trump a dunce, hedgehog, or a fox? We do know Trump is a man of many questions, a number of them rarely asked by past leaders. Yet, he is also a man who has reached some fairly basic political and policy conclusions that are not unprecedentedly novel, but rather have been mostly unspoken by establishment leaders and institutions, and even more rarely acted upon.

If Trump wins reelection, whatever the distribution of power in Congress, successfully realizing his *Restoration* ambitions will be equivalent to scaling Mt. Annapurna. It will take skill, experience, determination, courage, resilience, and a dedicated competence and effective group of support allies. Many imagine that climb. Few attempt it. Fewer succeed. The risks are high; the chances of success low; but it would be unwise to place a large bet against President Trump.

NOTE

1. Herbert Marcuse. 1964. *One-Dimensional Man: Studies in the Ideology of Advanced Industrial Society.* Boston: Beacon Press.

CONTENTS

Part I Preliminaries: The Real Psychology of the Trump Presidency

1 Building a Theory of Donald Trump and His Presidency — 3

2 In the Eye of the Hurricane: Strategies for Analyzing the Trump Presidency — 35

Part II Donald Trump's Presidential Leadership and Governing Style

3 The Paradoxical Foundations of the Trump Presidency: Causes and Consequences — 77

4 Donald Trump's Fight Club Presidency — 119

5 Leadership Style, Presidential Success, and Political Time — 159

xxvii

Part III   Psychiatry in the White House: Trump's Narcissism and "Fitness" for Office

6   President Trump's Narcissism Reconsidered   199

7   On President Trump's Psychological and Political
Fitness for Office   233

8   The Unexpected Trump   265

Part IV   The Trump Presidency in Practice

9   Prelude to a Unique Presidency: Preparation,
Expectations, and Judgment   301

10   Essentials of Leadership: The Core Sources
of Trump's Presidency   343

11   Conservative American Nationalism: The Trump
Doctrine in Theory and Practice   383

Part V   Political Transformation in the Balance

12   The Future of the Trump Presidency   419

Other Books by Stanley Renshon   467

References   469

Proper Name Index   535

Subject Index   539

PART I

Preliminaries: The Real Psychology of the Trump Presidency

CHAPTER 1

Building a Theory of Donald Trump and His Presidency

The United States has never had a president quite like Donald J. Trump. And, it is highly unlikely that there will be another one like him again.

He has been called, with good reason, "the most unorthodox president of modern times,"[1] and a "president unlike any other."[2] He is in many respects the Black Swan of the modern American presidency,[3] unique and unexpected, but also disproportionally consequential. And being consequential is Trump's presidential purpose—all in the service of what I argue in this analysis is an effort at *American Restoration.*

The fact that Trump's presidency is unprecedented, unexpected, and has already had substantial political and policy consequences does not necessarily mean that it will ultimately be successful. Mr. Trump's presidential ambitions are to reformulate, reform, and where necessary replace a number of the dominant policy and political paradigms that have governed American political life for the last half-century. His presidential purposes are essentially transformative, as well as reformist and restorative.

Trump's primary vehicles for successfully reaching those politically difficult and historically rare goals are his clearly observable and very distinctive presidential leadership style and equally unorthodox thinking patterns. Their foundations are a set of character traits and capacities along with habits of mind that go well beyond the narrow, hackneyed assertions that his narcissism is his only defining character trait.

© The Author(s) 2020
S. Renshon, *The Real Psychology of the Trump Presidency,*
The Evolving American Presidency,
https://doi.org/10.1007/978-3-030-45391-6_1

Yet, while his leadership style may be unique, its half-life and transferability may very well be limited.[4] Arguments have already been made by Trump's allies that even if he is successful during his presidency, "the real danger with Mr. Trump is that he may end up changing little."[5] It remains to be seen, given the substantial array for forces mobilized against his presidency, his own avoidable mistakes,[6] the unprecedented Coronavirus pandemic, the traumatic impact of the tragic death of George Floyd during a police stop and the peaceful demonstrations and riots that followed, and Trump's response to them both, along the magnitude of the tasks that he has set for himself and the country, whether President Trump will be "successful," and if so, how.

It has been clear from the president's first days in office that[7]:

> President Trump is moving at an unprecedented pace to change the direction of the country and reset America's place in the world. …If successful in making good on his vision, his presidency would be described as one of the most important and controversial of modern times—and no doubt one of the most contentious.

If.

Developing a Theory of Mr. Trump and His Presidency

This analysis is *not* an exploration that attempts to fit Trump's particular traits into a pre-existing a priori theoretical framework and typology of "presidential character."[8] That most well known of these theories has many demonstrated problems of conceptualization, evidence, and inference.[9] In any event, in Mr. Trump's case, there is so little examination of the real range of elements that comprise his psychology in reality that simply taking the reductionist singular characterizations of Trump's psychology and leadership style and putting them into a pre-existing theory would be a disservice.

The purpose of this analysis is theory building by *uncovering* core psychological elements in a deductive case study approach,[10] and to assess the evidence both for and against the tentative theories developed to understand and explain Mr. Trump and his presidency. It would then be possible to assemble the particular elements that comprise this president's psychology, ask how they are related, and examine how they affect the core elements of presidential performance—leadership and the judgment reflected in his choices.[11]

Ordinary social science addresses and builds on the "literature." Biographically based case studies like this one, using ordinary social science approaches to theory development and evidence, also build on the "literature," when available or relevant. Thus we examine in some detail notions of political time as they relate to Trump's presidential performance. We also delve quite deeply into the literature on the motivations of Trump supporters (see Chapter 10). We draw on diverse clinical theories of narcissism, both normal and pathological, to assess one major element of Trump's psychology (see Chapter 6) and use those theories to assess his psychological and political fitness for office (see Chapter 7). We also obviously draw on, throughout this analysis, studies of past presidencies and the theories of presidential leadership associated with them.

However, it is worth emphasizing that the primary "literature" available for an analysis of the Trump presidency is the enormous wealth of data generated by the Trump presidency itself. This effort then relies on assembling diverse data to inductively build a "theory of Trump and the Trump presidency." Those provisional formulations can then be used to gauge their utility in understanding the patterns of an unfolding presidency.

These efforts are meant to provide explanatory power and understanding of what we see President Trump doing as his presidency unfolds. They make use of a large range of data. One advantage of that approach is that when there are available facts that don't fit with an initial understanding, we are required make sense of them. These research strategies are likely to bring us closer to understanding the real man and his presidency. However, it is true that however much effort we put into developing and clarifying our theories and understandings, they will still remain provisional to some degree.

Analyzing President Trump While He Is Still in Office

This book is an "initial" analysis of Mr. Trump's presidency written as he completes almost four years in office, but not quite yet a full term. He may or may not serve another. His historical record and materials for the Trump archives and library are in the process of being enacted in real time. It is true that historical perspective and archival records can be grounds for revised understandings of any president, including Mr.

Trump, and they are obviously not available to scholars yet. Still, for reasons to be explained shortly, it is possible to reach some firmer more substantively based understanding of this complex man and presidency without waiting for his presidential library to open its doors.

This analysis breaks new ground in both its time frame and its conceptual framework. It does more than examine Mr. Trump's time in office at six months,[12] one,[13] or even two years,[14] highlighting the "highs" and "lows." It does that to some degree with its use of "event data" (see Chapter 2). However, this analysis spans Trump's life and personal development in search for patterns that can help us understand the man and his presidency.

FINDING CORE PATTERNS IN A KALEIDOSCOPIC PRESIDENCY

The framework of analysis that follows is made possible by the fact Mr. Trump is unusual in having governed with a leadership style that was entirely evident during both his presidential campaign and throughout his very public career as a business entrepreneur and empire builder. Not surprisingly, he has carried his unusual and unorthodox style into his presidency.

That is to be expected because these patterns and their underlying psychology have been developed and consolidated over a lifetime as a unique, singular CEO, and mostly successful career building an international business empire. As a result, his style and the psychological elements that support it have become firmly rooted and consolidated in this seventy-four year old president. They are key ingredients of his presidency, and likely to remain so.

Early in the Trump presidency the most informed observers could legitimately argue that "Trump Governs as He Campaigned: Unconventionally and Unpredictably."[15] Almost four years into Trump's first term, it is unclear if Trump's unpredictability is still as much of a shock and surprise as it was at the start of his campaign for the Republican nomination. Certainly, part of Trump's "unpredictability" is related to the fact that he ignored conventional rules in gaining the nomination and the presidency and continues to do so as president. Yet that does not mean there were no patterns in his behavior.

Policy and News at Trump Speed

One of the ways in which President Trump is unlike any previous American president is the way that he dominates the news cycle on a daily and almost an hourly basis. The president is the center of so many policy developments and news stories and analysis about them—the myriad debates regarding his handling of the Coronavirus,[16] his policy musings on homelessness,[17] the latest installment of Trump's first term long conflict with multiple Democratic investigations—including one dealing as the pandemic is unfolding with a focus on how the administration responded to the crisis,[18] his impeachment and acquittal,[19] the latest fight with his own party,[20] the latest firing of someone in his administration,[21] or a casual Christmas-eve conversation with a seven-year-old girl about whether she believes in Santa Claus—a question that revealed Trump's capacity to blunder across appropriate lines.[22] There are also the full array of policy and administrative initiations that the administration has undertaken in what we term the eight pillars of Trump policy reform (as he sees it)—the courts, economic growth and opportunity (including jobs and energy development), de-regulation, health care, immigration, foreign policy, trade, and lifting the fear of discussing many political debate topics (aka "political correctness"), all of which contain a great many discrete policies within those categories. All of these too are the subjects of endless rounds of Trump commentary and intensive opposition and debate as well.

The result is a kaleidoscopic tsunami of information that seems impervious to organization, much less understanding. You can think of this as Policy and News at Trump Speed.[23] It certainly makes it hard to keep up with the unfolding Trump presidency, but more importantly it presents challenges to understanding it.

Consider some of the headlines reflecting a view of the president as having slipped the constraints of the office and his former advisors, who some had hoped would manage and constrain him:

After Another Week of Chaos, Trump Repairs to Palm Beach. No One Knows What Comes Next[24]

White House shakeup shows Trump tired of hearing 'no' for an answer[25]

Trump Relishes Off-Script Approach[26]

Trump's bad week: A policy rollback, a political setback and a still-defiant president[27]

Reliable Allies Refuse to Defend a President Content With Chaos.[28]

Actually, Dan Balz of the *Washington Post* had the most insightful take on the turmoil and "chaos" regarding a batch of ongoing personnel and policy changes emanating from Mr. Trump[29]:

> There is no New Trump emerging here as this next phase begins. If anything, it is the reemergence of the old Trump, the pre-presidential Trump, who plays by his own rules and tries to rewrite the old ones he doesn't like. This is what made him rich as a business executive and won him the White House.

Exactly.

There is no wholly "new" Trump when it comes to his patterns of behavior. However, there might be a "new evolving Trump," as we argue there is, when one considers his presidential and life purposes in this stage of his life. I argue that his life's purpose has changed, although not necessarily for wholly altruistic reasons (see Chapter 6). One major task of the book is to understand and explain the "old" Mr. Trump and the "newer" presidential one, and how they both fit, or fail to fit, with the emerging office of the presidency and Mr. Trump's "*Restorative*" ambitions.

A Core Set of Dualisms at the Heart of the Trump Presidency

Complicating the analysis of President Trump and his presidency is the fact that there is a pervasive dualism in both. One is the tabloid-like presidency of Trumpian bombast and dire predictions of demise that have not yet to date come to pass. The other part of his presidency is a slow methodical effort to set in motion and consolidate a "reconstructive" presidency. As David Brooks put it[30]:

> It's almost as if there are two White Houses. There's the Potemkin White House, which we tend to focus on: Trump berserk in front of the TV, the lawyers working the Russian investigation and the press operation. Then there is the Invisible White House that you never hear about, which is getting more effective at managing around the distracted boss.

It's very questionable that President Trump is "distracted" and his staff is getting better in operating without him. The evidence suggests that in spite of Trump's reputation for being unable to focus, he can be a micro-manager[31] on issues where he wants to reach down into his government to get things done, like stripping medals given to prosecutors after they had, in his view, erroneously charged a Navy Seal for committing war crimes.[32]

The dualism at the heart of the Trump presidency reflects the fact the president and his administration often operate at two levels simultaneously. The examples are legion at both the personal and policy level. He is a man publicly criticized for using other people's money to fund his foundation, but he has a long record of helping people privately and anonymously outside of his public foundation (see Chapter 8). Trump's public bluster is often on display, but privately he can be and often is very gracious and charming.[33] He is man known from years of flashy tabloid exploits, who prefers to spend evenings at home.[34] He is well known to treat woman both as objects and equals.[35] He threatens North Korea with destruction, but travels around the world to meet its leader. He is a serial public provocateur who makes a number of safe moderate appointments.[36] He relentlessly and publicly attacked the Mueller investigation while almost wholly cooperating with those investigations behind the scenes.[37]

This is not a case of "Dr. Jekyll and Mr. Hyde are on their way to the White House," as one pundit wrote.[38] It is closer to reality to note that "Trump brings many different personas to Washington."[39] The evidence noted above suggests that is true, but there is more to it than that.

The results of the research analyzed herein suggests that beyond the innumerable anti-Trump caricatures and beneath his varied public personas there are a core set of basic patterns that anchor Trump's psychology. What then do the core dualisms noted just above reflect? They reflect a man and a psychology able to contain seemingly "opposite" perspectives on a range of things, that may or may not in reality really be opposite. It is the point of Walt Whitman's "containing multitudes" quote[40] that opened this book. Indeed it is one of the conclusions of the *Washington Post*'s deeply researched biography of the president: "Trump comes to this moment as a more complex man than is widely realized."[41]

The fact that Trump can publicly rail against the Mueller investigation for example while almost wholly cooperating with it, suggests that the reality principle is, in that case and others, firmly established in Trump's mind which does bear on his psychological fitness for office (see Chapter 7). Trump does feel, and there is evidence, that he and his administration were targeted on illegitimate legal grounds.[42] It is understandable that the president would be angry about the frequently asserted but unproven allegations of his being a traitor. What innocent person repeatedly and publicly accused of such criminal, disgraceful, and unforgivable behavior wouldn't be? On the other hand, the Muller investigation was a legal and duly authorized exercise of governmental power, and a failure to substantially respond to legitimate requests carried with it dire political and legal consequences. So, cooperate he did.

On a more personal level, when Trump first came to New York he frequented a number of night clubs on his evenings out and often dated beautiful women. Yet people who knew Trump then knew that he preferred homelife to nightlife, food to cuisine, and work to the playboy status he developed and cultivated. For all the hype around Trump's tabloid years, he is essentially a homebody. One recent analysis of how Trump spends his time noted,[43] "Early in this presidency, Trump's staff tried to nudge him out into the city more often for dinners or to attend events, but the plans always fell apart, said one of the former senior administration officials who called Trump a 'homebody'."

Or, consider his relationships with women. Leave aside at this point the allegations that Trump physically forced himself on women in non-consensual sexual advances. Not one of the allegations have been backed up by concrete evidence beyond the assertions. And when actual evidence has surfaced, it has disproved the allegations.[44] Looking instead at the object/equal treatment elements of the history of Trump's relationships with women simply reflect a common dualism. Men can find women attractive and also treat them fairly and with respect for their talents and skills. They can also see women through the lens of physical attractiveness. Did Trump do both? Yes. Did Trump have affairs while he was married? Yes. Did he still put women in positions of power and authority because of their abilities? Yes.

The point here, and it will be encountered again, is that Trump cannot be reduced to a single pattern of behavior—with women, his presidency, and much else. He is a man of many dimensions. The dualisms noted above are all real, but none of them alone is defining. Rather, they reflect a range of potential behaviors that Trump appears to be able to act upon without feeling either inauthentic or inhibited. They are part of his behavioral repertoire which is much wider than he is given credit for having at his disposal.

Yet, this is not a description of a presidential chameleon. There are, to repeat, a number of core elements to Trump's psychology that are fairly evident and which we will analyze. For example, too many causal observers among his critics conflate Trump's real narcissism with his brand thus missing the real range and motivations of his psychology. We hope to do better here.

In Search of the Real President Trump

Mr. Trump's bombastic, combative, and controversial leadership style has obviously given some credence to the many complaints lodged against him regarding his presidential demeanor and behavior. His public leadership style has never before been practiced in a modern presidency. His brash confrontational style (see Chapter 4) is a direct reflection of his psychology. It is also one that he sees as a necessary strategy given what he wants to accomplish and the widespread "resistance," a purposefully borrowed term of self-referral that inappropriately evokes the heroic men and women who during WW2 risked and sometimes experienced torture and death for opposing the Nazis,[45] arrayed against him. Analyzing the origins and relationship between these core elements of his presidential leadership style are essential to understanding his presidency. And understanding both the man and his presidency are the essential reasons for writing this book.

President Trump: A Prisoner of His Persona?

The dualisms at the heart of the Trump presidency suggest a somewhat unique issue that faces a psychoanalytically trained biographer of President Trump. That issue is distinguishing between Trump's psychology and his persona. The editors and reporters for the *Washington Post* who interviewed him at length of their book and related articles, "wanted more than anything to figure out how much of Trump's campaign manner was shtick and how much was real."[46] They were searching for the reality behind the "shtick." Yet, what if the "shtick" is a real part of Trump's psychology?

The point arises because Trump came into office with a very unusual background. Yes, he had no formal political experience, had not served in the military, and instead had a career in business, but that is not the point. What is more relevant is that Trump had a fifty-year career as the single, singular head of a vast and fast-moving business empire. There was no real organization chart and no detailed list of specific responsibilities. As Trump put it, "I prefer to come to work each day and just see what develops."[47] And that's exactly what he did.

Most careers are steeped in tradition, be they in law, politics, the military, business, or academia. They have a set of norms, expectations, routines, and paths to advancement. Yet, as the single and sole decision-maker in the Trump Organization, he ran the show. As a result, he developed a personal style that would be difficult to maintain in almost any traditional organizational setting. That style included flamboyance, combativeness, risk taking, rhetorical sleight of hand ("truthful hyperbole"), impulsiveness and flexibility that allowed him to pursue personal and business indulgences with cool calculation, enormous levels of hard work, creativity, and resilience in a peripatetic and wide-ranging business career.

This diverse and sometimes contradictory set of traits all existed in the same person, and they are all part of the style Trump developed over fifty-plus years in his unique position. It would be very surprising if they did not become a real part of his psychology. And herein lies an issue: What if the Trump persona that we can so easily observe is now a real part of psychology? That immediately raises two questions. Is Mr. Trump's psychology wholly explained by his persona? Critics would say yes, focusing on the most political and personally damaging items of the above list.

A more careful assessment would examine the full range of the Trump persona characteristics listed, and ask if there is evidence of any psychological elements that lie outside of this list. We argue in the analysis that follows that there are. One would then further ask which of these elements, person or persona, are related to Trump's political circumstances and his presidential style. We would then be in a better position to appreciate if there is room in Trump's presidency not for a "newer Trump" but of a different one.

Trump has said, "I won't change,"[48] and when he and his administration are under such relentless and continuing attack it may not be possible or wise for him to do so. There is however the danger that,

"Donald Trump may be turning himself into a captive inside the cage of his own very familiar persona."[49] In short, Mr. Trump, like any president, is advantaged when he is able to choose his response, not simply act on well-established patterns.

Here in lies a very core dilemma of Trump's presidential leadership. He and his administration are the focus of an enormous number and range of attacks. As a result, Trump's "fight club" persona and strategy, developed during his business career, serves a number of important purposes (see Chapter 4).

Yet, this observation leads to a core set of questions about President Trump that remain unresolved. They were directly put forward by Peggy Noonan several years ago[50]:

> Mr. Trump is a clever man with his finger on the pulse, but his political future depends on two big questions. The first is: Is he at all a good man? Underneath the foul mouthed flamboyance is he in it for America? The second: Is he fully stable? He acts like a nut, calling people bimbos, flying off the handle with grievances. Is he mature, reliable? Is he at all a steady hand?

It is at this point not difficult to answer the question of whether "he is in for America." We present evidence that he is, which does not, however, preclude deriving a sense of personal satisfaction, validation and other personal psychological benefits from his presidential efforts. The separate question Noonan asks—"Is he at all a good man?" asks a different question. Along with Trump's sometimes justifiable anger and clearly personal sensitivities to the unrelenting personal and political attacks against him and his administration, is there a part of Trump's psychology that remains apart from the combative persona he's developed and which has become a clear part of who he is? We present evidence in Chapter 8 (The Unexpected Trump) that there is.

However, in a milieu of constant attack, a combative president like Trump will respond as expected, combatively. That is one of the oppositions' purposes. They wish to continuously push Trump to appear "unpresidential." Doubtlessly, many Americans would prefer a "kinder, gentler" President Trump. However, those with that stance ultimately have to answer the question: what is a president to do when he, and his administration, are savagely and remorselessly attacked?

What Do You Make of a President Who...?

There is an expansiveness to the Trump persona that defies easy characterization. It is certainly more robust and consequential than the "Trump is unfit" narratives and memes that his critics push. Still, it is not easy to gain a firm fix on a president who takes great pride in his unpredictability.[51]

This analysis argues that Mr. Trump's real psychology and presidency is capable of being understood, even if not precisely predicted. Yet to do so one must be analytically willing to dive into the world of a very complex and contradictory man who purposely lived his life in a very public way, thereby providing the illusion that we know him well, when in fact there is much more to him that his public persona.

It may be true, as one report put it that, "All Presidents must contain multitudes."[52] Yet, Trump contains more than most, and certainly more than are reflected in the caricatures that are presented as Trump analysis. One critical biographer wondered: "What do you make of a man who, when he argues with women stoops to insulting their appearance?" To which another analyst might add, yes—but what do you also make of the fact that Trump is "spoken of highly by the many women he has hired into high level positions and worked successfully with over many years?[53]

That includes decades-long members of the Trump Organization's inner circle like Barbara Res (chosen by Trump to head of construction at his major building sites, a position which was unprecedented for a woman to have that that time). She wrote:

> He would always hire the person he thought was best without regard to gender. I know I never got a break like the one I got from Donald.[54]

Another was Louise Sunshine (Vice President of the Trump Organization from 1973 to 1985 involved in the development of Trump Tower and other major projects, and the growth of the "Trump brand").[55] Norma Foerderer was Trump's long time administrator and gate-keeper. Rhona Graff,[56] also worked for Trump over a decade before being promoted to the same slot when Ms. Foerderer retired in 2005.

As the *New York Times* put it, opening a window into another little-noted aspect of the Trump father–son relationship, "Mr. Trump's dedication to his secretary and hers to him is much like the relationship Fred C. Trump, his father, had with his secretary, Amy Luerssen, treating her like family."[57] Mr. Trump also apparently has had no difficulty in

1 BUILDING A THEORY OF DONALD TRUMP AND HIS PRESIDENCY 15

appointing women to high-level advisory positions in his administration.[58] As noted above, Trump seems equally capable of treating women both as objects and as equals.

We might further ask: what do you make of a man who has been publicly and roundly criticized for using other people's money to fund his own named charity,[59] and sometimes criticized in the press for being slow to make good on his promised personal charity promises.[60] Yet this very same man also once gave a dying child a check for $50,000.00 so that he could enjoy the last years of his life.[61] He gave thousands of dollars to a family whose hardships he read about in the papers—something his then long-time administrative assistant Norma Foerderer noted he did often.[62] Michael D'Antonio a frequent Trump critic and biographer writes that Trump agreed to a dying child's wish to be "fired" from *The Apprentice*, but when it came time to say those words, Trump couldn't bring himself to say those words to a dying child and instead gave him a check for several thousand dollars and told him "to go have the time of his life"?[63]

What do you make of a man who built a Manhattan real-estate empire based on nerve, ambition, innovation, and forging the necessary political connections mostly on his own after his father provided initial introductions and also financial help at key points in his career, and expanded it to global proportions. What do you make of a man who almost lost his empire, but weathered substantial economic difficulties, and emerged with a new innovative entrepreneurial idea-branding that vastly increased his success?

What do you make of a man who, at the same time wrote eighteen books (with help), many of which appeared on the *New York Times* bestsellers list and was the host and chief personality for twelve seasons of a very successful television series—*The Apprentice*, which made his name a household word and his brand synonymous with success?

And finally, what do you make of a man who, over decades, increasingly and publicly expressed his concern about the country's strength, direction, and leadership and decided in 2016 to seek the presidency against seventeen other candidates many of whom had national reputations and substantial political resources—and won? And what do you make of a political novice who beat Hillary Clinton, one of the most experienced, well-funded, widely supported modern Democratic candidates for the presidency?

One thing that can legitimately be made of such a person and president is that he is a man of tremendous talents along with his easily observable and obvious flaws. The analysis that follows will focus on both, along with some other traits and characteristics that are not so obvious. Trump deserves to be taken seriously not only because his talents are as real as his limitations, but also because both are an integral part of his presidential leadership style. And his presidency is proving to be as consequential as it is controversial.

ANALYZING PRESIDENT TRUMP: A WINDING ROAD WITH MANY PATHS

Many have been tempted to analyze Trump on a "what you see is what you get basis." One strand of this narrative analysis argues that[64]:

> There really are no Trump mysteries. His flaws aren't hidden away. He often attests to them himself, or demonstrates them publicly. For someone who cares so much about his image, and so assiduously crafts it, he's a relative open book.

There is a large element of truth in that observation. Yet, there is more to Mr. Trump's leadership style than serial bombast and a clearly observable, brash, and understandably controversial public persona. There is a pattern of motivation and thinking behind that behavior—one that reflects Trump's formative experiences and his understanding of the nature of life and his present political circumstances and what he hopes to accomplish in his presidency. This work analyzes both, and their relationship to each other.

President Trump: Beyond Psychological Caricature

As the very useful *Washington Post*'s biographical book reporting on Trump's background and candidacy put it[65]:

> We began this reporting on the theory that Trump, like everyone else is far more than his reputation or his brand...[we have discovered] that *the man elected as the 45th president is far more complex than his simple language might indicate*, that his motivations and values are informed by his parents and his upbringing, his victories and defeats and his life-long quest for love and acceptance.

1 BUILDING A THEORY OF DONALD TRUMP AND HIS PRESIDENCY 17

In short, in fundamentally human and psychological ways, Trump is really just like many of us.

That said, it is hard to think of a more useful summary of Freud's basic psychoanalytic framework than the second part of that *Washington Post* quote. The reporters who wrote the Trump book were interested in trying to establish basic facts around these elements. It is this analyst's and this book's purpose to try and use their and other factual reporting, wide-ranging interviews, and an extensive range of other information, to establish patterns that have explanatory power in understanding Mr. Trump and his presidency.

Tellingly, the conclusions of the *Washington Post* reporters who wrote the book, and this analyst who has spent the better part of five years carefully following Mr. Trump over a wide variety of circumstances and analyzing enormous amounts of data regarding him, have both reached the same conclusion. There is demonstrably more, much more, to Mr. Trump than the many shallow caricatures of him and his presidency.

As noted, there is much more to Mr. Trump's psychology than his obvious narcissism. This single trait is not synonymous with Trump's overall psychology. In so doing, we draw on an important distinction in the psychoanalytic and psychiatry literature between so-called "healthy"[66] and "pathological" narcissism. "Healthy narcissism" includes an absolutely normal wish to gain respect and validation for one's accomplishments. When that wish is stymied or denied, the person has the choice of slinking away to privately heal their wounds or fighting back for their own self-respect. Mr. Trump, throughout his life has always chosen the latter.

Ordinary healthy narcissism differs from what the psychiatric *Diagnostic and Statistical Manual* terms "narcissistic personality disorder" which Otto Kernberg, MD more simply terms "pathological narcissism."[67] The essential differences between the two are easy to grasp once the underlying theoretical distinctions are explained. Yet, Trump critics see only pathology and, as a result, put forward a wide variety of reasons, some psychological, some political, why Trump is "unfit" to hold office (see Chapter 7).

Finally, there is also much more to Trump's presidential purposes than assuaging his ego or building his brand to benefit himself financially in his post-presidential years—and even during them according to some. Mr. Trump has undertaken literally hundreds of policy initiatives, large and small, in diverse areas both domestically and abroad. Internationally, they could perhaps be grouped with some degree of accuracy under the concept of *America First* (see Chapter 11), but there is something more profound underlying that term and others that could be used.

MAKE AMERICA GREAT AGAIN: DONALD TRUMP'S HOPE AND CHANGE CANDIDACY

What did Donald Trump offer the American public with his candidacy? He certainly did not offer a sterling political résumé or a polished understanding of public policy. He did not offer soothing rhetoric or detailed policy plans. He did however, offer something more important in that election cycle. He offered a vision of American being better than it had become, and a leadership psychology that would not let traditional political dos and don'ts, that favored the status quo, stand in the way of his achieving it.

His was an unprecedented, brash, bold, bracing, disruptive, rude, and sometimes coarse candidacy. And those characteristics have become integral aspects of his presidency. In so being, he has unequivocally conveyed that this candidacy and presidency would be different. When Trump said, "America doesn't win anymore," he was referring to much more than being taken advantage of in trade deals. His deeper point was that American had lost the confidence and capacity to take care of itself and get things done that needed doing, both domestically and internationally.

Trump clearly felt America had a number of long-standing problems— jobs, the economy, trade, immigration, and an equally large and important set of foreign policy issues that had been allowed to fester and drift. He ran as the candidate who was serious about his intention to take them on and do something about them. For many Americans, this rekindled the hope that someone was really listening to their concerns about the direction of the country, and would do something about them. Hope and change indeed.

Campaign slogans, if they resonate with parts of the public as Trump's "Make America Great Again" did, capture an essential feature of presidential purpose for the public to interpret. They represent a promise not a policy blueprint. What are Trump's presidential purposes?

On first glance they appear to defy easy categorization. They span domestic and foreign policies. They encompass executive orders, myriad administrative initiatives in almost all of the government's executive departments, major presidential initiatives in foreign policy that are constitutionally within his arc of legal and political legitimacy, and successfully working first with his Republican majorities in the Congress, and then only the Senate, on appointing judges, budgetary blueprints that reset spending priorities, and the passage of major tax reform legislation.

During his first term in office Mr. Trump has riled his opponents with his domestic initiatives in: immigration policy and enforcement; energy production; domestic environmental policy regulatory reform; education reform; judicial appointments; emphasizing policies that create jobs in America, and in response to the Coronavirus pandemic trying to help the country to recover from its enormous losses.[68] He has done the same with a number of international policies including: withdrawing from several trade agreements and threatening to do so with NAFTA and South Korea; withdrawing from the Paris Climate agreements; loosening the restraints on the use of military force against ISIS and other terrorist groups; bombing Syria for crossing the red line he established about using chemical weapons; revising existing treaty understandings with our NATO allies; putting new pressures on oppositional regimes like North Korea, Iran, and Syria; cementing ties with traditional allies like Israel, Saudi Arabia, Japan, and India, addressing deficiencies in international organizations like WHO during the pandemic, and trying to maintain a working relationship with China while not avoiding criticisms about how it first handled the Coronavirus outbreak.

In all of these areas, one could add details about a range of changes to specific policies and practices. However, that would only underscore the fact that beneath the premature assertions that the Trump presidency is a failure, a narrative that began a mere month into his presidency,[69] this administration has been very busy. As *Atlantic Magazine*, no friend of the administration out it, "Trump Has Quietly Accomplished More Than It Appears."[70]

The question is: how do we understand Trump's many diverse initiatives in a variety of domestic and foreign policy areas? Are they really traditionally Republican or conservative after all? Are some, like his large infrastructure and immigration policy reform plans, more centrist and perhaps even a bit politically Democratic? And how are we to understand his unprecedented economic response to the pandemic that ignores decades of Republican economic orthodoxy?

Trump's Presidential Purpose: The Politics of American Restoration

All of Trump's diverse policy plans and initiatives share at their core one common purpose. I frame this core purpose as the *Politics of American Restoration*. That phrasing raises the obvious question: what exactly does President Trump want to restore? The answer put forward herein is this: Mr. Trump wants to restore an America where the premises of policies that have not worked as promised, or have become outdated are reviewed, revised, and if necessary, discarded. He wants to restore a confident "can do" spirit that helps America gets things done. He wants Americans to identify and act on a common and not parochial ethnic or racial identity interests—one core element of his *America First* rhetoric. And clearly, given the savage effects of the global pandemic, he wants to restore some sense of "normality" to American economic and ordinary life more generally. And he wants to reform the primary institutions both domestically (for example, the FBI and CDC) and internationally (for example, the WTO, WHO) that have an important impact on American economic and political life.

Above all, he wants to restore an America whose political leadership acts at all levels, but starting first with the president, to re-earn the trust of Americans by doing what he promised. That trust has been steadily lost over the last five decades by the political establishment. Indeed, a July 2019 poll found that 70% of Americans, an astounding number, say "they are angry at the nation's political and financial establishment."[71]

This last underlying presidential purpose is understandably somewhat ironic and surely paradoxical given the president's difficult relationship with political facts, formulations, interpretations, and rhetorical precision. How is it possible for the public to ever be able to trust this president when almost every word he says is subject to second guessing from official and self-appointed fact-checkers who always find his accuracy wanting—sometimes for good reason (see Chapter 10)? Trump is not betting his reelection on winning over the myriad "fact checkers" who find fault with his hyperbole and grasp of nuance; he is counting on something else.

President Trump is betting on his capacity to "deliver the goods," as he puts it in *The Art of the Deal*.[72] That now includes helping the country to weather the brutal consequences of the pandemic, and responding to bi-partisan wishes to reform some police practices.[73] He is betting that

1 BUILDING A THEORY OF DONALD TRUMP AND HIS PRESIDENCY 21

by doing so, he will be able to continue to change the basic policy narratives that have been the foundation of establishment-favored policies for decades. It is a large bet, but one entirely in keeping with Trump's lifelong level of ambition and risk taking.

President Trump in Political Time: A Reconstructive or Preemptive President?

President Trump's most basic presidential ambitions center around reversing the policies and assumptions that had resulted in decades of Americans feeling the country was moving in the wrong direction. To do so, he has pivoted away from what he considers to be the failed conventional policy wisdom of the last five decades. These include the view that unlimited immigration and limited enforcement of immigration laws has no downside, that low economic growth is the "new normal" and Americans should get used to it, that free trade is always a "win-win" for everyone, and that it is better not to insist on greater reciprocity abroad with American allies, or take a strong stance against adversaries.

These campaign positions were leadership signals, not coherent policies. They were meant to convey that Trump would be a different kind of president when it came to upholding and building on the conventional establishment policy consensus. And, he has been.

In almost four years in office Mr. Trump has angered his opponents with his domestic initiatives by: seriously enforcing immigration laws already passed by Congress and trying to stem immigration flows at the Southern border when Congress won't act; encouraging all forms of energy production including those involving coal, fracking, and offshore drilling; dramatically cutting back on regulatory burdens; reforming environmental policy regulations; encouraging educational reform in the form of school choice and charter schools; focusing on judicial appointments—not primarily from a left–right perspective, but from a philosophy of jurisprudence perspective emphasizing original intent and text; emphasizing policies that create jobs in America including plans for a very large set of infrastructure rebuilding initiatives; and most recently confronting China and American allies about their trade practices.

Internationally Trump has: withdrawn from the Transpacific Partnership Trade agreements and threatened to do so with NAFTA and the South Korean Trade Agreement; withdrawn from the Paris Climate Agreements; loosened the restraints on the use of military force against

ISIS (and other terrorist groups) that has helped to decimate them[74]; bombed Syria for crossing the red line he established about using chemical weapons—thereby reviving the important concept of reputation credibility[75]; revised existing treaty understandings with NATO allies leading to them spending more for their own defense[76] and focusing more on the threat of terror[77]—as Trump had insisted; putting new pressures on oppositional regimes like North Korea while opening up negotiations with them, Iran, and Syria; and cementing ties with traditional allies like Israel, Saudi Arabia, Japan, and India.

The point of this list is its existence, not its policy virtue. These policies, if they gain traction, may be successful or not. What is undeniable however, whatever their fate, is that they represent a substantial new set of policy departures.

President Trump's numerous policy and political initiatives in his first term in office make clear that he was very serious about revisiting, revising, and where he though necessary discarding the underlying policy architecture and accompanying narratives of the past several decades. In this quest, he clearly differs from Presidents Clinton (G.W.) Bush, and Obama who were all deeply establishment figures. Those three presidents were all generally versed in the policy narratives of their times and their parties. They all shared many policy premises even if they diverged on the specifics of the issues that arose from these core beliefs.

All three were ardent "free-traders." All three were ardent proponents of increased immigration. All three were ardent American internationalists and supported (Clinton and Obama more so and Bush somewhat less so), exercising American interests within the confines of international institutions. All three were, to varying degrees, supporters of expanding government's role to address a wide range of political, social, and economic issues, a form of a liberal domestic order. In short, they shared a number of core assumptions that formed a rough consensus underlying a basic establishment perspective. This is exactly the point at which candidate Trump parted company with them and almost every single one of the GOP's seventeen other candidates and certainly with the base and leadership of the Democratic Party.

President Trump in Political Time:
Reconstruction *or* Restoration?

In its ambitions, the Trump presidency clearly resembles, to use Stephen Skowronek's terms, a presidency of *reconstruction*.[78] That kind of presidency can take place when the "established regime and pre-established commitments of ideology and interest have, in the course of events, become vulnerable to direct repudiation as failed or irrelevant responses to the problems of the day," and further, that "there is a general political consensus that something fundamentally has gone wrong in the high affairs of state." This allows a president in these circumstances to attempt "the wholesale reconstruction of the standards of legitimate national government."

Yet, to date the reality of the Trump presidency is that it is, at present (again in Skowronek's terms) a *preemptive* presidency. Mr. Skowronek writes of these kinds of presidents that[79]:

> The distinctive thing about preemptive leaders is that they are not out to establish, uphold, or salvage any political orthodoxy. Theirs is an unabashedly mongrel politics. ...These leaders bid openly for a hybrid alternative. Their leadership stance provides them with considerable license to draw policy positions and political commitments from different sides of the issues of their day and to promote their recombination in a loosely synthesized mix.

This reads like a description of the Trump presidency. It seems clear that the iconoclastic disruptive presidency of Mr. Trump has moved the country into a new political time zone according to Skowronek's theory. Yet, it is unclear at this point exactly which political time zone that is. President Trump clearly aspires to have *reconstructive* presidency, but the most he has managed to date is to have a disruptive (*preemptive*) one. We take up the issue of how and under what circumstances President Trump could possibly emerge as a reconstructive leader, in Chapter 12.

This observation helps us to understand two key elements of the Trump presidency: why the opposition to Mr. Trump's presidency is so intense, and why Mr. Trump's fight-club presidency may be more politically consequential than simply a reflection of his psychology. In trying to move his presidency from *preemptive* to *reconstructive*, tough political fighting may not only be expected, but necessary. And if this is accurate, Mr. Trump's fight club presidency may not only be a matter of his psychology, which we argue it is, but of what he sees as a necessary political strategy.

Mr. Trump's Prospects for a Successful Presidency

Whether President Trump can survive the clear efforts by his many establishment and resistance enemies to checkmate his presidency or deny him reelection is unclear. Whether he can effectively politically harness his protean psychology to overcome those efforts is another. These two very basic questions lead to a third: can Mr. Trump have anything resembling a successful presidency?

The correct answer is: maybe. There was during Trump's first three years of office the ever- looming question of what, if anything, the Special Prosecutor looking into the Trump campaign's possible relationship to Russian interference in the 2016 presidential election would find. Anti-Trump opposition members hoped for the best, which in their view included clear evidence and formal charges of collusion with Russia to steal the election and evidence of obstruction of justice that could lead to successful articles of impeachment and Trump's removal by the Senate. In this they were sorely disappointed.[80]

President Trump, for his part, insisted that he has done absolutely nothing wrong and said that the accusation and investigations were partisan "witch hunts" designed to destroy the legitimacy of his presidency.[81] There is now evidence that he had a point.[82] In the end, the Mueller investigation provided no concrete evidence that Mr. Trump, or any of his senior advisors, colluded with Russian intelligence to influence the election.[83] NeverTrump opponents then put their hopes in the eighty-one current, ongoing Democratic House investigations of alleged administration wrongdoing,[84] with more new investigations being added by the week.[85] However, all of these together or individually were no more successful in providing a legitimate basis for removing Trump from office than the Mueller investigation did.[86]

Mr. Trump was still not "home free." He still faced and his to surmount an impeachment trial in the Senate passing on the two articles of impeachment voted on by the House along strict partisan lines. He also still faces public concern and scrutiny concerning his judgments and leadership in response to the medical and economic effects of the Coronavirus.[87] More recently he has faced a nation-wide convulsion of anger and revulsion in response to the video of police force that resulted in the death of an unarmed black man, George Lloyd, and the demonstrations both peaceful and violent that followed them. Critics have raised the question of whether it is possible to trust a president whom they have routinely and cavalierly branded as a racist, to address and help resolve the substantial racial disparities that effect the United States.

Mr. Trump's Home Alone Presidency

President Trump aspires to be, in Stephen Skowronek's terms, a reconstructive president. That is a rare accomplishment in American history, having happened only a few times during thankfully rare traumatic historical circumstances. Barack Obama was quite clear in his transformational intentions saying quite directly—"I want to transform this country."[88] Yet he failed to do so.

President Obama had two terms in which to set that transformation into motion, but was unable to consolidate that effort after losing control of Congress to the Republicans and a substantial number of American voters by presenting himself as a moderate and governing as a progressive. Those failed transformative efforts set the stage for Trump's 2016 election and his presidency has been aimed at dismantling both Obama's policies and their underlying presumptions.

In a highly politically divided, highly skewed partisan public, enacting policy much less policy and political transformation is a daunting task. President Trump is in an even worse position to accomplish transformation than was President Obama for several reasons including the pandemic. President Obama had his party almost fully united behind him and had the support of many traditional establishment institutions.

Trump does not have these resources available to him. He most certainly does not have the support of the news media and major civic organizations and institutions (see Chapter 3). And his circumstances for his first two years in office were not dramatically much better among many Republican leaders.

President Trump lacks a natural base of allies within the traditional leadership wings of the Republican Party, among conservatives, or within most major American civic institutions—of which the media is only the most obvious. He therefore occupies in some important respects a rather unique go-it-alone presidency that extensively relies on the executive powers of his office, and the force and resiliency of his own psychology, and ordinary Republicans.

Peggy Noonan captured President Trump's politically "home alone" dilemma in 2017 precisely[89]:

> Normally a new president has someone backing him up, someone publicly behind him. Mr. Obama had the mainstream media—the big broadcast networks, big newspapers, activists and intellectuals, pundits and columnists of the left—the whole shebang. He had a unified, passionate party. Mr. Trump in comparison has almost nothing. The mainstream legacy media oppose him, even hate him, and will not let up. The columnists, thinkers and magazines of the right were mostly NeverTrump; some came reluctantly to support him. His party is split or splitting. The new president has gradations of sympathy, respect or support from exactly one cable news channel, and some websites. He really has no one but those who voted for him.

Consider that last sentence for a moment; it is both striking and informative. It is striking because it is so unlike every other modern presidency, even Jimmy Carter whose "outsider" position seems to resemble Trump's circumstances, but really does not. It is informative because it provides one very clear explanation for why Mr. Trump's presidency faces such strong and effective headwinds. His own party's elected officials have been and remain to some degree ambivalent about his presidency, and act accordingly. Hence the president's tweeted complaint and lament that "Republicans, even some that were carried over the line on my back, do very little to protect their President."[90] That is true even though the post-2018 Senate is much more strongly pro-Trump than its 2016 predecessor. In a recent example, several Republican Senators joined Democrats in placing legal limits on Trump's ability to become involved in future military operations against Iran without Congressional approval.[91]

In the ordinary course of events Congressional members of the president's party do try to protect him both from opposition party critics and from legislative setbacks to his policies. That support is never unlimited—as Republicans' response to President Nixon's felonious behavior demonstrated. Nor does that support preclude more local focused reelection calculations by members of the president's party.

That said, it is rare to see the party in power take clear decisive public steps to limit their president's options as has happened with President Trump in several important areas.[92] Nor is it usual to have a senior senator of the President's party publicly rebuke the president's response

1 BUILDING A THEORY OF DONALD TRUMP AND HIS PRESIDENCY 27

to a controversial set of events (in Charlottesville), by saying, "The President has not yet been able to demonstrate the stability nor some of the competence that he needs to demonstrate in order to be successful."[93]

That criticism launched an ongoing public battle between President Trump and Senator Corker that spilled over into a very public fight when Senator Corker said that Trump's "Recklessness Threatens World War III," and then announced he would not seek reelection.[94] Republican Senator Jeff Flake publicly criticized President Trump while announcing that he too would not run for reelection.[95] In March of 2019, twelve Republican Senators joined their Democratic counterparts and voted against Trump's emergency declaration that allowed him to use 16.3 billion dollars in military funds to help build a Southern barrier.[96] More recently, a large number of House Republicans[97] have announced their retirements complicating Republican efforts to regain control of the House in 2020.

These Congressional actions and the public rebuke of Mr. Trump and his presidency by some senior members of his own party reflect a lack of confidence that President Trump will respect and adhere to the boundaries that they wish he would abide by—willful ignoring traditional covenants of presidential "decorum." Republicans in Congress are highly ambivalent about President Trump. He is increasingly a Republican president who does try to accomplish some traditional Republican goals—tax cuts, energy production, regulation reform, and staffing the courts with conservative judges.

On the other hand, he seems to some of them to be a mercurial policy maker whose specific views always seem to be in flux to some degree. Worse, from their standpoint, they are legitimately afraid that his rhetorical excesses and many public fights will scare away voters they might need for their elections and agendas. Trump remains extremely popular with ordinary Republicans and so there is a big risk in publicly opposing him—not the least of which is that he is not shy about picking fights with his party's leaders.

It is a tenuous base from which to become a successful reconstructive leader, but Mr. Trump has spent a lifetime overcoming expectations that it can't be done or he can't do it. This analysis honestly tries to addresses the Trump presidency fairly, but also seriously. One of the critically important reasons for doing so is found in an early profile of Trump on the campaign trail by a reporter for *Rolling Stone*—no supporter of his presidency, and worth quoting at some length[98]:

In all the hysteria, however, what's often missed are the qualities that brought Trump here. You don't do a fraction of what he's done in life—dominate New York real estate for decades, build the next grand Xanadus for the super-rich on the far shores of Dubai and Istanbul, run the prime-time ratings table for more than 10 years and earn a third (or sixth) fortune at it—without being immensely cunning and deft, a top-of-the-food chain killer. Over the course of 10 days and several close-in encounters, I got to peer behind the scrim of his bluster and self-mythos and get a very good look at the man. What I saw was enough to make me take him dead serious. If you're waiting for Trump to blow himself up in a Hindenburg of gaffes or hate speech, you're in for a long, cold fall and winter.

NOTES

1. Dan Balz. 2017. "Trump Governs as He Campaigned: Unconventionally and Unpredictably," *Washington Post*, April 28.
2. Karen Heller. 2018. "A President Unlike Any Other," *Washington Post*, January 19.
3. Nicholas Nassim. 2017. *The Black Swan: The Impact of the Highly Improbable*. New York: Random House.
4. Frank Bruno. 2016. "The Misery of the Mini-Trumps," *New York Times*, August 27.
5. Bobby Jindal. 2018. "A Look Ahead at the Post-Trump GOP," *Wall Street Journal*, July 31.
6. Peter Baker. 2019. "On Day 1,001, Trump Made It Clear: Being 'Presidential' Is Boring," *New York Times*, October 18.
7. Dan Balz. 2017. "Amid Distractions of His Own Creation, Trump Moves Swiftly to Change the Country Dramatically," *Washington Post*, January 28.
8. James David Barber. 1992. *The Presidential Character: Predicting Performance in the White House*, 4th ed. Englewood Cliffs, NJ: Prentice Hall.
9. Alexander L. George. 1974. "Review: Assessing Presidential Character," *World Politics*, Vol. 26, No. 2 (January), pp. 234–282.
10. Cf., Alexander L. George and Andrew Bennett. 2015. *Case Studies and Theory Development in the Social Sciences*. Cambridge, MA: MIT Press; see also Harry Eckstein. 2000. "Case Study and Theory in Political Science," in Roger Gomm, Martyn Hammersley, and Peter Foster (eds.), *Case Study Method: Key Issues, Key Texts*, Chapter 6. Newbury Park, CA: Sage.
11. Stanley Renshon. 1996. *The Psychological Assessment of Presidential Candidates*. New York: New York University Press, Chapter 8.
12. Steven J. Schier and Todd Eberly. 2017. *The Trump Presidency: Outsider in the Oval Office*. East Lanham, MD: Rowman & Littlefield.

13. Michael Nelson. 2018. *Trump's First Year*. Charlottesville, VA: University of Virginia Press.
14. Michael Nelson. 2019. *Trump: The First Two Years*. Charlottesville, VA: University of Virginia Press.
15. Balz 2017.
16. Donald J. Trump. 2020. "Remarks by President Trump in Meeting with African American Leaders," Cabinet Room, February 28. Donald Trump. 2020. "Remarks by President Trump, Vice President Pence, and Members of the Coronavirus Task Force in Press Conference," James S. Brady Press Briefing Room, February 27. Donald J. Trump. 2020. "Remarks by President Trump in Press Conference: Davos, Switzerland," January 22. Donald J. Trump. 2020. "Remarks by President Trump in State of the Union Address," U.S. Capital, November 4.
17. Scott Wilson. 2019. "Trump's Proposals to Tackle California Homelessness Face Local, Legal Obstacles," *Washington Post*, September 12.
18. Matt Zapotosky, Nick Miroff, and Ian Duncan. 2020. "U.S. Coronavirus Deaths Surge Past 4,600 as Officials Start to Compare Struggle with Italy's Outbreak," *Washington Post*, April 1.
19. Seung Min Kim. 2020. "In Historic Vote, Trump Acquitted of Impeachment Charges," *Washington Post*, February 5.
20. Jonathan Martin, Sheryl Gay Stolberg, and Alexander Burns. 2018. "Trump Policy Gyrations Threaten Fragile Republican Coalition," *New York Times*, December 21.
21. Annie Karni and Maggie Haberman. 2019. "Trump's Personal Assistant, Madeleine Westerhout, Steps Down," *New York Times*, August 29.
22. Daniel Victor. 2018. "Kids, Please Don't Read This Article on What Trump Said About Santa Claus," *New York Times*, December 25.
23. Stef W. Knight. 2017. "The Insane News Cycle of Trump's Presidency in 1 Chart," *Axios*, September 28; Jack Schaffer. 2018. "Drowning in News? Learn to Swim," *Politico*, March 12.
24. Mark Lander and Julie Hirschfeld Davis. 2018. "After Another Week of Chaos, Trump Repairs to Palm Beach: No One Knows What Comes Next," *New York Times*, March 23.
25. Jame Mason and James Oliphant. 2018. "White House Shakeup Shows Trump Tired of Hearing 'No' for an Answer," *Reuters*, March 13.
26. Peter Nicholas, Michael C. Bender, and Rebecca Ballhaus. 2018. "Trump Relishes Off-Script Approach," *Wall Street Journal*, March 23.
27. Dan Balz. 2018. "Trump's Bad Week: A Policy Rollback, a Political Setback and a Still-Defiant President," *Washington Post*, June 23.
28. Katie Rogers and Maggie Haberman. 2018. "Reliable Allies Refuse to Defend a President Content with Chaos," *New York Times*, December 21.

29. Dan Balz. 2018. "The Opening Act Was Tumultuous: Phase Two of Trump's Presidency Could Be Even More So," *Washington Post*, March 24.
30. David Brooks. 2018. "The Decline of Anti-Trumpism," *New York Times*, January 8.
31. Matthew Dallek. 2019. "In the Weeds," *Washington Post*, September 13.
32. Peter Baker. 2019. "Trump Orders Navy to Strip Medals from Prosecutors in War Crimes Trial," *New York Times*, July 31.
33. Mark Lander and Maggie Haberman. 2017. "Angry Trump Grilled His Generals About Troop Increase, Then Gave In," *New York Times*, August 21.
34. Maggie Haberman. 2017. "A Homebody Finds the Ultimate Home Office," *New York Times*, January 25.
35. Lauren Tuck. 2016. "Donald Trump Reportedly Treated Miss USA Contestants Like 'Property'," *Yahoo*, June 17; Liksa Belkin. 2015. "What's Up with Donald Trump and 'the Women'? Not What You Might Think," *Yahoo*, October 15.
36. Nick Timiraos. 2018. "While Trump Grumbles About Fed, His Picks Exude Pragmatism," *Wall Street Journal*, September 22.
37. Byron York. 2019. "From Former Trump Lawyer, Candid Talk About Mueller, Manafort, Sessions, Rosenstein, Collusion, Tweets, Privilege, and the Press," *Washington Examiner*, April 3.
38. Michael Gerson. 2016. "Dr. Jekyll and Mr. Hyde Are on Their Way to the White House," *Washington Post*, December 17.
39. Jenna Johnson. 2017. "Trump Brings Many Different Personas to Washington," *Washington Post*, January 20.
40. Walt Whitman, "Song of Myself (1892 Version)."
41. Michael Kranish. 2017. "A Fierce Will to Win Pushed Donald Trump to the Top," *Washington Post*, January 19.
42. FISA Judge Rosemary Collyer responding to a major IG report on the DOJ's application for surveillance found "troubling instances in which FBI personnel provided information" to the court "which was unsupported or contradicted by information in their possession." Collyer quoted in Editorial. 2019. "The FISA Judge Strikes Back," *Wall Street Journal*, December 17. See also Charles Savage. 2019. "Court Orders F.B.I. to Fix National Security Wiretaps After Damning Report," *New York Times*, December 17; United States Foreign Intelligence Surveillance Court. 2019. LeeAnn Flynn Hall, Clerk of Court. "In RE Accuracy Concerns Regarding Docket No. Misc. 19-02 FBI Matters Submitted to the FISC," Washington, DC, December 17. https://www.fisc.uscourts.gov/sites/def ault/files/MIsc%2019%2002%20191217.pdf.
43. Nancy Cook. 2019. "Forget the Oval: The Real Trump Action Is in the Residence," *Politico*, November 24.

1 BUILDING A THEORY OF DONALD TRUMP AND HIS PRESIDENCY   31

44. Beth Reinhard. 2019. "Alva Johnson, Former Campaign Staffer, Drops Lawsuit Accusing Trump of Kissing Her Without Her Consent," *Washington Post*, September 5.
45. I am indebted to Peter Suedfeld for this observation.
46. Marc Fisher and Michael Kranish. 2016. "The Trump We Saw: Populist, Frustrating, Naive, Wise, Forever on the Make, "*Washington Post*, August 12, p. 1.
47. Donald J. Trump [with Tony Schwartz]. 1987. *Trump: The Art of the Deal*. New York: Random House.
48. Candidate Donald Trump quoted in Noah Bierman. 2016. "A Testy Donald Trump Lashes Out at News Media and Says, 'I'm Not Changing'," *Los Angeles Times*, May 31.
49. Daniel Henninger. 2016. Trump's MAD," *Wall Street Journal*, June 1. Jeremy Herb. 2017. "Trump Hasn't Demonstrated the Stability or Competence to Be Successful," *CNN*, August 18.
50. Peggy Noonan. 2017. "President Trump Declares Independence," *Wall Street Journal*, January 20.
51. Peter Baker. 2019. "As Trump Swerves on Trade War, It's Whiplash for the Rest of the World," *New York Times*, August 27.
52. Michael Scherer and Zeke J. Miller. 2017. "TIME Exclusive: Donald Trump After Hours," *Time*, May 12.
53. Francis Stead Sellers. 2015. "Donald Trump, a Champion of Women? His Female Employees Think So," *Washington Post*, November 24.
54. Barbara A. Res. 2016. "Donald Trump, My Boss: The Billionaire Developer Gave Women Like Me a Chance, But He Also Leered at Attractive Employees and Only Let the Prettiest Secretaries Greet Guests and Serve Coffee," *New York Daily News*, February 9. See also Barbara A. Res. 2013. *All Alone on the 68th Floor: How One Woman Changed the Face of Construction*, 2nd ed. New York: CreateSpace Independent Publishing Platform and Jason M. Breslow. 2016. "The FRONTLINE Interview: Barbara Res," *PBS*, September 27.
55. Callie Wiser. 2016. "The FRONTLINE Interview: Louise Sunshine," *PBS* FrontLine, September 27.
56. Barbara Nelson. 2004. "Trump's Right Hand a Star in Own Right," *Real Estate Weekly*, August 4.
57. Jason Horowitz. 2017. "Back Channel to Trump: Loyal Aide in Trump Tower Acts as Gatekeeper," *New York Times*, March 27.
58. Emily Ward. 2019. "Trump Has More Women as Top Advisers Than Obama, Bush, or Clinton," *Washington Times*, March 22.
59. David A. Fahrenthold. 2016. "Trump Promised Millions to Charity: We Found Less Than $10,000 Over 7 years," *Washington Post*, June 28.
60. David A. Fahrenthold. 2016. "Trump Boasts About His Philanthropy: But His Giving Falls Short of His Words," *Washington Post*, October

29. The reporter's story directly implied that Mr. Trump pledged the money but did not give it until prodded to do so by his, and other reporters' questions. Mr. Trump called the accusation "nasty" and said his organization needed to vet charity recipients before sending checks.

61. Michael D'Antonio. 2015. "Donald Trump's Long Publicity Con," *Daily Beast*, November 28, p. 11.

62. William E. Geist. 1984. "The Expanding Empire of Donald Trump," *New York Times*, April 8.

63. Trump quoted in Michael D'Antonio. 2019. *Never Enough: Donald Trump and the Pursuit of Success*. New York: Thomas Dunne/St. Martin's Press, p. 264.

64. Rich Lowry. 2019. "There Are No Trump Mysteries," *Politico*, May 8.

65. Michael Kranish and Marc Fisher. 2019. *Trump Revealed: The Definitive Biography of the 45th President of the United States*. New York: Scribner, vii, emphasis added.

66. Cf. Heinz Kohut, MD. 1971. *The Analysis of the Self: A Systematic Approach to the Psychoanalytic Treatment of Narcissistic Personality Disorders*. New York: International University Press; Heinz Kohut, MD. 1977. *The Restoration of the Self*. New York: International University Press.

67. Cf. Otto Kernberg, MD. 1975. *Borderline Conditions and Pathological Narcissism*. New York: Jason Aronson, 1975; Otto Kernberg, MD. 1980. *Internal World and External Reality: Object Relations Theory Applied*. New York: Jason Aronson, p. 14.

68. Jeff Stein and Robert Costa 2020. "White House Readies Push to Slash Regulations as Major Part of Its Coronavirus Economic Recovery Plan," *Washington Post*, April 21.

69. Cf. Fareed Zakaria. 2017. "Trump Is Putting on a Great Circus, But What About His Promises?" *Washington Post*, February 16; see also Timothy Eagan. 2017. "One-Month Report Card," *New York Times*, February 17.

70. David A. Graham. 2017. "Trump Has Quietly Accomplished More Than It Appears," *The Atlantic*, August 2; see also more recently Delroy Murdock. 2017. "This Thanksgiving, Thank Donald J. Trump," *National Review*, November 23.

71. Carrie Dann. 2019. "'A Deep and Boiling Anger': NBC/WSJ Poll Finds a Pessimistic America Despite Current Economic Satisfaction," *ABC*, August 25.

72. Trump [with Schwartz] 1987.

73. Donald J. Trump. 2020e. "Remarks by President Trump at Signing of an Executive Order on Safe Policing for Safe Communities," *The White House*, June 16.

74. Max Boot. 2017. "The First Victory Over ISIS," *Commentary*, November 13.

75. Jonathan Renshon, Allan Dafoe, and Paul Huth. 2018. "Leader Influence and Reputation Formation in World Politics," *American Journal of Political Science*, Vol. 62, No. 2, pp. 325–339.
76. Julian Robinson. 2017. "NATO Allies—Excluding the US—Will Increase Defence Spending by 4.3% in Victory for Donald Trump After He Warned Member States 'Must Finally Contribute Their Fair Share'," *Daily Mail*, June 29.
77. Press conference. 2017. NATO Secretary General Jens Stoltenberg ahead of the meeting of NATO Defence Ministers, June 28.
78. Stephen Skowronek. 1977. *The Politics That Presidents Make: Leadership from John Adams to Bill Clinton*, revised ed. Cambridge, MA: Belknap Press, p. 36.
79. Skowronek 1977, p. 449.
80. Carrie Johnson. 2017. "Robert Mueller May Not Be the Savior the Anti-Trump Internet Is Hoping For," *NPR*, August 17.
81. Julie Hirschfeld Davis. 2017. "Trump Calls Congressional Inquiry a 'Witch Hunt'," *New York Times*, March 31.
82. *New York Times*. 2019. "Office of the Inspector General Report on the Russian Investigation." New York.
83. Cf., Conrad Black. 2017. "Disgraceful Charade Unfolds In Battle Over Evidence Twixt Mueller and Congress," *New York Sun*, October 11.
84. Alex Moe. 2019. "House Investigations of Trump and His Administration: The Full List," *NBC*, May 27.
85. Olicia Beavers. 2020. "Democrats to Plow Ahead with Trump Probes Post-Acquittal," *The Hill*, February 8.
86. Johnson 2017.
87. Matt Egan. 2020. "Coronavirus could cost Trump the election, Goldman Sachs Warns," *CNN Business*, February 27.
88. Obama quoted in Richard Wolffe. 2009. *Renegade: The Making of a President*. New York: Crown, p. 67; see also Stanley A. Renshon. 2012. "Foreign Policy Legacies of American Presidents," in Timothy J. Lynch (ed.), *Oxford Encyclopedia of American Military and Diplomatic History*, Chapter 4. Cambridge and New York: Oxford University Press.
89. Peggy Noonan. 2017. "President Trump Declares Independence," *Wall Street Journal*, January 20.
90. https://twitter.com/realDonaldTrump/status/889217183930351621.
91. Catie Edmondson. 2020. "In Bipartisan Bid to Restrain Trump, Senate Passes Iran War Powers Resolution," *New York Times*, February 13.
92. Cf., "On Thursday, before leaving on a month-long recess, the Senate set up a system to prevent the president from appointing senior administration officials to posts that require confirmation in the senator's absence." See Jennifer Steinhaur. 2020. "With Few Wins in Congress, Republicans Agree on Need to Agree," *New York Times,* August, 4; Aaron Blake.

2017. "Republicans Are Starting to Draw Red Lines on Trump Firing Sessions and Mueller," *Washington Post*, July 27; and Mike DeBonis and Karoun Demirjian. 2017. "House Passes Russia Sanctions Bill, Setting up Veto Dilemma for Trump," *Washington Post*, July 25.

93. Senator Corker (R-TN) quoted in Jeremy Herb. 2017. "Trump Hasn't Demonstrated the Stability or Competence to Be Successful," *CNN*, August 18.

94. Jonathan Martin and Mark Lander. 2017. "Bob Corker Says Trump's Recklessness Threatens World War III," *New York Times*, October 8.

95. Sheryl Gay Stolberg. 2017. "Jeff Flake, a Fierce Trump Critic, Will Not Seek Re-Election for Senate," *New York Times*, October 27.

96. Alexander Bolton. 2020. "12 Republican Senators Defy Trump on Emergency Declaration," *The Hill*, March 14.

97. Deidre Walsh. 2019. "GOP Retirements Spike, Diminishing Hope of Retaking House Majority in 2020," *NPR*, September 6.

98. Paul Solotaroff. 2015. "Trump Seriously: On the Trail with the GOP's Tough Guy," *Rolling Stone*, September 9.

CHAPTER 2

In the Eye of the Hurricane: Strategies for Analyzing the Trump Presidency

After a half century in the public eye, innumerable news stories and commentaries about him, a number of biographies and countless interviews, Trump remains a mystery, even to those who might be thought of as knowing him best. Ivanka Trump, was asked recently by a Trump biographer whether she had figured her ex-husband out. At first she answered "'Yea, I figured it out,' but then added 'Well, I really don't know'."[1] Liz Smith, a long-time Trump confidant and fixture on the *New York News* gossip scene says more bluntly, "I've known him forever and I still can't figure him out."[2] It may turn out to be true that, "Mr. Trump himself is a wild card, in some ways an incalculable president."[3]

Analyzing any president "at a distance," which to say relying on publicly available information, presents the researcher with a number of well-known issues. Chief among them are issues of evidence and its extensiveness, theoretical validity and reliability, and an array of evaluative concerns like politically saturated confirmation bias. These same issues apply in organizing information into explanatory categories, and from there attempting to develop theories of a president's psychology and leadership style. There is also in Trump's case, as noted, simply the enormous amount of information this presidency has generated. It is difficult to keep up with, much less to organize and then take a step back in order to analyze.

© The Author(s) 2020
S. Renshon, *The Real Psychology of the Trump Presidency*,
The Evolving American Presidency,
https://doi.org/10.1007/978-3-030-45391-6_2

This analysis argues that Mr. Trump's real psychology and presidency are capable of being understood, even if not precisely predicted. Yet to do so, one must be willing and able to dive into an ocean of information and misinformation while attempting find and make use of potential evidence that helps to build an accurate understanding of this complex, controversial man and presidency. These tasks must be accomplished while also being constantly buffeted by the raw emotions that Trump inspires. That requires engaging, as anyone writing about this president must, the fierce and more subtle anti-Trump narratives and memes that permeate analyses of this presidency.

Analyzing Trump's Presidential Leadership: Swimming Against the Narrative Tide

Most purported Trump analyses take the form of politically purposeful narratives, not real theories. A narrative is a motivated assembly of carefully selected and proffered facts along with their interpretation that seeks to convey a truth congenial for the purpose that the narrative was created to convey. A meme can be considered a mini-narrative with the same purpose and structure, only shorter. Narratives can be thought of as a kind of distorted pseudo-scholarship, memes their even less substantive imitation. Ubiquitous Trump buzzwords like "narcissistic" or "unfit" may be thought of as politicized terms that come with their own pre-packaged narratives and the associated memes that can serve as building blocks for them.

Narratives are not synonymous with reality and bear no a priori relationship with it. Indeed, narrative is to truth what Akira Kurosawa's movie classic masterpiece *Rashomon*[4] is to reality. Yet a narrative's purposeful assembly often for partisan purposes does not diminish its political power. As a recent anti-Trump article headline worried, "That is what Power Looks like: As Trump Prepares for 2020, Democrats Are Losing the Only Fight That Matters."[5] What is that fight? The fight is over commanding attention and thus being able to put your narrative front and center to the exclusion of others.

Fact-Checking the "Truth"

It is not the case that all the anti-Trump narratives and memes are wholly without any factual foundation, or that there is no truth whatsoever to them. Rather, very much like Trump's own use of "truthful hyperbole," there are factual elements in some of them, but they by no means provide "the truth, the whole truth, and nothing but the truth." Rather they provide a very carefully constructed version of a truth.

Consider the widely mocked point made by Trump advisor Kellyanne Conway about "alternative facts"[6] to which her *NBC Meet the Press* host Chuck Todd erroneously replied, "Look, alternative facts are not facts they're falsehoods." That is clearly incorrect. If, as Miss Conway clearly meant to covey, every set of circumstances has multiple facts connected with it, she is most assuredly right. The truth or falsity of any particular fact remains to be determined, but being part of a package of factual understandings does not *ipso facto* make any specific element false. Nor does it make it true.

In the social sciences and political, economic, and cultural life no single fact is, by itself, dispositive. The current craze for fact-checks (see Chapter 10) will not rescue them from this reality. Facts don't speak for themselves. Fact check compilers purposefully assemble some facts, and their interpretation into narratives. Those facts do not speak for themselves so much as retell a story that is dependent on what "facts" are or not used, the views of the "experts" called upon to explain them, or the stance of the institutions that fund or support the efforts.

The same is true of many news reports and certainly viewpoint analyses. Anti-Trump narratives and memes often proclaim the centrality of one, or a few, isolated factual elements of dubious relevance or validity, and draw direst implications from them for the Trump presidency. So, for example, it is frequently asserted that Trump is "authoritarian" or has an "authoritarian streak." It is rarely clear just what this means. Does it reflect his preference for forceful statements? Does it reflect his preferences to get his own way on core policy matters like building an effective physical barrier at the Southern border? Is it his tendency, as is the case with the physical barrier, to keep trying to gain policy traction even when he suffers setbacks, and keep at it until he makes some progress?

A fair-minded deconstruction of a "Trump fact," would ask if there were other possibly relevant facts. Analysis of "Trump facts" would be furthered by having more context or considering alternative explanations. Many checks fact are, in reality, continuations of policy debates by another name. The recent *Washington Post* fact check of Trump's 2020 SOTU address began by noting that it "was chock-full of stretched facts and dubious figures."[7] Trump's penchant for hyperbole ("The best economy in our history") lends itself to easy debunking,[8] without acknowledging the various metrics by which the economy could be judged, and professional debate on them—in addition to the actual figures.

The fact check criticizes Trump for claiming credit for gains "begun in the Obama administration." Fair enough. Yet that eludes answering the question of whose policies were more associated with those developments. When Trump says: "Thanks to our bold regulatory reduction campaign, the United States has become the number one producer of oil and natural gas in the world, by far," the check fact criticizes that by saying "The notion that a revolution in energy began under the Trump administration is wrong." In the criticized quote Trump doesn't say that he "began" the energy revolution; he simply touts his presidency's contribution to that development.

When Trump mentions "gaining 12,000 new factories," the check fact replies that "'Factories' conjures up images of smokestacks and production lines, but the data set Trump cited is not really about factories." It notes in criticism, "But more than 80 percent of these 'manufacturing establishments' employ five or fewer people." Is Trump's number accurate though? Yes; the fact check notes that, "The data show that United States gained nearly 12,000 additional 'manufacturing establishments' between the first quarter of 2017 through the second quarter of 2019." So Trump's data were accurate. They simply didn't comport with the fact checker's view of how one ought to think of a "real factory."

Or consider Trump's statement: "Forty million American families have an average $2,200 extra thanks to our child tax credit." The *WP* fact check responds: "This is an example of Trump using correct numbers, *but* he gives too much credit to himself and his Republican colleagues" (emphasis added). That "but" signals we are about to leave factual assessment for political debates about the allocation of credit. All of these kinds of disagreements go in the *Post*'s widely publicized list of Trump's "false and misleading claims." Note: not false *or* misleading, but both false *and* misleading.

Some will be surprised to find that we are not on inviolate factual grounds if we depend on patterns of facts assembled with legitimate social science techniques like survey research. In reality, those techniques still contain areas in which researchers' choices and interpretations make a difference. As a result, while these "objective" measures do have legitimacy, they do not merit unlimited claims to accuracy and validity. We see evidence of this, analyzed in Chapter 10, in connection with efforts to portray Trump supporters as being suffused with "Racial Resentment."

Given that there are no single dispositive facts to resolve social and political debates, the focus on finding real understanding and some substantial degree of truth value, lie more in the overall integrity of the proofs than in the individual facts presented. The question then is not only is this fact "true" or challenged by deficiencies of one form or another. The real issue of truth value turns on which facts are assembled and which left out, how fairly the facts are presented, how they are characterized or mischaracterized, the weight of evidence either way, and the alternative formulations that were considered and evaluated.

The Downside of Politically Constructed Narratives and Memes: Misdirected Analysis

Mr. Trump apparently watches more political news and commentary shows than any other modern president. Leave aside momentarily, the characterization that he is "addicted" to doing so. That raises the specter of uncontrolled or uncontrollable impulses for which no evidence is presented. It is clear that he does watch news and commentary shows and gains some sense of the American political pulse from doing so. Yet, there are other benefits to these streams of political information gathering. Consider Mr. Trump's self-appointed role as "narrator-in-chief."

The *Washington Post* headline, "The narrator in chief: Trump opines on the 2020 Democrats—and so much more" captures something important about Trump's presidential leadership.[9] Trump has not only become the center of his presidency, as has been the case for almost all other modern presidents. The president has also made himself the public center of commentary and analysis of his presidency to an unprecedented degree.

This is a unique presidential role and it has provided enormous amounts of Trump commentary. What the president thinks on any given matter is rarely a secret. Trump also uses his unique vantage point for self-defense. It might be Trump defending himself for days[10] over what others termed an erroneous inclusion of Alabama in a hurricane warning.[11] Or it could entail Trump calling presidential attention to a *Washington Post* story on his administration's "lost opportunities" during the summer[12] that failed to mention twenty-two other summer initiatives that the administration could reasonably count as "successes."[13] The point here is that in these, and too numerous to count other examples,

Trump has emerged as the most highly visible and vociferous defender of his own presidency. This is no strategic accident. There is no end or any limits to the accusations that are made against the president and his administration. In response, Trump has a choice. He can allow the many thousands of accusations, many quite ugly, to go unanswered, accumulate, and in so doing acquire some standing as "truth." Or, take them on as they come, providing a counter narrative and perspective and in so doing deprive them of uncontested claims to be true. Trump and his opposition detractors are locked into a rhetorical arms race.

It is easy to shoehorn this observation into a "Trump is narcissistic," or "Trump has a thin skin," or likes to fight narratives and their associated memes. Yet, doing so misses an important element of its purpose. In a 24/7 rapid-fire news world filled with daily crescendos of often savage anti-Trump narratives and memes, traditional responses to this kind of onslaught would be too little, too late, and too ineffective as counterweights. Trump's tweets have their downsides (see Chapter 10), but they, along with his unusual availability for non-formal press conference like venues, allow Trump to counter his attackers in real time. That is duly reported by the press that repeats and thus extends Trump's counterpoints and claims.

Consider the numerous critical news reports and commentary that appeared,[14] prematurely as it turned out, as President Trump threatened Mexico with tariffs if they didn't provide more help to the United States to stem the tide of migrants passing through their country. A number of analyses immediately appeared that argued "nothing new here."[15] One anti-Trump pundit, Daniel Drezner, complimented himself in print on his own expertise,[16] and went on to say in a typical observation, "Despite the threat of tariffs, however, it appears that Mexico agreed to little more than moves it had already agreed to in previous rounds of negotiations." Subsequent events showed that these instant analyses were wrong.[17]

The anti-Trump memes and narratives and the news stories written with them in mind are meant to counter, delay, and delegitimize Trump's presidency. Trump has pushed back, repeatedly and hard against many of them, at a minimum not allowing them to stand uncontested. The result is a fight-club presidency (see Chapter 4) that is difficult for many people, even those who support his policies, to bear. It is an open question whether Trump's presidential results can overcome Americans' desire for political peace.[18]

TRUMP AND CONSPIRACY THEORIES

Critics say Trump is a president who "needs conspiracy theories."[19] Why? Critics say, "These baseless theories are a way for Trump to explain away his problems and undercut opponents. Beyond that, though, they seem to serve distinct emotional needs, feeding a narcissistic ego that cold reality won't satisfy." In short, Trump conjures up conspiracies to buttress his fragile ego because of his narcissistic pathology.

Before examining these claims (see Chapter 6) it is perhaps best to start with the definition and nature of conspiracies. One useful definition is, "A secret plan by a group to do something unlawful or harmful."[20] An important and related, but not synonymous question is whether a conspiracy allegation is either true, false, or something in between. As it turns out, it is not as easy as one might think to place a belief or conviction into one or another of these categories.

Illegals Voting?

First, conspiracy thinking can be distinguished from beliefs that according to almost all available evidence are factually wrong. Trump's repeated assertion that millions of people voted illegally in the 2016 presidential elections, is one of those claims for which the term "debunked" seems well suited.[21] It is based on what can only be accurately labeled as speculation even given the equivocal accuracy of many voter rolls.[22] The Pew Foundation estimated that[23]: "Approximately 24 million—one of every eight—voter registrations in the United States are no longer valid or are significantly inaccurate; More than 1.8 million deceased individuals are listed as voters; Approximately 2.75 million people have registrations in more than one state." It is, of course, quite a factual distance to travel in order to use those numbers as the basis for any specific claim of illegal voting. However, Trump's illegal voter claim is not a conspiracy claim because it involves no coordinated effort on the part of a group.

Trump and "Birtherism"

There are other more clearly conspiratorial Trump claims. There is his association with "Birtherism." That is the idea, in its various forms, that President Obama was not an American citizen and thus ineligible to be president or that he was not a "real" American—a claim that rests on his attributed Muslim religion or the time during his "formative years" that he had spent living out of the country. These are, in their various forms bona fide conspiracy theories, and Trump did push them by repeatedly asking Obama to produce his long-form birth certificate—which he eventually did. Trump could then claim he was only asking for documentation because "questions had been raised."

Why did Trump push getting Obama's long-form birth certificate from State Hawaiian officials? The go-to explanation on the left was Trump's racism.[24] However, the most reasonable and direct answer is that Trump pushed getting the documentation for pure political calculation reasons.

At the time that the "birther" allegations were making the rounds on both pro-Hillary[25] and conservative anti-Obama sites,[26] Trump was gearing up to seriously consider making a presidential run. He knew he had little standing or few allies among ordinary Republicans of conservatives and was looking to gain some traction, somewhere. The out of the mainstream conservative fringes were a starting point. His efforts signaled that he wasn't afraid to be associated with raising fringe questions. However, he did so in a way that did not allow him to claim some higher ground. After all, he was only looking for evidence to answer public questions. Trump could also then claim some legitimacy and success as Obama did eventually release the long-form of his birth certificate in response to repeated inquiries.

Did Trump actually believe that Obama was not born in the United States? Did he believe it was true, or perhaps just a possibility? That's a hard question to answer one way or another. It's fair to say that he clearly entertained the idea, and that his own political calculations were part of his thinking in going public with them.

Spying on the Trump Administration?

We are on much more solid evidentiary ground in asking whether Trump really believes some of the other things that critics routinely label as "debunked" conspiracy theories. Peter Nicholas' broadside against Trump's conspiracy theorizing noted above, mentions several. Among them he includes that (emphasis in original): "*Barack Obama himself might have ordered spies to infiltrate Trump's campaign. Thousands of Never Trumpers have been plotting against him since he took office.*"

Nicholas was writing in late 2019. He was aware of the unfolding evidence regarding unprofessional and possibly illegal behavior at the top levels of the FBI. That evidence concerned the defective applications for surveillance of Trump administration personnel to the nation's FISA court. That court issued "a highly unusual public rebuke of the FBI for mistakes,"[27] after having been misled into granting several such applications. Before the Justice Department Report on the FBI's failures, Trump complained that his administration had been "spied on," and that assertion was considered a "false claim" even though it was clearly true. The question of whether there was an illegal coordinated attempt behind the numerous "errors" cited in the Inspector's General's Report, in effect a conspiracy in the ordinary legal sense of that term, is now the subject of a major DOJ investigation conducted by US Attorney John Durham.[28]

Before the Inspector General's inquiry about the FISA court applications and the FISA Court's public rebuke of the FBI for having misled it in seeking warrants to spy on Trump administration personnel, there was no public evidence to fairly judge Trump's spying claims. There is now, and it is not easily dismissed. Trump's claim that, as Peter Nicholas put it, "*Barack Obama himself might have ordered spies to infiltrate Trump's campaign*" was quickly, but somewhat prematurely, dismissed as "false." It was not.[29]

About Those NeverTrump Plots Against the President and His Administration

Nichols lists the idea that "*Thousands of Never Trumpers have been plotting against him since he took office*" as one of the many false conspiracy theories that Trump espouses. This is a surprising assertion given that his article was published on November 29, 2019 and there was substantial evidence before it was published that his assertion was just plain wrong. The author should have known it.

The widely discussed *New York Times* op-ed by Anonymous, a senior administration official who was staying in place to thwart the administration, was published on September 5, 2008. Bob Woodward's book *Fear: Trump in the White House*, which detailed senior administration officials removing documents from Trump's desk so he would forget about them and not further implement his policies was published on September 11, 2018. As documented in Chapter 3, there were also numerous efforts across the political landscape, at all levels of government, by civic, news, and other organizations, of both a personal and official nature to retard, sabotage, and delegitimize the Trump presidency.

The overwhelming publicly available evidence is that individuals and institutions who were opposed to Trump did try to cripple his presidency and drive him out of office. Was it a secret conspiracy? No. It was actually quite public and reported at the time. Was it a coordinated effort? Not directly, although each effort that has been publicly detailed sprang from the same premises, that Trump is dangerous, bad, pathological, etc. and must be stopped. Were those involved in such efforts in touch with each other? In a number of documented cases, yes. In general, no. They didn't need to be. They all knew the views they shared and their commitments. How those would play out depended on individual circumstances and institutions. As noted in Chapter 3, no "deep state" was needed as a central organizing entity.

One is reminded here of the old psychological joke; just because you're paranoid, it doesn't mean they aren't out to get you. Trump has said of himself that he is not a trusting person. Given the competitive nature of his business career and the levels of ambition and wealth at which he operated, one would have to be careful in operating on the basis of being trusting. Trump could not assume, and didn't, that others outside of his family had his best interests at heart. Trump was used to being laughed at in business and politics. He was used to having others constantly trying to best him in business or politics. He was very used to people wanting something from him because he is rich and powerful. This left Trump with the feeling that real friends were few and he had to protect himself.

After almost four years of relentless opposition, with more on the horizon even after his acquittal on impeachment charges,[30] Trump could understandably think that many people were out to get him. A number of people were and are. This is less a conspiracy theory than just a plain fact.

Analyzing Trump: Beyond Single Explanations and Caricature

The Trump presidency cannot be well analyzed without taking into account the strong emotional and political currents that have arisen in response to his election. These strong currents distort much of the commentary and analysis surrounding the Trump presidency. Into this political and emotional maelstrom, any analyst enters with care.

Defending Trump?

A major problem with much of what is written about Trump and his presidency is not only that it is biased and reductionist, but also often just plain wrong. Such analyses are simply unreliable guides to understanding the real man and his purposes. Fair-minded efforts to clear a path "through the tangle of…underbrush that impedes more and better inquiry,"[31] to use Fred Greenstein's felicitous phrasing, are sorely needed.

It is clear that many characterizations of Mr. Trump are overly broad and deeply flawed. In practice this means characterizations that are substantively narrow and evidentiary shallow. Critics for example, emphasize Trump's "pathological narcissism," while not mentioning or analyzing the possible impact of "ordinary" narcissism. Trump critiques frequently take the form of beginning with explanatory conclusions and adding a preferred fact or two that support the premises with which the author began. Or, it can entail listing single sentence litanies of policies with which the person disapproves as evidence for the conclusion with which they began. Other facts, or alternative explanations that contradict a preferred formulation are simply not mentioned or engaged. In so doing, one avoids the need to weigh the different strands of evidence and, where necessary, modify the formulations.

Any attempt at fair minded analysis, given the amount of misinformation and strong anti-Trump feelings, must examine and where necessary challenge the many shallow efforts to disparage and delegitimize Trump and his presidency. Putting forward in their place more substantive grounded formulations will seem to many Trump critics to be "defending" or "normalizing" Trump and his presidency. That is not their purpose.

Utilizing a wider array of information and understandings creates a rather large "correcting the record" dilemma for any analysis that seeks to be scholarly, in the general understanding of that word. Considering a *range* of data and not only the information that supports the point of view that you begin with will, of necessity, involve some revisionism. Such an analysis may result in changing an established, but incorrect understanding of Mr. Trump.

Much of the conventional wisdom regarding Mr. Trump is substantive, conceptually, theoretically, and evidentially weak. The purpose of this book is to provide a fuller, fairer, more substantive, theoretically and factually grounded portrait of Mr. Trump and his presidency. That will require some revision to Trump-related conventional wisdom. That could easily result in accusations that such analysis is an effort to defend the indefensible. That is not the purpose of this analysis. It is important to be clear that the analysis that follows is not meant to convey the author's personal approval of the president or his presidency.

That said, there is no escaping the "correcting the record" consequences of examining a wider range for data and information than has been ordinarily examined in trying to analyze and understand the Trump presidency. There are several clear examples below of the ways in which narrow, often erroneous views of this president and the evidence to support them lead us astray. So, for example, it does matter that there is little documented evidence that Trump's father repeatedly told him he had to be a "killer." It does matter that Trump's father did repeatedly tell him it was important to "love what you do." The latter is almost never reported. That doesn't keep Trump critics from using the poorly documented and often asserted "killer" factoid to make an erroneous point about Mr. Trump's character and as an explanation for the derogatory characterizations that critics wish to make.

Later in this analysis (Chapter 6), we examine the issue of Mr. Trump's narcissism, which is certainly a psychological fact. The question is not whether Mr. Trump has narcissistic elements in his psychology, he obviously does, but rather their nature. Are they a reflection of "ordinary narcissism," or of the much more troubling variety of "malignant narcissism," posited by so many Trump critics?

In order to try and answer that crucial question, one needs to examine whether Trump displays the characteristics of the more "malignant" type—for example, lacking any semblance of empathy or the ability to express care or concern for other people (see Chapter 8 for an examination these particular elements). There is and this analysis presents evidence that this is factually not the case. What then is an analyst to do? If you present that counter evidence, you are certainly "correcting the record" and undercutting a dominant narrative, e.g., Trump is a dangerous, sociopathic "malignant narcissist."[32] Such an analysis might easily be construed as "normalizing" what critics see as an "abnormal" Mr. Trump, and it may. It might also be humanizing him as well, and that too is anathema to Trump critics. However, these are not legitimate reasons to avoid more substantive based and accurate analysis.

Mr. Trump is a complex man, not a one-dimensional evil, pathological stick figure. Yet, Mr. Trump's brash argumentative hyperbole can be off-putting to any moderate. His egregious generalizations about Mexicans that began his campaign would make any fair-minded person wince, even if the generalization contained some amount of factual accuracy. Illegal aliens do commit serious felonies. Trump's caustic comments about John McCain and preferring military personnel who didn't get captured was an ugly personal insult against a man who served his country honorably and heroically during the Vietnam War regardless of the enmity that developed later between those two men on policy grounds.

On the other hand, his response to the many people like Democratic Representative John Lewis who publicly called Trump's presidency illegitimate was another matter. Trump responded with understandable anger to Khizr Khan, the "Gold Star" father of a soldier killed in battle, who publicly attacked Trump in front of millions of viewers at the Democratic national convention. Trump's gratuitous swipe at Kahn's wife was not so understandable, except as an example of Trump's inability to restrain himself when he should and his susceptibility to stereotypes,[33] some of which are not devoid of small elements of accuracy.

Still, we can ask, what kind of response is "normal" or reflects established norms of "presidential demeanor" when the former head of the CIA calls the president's behavior at a Soviet–US press conference "nothing short of treasonous"?[34] What is the normal response when the accusation is boldly asserted in a *New York Times* opinion column calling Trump a "Treasonous Traitor"?[35] And what is the normal response when another Pulitzer Prize *New York Times* columnist informs us about Trump that, "There is the Smell of Treason in the Air,"[36] and the much lauded senior professor of international studies at Johns Hopkins, Eliot Cohen, tweets his apparent agreement.[37]

Not fighting back when you, and your family are personally, publicly, and repeatedly attacked with those kinds of ugly and factually unsupported accusations has political costs and consequences. It also carries enormous costs for one's sense of personal integrity and sense of self. What kind of husband, whether he is president or not, remains silent in the face of public accusations that his wife was a prostitute?[38] Analyzing those costs and consequences, including the benefits of fighting back is neither to condone or support the general response (and certainly not each instance of it), but to understand them, and in doing so make better sense of Mr. Trump's psychology and presidency.

On the Nature of Trump Evidence: Q & As, Interviews, Reported Quotes

Revealing or informative quotations from principals are a cornerstone of biographical analysis, and of the kind of political and psychological framework employed herein. Such data comes in many forms for President Trump—in set speeches and ad hoc rally remarks, an unprecedented number of media interviews—both historical and contemporary, and interviews conducted with others over the decades that have some bearing on Mr. Trump's thinking or behavior. It is a large body of data, but of unequal quality. Some of it is useful, some of it is poor, and of some of it is useless.

Interviewing the President: Two Informative Examples

The number of Trump interviews now easily runs into four and perhaps five figures. The most important for a project like this are extended interviews, accompanied by transcripts, that press Mr. Trump not only to comment on current or past events, but that also explore his thinking about them. Often these interviews are written up as news stores or analyses and it is at that point that a reporter's own Trump narratives and memes sometimes enter into the analysis. For that reason, it is preferable for the researcher to read the Q&A transcripts and come to his or her own conclusions.

Still, there are lessons to be learned from the work of seasoned Trump interviewers. One of a seasoned team of *New York Times* reporters who interviewed Trump a number of times had this to say about those interviews[39]:

> With other presidents, we sometimes struggled to find nuggets of news in an interview; with Mr. Trump we were overwhelmed...
>
> I have now interviewed seven presidents some in office, some after they left office and with Mr. Trump the experience is strikingly different in almost every respect...
>
> Clearly he was conscious that some things would be problematic if quoted, so it is fair to conclude that the provocative things he said on the record were intentionally so...
>
> Unlike with other presidents, though, there was no need to knock him off the script. *He happily answered every question we asked, even if it would*

ultimately overshadow the designated messages of the day in this case health care and made-in-America economics...

With Mr. Trump, the conversation is more rat-a-tat. He doesn't mind if you interject. But he tends to veer wildly from thought to thought, moving on before you've fully explored what he just said. For all the troubles of his presidency...we found him in a relaxed, upbeat mood. There was none of the fiery media bashing that marks his public appearances. Is that, then, shtick to fire up the base, or genuine grievance? Probably a measure of both.

Another particularly useful example of this kind of data are the twenty-five interviews with Trump and others important in his personal and work life at various times (with twenty hours of interviews with Trump alone), conducted by *Washington Post* reporters for the newspaper's Trump book. These are archived and publicly available.[40] These kinds of interviews are very useful because the reporters are well informed about Trump's life and the interviews are long enough for many follow up questions.

The *Washington Post* reporters also had an important core purpose to their interviews. Their paper was extremely unlikely to endorse Trump. So "the only value of the interview was to see if the editors and columnists could press Trump on his more extreme statements and test whether he really knew his stuff."[41] What they found and concluded is worth noting. They "emerged thinking that they had seen the genuine Trump—a man certain of his views, hugely confident in his abilities, not terribly well informed, quick to take offense, and authentically perplexed by suspicions that he had motives other than making America great again."[42]

In short, they found a man and president much more complex than his caricatures, yet not entirely unconnected to observations associated with some of his critics' reasonable concerns.

On the Nature of Trump Evidence-Events Data

This analysis makes abundant use of events data. Like other forms of evidence used herein, news reports, interviews and Q&A's, they are used purposefully and clearly footnoted. Why? Given the controversial nature of the Trump presidency and the fact that almost everything he or his administration says or does is subject to debate and often dispute, it is especially important for any Trump analysis to provide copiously referenced source data so that the reader may draw their own judgments about the evidence.

These data are single and multiple cross-checked news reports and other contemporaneous accounts of Trump's policy and political choices and his own expressed understanding of his actions in interviews. They include a concentrated focus on the unusually large number of Mr. Trump's own commentaries on his presidency, themselves primary data, given in numerous interviews, off the cuff remarks and more formal presentations. We pay close attention as well to the many well documented instances of administration choices and initiatives.

Clearly no scholar can afford to take every statement that Mr. Trump makes at face value. His consistent use of "truthful hyperbole,"[43] coupled with his meandering thinking and speaking style that we analyze in Chapter 10, requires caution and attention. On the other hand, a careful examination of Trump's Q&A exchanges with knowledgeable and often critical interviewers like those of the *Washington Post*[44] and the *New York Times*[45] (among others) provide often surprising insights into Mr. Trump's thinking, about himself and his presidency.

Clearly, not only must Mr. Trump's interviews be cross-checked with other interviews, but also with the actual actions of the president and his administration. And these events data must not only be cross-checked by examining multiple events accounts, they must also be cross-checked against Mr. Trump's many and sometimes conflicting observations about and explanations of them. Only by doing so will it be possible to uncover and substantiate the patterns that will allow us to make tentative theoretical formations about Mr. Trump and his presidency.

One reason to use events data is to document that a particular event, or set of events occurred. For a president as controversial as Mr. Trump where even the most basic facts are often in dispute or politicized, this allows readers to examine the sources of evidence used herein and, again, reach their own conclusions. However, the point is not only to provide readers with a factual touchstone for some elements of the analysis. Nor is it to provide a description of all the newsworthy events that have taken place during the first four years of Trump presidency. These data are also used as a base from which to draw some clear theoretical elements of Trump's presidential leadership and performance and examine their development over time including the decades before he became president.

Many of the events data used herein follow the same set of events over time. That often allows some clarification that reframes and leads to a better understanding. For example, it was widely reported that French President Macron's invitation to Iranian Foreign Minister Mohammad

Javad Zarif to join the G-7 Summit in Biarritz, France was a public slap to the president. It produced a headline—"Iran's Zarif makes surprise trip to G-7, catching Trump off-guard,"[46] that became a meme—that resulted in another mistaken headline, "Trump finds himself on his heels and fumbling at G-7."[47]

The reality was quite different. At his joint press conference with President Trump, President Macron had this to say: "So we coordinated our efforts and we reached the decision to bring together the foreign ministers—the Foreign Minister of Iran, who had a meeting with the French Foreign Minister. So I informed, before making it [the invitation]—I informed President Trump that it was my idea."[48]

It would have been an extreme and public provocation to a president who doesn't respond quietly to being disrespected to have sprung the Iranian Foreign Minister's visit on Mr. Trump. And for what possible purpose? Mr. Macron is already the titular de facto leader of the establishment G-7 group. Following that story over time not only provided correction to a set of mistaken first impressions and memes, it provided some insight into the real relationship Trump has with a major allied leader.

Sometimes following an important story over a long period of time is essential as well as informative. Consider the "trade war" between China and the United States that has unfolded over several years of the Trump presidency. It is a direct policy descendent of trade complaints Trump has publicly expressed for decades (then with Japan in the leading culprit role). At one level, events in this category give a set of observations about US–China economic relations. At another level, it is a set of observations about adjusting the changing strategic international relationships between two major world powers. At yet another level, they provide a set of observations about Trump's maximum pressure leadership strategies that are also on display with Iran, Mexico, and Guatemala on immigration, and Democrats more generally as a counter to their numerous congressional probes.

Following those trade negotiations more closely provides data on Trump's persistence, his willingness and ability to stand apart from the economic anxieties and criticisms that the fight produces, including some among his own supporters (e.g., farmers),[49] and some information on his long vs short term perspective. Along the way, one can learn a great deal about the complex nature and variable impacts of tariffs. One can then better understand to what degree, and under what circumstances they represent a real "tax" on American consumers (that varies).[50] And a focus on these kinds of issues over time, also allows consideration of the relative value of weighting them primarily as an economic issue or whether there are other frames of analysis that need to be also taken into account (national security being one; trade fairness and reciprocity issues being another).

The tariff issues discussed above are emblematic of the many different kinds of issues that someone writing about the Trump presidency must analyze. Trying to do so conscientiously does not turn a political scientist or psychoanalyst into a trained economist. It does however, allow that person to be better able to understand what's at stake in this important Trump presidency issue.

Events data are not, of course, synonymous with "the literature"— that body of professional evidence and debate that informs analysis of particular theoretical or empirical questions. The dilemma for a psychologically-minded Trump analyst is that his presidency is so distinctive and controversial, the theoretical characterization about him so often narrow and partisan as we detail in this chapter, and the understanding of presidential psychology so rudimentary[51] that any appeals to the "literature" are in danger of being unsuitably derivative, premature, and counterproductive.

This analysis does make use of the literature—on narcissism, on presidential time, on racial resentment theory as appropriate. Yet, in many important aspects of the Trump presidency—for example, his fight club mentality, there is no precedent and thus no literature. As noted in Chapter 1, the primary "literature" available for an analysis of the Trump presidency is the enormous wealth of data generated by the Trump presidency itself. This analysis uses existing professional literature when it can, but works to develop new Trump presidency-based literature where necessary.

Varieties of Anti-Trump Analysis

Anyone who spends much time trying to analyze the Trump presidency inevitably, unavoidably, and repeatedly comes into contact with anti-Trump analysis. Sometimes that bias is subtle. Frequently, it is overt. Most often it is obvious.

One question for a researcher is what to do about it. It would be relatively easy to write the equivalent of the twenty-four volumes of Freud's

Standard Edition[52] devoted to errors of Trump reporting. That is a waste of time and purpose here. Yet, it is worthwhile and sometimes necessary to provide some illustrations in areas that have an impact on the analysis that follows.

Correcting the Biographical Record

There are by now a number of biographical treatments of Trump and they can be arrayed on a continuum from useful to awful. Among the most useful are Jerome Tuccille's,[53] and Gwenda Blair's,[54] although she emerged as a willing participant in a gathering of anti-Trump biographers for an extended round robin of Trump bashing.[55] *The Washington Post* biography is also extremely useful,[56] and contains little of the anti-Trump slanted reporting of the newspaper. Its online transcriptions of Trump and Trump related interviews, already noted, are a treasure trove of Trump primary data.

Timothy O'Brien's original Trump biography contained none of the author's post publication anti-Trump writings and harsh criticisms of those who support him[57] at least before the paperback reissue of his book with a new stridently anti-Trump introduction,[58] and is therefore also useful. It is especially so on Trump's net worth debate and on Trump's bankruptcies, though at points it loses substance as it strains to be amusing[59]—which, admittedly, it sometimes is.

Others Trump biographies are simply awful.

One intensely anti-Trump biographer recently published a psychiatric diatribe whose book structure can be summarized as devoting one chapter each to a list of Trump pathologies. His list of Trump traits to be covered include[60]:

Narcissist. Liar. Racist. Sexist. Adulterer. Baby. Hypocrite. Chiseler. Tax cheat. Outlaw. Psychopath. Paranoid. Fraud. Ignorant. Vengeful. Delusional. Arrogant. Greedy. Contemptuous. Unsympathetic. Learning disabled. Cruel. Obstructer of Justice. Threat to the constitution. Traitor.

The book makes clear that Trump is guilty to all counts. The author goes on say, "My task is not only to appreciate the full list but also to ignore the big picture and focus on a single pathology at a time." I can think of no better formula for producing a determinedly biased, shallow psychiatric hatchet job, which this book most assuredly is.

Finally, at least one published Trump biography contained so many mistakes and unsupported personal accusations against Trump and his family, including a rape charge against Mr. Trump and an unproven accusation that his father Fred was a serial philanderer,[61] that the original publisher, W. W. Norton, refused to reissue the book when Trump became president. The reissue of the book is self-published.[62]

That book contains clearly manufactured verbatim discussions between Donald and his father Fred that supposedly took place[63] in the privacy of Trump's penthouse office. The author was clearly not present. In one of the ugliest accusations made by the author, he recalls Fred Trump, eating a hotdog at a Coney island spot with his "Secretary-Mistress" and saying out loud of a plane carrying his son Donald somewhere: "I hope his plane crashes."[64] That publicly expressed filial death wish is literally astounding for many reasons, not the least of which it is contradicted by decades of evidence of Fred's great love and respect for his son and his well-documented lifelong effort to help him.

One of the Hunt book's chief disservice to Trump biography, among many, however, lies in emphasizing the reportedly verbatim discussions in which Fred is quoted as telling his son Donald, repeatedly, "you are a killer! You are a king."[65] Other anti-Trump biographers repeat that quote[66] because it fits in so well with the meme that Trump is a narcissistic, entitled, vicious practitioner of a zero-sum childhood, career, and now presidency. Trump himself mentions the phrase only once, in passing, in all his writings and interviews. That single mention is in connection with his father trying to raise his spirits during his son's dark days of staring into his partially self-made economic abyss.[67] Fred's most important life lesson to his son which Donald repeats and writes about (see below) often is "love your work." This is another illustration of the ways in which a focus on a preferred, but erroneous, narrative or meme leads real analysis astray.

Finally, a number of books about Trump are essentially anti-Trump diatribes. One clear example is David Kay Johnson, the title of whose recent book, *It's Even Worse Than You Think: What the Trump Administration Is Doing to America*[68] gives ample evidence of its premises. The first part of the book begins with repeating almost every political and financial accusation made against the president. They are all stated as facts, with no effort to bring any evidence that would run counter to the accusation. There is no effort bring forward or weigh diverse strands of evidence, and no effort made to consider alternative explanations. Why bother if the operating assumption is that Trump is a criminal? Example: Trump built buildings out of concrete. The concrete industry in New York was controlled by organized crime. Therefore, Trump consorted and worked with known criminals, Q.E.D.

The Real Father to Son Life Lesson: Love What You Do

Trump watched and learned a great many things about business and life from his father. One of the most important, according to Trump, was the importance of loving what you do. In accepting the Horatio Alger Award for overcoming adversity Fred is quoted by the *Washington Post* as saying[69]:

> you must like what you do. You must pick out the right business or profession. You must learn all about it. ...Nine out of 10 people don't like what they do. And in not liking what they do, they lose enthusiasm, they go from job to job, and ultimately become a nothing.

Trump has said many times that it is important to love what you do. In one book he wrote of his father,[70] "You know what I really learned from him?...He loved working. He was a happy guy." In another he wrote[71]: "my father would say to me, 'The most important thing in life is to love what you're doing, because that's the only way you'll ever be good at it'." In short, there is ample evidence of the "love your work" as a favorite father–son truism. There is little evidence on the record that Fred repeatedly admonished his son to be a "killer" and "king."

REPORTING THE TRUMP PRESIDENCY

Trump and his presidency are viewed though a cauldron of such intense feelings that two of America's major newspaper have taken the position that the ordinary standards of news reporting shouldn't apply to the president. Jim Ruttenberg wrote on *The New York Times*' front page[72]:

> If you're a working journalist and you believe that Donald J. Trump is a demagogue playing to the nation's worst racist and nationalistic tendencies, that he cozies up to anti-American dictators and that he would be dangerous with control of the United States nuclear codes, how the heck are you supposed to cover him?

Because if you believe all of those things, you have to throw out the textbook American journalism has been using for the better part of the past half-century, if not longer, and approach it in a way you've never approached anything in your career. *If you view a Trump presidency as something that's potentially dangerous, then your reporting is going to reflect that.*

The *Washington Post*'s chief media columnist Margaret Sullivan soon followed suit. She noted a Harvard study[73] that details the almost wholly negative coverage of the first year of the Trump Presidency, and then goes on to write[74]:

Trump's press coverage has been a political nightmare. Isn't that terribly unfair? Here's my carefully nuanced answer: Hell, no. That's because when we consider negative vs. positive coverage of an elected official, we're asking the wrong question.

Her point, and it is a fair one, is that no president is owed positive coverage in the interest of abstract ideas of fairness, if what they do isn't positive. She goes on:

The president's supporters often say his accomplishments get short shrift. But let's face it: Politicians have no right to expect equally balanced positive and negative coverage, or anything close to it. If a president is doing a rotten job, it's the duty of the press to report how and why he's doing a rotten job.

Being "owed" positive coverage is one thing, taking as a premise that Trump is doing a "rotten job" and that must be reported is quite another. In Sullivan's premise and view, Trump deserves all the negative coverage he receives.

And therein lies her fallacy. It is also the basic fallacy of the legions of reporters, pundits, analysts, and academics whose adversarial stance toward the president and his administration are much more consistent with the premises and outlook of the anti-Trump opposition than they are with the traditional information gathering and analysis roles they present themselves as still doing. It is true that no president is owed positive coverage. However, every president, and this includes Mr. Trump, is owed an effort to consider and evaluate a range of information about an issue or circumstance that is reported or analyzed—including information that contradicts the narrative being developed. Every president deserves a consideration of alternative explanations for the narratives or facts assembled. And every president, even and perhaps especially because of the controversial nature of his policy ambitions, deserves the assumption of fair-minded analysis.

Miss Sullivan has recently gone farther in this adversarial anti-Trump direction. In a piece entitled "We have entered the Trump Unbound era and journalists need to step it up," she recommends[75]:

> In this new era, Trump has declared himself the nation's chief law enforcement official. He has pardoned a raft of corrupt officials. He has exacted revenge on those he sees as his impeachment enemies—Lt. Col. Alexander Vindman, the decorated military veteran and national security staffer; and Gordon Sondland, Trump's own handpicked ambassador to the European Union—simply because they testified under subpoena to what they knew about the White House's dealings with Ukraine.
>
> In other words, we are in entirely new territory now. Should the news media continue as usual? Should it retain its own traditions as the nation slides toward autocracy? Should it treat the Trump presidency as pretty much the usual thing, with a few more fact-checks and the occasional use of a word like "lie"?
>
> *No. We need a new and better approach if we're going to do our jobs adequately.*
>
> *First, we need to abandon neutrality-at-all-costs journalism, to replace it with something more suited to the moment.*

Every single assertion above is a conclusion embedded in a set of Miss Sullivan's anti-Trump assumptions. They are clearly her views. However, they are not correct simply because she forcefully asserts them, as to take but one example her conclusions about Lt. Col. Alexander Vindman (see Chapter 12).

Mr. Trump is owed the presumption that he is *not* guilty, whatever the accusation, before a fair effort to ascertain and evaluate the range of facts and not just state a conclusion, is honestly undertaken. If that were done, readers would never read the following:

> Donald Trump Is Guilty. The only remaining question is what exactly he's guilty of.[76]
>
> or

"Do you think the president and his family are using the office to enrich themselves?" Goldman asked Walter Shaub, former director of the Office of Government Ethics (OGE), "You can't be sure, *and so it almost doesn't matter whether they are profiting or not.*"[77]

or

I also wonder: What's with all the private "executive time" on his daily White House schedule, when he's off by himself, unobserved and unobservable? He could be hooked up to a dialysis machine. He could be receiving transfusions. *I don't have evidence of either. But who needs proof when you have suspicions?*[78]

or

When this administration makes contentious decisions—such as awarding a 10 billion Pentagon Contract to Microsoft instead of Amazon, or probing the origins of an investigation into Russia's attack on the 2016 election—*the presumption of goodwill has been replaced by a presumption of ill will and illegality.*[79]

Exactly. Of course. When the standard operating assumption of many (though certainly not all) who write about Trump is that he "*is one of those extraordinary individuals about whom there is absolutely nothing good to say,*"[80] our capacity to understand this unique man and presidency are unnecessarily diminished.

Correcting the Reporting Record

Much of the news coverage of the president and his administration since he has been in office has been relentlessly negative.[81] Some of this is a by-product of the Watergate and Vietnam era that damaged the assumption of presidential competence and credibility. That period also understandably instilled in some members of the press the view that they should be the public's advocate and speak truth, as they saw it, to power. Some of it is a by-product of Mr. Trump's own leadership style which is very combative, assertive, and deeply imprecise. And no small part of it reflects a visceral level policy and personal dislike of what Trump and his administration are trying to accomplish.

The result is literally an ongoing narrative civil war fought out in the public arena through news and think tank commentary, analysis, opinion, reports, and newspaper stories that are beginning to become increasingly difficult to distinguish, and Trump's response to them. In what stories are covered as news, the range of analysis put forward in reports, the particular facts that are and are not included, their interpretation, the nature and range of conclusions that are drawn, the line between narrative and news is becoming blurred. Certainly, as noted, the line between narrative analysis and "truth" has become increasingly equivocal and difficult to establish.

Complicating these issues is the fact that adapting an anti-Trump stance can be a career booster. Well known *New York Times* columnist David Brooks acknowledged in an interview, "I want to drive traffic. How do I drive traffic? I write something nasty about Donald Trump."[82] In that interview, he is simply reporting what he does as a fact of publishing life.

Others are less reluctant. Some are seeking redemption for their past mistakes of helping or supporting Trump.[83] Others recognize their clear anti-Trump bias, but simply don't care. In a *New York Times* opinion piece Republican establishment figure Peter Wehner writes[84]:

> I know it's a struggle for me to see Mr. Trump, whom I consider to be malicious, in a disinterested way. I know, too, that I'm quick—most Republicans would say much too quick—to home in on his failures, to focus on the things he does that confirm my concerns about him. That doesn't necessarily mean, of course, that my judgments about Mr. Trump aren't in the main correct. I believe they are. History will sort out whose judgments were vindicated and whose were not. *I'm simply saying that for me to see Mr. Trump from a distance, dispassionately, is impossible. So my views of him, even if they are basically accurate, are also incomplete and probably distorted.*

His public admission of rampant anti-Trump bias, which is in his view, essentially accurate, has not resulted in any change in either his writing or perspective. Why should it? He believes his biases are essentially correct.

It is certainly possible to find biased pro-Trump viewpoints as well, though they are far fewer in number and are much less likely to appear on the pages of the countries' major national newspapers or be seen on the country's major networks. If it were just a matter of numbers of biased pro- or anti-Trump views, there would still be an issue, but it would be more of a they-said vs they-said issue rather than part of a larger more difficult and divisive set of questions. The real major issue of Trump coverage and analysis concerns the stance of the country's major new and media organizations in reporting the latest set of Trump allegations. There have been enormous numbers of them over the past four years and the harsh characterizations and implications drawn from them are the rule, rarely the exception.

"Sources Say"

A fairly substantial number of "bombshell" reports about Trump have just been plain wrong.[85] There is no purpose in reporting the many that are in my files and widely available. However, one illustration may perhaps serve as a proxy for the many and the specific issues raised about a not insignificant amount of Trump reporting.

One widely discussed report said that Russians oligarch close to Vladimir Putin had co-signed major loans to Trump from Deutsche Bank.[86] If true, that would have been the "smoking gun" proving that Trump was personally and politically in debt to the Russians. The public accuser, Lawrence O'Donnell, relied on one source who, it turned out, had not actually seen the documents involved. Mr. O'Donnell retracted his allegation, but with the joint caveat and innuendo that "we don't know if the information is inaccurate."

This clearly questionable accusation highlights a major problem with reporting on the Trump presidency that is so ubiquitous that it is hardly mentioned much less analyzed. That issue concerns the sources used for much reporting—their anonymity, the motives of the sources, and their actual closeness to the material that they give and which is authoritatively reported.

Consider another "bombshell" report. A "whistleblower" alleged that President Trump in a telephone call made a "promise" to a foreign leader if he would reopen a criminal investigation on one of Trump's Democratic presidential nominee's son's work in that country, that Trump would free up aid money. Translation: Trump promised a quid pro quo to a foreign leader in a phone conversation if they would dig up dirt on one his possible presidential campaign rivals.[87] There were, for this bombshell too, immediate calls for Trump's impeachment,[88] including by Elizabeth Warren one of Democrat's major presidential contenders before she withdrew from the nomination race.[89] And in fact accusation did serve as the basis for one Article of Impeachment.

However, among the problems with that accusation, as Trump himself pointed out, "Is anybody dumb enough to believe that I would say something inappropriate with a foreign leader while on such a potentially 'heavily populated' call?"[90] All of the president's calls to foreign leaders are listened into by members of the intelligence and foreign policy communities of both parties to the call.

The "bombshell" was further undercut with the emergence of information that[91]:

> The whistleblower didn't have direct knowledge of the communications, an official briefed on the matter told *CNN*. Instead, the whistleblower's concerns came in part from learning information that was not obtained during the course of their work, and those details have played a role in the administration's determination that the complaint didn't fit the reporting requirements under the intelligence whistleblower law, the official said.

Trump released an actual transcript of the call, and its interpretation became a matter of impeachment level debate. How that person "learned" the information, from whom, and what specifically it actually consisted of remained unclear. However, it is far removed from a complaint from an actual person who had first person knowledge of what was said. The need to any complainant to have first-hand knowledge in order to make such an accusation was quietly changed before the accusation was acted upon. The fact then emerged that Trump's accuser had coordinated his complaint with the chair and staff of the House Democratic committee tasked with drawing up Articles of Impeachment against Trump.[92]

The use of confidential sources for news reports is itself hardly newsworthy. What makes it worth noting in the case of the Trump presidency is the unprecedented level of use of such sources. There are many who occupy a position of some kind, somewhere in the administration and who are strongly opposed to its policies. They include not only the permanent non-political staff of major agencies who develop an investment in how things have been done by most presidents of either party before Trump, with the exception of Reagan. They include many Republicans throughout the administration who have and continue to oppose Trump policies.

The avatar of this genre of sourcing is an anonymous op-ed in the *New York Times*, whose headline announced: "I Am Part of the Resistance Inside the Trump Administration."[93] That person goes on to say, "I work for the president but like-minded colleagues and I have vowed to thwart parts of his agenda and his worst inclinations." That is only the most public tip of a very large cadre of people tapped by reporters to provide damaging, if true, details regarding the administration. The veracity of their reports can't be examined because of anonymity concerns. Accusations therefore are simply stated, accepted as fact, and used to develop and legitimize anti-Trump narratives and memes.

The sources for these stories are varied and their ability to authoritatively report what they anonymously tell reporters is unknown. The impact of their motivations on what they report is unexamined and incapable of being assessed even if there were the will to do so. Sometimes critical reports are based on "two sources," unnamed and not otherwise identified as part of the administration.[94] Or, there are news reports based on "according to three people familiar with the situation."[95] Then there are stories about what the president may, or may not have said, "according to a source familiar with their conversation."[96] Familiar with the situation or conversation? How so? We don't know and are not told.

There are also: "one person with knowledge of their thinking said …"[97] or "familiar with his [the president's] response,"[98] or "people briefed on the meeting said …,[99] or "according to one of Trump's advisers,"[100] and the ubiquitous "according to a White House official who spoke on the condition of anonymity to discuss internal deliberations."[101] To give some idea of the enormous numbers involved in the use of the term "advisor" or "official," there are over 200 people assigned to the president's national security staff alone[102]—all of whom could be said to "advise" the president, or be listed as "officials." Other executive agencies add hundreds more to these numbers. Who are these people and why do their reported comments run almost wholly in the direction of criticizing the president, even if, and that is a big if, they are reporting accurately?

It is true that in the past, White House officials give briefings on "background" with the stipulation that their names or titles not be used. It is also true that in the 1990s as a private citizen Trump gave "off the record remarks to the *New York Daily News*."[103] Yet it is now almost three decades later, Mr. Trump is president, and the news reports noted above all go one direction. They are uniformly critical in one way or another of the president. Anonymity protects sources, but is also allows the harshest accusations to be made without factual evaluation.

Bias by Omission

The anti-Trump slanting of seemingly objective news stories can be subtle and hard to discern, primarily because it requires the average interested reader to have at their fingertips relevant material that should have been but wasn't included in the article. Consider in that regard, the news story regarding Trump's "lost opportunities" during the summer of 2019[104] that failed to mention twenty-two summer initiatives that the administration could reasonably count as "successes."[105]

One reporter from the *Washington Post* countered that the paper had indeed covered all of these initiatives over the past four months, at the time they were undertaken and that was accurate.[106] Yet, the Post's "Trump's lost summer" story was meant to be an overall evaluation of those efforts. That was difficult to do when the majority of the administration initiatives were not brought up in that context for consideration. The "we already covered it response" is a bit disingenuous since it assumes people read and or remember what had been written months before, which is unlikely. An article framed by the lost summer/missed opportunity narratives embedded owed its readers a fuller accounting.

In responding to the *Washington Post*'s summary of Trump's "lost summer opportunity, the administration responded:

in a "news" article about Trump's summer accomplishments, the *Post* not only chose to ignore, but refused to cite 84% of the president's *actual* summer accomplishments. Respectable, reputable, responsible news reporters would have listed those, gathered opinions from sources with diverse perspectives, and presented all of this information to their readers so they could develop their own opinions. Doing so would be a valuable, nonpartisan service to all Americans from across the political spectrum.

The administration had a point.

Or consider how a headline can slant a story. One recent one read: "Pence seizes control of coronavirus response amid criticism of his qualifications."[107] Criticisms of Pence's scientific background is expected and legitimate, although the asserted criticisms are simply presented as facts and are not analyzed in the story itself. However, the "seized control" phrase is puzzling. Pence did not "seize control," a characterization buttressed by the claims of two anonymous "officials." He was assigned by the president to coordinate a nation-wide and global response, including taking both responsive and preventative steps to contain the virus and helping to keep the public accurately informed.

The unfolding of the Coronavirus epidemic is a vast unfolding story that includes many examples of individuals giving their point of view, many of which, not unexpectedly in a very large story such as this one, diverge. In such circumstances there is a great deal of misinformation, speculation, and premature conclusions being drawn. Trying to bring some factual order and accuracy in such circumstances is a needed, necessary, and legitimate public step.

This Book's Strategy of Analysis

While focusing on individual presidents, either singularly or on a comparative basis, we follow Harold Lasswell's early insight about such frames of analysis[108]: "We want to discover what developmental traits are significance for the mature," and further that "the life history is a natural history and a life history is concerned with facts that are *developmentally* significant." Lasswell is arguing that a leader's present behavior is rooted in the past, but that not every developmental fact is relevant.

Informed by psychoanalytic theory, this is an analysis of Trump's psychology, its development and its presidential consequences. It pays close attention to reoccurring patterns and unique milestones, important relationships and critical inflection points in Trump's developmental history.

Many people influence a president's life and Trump is no exception to that rule. What is unusual about Trump is that his father Fred clearly played an outsized role in his son's life as mentor, model, ideal, business partner, life guide and sometimes goad, life-long supporter, and enormously proud parent. His mother Mary was the linchpin of Trump family life and a supportive and consistent presence and homemaker to her children. Trump remembers her fondly[109] and has spoken or written about her many times with affection. He said that he was able to count on her steady presence so much that it wasn't until later, after he had experienced a lot more of life's vicissitudes that he came to realize how important and unusual their relationship was.

In a Mother's Day interview about his mother, Trump said:

"I had a great mom. I loved my mom and she loved me, which … is probably not easy to do…"She was so good to me. I couldn't do any wrong, which is a big problem. Maybe that's why I ended up the way I ended up. I don't know. I couldn't do any wrong in her eyes."[110]

Psychoanalysts have a term for this, "unconditional love" which, from the work of Freud has been recognized as one of the most precious experiences that a parent can give to a child.

Prudence Gourguechon, former president of the American Psychoanalytic Association is quoted in one of the few efforts to try and fill in the thin public records of Mary Trump's life and impact as saying,[111] that a solid relationship with "what we sometimes call an ordinary, devoted mother" establishes a foundation on which critical character architecture can be built. That seems to have been at the least the case for Mary Trump's impact on her son.

Donald Trump's family experience was lived out along a continuum anchored by two very different poles. One pole was the hard driven and resilient ambition of Trump's father determined to make his way and his mark in the larger world. The other, was the comparatively calm steady presence of his mother who gave her son the developmental gift of unconditional love. These very different developmental anchors and their associated experiences defined and help to shape Donald's Trump's character and emotional life.

Mary Trump left little in the way of a public record of her family life or the nature of her relationships with her husband and children. As a result, only small fragments of information about her life are available for analysis. It seems prudent therefore not to speculate on the basis of dimly remembered snippets of wholly inadequate information as one anti-Trump biographer had done.

He claims, without much evidence, insight into Mary Trump's reported "remoteness" and being "disengaged," and further, on her "absence from his [Trump's] presence growing up." Trump's Mother Days' remembrance certainly doesn't seem to reflect that understanding at all. All of this author's anti-Trump speculations are in the service of attempting "to create a distinctive picture of how her conduct as mother could have contributed to Trump's tendency to lie, to brag, to bully and to evade taking responsibility for these and other behaviors." In this author's view Trump is guilty of an array of pathological behaviors—"psychopath, racist, threat to the constitution, traitor"—and this is just a partial list. And since this biased psychiatric biographer knows that mothers help set the course of their children's development, Mary Trump must also be guilty as charged. That is the case—even if the "evidence" consists of limited, fragmentary, and unvalidated information coupled with ample amounts of psychiatric speculation, venom, and hubris.[112]

Toward a Strategy of Trump Analysis

Trump reacts, often in the moment, to the information and people around him. He came to office with no well-formed ideology, a basic and evolving understanding of history and government, and a clear goal of using his business experience. He is "extremely confident in his own judgment, often willing to act alone, to take risks, even when those around him plead caution."[113] He is a president whose leadership is often obscured by a whirlwind of presidential motion, not all of it consistent or productive, and much of it controversial.

President Trump's behavior however is not random. As a result, understanding this seeming mercurial president requires no special departure from conventional forms of scholarship. One identifies core questions, gathers diverse streams of information and the data relevant to them, evaluates and weighs the evidence, develops formulations, tests them against the evidence and, where necessary, modifies them. Then, all these elements can be assembled in a theoretical package that helps us to understand the president and his presidency. During that process, alternative explanations can be seriously considered. There is nothing mysterious about the strategy of this kind of analysis because it makes use of psychoanalytic theory. The procedure is that same as it is for every other form of evidence-based analysis. All such procedures are scholarly at their core.

If these basic principles of sound research are followed, it would then be possible to draw together a meaningful composite psychological and political portrait of Mr. Trump and his presidency.. That kind of portrait would capture, as it will for any person including President Trump, an array of psychological elements that come into play in one for set of circumstances but may not in another. It will also capture a set of psychological factors that might be an advantage for presidential success and those that weigh against it. It might even capture a set of traits like ambition that can be favorable (or not) depending on their level, nature, and use.

The purpose of such an analysis is not to relate Trump's every characteristic to his childhood. That was the previously reigning caricature of psychoanalytic theory. Nor, as noted, is it the purpose of this analysis to reduce Trump's presidency to his psychology. Rather the purpose to uncover the core patterns of the president's psychology and style, trace their origin and development through his childhood and adulthood, and then carefully examine how these patterns play out in his presidential leadership and policy ambitions.

Nor, most definitely, is the point of this analysis to provide a psychiatric diagnosis of Trump. That would result in making the target of the analysis a narrow search for Trump pathology, for which there are already too many eager anti-Trump "mental health professionals, and others, providing a seemingly endless stream of repetitious psychiatric accusations." It would also be ethically questionable according to the American Psychiatric Association's Goldwater rule prohibition, about which I have written, which analyzed the misnamed and infamous *Fact Magazine* article on Goldwater's psychiatric suitability see Chapter 8).[114] The much more prosaic purpose here it to understand Trump and offer a psychologically framed portrait of his presidency, not a psychiatric diagnosis of his mental health.

Can an analysis "at a distance" be substantive, accurate, and fair? Can it provide a useful set of theories and observations based on the substantial evidence that is made available within these pages to be understand the subjects of its focus? I will leave that judgment to the book's readers.

NOTES

1. Ivanka Trump quoted in Michael D'Antonio. 2019. *Never Enough: Donald Trump and the Pursuit of Success*. New York: Thomas Dunne/St. Martin's Press, p. 264.
2. Liz Smith quoted in Michael D'Antonio. 2019. *Never Enough: Donald Trump and the Pursuit of Success*. New York: Thomas Dunne/St. Martin's Press, p. 264.
3. Holman Jr. Jenkins. 2016. "Trump's Market Mandate: Green Shoots Say the President-Elect Is the Real 'Hope and Change' Candidate," *Wall Street Journal*, December 20.
4. https://www.imdb.com/title/tt0042876/.
5. Peter Hamby. 2018. "'That Is What Power Looks Like': As Trump Prepares for 2020, Democrats Are Losing the Only Fight That Matters," *Vanity Fair*, May 26.
6. Conway quoted in *Meet the Press* interview, December 3, 2017.
7. Glenn Kessler, Salvador Rizzo, and Sarah Cahlan. 2020 "Fact-Checking President Trump's 2020 State of the Union address," *Washington Post*, February 4.

8. Ronald Kessler. 2018. "The Real Donald Trump," *The Daily Caller*, April 23.
9. Ashley Parker and Robert Costa. 2019. "The Narrator in Chief: Trump Opines on the 2020 Democrats—And so Much More," *Washington Post*, May 20.
10. Daniel Chaitin. 2019. "Coast Guard Rear Admiral Defends Trump from Storm of Backlash After Alabama Forecast," *Washington Examiner*, September 5.
11. John Wagner and Felicia Sonmez. 2019. "Trump Continues to Push Erroneous Claim About Alabama as Dorian Lashes Carolinas," *Washington Post*, September 5.
12. Philip Rucker and Ashley Parker. 2019. "Trump's Lost Summer: Aides Claim Victory, But Others See Incompetence and Intolerance," *Washington Post*, September 1.
13. Stephanie Grisham and Hogan Gidley. 2019. "The *Washington Post*'s Lost Summer," *Washington Examiner*, September 5.
14. Michael D. Shear and Maggie Haberman. 2019. "Mexico Agreed to Take Border Actions Months Before Trump Announced Tariff Deal," *New York Times*, June 8.
15. Cf., "Despite the Threat of Tariffs, However, It Appears That Mexico Agreed to Little More Than Moves It Had Already Agreed to in Previous Rounds of Negotiations." Daniel W. Drezner. 2019. "An Open Letter to Donald Trump from an Expert on Economic Coercion: I Know Some Things About How Economic Coercion Works—Trump Knows Fewer Things," *Washington Post*, June 11.
16. Cf., "I know some things about how economic coercion works: Trump knows fewer things." See Daniel W. Drezner. 2019. "An Open Letter to Donald Trump from an Expert on Economic Coercion," *Washington Post*, June 11.
17. Nick Miroff, Kevin Sieff, and John Wagner. 2019. "How Mexico Talked Trump Out of Tariff Threat with Immigration Crackdown Pact," *Washington Post*, June 10; Juan Montes. 2019. "In Mexico's South, Police Check Buses, Trains in Migrant Crackdown," *Wall Street Journal*, June 10.
18. Rich Lowry. 2019. "Trump Better Hope Voters Don't Tire of All the Drama," *New York Post*, August 22.
19. Peter Nicholas. 2019. "Trump Needs Conspiracy Theories," *The Atlantic*, November 29.
20. https://www.lexico.com/en/definition/conspiracy.
21. Cassie Hunt. 2017. "Trump Again Makes Debunked Claim: 'Illegals' Cost Me Popular Vote," *NBC News*, January 23.

22. For the debate on illegal voting see Jesse Richman and David Earnest. 2014. "Could Non-Citizens Decide the November Election?" *Washington Post*, October 24; John Ahlquist and Scott Gehlbach. 2014. "What Can We Learn About the Electoral Behavior of Non-Citizens from a Survey Designed to Learn About Citizens?" *Washington Post*, October 28; and Michael Tesler. 2014. "Methodological Challenges Affect Study of Non-Citizens' Voting," *Washington Post*, October 27.
23. The Pew Center on the States. 2012. "Inaccurate, Costly, and Inefficient: Evidence That America's Voter Registration System Needs an Upgrade," Policy Brief, February.
24. German Lopez. 2020. "Trump Is Still Reportedly Pushing His Racist 'Birther' Conspiracy Theory About Obama," *Vox*, November 29.
25. Ben Smith and Byron Tau. 2011. "Birtherism: Where It All began," *Politico*, April 22. A March 19, 2007 memo from Mark Penn, senior Clinton campaign advisor discussed Obama's "Lack of American Roots," and suggested ways to make an issue of it. See Joshia Green. 2008. "Penn Strategy Memo, March 19, 2007," *The Atlantic*, August 11.
26. David Weigel. 2016. "Why Are People Giving Jill Stein Millions of Dollars for an Election Recount?" *Washington Post*, November 24.
27. Pete Williams. 2019. "Secret FISCA Court Issues a Highly Unusual Public Rebuke of the FBI for Mistakes," *NBC News*, December 17.
28. Katie Benner and Adam Goldman. 2019. "Justice Dept. Is Said to Open Criminal Inquiry Into Its Own Russia Investigation," *New York Times*, October 24; see also Jarrett 2019. Laura Jarrett. 2019. "Top Federal Prosecutor in Connecticut to Review Origins of Russia Probe," *CNN*, May 14; Aruna Viswanatha, Warren P. Strobel, and Sadie Gurman. 2020. "Investigation into Origins of Trump-Russia Probe Continues Despite Coronavirus," *Wall Street Journal*, April 2.
29. Cf., Jonathan Turley. 2020. "More Willful blindness by the media on spying by Obama administration," *The Hill*, July 25.
30. Oliva Deasvers. 2020. "Democrats to plow ahead with Trump probes post-acquittal," *The Hill*, February 8.
31. Fred I. Greenstein. 1967. "The Impact of Personality on Politics: An Attempt to Clear Away Underbrush," *American Political Science Review*, Vol. 61, No. 3, p. 630.
32. Lance Dodes, MD. 2017. "Sociopathy," in Bandy Lee (ed.), *The Dangerous Case of Donald Trump: 27 Psychiatrists and Mental Health Experts Assess a President*, 83–92. New York: St. Martin's Press.
33. Cf., Speaking of the Iranian nuclear deal, Trump said: "It was a terrible negotiation. It was negotiated by people that are poor negotiators against great negotiators. Persians being great negotiators, okay? It's one of those things. You might be Persian. But the Iranians, frankly, are great negotiators." See Bob Woodward and Robert Costa. 2016. "Transcript:

Donald Trump Interview with Bob Woodward and Robert Costa," *Washington Post*, April 2.

34. https://twitter.com/johnbrennan/status/1018885971104985093 [July 16, 2018].

35. Charles Blow. 2018. "Trump, Treasonous Traitor," *New York Times*, July 15.

36. Nicholas Kristoff. 2017. "There's a Smell of Treason in the Air," *New York Times*, March 23.

37. https://twitter.com/eliotacohen/status/1018909576975081475?lang=en [July 16, 2018].

38. Kelsey Sutton. 2017. "Maryland Blogger Settles Defamation Lawsuit Brought by Melania Trump," *Politico*, February 7.

39. Peter Baker. 2017. "The New Presidential Interview," *New York Times*, July 24; see also Marc Fisher and Michael Kranish. 2016. "Trump Interview," *Washington Post*, June 9.

40. https://www.washingtonpost.com/graphics/politics/trump-revealed-book-reporting-archive/.

41. Fisher and Kranish 2016, p. 10.

42. Fisher and Kranish 2016, p. 11.

43. Donald J. Trump (with Tony Schwartz). 1987. *Trump: The Art of the Deal*. New York: Random House, p. 58.

44. See "Trump Revealed: The Reporting Archive," *Washington Post*, August 30, 2016.

45. Representative NYT interviews can be found at "Excerpts from Trump's interview with the *New York Times*," *New York Times*, December 28, 2017 and "Excerpts from the Time's Interview with Trump," *New York Times*, July 19, 2017.

46. Michael Birnbaum and Toluse Olorunnipa. 2019. "Iran's Zarif makes surprise trip to G-7," *Washington Post*, August 25.

47. Aaron Blake. 2019. "Trump Finds Himself on His Heels and Fumbling at G-7," *Washington Post*, August 25.

48. Macron quoted in Donald, J. Trump, 2019. "Remarks by President Trump and President Macron of France in Joint Press Conference," Biarritz, France, August 26.

49. Alan Rappeport, Jeanna Smialek, and Nelson D. Schwartz. 2019. "Trump Plans More Tariffs for China. You'll Feel This Round," *New York Times*, August 2.

50. Alberto Cavallo, Gita Gopinath, Brent Neiman, and Jenny Tang. 2019. "Tariff Pass through at the Border and at the Store: Evidence from US Trade Policy," NBER Working Paper No. 26396, October.

51. Alexander L. George 1974. "Review: Assessing Presidential Character," *World Politics*, Vol. 26, No. 2 (January), pp. 234–282.

52. Sigmund Freud. 1968. *The Standard Edition of the Complete Psychological Works of Sigmund Freud, 1968–1974*. London: Hogarth Press.
53. Jerome Tuccille. 1985. *Trump: The Saga of America's Most Powerful Real Estate Baron*. New York: Donald I. Fine. Tuccille's biography is the first book-length Trump effort and is distinguished for his earnest effort to assemble and check then known facts, that have in some case been superseded by more recent efforts.
54. Gwenda Blair. 2000. *The Trumps: Three Generations That Built an Empire*. New York: Simon & Schuster; see also Gwenda Blair. 2005. *Donald Trump: Master Apprentice*. New York: Simon & Shuster..
55. Susan B. Glasser and Michael Kruse. 2016. "I Think He's a Very Dangerous Man for the Next Three or Four Weeks," *Politico*, October 12.
56. Kranish and Fisher 2016.
57. O'Brien quoted in Glasser and Kruse 2016, *passim*.
58. Lozada, Carlos. 2016. "A biographer sums up Donald Trump in a single, devastating 210-word sentence," *Washington Post*, June 8.
59. Timothy L. O'Brien. 2015. *Trump Nation: The Art of Being the Donald*. New York: Grand Central Publishing, p. 93. Of the Koch–Trump feud he writes, "every so often the entire city gets lucky enough to have front row seats when two well known people decide to duke it out publicly and fill Manhattan with the clattering, unavoidable din of gargantuan babies' rattles."
60. Justin A. Frank. 2018. *Trump on the Couch: Inside the Mind of the President*. New York Avery, p. xxi.
61. Harry Hurt III. 2016. *Lost Tycoon: The Many lives of Donald Trump*. Brattleboro, VT: Echo Print Books & Media, loc. 1084.
62. Hurt 2016.
63. Hurt 2016, Chapter 3.
64. Hunt quoting Fred Trump in Glasser and Krause 2016.
65. Hurt 2016, loc. 82, loc. 97, loc. 191, loc. 1072.
66. Michael D'Antonio. 2019. *Never Enough: Donald Trump and the Pursuit of Success*. New York: Thomas Dunne/St. Martin's Press, p. xvii; Gwenda Blair. 2005. *Donald Trump: Master Apprentice*. New York: Simon & Shuster, pp. 7, 244.
67. Donald J, Trump (with Meredith McIver). 2004. *Trump: How to Get Rich*. New York: Ballantine Books, p. xvi.
68. David Kay Johnson. 2018. *It's Even Worse Than You Think: What the Trump Administration Is Doing to America*. New York: Simon & Shuster.
69. Fred Trump quoted in Fisher and Kranish 2016.
70. Donald J. Trump and Bill Zanker. 2007. *Think Big and Kick Ass in Business and Life*. New York: HarperCollins, pp. 47–48.

71. Fred Trump quoted in Trump (with Schwartz) 1987, p. 67.
72. Jim Ruttenberg. 2016. "Trump Is Testing the Norms of Objectivity in Journalism," *New York Times*, August 7, emphasis added.
73. Thomas E. Patterson. 2017. "News Coverage of Donald Trump's First 100 Days," John F. Kennedy School of Government, September 2017.
74. Margaret Sullivan. 2017. "Is Media Coverage of Trump Too Negative? You're Asking the Wrong Question," *Washington Post*, June 11.
75. Margaret Sullivan. 2020. "We Have Entered the Trump Unbound Era and Journalists Need to Step It Up," *Washington Post*, February 23.
76. Max Boot. 2017. "Donald Trump Is Guilty: The Only Remaining Question Is What Exactly He's Guilty Of," *Washington Post*, December 5.
77. Shaub quoted in Julianna Goldman. 2017. Office of Government Ethics Resigns, "*CBS News*, July 6, emphasis added.
78. Frank Bruni. 2017. "The Week When President Trump Resigned," *New York Times*, August 18, emphasis added.
79. Max Boot. 2019. "Trump Is Trashing the Rule of Law to Stay in Power," *Washington Post*, April 9, emphasis added.
80. Gabriel Schoenfeld. 2019. "'F: Demagogue Fail,' Grading President Donald Trump in His Second Year," *USA TODAY*, January 18, emphasis added.
81. Patterson 2017; Stephe J. Farnsworth, S. Robert Lichter, and Roland Schatz. 2017. "News Coverage of Trump Is Really, Really Negative: Even on Fox News," *Washington Post*, February 28; Jennifer Harper. 2018. "Unprecedented Hostility: Broadcast Coverage of President Trump Still 90% Negative, Says Study," *Washington Times*, March 6.
82. Brooks quoted in David Brody. 2019. "New York Columnist David Brooks admits to CBN News That Targeting Trump Is 'Good for Business,'" *CBN*, June 17 [at 4:11 on the interview tape].
83. Cf., "I Feel a Deep Sense of Remorse, Donald Trump's Ghostwriter Says," Schwartz quoted in David Rappaport. 2016. "I Feel a Deep Sense of Remorse, Donald Trump's Ghostwriter Says," *New York Times*, July 18.
84. Peter Wehner. 2017. "Seeing Trump Through the Glass Darkly," *New York Times*, October 7, emphasis added.
85. Glenn Greenwald. 2019. "Beyond BuzzFeed: The 10 Worst, Most Embarrassing U.S. Media Failures on the Trump-Russia Story," *The Intercept*, January 20.
86. Tom Porter. 2019. "MSNBC's O'Donnell Said He 'Shouldn't Have Reported' His On-Air Claim That Trump Has Loans with Deutsche Bank Backed by 'Russian Billionaires Close to Vladimir Putin,'" *Business Insider*, August 28.

87. Greg Miller, Ellen Nakashima, and Shane Harris. 2019. "Trump's Communications with Foreign Leader Are Part of Whistleblower Complaint That Spurred Standoff Between Spy Chief and Congress, Former Officials Say," *Washington Post*, September 18.
88. George T. Conway III and Neal Katyal. 2019. "Trump Has Done Plenty to Warrant Impeachment: But the Ukraine Allegations Are Over the Top," *Washington Post*, September 20.
89. Daniella Diaz. 2019. "Warren: 'Congress Is Complicit' by Failing to Start Impeachment Proceedings Against Trump," *CNN*, September 21.
90. https://twitter.com/realdonaldtrump/status/1174696521914339328.
91. Stephen Collinson. 2019. "New Revelations Deepen Scandal Over Trump Whistleblower Complaint," *CNN*, September 20.
92. Julian E. Barnes, Michael Schmidt, and Matthew Rosenberg. 2019. "Schiff Got Early Account of Accusations as Whistle-Blower's Concerns Grew," *New York Times*, October 2.
93. Anonymous. 2018. "I Am Part of the Resistance Inside the Trump Administration, "*New York Times*, September 5.
94. Cf., Jake Tapper. 2019. "Trump Pushed to Close El Paso Border, Told Admin Officials to Resume Family Separations and Agents Not to Admit Migrants"; "Behind the Scenes, Two Sources Told *CNN*, the President Told Border Agents to Not Let Migrants In," *CNN*, April 9.
95. Anita Kumar, Gabby Orr, and Daniel Lippman. 2019. "Stephen Miller Pressuring Trump Officials Amid Immigration Shakeups," *Politico*, April 8.
96. Anita Kumar and Andrew Restuccia. 2019. "Barrage of Setbacks Spoils Trump's Post-Mueller Reset," *Politico*, March 4.
97. Ashley Parker, Ellen Nakashima, Devlin Barrett, and Carol D. Leonnig. 2019. "Potentially Damaging Information in Mueller Report Ushers in New Political Fight," *Washington Post*, April 4.
98. Lachian Markay, Bruce Ackerman, and Erin Banco. 2018. "We See Ourselves as Rebels, Trump's Internal Resistance," *Daily Beast*, September 6.
99. Jonathan Martin, Alexander Burns, and Maggie Haberman. 2018. "Trump's Role in Midterm Elections Roils Republicans," *New York Times*, April 28.
100. Ashley Parker, Philip Rucker, and Josh Dawsey. 2018. "'Not in a Punch-Back Mode': Why Trump Has Been Largely Silent on Stormy Daniels," *Washington Post*, March 26.
101. Toluse Olorunnipa and Josh Dawsay. 2019. "'What I Said Was Accurate!': Trump Stays Fixated on His Alabama Error as Hurricane Pounds the Carolinas," *Washington Post*, September 5.
102. Jennifer Jacobs and Justin Sink. 2019. "Trump Orders Cut to National Security Staff After Whistle-Blower," *Bloomberg News*, October 5.

103. Megan Keller. 2018. "Reporters Fire Back at Trump for Ripping 'Anonymous Sources,'" *The Hill*, August 29.
104. Rucker and Parker 2019.
105. Grisham and Gidley 2019.
106. Philip Bump. 2019. "The White House Thinks the Post Ignored Trump's Summertime Successes: So, About That," *Washington Post*, September 6.
107. Toluse Olorunnipa, Josh Dawsey, and Yasmeen Abutaleb. 2020. "Pence Seizes Control of Coronavirus Response Amid Criticism of His Qualifications," *Washington Post*, February 27.
108. Harold D. Lasswell. 1930. *Psychopathology and Politics*. Chicago: University of Chicago Press, pp. 8, 9.
109. Cf., See Marc Fisher and Michael Kranish. 2016. "Interview with Donald Trump," *Washington Post*, April 21.
110. Donald Trump quoted in Deb Riechmann. 2020. "Trump says in his mother's eyes, he 'could do no wrong'." Associated Press, May 8.
111. Gourguechon quoted in Michael Krase. 2017. "The Mystery of Mary Trump," *Politico*, November/December.
112. Justin A. Frank. 2020. *Trump on the Couch: Inside the Mind of Donald Trump*. New York: Avery, pp. xxi, 6, 10.
113. Michael Scherer and Zeke J. Miller. 2017. "*TIME* Exclusive: Donald Trump After Hours," *Time*, May 12.
114. Stanley A. Renshon 1996. *The Psychological Assessment of Presidential Candidates*. New York: New York University Press, Chapter 5 [Assessment at a Distance: A Cautionary Case Study of the 1964 Presidential Campaign].

PART II

Donald Trump's Presidential Leadership and Governing Style

CHAPTER 3

The Paradoxical Foundations of the Trump Presidency: Causes and Consequences

President Trump entered a powerful office with an ambivalent history. There is no doubt that the presidency is, as it was conceived and as it has developed, a unique, core, and perhaps Archimedean institution of the American political system. However, the Constitutional Convention debated that office in the shadow of two clear cautionary experiences, the succession from Great Britain and its despotic King George, and the clear failure of the Articles of Confederation[1] to provide a viable framework for the effective governance of the former colonies. The framers felt that a robust executive was important, but they feared that the accumulation of power in that office might undermine the constitutional republic of which it was a part.

That concern led to many suggestions meant to contain the presidency including mandating the number and length of presidential terms, the scope of the office's powers, and the provisions for either a single or multiple executive/s. In the end, Hamilton's goal of having "energy in the executive" won approval,[2] and the country has been dealing with the paradoxical consequences ever since.

This chapter is a revised version of a talk delivered at New York University on May 24, 2017. The author wishes to thank members of the Oasis Club who attended and offered their observations.

© The Author(s) 2020
S. Renshon, *The Real Psychology of the Trump Presidency*,
The Evolving American Presidency,
https://doi.org/10.1007/978-3-030-45391-6_3

77

Clear, demonstrable, or unusual "energy in the executive" proved more the exception than the rule for most of the presidencys' premodern period. Obviously several presidents during this period faced steep national and political challenges (e.g., Abraham Lincoln), and a few were very energetic regardless of the challenges they faced (e.g., Theodore Roosevelt). Yet the real test of the presumption that the presidency needed "energy" became clearer as the United States assumed a larger role in the world during and especially after World War II and when, somewhat in tandem, the public began to expect more, economically and in other policy areas, from the presidency.

One response to these rising presidential expectations was the creation of the Brownlow Committee,[3] appointed by President Roosevelt in March of 1936. Congress did not endorse the committee's 1937 report because of the broad reorganization powers it granted to the president. However, a modified version of that plan was adapted two years later and became the administrative foundation of the modern presidency.

The importance of the Brownlow Report lies in the increasingly obvious reality, certainly to President Roosevelt and his academic and political advisors, that the presidency was increasingly expected to do more and needed the tools to successfully accomplish those expanding purposes. And recall that this was before Franklin Roosevelt needed to respond to the Depression and the military rise of Germany and Japan. All the presidents who followed Roosevelt became responsible both for American national and economic security. The expectations that surround the modern presidency are nowhere better captured than in Richard Neustadt's telling observation[4]:

> A President may retain liberty, in Woodrow Wilson's phrase, "to be as big a man as he can." But nowadays he cannot be as small as he might like.

As a result of the inevitable gap between increasing public expectations and presidential performance, the history of the modern presidency has been permeated by hyperbole and disappointment. In a classic 1973 book, *The Imperial Presidency,* too much presidential power was the worry.[5] By 1984, another classic study framed the debate in this way: *The Personal Presidency: Power Invested, Promise Unfulfilled.*[6] By 2008, concern with the state of the presidency and the expectations surrounding it were well summarized by this title: *The Cult of the Presidency: America's Dangerous Devotion to Executive Power.*[7] By 2017, a book entitled *The Impossible*

Presidency[8], pictured a president looking down at his desk in seeming despair. By 2020, another presidency book with a despondent president on its cover was simply entitled *The Hardest Job in the World*.[9]

Ambivalence toward, and disappointment in, the presidency has not been the only major political problem for that office, its occupants, and the country. Propelled by unrealistic public expectations, fueled by the understandable, indeed in some ways required, ambitions of presidents and candidates alike, and undercut by the failure of many proposed policy solutions to work as promised, the public's trust in government has dramatically declined over several decades. These elements set the political premises of many Americans for the 2016 presidential election.

2016: A Dire Election for Both Sides

The 2016 presidential election was a watershed event in American politics. It was unusually fraught, consequential, and extremely controversial in large part because it resulted in the unexpected Donald Trump presidency. Understanding that election and examining why Trump won is essential in understanding the man, his presidency, and the response to them.

Both Republicans and Democrats framed the 2016 presidential election in dire, even apocalyptic language. Leading up to the election, Trump opponents from the left, right and center, and not only the fringe said he was: "a lowlife degenerate with the temperament of a 10-year-old and the moral compass of a severely wayward teen,"[10] a "human leech," and a "racist" (Democratic Senate Minority Leader Harry Reid)[11] a clown,[12] the "most dangerous man in the world,"[13] a racist psychopath, a monster,[14] a dangerous maniac, "not a patriot" (former CIA Director Michael Morell), a "danger," and a "cancer" (Hillary Clinton),[15] a person "who makes people want to wrench" (Francois Hollande, President of France),[16] "unfit to serve" as the nation's 45th president (President Barack Obama),[17] a "faker—How has he gotten away with not turning over his tax returns?" (Justice Ruth Bader Ginsburg),[18] a threat to American democracy,[19] a raving lunatic,[20] and a racist imbecile[21] among many other similar characterizations. After his election the vehemence of the denunciations became, if anything, harsher (Cf., the evergreen accusation that Trump is like Hitler),[22] more hyperbolic,[23] and more personal (he is a "deranged animal").[24]

Trump supporters also came in for their share of harsh characterizations during the campaign.[25] However, the actual views of Trump supporters were largely missing from election reporting while it was ongoing. Even now, much analysis that presents itself as explaining Trump voters focuses on their presumed racial resentments. economic marginality, and loss of cultural status. We explore these proposed, and mistaken, explanations of Trump supporters in some detail in Chapter 10, and argue that the real explanations for their support lie elsewhere.

A "Fight or Die" vs "More of the Same" Election

Some Trump supporters saw the presidential contest as "The Flight 93 Election."[26] That characterization is both the title of a thoughtful paper that appeared in a scholarly conservative journal of ideas, *The Claremont Review of Books*, and a metaphor for the essential nature of the election as a fight-or-die election.[27] Flight 93 was one of the flights taken over by the 9/11 terrorists. Some of the passengers on board, through their cellphone contact with the outside world, learned what was taking place, and decided to rush the cockpit. They did, wrestling control from the hijackers, but at the price of their lives and the lives of everyone else on that plane.

No argument is being made here that many, or any, ordinary Trump supporters read this article and recognized that it reflected their feelings and views. The *CRB* is a small niche publication, and its influence is primarily felt in the upper reaches of the conservative intellectual stratosphere. Nonetheless, the article holds interest because it clearly articulates the "sense," and that term is deliberately used here, that many Trump voters expressed, though not in highly articulated or well refined form.

They were worried and upset about the direction of the country. They felt they were being ignored or disdained by establishment figures on both sides of the political aisle. At their core, these feelings were not generally motivated by the racist, status, or economic marginality attributed to them, but by the feeling that they and their views and been ignored and ridiculed, and that they were Americans too and their views ought to be heard and taken into account.

Consider the election of Mrs. Clinton from their perspective. Had Hillary Clinton won, the country would have had another four years, and perhaps eight, of further efforts at its progressive transformation, promised and begun by President Obama. This would almost certainly have been locked into place by progressive appointments to the Supreme Court and federal courts at every level, as Trump has done.

Recall too, at the time of the 2016 election, the United States had been through decades of political, social, cultural, and economic upheaval. A number of these changes were clear improvements over past practices, in voting and civil rights for example. Yet others did not really solve old problems while generating new ones. One result of this divergence was that increasingly harsh policy debates collectively ushered in a long period of ever more strident politics. The country has now reached the contemporaneous apogee of stark partisan separations on almost every issue that gets polled.[28]

Had Mrs. Clinton won the election then, she would have been a president of *articulation* in Skowronek's useful framework.[29] In his words, presidents of articulation: "continue the good works of the past and demonstrate the vitality of the established order in changing times."

For those voters who didn't support the country's progressive transformation, and who thought that the country was "going in the wrong direction," Mrs. Clinton's very likely election was an extremely troubling possibility. It was for many millions of American voters sufficiently unsettling to lead them to take an enormous risk by voting for a brash, pugnacious, inexperienced presidential candidate who promised, and seemed willing and able, to upend the conventional political assumptions of the past several decades.

Trump's unexpected victory was clearly difficult for many commentators, Americans, and even members of his own party to take seriously.[30] The specifics of an actual Trump presidency were even more difficult to imagine. His election put into office a candidate with no real political experience, no in-depth understanding of policy issues—including those he championed, and a man whose temperament seemed to range from aggressive to bombastic.

Many of his stated policy positions were directly opposed to the firmly established narrative consensus that Democrats, Republicans, and conservative establishment leadership figures, and those in Federal and State bureaucracies charged with carrying them out, had generally favored for decades. Mr. Trump was aiming for nothing less than a presidency of *reconstruction*.[31] *Reconstructive* presidents, recall, lead from a stance of, "opposition to the previously established regime, and pre-established commitments to ideology and interests that have in the course of events, become vulnerable to direct repudiation or failed as irrelevant responses to the problems of the day." *Reconstructive* presidents, like Trump aspires to be, believe that the old paradigms and their supporting narratives no longer work as promised, if they ever did, and that it is therefore time to reform or discard them.

One question raised by this analysis is whether Trump's *reconstructive* ambitions are possible, or whether he will finish his time in office as anything more than a *preemptive* president. Recall that according to Skowronek, *preemptive* presidents[32]

> have the freedom of their independence from established commitments, but unlike presidents in the politics of reconstruction, their repudiative authority is manifestly limited by the political, institutional, and ideological support that the old establishment maintains ... These presidents will be in effect probing for reconstructive possibilities without clear warrant for breaking clean with the past.

The problem of Trump's presidential aspirations is that he may want to be a *reconstructive* president, but firmly established policy assumptions, embraced by political leaders on both sides of the political aisle, many major political, civic, and partisan institutions, and a substantial part of the voting public that have supported them for many decades make that ambition extremely difficult to accomplish, at best.

THE 2016 PRESIDENTIAL ELECTION: A NATION FACING A TRUST IN GOVERNMENT CRISIS

Mr. Trump's presidential campaign unfolded in a country that faced an enormous political and policy fork in the road. Decades of promised policy solutions had failed to live up to the assurances given to pass them. At the same time, the country had become increasingly and bitterly divided along partisan, political, and cultural lines.

These growing divisions both paralleled and had been preceded by the relentless decline in the public's faith in the honesty, integrity, and competence of the national leaders of both parties, and the country's major political and civic institutions. Trust in government, measured by the assumption that government will "do the right thing" "almost all" or "most of the time" had declined from 73% in 1958 to about 17% in 2019.[33] Moreover, Americans' trust in their major institutions—including banks, news media, congress, organized religion, and others, had fared no better. The average level of confidence in major American institutions was about 14%.[34] Even more directly relevant, in 2015 just three in ten Americans believed that their views are represented in Washington, according to a *CNN/ORC* poll.[35] A 2019 national survey found that 70 percent of its respondents felt a "deep and boiling anger" at the American political establishment.[36]

Approaching the 2016 presidential election, Americans were faced with four overlapping political crises. Many had lost confidence over many years in their three branches of government,[37] their political leaders, and many of their institutions. They had lost confidence in the many unfulfilled assurances that government policies would work as promised.[38] They had begun to withdraw from common political outlooks in search of those more compatible with their specific views, a tendency mirrored in almost every major political and civic institution. And they faced a presidential election in which almost all the candidates from both parties promised the equivalent of more of the same, except for one.

Mr. Trump's surprising victory in the Republican primary meant that the public then faced a presidential election with two very different candidates. One promised to consolidate and extend the progressive policy programs and underlying policy premises of the last eight years of the Obama presidency, becoming in essence a presidency of *articulation* in Skowronek's terms. The other ran on a platform of challenging, modifying, and if necessary discarding much of what had been accepted as conventional policy wisdom for the past four decades, a *reconstructive* presidency, again in Skowronek's terms. Trump ran his campaign in a way that signaled that he was entirely ready, willing, and capable of doing what he promised.

Why Trump Won: Missing the Forest and the Trees

How was a candidate like Donald Trump with no previous political experience, little in the way of thought-through policy ideas, a loud, brash, combative brawler, rude—and sometimes crude man, with an incessantly self-promoting public persona, able to vanquish seventeen rivals, some of whom were real political heavyweights to become the Republican Party's nominee? How, when he had done that, was he able to defeat a smart, politically experienced, well-financed presidential candidate with impeccable establishment credentials who would, if she won, become the country's first woman president? Many answers to that question have been put forward.

Rounding Up the Usual Suspects: Neglecting the Crucial Trust Issue

Hillary Clinton provided her own views on those questions.[39] Others added theirs. For example, one clearly reductionist explanation was that voters who had backed Obama and then voted for Trump had come into contact with and believed to be true (at least) one news item that was factually incorrect.[40] The most frequent answer however, was to look to the deficits of Mr. Trump's supporters.

They are, it was alleged, low information voters[41] and thus easily conned.[42] Moreover, they are, take your pick—racist,[43] xenophobic, and nativist,[44] economically marginal,[45] supporters of "social dominance" along with prejudice and lack of intergroup contact, as well as feeling relatively deprived,[46] worried about keeping their white privilege,[47] authoritarians looking for a Hitler-like leader who can make a complex world simple again,[48] or just too plain ignorant[49] or deplorable[50] to know that their real interests, economic and otherwise, were better served by Mrs. Clinton and the Democrats.[51]

The above list underscores a very basic error regarding these formulations. The nature of that error is found in the assumptions embedded in a paper that presents itself as the result of academic research[52] and which is titled, "The One Weird Trait That Predicts Whether You're a Trump Supporter."[53] That trait is being "authoritarian," measured by a respondent's support for varying child-rearing philosophies. The nature of the error is made very clear by the fact that over sixty-two million Americans voted for Trump. Voters supported Trump sometimes mostly for one reason, others supported him for several reasons combined. These Trump voters included a substantial number of those who had voted for President Obama in previous elections. Their votes could not be explained or predicted by one trait—authoritarianism, "weird" or not.

Were all of these former Obama voters "authoritarian" as "*the* trait" that predicts Trump support maintains? Touching on other factors on that list, were all the former Obama voters looking for an American Hitler? Or, were all former Obama voters who voted for Trump "low information," "racist," "nativist," "economically marginal," "ignorant" voters? To state the assumption so directly is to underscore the ludicrousness of these single factor explanations.

Trump's Victory: An Alternative Explanation to Consider

There is however, an alternative formulation about Mr. Trump's victory and his supporters to consider. It begins with the general loss of public confidence in the country's political and civic institutions and their political leadership. In July of 2016 before the presidential election, 82 percent of those surveyed said the country was going in the wrong direction. In the months immediately before the election that number stayed in the 70% range.[54] The *Wall Street Journal* noted[55] "Americans have been disheartened for so long about the nation's course that it is easy to miss a landmark in the new *Wall Street Journal/NBC* News poll: Nearly three-quarters of voters believe the nation has gone off on the wrong track, *the highest mark of pessimism in three years.*"

On several major issues—immigration, trade, and foreign policy—for example, many establishment Democrats, Republicans, and conservatives had blended their shared assumptions into conventional wisdom whose premises were rarely or seriously examined. So, for example, establishment figures from all sides of the political spectrum asserted that mass immigration and "free trade" were good policies without much downside. Therefore the more immigration or trade the country had the better. Establishment supporters of these and other policies might offer a tweak here or a caveat there, but generally they didn't question the supposedly unalloyed benefits they presented these policies as having. Alternative views struggled to be part of the debate, if they were heard at all.

In these and other areas, establishment figures in their respective political camps were certain they knew what was right and acted accordingly. They marginalized public disquiet by either ignoring it, insisting there was a "consensus" for their views, touting the advocacy research of like-minded experts or, when that failed, as it did for example with immigration policy, simply accusing ordinary Americans of xenophobia and racism.

Not surprisingly, as a *Washington Post* headline put it reporting on one study of the country's political leaders, "Washington's 'governing elite' think Americans are morons."[56] A major television network producer was caught on tape saying that American voters are "stupid as sh-t."[57] One well regarded establishment writer and pundit, James Traub, wrote an article entitled: "It's time for the Elites to Rise Up Against the Ignorant Masses."[58] There is evidence that Traub's suggested revolt against the so-called "ignorant masses," had actually been in process for some time.[59]

What stands out in all these sentiments is the disdain of ordinary Americans they reflect. What also stands out in these views is the accompanying assumption that these ordinary Americans don't know what is really best for them and therefore shouldn't be allowed to simply follow or make their own choices. That strain of mainstream thinking continues with one political scientist suggesting in a recent viewpoint piece entitled, "It's time to switch to preference preferences,"[60] which suggests that ordinary voters cede their choice of potential presidential nominees through ranked voting to "party elites";

> A process in which intermediate representatives—elected delegates who understand the priorities of their constituents—can bargain without being bound to specific candidates might actually produce nominees that better reflect what voters want.

Translation: Each voter express his/her multiple preferences, but party elites choose the actual candidate. Preferably, from this standpoint, Americans hobbled by the false consciousness of their own views would be managed or traduced into accepting what establishment figures agreed was the preferred candidate or policy.

"Elite" disrespect for the views of ordinary Americans, even at the presidential level, was expressed by President Obama[61] and Hillary Clinton,[62] and has been evident for many years. As a result, many ordinary Americans have become increasingly alienated from ordinary politics because of the disdain with which establishment "elites" of both parties have held them and their views. They have also become alienated because of the misrepresentations put forward to further establishment policies, and the broken promises they had endured. Obama's promise that "if you like your health insurance you can keep it" being the most emblematic example of this point.[63]

The "system is rigged" was not only a battle cry of Trump and Sanders supporters during the election, it has been slowly but increasingly seen as a fact of American political life by ordinary people.

Donald Trump's Hope and Change Candidacy

Before the Trump candidacy, Americans who felt alienated from the status quo had little recourse. Trump's candidacy was the only one that offered a different, very different approach to the establishment assumptions that had governed American politics, sometimes for better, but often for worse in the view of many, during the last four decades.

He spoke out loudly, and without much restraint, about the things that he felt had gone wrong and needed to be changed. He was, as noted, unprecedentedly brash, bold, bracing, along with being a rude, and sometimes coarse candidate. In being so unequivocally disruptive of convention he conveyed that this candidacy was different. When Trump said, "America doesn't win anymore," he was referring to much more than being taken advantage of in trade deals. His deeper point was that American had lost the confidence and capacity to take care of itself and get things done that needed doing.

Trump's factual grasp of policy was minimal, and his rhetoric was frequently unsettling. Yet he seemed to be giving voice to some essential understandings that many people shared even in inchoate form. More importantly, he demonstrated during his candidacy he would not be deterred by harsh, even withering and very personal and political criticism of his policies or style by his opponents as previous Republican candidates had been. Nor would he be deterred by a two-year-long investigation of his alleged collusion with Russia to win the election. He would also not be deterred by allegations based on second- and third-hand information that he offered a quid pro quo to a foreign leader—by offering foreign aid in return for getting dirt on an opponent that resulted in one of the two articles of impeachment to remove him from office. Trump also demonstrated that he would plunge ahead, overcoming his own missteps and the inadequacy and failings of multiple Federal and State governments and institutions to immediately respond to the unprecedented Coronavirus pandemic, to help the country weather that ferocious public health and economic storm.

Trump ran as the candidate and governed as a president who was serious about his intention to take on the problems he saw and do something about them. For many Americans, this rekindled the hope that someone was really listening to their concerns about the direction of the country, and would do something about them. As a result, many millions of primary voters were willing to take a chance. Thus, when the actual votes were counted after election day, sixty million plus Americans had been willing to take a chance on Trump.

The Presidential Campaign: A Stark Choice

What Trump offered America was clear, but what about Hillary Clinton? Everybody who runs wants to be president, but that is not enough. An honest answer to the question of why you want to be president is necessary. Ordinarily, you have to believe yourself to be, and find a way to say, that you're qualified without sounding arrogant or entitled. Yet, you also have to have a reason beyond ego that connects your candidacy to the concerns and hopes of the voting public. That is easier said than done.

Some presidential candidates flounder on even that most basic question. In 1979 Ted Kennedy was the overwhelming favorite to win the Democratic Party nomination. Yet, during the course of an awkward five-minute interview he was unable to answer that basic but profound question of why he wanted to be president, and his candidacy was essentially over.[64]

Sometimes a real and obvious rationale for a presidential run can't easily be said. Hillary Clinton's 2016 campaign offers a case in point. Mrs. Clinton was a smart thoughtful candidate whose political résumé dwarfed Donald Trump's. Her vast knowledge of policy, acquired over her long career of public service did the same.

There was no doubt that she was better qualified to be president, on those traditional metrics, than her opponent. Yet, that still left her with the need to find a suitable purpose for her candidacy and for her presidency. That is precisely where she ran into trouble.

It is fashionable to criticize Mrs. Clinton's increasing fraught and consultant driven search for a campaign theme that would encapsulate the purposes of her presidency, as President Trump's slogan "Make America Great Again" did for his."[65] Yet that would miss an important point. It is true that Mrs. Clinton poll-tested eighty possible themes for her campaign, several of which were actually used then discarded.[66] "Stronger Together" and "I'm With Her" emerged as Mrs. Clinton's preferred slogans. Yet, neither provided any rationale or insight into her policy purposes if she won the election.

And why would they? Mrs. Clinton was running on her résumé and the assumption that what America needed after four years of a very liberal Democratic presidency was more of the same. More nuanced perhaps. Reframed in different terms certainly; "ordinary Americans" rather than the "middle class." Yet she was at heart, and authentically in reality,[67] another deeply establishment figure who would pursue the very same kinds of progressive government-centered policies as her predecessor and which many voters had grown increasingly suspicious and skeptical of supporting. Her difficulties remind us that it is not authenticity per se that voters want, but authenticity of a particular kind—in the service of policies and views that they support.

It wasn't Mrs. Clinton's campaign slogan troubles that did her in. It was her basic stance toward her presidency's purposes that was fatal. She never questioned the long-established establishment policy narratives and strategies that she championed and which had represented her whole career. As a result, she lost to Trump's 2016 version of a hope and change candidacy.

THE 2009 TEA PARTY MOVEMENT: A MISSED OPPORTUNITY?

The Trump–Clinton presidential match-up in 2016 was the culmination of decades of lost opportunities to take a second look at some of the dominant assumptions and policies that caused many American to distrust their leaders, their talking points, their honesty, and the effectiveness of their policies—and to make some real changes. The third party candidacy of Ross Perot in the 1992 and again in the 1996 presidential elections were the first real note from the canary in the political coal mine. Perot ran on a platform of ending the outsourcing of American jobs, a theme that was a large part of Trump's platform and appeal. Perot won almost 19% of the popular vote from across the political spectrum and did especially well with independents. In 1996 his popular vote dropped to 8.4% and his challenge to the consensus establishment policies of the Democrats and Republicans faded.

Yet the forces that sustained a Perot candidacy soon reappeared in the form of the Tea Party movement. That began as a real grass-roots movement fueled by the distrust of both parties and their establishment validated policies. They issued their own "Contract with America" that consisted of the following points[68]: (1) protect the Constitution; (2) reject cap and trade regulation of climate-warming gases; (3) demand a balanced budget; (4) enact fundamental tax reform; (5) restore fiscal responsibility and constitutionally limited government in Washington; (6) end runaway government spending; (7) defund, repeal, and replace government-run health care; (8) pass an "all-of-the-above" energy policy (referring, in part, to the exploration of domestic energy reserves); (9)

stop the pork; and (10) stop the tax hikes. It's easy to see many, though not all, of these contract items as an easy fit with President Trump's *reconstructive* ambitions that I analyze as his *Politics of American Restoration* agenda.

The Tea Party movement struggled to make the transition from "fringe" to mainstream which meant having a "national convention" and developing an organizational structure to elect candidates to local and state office.[69] The natural consistency of the Tea Party movement was the Republican Party, although there were large strains between the two because of the establishment policies of the latter.[70] At the height of the Tea Party movement one survey found that four in ten members were Democrats or independents.[71]

Tea Party supporters were erroneously branded as racist,[72] much as Mr. Trump's supporters have been. Yet, the *New York Times*, along with *CBS*, conducted a major national poll of Tea Party followers[73] and found no evidence of that. They did find a great deal of concern over what Tea Party supporters saw as President Obama's liberal policies On these and other grounds, the *Times* write up is worth noting in some detail[74]:

> Tea Party supporters are wealthier and more well-educated than the general public, *and are no more or less afraid of falling into a lower socioeconomic class.*
>
> They hold more conservative views on a range of issues than Republicans generally. They are also more likely to describe themselves as "very conservative" and President Obama as "very liberal."
>
> Tea Party supporters' fierce animosity toward Washington, and the president in particular, is rooted in deep pessimism about the direction of the country and the conviction that the policies of the Obama administration are disproportionately directed at helping the poor rather than the middle class or the rich."
>
> The overwhelming majority of supporters say Mr. Obama does not share the values most Americans live by *and that he does not understand the problems of people like themselves.*
>
> [W]hile most Republicans say they are "dissatisfied" with Washington, Tea Party supporters are more likely to classify themselves as "angry."
>
> Asked what they are angry about, Tea Party supporters offered three main concerns: the recent health care overhaul, government spending and *a feeling that their opinions are not represented in Washington.*

Ultimately, the energy of the movement eventually fizzled and its impact receded. Writing in 2014, Ross Douthat noted that the Tea Party essentially failed in gaining permanent public traction because it failed to ally itself with a successful Republican presidential candidate. As he put it then[75]:

> A Rubio victory would probably make the Tea Party seem a little less ideological in hindsight, a little more middle American and populist, and more like a course correction after George W. Bush's compassionate conservatism's than a transformative event ... A Cruz triumph would lend itself to a more ideological reading of the Tea Party's impact ... A Paul victory would write a starkly libertarian conclusion to the Tea Party's story, making it seem much more revolutionary, a true break with both Reagan's and Bushism, with an uncertain future waiting beyond. ... And what about a *Jeb Bush* victory, you say? Well, then maybe it will be time to talk, not about the Tea Party's unsettled legacy, but about its actual defeat.

Enter Donald Trump. Using survey data from 2014–2018, Pew Research Center analysts found "A decade after the tea party emerged as a political force, its former supporters are some of Donald Trump's most stalwart Republican supporters."[76]

An Unexpected and Shocking Presidency

Trump's election victory surprised most of the country,[77] including many of his supporters,[78] the world at large,[79] and at some points, even Trump himself.[80] And he won by the smallest of vote margins[81]:

> Donald Trump owes his victory in the Electoral College to three states he won by the smallest number of votes: Pennsylvania, Wisconsin, and Michigan. So, it's fair to say that the 2016 presidential election was decided by about 77,000 votes out of than 136 million ballots cast.

The surprise and shock generated by the election were reflected in the headlines of two of the country's major newspapers: "President-elect Donald Trump's cataclysmic, history-making upset,"[82] and "Donald Trump is Elected President in Stunning Repudiation of the Establishment."[83] Almost four years into Trump's presidency that sense of shock has somewhat receded. In its place there has been a surge of genuine and widespread antipathy toward this president and his administration from establishment leaders and their supporters from most corners of the political spectrum. His opponents are certain that his will be a failed presidency[84] and have done everything in their power to make that hope a reality.

Mr. Trump's presidential leadership style has exacerbated some of his difficulties. His presidency has been a blur of bold provocative presidential actions (on trade,[85] relationships with allies being squeezed by great power competitors,[86] or homelessness in California)[87]; botched initiatives,[88] dramatic setbacks,[89] Perils of Pauline recoveries,[90] singular and important accomplishments,[91] strategic reversals of long held positions,[92] provocative escalations of crisis against long standing nemesis countries[93] that can be abruptly reversed to hold summits with that country's leader Kim Jong-un,[94] an early unexpected, and unfulfilled pivot to work with Democrats on some issues at the expense of the Republican caucus, and rhetorical missteps[95] and wildly and willfully misinterpreted suggestions[96] during his expansive Coronavirus task force press conferences.

While this whirlwind of activity and necessary presidential learning is taking place he has had to deal with a two year major Special Council investigation of his candidacy and first months in office, followed by the voting of two articles of impeachment by Congressional Democrats and a Senate trial ending in acquittal on both counts, and then a major international pandemic followed by wide-spread anti-police racism demonstrations, both peaceful and violent, and efforts to topple historic statues whose politics the demonstrators disliked.

Mr. Trump has responded to the movement of intense opposition to him personally, to his presidency, and his policy ideas meant to fight, delay, and ultimately defeat his presidency by fighting back. He has repeatedly and publicly attacked his many opponents while touting his administration's accomplishments, not always accurately, as he sought to gain political traction on his presidencys' ambitions. These include, somewhat paradoxically, an attempt to bring Americans together around his restorative vision that I characterize as the *Politics of American Restoration*.

That vision and the policies that flow from it are meant to help restore what Trump views as Americans' lost confidence in their government, institutions, and leaders. One puzzling paradox of the Trump presidency, covered in the chapters that follow, is how it is possible to bring people together around his vision of *American Restoration* while fighting an all-out political war against your opponents? Another is how a president given to speaking imprecisely and in hyperbole as well as prose can restore the public's trust in government?

Trump's Presidential Demeanor and the Guardrails of Democracy Argument

Trump's lack of traditional presidential demeanor, his determination to revise, reform, or reverse decades of policy assumptions, and his willingness to fight back against his opponents always bluntly and sometimes brutally has led his opponents to the view him as an existential threat to American democracy. In one article's title words: "Donald Trump Isn't Julius Caesar. He's Republic-Killer Tiberius Gracchus."[97] The chief narrative metaphor for that view is the "guardrails of democracy" argument.

Narrative Guardrails and Trump's President's Leadership Style

That argument is put forward most directly by anti-Trump pundit David Frum.[98] He names seven such guardrails. They include: (1) expectations about how a candidate for president of the United States should speak and act; (2) the expectation of some measure of trustworthiness in politicians; (3) the view that a potential president should possess deep—or at least adequate—knowledge of public affairs; (4) the view that a president ought to have a coherent ideology. Hardline conservatives would surely reject a candidate who barely understood what a principle was! Anti-compromise Republicans would certainly recoil from a candidate who advertised himself as a deal-maker!; (5) the primacy of national security concerns; (6) deep belief in tolerance and non-discrimination for Americans of all faiths, creeds, and origins that also once functioned as a guardrail against destructive politics; and (7) loyalty to the nation as a whole.

In Frum's view, Trump is primarily and uniquely responsible for bending or breaking each of these norms, and thus placing American democracy in direct and dire danger. Frum's list contains some fair points. It is preferable if presidents have adequate knowledge of public affairs, although such knowledge in the past has not kept presidents from making serious policy mistakes, or being advised to do so. It would also be preferable for presidents to generally publicly speak and act at a level consistent with the stature of the office, although speaking softly or not at all in response to repeated vicious personal and political attacks can understandably be seen as a form of unilateral disarmament and a failure of nerve, self-respect, and commitment to the issues that bind your supporters to you.

Frum's ideology guardrail argument is an odd one. Strong ideological conviction on either the left (Obama) or right (Reagan) is about policy direction not democracy. Pragmatic non-strong ideological (Eisenhower) policy preferences have been thought to be the basis of more bi-partisan policies which are assumed to be preferable and sometimes, but not always, are. At any rate, there is a strong argument to be made that Trump for all his "deal making" in pursuit of his *Restoration* agenda is governing in many respects as a true, somewhat ordinary conservative Republican.[99]

The importance of national security as a guardrail of American national security being compromised by Trump is also a bit odd. If you believe though, as Frum apparently does that, "Again and again, Trump has acted in ways that align with the interests of foreign states, raising questions about his motives"[100] his criticism makes sense. Frum makes it clear that he thinks Trump has sold out his country to further his business interests. That's an accusation of treason hiding behind the fig-leaf of the somewhat vague phrase "raising questions about his motives." Perhaps Mr. Frum can explain how the administration's successful years' long hunt to track down and eliminate ISIS leader Abu Bakr al-Baghdadi fits in with Trump's business plan.[101]

Frum's worrying about Trump destroying the guardrail of tolerance and non-discrimination for Americans of all faiths, creeds, and origins is also puzzling. Narrative accusations that Trump is a racist are constructed from his complaints that have nothing to do with race. His broadside against four Congresswomen who criticized this county, its history, and its policies was immediately branded by his critics as racist.[102] Two words Trump used out of many, specifically "go home,"[103] were repeatedly cited without mentioning the other 119 words that made up Trump's tweet. One mainstream columnist, The *Washington Post*'s Kathleen Parker accused Trump of inviting a "rhetorical race war."[104]

His actual tweet of advice to those critics read[105]:

> So interesting to see "Progressive" Democrat Congresswomen, who originally came from countries whose governments are a complete and total catastrophe, the worst, most corrupt and inept anywhere in the world

(if they even have a functioning government at all), now loudly … and viciously telling the people of the United States, the greatest and most powerful Nation on earth, how our government is to be run. Why don't they go back and help fix the totally broken and crime infested places from which they came? Then come back and show us how … it is done. These places need your help badly, you can't leave fast enough. I'm sure that Nancy Pelosi would be very happy to quickly work out free travel arrangements!

How would one know this is racist and not a critique of progressive complaints about the country? Well, as the *New York Times* emphasizes, "All but one are American-born, but all are women of color."[106] What of the fact that the tweet clearly emphasizes returning to their countries of original origin, see how they are run, returning to the United States, and reporting back to Americans how things should be done? No matter, unnamed experts say that, "The president's words reflected a love-it-or-leave-it sentiment … [that] has animated a sense of xenophobia since the dawn of the republic." This is not the first time that an essentially conservative political critique of a liberal political position has been equated with racism.

Finally, it is clearly preferable for presidents to have a degree of factual trustworthiness. It is however, unclear how Trump's general rhetorical imprecision and looseness with factual details, embellishments of his preferred facts to all the facts in a particular circumstance, or his stubborn repetition of what he believes to be true even though the weight of "expert" opinion is against his views count in the calculation of factual trustworthiness. Many listening to Trump are likely to simply factor in a "rhetorical discount" to what he says.

We noted the issues of fact-checking the truth in the last chapter and will take up the broader issue of Trump and the truth in Chapter 10. One might also wonder how Trump's rhetorical and factual imprecision stacks up against decades of false facts and narratives in support for others president's preferred policies ("if you like your health care you can keep it" being one iconic example of these misrepresentations). We might also ask how Trump's effort to keep his major campaign promises—his "promise keeper" approach to restoring public trust (see Chapters 4, 5, 10, and 12) will weigh in the balance of his clear rhetorical excesses.

The Guardrails of Democracy Narrative in Comparative International Perspective

The guardrails of democracy narrative also has an international and comparative component to it. Two recent comparative politics books chart what they view as the worldwide decline of democracies, and support for them, including the United States.

One, recently published by Harvard University Press, argues that "The world is in turmoil. From Russia, Turkey, and Egypt *to the United States, authoritarian populists have seized power*. As a result, democracy itself may now be at risk."[107] One does not have to search very far to learn who that authoritarian populist is in the United States. Mounk argues that Trump, "is following the same playbook as other authoritarian populists around the world. He's just bad at it—so far."[108]

The other recent comparative study explores the same themes,[109] the decline of democracy worldwide including in the United Sates. Here as well, that theme has found its American authoritarian avatar in the presidency of Donald Trump. The authors write[110]:

> An essential test for democracies is not whether such figures emerge but whether political leaders, and especially political parties, work to prevent them from gaining power in the first place—by keeping them off mainstream party tickets, refusing to endorse or align with them and, when necessary, making common cause with rivals in support of democratic candidates. America failed the first test in November 2016, when we elected a president with a dubious allegiance to democratic norms.

The authors' repeated claim that Trump is, or threatens to become dictator or would like to be one is a staple of the Trump opposition.[111] It's not hard to find overwrought mainstream illustrations. Max Boot writes, "Trump trashes the rule of law to stay in power."[112] Thomas Friedman writes[113]:

> you had to ask whether we really can survive two more years of Trump as president, whether this man and his *demented behavior*—which will get only worse as the Mueller investigation concludes—*are going to destabilize our country, our markets, our key institutions and, by extension, the world*. And therefore his removal from office now has to be on the table ... if there is not a radical change in how he conducts himself—and I think that

is unlikely—the party's leadership will have no choice but to press for his resignation or join calls for his impeachment.

Or, more simply, "Yes, Trump is a fascist."[114] As the chairman of the House Judiciary Committee put it, "The very system of government of the United States, the system of limited power, the system of not having a president as a dictator, is very much at stake."[115]

The Guardrails of Democracy Narrative in Reality

The problem with all of these Trump as dictator or despot narratives is that they make accusations and characterizations, but fail to produce or examine much evidence. For example Greg Ip at the *WSJ* writing about Trump being forced to back down during the government shutdown over border wall funding writes[116]:

> The shutdown is the latest evidence that, so far, those institutions are constraining Mr. Trump, just as they constrained his predecessors ... In fact, Mr. Trump didn't really lose to the Democrats; he lost to James Madison.

The same loud complaints from the president which were followed by accepting a court's determination regarding his policies is easily documented in the field of immigration policy. For example, one major headline read[117]: "In a blow to Trump's immigration agenda, federal judge blocks asylum ban for migrants who enter illegally from Mexico." What did Trump do next? Ignore the court decision? No. Did he secretly have his policies carried out? No. The *Washington Post* reports that he did what every president in his circumstances would do when having to deal with an adverse court decision, he appealed. To wit: "The Trump administration said Tuesday it will continue to press the matter in court."

The set of circumstances arose when the Supreme Court ruled that the Trump Administration had to provide a more comprehensive rationale for ending the DACA program and returned it to the lower courts for that to happen. They did not rule against the legality of ending that program. What did the Trump administration then do? It said that it would in the words of Acting DHS Secretary Chad Wolf:[118]

> WOLF: ... we know that the DACA program is unlawful. The Supreme Court even this week did not say that the program was lawful. And

in fact, they said that the department has the ability to rescind the program....

MARGARET BRENNAN: So what—those work visas—will continue to be renewed and there won't be forcible deportations. Is that what you're saying?

WOLF: Absolutely. We'll continue the program as we have over the past two years, continuing to renew those.

In short, again as it had in the travel ban setback noted below, the Trump administration followed the court's orders and made it clear that it would provide the court with what it said it needed.

The same dynamic played out earlier in the Trump administration's ill-prepared roll out of restrictions on travel from seven Muslim majority counties. Several lower courts ruled against various parts of the Trump policy.[119] Again, what did Trump do?

Trump did what every president in his circumstances would do. He fought the adverse decision up the constitutional ladder until it got to the Supreme Court (not all presidential setbacks in court cases do go that high, of course). The Supreme Court ruled in his favor.[120] While doing that, he continued to implement the parts of the policy that the court had ruled were legal, and appealed the adverse decision regarding the rest. That is typical presidential behavior.

What did groups opposed to Trump's immigration policies do after the Supreme Court ruled in his favor? They filed a revised set of lawsuits seeking a new hearing.[121] It's the American way of political conflict resolution and Mr. Trump clearly accepts these limits—while complaining loudly about them.

Hasn't Trump stretched the boundaries of the constitutional permissible in a number of his acts as president? Yes, but in that he is no different than almost every modern president, who test the contours and limits of their political power. Understanding this element in the Trump presidency requires an acquaintance with Richard Neustadt,[122] not Sigmund Freud.

Opposition to the Trump Presidency: By Any Means Necessary

One of the most basic personal and political circumstances facing and shaping the Trump presidency is the enormous, and in many ways unprecedented range, depth, and persistence of the opposition to it. This is one major reason why Mr. Trump has adapted a "fight club presidency" leadership style (see Chapter 4). It's a strategy meant to preserve any chance of accomplishing his presidency's *Restoration* ambitions. Yet, is important to take a step back and view the depth, range, and determination of the opposition's efforts to impede or derail his presidency in order to fairly and fully understand Trump's response to it.

The enormous cascade of anti-Trump opposition actions has become such a part of contemporary American political life that its incredible nature has been hidden in plain sight. It is simply taken for granted. However, it should not be and deserves some substantive attention.

Any real analysis of the Trump presidency and Trump's presidential leadership must take into account the full range of the opposition against his presidency—its determination, relentlessness, and sometimes its viciousness.[123] It is a basic fact of political life, much like gravity is in real life, that frames every aspect of Trump's presidency. A fuller understanding of the enormity of the opposition's nature and strategies also helps to throw light on two other important issues. First, it helps in accessing the prospects for "success" of the Trump presidency. Second, it raises the question of what it takes psychologically and politically for a president to cope with such a determined onslaught.

In the opposition to Trump audit that follows I make no assumptions as to whether or not Trump's presidency merits the treatment it receives. Nor does the analysis that follows assume that many of the tools that the opposition uses are illegitimate, except for ugly personal smears against Mr. Trump, his family, and supporters. That holds as well for the unsubstantiated hyperbolic accusations like Trump's supposed treason or the idea that he suggested that Americans drink bleach to cure the Coronavirus that are treated as facts in some quarters. It is simply a list that allows one to gain some sense of the full range and impact of opposition to Trump and his presidency, which is clearly a very basic element his governing circumstances.

The purpose of detailing with the determination, depth, and range of Trump's opposition here is not to cast the president as a blameless victim. His provocative rhetoric and blunt counterattacks are clearly part of his political strategy and have obviously helped to incite his opponents. That is likely one of their purposes. Still, that said, the frequency, emotional ferocity, personal nature, and depth of the anxiety, rage, and hatred that the president and his policies bring out in many of his opponents, are unprecedented in modern political life. They have made necessary a

100 S. RENSHON

powerful response if Mr. Trump's *Restoration* ambitions are to have any chance of success.

Using Every Tool Available

Shortly after Mr. Trump assumed office, a *New York Times* major story captured in this headline the shape of the next four years, and perhaps beyond—"Weakened Democrats Bow to Voters, Opting for Total War on Trump."[124]

Opponents of Mr. Trump and his presidency have used many tools at their disposal to delay, delegitimize, or stymie Mr. Trump and his presidency. These include: introducing a Senate bill in 2016 that would make having a presidential "conflict of interest" an impeachment level offense,[125] policy and political roadblocks put in place by the Obama administration to impede the Trump presidency,[126] third-party voter recounts to reverse the election results,[127] pressure on presidential electors to not vote for Trump,[128] efforts to close down the Electoral College so that Trump cannot win reelection based on its vote aggregation model,[129] baseless and unsubstantiated accusations after two-plus years of intensive investigation that Mr. Trump aided Russia in hacking the 2016 presidential election,[130] myriad orchestrated displays of demonstrations in the streets[131] and in public meetings,[132] "strike forces" for former Obama officials to oppose Trump policies in the 2018 and 2020 elections,[133] unprecedented congressional slowdowns in approving administration personnel,[134] waves of coordinated legal challenges to Trump's policies at the state, local, and national levels,[135] a blizzard of personal and economic lawsuits against Trump[136] and his family,[137] and sensational but unverifiable Anonymous leaks of Trump's alleged malfeasance and criminal behavior as president.[138]

There were as well campaigns of outright opposition against Mr. Trump by employees of several major government agencies including the EPA, the State Department, the National Security Council[139] and others using cloaking devices to cover their electronic tracks as they "organize letters, talk strategy, or contact media outlets and other groups to express their dissent."[140] A major *Washington Post* news report found that[141]:

> Less than two weeks into Trump's administration, *federal workers are in regular consultation with recently departed Obama-era political appointees*

3 THE PARADOXICAL FOUNDATIONS OF THE TRUMP PRESIDENCY ... 101

about what they can do to push back against the new president's initiatives. Some federal employees have set up social media accounts to anonymously leak word of changes that Trump appointees are trying to make.

The "deep state" of conservative ire consisting of senior level officials at the FBI and intelligence agencies may or may not be an apt term.[142] However, there is little doubt that the term fits, both as a description of operations beneath the surface and the efforts of like-minded people throughout the vast federal bureaucracy. During the last election, 95% of the political donations from federal employees went to Hillary Clinton.[143]

Opposition to Trump has begun transitioning into a specifically "De-trumpifiction Agenda" whose goal is to legally overturn a wide range of Trump initiatives.[144] Anti-Trump opponents, including Kamala Harris and other former Democratic presidential nominees, have said they would be open to increasing the number of justices on the Supreme court so that Trump's right center majority can be overcome.[145] Elizabeth Warren[146] and others have also argued in favor of, and supported legislative steps, to take away the country's electoral college role (via the National Popular Vote Interstate Compact), thus by-passing while negating the Constitution and making the presidential vote into a popular referendum.

Additionally, given the Congressional impeachment investigations that have recently concluded with Trump's Senate trial and acquittal, it is interesting to note that on January 26, 2017 very shortly after Trump had just assumed office, 62% of Democrats supported impeaching him.[147] Along similar lines, the *New York Times* reported that Trump had, "been seriously threatened with impeachment since before his inauguration," and "Mr. Trump's critics began discussing impeachment within days of his election because of various ethical issues and Russia's interference in the 2016 campaign."[148] Indeed on the very day Trump was inaugurated, the *Washington Post* published a story with the following headline: "The campaign to impeach President Trump has begun."[149]

As noted, in 2016, after having just entered office, Elizabeth Warren (D-MA) introduced a bill that would have made it an impeachable offense if Trump failed "to declare conflicts of interest between his new presidential role and his business empire."[150] Those worried about not being able to successfully impeach Trump were advised to impeach his whole cabinet.[151] Those worried about not being able to impeach all of Trump's cabinet officials were advised by Max Boot to settle for impeaching Pence, Pompeo, and Barr.[152]

It seems like a fair observation that Trump's critics have been searching for a way to keep Trump from having his election victory certified and once it was to find a way to remove him from office from the very start of his presidency and even before. For all the talk of Trump bending or breaking the "guardrails of democracy," he has scrupulously adhered to the law in the form of court rulings that have gone against him, even while clearly not treating so-called "settled norms"[153] as legal obligations. The suggestions detailed above reflect the lengths to which anti-Trump civic and political leaders are willing to abandon several obvious guardrails of democracy in their quest to try and negate the results of the 2016 presidential election and Trump's presidency.

Less Legitimate Tools of Trump Opposition

Occupying another level of resistance are the multiple and public accusations that Mr. Trump should be publicly censured for failing to say expected things.[154] More serious are the accusations that he has committed treasonous actions—impeachable offenses. Of course, if true, these accusations of treason would lead him to be removed from office. In one such set of accusations, Mr. Trump's March 6, 2107 executive order increasing the vetting of persons coming from countries with large radical jihadist presences, a *New York Times* opinion piece by two vociferous critics of Mr. Trump characterized that decision as having been made to spare countries in which he had business interests.[155]

That unsubstantiated accusation essentially accuses Mr. Trump of compromising the safety and security of this country so that he can continue to make a profit. It is a cruder variation of the equally baseless but ubiquitous, "He's in it [the presidency] for the money" narrative.[156] That is an accusation repeatedly put forward by many Trump opponents, including two often-quoted anti-Trump biographers, Michael D'Antonio[157] and Timothy O'Brien[158] on the basis on no other evidence than their own assertions.

It's an accusation that is often brought up whenever critics have a policy disagreement with the president. When Trump decided to reposition American troops in Northern Syria (discussed in Chapter 5) as part of his long term effort to withdraw American troops, his family's business interests in Turkey, and thus the "in for the money" accusation resurfaced. "Donald Trump's longtime business connections in Turkey back in the spotlight," read the headline.[159] More recently accusatory innuendoes have been put forward questioning Trump's personal economic interest in hydroxychloroquine or his stated wish to help the cruise ship industry recover from the effects of the pandemic.[160]

It is a small step from believing these, and the many other charges leveled against the president, to the view that he is "unfit" for office because as one analysis put it, "Donald Trump's narcissism makes it impossible for him to carry out the duties of the presidency in the way the Constitution requires."[161] Therefore he must be removed from office—by whatever means and methods available, certainly before he has a chance to run for and possibly gain reelection. The suggested political vehicles to accomplish this are that he be declared psychologically unfit to continue in office (discussed in Chapter 7) and removed via the procedures outlined in the 25th Amendment,[162] or through the process of impeachment that failed.[163] These are the major political vehicles discussed and in the case of impeachment, acted upon. However, removal efforts are by no means limited to these.

Less traditional and legitimate opposition tools are also used on a daily basis. They include the orchestrated campaigns of leaks, innuendoes, and unsupported accusations. They include very nasty personal and political smears against Trump (he's a "treasonous traitor")[164] and his family ("Melanie worked as a prostitute and had a nervous breakdown during the campaign").[165] Many of Trump's opponents believe that every accusation against Trump has merit, that the president should be removed from office by any means possible, and that whoever supports him, including his family,[166] should be publicly targeted. Many of the unsubstantiated accusations and smears have become staples on national media networks, radio shows, and major news outlets until their factual integrity can no longer be sustained. Then new ugly personal accusations spring up to take their place. The purpose of these efforts is not to "speak truth to power," but to ensure that "power" (President Trump) is no longer around to speak and if it is, it will be seen and heard as wholly illegitimate.

The level of hatred against Trump is clearly reflected in a number of mainstream quarters of the opposition. Making the leap from classic literature to modern political life, the New York's Public Theater staged a revival of *Julius Caesar* with a "Trump like figure" as the traditional ruler.[167] "Its depiction of a petulant, blondish Caesar in a blue suit, complete with gold bathtub and a pouty Slavic wife, takes onstage Trump-trolling to a startling new level."[168] According to the *New York Times* review there is little doubt the play's object was Trump. The following year, making the transition from fiction to contemporary politics, the *New York Times* invited five authors to imagine the end of the Trump presidency in short stories, one of which depicted Trump's assassination.[169] And in making the transition of wish to real life (not reality) a number of public figures including Democratic presidential candidate Kamala Harris have either "joked" about killing the president,[170] or simply wished straightforwardly for Trump's assassination.[171]

No claim is being made here that the wish will prove to be father to the deed, as Freud thought happened in many of the cases he treated. The point is more simply that sometimes a cigar really is just a cigar—or in these cases, the wish is simply the wish. That tells us something chilling about the murderous level of rage that Trump induces in some of our mainstream institutions and leaders.

Is the "Resistance" Trump's Fault?

This analysis has used a number of adjectives to describe aspects of Trump's presidential demeanor and leadership style. Loud, brash, combative, rude, and sometimes crude were some of them, and there is ample evidence that these characterizations are factually accurate. That fact acknowledged, the question arises as to whether it is Trump's demeanor, style, or policies and *Restoration* presidential goals that are the real issue for the Trump opposition. It is likely that all three play a role, but their standing as a basis for opposing Trump by any means necessary, including the less savory, less legitimate parts of that effort, differ.

Mr. Trump's demeanor is certainly not presidential in any sense that term has been used before. There has never been a modern president who is not afraid to publicly be the rhetorical equivalent of a bare knuckled brawler. It is certainly understandable that this style would be an off-putting feature of the Trump presidency, even for those who support his policies.

Nonetheless, it was clear during the nomination process and the election contest that this was a clear feature of Trump's psychology and style that was unlikely to disappear. Whatever the level of discomfort or distaste with Trump's demeanor by supporters or opponents, he was legally and legitimately elected with this characteristic in plain sight. Not unimportantly, in that very important survey question—"cares about people like me," Trump's fighting demeanor was evidence to many that he would.

Many Trump voters believed that his "no holds barred" approach to political combat showed that he would not be intimidated or dissuaded by the kind of attacks, for example, being called racist, that had been successfully used against Republican candidates repeatedly in the past. For these supporters, any discomfort they felt was less central than the fact that Trump would really fight for the views they felt deserved a hearing. That expectation proved to be correct, and is a crucial part of their emotional connection with him.

The Question of Policy as a Source of the Opposition to President Trump

Trump's version of Skowronek's *reconstructive* presidency is the *Politics of American Restoration.* That set of policy ambitions seeks to review, revise, and where necessary discard policy assumptions and their underlying premises that have governed establishment policy thinking for decades. Obviously, those policies and premises have acquired many powerful stakeholders over time. The standing and stature of both the stakeholders and the policies are intertwined and any attempt to really revise or discard them is likely to meet with fierce opposition and has done so.

No argument is being made here that Trump is correct in his policy views. A more basic point is being made. In trade, immigration, regulation, foreign policy and a large number of domestic and international areas, Trump has set out to change the narrative understanding and the policies that emanate from them. Not surprisingly, stakes holders in all of these areas, both individually and collectively have fought Trump's efforts. This amounts to ordinary, basic, expected, and wholly understandable *political* behavior.

Individuals and groups do fight to preserve their interests. Yet, there have also been many repeated less legitimate efforts to derail Trump's presidency through harsh, unsubstantiated accusations of psychological (cf., "malignant narcissism" and/or political unfitness (cf., Trump is a "Nazi," or a "traitor" who has committed "treason") already noted. All of this is taking place as the November 2020 presidential election is coming into view.

The fast-tracking of Trump's impeachment was designed to come to a conclusion before Americans could express their views on a second Trump term. One question is why? One reason is that the fast track to impeachment was more likely designed to damage Trump during the election, rather than actually successfully remove him.[172]

The level of opposition vehemence and the determined search, literally, for any means to remove Trump from office suggest there is more than his demeanor or even his style that independently fuels this level of anger and anxiety. These enter into the opposition's response, but it is mostly what Trump is trying to do, not his presidential demeanor or lack thereof that is the major issue.

NOTES

1. Cf., Alexander Hamilton. 1787. "The Insufficiency of the Present Confederation to Preserve the Union," *Federalist* No. 15, December 1. Federalist Papers No. 16–22, some written with James Madison, take up the same subject.
2. Alexander Hamilton. 1788. "The Executive Department Further Considered," *Federalist* No. 70, March 18.
3. J. W. Fesler. 1987. "The Brownlow Committee Fifty Years Later," *Public Administration Review*, 47, 291–296; see also Fredrick C. Moser. 1988. *The President Needs Help.* Lanham, MD: University Press of America.
4. Richard Neustadt. 1990. *Presidential Power and the Modern Presidents: The Politics of Leadership From Roosevelt to Reagan.* New York: Free Press, p. 6.
5. Arthur M. Schlessinger Jr. 1973. *The Imperial Presidency.* New York: Houghton Mifflin.
6. Theodore Lowi. 1984. *The Personal Presidency: Power Invested, Promise Unfulfilled.* New York: Cornell University Press.
7. Gene Healy. 2008. *The Cult of the Presidency: America's Dangerous Devotion to Executive Power.* Washington, DC: CATO Institute.
8. Jeremi Suri. 2017. *The Impossible Presidency: The Rise and Fall of America's Highest Office.* New York: Basic Books.
9. John Dickerson. 2020. *The Hardest Job in the World: The American Presidency.* New York: Random House.
10. Charles Blow. 2016. "Trump Is an Existential Threat," *New York Times*, November 3.
11. Ted Barrett. 2016. "Harry Reid Calls Donald Trump 'A Racist'," *CNN*, September 26.
12. Jason Zengerle. 2015. "Donald Trump Being a Clown Is Bad for Hillary," *GQ*, October 27.

13. Jorge Benitez. 2016. "Why Trump Is Now the Most Dangerous Man in the World," *The Hill*, August 8.
14. Erin C. Cassese. 2016. "Here Are 3 Insights Into Why Some People Think Trump Is a 'Monster,'" *Washington Post*, October 31.
15. Ian Schwartz. 2016. "Hillary Confronted on 'Super Predator' Term on Black Radio Show; Calls Trump 'Dangerous,' 'Cancer'," *Real Clear Politics*, April 18.
16. Aurelien Breeden. 2016. "France's President Says Trump's 'Excesses' Make People 'Want to Retch'," *New York Times*, August 3.
17. Michael D. Shear and Nick Coransaniti. 2016. "Obama Says Republicans Should Withdraw Support for Trump," *New York Times*, August 2.
18. Joan Biskupic. 2016. "Justice Ruth Bader Ginsburg Calls Trump a 'Faker,' He Says She Should Resign," *CNN*, July 13.
19. Editorial. 2016. "Donald Trump Is a Unique Threat to American Democracy," *Washington Post*, July 22.
20. Jennifer Rubin. 2016. "Trump Spews Crazy Talk—And He's Not Alone," *Washington Post*, October 14.
21. Simon Romeroaug. 2015. "Trump Hotel Goes Up, and His Latino Views Barely Raise Eyebrows," *New York Times*, August 30.
22. Rich Lowry. 2018. "The Tawdry and Dumb Nazi Charge," *Politico*, June 27.
23. Cf. Helana Wright. 2017. "Donald Trump Is a Threat to Survival of Life on Earth: If Nuclear War Doesn't Get Us, Falling Oxygen Levels Will," *Newsweek*, September 24.
24. Cf., Alyssa Mastromonaco, a former deputy chief of staff to President Barack Obama quoted in Calvin Woodward. 2017. "Trump's Claim About Predecessors, Fallen Troops Disputed," *Associated Press*, October 17.
25. James Poulos. 2015. "Why Americans Secretly Love a Gladiatorial Blowhard Like Donald Trump," *The Week*, June 19.
26. Publius Decius Mus [Michael Anton]. 2016. "The Flight 93 Election," *Claremont Review of Books*, September 5.
27. Jennifer Schuessler. 2017. "'Charge the Cockpit or You Die': Behind an Incendiary Case for Trump," *New York Times*, February 20.
28. Carroll Doherty Dimock, Jocelyn Kiley, and Russ Oates 2014. "Political Polarization in the American Public," *Pew*, June 12.
29. Stephen Skowronek. 1977. *The Politics That Presidents Make: Leadership from John Adams to Bill Clinton*, revised ed. Cambridge, MA: Belknap Press.
30. Paul Kane. 2016. "One Reason the GOP Health Bill Is a Mess: No One Thought Trump Would Win," *Washington Post*, July 6.
31. Skowronek 1977, pp. 36–37.
32. Skowronek 1977, pp. 43–44.

33. Pew Research Center. 2017. "Public Trust in Government: 1958–2017," May 3; Pew Research Center. 2019. "Trump's Staunch GOP Supporters Have Roots in the Tea Party," May.
34. Jim Norman. 2016. "Americans' Confidence in Institutions Stays Low," Gallup, June 1–5. Norman reported that Americans' average confidence in fourteen institutions was at 32%.
35. *CNN/ORC* poll, July 22–25, 2015. http://i2.cdn.turner.com/CNN/2015/images/07/26/72715CNNorc.pdf.
36. Carrie Dann. 2019. "'A Deep and Boiling Anger': *NBC/WSJ* Poll Finds a Pessimistic America Despite Current Economic Satisfaction," *ABC*, August 25.
37. Justin McCarthy. 2014. "Americans Losing Confidence in All Branches of U.S. Gov't," Gallup, June 30.
38. Cf., Kate Davidson. 2016. "New Laws Haven't Made Big Banks Safer, Paper by Lawrence Summers Says," *Wall Street Journal*, September 15.
39. Jonathan Allen. 2017. "Clinton Blames Herself, and Many Others," *Politico*, September 11.
40. Richard Gunther, Paul A. Beck, and Erik C. Nisbet. 2018. "Fake News May Have Contributed to Trump's 2016 Victory," Unpublished Paper, March 8.
41. Richard Fording and Sanford Schram. 2016. "'Low Information Voters' Are a Crucial Part of Trump's Support," *Washington Post*, November 7.
42. Paul Waldman. 2016. "If You Voted for Trump Because He's 'Anti-Establishment,' Guess What: You Got Conned," *Washington Post*, November 16.
43. Thomas Wood. 2016. "Racism Motivated Trump Voters More Than Authoritarianism," *Washington Post*, April 17.
44. Curtis Wilkie. 2014. "The South's Lesson for the Tea Party," *New York Times*, August 12.
45. William Galston. 2015. "The Bleak Reality Driving Trump's Rise," *Wall Street Journal*, December 15.
46. Thomas F. Pettigrew. 2017. "Social Psychological Perspectives on Trump Supporters," *Journal of Social and Political Psychology*, Vol. 5, No. 1, pp. 107–116.
47. Allison Skinner.2017. "Trump Voters Were Scared: Increasing Diversity Might Make Americans More Xenophobic," *Salon*, January 10.
48. Matthew MacWilliams. 2016. *The Rise of Trump: America's Authoritarian Spring*. Amherst, MA: Amherst University Press.
49. Jason Brennan. 2016. "Trump Won Because Voters Are Ignorant, Literally," *Foreign Policy*, November 10.
50. Amy Chozick. 2016. "Hillary Clinton Calls Many Trump Backers 'Deplorables,' and G.O.P. Pounces," *New York Times*, September 2.

3 THE PARADOXICAL FOUNDATIONS OF THE TRUMP PRESIDENCY ... 109

51. Amanda Taub. 2017. "Why Americans Vote 'Against Their Interest': Partisanship," *New York Times*, April 12; Catherine Rampell. 2016. "Why the White Working Class Votes Against Itself," *Washington Post*, December 22.
52. Matthew MacWilliams. 2016. *The Rise of Trump: America's Authoritarian Spring*. Amherst, MA: Amherst University Press.
53. Matthew MacWilliams. 2016. "The One Weird Trait That Predicts Whether You're a Trump Supporter," *Politico*, January 17.
54. "Satisfaction with the United States," Gallup, 2016. https://news.gallup.com/poll/1669/general-mood-country.aspx.
55. Aaron Zitner. 2016. "U.S. Seen on Wrong Track by Nearly Three-Quarters of Voters," *Wall Street Journal*, July 17, emphasis added.
56. Cf., Jeff Guo. 2016. "Washington's 'Governing Elite' Think Americans Are Morons," *Washington Post*, October 5. The book being reviewed in that article is: Jennifer Bachner and Benjamin Ginsberg. 2016. *What Washington Gets Wrong: The Unelected Officials Who Actually Run the Government and Their Misconceptions about the American People*. Amherst, NY: Prometheus Books.
57. Joe Concha. 2017. "*CNN* Producer on New O'Keefe Video: Voters Are 'Stupid,' Trump Is 'Crazy'," *The Hill*, June 30.
58. James Traub. 2016. "It's Time for the Elites to Rise Up Against the Ignorant Masses," *Foreign Policy*, June 28.
59. Frederick F. Siegel. 2014. *The Revolt Against the Masses: How Liberalism Has Undermined the Middle Class*. Washington, DC: Encounter Books.
60. Julie Azari. 2020. "It's Time to Switch to Preferences," *Washington Post*, February 18. The original headline of the piece, since changed, was, "It's time to give elites a bigger say in choosing the president."
61. Flower Mayhill. 2011. "Obama: No Surprise That Hard-Pressed Pennsylvanians Turn Bitter," *Huffpost*, May 25.
62. Editorial. 2018. "Hillary Leans Out," *Wall Street Journal*, March 13.
63. Aaron Blake. 2013. "Politifact Awards 'Lie of the Year' to Obama," *Washington Post*, December 12.
64. Chris Whipple. 2019 "Kennedy: The Day the Presidency Was Lost," *ABC News*, August 31. The actual interview segment can be seen at https://www.youtube.com/watch?v=e5TkhNWPspM.
65. Karen Tumulty of the *Washington Post* conduced a phone interview with the president on how he came up with the slogan on July 13, 2017. It can be found on line at https://www.washingtonpost.com/videopolitics/donald-trumps-interview-about-make-america-great-again-in-6-parts/2017/01/18/3056868a-dd39-11e6-8902-610fe486791c_video.html?utm_term=.7b218d2b5446.
66. Gregory Krieg. 2016. "Hillary Clinton's Would-Be Campaign Slogans, Ranked," *CNN*, October 19.

67. Jeff Greenfield. 2017. "The Strange Authenticity of Hillary Clinton," *Politico*, September 20.
68. Bernie Beker. 2010. "A Revised Contract for America, Minus 'With' and Newt," *New York Times*, April 14.
69. Kate Zernike. 2010a. "Tea Party Looks to Move From Fringe to Force," *New York Times*, February 7.
70. Kate Zernike. 2010b. "Republicans Strain to Ride Tea Party Tiger," *New York Times*, January 23.
71. Sean J. Miller. 2010. "Survey: Four in 10 Tea Party Members are Democrats or Independents," *The Hill*, April 4.
72. Liberal columnist John Judis writes in the left-center *New Republic* "The Tea Party Movement Isn't Racist." See John Judis. 2010. "The Tea Party Movement Isn't Racist," *The New Republic*, June 2.
73. https://www.nytimes.com/interactive/projects/documents/new-york-timescbs-news-poll-national-survey-of-tea-party-supporters. See also Lydia Saad. 2010. "Tea Partiers Are Fairly Mainstream in Their Demographics," Gallup, April 5.
74. Kate Zernike and Megan Thee-Brenan. 2010. "Poll Finds Tea Party Backers Wealthier and More Educated," *New York Times*, April 14, emphasis added.
75. Ross Douthat. 2014. "The Tea Party Legacy," *New York Times*, May 24, emphasis in original.
76. *Pew* 2019.
77. David Lauter. 2016. "Trump's Victory Surprised Americans, Most Accept His Victory as Legitimate," *Los Angeles Times*, November 13.
78. Cf., "The Gallup Poll Records That 62% of Trump Voters Were Surprised at His Victory." See Jim Norman. 2017. "Trump Victory Surprises Americans; Four in 10 Afraid," Gallup, November 11.
79. Kim Hjelmgaard. 2016. "Total Global Disbelief as Trump Is Elected President," *USA TODAY*, November 9.
80. Cf., "And then one poll included me, and I didn't do that well. I was down at like 3 percent. I said to my wife, 'I don't think I can run. I'm down at 3 percent'." Trump quoted in "Transcript: Donald Trump Interview with Bob Woodward and Robert Costa," 2016. *Washington Post*, April 2.
81. William Kristol. 2017. "The Election Came Down to 77,744 Votes in Pennsylvania, Wisconsin, and Michigan (Updated)," *Weekly Standard*, August 21.
82. Chris Cillizza. 2016. "President-Elect Donald Trump's Cataclysmic, History-Making Upset," *Washington Post*, November 9.
83. Matt Flegenheimer and Michael Barbaro. 2016. "Donald Trump Is Elected President in Stunning Repudiation of the Establishment," *New York Times*, November 9.

84. Julian Z. Zelizer. 2018. "Trump Just Put Himself in a Political Red Zone," *CNN*, April 5.
85. Anne Gearon, Philip Rucker, and Simon Denyer 2016. "Trump's Taiwan Phone Call Was Long Planned, Say People Who Were Involved," *Washington Post*, December 4.
86. Jim Tankersley. 2017. "Trump's Tariffs Keep Allies, Markets and Industry Guessing," *New York Times*, March 24.
87. Scott Wilson. 2019. "Trump's Proposals to Tackle California Homelessness Face Local, Legal Obstacles," *Washington Post*, September 12.
88. Cf., Yeganeh Torbati, Jeff Mason, and Mica Rosenberg. 2017. "Chaos, Anger as Trump Order Halts Some Muslim Immigrants," *Reuters*, January 29.
89. Jennifer Sinco Kelleher. 2017. "Judge in Hawaii Extends Order Blocking Trump's Travel Plan," *Associated Press*, March 30. Kristina Peterson, Michelle Hackman, and Siobhan Hughes. 2017. "'Skinny' Repeal of Obamacare Fails in Senate," *Wall Street Journal*, July 28.
90. Lawrenec Hurley and Andrew Chung. 2017. "In Victory for Trump, U.S. Supreme Court Revives His Travel Ban," *Reuters*, July 26.
91. Bent Kendall and Jess Bravin. 2016. "Justice Neil Gorsuch Leans Conservative, Fulfilling Expectations," *Wall Street Journal*, June 27; Julie Watson and Cedar Attanasio. 2019. "Trump Administration Puts Tough New Asylum Rule into Effect," *Washington Post*, September 12.
92. Ian Talley. 2017. "Donald Trump's Campaign Vow: Reversal on Yuan Bets on the Long Game with China," *Wall Street Journal*, April 12.
93. The most obvious example is his rhetoric against North Korea: see Peter Baker and Choe Sang-Hun. 2017. "Trump Threatens Fire and Fury Against North Korea if It Endangers U.S.," *New York Times*, August 8; Joe Pramuk. 2017. "Trump: Maybe 'Fire and Fury' Statement on North Korea Wasn't Tough Enough," *ABC News*, August 10.
94. Timothy W. Martin, 2019. "In Talks with North Korea, U.S. Faces New Chessboard," *Wall Street Journal*, September 10.
95. At one such press conference Trump asserted that it was his decision alone as to whether or not States could or should reopen. That overstated his authority in the country's federal system. See Donald J. Trump. 2020. "Remarks by President Trump, Vice President Pence, and Members of the Coronavirus Task Force in Press Briefing," James S. Brady Press Briefing Room, April 14; see also David B. Rivkin Jr. and Lee A. Casey. 2020. "Presidential Power Is Limited But Vast," *Wall Street Journal*, April 15.
96. At another task force press conference, Trump asked questions of his medical team as to whether some form of bleaching regime could be developed to help dampen the virus's spread. Critics immediately accused

him of suggesting the bizarre view that people should ingest bleach. In response, Trump floated the suggestion his questions were meant to be "sarcastic" instead of legitimate inquiries given the reports on ultra-violent light and bleaching for cleaning virus contaminated surfaces that his medical team had just presented. See Donald J. Trump. 2020. "Remarks by President Trump, Vice President Pence, and Members of the Coronavirus Task Force in Press Briefing", James S. Brady Press Briefing Room, April 23; see also Kathryn Watson. 2020. "Trump Says He Was Being Sarcastic When He Floated Idea of Disinfectant as a Coronavirus Treatment," *CBS News*, April 24, and Ryan Saavedra. 2020. "FACT CHECK: No, Trump Did Not Tell People To 'Inject Themselves With Disinfectant' Or 'Drink Bleach'," *DailyWire*, April 24.

97. Max Burns. 2019. "Donald Trump Isn't Julius Caesar. He's Republic-Killer Tiberius Gracchus." *Daily Beast*, October 13.

98. David Frum. 2016. "The Seven Broken Guardrails of Democracy," *The Atlantic*, May 31.

99. Cf., Trump recently signed two Executive Orders regulating administrative overreach that, "gravely undermines our constitutional system of government." See Hugh Hewitt. 2019. "Why Do Conservatives Support Trump? Because He Implements Conservative Policies," *Washington Post*, October 12.

100. David Frum. 2018. *Trumpocracy: The Corruption of the American Republic*. New York: Harper.

101. Missy Ryan, John Dawsey, Dan Lamothe, and John Hudson. 2019. "How Trump Decided to Kill a Top Iranian General," *Washington Post*, January 3.

102. Matthew Yglesias. 2019. "Trump's Racist Tirades Against 'the Squad,' Explained," *Vox*, July 18.

103. Colin Dwyer. 2019. "'Go Back Where You Came From': The Long Rhetorical Roots Of Trump's Racist Tweets," *NPR*, July 15.

104. Kathleen Parker. 2019. "Donald Trump's Rhetorical Race War," *Washington Post*, July 31.

105. https://twitter.com/realDonaldTrump/status/1150381396994723841 emphasis added.

106. Katie Rogers. 2019. "The Painful Roots of Trump's 'Go Back' Comment," *New York Times*, July 16.

107. Yascha Mounk. 2018. *The People vs. Democracy: Why Our Freedom Is in Danger and How to Save It*. Cambridge, MA, Harvard University Press, emphasis added.

108. Yascha Mounk. 2018. "Why Isn't Trump President for Life Yet?," *Slate*, March 18.

109. Steven Levitsky and Daniel Ziblatt. 2018. *How Democracies Die*. New York: Crown.
110. Steven Levitsky and Daniel Ziblatt. 2018. "This Is How Democracies Die,"? *Guardian*, January 21.
111. Brian Klass. 2017. *The Despot's Apprentice: Donald Trump's Attack on Democracy*. London: C. Hurst.
112. Max Boot. 2019. "Trump Is Trashing the Rule of Law to Stay in Power," *Washington Post*, April 9.
113. Thomas Friedman. 2018. "Time for G.O.P. to Threaten to Fire Trump," *New York Times*, December 24.
114. Jasmil Smith. 2015. "Yes, Donald Trump Is a Fascist," *The New Republic*, November 29.
115. Nadler quoted in Brooke Singman. 2019. "Nadler Likens Trump to 'Dictator,' Threatens Barr with Contempt After Hearing Boycott," *Fox News*, May 2.
116. Greg Ip. 2019. "Shutdown Shows American Institutions Are Alive and Kicking," *Wall Street Journal*, January 30.
117. Maria Sacchetti and Isaac Stanley-Becker. 2018. "In Blow to Trump's Immigration Agenda, Federal Judge Blocks Asylum Ban for Migrants Who Enter Illegally from Mexico," *Washington Post*, November 20.
118. Transcript: Acting Secretary Chad Wolf on "Face the Nation," *CBS*, June 21, 2020].
119. Vivian Yee. 2017. "Judge Temporarily Halts New Version of Trump's Travel Ban," *New York Times*, October 17.
120. Adam Liptak and Michael D. Shear. 2018. "Trump's Travel Ban Is Upheld by Supreme Court," *New York Times*, June 26.
121. Zoe Tilman. 2019. "The Court Fight Over Trump's Travel Ban Isn't Over," *Buzzfeed*, May 3.
122. Neustadt 1990.
123. Individual Trump supporters have been guilty of assault, as have Resistance supporters. One Trump supporter drove a car into a crowd killing a bystander. A Trump opposition supporter drove his car into a Republican Voting registration booth, but there were no fatalities. These individual, unhinged acts differ from the systematic efforts described in the text.
124. Jonathan Martin and Alexander Burns. 2017. "Weakened Democrats Bow to Voters, Opting for Total War on Trump," *New York Times*, February 23.
125. Will Worley. 2016. "Donald Trump Faces Impeachment if New Conflicts of Interest Bill Passed," *The Independent*, December 16.
126. Michael D. Shear. 2016. "Obama's Last Days: Aiding Trump Transition, But Erecting Policy Roadblocks," *New York Times*, December 31.
127. David Weigel. 2016. "Why Are People Giving Jill Stein Millions of Dollars for an Election Recount?" *Washington Post*, November 24.

128. Kimberlee Kruesi and Bill Barrow. 2016. "Trump Opponents Try to Beat Him at the Electoral College," *Associated Press*, November 19; see also Todd Unger. 2016. "Local Electors Face Mounting Pressure to Not Vote for Trump," *WFAA 8 NBC*, November 17.

129. Sam Weber and Laura Fong. 2016. "This System Calls for Popular Vote to Determine Winner," *PBS*, November 6; Matthew Olsen and Benjamin Haas. 2017. "The Electoral College Is a National Security Threat," *Politico*, September 20.

130. Madeline Conway. 2017. "Schiff: There Is Now 'More Than Circumstantial Evidence' of Trump–Russia Collusion," *Politico*, March 22.

131. Evan Osnos. 2016. "The Gathering Storm of Protest Against Trump," *New Yorker*, November 17; see also Erik Kirschbaumk. 2017. "Protests Against Trump Are Unrolled Around the World Saturday," *Los Angeles Times*, February 4.

132. Josh Hicks. 2017. "Activists Disrupt Hearing to Demand That Hogan Oppose Trump," *Washington Post*, February 22.

133. Anne Gearan. 2018. "Democrats Marshal Strike Force to Counter Trump on National Security in 2018, 2020 Elections," *Washington Post*, February 27.

134. Carl Hulse. 2017. "Democrats Perfect Art of Delay While Republicans Fume Over Trump Nominees," *New York Times*, July 17.

135. Charles Savage. 2017. "Liberal Lawyers Plan Wave of Resistance to Trump Policies," *New York Times*, January 30.

136. Cf., Jonathan O'Connell. 2017. "Wine Bar Owners Sue President Trump, Saying D.C. Hotel Unfairly Takes Away Business," *Washington Post*, March 9.

137. Cf., Matea Gold. 2017. "As Ivanka Trump's White House Role Expands, Her Company Is Sued for Unfair Competition," *Washington Post*, March 21.

138. Cf., Brian Ross and Matthew Mosk. 2017. "Source of Key Trump Dossier Claims," *ABC News*, January 30; see also Rosalind S. Helderman and Tom Hamberger. 2016. "Who Is 'Source D'? The Man Said to Be Behind the Trump-Russia Dossier's Most Salacious Claim," *Washington Post*, March 29.

139. Nahal Toosi. 2019. "Inside the Chaotic Early Days of Trump's Foreign Policy," *Politico*, March 1.

140. Andrew Restuccia, Marianne Levine, and Nahal Toosi. 2017. "Federal Workers Turn to Encryption to Thwart Trump," *Politico*, February 2.

141. Juliet Eilperin, Lisa Rein, and Marc Fisher. 2017. "Resistance from Within: Federal Workers Push Back Against Trump," *Washington Post*, January 31.

3 THE PARADOXICAL FOUNDATIONS OF THE TRUMP PRESIDENCY ... 115

142. James B. Stewart. 2019. *Deep State: Trump, the FBI, and the Rule of Law*. New York: Penguin Press.
143. Jonathan Swan. 2016. "Government Workers Shun Trump, Give Big Money to Clinton," *The Hill*, October 26.
144. Michelle Goldberg. 2018. "The De-Trumpification Agenda," The *New York Times*, February 28.
145. Rashaan Ayesh and Ursula Perano. 2019. Court Packing: Where the 2020 Candidates Stand," Axios, October 2.
146. Gregory Krieg. 2019. "Warren Backs Plan to Get Rid of the Electoral College," *CNN*, March 18.
147. Public Policy Polling. 2017. "Americans Think Trump Will Be Worst President Since Nixon," January 26, p. 28.
148. Peter Baker. 2019. "Trump Makes Clear He's Ready for a Fight He Has Long Anticipated," *New York Times*, September 24.
149. Matea Gold. 2017. "The Campaign to Impeach President Trump Has Begun," *Washington Post*, January 20.
150. Worley 2016.
151. Garrett Epps. 2019. "Can't Impeach Trump? Go After His Cabinet," *The Atlantic*, July 16.
152. Max Boot. 2019. "Pence, Pompeo and Barr Deserve to Be Impeached, Too," *Washington Post*, October 9.
153. Frum 2016.
154. Legislation introduced into Congress demanded that Mr. Trump be formally censured for saying that 'both sides' are to blame for a violent encounter between white supremacists and neo-Nazis and the activists who showed up to protest them. See Leslie Clark. 2017. "Democrats Move to Formally Censure Trump Over Charlottesville," *McCatchy*, August 16; Cristina Marcos. 2017. "House Dems Push to Censure Trump Over Charlottesville Response," *The Hill*, August 16. The full draft of the Censure bill can be found in NeverTrump *Washington Post* columnist Jennifer Rubin's column. See Jennifer Rubin. 2017. "Every Republican Must Sign a Censure of the President," *Washington Post*, August 16.
155. Richard W. Painter and Norman L. Eisen. 2017. "Who Hasn't Trump Banned? People From Places Where He's Done Business," *New York Times*, January 29.
156. Cody Cain. 2016. "Marketer-in-Chief: Is Donald Trump Only Running for President to Exploit the Business Opportunities?" *Salon*, July 10.
157. "I don't think that he could keep himself from inquiring about the performance of these businesses any more than he can keep himself from tweeting," Mr. D'Antonio said. "It is just too vital to his identity. Profit is the way he has always measured himself. I don't see how he can stop." D'Antonio quoted in Megan Twohey, Russ Buettner, and

Steve Eder. 2016. "Inside the Trump Organization, the Company That Has Run Trump's Big World," *New York Times*, December 25.

158. On Mr. Trump's being able to step back from his pursuit of profits, Mr. O'Brien opined, "Oh my god, it'll be the first thing on his mind when he wakes up in the morning." O'Brien quoted in Darren Samuelsohn and Josh Dawsey. 2016. "Trump Lays Out Limits of Business Involvement," *Politico*, December 16.

159. Heidi Przybyla and Anna Schecter. 2019. "Donald Trump's Longtime Business Connections in Turkey Back in the Spotlight," *NBC News*, October 9.

160. Neither of these accusations is factually sustainable. Mr. Trump's blind trusts hold an absolutely miniscule amount of drug company shares and the cruise ship industry did not received money from the federal government, because as Trump noted, they were not American registered companies. See Josh Dawsey, Jonathan O'Connell, and Ashley Parker. 2020. "Coronavirus Pandemic Tests Clout of Cruise Industry and Its Long-Standing Ties to Trump," *Washington Post*, March 12; Peter Baker, Katie Rogers David Enrich, and Maggie Haberman. 2020. "Trump's Aggressive Advocacy of Malaria Drug for Treating Coronavirus Divides Medical Community," *New York Times*, April 6. Trump's supposed profiting on the drug is debunked by the left-center website *Vox* as well as *Forbes*. See Sean Collins. 2020. "Trump's Promotion of Unproven Drugs Is Cause for Alarm, But Not Because He's Making Money Off It," *Vox*, April 7, and Lisette Voytko. 2020. "Trump Has 'Small,' 'Distant Link' to Sanofi, French Drugmaker of Hydroxychloroquine," *Forbes*, April 7.

161. George T. Conway III. 2019. "Unfit for Office." *The Atlantic*, October 3; see also David Rothkopf. 2017. "The Greatest Threat Facing the United States Is Its Own President," *Washington Post*, July 4. Both Conway and Rothkopf's indictment of President Trump's "fitness," employs the litany approach to supporting his assertions in which single sentences of references to Trump's policies are aggregated to make the unfit claim.

162. Phil McCauslandl. 2017. "Democratic Bill Lays the Groundwork to Remove Trump from Office," *NBC News*, July 3; see also Michael Isikoff. 2017. "Bill to Create Panel That Could Remove Trump from Office Quietly Picks Up Democratic Support," *Yahoo News*, June 20.

163. Laurence H. Tribe. 2017. "Trump Must Be Impeached: Here's Why," *Washington Post*, May 13; Christine Mai-Duc. 2017. "Rep. Brad Sherman Introduces Articles of Impeachment Against Trump," *Los Angeles Times*, July 2.

164. Charles Blow. 2018. "Trump, Treasonous Traitor," *New York Times*, July 15.

165. Kelsey Sutton. 2017. "Maryland Blogger Settles Defamation Lawsuit Brought by Melania Trump," *Politico*, February 7.
166. Rachel Abrams. 2017. "Nordstrom Drops Ivanka Trump Brand From Its Stores," *New York Times*, February 2.
167. Liam Stack. 2017. "Et Tu, Delta? Shakespeare in the Park Sponsors Withdraw From Trump-Like 'Julius Caesar," *New York Times*, June 11.
168. Jesse Green. 2017. "Review: Can Trump Survive in Caesar's Palace?" *New York Times*, June 9.
169. Zoë Sharp, 2018. "How It Ends," *New York Times*, October 23.
170. Michelle Robertson. 2018. "Sen. Kamala Harris Ruffles Feathers with 'Trump Death Joke' on 'Ellen' Show," *San Francisco Gate*, April 5.
171. Brandon Carter. 2017. "Missouri State Senator Posts, Deletes Comment 'Hoping' for Trump's Assassination," *The Hill*, September 18.
172. Charles Lipson. 2019. "What Pelosi Really Wants From Impeachment," *Real Clear Politics*, October 15.

CHAPTER 4

Donald Trump's Fight Club Presidency

Mr. Trump's election provoked a fierce backlash from all those who opposed his election and were anxious and angry by his support of policies they rejected. A *Politico* headline made the point directly: "Democrats launch scorched-earth strategy against Trump."[1] Officially then, the opposition is associated with the Democratic Party, but it is much more widespread than that. It includes quite large and diverse groups: establishment liberals, establishment Republicans and conservatives, and all of their numerous allies embedded in America's major cultural and political institutions including the media, the federal bureaucracy, and executive branch departments.

The question naturally arises: what would President Trump do in response to the unprecedented opposition to his presidency's legitimacy and purposes? Would he ignore his critics and act "presidential," or engage his enemies? And if so, how? The answer was not long in coming, and anyone familiar with Mr. Trump's history and psychology would not be surprised. He fought back hard—often in unprecedented ways for an American president.

One obvious conclusion to draw is that Mr. Trump's combativeness is an important element in his psychology and performs important functions in his presidential leadership and governing style. However, a psychoanalytically informed analysis of Mr. Trump and his presidency is not only

© The Author(s) 2020
S. Renshon, *The Real Psychology of the Trump Presidency*,
The Evolving American Presidency,
https://doi.org/10.1007/978-3-030-45391-6_4

119

interested in the obvious existence of his combative nature, but also how and why it developed, and its political and psychological purposes.

Winning the presidency did not have much effect on the president's willingness to engage in rhetorical political combat with his opponents. Mr. Trump simply ignored calls to be more "presidential." Many voters who support him would like him to stop his tweet fights and combative commentary because they feel it hurts his agenda.[2] Many more would like him to tone them down[3] because they don't like public political conflict and prefer their presidents to reach for "bi-partisanship."[4] His opponents would like him to give up his Twitter account because it would effectively silence him. Trump is aware of that danger and has said; "They want to take away my voice,"[5] and the reason is quite clear in his mind; "[It is the] Only way for me to get the truth out!"[6]

The advice to the president to tone down his rhetoric has merit. The president tends to personalize many of his rhetorical comments against his opponents. That can be, but not always is, unnecessary and counterproductive. There is a long list of these mistakes.

John McCain was an American hero when he refused to break after he was captured and tortured during the Vietnam War. He refused to allow himself to be repatriated before others also being held. It is also true that he later sabotaged President Trump's effort to repeal "Obamacare," and played a role in the dissemination of the now largely discredited Steele Dossier.[7] However, it would have certainly been possible for President Trump to have honored McCain's heroic war behavior, which Trump didn't, and complain about his scuttling efforts to rescind Obamacare and his role in passing on the Steele Dossier. So too, it is wholly appropriate, if that's what you think, to publicly call Republican Senator Mitt Romney a "pompous ass."[8] Yet it is also possible to criticize a rival presidential candidate without, as Trump did in 2015, doing so with Carly Fiorina on the basis of her looks.[9]

In short, it is possible to wage a "few holds barred," not a "no holds barred" battle against your opponents and enemies while maintaining some level of restraint. That can be done even while you fight back with a level of force and directness that will of necessity violate the norms of past presidencies that did not have to deal with the unrelenting level of personal and political opposition, magnified and amplified by the new communications environment that Trump faces. This is a distinction that Trump has yet to act upon.

4 DONALD TRUMP'S FIGHT CLUB PRESIDENCY 121

That said, fighting back against relentless, determined, and highly motivated enemies and opponents is a central core of Mr. Trump's psychology. It is also an understandable response, even if rarely carried out with restraint. It is at least as important a part of his psychology as the obvious narcissistic elements in his psychology.

Presidential Demeanor and Mr. Trump's Fight Club Presidency

The question of conventional notions of decorum and Mr. Trump's repeated violations of them bring into sharper relief a basic element of his leadership and governing style. It is not only just *what* President Trump hopes to accomplish in his presidency, but also *how* he goes about trying to accomplish it.

The distinction is well captured in this analysis[10]:

> The difference in style between Mr. Trump and Washingtonians is obvious. D.C. is a conventional, boring place. Washingtonians follow procedure. Presidents, senators, congressmen and judges are all expected to play to type, to intone the obligatory phrases and clichés, to nod their heads at the appropriate occasions, and, above all, to not disrupt the established order ...
>
> To say that Donald Trump challenges this consensus is an understatement. Not only is he politically incorrect, but his manner, habits and language run against everything Washington professionals in particular ... have been taught to believe is right and good.

President Trump has challenged notions of presidential demeanor on many occasions and in many ways. He has upended conventional protocol, spoken sharply and personally about his opponents, and only occasionally measured up to what has traditionally been considered "presidential."[11] Indeed, after almost four years in office, Mr. Trump has crossed so many lines, discarded so many conventions, and said and done so many things that other presidents would not have that he has "radically shifted the understanding of what is standard in the White House."[12]

That new terrain of presidential demeanor has sometimes led to mistakes in analyzing it. One thousand days into his presidency for example, a news report mistook Trump's playful rally riffs with supporters as being a deep reason for his lack of presidential decorum—"On Day

1,001, Trump Made It Clear: Being 'Presidential' Is Boring.'"[13] It is true that Trump likes to keep his supporters connected to what he does and his many tweets and rallies are an effective way to develop and cement that emotional bond. It is also true that providing some anticipation and familiarity with established routines at rallies with supporters furthers that connection. Fighting back is also an effort to solidify those emotional and political connections and furthers the chance to accomplish presidential purposes.

It is clear that Trump enjoys these rallies. He is actually having some fun, which if you look back in his history is something he mentions is important to him (see Chapter 6). Trump's feigned boredom with presidential expectations has little to do with it.

Trump's breaches of conventional expectations of presidential decorum are cause for opprobrium and alarm among Trump opponents. They believe "guardrails of democracy" are being breached.[14] Those, as noted, are *theorized* conventions of behavior and procedure that mark the boundaries that Trump critics believe help to contain, constrain, and normalize presidential power,[15] especially if that president is named Trump.

Trump critics have varied complaints. For some, "Every vote cast for Donald Trump was a vote for vulgarity."[16] Others insist that, "If by now you don't find Donald Trump appalling, you're appalling."[17] For others he crossed the guardrail line by "refusing to release his tax returns, bragging about his penis size, feuding with the Muslim father of a fallen American soldier and choosing puerility over poetry at nearly every meaningful moment."[18] For others, it is the ongoing tweet fights with a large number and substantial range of opponents.[19] The nature and content of guardrails viewed as essential are clearly flexible and variable. However, as noted with legal setbacks to his immigration policies, Trump is certainly able to, and has, worked within the real constitutional guardrails that protect American Democracy.

Donald Trump's Fight Club Psychology: Origins and Motivations

Clearly, any analysis of President's Trump's leadership style has to begin with the obvious fact of his capacity for pugnacity. If there's one thing that the world has learned about Donald Trump is that he is a fighter. Yet in Trump's view he is a counter puncher who is only hitting back after he

4 DONALD TRUMP'S FIGHT CLUB PRESIDENCY   123

has been hit first. In an early interview, asked about his pugnacious style, Trump said[20]:

> this is a campaign. And usually and I think you know this better than anybody. I'm responding to them. I'm a counter-puncher. I think at every single instance I hit. For instance, Walker is very nice to me. All of a sudden, he hit me and I hit him back. All of these guys, Rubio is very nice to me. Couldn't have been nicer. All of a sudden a week ago, he started hitting me, I hit him back.

The list of Mr. Trump's public fights since becoming president (and before) is a long one.[21] However, an examination of Trump's many public fights over the years suggests he is being accurate in his view that he only fights back when being attacked. The caveat here is that what other people view as legitimate, if critical, observations, Mr. Trump often, and not always entirely inappropriately, construes as personal attacks rather than policy disagreements. It is unclear for example, whether Trump distinguishes the former from the latter when he refers to opponents like Scott Walker during the presidential nominating campaign being "very nice to me."

How a Willingness and Capacity to Fight Helped Trump Win the Republican Presidential Nomination

The Democrats nominated Hillary Clinton and Republicans fielded a large group of candidates that were heavy on establishment credentials and experience. Many of them had considerable and formidable political assets, but each had fatal flaws that Mr. Trump saw and exploited.

Consider the fate of Jeb Bush. He was an experienced moderate establishment Republican candidate with enormous political and financial resources. However, he proved himself to be very far out of sync with the wishes of many American voters by famously and ineffectively campaigning as a "joyful tortoise."[22] That self-characterization was flawed in two fatal ways.

First, what disaffected Americans wanted was someone who shared their distress at what was happening to them and their country, not a "happy warrior." And they wanted someone who would do something about their distress now, not a tortoise joyfully dawdling along with no sense of urgency on their behalf. Trump's characterization of Mr. Bush as a "low energy" candidate delivered a *coup de grâce*, in part because it fit remarkable well with Mr. Bush's own view of his campaign.

Of all the seventeen GOP candidates, only Donald Trump recognized what was motivating many Americans and what they wanted from their next president. They wanted a dramatic change in the status quo. He responded, in his own unique way, directly to that wish. Mr. Trump's gift for branding both his political insights and his opponents clearly had its advantages in the nomination fight and general election.

However, two important elements get lost in the focus on Trump's bombast. First, Trump alone among the candidates realized what many Americans were looking for someone who would really fight for them. Second, and equally important, Mr. Trump had the psychological willingness and capacity to act on that insight. Mr. Trump's stature-shrinking characterizations of the other candidates signaled that he was a different kind of campaigner. He was one who would go for the political jugular as often as necessary, previous ideas of decorum be damned. He was forceful, profane, and willing to say what many thought about a range of subjects that had become taboo to discuss outside of establishment-approved ways. In so doing, Mr. Trump gave many Americans the idea that he would put those qualities to work on their behalf. That was precisely what many of them wanted.

The Psychological Foundations of Trump's Fighting Style: Recognition and Respect

A first point to be made about the serial public fight-club dimension of Trump's style of presidential leadership and governance is that it is a response to criticism that either does not acknowledge or directly disparages what Trump feels are his legitimate accomplishments. This is not a matter of acknowledging Trump's well known penchant for hyperbole.[23] It is well known that Trump feels that, "a little hyperbole never hurts. People want to believe that something is the biggest and the greatest and the most spectacular." Trump frequently obliges this expectation and the various "fact check" efforts have to work hard just to keep up.

Less often acknowledged is what comes after that oft-repeated quote. Trump continues "you can do a wonderful promotion and get all kinds of press, and you can throw in a little hyperbole, *but if you don't deliver the goods, people will eventually catch on.*"[24] This is Trump's promise keeper strategy for restoring some measure of public trust.

Trump's serial hyperbole merits the public reality discount it gets from his supporters, though not always from his critics. They often take Trump literally but not seriously.[25] What would taking Trump seriously entail? It might take the form of simply acknowledging that Trump has built a generally successful major worldwide business empire,[26] instead of more narrowly focusing on the setbacks he's endured along the way.[27]

It is Trump's setbacks, real and imagined, that dominate Trump career coverage. One overview of Trump's thirty-year effort to develop a major project on the largest undeveloped land parcel in New York City (site of the old Pennsylvania rail lines property) announced that this project, and "certainly not a political office of any kind," was to be Trump's legacy.[28] With equal certainty the author also announced: "*Trump failed*" because the vision he started with changed over a thirty-year period of the parcel's development. That time period however, required Trump to deal with changes in an enormously complex thicket of social and governmental interests, the realities of multiple bureaucratic agencies whose approval was needed and whose personnel changed, changes in the New York political leadership, disciplined, well-funded and committed opposition, and economic upturns and downturns.

It is not until one reads very deeply into this very long 4500 word article that one learns that according to the author, "*Trump found a way to win after all—with the help, remarkably, of enemies he converted to allies.*" How did he do that? By modifying his vision and designs to work with those who had opposed him, a reflection of the flexibility that characterizes his decision style then and now. In other words the flexibility that allowed Trump to "win," was the very basis of the article's conclusion that he had "failed."

Taking Trump politically seriously might take the form of noting that whatever its real or imaged drawbacks, the Trump administration did get passed "the most far-reaching overhaul of the U.S. tax system *in decades*."[29] It might take the form of noting that it has made substantial strides in enforcing immigration laws already passed but ignored or downplayed over a number of years. It might take the form of acknowledging that Trump is the only recent American president who has directly taken on Chinese trade and economic strategies meant to further their international ascendency and tried to check them. Or it simply might take a

126   S. RENSHON

Princeton history professor allowing an administration of which he disapproves more than a year in office before concluding that it is "a colossal failure."[30]

TRUMP'S FIGHT FOR RECOGNITION

The wish to be recognized for one's achievements is a very ordinary part of human psychology in societies like that of the United States that value individualism, ambition, and ardent efforts to realize your goals. That wish can be frustrated in many ways. A person can fall short of achievement that calls for recognition. Or, they can achieve a great deal and for a variety of reasons not be recognized for their accomplishments.

That is what happened to Othmar H. Ammann, the gifted and enormously accomplished architect[31] of the massive, and for its time, unprecedented Verrazano-Narrows Bridge. That bridge joined Staten Island and Brooklyn and was the longest and highest suspension bridge in the world. The 1964 gala opening ceremony included 1500 officials, fifty-two black limousines and numerous dignitaries including Robert Moses, Cardinal Spellman, Mayor Wagner, and Governor Rockefeller among many others.

It also included then eighteen-year old Donald Trump who was in attendance with his father. What happened that day to the architect during the celebration of his work and creation made a lasting impression on Trump. He carried the lesson of that impression into his adulthood and on into his presidency.

Gwenda Blair, one of Trump's better biographers, wrote of that incident[32]:

> it was an obvious occasion for politicians to deliver remarks and receive applause. But what Donald noted was that Othmar Hermann Ammann, the 85-year old Swiss-born immigrant who designed the bridge, was alone and ignored. "I realized then, and there something I would never forget" the young developer-to-be told a reporter many years later. "I don't want to be made anybody's sucker."

A retrospective on the then contemporary descriptions of those events notes that, "In the bleachers, in the second row, quietly sat Othmar H. Ammann, arguably the world's greatest bridge engineer. He sat inconspicuously in the crowd, rising only once to acknowledge the praise Wagner

4 DONALD TRUMP'S FIGHT CLUB PRESIDENCY   127

heaped upon him." Actually, the praise was delivered by Robert Moses,[33] legendary New York City builder and the master of ceremonies with one startling omission as he introduced the architect to the assembled crowd[34]:

> "I now ask that one of the significant great men of our time—modest, unassuming and too often overlooked on such grandiose occasions—stand and be recognized ... It may be that in the midst of so many celebrities, you don't even know who he is," Mr. Moses continued, as the crowd applauded. "My friends, I ask that you now look upon the greatest living bridge engineer, perhaps the greatest of all time ..." There was more applause, *but Mr. Moses forgot to mention his name.* Mr. Ammann sat quietly down, again lost in the second row of the grandstand.

In fact, Trump's fuller response in a 1980 interview,[35] not reported by Blair, ties the impact of this incident directly to the failure of the acknowledgments to specifically mention the architect's name. Trump said during that interview[36]:

> In a corner, just standing there in the rain, is this man, this 85-year-old engineer who came from Sweden (sic) and designed this bridge, who poured his heart into it, and nobody even mentioned his name. I realized then and there, that if you let people treat you how they want, you'll be made a fool.

To Trump, it was the architect who designed the bridge and oversaw its construction who was the indispensable, knowledgeable, and practical visionary responsible for this monument of accomplishment. Trump's identification with the bridge's architect was no accident. It was as a future builder of innovative and spectacular projects that Trump envisioned himself as he looked out on the New York skyline from Queens as a young adult, and dreamed of changing Manhattan's skyline.

In reality, given Trump's deal-making concerns with the bottom line and his emphasis on his net worth, often magnified, as a reflection of his success, it wasn't only making money that focused his gaze across the river. If he had only wanted to make money, Trump could have joined his father every day at his small non-descript office on Avenue Z in the Coney Island section of Brooklyn and continued the strategy of the quiet and successful accumulation and sales of properties wherever an opportunity arose that made his father a multi-millionaire.

Trump clearly wanted something more out of his life than money. He wanted more than the kind of success that being rich indicated. He wanted to do exciting (to him), innovative, large-scale projects that took substantial talent and drive to accomplish. He wanted projects which when completed would stand out as enormous monuments to those characteristics and that would earn well-deserved recognition for the person responsible for carrying them out.

As the major architect for Trump's Commodore building project, Derr Scutt once put it,[37] "If it's not impossible, he doesn't want to do it. It's not interesting to him." Trump himself said in speaking of the complex assembling of the land parcels on which he built his signature Atlantic City casino, "I have an almost perverse attraction to complicated deals partially because they tend to be more interesting ..."[38] It was the enormity of the challenge that partially motivated Trump, and reimaging the New York skyline was a dream worthy of that challenge. So is the *Politics of American Restoration*.

As Trump put it in remembering a conversation with his father who wanted him to stay and work in Queens and Brooklyn:

> I gotta go into Manhattan. I gotta build those big buildings. I gotta do it, Dad. I've gotta do it.[39]

Having done that and much more, and having received little credit or recognition for those accomplishments it is not surprising that in announcing his presidential run he would echo the lessons he learned more than a half century before at the Verrazano Bridge opening:

> But they all said, a lot of the pundits on television, "Well, Donald will never run, and one of the main reasons is he's private and he's probably not as successful as everybody thinks." So I said to myself, you know, nobody's ever going to know unless I run, because I'm really proud of my success. I really am.

Trump's Fight for Respect

Trump's fighting response however, is not only a matter of others not acknowledging his accomplishments. It is also a matter of his wishing to be taken *seriously* as person and as a major player with important contributions to make in the fields that he has entered, including politics. This

4 DONALD TRUMP'S FIGHT CLUB PRESIDENCY 129

may seem like a distinction without much difference, but psychologically it is important.

As a young adult, Trump began his business career in the New York City real estate business against his father's wishes. His father, Fred Trump, a major real estate developer in Brooklyn and Queens, thought the idea was "crazy."[40] Trump says that his father told him[41]: Donald, don't go into Manhattan. That's the big leagues. We don't know anything about that. Don't do it.

His father warned him that the major players in Manhattan were not hospitable to "our kind of people," and he was right. One analysis at the time noted that Mr. Trump was "a young man in an older man's business." Sam LeFrak, one of big players in the Manhattan real-estate market was quoted as saying of Mr. Trump, "the kid only knows how to talk not build." "Soon, everyone, not just the LeFraks were sneering."[42] At first, "senior realty titans scoffed, believing that braggadocio was the sum and substance of the blond, blue-eyed, six-footer who wore maroon suits and matching loafers, frequented Elaine's and Regine's in the company of fashion models,"[43] but through sheer determination, entrepreneurial flair, and eventual results, he proved them mistaken.

The responses to Trump's political interests were no less patronizing and dismissive. At the 2011 White House Correspondent's Dinner, President Obama publicly mocked, Mr. Trump.[44] This led some reporters to ask whether that experience was responsible for Trump's presidential campaign.[45] Similarly, at the 2016 Alfred E. Smith Memorial Foundation Dinner, Mr. Trump was "Heckled by New York Elite at Charity Dinner" as the *New York Times* headline put it for some of his remarks about Hilary Clinton.[46] Her speech contained similarly sharp lines against Mr. Trump that were applauded. It is unlikely however, that these examples for public "roasting" in humorous venues were directly responsible for Trump's presidential candidacy. Trump had agreed to be the subject of a comedy roast in 2011, the same year as the White House Correspondent's dinner and took the "insults" well.[47]

Respect however, continued to elude Trump. Mitt Romney wanted campaign contributions from him and the endorsement of his own candidacy, but never took Trump seriously. He took steps to make sure they weren't photographed together when he visited Trump Towers in 2011, entering and exiting discreetly, with no cameras on hand to capture the event.[48] And at a campaign event to showcase Mr. Trump's endorsement of Mr. Romney's candidacy in 2012, his campaign put up blue curtains around the ballroom where the endorsement took place, so that Mr. Romney did not appear to be standing "in a burlesque house or one of Saddam's palaces."[49]

As Trump himself said, "I realized that unless I actually ran, I wouldn't be taken seriously."[50] The questions to be answered are "taken seriously" in what way, and for what reasons? Given the reality of Trump's narcissism as one obvious element of his psychology, it is plausible, but inaccurate, to see his realization as a wish to be taken seriously in order to make himself feel important. A more plausible explanation is Trump's wish to be taken seriously as a result of what he felt that he has accomplished and for which he has received scant, if any credit, especially from those opposing him. We will take up these issues at greater length in Chapter 6.

The Early Family Origins of a Presidential Style

The quest for recognition and being taken seriously can spring primarily from either an effort to validate self-esteem (a manifestation of ordinary narcissism), or as an acknowledgement of accomplishment, or more frequently both. Trump's concern for being taken seriously in politics echoes his quest to be taken seriously as a major player in Manhattan real-estate circles. Both were a reflection of his view that his accomplishments were legitimate and entitled to some recognition. In politics he had courted and been courted, but it was his views on trade, the "free rides" of some allies, and American military involvement that he though accurate and deserving of the hearing they would get if he had a real political voice.

That still leaves the question of how the quest for validation became so strongly linked with fighting for what he felt he had earned. The answer begins with his relationship to his father Fred.

FATHER AND SON

Mr. Trump's father was a very hard working, productive, and successful real-estate developer in Queens and Brooklyn. There is no doubt that he loved his children, but he achieved his success by, among other things, his determination and single mindedness. Trump said of him, "He was a strong, strict father, a no-nonsense kind of guy."[51] And those traits helped make him a disciplinarian as a father. According to his father Fred, Donald Trump was, "a pretty rough fellow when he was small."[52]

Not surprisingly father and son clashed over rules of deportment. Trump was by his own admission a rebellious and occasionally a disruptive young man. Young Donald was a boisterous adolescent, prone to testing boundaries, especially his father's rules. He and his best friend sometimes quietly left Queens to explore the "wilds" of New York City for a day of fun including such risk-taking adventures as riding on the small platforms separating the cars of the subway. His father was hard-working, ambitious, learn-the-rules-of-success-and-apply-them kind of guy. Not surprising, Fred Trump came to see part of his fatherly role as needing to calm his son down and, as Trump remembers his father putting it, "taking the lumps out."[53]

Trump recalled[54]:

> I was very bad. That's why my parents sent me to a military academy. I was rebellious. Not violent or anything, but I wasn't exactly well behaved. I once gave one of my teachers a black eye. I talked back to my parents and to people in general. Perhaps it was more like bratty behavior, but I certainly wasn't the perfect child.

Yet, Donald Trump stood his ground against his father. In Trump's own words:

> [I was] never intimidated by my father the way most people were. I stood up to him, and he respected that.[55]

Anti-Trump pundits and aspiring but untrained Sigmund Freud amateurs, like Tony Schwartz, who helped write Trump's bestseller *The Art of the Deal* and has publicly expressed a "deep sense of remorse"[56] for having done so, provide little help in understanding that father and son relationship. Schwartz has written: "Refusing to accept blame or admit uncertainty is a habit he [Trump] developed early in life to protect himself from a brutal father, whose withering criticism he had watched drive his older brother, Fred Jr., to alcoholism and an early death."[57] Elsewhere he has written, "He [Trump] had a very brutal childhood. That's a fact."[58]

Leaving aside the ugly and unsubstantiated accusation that Trump's father was responsible for his son Fred Jr's death due to alcoholism,

Fred Trump's "brutality" is not a fact. It's a characterization and not an accurate one at that.

The same holds for Trump's niece's supposed exposé consisting almost entirely of her own bitter revenge saturated allegations to get back at her uncle, the president, that had its roots in a bitter family feud over money.[59] She alleges, based on no evidence than her own assertions, that the president suffered "child abuse" at the hands of his father because Fred Trump wanted obedience and Donald was forced to give it to him. These alleged experiences "scarred Trump for life" and turned him into a Frankenstein monster, "but without the conscience."[60] Subtle.

According to the *Washington Post*, "Mary Trump has long been estranged from the family after a dispute over her inheritance and other matters."[61]

Also, according to the *Washington Post*,[62] when Fred Trump died the niece, "Mary and her brother had hoped they would get an amount close to what would have gone to their father, if he had lived, but they learned they were due to receive a lesser amount, and a probate fight ensued, court records show. In an interview she gave a decade ago, Trump's niece acknowledged.[63]

> Given this family, *it would be utterly naive to say it has nothing to do with money*. But for both me and my brother, it has much more to do with that our father [Fred Jr.] be recognized..

With a larger portion of Fred Trump's estate.

In reality, Trump's father loved his son and was at his side helping him throughout a lifetime of financial, political, and personal ups and downs. It was Fred who gave his son the seed money to begin to realize his Manhattan real-estate aspirations. It was Fred who once bought a million dollars of casino chips, that he didn't play, to provide his son with a needed cash infusion. It was Fred who helped his son get the necessary political backing from then Mayor Beame for his first big effort in Manhattan. Fred was proud of all that his son accomplished and said so, publicly many times.

Were there tensions between the two very strong willed men? Of course, some have been noted above. Yet there is no doubt Fred loved and trusted his son. Donald Trump was the only person his father ever let sign company checks on his own. And, as noted, Fred Trump provided his son with financial, political, and emotional support over the course of both their lives.

It is also true that Trump loved his father. In one of many such interviews Trump recalled his father lovingly[64]: "My father passed away recently, and he was something very special. He was somebody, to me, very special." In another more recent interview with the *Washington Post*, he said, "I had a great father."[65] There are many more Trump tributes to his father of which these are only a sampling.

Clashes with his father were certainly one part of Donald Trump's development. Yet deep mutual love and affection were the primary foundation of their relationship. Indeed, it is not too far afield to suggest that Thump not only loved his father, but also idealized him. Stanley Leibowitz who was the rental agent for one of Fred Trump's large properties recalled, "his father was his idol, anytime he would come into the building Donald would be with him."[66] One of Trump's high school friends recalled that[67]:

> During rides home from school on a Port Authority bus, the young Donald would point out all the buildings built by his father. "We'd go through Queens and he'd say, 'My dad, he built all those homes over there'." He'd look out, very proud.

Trump's development was, as noted in Chapter 2, anchored by two powerful emotional poles. The first, according to Trump, was his mother's unconditional love, even as Trump was, by his own admission, not an easy child to raise. The second pole was anchored by his determined, hardworking, no-nonsense father who was devoted to his son throughout his life, and who Trump loved and most likely idealized. Mr. Trump has been trying to reconcile his own psychology within that continuum his whole adult life.

TRUMP'S FIRST REAL POLITICAL FIGHT

Trump's early fight-back experience with his father were followed by another set of seminal formative psychological experiences. In his first years as a principle in his father's real estate business, he fought back hard[68] against government accusations that the Trump organization had discriminated against minorities. Reading through the news reports and court transcripts,[69] it is a complex case.

There was some evidence of racial steering, that Trump denied. There was the issue of the government wanting tenants to be able to use welfare checks as indicators of their income, a position that Trump did not accept. There also was the nowhere stated rationale that most of Trump's tenants were working-class people with their own views of who their neighbors should be at a time when racial prejudice had not yet substantially faded from national consciousness. These issues were fought out in hearings and a Consent Agreement reached in which both sides claimed vindication of their positions.

Our primary interest in these events, given the conflicting evidence and no-fault settlement, is what Trump actually did in response to the charges. His was the only real-estate company, of which there were a number, that was sued by the government and fought back. Trump enlisted Roy Cohn, a smart and extremely aggressive attorney, and they fought over several years, finally agreeing to sign a "consent order" that admitted no wrongdoing.

James David Barber has called our attention to the importance of a president's young adult developmental experiences in his "first independent political success." That is the time or set of circumstances that a president, in this case Trump, stepped into a primary role as a young adult and forged a strategy and a style.[70] That federal discrimination charge and Trump's decision to fight instead of settle cemented the lesson he learned dealing with his father growing up—don't just acquiesce, fight back. It also set the stage for Trump's hard fought and tumultuous business rise, his abrupt stumbles, and the eventual resurrection of his business empire against tough odds. Trump has been, from his childhood and into and through his adulthood, a "fighter," and it is not at all surprising that he carried that style and the psychology that underlay it, into the White House.

Fighting for American Restoration

Donald Trump's "fight club presidency" owes its expression to several recent political developments, as well as to its psychological origins. One factor is the rise of partisanship in the American public that now permeates many of the country's political and civic institutions and organizations. There is also the "war room" mentality of both political parties as they struggle for advantage and control. Accompanying that has been the decline of conventional standards of campaign etiquette and decorum to a more no-holds barred, whatever it takes to win, approach.

The Trump presidency may be the contemporary apogee of these elements, but they all preceded him. What did not precede him, and is the more immediate cause of his response is his opposition's by any means necessary campaign to deny him the Republican nomination, the presidency, and once he won that office, political legitimacy (see Chapter 3). There is no need to use the buzzword, "deep state" to describe this development.[71] It is neither accurate nor necessary to argue that those who point to the opposition's ascendancy are conspiracy theorists.[72] As noted in Chapter 3, no hidden central command is needed because adherents throughout the country's major governmental, political, civic, and other institutions share the same general perspectives, Trump antipathies, and act accordingly.

It is not hyperbole to say that Mr. Trump, his presidency, and above all his efforts to revise and where he thinks necessary overturn, decades of conventional policy assumptions are under siege and constant, forceful attack. From the perspective of those who hold Trump opposition views, this is neither surprising, nor illegitimate. They see Mr. Trump and his presidential policy ambitions as ill-informed and wrong. They also believe Mr. Trump to be simply, "the worst, most dangerous president in modern history."[73]

Mr. Trump, his supporters, and the opposition all agree that the latter will stop at nothing to keep him from bringing about his presidential policy purposes (*American Restoration*). They think their opposition is necessary and warranted. Trump and his supporters strongly believe that the country needs to implement the policies that he was legitimately elected to put into place. This politically primal conflict raises a more basic theoretical set of questions. Can entrenched policy paradigms be changed in the face of strong opposition and do Trump's presidential strategies offer a strategy to effectively do so? We take up these questions in Chapter 12.

Recall that in Skowronek's terms, Mr. Trump is aiming for a *reconstructive* presidency, but so far has only been able to achieve a *preemptive* one. The latter according to Skowronek: "Like all opposition leaders, these presidents have the freedom of their independence from established commitments, but unlike presidents in the politics of reconstruction, their repudiative authority is manifestly limited by the political, institutional, and ideological supports that the old establishment maintains …"[74] That seems like a very apt description of where the Trump presidency now stands—lots of disruption, less consolidated reconstruction.

However, the question is not only where the Trump presidency is now, but also where it wants to go, and how the president thinks he might get there. Mr. Trump's core presidential ambitions, the *Politics of American Restoration*, require him to take on the conventionally accepted policy paradigms that he wishes to revise or replace. His task is not a matter of taking on only one policy area, but a number of them both domestic and foreign. Recall there are the eight pillars of Trump policy reform (as he sees it)—the courts, economic growth and opportunity (including jobs and energy development), de-regulation, health care, immigration, foreign policy, trade, and lifting the fear of discussing many political debate topics (aka "political correctness") all containing a great many discrete policies within those categories. These are not small bore policies. Together they represent a vast historic effort at *Restoration*. Fierce, determined political opposition is to be expected in these circumstances and that is precisely what Mr. Trump and his presidency have faced.

How Limited Are Trump's Restoration *Prospects?*

Given his *Restoration* ambitions, are President Trump's options for eventual success limited and difficult to achieve? Yes. In the best of all democratic worlds—that of deliberative democratic theory,[75] he would place his ideas—on immigration, taxes, job creation, regulation, climate, trade, ISIS, Syria, Russia, Iran, and a host of other policy issues into public debate and win over Americans to his perspective over time. This sounds like a deliberative democratic fantasy and it is.

Many basic and obvious considerations mitigate against this strategy for any president, and especially one who aspires to *Reconstruction*. First and most obviously, the current state of American politics in no way resembles university or privately sponsored (e.g., IQ2 debates)[76] exercises in deliberative democracy. In those highly regulated venues each side keeps to its allotted time, conventions of decorum are scrupulously observed, moderators are even-handed and fair, and the audience aside from being interested in the one issue (not many) that is typically debated are respectful of the idea of real, fair debate and its rules.

None of these circumstances exist in the real contemporary world of American political life and debate. Presidential time in office is relatively short and even failing paradigms take time to lose their credibility, in non-catastrophic circumstances. In such situations, they still are able to retain some of their power past their demonstrated effectiveness because of inertia and the support of those who profit from supporting the *status quo* in terms of power and prestige.

Gathering support for new approaches or paradigms requires public experience with these policies as well as debate. Public experience require examples, which in turn require operating policies in order to make judgments. These new policies must be enacted in a political not a debating context in which the consequences include loss of power, status, and the viscerally divisive political view that sees the new policies either as long overdue or downright dangerous.

Trump is also at another great "deliberative disadvantage." He is seeking to revise or discard policy paradigms that many establishment Republicans, Democrats, and even many conservatives have come to accept, if not support. As a result, Trump is therefore not only going against the policy grain of progressive Democratic views but also the views of many establishment figures in his own party. Obviously that bi-partisan agreement contains no assumption that these paradigms are effective policies, or that they can't be revised to be better. It does mean that Trump cannot fully count on the united support of his party for many of his *Restoration* initiatives any more than he can count on getting a respectful and fair hearing from Trump opponents and their major supporters across American public and civic institutions.

The Psychological and Political Functions of Fighting Back

Trump's presidential ambitions are up against a "by any means necessary" opposition. What's a combative, never give up president who strongly believes in his *Restoration* policies to do? Fight.

Trump's fight club presidency is designed to enact some of his policy views, so that the American public may actually judge them. It is a good illustration of an important element of a president's basic psychology directly meeting the nature of the political moment. Trump's combative nature and leadership style are arguably exactly the kind of character traits that are necessary if Trump is to have a chance of succeeding with his *Restoration* presidential agenda given the nature, power, and level of opposition of all those arrayed against him. There is however, more to Trump's fight club presidency than having a chance to enact his vision of *American Restoration*, as important as that is for him. There are more personal issues involved, among them self-respect and validation.

FIGHTING BACK AS A FORM OF SELF-RESPECT AND POLITICAL SELF-VALIDATION

Mr. Trump has a long personal history of fighting back beginning with his father, a formidable man with strong views. Yet there is much more to his fighting back than that. Mr. Trump's willingness to fight back has made him a champion of his supporters and helped to stimulate the anger of his opponents. His core supporters expect him to do just that, and they approve of it.[77] They feel, not incorrectly, that in fighting for his presidency he is fighting for them.

Yet, fighting back serves other more personal purposes as well. The president's fights also function as a form of emotional self-validation and a protector of the crucial sense of personal integrity. As one observer noted, "The president's much-maligned Twitter stream provides a modern way to self-validate. Anything he says registers thousands of likes, thousands of retweets and, over time, millions of new followers."[78] That, obviously, provides a strong basis for knowing that you are not alone in seeking to put into place your policy plans. Yet, it also reaffirms a sense of personal integrity—that consists of persevering under incredibly difficulty circumstances and not giving up in response to severe and unrelenting hostility.

Fighting back also provides an emotional shield against the political and emotional onslaught directed against him and his administration. That onslaught has inflicted a large psychological price on the administration, and is meant to do so. Early in the president's term then White House Press Secretary Sean Spicer described the unrelenting negative coverage of the Trump White House as "demoralizing." He then went on to say: "And it's unbelievably frustrating when you're continually told its [administration policies are] not big enough; it's not good enough. You can't win."[79] That was part of its purpose.

The same dynamic was on view in the relentless assault against other Trump appointees. For example Scott Pruitt, Trump's EPA Administrator was said to have resigned "as a result of a very large number of investigations brought about by numerous accusations of ethics and management lapses."[80] All of the accusations were discussed in the nation's newspapers before any conclusions could be reached as to their factual accuracy as a result of a formal investigation, with one exception. The GAO did find that "the E.P.A. had not notified Congress as required before spending more than $5,000 on office equipment."[81] In this case, the charge was for a sound proof phone booth for confidential conversations that was purchased. A lapse in procedural requirements? Yes. However, was that notification error an act of such corruptive or misuse of power magnitude as to require firing or resignation? Hardly.

The many other allegations against Mr. Pruitt had not been officially examined or investigated at the time he announced his resignation. A *Washington Post* headline read "Scott Pruitt steps down as EPA head after ethics, management scandals." A more accurate headline would have read (emphasis added): "Scott Pruitt steps down as EPA head after *allegations* of ethics, management scandals."[82]

Given their large number and the wide range of allegation made, it seems fair to suggest that the examination and resolution of the barrage of accusations on the merits of each case was not their real point. Mr. Pruitt's resignation letter contained the ordinary odes to his honor at having served the president, but added this personal point: "However, the unrelenting attacks on me personally, my family, are unprecedented, and have taken a sizable toll on all of us."[83] And again, as was noted above in connection with Sean Spicer's lament about being demoralized, that is one of the purposes of the barrage against all things Trump.

No Trump administration official has been immune to this tactic, even those who like former Chief of Staff John Kelly who was originally welcomed as a constraint on Mr. Trump before it became clear that the two shared some similar policy views.[84] He is alleged to have called Mr. Trump an "idiot,"[85] a report he strongly denied.[86] That was reminiscent of an earlier allegation made that former Secretary of State Tillerson had reportedly called Trump a "moron."[87] Mr. Kelly has been the subject of repeated speculations that he would resign in protest against Mr. Trump's policies or his own supposed marginalization.[88] He eventually did[89] over disagreements with Trump's decision to withdraw some American troops from Syria.

Yet before leaving, in an interview with *NPR* on press coverage of him and the White House, he had this to say[90]:

> Working in the White House is the hardest thing I've ever done in my life, bar none. Well, first, with all due respect to people like yourselves, I was not ready for the press that covers a White House ... When I was

working in the Pentagon at a higher level, senior level the Pentagon press corps were really good to work with … This is vastly different. This is—*it's personal, it's vicious.*

In that same interview Mr. Kelly related this startling exchange with a reporter (emphasis added):

> I did my first [interview] off the record — that was immediately violated. But after about six weeks in a job one of the reporters said to me, "Look you were our worst nightmare. This place was a clown show before you showed up. We didn't think this president would last a year [or] 18 months. *Now that you're here, there's order to the place. The leaks all but went away. So, sorry but you got to go.*" So here I am, sitting, still here.

Mr. Kelly is known as an honest and straightforward man so the vignette carries some weight. It also fits in with the "by any means necessary" barrage of accusations mounted against the president and his administration noted above. It is also consistent with repeated public calls for anyone who works for Mr. Trump to immediately resign.[91]

THE CAPACITY TO FIGHT BACK AND PRESIDENTIAL RESILIENCE

One purpose of noting these unrestricted, unrestrained, and to date inexhaustible efforts to emotionally and politically cripple his presidency, is to underscore their existence as a fact of political life to be reckoned with by President Trump. Any president with *Reconstruction* ambitions, as Mr. Trump has, had better be prepared for unrelenting conflict. Deeply entrenched policy premises and the power associated with being their institutional representatives are not going to be given up without a fight, one that is being waged, as documented, by any means possible or necessary.

Mr. Trump's psychology, childhood, and career, have given him ample preparation for this onslaught. However, that is not the only point of the above evidence. Critics of President Trump assert that he cannot handle the stresses of the presidency and wilts under pressure. Maureen Dowd opined that, "He is not built for this hostile environment and it shows in his deteriorating psychological state."[92] That was said in 2017. The *New York Times* editorialized that, "Mr. Trump may be a more tender soul, or less resilient." In any case, "he can't seem to take the heat."[93] That view gained traction in the wake of Mr. Trump's decision to abandon his shutdown of the government to get financial backing for building new additions to his border barrier.[94]

Actually, the great preponderance of the evidence points in the opposite direction. In one news article, Jeffrey Tulis, a government professor at the University of Texas is quoted as saying of Trump, "He caves when people are tough with him,"[95] though several of the examples used in that article undercut Tulis' view. There are so many examples of Trump sticking to his policy views—immigration enforcement, the Iranian nuclear deal, the trade deals with Mexico and China, withdrawing most troops from northern Syria and downsizing American forces in Afghanistan that one would have thought that the "cave in" theory would have died of factual causes. However it has not, as recent characterizations that Mr. Trump "caved into Turkey's wish to have a buffer zone in northern Syria suggest."[96]

The ability to persist in the face of extreme adversity is a real part of Mr. Trump's psychology, honed during a business career that brought him face to face with his own personal economic Armageddon. His determined capacity to persist and overcome adversity has been noticed, but not analyzed. The psychological term for this is resilience. Two *New York Times* reporters note that, "Over the years, Mr. Trump has proved to be a resilient operator ..."[97] and they are among the few that have acknowledged this trait.[98]

Trump has had to absorb unrelenting public criticisms and the harshest kind of personal accusations that began once he became the Republican nominee on May 4, 2016.[99] During that time he has railed against what he sees as the unfairness and injustice of these attacks but on a completely separate track has stayed focused on what he wants to accomplish, a prime example of Trump being able to lead and govern simultaneously on two very different tracks.

President Trump has endured four years of the most extraordinary antipathy to him, his ideas, and his administration. That opposition continues unabated and is almost certain to continue into a second Trump term, if he gets one. Yet, it is clear that Mr. Trump has the capacity and determination to keep on going against gale force political headwinds without flagging or allowing the onslaught against him to drain him of motivation.

This is, if you are a Trump supporter, something to be applauded. If you are a Trump opponent it is a cause for despair to be viewed as a calamity.[100] But psychologically, it does seem to be a fact.

Mr. Trump's "fight-club presidency" is clearly not what Richard Neustadt had in mind with his observations regarding the importance of presidential "self-help."[101] However, Trump's so far undiminished fight back psychology clearly qualifies for inclusion in that category. Its self-help aspects include allowing the possibility of presidential success in his *Restoration* efforts as well as keeping the president on a more even emotional keel. This seems like an odd and certainly paradoxical observation given Mr. Trump's frequent public and private outbursts of frustration. Yet the fact remains that for all the emotional turmoil in his presidency, President Trump carries on advancing his many policy purposes as best he can in the circumstances. Passivity in the face of relentless assault can easily be experienced as not being self-respecting, and can easily become de-motivating. Passivity is, at any rate, not a discernible element of Mr. Trump's psychology.

The Hidden Dimension of Trump's Fighting Style: Freedom and Creativity

Freedom and creativity are not two words that immediately seem applicable to either the president or his fighting style. However, I want to suggest here that they are. In order to be able to fight you have to feel free to do so. That means you need fighting skills, but also importantly a level of psychological comfort with conflict, sometimes at a very elevated level.

There is no doubt that Trump reached a high level of fighting comfort early in his adulthood that was an integral part his subsequent career. A book detailing the history of Trump's fights with politicians and community leaders[102] would be a long one. Yet that alone doesn't explain Trump's success in utilizing this tool both in his business and political career.

It is at this point that freedom enters the explanation. In 1966 the psychologist Jack Brehm published an important book entitled *A Theory of Psychological Reactance*.[103] His theory was that having freedom and choice were extremely important to some people and that the prospect of having either taken away would stimulate a fight to retain them. Trump appears one of those people for whom Brehm's theory fits.

4 DONALD TRUMP'S FIGHT CLUB PRESIDENCY   143

Recall that Trump's father originally opposed his dream to become a Manhattan real estate developer. Trump went ahead anyway. Recall that the big real estate players there didn't think much of his ability to succeed. Yet succeed he did. Recall that politicians were willing to take his money but not be seen with him. Today he is president of the United States. Small wonder that at one point during a campaign event a town hall voter asked Trump[104]:

> "have you ever been told no?" He responded: "My whole life really has been a 'no' and I fought through it."

Clearly Trump rarely, if ever, took no for a final answer. Equally important, he built a career and an organization in which he didn't have to. The Trump Organization was vast in its reach and ambitions, but diminutive in the number of key personnel at the higher levels of the organization. At the pyramid's apex stood the singular and unique Mr. Trump. He was not one of many or even one of the few. He stood alone at the top and his ambitions, style, skills, and foibles, for better and worse, were allowed and given free reign.

That meant that Trump was free to fight, and he did. Yet that freedom also had one more implication. It allowed him to be creative. And he was.

Trump's creativity, his ability to chart a successful course to his goals outside of conventional paths was clearly on display during his presidential campaign. However that capacity had not mysteriously or unexpectedly arisen then. Trump had a long history of vision and innovation in his business career.

Discussing some of the differences between himself and his father Trump said, "But if I had an edge over my father, it might have been in concepts—the concept of a building."[105] Trump once told one of his biographers, "I won't make a deal just to make a profit. It has to have flair."[106]

There was the innovation of the facade of Trump's Grand Hyatt Hotel fusing mirrored glass onto the skeleton of the Commodore Hotel adjoining Grand Central Terminal. There was the innovation of the Atrium at Trump Towers—a vertical shopping mall rendered in peach marble and bronze with an 80-foot cascading waterfall. There was even innovation in the financing of some of his New York City projects.

All of these projects reflected Trump's successful capacity for salesmanship. They also reflected his detailed knowledge of unusual finance opportunities both public (the New York State Urban Development Corporation) and private (Equitable Life). Trump had an eye for undervalued properties with great potential that, when coupled with his vision, elevated their value. He also had an ability to harness his determination to carry on with these major projects, even if as in the case of Trump projects on the Upper West Side of New York, it took decades (see Chapter 8 for details on these innovations).[107]

Critics have confused Trump's boorish behavior, which is real enough, with assumptions that he is not only ignorant, but stupid (we take up the question of whether Trump is a dunce, a hedgehog, or a fox in Chapter 12). In so doing, they miss the bold, brash, unprecedented transgressive innovation that underlies some of Trump's success. For example, many sexual accusations were made directly against Trump by Hillary Clinton supporters and were alluded to by Mrs. Clinton. Trump could have protested and denied them, which he did, and let it go that, which he didn't.

Who else could have thought of assembling and show casing a group of women who had accused President Clinton of inappropriate sexual behavior toward them immediately before a debate with Hillary Clinton?[108] More to the point, who else would have done it? It was a bold, conventionally crass, but also a powerful and public signal of a fundamental psychological fact about Trump. He can not only think innovatively and ruthlessly, but also act in the same way, regardless of conventional decorum.

A slightly less contentious example of the same transgressive stance occurred during one of Trump's daily Coronavirus task force briefings. Mr. Trump had been criticized by some governors who accepted large amounts of federal aid and thanked Trump privately while complaining about him publicly in local news interviews. Some reporters at the briefings consistently raised these points of criticisms and framed a narrative that suggested Trump had been negligent or neglectful. In response, Trump began one such press conference with a several-minutes video presentation of these very same governors, and others praising his responsiveness.[109]

Again, many in these circumstances might have had Trump's annoyed or angry feelings, but it's difficult to imagine another modern president or candidate having that reel put together and using it to begin a national press conference. One anticipates that Tara Reade, who has filed a credible sexual assault claim against Joe Biden[110] will possibly become part in some directly physically present way in the fall Biden–Trump debates.

Interestingly, when asked during a contentious news conference by a reporter why he "felt the need to antagonize people," "why antagonize?" Trump responded rhetorically, "Because I don't care."[111] Actually, though, he does.

In an interview with the *New York Times*, Trump had this to say[112]: *"you know it would be, to me, a great achievement if I could come back here in a year or two years and say—and have a lot of the folks here say, 'You've done a great job.' And I don't mean just a conservative job, 'cause I'm not talking conservative. I mean just, we've done a good job."*

Here, Mr. Trump who has built his presidency in part around fighting that he sees as liberal bias, expresses the wish that he will be able one day to return to the *New York Times*, a bastion of liberal opposition, and have them agree that his efforts have been worthwhile. Could there be a more obvious example of Trump's need for validation for his accomplishments, even from his opponents?

Yet, Trump's basic self-insight about not caring is accurate to a substantial degree. He is able, psychologically, to stand and remain apart, if necessary. This helps explain how he was able to withstand enormous pressures from domestic interest groups and international allies and withdraw from the Paris Climate accords, among other Trump policy initiatives. One news analysis report called it:

> a remarkable rebuke to fellow heads-of-state, climate activists, corporate executives and members of the president's own staff, all of whom failed this week to change Mr. Trump's mind with an intense, last-minute lobbying blitz … In recent days, Mr. Trump withstood withering criticism from European counterparts who accused him of shirking America's role as a global leader and America's responsibility as the world's second largest emitter of planet-warming greenhouse gasses.[113]

It also helps explain how he was able to impose steel tariffs,[114] while defying allies both at home and abroad[115] and losing the chairman of his economic council as a result.[116] Being able to stand apart helps explain why he had little trouble taking some public positions against his stalwart supporters the NRA[117] after another terrible school shooting incident although he did not fully follow through on all the issues he mentioned, or breaking decades of foreign policy precedents by agreeing to meet directly with North Korean leader Kim Jong-un,[118] or drawing down American troop levels in Afghanistan and phrasing out troops in Syria.[119]

These counter conventional initiatives are being noted, not analyzed on substantive policy grounds. No approval or disapproval is either intended or implied. They are put forward in support of a different kind of analytical observation. As one 1983 profile noted, "Mr. Trump has operated as a lone wolf in Manhattan for nearly the last decade."[120] Add thirty-five years to that decade, substitute White House for Manhattan, and add his singular determination to act on what he thinks, and you have an important element of the Trump presidency.

Trump as a Reflexive Counter Puncher: A Downside to Trump's Leadership Style

Mr. Trump's inability to master aspects of his own psychology has helped his opponents at the expense of his presidency. Opposition to the Trump presidency is real, ferocious, and unrelenting. He has chosen as a matter of political necessity, and his own psychology, to fight back.

This is understandable given Mr. Trump's psychology and circumstances. Yet, as necessary and politically and psychologically functional as that response might be, it is still in need of line drawing, boundaries, and putting first things first. Mr. Trump has difficulty in drawing those distinctions.

Mr. Trump was correct, for example, in his assertion that first responders to the devastation caused by Hurricane Maria in Puerto Rico couldn't stay there forever.[121] However he could have coupled that obvious and accepted fact with a pledge to be there for that island, even after first responders left. He did say that the next day[122] after he had been accused of "abandoning" the island.[123]

It is unclear whether his original statement was a result of his view that he was criticized and being pushed to make commitments by the leadership of the island that had a long history of incompetence and corruption issues[124] and wanted to lay down a limits marker. What is clear is that whatever issues he envisioned down the road with the outspokenly anti-Trump Democratic mayor of San Juan or other members of the country's political class, the primary sufferers from the storm were ordinary people and they needed his reassurance, not his future limits marker. "We'll be

4 DONALD TRUMP'S FIGHT CLUB PRESIDENCY   147

there with you as recovery proceeds" would have been a perfectly appropriate and reassuring message without, however committing the president to any particular specifics.

Trump has a visceral aversion to being criticized, pushed, and hemmed in by political leaders and advisors whose competence and motives he doesn't trust. That is a rather long list and stems from Trump's stated view that advisors and others who offer their views often have their own self-interests in mind. Usually, as was the case for the remedial foreign policy seminar arranged for him by some of his chief advisors (see Chapter 12), it is to get him to abandon his views. This well-honed suspicion often leads him to push his focus away from where it ought to have concentrated, as in the Puerto Rican case.

Trump's well-honed "fight-back" tendencies getting in the way of a more appropriate response can be seen in his response to criticism of his condolence call to the family of a Marine killed in combat. A Democratic Congresswoman who was in the car when the call came criticized Mr. Trump for being "insensitive." He of course pushed back.[125]

Whether the family was right to misunderstand the sentiments that Trump was trying to convey or not, it was their grief not their understanding or misunderstanding of Mr. Trump's sentiments that was the point. As one thoughtful critic wrote, Trump could have easily just said, "I really didn't mean it the way you heard it and it pains me to think that I've in any way added to your distress. Please accept my apology and deepest condolences."[126] Instead his reflexive pattern of fighting got him into a fight with a Democratic congresswoman who was a Trump opponent, but whose motivations were not the issue.

Trump: Learning How to Be a President

What accounts for these lapses? For critics, the answer is easy. Mr. Trump is a rude, self-centered man who lacks a shred of empathy, as you would expect of someone who is a "malignant narcissist." For such people, there are no boundaries, only the aggrandizement of their own needy impulses. Trump's critics say he's all ego, misunderstanding Freud's term for the psychological agency that helps us all navigate the world though the operation of the "Reality Principle." They mean Trump's conduct is governed by the "Pleasure Principle," and that he has an Id-dominated psychology.

Mistaken nomenclature aside, there is a very large body of evidence that contradicts these assertions. The hardly Trump-friendly *Washington*

Post reported that Trump's visceral reactions to pictures of the Syrians gassed by their government ("Horrible' pictures of suffering moved Trump to action on Syria"[127]) led him to approve bombing raids against that country's government. Trump has spoken publicly, directly, and movingly about his sorrow when meeting the caskets of soldiers killed in the line of duty.[128] There is his behind the scenes charitable help to those in distress noted in Chapter 1, and in the section on the "Unexpected Trump" (see Chapter 8).

In short, rather than the "malignant narcissist" of anti-Trump opposition distortions, there is a complex man capable of feeling and expressing regret, sorrow, and empathy. Again, there is more, much more to Mr. Trump than his caricature.

A more likely and useful explanation of Trump's difficulty in drawing and keeping within lines, even as he operates outside of the ordinary limits of what we have come to expect in our modern president's typical behavior comes from experience as owner, developer, and sole real decision maker of the Trump Organization. As noted, Trump had many decades of experience being the sole person in charge of his empire and ultimately was responsible for the decisions he made, for better or worse. Any close examination of his business and personal life makes clear his interest, for branding and personal reasons, in living out many aspects of his very rich, some think glamorous life. He has done so very publicly. He has indulged both his unconventional business strategies, personal life, and his tendency often for branding purposes, to keep score by accumulation.

The key word here however, is unconventional. Trump succeeded, when he did, by being different and doing things in unexpected ways. Whether it was gaining a commitment from the Penn Central railroad for the land he acquired or his forays into wrestling or buying a football team, Trump found a way to do what he wanted. Sometimes that was a successful strategy, others times it was not, but the key point is that being unconventional became a fixture of his decision making.

The presidency provided quite a reality shock to that strategy. It's a truism that Trump had no political experience in political office before becoming president, but less attention has been paid to exactly what that means in Trump's case. What it means is a gap in understanding exactly how things work when you are president.

Dwight Eisenhower ran into the same difficulties. As Supreme Allied Commander he had whole institutions designed to carry out his orders.

Once in the White House he was surprised to find that his orders didn't carry themselves out and that he needed to find ways to follow through.[129] Trump's knowing how things worked was different. He continually chafed against restrictions that were both administrative and legal. "Why can't I do that" was a constant complaint. Rex Tillerson, Trump's former Secretary of State in his testimony to Congressional investigators had this exchange[130]:

BY SR. DEMOCRATIC COUNSEL:

Q: So, sir, in that same interview, you said publicly that you frequently had to say to the President: "I understand what you want to do, but you can't do it that way, it violates the law." How many times did that happen?

A: Well, let me try to answer it this way, and first, I'm going to just say right up front, *the President never asked me to violate the law, okay. So, I want to be clear, that that statement doesn't get misinterpreted by anyone.* A lot of these—a lot of the early issues had to do with immigration policy, actions, implementation. And, you know, I shared the President's endpoint objective. *It was how do you want to get it done, you know. And he was—often times wanted to do it: Boom, you know, this is it. Let's issue this.* And I'm not a lawyer, so let me be clear on that, too, I'm not a lawyer, so it wasn't fair of me to be giving him legal advice. But I knew a bit about immigration laws. *And so on occasion I would have to say to him: Well, we can't do it that way. And I think I said, you know: It's going to get challenged in the court and you're going to lose, you know.*

Like every president before him, Trump has had to learn how to be a president. The specific issues for each president differ, but they all must contend with the gap between their expectations and the nature of the office as it is when they enter it. Trump is no exception to this.

NOTES

1. Gabriel Debenedetti. 2017. "Democrats Launch Scorched-Earth Strategy Against Trump," *Politico*, January 26.
2. Dana Blanton. 2017. "*Fox News* Poll: Voters Say Trump's Tweets Hurting Agenda," *Fox News*, June 28.

3. Stephanie McNeil. 2017. "Trump Supporters Love Everything He's Doing, But Some Think He Could Cool It on the Tweets," *Buzz Feed*, July 25.
4. See Danti Chinni. 2017. "Trump's Twitter Habit Gets Low Approval Rating from Both Parties," *WSJ*, September 26. The data reported in this article show that Trump's use of Twitter to communicate with the American people generally receives low levels of support, though that varies somewhat by partisanship. However, over 70% of the sample supports him tweeting when "he was agreeing with congressional Democrats on legislation." See also David Byler. 2018. "Trump's Trump-iest Tweets Aren't Popular," *Weekly Standard*, July 19.
5. Trump quoted in Mark Leibovich. 2017. "This Town Melts Down," *New York Times*, July 11.
6. https://twitter.com/realdonaldtrump/status/892383242535481344? lang=en.
7. Tom Hamberger and Rosaland S. Helderman. 2018. "Hero or Hired Gun? How a British Former Spy Became a Flash Point in the Russia Investigation," *Washington Post*, February 6; see also John McCain with Mark Salter. 2018. *The Restless Wave: Good Times, Just Causes, Great Fights, and Other Appreciations*. New York: Simon & Shuster.
8. Andrea Shalal and Davikd Brjunnstrom. 2019. "Et tu, Mitt? Trump Blasts Republican Senator as Impeachment Battle Heats Up," *Reuters*, October 5.
9. Jessica Estapa. 2015. "Donald Trump on Carly Fiorina: 'Look at That Face!'" *USA TODAY*, September 10.
10. Matthew Continetti. 2017. "Trump Goes Rogue," *New York Times*, July 31.
11. David M. Shribman. 2017. "Trump Mixes Up the Parties, Raises Questions," *Post-Gazette*, June 18.
12. Peter Baker. 2017. "For Trump, a Year of Reinventing the Presidency," *New York Times*, December 31; See also Max Boot. 2017. "Let's Count the Ways Donald Trump Has Gone Where No President Has Gone Before," *Los Angeles Times*, April 4.
13. Peter Baker. 2019. "On Day 1,001, Trump Made It Clear: Being 'Presidential' Is Boring," *New York Times*, October 18.
14. David Frum. 2017. "It's Not over Yet for Donald Trump," *The Atlantic*, April 1; see also Editorial. 1993. "No Guardrails," *Wall Street Journal*, March 18.
15. Timothy L. O'Brien. 2017. "Defining 'Presidential' Downward," *Bloomberg*, July 20.
16. Brett Stephens. 2017. "The 'No Guardrails' Presidency," *New York Times*, July 28.

4 DONALD TRUMP'S FIGHT CLUB PRESIDENCY 151

17. Brett Stephens. 2015. "The Donald and the Demagogues," *Wall Street Journal*, August 31.
18. Frank Bruni. 2017. "The Week When President Trump Resigned," *New York Times*, August 18.
19. Jasmine C. Lee and Kevin Quealy. 2018. "The 425 People, Places and Things Donald Trump Has Insulted on Twitter: A Complete List," *New York Times*, January 3.
20. Erwin Burnett. 2015. "OUTFRONT: Interview with Donald Trump," *CNN*, September 28.
21. Jasmine C. Lee and Kevin Quealy. 2017. "Trump Is on Track to Insult 650 People, Places and Things on Twitter by the End of His First Term," *New York Times*, July 26.
22. Adam C. Smith. 2015. "Jeb Bush: 'I'm a Joyful Tortoise' in Long, Acrimonious Race," *Tampa Bay Times*, July 27.
23. Donald J. Trump (with Tony Schwartz). 1987. *Trump: The Art of the Deal*. New York: Random House, p. 58.
24. Ibid., p. 60, emphasis added.
25. Salena Zito. 2016. "Taking Trump Seriously, Not Literally," *The Atlantic*, September 23.
26. Steve Eder and Alica Parlapiano. 2016. "Donald Trump's Ventures Began with a Lot of Hype. Here's How They Turned Out," *New York Times*, October 6.
27. Cf., Timothy L. O'Brien. 2016. "How Trump Bungled the Deal of a Lifetime," *Bloomberg*, January 27.
28. The quotes that follow are drawn from Michael Kruse. 2018. "The Lost City of Trump," *Politico*, July–August, emphasis added.
29. Louise Radnofsky. 2017. "Trump Signs Sweeping Tax Overhaul into Law," *Wall Street Journal*, December 22, emphasis added.
30. Sean Wilentz. 2018. "They Were Bad: He May Be Worse," *New York Times*, January 20.
31. He was also the chief engineer of the Port Authority of New York and the Triborough Bridge and Tunnel Authority, he oversaw the building of the Lincoln Tunnel, the Outerbridge Crossing and the Bronx-Whitestone, Throgs Neck, Triborough, Bayonne, and Goethals Bridges.
32. Gwenda Blair. 2005. *Donald Trump: Master Apprentice*. New York: Simon & Shuster, p. 15.
33. There is also some disagreement as to whether it was sunny or raining. See Arthur Goldwag. 2015. "Putting Donald Trump on the Couch," *New York Times*, September 1.
34. Gay Talese. 1964. "Verrazano Bridge Opened to Traffic," *New York Times*, November 2, emphasis added; see also Jerome Tuccille. 1985.

Trump: The Saga of America's Most Powerful Real Estate Baron. New York: Donald I. Fine, p. 17.
35. Howard Blum. 1980. "Trump: The Development of a Manhattan Developer." *New York Times*, August 26.
36. Goldwag 2015.
37. Quoted in Marie Brenner. 1980. "Trumping the Town," *New York Magazine*, November 17, pp. 35–36.
38. Donald J. Trump (with Tony Schwartz). 1987. p. 200.
39. *Time*. 2015. "Here's Donald Trump's Presidential Announcement Speech," June 16.
40. Trump quoted in Michael Kranish. 2017. "A Fierce Will to Win Pushed Donald Trump to the Top," *Washington Post*, January 19.
41. Trump Presidential Announcement Speech. 2015. *Time Magazine*, June 16.
42. Brenner 1980, p. 27.
43. Marilyn Bender. 1983. "The Empire and Ego of Donald Trump," *New York Times*, August 7.
44. Maggie Haberman and Alexander Burns. 2016. "Donald Trump's Presidential Run Began in an Effort to Gain Stature," *New York Times*, March 12.
45. Emily Heil. 2016. "Is Obama's 2011 White House Correspondents' Dinner Burn to Blame for Trump's Campaign?" *Washington Post*, February 10; Roxanne Roberts. 2016. "I Sat Next to Donald Trump at the Infamous 2011 White House Correspondents' Dinner," *Washington Post*, April 28.
46. Mat Flegenheimer and Ashley Parker. 2016. "Heckled by New York Elite at Charity Dinner," *New York Times*, October 20.
47. Chris Barton. 2018. "Revisiting Comdy Central's 'Roast of Donald Trump,' When 'President Trump' Was a Punchline and Trump Could Take a Joke," *Los Angeles Times*, April 27.
48. Haberman and Burns 2016.
49. Ibid.
50. Trump quoted in Haberman and Burns. 2016.
51. Trump quoted in Glenn Plaskin. 1990. "Playboy Interview: Donald Trump (1990)," *Playboy*.
52. Fred Trump quoted in Bender 1983.
53. Trump quoted in Nancy Benak. 2016. "For Trump, It's About America's Ego—And His Own," *Associated Press*, July 16.
54. Trump quoted in Plaskin 1990.
55. Trump quoted in Tim Stanley. 2016. "Introducing the Real Donald Trump: A Careful Plotter and Media Master Who Is Far More Intelligent Than He Seems," *The Telegraph*, July 18.

4 DONALD TRUMP'S FIGHT CLUB PRESIDENCY 153

56. Schwartz quoted in Alan Rappeport. 2016. "I Feel a Deep Sense of Remorse Donald Trump's Ghostwriter Says," *New York Times*, July 18.
57. Tony Schwartz. 2019. "Why Trump Can't Change, No Matter What the Consequences Are," *Washington Post*, October 18.
58. Schwartz quoted in Jon Wiener. 2017. "Trump's Ghostwriter Says the President Is Now in Survival Mode," *The Nation*, November 3.
59. Mary L. Trump. 2020. *Too Much and Never Enough: How My Family Created the World's Most Dangerous Man*. New York: Simon & Shuster.
60. Daniel Bates. 2020. "EXCLUSIVE: Donald Trump Was a Victim of 'Child Abuse' at the Hands of His Father, Who 'Caused Him Terror That Would Scar Him for Life', Claims President's Niece Who Believes He Could Be a 'Sociopath' in Explosive Memoir," *Daily Mail*, July 7.
61. Shane Harris and Michael Kranish. 2020. "Trump's Worldview Forged by Neglect and Trauma at Home, His Niece Says in New Book," *Washington Post*, July 7.
62. Michael Kranish. 2020. "Mary Trump Once Stood up to Her Uncle Donald. Now Her Book Describes a 'Nightmare' of Family Dysfunction," *Washington Post*, July 2.
63. Heidi Evans. 2000. "INSIDE TRUMPS' BITTER BATTLE Nephew's Ailing Baby Caught in the Middle," *Daily News*, December 19.
64. Trump quoted in Dianne Sawyer. 2009. "Interview with Donald Trump," *NBC* (Good Morning America), December 2.
65. Trump quoted in Marc Fisher and Michael Kranish. 2016. "The Trump We Saw: Populist, Frustrating, Naive, Wise, Forever on the Make," *Washington Post*, August 12.
66. Leibowitz quoted in Jonathan Miller and Steve Elder. 2016. "'No Vacancies' for Blacks: How Donald Trump Got His Start, and Was First Accused of Bias," *New York Times*, August 27.
67. William Specht quoted in Matt Viser. 2015. "Even in College, Donald Trump Was Brash," *Boston Globe*, August 28.
68. Noah Bierman and Joseph Tanfani. 2016. "As a Young Donald Trump Began His Real Estate Career, He Fought Hard Against Allegations of Racial Bias," *Los Angeles Times*, August 15.
69. Michael Kranish. 2017. "A Fierce Will to Win Pushed Donald Trump to the Top," *Washington Post*, January 19.
70. James David Barber. 2017. *The Presidential Character: Predicting Performance in the White House*, 4th ed. Englewood Cliffs, NJ: Prentice Hall.
71. Amanda Taub and Max Fisher. 2017. "As Leaks Multiply, Fears of a 'Deep State' in America," *New York Times*, February 16; see also Julie Hirschfeld Davis. 2017. "Rumblings of a 'Deep State' Undermining Trump? It Was Once a Foreign Concept," *New York Times*, March 6.

72. Michael Crowley. 2017. "The Deep State Is Real," *Politico*, September–October; see also Ed Rogers. 2017. "The 'Deep State' Is Real: The 'Alt Right' Is Fake,' *Washington Post*, February 21.
73. Editorial. 2019. "Undoing the Great Mistake of 2016," *Los Angeles Times*, October 20.
74. Stephen Skowronek. 1977. The Politics That Presidents Make. *Leadership from John Adams to Bill Clinton, Revised Edition*. Cambridge, MA: Belknap Press, p. 43.
75. James Bohman and William Rehg (eds.). 1997. *Deliberative Democracy: Essays on Reason and Politics*. Cambridge, MA: MIT Press; see also Amy Gutmann. 2009. *Why Deliberative Democracy?* Princeton NJ: Princeton University Press; and James S. Fishkin. 2009. *When the People Speak: Deliberative Democracy and Public Consultation*. Oxford: Oxford University Press.
76. https://www.intelligencesquaredus.org/news/blog.
77. Evan Sayet. 2017. "He Fights," *Townhall*, July 13.
78. Randall Lane. 2017. "Inside Trump's Head: An Exclusive Interview with the President, and the Single Theory That Explains Everything," *Forbes*, October 10.
79. Spicer quoted in Lisa Hagen. 2017. "Spicer: 'Negative' Trump Coverage Is 'Demoralizing,'" *The Hill*, January 23.
80. Lisa Friedman. 2018. "The Investigations That Led to Scott Pruitt's Resignation," *New York Times*, April 18.
81. Lisa Friedman. 2018. "E.P.A. Chief's $43,000 Phone Booth Broke the Law, Congressional Auditors Say," *New York Times*, April 16.
82. Dennis Brady and Juliet Eilperin. 2018. "Scott Pruitt Steps Down as EPA Head After Ethics, Management Scandals," *Washington Post*, July 5.
83. Scott Prewitt. 2018. "Scott Pruitt's Resignation Letter," *Washington Post*, July 5.
84. Peter Baker. 2017. "For Trump, a Year of Reinventing the Presidency," *New York Times*, December 31.
85. Carol E. Lee, Courtney Kube, Kristen Welker, and Stephanie Ruhle. 2018. "Kelly Thinks He's Saving U.S. from Disaster, Calls Trump 'Idiot,' Say White House Staffers," *NBC News*, April 30.
86. Josh Dawsey. 2018. "Kelly Denies Calling Trump an 'Idiot,' Says News Report Is 'Pathetic Attempt to Smear People,'" *Washington Post*, April 3.
87. Carol E. Lee, Kristen Welker, Stephanie Ruhle, and Dafna Linzer. 2017. "Tillerson's Fury at Trump Required an Intervention from Pence," *NBC News*, October 4.
88. Jonathan Swan. 2018. "John Kelly Blew Up at Trump in Oval Office Meeting, Threatened to Quit," *Axios*, April 7.

89. Kim Seung Min and John Dawsey. 2018. "Chief of Staff John Kelly to Leave White House by End of Month, Trump Says," *Washington Post*, December 8.

90. John Kelly. 2018 "Transcript: White House Chief of Staff John Kelly's Interview with NPR," *NPR*, May 11, emphasis added.

91. Ruth Marcus. 2018. "If You Work for Trump, Quit Now," *Washington Post*, July 16; Brett Stevens. 2018. "Resign, Mike Pompeo. Resign, John Bolton," *New York Times*, July 19.

92. Maureen Dowd. 2017. "Cruella de Trump," *New York Times*, July 1.

93. Editorial. 2017. "President Trump, Melting Under Criticism," *New York Times*, June 30.

94. Maggie Astor. 2019. "Did Trump Cave on the Wall? Some Conservatives Say Yes," *New York Times*, January 25; see also Marc Fisher. 2019. "Bluster, Bombast, Backing Down: What Happens When Someone Says No to Trump? *Washington Post*, January 24.

95. Tulis quoted in Marc Fisher. 2019. "Bluster, Bombast, Backing Down: What Happens When Someone Says No to Trump?" *Washington Post*, January 24.

96. David E. Sanger and Eric Schmitt. 2019. "In 'Cave-In,' Trump Cease-Fire Cements Turkey's Gains in Syria," *New York Times*, October 17.

97. Glenn Thrush and Maggie Haberman. 2017. "Trump the Dealmaker Projects Bravado, But Behind the Scenes, Faces Rare Self-Doubt," *New York Times*, March 23.

98. Mike Allen and Jonathan Swan. 2017. "Exasperated Trump WH Staff Admit His Special Resilience," *Axios*, May 20; see also Maggie Haberman and Katie Rogers. 2018. "'Drama, Action, Emotional Power': As Exhausted Aides Eye the Exits, Trump Is Re-energized," *New York Times*, June 10; and Niall Strange. 2018. "The Memo: Dems Grapple with Trump's Resilience," *The Hill*, July 24.

99. Steve Collinson. 2016. "Donald Trump: Presumptive GOP Nominee; Sanders Takes Indiana," *CNN*, May 4.

100. Robert Costa and Phillip Rucker. 2020. "'Tempted to Despair': Trump's Resilience Causes Democrats to Sound the Alarm," *Washington Post*, February 8.

101. Richard Neustadt. 1990. *Presidential Power and the Modern Presidents: The Politics of Leadership from Roosevelt to Reagan*. New York: Free Press, pp. 102, 144, 295.

102. Eliot Brown. 2018. "Remember Trump City?" *New York Observer*, August 5.

103. Jack Brehm. 1996. *A Theory of Psychological Reactance*. New York: Academic Press.

104. Trump quoted in Jeremy Diamond. 2015. "Donald Trump Describes Father's 'Small Loan': $1 Million," *CNN*, October 27.

105. Trump quoted in Plaskin. 1990.
106. Trump quoted in Wayne Barnett. 2015. "How a Young Donald Trump Forced His Way from Avenue Z to Manhattan," *Village Voice*, July 20.
107. Bender 1983.
108. Liam Stack. 2016. "Donald Trump Featured Paula Jones and 2 Other Women Who Accused Bill Clinton of Sexual Assault," *New York Times*, October 9.
109. Donald J. Trump. 2020. "Remarks by President Trump, Vice President Pence, and Members of the Coronavirus Task Force," in *Press Briefing, James S. Brady Press Briefing Room*, April 14.
110. Monica Hesse. 2020. "Tara Reade, Joe Biden and the Limitations of Journalism," *Washington Post*, April 16.
111. Donald J. Trump, 2019. "Trump in Press Conference Osaka, Japan," June 29.
112. *New York Times*. 2016. "Donald Trump's *New York Times* Interview: Full Transcript," *New York Times*, November 23.
113. A. J. Brad, Plumer Chavar, and Susan Joan Archer. 2017, "U.S. to Leave Paris Climate Accord: What Happens Now?" *New York Times*, June 1.
114. Ana Swanson. 2018. "Trump to Impose Sweeping Steel and Aluminum Tariffs," *New York Times*, March 1.
115. Peter Baker and Ana Swanson. 2018. "Trump Authorizes Tariffs, Defying Allies at Home and Abroad," *New York Times*, March 8.
116. Kate Kelly and Maggie Haberman. 2018. "Gary Cohn Says He Will Resign as Trump's Top Economic Adviser," *New York Times*, March 6.
117. Rachel Wolfe, "President Trump Bucks the Republican Party on Gun Control: Full Transcript," *Vox*, February 28.
118. Peter Baker. 2018. "Trump's Meeting with Kim Jong-un Is Another Pledge to Do What Nobody Else Can," *New York Times*, March 8; see also Michael Crowley. 2018. "Trump's Shock and Awe Foreign Policy," *Politico*, March 9.
119. Michael Crowley. 2019. "In Bracing Terms, Trump Invokes War's Human Toll to Defend His Policies," *New York Times*, October 19.
120. Bender 1983.
121. Frances Robles. 2017. "Emergency Manager Resigns in Puerto Rico; Army Ends Its Mission," *New York Times*, November 10.
122. Peter Baker. 2017. "For Trump, a Year of Reinventing the Presidency," *New York Times*, December 31.
123. Eugene Robinson. 2017. "Abandoning Puerto Rico Would Be an Impeachable Offense," *Washington Post*, October 12.
124. Jeff Stein. 2019. "FBI Makes Arrests in Puerto Rico Corruption Scandal, Prompting Calls for Governor's Ouster and Concerns About Billions in Storm Aid," *Washington Post*, July 10.

125. Mark Lander and Yamiche Alcindor. 2018. Trump's Condolence Call to Soldier's Widow Ignites an Imbroglio," *New York Times*, October 18.
126. Rich Lowry. 2017. "The Out That Trump Never Permits Himself," *National Review*, October 20.
127. Ashley Parker, David Nakamura, and Dan Lamothe. 2019. "'Horrible' Pictures of Suffering Moved Trump to Action on Syria," *Washington Post*, April 7.
128. Michael Crowley. 2019. "Debate Flares Over Afghanistan as Trump Considers Troop Withdrawal," *New York Times*, August 16.
129. Richard Neustadt. 1990. *Presidential Power and the Modern Presidents: The Politics of Leadership from Roosevelt to Reagan*. New York: Free Press.
130. "Transcript of Interview with Former Secretary of State Rex Tillerson." 2019. House Committee on Foreign Affairs, June 27, p. 117, emphasis added.

CHAPTER 5

Leadership Style, Presidential Success, and Political Time

Demeanor is part of leadership style but they are not synonymous. Style refers to more basic characteristics of presidential leadership and reflects a president's general approach to his responsibilities. We have already noted several of them for Trump—an ability to stand apart and alone if necessary on policy decisions, a capacity to fight back leading to what I term his "fight club presidency," a dislike of being hemmed in by conventional policy expectations or advice, and the wish to retain maximum flexibility to ultimately reach his policy goals.

This last stylist leadership element is often mischaracterized by both Trump and his critics as his wishing to be "unpredictable." Trump has said, "I don't want people to know exactly what I'm doing—or thinking. I like being unpredictable. It keeps them off balance."[1] There is no doubt that Trump likes to surprise people, including his supporters, in part to avoid being easily pigeonholed, and in part to keep his opponents off balance. Those, however, are not the most important aspects of this trait.

UNPREDICTABILITY AND POLICY FLEXIBILITY

The real *Art of the Deal* reflects the importance of the maximization of flexibility for Trump. He repeatedly demonstrated in his well-documented New York real estate years what is involved. You must first gain a sense of the complex and often disparate elements that will be

© The Author(s) 2020
S. Renshon, *The Real Psychology of the Trump Presidency*,
The Evolving American Presidency,
https://doi.org/10.1007/978-3-030-45391-6_5

necessary to complete a deal. Then you must slowly, and often quietly, begin to assemble those elements necessary to possibly succeed. You must be able to move from one to another element as necessary including having a number of Plan Bs in mind when plans to accomplish elements that cannot be nailed down or reach a dead end must be bypassed or modified. In short, you must be smart enough to see what needs to be done and flexible and ready to change direction as necessary to accomplish your goals.

Metaphorically, imagine working on several large jigsaw puzzles at the same time. Imagine that while working on one or more of them there are portions you've assembled that suddenly no longer fit together. Further, imagine that others working on the same puzzles are trying to block you from assembling your other pieces. They do so in part by trying to enlist others to do the same, including the judges that decide if the final assembly is correct. Finally, imagine that the final puzzle solution may, or more likely may not, completely resemble the picture on the cover of the puzzle box from which you are working.

In basic form, the above are features of many of the large complex Trump real estate and business initiatives, and a fair metaphor for trying to pursue presidential policy goals in the American political system while facing enormous levels of opposition. These elements are at the core of President Trump's leadership style.

Donald Trump: A New Kind of American President

It is clear that Mr. Trump is a new kind of president, one never before seen in the White House. His uniqueness is captured in the *New York Times* headline, "For Trump, a Year of Reinventing the Presidency." That article makes the point that, "In ways that were once unimaginable, President Trump has discarded the conventions and norms established by his predecessors."[2]

The obvious manifestations of these discarded conventions include behavior that has traditionally been summarized by the term presidential demeanor. This term reflects the conventional, and long held assumption, that a president's behavior in office will follow certain set scripts and traditions. A president's (or candidate's) adherence to them is then taken to be, somewhat circularly, one indicator of how emotionally, temperamentally, and politically fit a person is to hold that office. On those grounds, considered alone, President Trump has clearly flunked that test.

Failing Presidential Demeanor: The Unexpected Becomes Expected

President Trump is brash, sometimes crude, and can be by his own admission nasty.[3] He is endlessly argumentative and combative, almost always self-promoting in the face of his belief that he receives insufficient credit for his accomplishments, insisting loudly and publicly on doing things his way regardless of how they have been done before, and often saying what he thinks regardless of its overall or specific accuracy.

Trump does not shrink from saying what he thinks even when it is unexpected and, to many, unacceptable. For example, consider his response to a dual protest march in Charlottesville, VA that turned violent because of outside protestors from both sides of the political spectrum. Mr. Trump said that people who peacefully marched in favor of keeping a statue of Robert E. Lee in their city park and those who peacefully protested that idea were both "very fine people."[4] That violated the expectation that he should limit himself to condemning the Neo-Nazis who came into town to demonstrate there, and his remarks were widely and repeatedly misreported and mischaracterized. They still are.

Nor has Trump always said the obvious and necessary in a timely manner. He publicly praised an aide for his work while he was being forced to resign over allegations of spousal abuse.[5] He then tweeted his concern about the lack of due process that frequently accompanies sexually charged allegations, a fair and somewhat anodyne point.[6] That became more controversial however when he delayed stating that he was against such behavior for a week.[7]

These and similar examples clearly reflect Trump's determination to speak his mind regardless of controversy or expectations. Yet, they also reflect the president's clear willingness, and apparent relish in defying expectations. That seems to be especially the case when speaking out is at the expense of critics whom he does not consider to have the standing to act as the moral, political, or substantive arbiters of his behavior. His supporters cheer Trump's return of establishment disdain, but for many ordinary Americans his behavior in these kinds of circumstances is unsettling and even disturbing.

In the Eyes of the Beholder: Mr. Trump's Presidential Demeanor

As controversial as Trump's decided lack of conventional presidential demeanor is, it has had mixed consequences for his presidency. For some, on both sides of the political divide, it is a reflection of the fact that Trump seems to prefer fighting to governing and has essentially abandoned the idea of having what many would consider, and prefer, what used to be a "normal presidency".[8] However, a "normal" presidency in the country's current political circumstances may not be possible, especially if your presidential purpose, like Trump's, is *American Restoration*—a *reconstructive* presidential goal in Skowronek's terms.[9]

NeverTrump opponents from all points of the political spectrum fervently oppose him. Among this group are those who believe that the frequency and nature of Trump's public fights and lack of presidential decorum are prima facie evidence that he suffers from a "dangerous mental illness" and should be removed from office.[10] Yet other voters have come see this unorthodox and unprecedented style as Trump just being Trump.

It is still is not preferred behavior, but over time, it has become less disorienting. In this group, evaluations of Trump may now be seen in the context of some Trump policy accomplishments publicly centered on the economy,[11] and other policy areas like his handling of the Coronavirus pandemic. This is likely one reason why even early on in his presidency polls found that even if Mr. Trump himself flunks popularity polls, his policy measures are more popular with voters than he is.[12] That is likely one reason that although Mr. Trump personally has historically low approval ratings, after almost four years in office, they were, for a time, on the rise,[13] and recently reached a high of 49% before again retreating.[14]

For many Trump supporters, of course, it is exactly his willingness to flout convention by not following Marquis of Queensbury rules when being attacked and continuously taking on establishment policy conventions, that make him a president who inspires their hope and trust.

As one analysis put it[15]:

> His most loyal supporters back him because of, not despite, his brash behavior. He would not be in the Oval Office today had he followed a conventional path or listened to the advisers telling him to tone down

his rhetoric and discipline his behavior. If Republican primary voters had wanted a border wall, tax cuts and sound judges without the drama, they could have picked Ted Cruz. Instead they elected Mr. Trump for exactly the reasons that the mainstream media, late-night comics, and party elites cannot stand him.

As one supportive analysis put it: "Donald Trump is Teaching Republicans How to Fight."[16] Or, as one member of pro-Trump voter's group put it while being interviewed: "I think [I got] exactly what I voted for."[17]

Any fair assessment of Trump's presidential demeanor would have to include evidence that he is perfectly capable of normal presidential behavior. He has paid presidential visits to wounded soldiers at Walter Reed.[18] He has traveled to Andrews Air Force base to pay his respects to soldiers killed in an Afghanistan helicopter crash.[19] He has spoken to the country in the aftermath of the killing of seventeen students in Florida with words of compassion and empathy.[20] He met with families and students connected with that tragedy and listened and responded to their outpouring of anger and grief with efforts at consoling and promises to find a solution.[21] He visited flood-ravaged Texas with words of encouragement and federal aid.[22] He gave a well-received speech to a joint session of Congress,[23] and delivered a perfectly normal first State of the Union address in 2018[24] that was approved of by 75% of those who saw it[25] and an equally normal 2020 State of the Union address after his impeachment.[26] And he conducted an "extraordinary,"[27] full-scale cabinet meeting and debate with members of both parties present on immigration that was carried live for over an hour.

Mr. Trump's Two Presidencies

The point of noting these clearly more "normal," even ordinary, examples of presidential demeanor is to underscore the point that Trump is clearly capable of being both "presidential," and of unequivocally failing the demeanor test. Since he is capable of doing both, the question arises: what accounts for his choices to do one or the other?

Is President Trump's leadership style a reflection of some kind of split personality—a Dr. Jekyll/Mr. Hyde psychology over which he has no control and which comes upon him suddenly, as one analysis suggested?[28] Or, as another pundit reaching for the same metaphor while disclaiming any intention of "attempting a clinical diagnosis" asked, do we see unfolding the "emerging outlines of a bipolar presidency"?[29]

That phrasing is unhelpful since "bipolar" is a clinical term that refers to alternating states of mania and depression. Nowhere is there evidence of this psychiatric syndrome in Mr. Trump himself or in his presidency more generally. Still, as the above discussion of Trump's presidential demeanor makes clear, there are two strong very publicly visible currents operating in tandem in the Trump presidency.

One is most easily mischaracterized as Trump's tabloid presidency. In this narrative strand, the latest "explosive" Trump speculations (almost all anonymously sourced), accusations (many by self-interested parties), changes in personnel for whatever reasons, or Trump's fighting tweets in response briefly explode across the media world. They inspire predictions of disastrous consequences for Mr. Trump and his presidency[30] that eventually fade from public view and are replaced by the next round of dire speculations. The result is a presidency that seems, from many headlines, to be a continuous melodrama unfolding under numerous "Swords of Damocles" as reported by *The National Inquirer* of supermarket checkout fame, with elements of the *Jerry Springer Show* thrown in.[31]

The focus of this seemingly "tabloid" dimension captures a real and obvious element of the Trump presidency. Yet, doing so runs the danger of ignoring, what amounts to Trump's parallel presidency, a serious effort at building a *Reconstructive* presidency.[32] We will shortly note a number of Trump initiatives that fit this category.

Almost any week's headlines underscore the distinction. One week's headlines and news reports exploded over a Department of Justice recommendation that suggested sentencing guidelines for convicted felon Roger Stone were too harsh for a first time, non-violent offender.[33] It is a legitimate news story but major news outlets were soon full of reports[34] and critical op-eds[35] casting doubt on the integrity of the Justice Department and the Attorney General. Meanwhile the *New York Times* reported: "Trump Gives Conditional Go Ahead on Peace Deal With Taliban, Officials Say."[36] There had been a prior abortive effort, and a final tentative deal was subsequently announced.[37] Whether it will work as hoped remains to be seen and evaluated. However these developments perhaps ending an eighteen-year war, appeared substantial. And they unfolded at the very same time that Trump's tabloid presidency was getting full front page treatment in many major newspaper and network news reports.

A Downside of Trump's Flexible Style and Dual Presidency

Trump's highly flexible style has been the source of legitimate criticism. His decision to move some American troops in Syria away from an area in which Turkey was going to establish a buffer zone between it and the Kurdish militias that had fought alongside the United States against ISIS caused anxiety among those who didn't support what they thought Trump was doing. It also caused confusion among those who weren't informed beforehand and didn't fully understand the rationale for the decision.[38] (We further take up this Syria decision in connection with an assumed establishment "foreign policy consensus" in Chapter 12.)

Trump did provide several rationales.[39] They included keeping a campaign promise to withdraw from unnecessary and ill-advised ("ridiculous endless wars, many of them tribal" in his view) military deployments in war zones in which the United States had no top level strategic interests, economic considerations, and recognizing Turkey's point that there are important distinctions among different Kurdish groups[40] that make it dangerous to consider allowing tens of thousands of Syrian refugees to make permanent homes in Turkish territories. That situation was exacerbated by the European Union's refusal to repatriate captured ISIS fighters from its counties.

Trump failed to recognize or appreciate that some explanation, even if it was not accepted by critics, was necessary to forestall the anxiety and confusion that accompanied what many felt was an abrupt and unexpected decision. It was not the first time. In failing to give the stakeholders a public explanation, Trump was reprising the error that accompanied his roll out of his executive order for enhanced screening for those entering the country from a number of Muslim majority countries already flagged as requiring more attention because of terrorism concerns.

"Act first, let explanations catch up later," is a recipe for dysfunctional presidential leadership and heightened public anxiety.

Why Trump Survives

The problems that the Trump presidency faces in having a successful presidency are many and varied. There are the enormous headwinds generated by the opposition to Trump and antipathy toward him in many major political, civic, religious, media, legal, and other national organizations.

They are allied with the views of millions of voters for whom anything Trump is anathema. The collective purpose of these opponents is to raise whatever issues they can, whenever they can, and in any manner they can to slow, sidetrack, damage, or otherwise impede the Trump presidency. And they have been successful to some degree in doing so. Their opposition has contributed to the sputtering, sometimes faltering ability of Trump's presidency to have anything like a "normal" presidency that can built on its own successful efforts. And, of course, the Coronavirus pandemic, the nation-wide demonstrations in the aftermath of the death of George Floyd, and the spasms of historical statue destruction of have totally upended "normal" pre-election politics.

What opponents have not been able to do so far is to completely derail Trump's presidency. There are several reasons why they have failed in this quest. It is worth exploring why they have not completely succeeded, for what it reflects about that effort and the president.

One can look first to institutional explanations. Those would include the lack of a groundswell of public support for removing the president through repeated "bombshell" revelations that did not hold up. The fact is that the Mueller investigation did not find evidence of criminal collusion and Mr. Mueller's Congressional appearance "fell flat."[41] The House's impeachment case was dramatic but was not successful in removing Trump from office. A number of congressional Democrats were originally ambivalent about impeachment,[42] but ultimately decided to go ahead in spite of the low probability of ultimate success out of either conviction, election calculation, or both.

Attention is also due to Trump's strategy and the fact that Trump made it very clear that he would not cooperate with the House's impeachment investigation—and didn't.[43] Multiple Congressional subpoenas and investigations[44] produced numerous unresolved lawsuits, not substantiated charges.[45] Oddly and somewhat paradoxically, Trump's decision to contest many of these House efforts in court, was the basis before there was a court decision on these suits, of the Second Article of Impeachment: "Obstruction of Congress." Many of the serious accusations against the president and his administration, like the "criminal intent" of the president's Ukraine call have remained at the level of ultimately unsubstantiated accusation narrative.[46] One can also look at the intense, stable, if moderate levels of Trump's support. Throughout almost four years of the Trump presidency his supporters have not wavered and in the

5 LEADERSHIP STYLE, PRESIDENTIAL SUCCESS AND POLITICAL TIME 167

impeachment proceedings, his House and Senate party members, with one exception, supported him.

Aside from these situational factors, there is first and foremost Trump himself. He is a fighter, and when necessary a brawler, and has been one his whole life. Fighting is deeply woven into the life he has chosen to live. Whether in the courts or the tabloids, whether against government accusations of bias in his family's housing projects that he rejected, whether against business competitors, creditors, or his ex-wives, fighting back is by now a routine response to the numerous and diverse people and agencies who have gone after him.

It is not a life that many would choose to live or have the ability to do so even if they so chose. The young Donald Trump who stared across at Manhattan skyline from Queens wanted to change its skyline while building an empire. It's not a real dream for mildly ambitious or quietly low key people, and Trump is neither.

Second, Mr. Trump has enormous energy, and has had ever since he entered adulthood. It's well known that he is not a person who needs or gets eight hours of sleep a night. He is not known to take afternoon naps as several presidents have done. In short, he still has, at his age an enormous store of energy that allows him to draw upon personal resources, including time to get things done. This is not to say that everything he decides he might want to do with that time is well thought through or worthwhile. It is only to say that his energy is a time and opportunity resource.

Coupled with his energy is Trump's enormous resilience. That he can stand against the enormous level of personal and political abuse that has been aimed at him as president, and keep his focus on his purposes while fighting back is a capacity worth underscoring. Trump complains a great deal about his treatment by Democrats, the press, and others who are part of the anti-Trump opposition. Ordinarily opposition to a president's policies that one does not support is part of American political life, and entirely normal. Yet, as noted (see Chapter 3), opposition to Trump goes beyond "normal" politics.

No modern president has been subjected to the all-out public and behind the scenes private assaults waged every hour of every day in a 24/7 national and international news cycle and enlisting every source of public or private opposition that can be found and utilized at every level of government and which began as soon as Trump won the Republican nomination. Only Abraham Lincoln had to endure this level of hatred because of his determined efforts to save the Union, which he did—but for which he was assassinated. In today's hard wired media environment, harsh and often vicious accusations, can be made more directly and multiplied indefinitely repeatedly reinforcing Trump hatred on a daily basis.

This modern level of political and persona rancor raises important psychological and political questions for Trump. Aside from the implications of the rancor for both for assessments of Trump's psychological and political "fitness" for office (see Chapter 7) and Trump's chances for success, if any, for his presidency, there is another. How does he cope?

Trump has spent a lifetime battling back. If there ever was a president prepared by his previous life to withstand and fight back against a no-holds barred assault, Trump is that president. Yet, there is more to Trump's response than ingrained habit.

Fighting back against what one considers unfair assaults is also a form, as noted, of "self-help" in Neustadt's term. It is also self-affirming. It reflects a refusal just "to take it." That in itself helps avoid the feelings of emotional deflation and self-reproach that can accompany not taking action when it is needed.

There is for Trump, however, a sense of wistfulness and regret that his presidency has turned out this way. Return momentarily to Trump's interview with critical members of the *Washington Post* editorial board. They wrote of Trump after their interviews that they found him to be "authentically perplexed by suspicions that he had motives other than making America great again."[47] In Trump's mind, he genuinely believes that he has America's best interests at heart, wants to do a good job, and believes that he has, even though he feels he hasn't received much credit for what he feels he has accomplished.

In a joint news conference with President Niinistö of the Republic of Finland, Trump said[48]:

> So the political storm—I've lived with it from the day I got elected. I've done more—and this administration has done more than any administration in the history of this country in the first two and a half years. *I'm used to it. For me, it's like putting on a suit in the morning.*

When asked how he personally responds to the relentless personal and political attacks against him, his presidency, and all things Trump and in the daily combat with Democrats, the media, and his presidency, he

5 LEADERSHIP STYLE, PRESIDENTIAL SUCCESS AND POLITICAL TIME   169

replied: "It sounds strange to say I'm energized, but I love it, I love it."[49]

Perhaps he is "energized," but that's not all there is. A few days later in a Q&A with reporters, there was this[50]:

> we won on the Mueller scam. That was a whole big deal. That lasted for two and a half years. *We had a few days of peace and then, all of a sudden, they came up with this one [the Ukrainian call]. But I guess it's just part of my life.*

"I guess it's just a part of my life" is partially wistful ("we had a few days of peace") and partially regret and resignation. Trump is clearly not emotionally impervious to the trauma of his presidential circumstances, yet he will continue to fight on. Why?

At one level, he will fight on because he really thinks he did nothing wrong in the call to the president of the Ukraine that others are characterizing as offering foreign aid to get dirt on his opponent. Relatedly, he believes, with some legitimacy, that his opponents have tried to keep him out of office, or remove him from it since he was elected. Quitting would be an admission that opponents bested him and forced him to give up. That would be a colossal public admission of personal failure and is very unlikely to happen.

Never give up is, if anything, more of a Trump family motto and rule to live by than even love what you do. At Fred Trump's memorial service, his favorite poem "Don't Quit,"[51] both a motto and a reflection of his drive to be successful by overcoming Depression-era related setbacks, was read by one of his daughters.[52] When Donald Trump had a family crest designed, its Latin motto was: *numquam concedere* [Never Give in].[53]

In a 2015 interview with *Time*, Trump was asked his long shot candidacy: What's the most significant learning experience in your life?[54] He replied:

> *Trump*: I will say this, over my lifetime I've seen a lot of very smart people who were quitters. They never made it. And I've seen people that weren't as smart who never ever, ever gave up. And those were the people that made it. And I've seen it to this day ... And the ones that are the biggest people are the people that never gave up. It's something I've just observed over the years.
> *Time*: So I take it you're not giving up.

Trump: No, I don't give up.

Never Give Up is as well part of the title of one of Trump's many books,[55] and more importantly it is an outlook that has guided him through life. It has also helped him to achieve the success he has and overcome substantial economic adversity. The *Washington Post* headline almost captured this insight with their headline: "A fierce will to win pushed Donald Trump to the top."[56] Substitute "succeed" for "win" and "never give up" for "fierce will" and you have a real insight for a headline.

Speaking to reporters on the south lawn who raised the parallel between his possible impeachment and Richard Nixon's, Trump had this to say[57]:

> When you look at past impeachments, whether it was President Clinton or—I guess President Nixon never got there. *He left. I don't leave. A big difference. I don't leave.*

A Potentially Very Consequential Presidency: Slowly and Haltingly Gathers Momentum

Mr. Trump's ambitions to be a *reconstructive* president in the service of *American Restoration* represent a Mt. Everest level of political success, even in the most congenial of political circumstances, which Mr. Trump's are not. Therefore, it is not surprising that by many critics' measures and also Mr. Trump's numerously expressed frustrations, his *Reconstructive* ambitions began slowly and haltingly. At this point however, his critics now find it hard to repeat the narrative they adopted from the start, that Trump "doesn't have any meaningful accomplishments"[58] or that "he is becoming a failed president."[59]

Yet, it is clear that the President has not been successful to the degree that he had hoped. Mr. Trump's early frustration with his party's inability to unite and pass major legislation is consistent with that view.[60] Certainly, having his party lose control of the House in the 2018 midterm elections did nothing to further his presidency's major legislative prospects.

Trump's Slow Start: Success by Other Means?

The slow, sometimes stumbling start to the Trump presidency is attributable to several factors. There is primarily Trump's own lack of real political governing experience. That is not his fault, but it is a fact and did have consequences. There is also the need to learn how to fit his style with his and the country's political circumstances. And, of course, there is the daily drama of the latest opposition-inspired daily dramatic fireworks.

There is as well, the continuing search of ways to resolve a primary governing issue for Trump—developing cadres of advisors and "officials" on whom he can count. An early and to some degree continuing loss of momentum has been one by-product of Trump's search for good senior advisors, those who are able to fit within Trump's range of views and his style. There is also Mr. Trump's own style of decision making that maximizes his options, but also leaves members of his administration uncertain and puzzled as to his intent and direction. Trump has every right to insist on having the degree of flexibility he wants, but a maturing president might also recognize that his more senior advisors and officials might function more effectively on his behalf with some anticipatory knowledge.

Almost four years into his administration it seems fair to say that Mr. Trump has grasped the essentials of governing, while still insisting on doing so within the framework of his leadership style. He has very gradually assembled a working team in major administrative and political power centers—at Homeland Security, several more recent Chiefs of Staff, the Department of State and the Department of Justice to name several key areas. The one place where he has not made much headway, except for survival, is in blunting the determined efforts of the anti-Trump opposition. Trump's last year in office is every bit as conflictual on a daily basis as his first three. Given the continued post-impeachment all-out war against Trump that impeachment proceedings have helped to maintain, and Trump's response to the Coronavirus pandemic and the mass demonstrations that followed George Floyd's death, most peaceful, but many violent, the last months of the Trump's first term are likely to be tumultuous because they represent the last chance to prevent his possible reelection.

These represent substantial roadblocks to presidential success as that term is usually understood. There are however, a number of possible metrics by which to judge presidential success. Enacting major legislation is certainly one, but not the only such measure.

The Major Legislation Success Metric

A standard metric of presidential success is major legislation passed in Congress. By this traditional measure Mr. Trump has not achieved much of his legislative agenda. He has achieved only one major legislative victory that could in any sense be considered major, his tax cut legislation.[61] He has also achieved a somewhat less than major, but still important, legislative accomplishment in 2018—his criminal justice reform bill.[62] The four major economic bi-partisan support packages signed by Trump in response to the pandemic are "successes" in some sense of that word, but the dire circumstances that led to them are no cause for political celebration.

Trump was not successful in another major legislative effort—the repeal and replacement of President Obama's signature health care legislation. And the on-again, off-again efforts to reform immigration policy have yielded no discernible legislative results.[63] If legislative accomplishments were the sole metric of presidential success, Mr. Trump's presidency would be modest at best, although nowhere near the failure that his critics have characterized it as being almost as soon as it began.[64]

Over time, critics and pundits have added additional items to President Trump's "setback" list.[65] Some of the "setback" additions are not legislative, but political. It remains to be seen whether they will prove enduring or consequential. The twists and turns of the Russia–Trump collusions allegations and investigations are a good case in point.[66] They reached a legal and political dead end and were made part of the two impeachment articles drawn up in the House.

Trump's acquittal on both impeachment counts leaves both him and his Democratic opposition in a state of emotional and political limbo going forward. Feelings are running understandably high for both. Democrats are angry, anxious, disappointed, and frustrated at the outcome. Trump is feeling relief, vindication, and anger at having been put though "hell" as he put it,[67] for a vindication he thought he deserved and should never have had to fight to get.

Democrats are torn between more Trump investigations which Trump will publicly berate, and to some extent possibly ignore, and concentrating on their policies. There has also been speculation regarding the unlikely possibility of further impeachment articles. The president has already claimed some openness to working with Democrats, doubtless on his own terms, but has expressed puzzlement as to whether Democrats are interested or capable for doing so. Political need has overcome worse circumstances, but powerful emotions often interfere with self-interest. And, as noted, the Coronavirus pandemic, anti-police bias demonstrations, and destructive assaults on American historical statues and figures have upended these and other traditional pre-election considerations.

Every administration experiences political, legal, or administrative setbacks in pursuing its policies, so their existence in the Trump administration isn't novel. The more important question is whether a president has the determination and finds the means to continue toward his goals and eventually gain some traction on achieving them, as Mr. Trump has been in building an effective barrier along parts of America's southern border.

Still, President Trump's legislative accomplishments are meager, and he is unlikely to add to much in his last year of his first term, given the strong feelings on both sides that his impeachment and acquittal have generated, and the disruptions caused by the pandemic. However, legislative success is not the only important metric of presidential success. This may especially apply to a president who wants to transform conventional policy, political, and governance narratives and replace them with the *Politics of American Restoration.*

PRESIDENTIAL SUCCESS: OTHER METRICS

Obscured by raging rhetorical and political conflict, the Trump presidency has been slowly accumulating substantial accomplishments. Some of these initiatives have the potential to ultimately result in a sea change in American politics. The obvious place to begin looking for these kinds of accomplishments would be in Trump's executive and administrative initiatives on behalf of his ambitions in both domestic and foreign policy.

Some obvious and important illustrations of these efforts are to be found in the large regulatory reforms undertaken by the Trump administration,[68] but there are many others. These include revisions of a major carbon emission rule put into place by the Obama Administration.[69] They include myriad changes to immigration enforcement procedures, large and small,[70] that have resulted in all categories of illegal entrants being subject to removal.[71] They have also included a number of lawsuits against cities and jurisdictions that do not cooperate with ICE (Immigration and Customs Enforcement).[72]

They include numerous efforts to reform the American health care system including efforts to lower drug prices,[73] expanded health care options,[74] while still trying to rescind and replace Obamacare.[75] They include new work rules for able-bodied welfare recipients[76] and Medicare recipients.[77] They include two executive orders that aim to bring more transparency to federal agency regulations ending rulings from agencies made to provide "guidance" that is cited in blogs, letters, and brochures but not approved as official policy.[78] They include a downsizing of the federal workforce[79] and revisions to its promotion and retention rules.[80] They include moving administrative functions and personnel out of Washington closer to areas they serve.[81] More efforts along those lines may be in some bureaucratic futures.[82]

No consideration of Trump's presidency can overlook his success in placing his own stamp on the American judicial system. His successful nomination and placement of Justice Brett M. Kavanaugh under very difficult circumstances, and Justice Neal Gorsuch on the Supreme Court, has received enormous attention and legitimately so. Every presidential appointment to the Supreme Court carries potentially major long term judicial consequences. Mr. Gorsuch has filled a very important slot,[83] and Justice Kavanaugh's successful appointment shifted the court's center of gravity.

President Trump has also been successful in placing a large number of judges below the Supreme Court level that will affect the shape of judicial decisions for decades to come. As of June 2020, that number is 200 Federal judges[84] along with his two Supreme Court Justices. He is remaking the federal judiciary,[85] not only along the traditional liberal conservative lines, but also by paying close attention to potential judges' response to the issue of shrinking the administrative state.[86]

Mr. Trump has made the economy and creating jobs a top priority and signaled his personal involvement in that process even before he took office.[87] The economic optimism that his presidency has generated has been reflected in a sometimes volatile stock market because of China trade, impeachment tensions, and the pandemic's severe economic impact. Yet, it has generally been a "bull market,"[88] itself a reflection of the "Spirit of Optimism" that the president touts. Job report figures are more empirically grounded than "optimism," and these have been encouraging with the unemployment rate hitting a fifty-year low,[89] until the pandemic hit. The same is true of over all measures of economic productivity—the GNP.[90] The impact of the coronavirus pandemic has had a dramatic effect on the stock market,[91] but its longer-term economic effects remain unclear.

In the area of foreign policy, President Trump had twice threatened to certify that Iran was not in compliance with its treaty obligations[92] and then did so, withdrawing from the agreement.[93] He has followed the same general strategy in ending President Obama's executive order on Deferred Action for Childhood Arrivals (DACA) calling on Congress to pass legislation that would save and legally secure that program,[94] while adding his own list of immigration policy preferences to be considered in any negotiation.[95] In these efforts President Trump tries to place himself in the position supporting traditional sources of legislative authority rather than simply issuing an executive order reversing President Obama's DACA executive order,[96] and letting that be the end of it. Concerns that Trump is governing primarily by executive actions to the detriment of democratic institutions need to take these actions into account.[97]

In other foreign policy initiatives, Trump has loosened the constraints on military initiatives in theaters of combat.[98] This appears to have made a substantial contribution to the dramatic change in the fortunes of ISIS.[99] He has bombed Syria when it violated a "red line" against the use of chemical weapons.[100] He has forcefully confronted North Korea rhetorically[101] which set the stage for a series of summits and lower level talks that helped cool rising tensions between the two powers.[102] He also increased pressure on China[103] that helped to bring North Korea to the negotiating table, though not to any agreement. In the meantime, he has also sent clear and obvious military signals[104] to lay the groundwork of a possible regional bargain to which North Korea might adhere.[105] And lastly, in response to clear indications that the Iranians were responsible for a drone attack on Saudi Oil processing facilities,[106] he ultimately chose not to respond with military force, but with increased economic sanctions,[107] and cyberattacks against Iranian intelligence assets.[108]

Mr. Trump has withdrawn from the Paris Climate accords,[109] and the Trans-Pacific Partnership Trade deal[110] over vehement domestic and international opposition. He has confronted China with stiff tariffs to protest its unfair trade practices,[111] a conflict that stretched over two years[112] before a Phase I accord was signed.[113] He has also used the threat[114] to withdraw from NAFTA (North American Free Trade Agreement) to renegotiate a revised agreement with Mexico and Canada.[115] That new agreement (USMCA, United States–Mexico–Canada Agreement) has now been signed into law. Mr. Trump has now turned his attention to a major trade renegotiation with the EU.[116] He has refused to appointment new members of the World Trade Organization until their dispute mechanism is made fairer.[117]

These, and similar confrontations, undertaken with eventual negotiation and agreement in mind are politically difficult to undertake as the China trade conflict most clearly demonstrates. And they have, of necessity, been put on hold, to respond to the pandemic. Trump has rarely shied away from taking the public steps, often against enormous opposition, signaling that he is able and willing to stand apart and alone, if necessary against deeply held policy narrative conventional wisdom. His "against the grain" stance has produced some surprising results in his first term.

One report on Trump's several trips to the yearly G-20 meetings observed that "If anything, Mr. Trump's two forays overseas have shown that some leaders are bending toward his positions, not the reverse."[118] We can see some evidence in Trump's success in getting some American allies to commit substantially more resources to their own defense. If you are going to be a consequential perhaps even a *Restoration* president and your presidency's ambition is changing the country's dominant political and policy narratives, always getting along with, and being praised by, traditional national and international "elites" cannot be at the top of your emotional wish list.

The list above of Trump initiatives is not mean to be comprehensive. Rather the list is meant to make one basic point. In these, and in other matters both large[119] and small,[120] the Trump administration has been extremely active and consequential. This fact has been obscured in plain sight in a sea of bombast and controversy. Trump may well have, as one opposition outlet wrote, "Quietly Accomplished More Than It Appears."[121] Yet, an even more revealing headline appeared in the *Washington Post* that captures the dual level "hidden in plain sight" progress of the Trump Presidency, "While eyes are on Russia, Sessions dramatically reshapes the Justice Department."[122]

The Trump Presidency: Stuck in Political Time?

Mr. Trump's presidency has the potential to be extremely consequential. His election by itself has disrupted the expected unfolding of "political time" that Skowronek has posited in his major work on the politics that presidents make.[123] One virtue of that work is that it specifically locates the potential success and effectiveness of any given presidency squarely within a very large, basic, and crucial question: are the presumptions and consequences of the major policy and political narratives that govern political life effectively working as publicly promised? Or, are the assumptions, promises, and dominant narratives increasingly being questioned by the general public who are then increasingly open to more realistic and effective alternatives?

Had Hillary Clinton won the presidential election, hers would have been in Skowronek's theoretical framework a presidency of *articulation*. There, the new president builds on the dominant political and policy paradigms their predecessors have helped to establish,[124] and tries to further deepen and solidify them. Instead, her election loss and the iconoclastic disruptive presidency of Mr. Trump have moved the country into a new political time zone according to Skowronek's theory. However, it is unclear at this point exactly which one it is.

A RECONSTRUCTIVE PRESIDENCY?

The Trump presidency looks in some ways very similar to the major *reconstructive* presidencies. That kind of presidency can take place, as noted, when the "established regime and pre-established commitments of ideology and interest have, in the course of events, become vulnerable to direct repudiation as failed or irrelevant responses to the problems of the day."[125] Further, they occur when "there is a general political consensus that something fundamentally has gone wrong in the high affairs of state."[126] In these political circumstances, "the order-creating capacities of the presidency were realized full vent in the wholesale reconstruction of the standards of legitimate national government."[127]

Reconstructive presidents, Skowronek says, "each set out to retrieve from a far distant, even mythical past, fundamental values that they claim have been lost in the indulgencies of the received order."[128] "Make America Great Again" indeed![129] That certainly sounds like an accurate description of a part of the set of circumstances that aided Mr. Trump's election, although Mr. Skowronek does not seem to think so.

He is clearly a supporter of the Obama presidency, calling him at one point, "in many ways the perfect president for the moment."[130] Further in that same interview he says of Trump's unlikely status as a *reconstructive* president:

you cannot transform the system without irrefutable evidence that there is no viable alternative. Without a prior disjunction—essentially, a crisis in the reigning orthodoxy of government—demonstrating that the old order is beyond repair, the president won't be able to seize control of the meaning of his changes. You can't reconstruct politics if there is not more or less a consensus that what came before was a complete and systemic failure.

Mr. Skowronek's metrics for *reconstructive* presidencies are somewhat extreme. Does the phrase "without irrefutable evidence that there is no viable alternative" refers to a disjuncture that requires a conclusive demonstration that the "old order is beyond repair?" The equivalent of a worldwide depression that helped elect FDR is exceedingly rare. Many important "disjunctures" don't have a dramatic, immediate catastrophic effect to demonstrate regime bankruptcy conclusively. Lincoln's rescue of the Union was many years in the making. So too, the continued decline in the country's trust in government, its institutions, and the effectiveness of policy promises over the last forty years would certain seems to qualify as a crisis, albeit one hidden quietly in plain sight. Moreover, requiring a "more or less consensus that what came before was a complete and systemic failure" also seems somewhat extreme. Inertia, and lack of clear alternatives often result in failed or failing governing paradigms to continue. That is the situation that President Trump faces.

Efforts at various reforms have not changed the basic policy premises on which the governing establishment has continued in power, because there is little political appetite to really examine their foundation or dramatically change them. As a result, few changes in assumptions or direction are discussed or tried. It's clear that the 62 million-plus votes that Trump received for president are certainly less than a national consensus. Yet they would certainly argue, along with President Trump, that the *status quo* consensus, to the extent it was simply not habit and lethargy is no longer substantially supportable. In any event, because of the Trump presidency a process of reconstruction has begun nonetheless. Its fate is the real question.

Skowronek writes that "only presidents who can effectively fuse power and authority in the reproduction of the political order" can become reconstructive presidents.[131] In part, this is because these national moments give rise to an "expansive authority to repudiate the established government formulas."[132] However, Skowronek also cautions that "Presidents stand preeminent in American politics when government has been most thoroughly discredited, and when political resistance to the presidency is weakest."[133]

These elements of political time that favor *reconstructive* presidencies in Skowronek's theory are clearly not yet evident in Mr. Trump's political time in office. To begin with the obvious, the major domestic and foreign policy paradigms that Mr. Trump is seeking to update, negate, or replace are far from "thoroughly discredited." They are under skeptical siege from Americans who doubt their premises and effectiveness, but a large portion of establishment leaders and institutions—Republican, Democratic, and conservative and various government bureaucracies still substantially embrace them.

In order to preserve what they think are their superior policies, paradigms, and the political and moral authority that comes with them, establishment members of the opposition have literally, as noted, declared all-out war on the Trump presidency.[134] They have done so in a variety of ways including mounting an intensive effort to legally overturn any of the president's legislative or executive accomplishments,[135] and moving very rapidly to impeach the president,[136] and criticizing almost every aspect of his response to the pandemic. The president, as noted, has returned their fire,[137] even more forcefully so after his Impeachment acquittal.[138] It is therefore quite obvious that a second of Mr. Skowronek's preconditions for a *reconstructive* presidency, resistance to the (Trump) presidency is "weakest" is simply not the case. There is an enraged, highly motivated, well connected, and powerful opposition waging a war against the Trump presidency across the country's political, legislative, judicial, cultural, economic, and social domains. It has not abated. Still, as Chapter 12 argues it is possible to change entrenched paradigms in the absence of catastrophic circumstances and Mr. Trump has made some small progress in that direction.

A Nascent *Reconstructive* Presidency?

Mr. Trump's nascent policy and narrative alternatives are themselves in the process of development and are not yet fully established options that have proved themselves effective, much less preferred. Whether or not he is able to establish and consolidate them will have a lot to do with whether he can gain a second term, and what the distribution of Congressional power will be if he does (see Chapter 12). Only if Trump gains a second term and his approaches to presidential leadership and policies bear fruit

180   S. RENSHON

would he then be in a position to move towards a real *reconstructive* presidency.

Mr. Trump successfully mobilizes his supporters. Yet, he has not been to date an effective articulator of the larger goals they both peruse. If you examine several of Mr. Trump's "set" speeches, say his dark inaugural address[139] and his sunnier uplifting address, promising a "renewal of the American Spirit,"[140] to a joint session of Congress in 2017[141] you find the continuum of dire circumstances and sunny can-do optimism that frame his presidential rhetoric. What you will not find is a clear concise, easy to understand and remember statement of his purpose.

Part of the issue is that Trump is a president focused on action, not rhetoric. Yet, there is not yet a clearly articulated sense of the purpose of Trump's presidency, as Ronald Reagan's years of immersion in basic conservative politics and policy allowed him to have and articulate. Reagan had the essential distillation of his views that his advisors referred to as "The Speech."[142] Trump has his tweets,[143] which are the free associations of his presidency and his political rallies in which he effortlessly rifts on his current thoughts. Both are revealing of his thinking, but they are far from the refined essence of purpose that provides an easy to understand key to Trump's long-term presidential ambitions.

A Preemptive Presidency?

In the foreseeable future, Mr. Trump will have to be content with what Skowronek calls a *preemptive* presidency. We noted that those presidencies have oppositional leaders at their helm, and "Like all opposition leaders, these presidents have the freedom of their independence from established commitments, but unlike presidents in the politics of reconstruction, their repudiative authority is manifestly limited by the political, institutional, and ideological supports that the old establishment maintains ..."[144] This is an apt description of the political circumstances in which President Trump finds himself. He promised and was elected by his followers to dramatically change the country's dominant political and policy practices. Yet in undertaking these goals he has had to constantly defend himself and his policy aspirations from those who will lose status and power if he is successful.

Mr. Skowronek writes that[145]:

5 LEADERSHIP STYLE, PRESIDENTIAL SUCCESS AND POLITICAL TIME 181

> The distinctive thing about preemptive leaders is that they are not out to establish, uphold, or salvage any political orthodoxy. Theirs is an unabashedly mongrel politics ... These leaders bid openly for a hybrid alternative. Their leadership stance provides them with considerable license to draw policy positions and political commitments from different sides of the issues of their day and to promote their recombination in a loosely synthesized mix.

This formulation does not seem to aptly or amply capture the essence of Mr. Trump's real challenge to established narratives. Mr. Trump *is* aiming to establish a new "political orthodoxy." He is not seeking some "mongrel" amalgam. Rather he is attempting to reorientate the basic views of the Republican Party away from its establishment Wall Street, county club anchors to a more working-class perspective. This is exactly the kind of basic party reorientation of which Azari says, "This kind of personalistic leadership is more strongly associated with reconstructive leadership."[146]

There is a policy mix in Trump's *Restoration* efforts. There is his straightforward "law and order approach to crime,"[147] and immigration enforcement.[148] There is the ruthless annihilation strategy to combat ISIS and its terrorist's supporters.[149] There are his efforts to modify trade deals to take account of the nation's workers, a stance traditionally associated with labor unions in the United States.[150] There are his plans, mentioned occasionally, to invest heavily in national infrastructure policies traditionally favored by big government Democrats and big business Republicans.[151]

These and other policies do represent some blend of "left" and "right." Yet, they are in essence, individually and collectively, broadsides against the long-standing and entrenched policy preferences, narratives, and assumptions of establishment figures from *both* sides of the political spectrum. Democrats know that Mr. Trump is not one of them. A number of conservative intellectuals are sure he isn't really one of them either,[152] a position that hardened in the wake of the controversies surrounding the Trump–Putin meeting in Helsinki.[153] The Republican establishment supports some (reduce taxes), but by no means all (make trade "fair," enforce immigration laws) of Trump's policies. They remain skittish about a number of his leadership qualities including his trustworthiness, temperament, and knowledge.[154] And given the deep disagreement between conservatives and establishment GOP leaders in Congress, and between ordinary Americans who support the GOP and their establishment leaders, Mr. Trump is, in some important ways a still a "home-alone" president attempting to both reorient and reunite one of the country's major political parties.

COULD TRUMP'S *PREEMPTIVE* PRESIDENCY BECOME *RECONSTRUCTIVE?*

Fractious Republican and Democratic opposition aside, it is well to keep in mind that in an "Afterword" to the 1997 edition of his book, Skowronek writes this about preemptive presidents[155]:

> Efforts to chart a third way in American politics have not only been marked by extraordinary variety, but also by extreme volatility. Preemptive leaders appear as wildcards in presidential history; they intrude sui generis into our national politics with inconsistent and often explosive results.

Although written well before Mr. Trump and his wife descended the escalator to formally announce his candidacy, Skowronek's "Afterword" cautions about preemptive leaders seems like an eerily prescient description of Trump's first term.

One reason that Mr. Skowronek does not view Mr. Trump as a *reconstructive* leader[156] is because that role is harder to successfully occupy given the growth of the administrative state and because of Mr. Trump's first-year difficulties in office. Skowronek does not take up the question of whether a *preemptive* president can, through dint of a protean psychology and changes in his circumstance become a *reconstructive* president. That is the major question that now faces Trump's presidential ambitions. It is worth considering the possibility.

Mr. Trump may survive his formidable opposition to win another term. In those circumstances he would have eight years to develop and demonstrate the usefulness of his approach to presidential leadership, politics, and policies. Those eight years might in turn earn enough support for the next president, perhaps another Republican, to have a presidency of articulation.

Conclusion: Promise Keepers: Trump's Strategy of Restoring Public Trust

In Chapter 3 we noted a rather large paradox at the core of the president's *Restoration* ambitions. How can a president who is given to flights of rhetorical and factual hyperbole regain the trust of the American public? Trump's rhetorical assertions are not always accurate. Neither is his grasp of the specific debates that underlie the policy areas that he wants to change.

Understanding Trump's thinking requires a meandering journey through assumptions, associations, fragments of facts and analysis, misstatements, and sometimes surprisingly keen insights. Yet, in the end, Trump's free-wheeling stream of consciousness rests on his conveying what he thinks of as policy essences rather than the kind of layers of arguments that would win a debate at the Cambridge Union (see Chapter 10).

President Trump's copious outpouring of tweets, threats, commentary, initiatives, policies, and generally what we have termed Policy and News at Trump Speed is a basic element of the Trump presidency. They serve a core purpose beyond presidential defense. That purpose is to remind Americans that much if not everything they have taken for granted as being true, fair, accurate, and the basis for developing conventional policy needs to be reexamined, rethought, modified, and where necessary discarded.

Moreover, it is possible to discern progress in a number of areas. NATO payment levels for their own defense[157] has increased for the "fourth year in a row following Trump pressure."[158] NATO has also undertaken to update the mission of an alliance formed to combat circumstances over sixty years ago.[159] The view that trade agreements have a downside is getting a hearing among members of the establishment.[160] New, improved trade deals are being negotiated and signed.

Many Americans also would like to see immigration laws already passed by Congress enforced and not voided by creative administrative loopholes. That is being done. They would like to see unnecessary and onerous regulations reduced. That is being done. They would like to see a military strong enough and willing enough to use its strength not to have to do so. That is being done. They would like to see a president who does not look down on ordinary people and who, over the years, has shown evidence of being personally comfortable with a diverse range of Americans despite his tendency to sometimes reach for conventional group stereotypes.[161] That too, is part of Trump's leadership style and policy ambitions.

In these kernels of policy essences are Trump's possible road to a *Restoration* (née *reconstructive*) presidency. Therein lies the solution to an apparent basic paradox of the Trump presidency. How is a fact- and accuracy-challenged presidential purveyor of hyperbole going to restore public trust?

Promise Keeping

The answer is presidential promise keeping. Whether it is withdrawing from a trade or climate treaty, paring back regulations, insisting that NATO pay its "fair share," "enforcing immigration laws," or the literally dozens and dozens of other Trump Administration initiations undertaken, they are all consistent with the direction and premises of Trump's promises. Those who take him seriously, but not literally, know it.

If you look at the Trust in Government figures for the Reagan presidency period you will notice an uptick in the level of public trust, not to the levels of the Eisenhower years, but an increase none the less. I attribute this not to Reagan's conservative philosophy per se, but to his honesty in expressing his views and trying to acting on them.

A recent analysis of Trump noted, "He's not the first to argue for tariffs, border security and an embassy move—only the first to deliver."[162] Another *New York Times* analysis of Trump's foreign policies noted, "Above all, Mr. Trump has taken pride in delivering on his campaign promises."[163] Even severe critics of the president who accuse him of lying "prodigiously" continue by noting that, "but when it comes to campaign promises on immigration, trade, and other issues, he's working hard to keep them."[164]

After more than three years in office, it is clear that Trump does much better in keeping his promises than in speaking accurately about them.[165] His redeployment of American troops in northern Syria was a clear part of keeping a campaign promise.[166] The explanations of his thinking were not easy for him to articulate much less to convey to the general public.

Therein lies the possible resolution, and the dilemma, of what must count as one of the most deeply paradoxical and ironic elements of the Trump presidency to date. It is that Trump is positioning himself as "truth-teller-in-chief" regarding his presidency's promises as a means of restoring public trust in government by doing so. That is Trump's political strategy and path to his presidential dream of *American Restoration*.

NOTES

1. Donald J. Trump. 2015. *Great Again: How to Fix Our Crippled America*. New York: Threshold Editions, p. 46.
2. Peter Baker. 2017. "For Trump, a Year of Reinventing the Presidency," *New York Times*, December 31. That article asks: "Will that change the institution permanently?" Our starting point is the first observation, the last question is too premature to try and answer.
3. In speaking about Hillary Clinton during the 2016 presidential campaign, Trump said "She's nasty, but I can be nastier than she ever can be." Trump quoted in Patrick Healy and Maggie Haberman 2016, "Donald Trump Opens New Line of Attack on Hillary Clinton: Her Marriage," *New York Times*, September 30.
4. President Trump did *not* include neo-Nazi group within the category of "very fine people." See "Trump's News Conference in New York: Video and Transcript," *New York Times*, August 15, 2017.
5. Maggie Haberman, Julie Hirschfeld, and Michael S. Schmidt. 2018. "Kelly Says He's Willing to Resign as Abuse Scandal Roils White House," *New York Times*, February 9.
6. Mark Lander. 2018. "On Foreign Policy, President Trump Reverts to Candidate Trump," *New York Times*, April 3.
7. Julie Davis, Julie Hirschfeld, and Maggie Haberman. 2018. "Trump, a Week After Porter Resigned, Says He's 'Totally Opposed' to Spousal Abuse," *New York Times*, February 14.
8. Frank Bruni. 2017. "The Week When President Trump Resigned," *New York Times*, August 18; see also Karl Rove. 2018. "Trump Wastes Another Weekend," *Wall Street Journal*, February 21.
9. Stephen Skowronek. 1977. *The Politics That Presidents Make: Leadership from John Adams to Bill Clinton*, revised ed. Cambridge, MA: Belknap Press.
10. Mary Bulman. 2017. "Donald Trump Has 'Dangerous Mental Illness', Say Psychiatry Experts at Yale Conference," *The Independent*, April 21; see also Bandy X. Lee et al. 2017. *The Dangerous Case of Donald Trump: 27 Psychiatrists and Mental Health Experts Assess a President*. New York: Thomas Dunne Books.
11. John Wagner. 2017. "Trump Signs Sweeping Tax Bill into Law," *Washington Post*, December 22.
12. Charlotte Allen. 2017. "Trump Month One: Success for His Supporters," *USA TODAY*, February 17.

13. Alex Roarty. 2018. "Internal Dem Polling Shows Trump's Standing on the Rise,' *McClatchy*, February 13; see also David A. Graham. 2018. "What's Behind Trump's Rising Popularity?" *The Atlantic*, February 14.
14. Jeffrey M. Jones. 2020. "Trump Job Approval at Personal Best 49%," *Gallup*, February 4.
15. Bobby Jindal. 2017. "Trump's Style Is His Substance," *Wall Street Journal*, February 14.
16. Michael Goodwin. 2018. "Donald Trump Is Teaching Republicans How to Fight," *New York Post*, January 30.
17. Ian Schwartz. 2018. "CNN Focus Group of Trump Voters: 'Exactly What I Voted for'," *Real Clear Politics*, February 13.
18. Zeke Miler. 2017. "Trump Pays Holiday Visit to Wounded Troops at Walter Reed," *Associated Press*, December 21.
19. Darlene Superville. 2019. "Trump Travels to Dover to Pay Respect to Soldiers Killed in Afghanistan Helicopter Crash," *Associated Press*, November 21.
20. Donald J. Trump. 2018. "Statement by President Trump on the Shooting in Parkland, Florida," *The White House*, February 15.
21. "President Donald Trump Meets with Teachers, Students Affected by School Shootings," *YouTube*, February 22, 2018. https://www.youtube.com/watch?v=6GVISsXd9mU [at: 110:2].
22. Glenn Thrush. 2017. "Trump, in Texas, Calls Harvey Recovery Response Effort a Real Team Effort," *New York Times*, August 29.
23. Jennifer De Pinto, Fred Backus, Kabir Khanna, and Anthony Salvanto. 2018. "Viewers approve of Trump's First State of the Union Address," *CBS News*, January 30.
24. Donald J. Trump. 2018. "Remarks by President Trump in State of the Union Address," *The White House*, January 30.
25. De Pinto et al. 2018.
26. Donald J. Trump. 2020. "Remarks by President Trump in State of the Union Address," U.S. Capital, February 4.
27. Cf. "The White House meeting was extraordinary, an extended negotiating session that was televised by the news channels." See Julie Hirschfield Davis. 2018. "Trump Appears to Endorse Path to Citizenship for Millions of Immigrants," *New York Times*, January 9; and also Donald J. Trump. 2018. "Remarks by President Trump in Meeting with Bipartisan Members of Congress on Immigration," *The White House*, January 9.
28. Tina Nguyen. 2016. "5 Signs Donald Trump Is Having a Full-Blown Identity Crisis," *Vanity Fair*, April 22.
29. Michael Gerson. 2016. "Dr. Jekyll and Mr. Hyde Are on Their Way to the White House," *Washington Post*, December 17; Michael Gerson.

2016. "Trump Spirals into Ideological Psychosis," *Washington Post*, October 17.

30. Philip Rucker, Ashley Parker, and Josh Dawsey. 2018. "'Pure Madness': Dark Days Inside the White House as Trump Shocks and Rages," *Washington Post*, March 3.

31. Drian Moylan. 2016. "The *Jerry Springer Show* Turns 25: The 10 Most Outrageous Moments," *The Guardian*, September 29.

32. Skowronek 1977, p. 36.

33. Aruna Viswanatha. 2020. "The Dispute over Roger Stone's Recommended Sentence Explained," *Wall Street Journal*, February 19.

34. Cf., Aaron Blake. 2020. "As Trump Claims a Win on Iran, He Accuses Obama of Funding Its Attacks," *Washington Post*, January 8.

35. Nancy Gertner. 2020. "Stone Case Lays Bare Barr's Not so Just Justice Department," *Boston Globe*, February 19.

36. Mujib Mashal and Lara Jakes. 2020. "Trump Gives Conditional Go Ahead on Peace Deal with Taliban, Officials Say," *New York Times*, March 4.

37. Abdul Qadir Sediqi and Alexander Corwall. 2020. "U.S.–Taliban Sign Historic Troop Withdrawal Deal in Doha," *Reuters*, February 29; Mujib Mashal. 2020. "Taliban and U.S. Strike Deal to Withdraw American Troops from Afghanistan," *New York Times*, February 29.

38. Nick Wadhams and Glen Carey. 2019. "Trump's Confounding Syria Moves Again Spur Policy Confusion," *Bloomberg News*, October 8.

39. Donald J. Trump. 2019. "Remarks by President Trump in Briefing with Military Leaders," The Cabinet Room, October 7.

40. Megan Specia. 2019. "Why Is Turkey Fighting the Kurds in Syria?" *New York Times*, October 9; Michael Duran and Michael A. Reynolds. 2019. "Turkey Has Legitimate Grievances Against the U.S.," *Wall Street Journal*, October 9.

41. Rachael Blade and Mike DeBonis. 2019. "Democrats Struggle to Figure Out Next Move Against Trump After Mueller Hearing Falls Flat," *Washington Post*, July 25.

42. Mike DeBonis and Amber Phillips. 2019. "For House Democrats, Impeachment Probe Widens the Divide They Hoped to Bridge," *Washington Post*, October 5; Sarah Ferris. 2019. "Moderate Democrats Warn Pelosi of Impeachment Obsession," *Politico*, September 15.

43. Nick Fandos, Peter Baker, Michael S. Schmidt, and Maggie Haberman. 2019. "White House Declares War on Impeachment Inquiry, Claiming Effort to Undo Trump's Election," *New York Times*, October 8.

44. Nicholas Fandos. 2019. "House Committee to Issue Blitz of Subpoenas, Raising Heat on Trump," *New York Times*, July 9.

45. Rachael Blade. 2019. "'A Lack of Urgency': Democrats Frustrated as House Investigators Struggle to Unearth Major Revelations About Trump," *Washington Post*, July 23.

46. Paul Sperry. 2020. "Impeachment's Fail Was No Proof of Trump 2020 Motive," *Real Clear Investigations*, February 10.
47. Marc Fisher and Michael Kranish. 2016. "The Trump We Saw: Populist, Frustrating, Naive, Wise, Forever on the Make," *Washington Post*, August 12.
48. Donald J. Trump. 2019. "Remarks by President Trump and President Niinistö of the Republic of Finland in Joint Press Conference," The White House, October 2.
49. Trump quoted in Michael Goodwin. 2019. "Trump Talks Impeachment, Dems and de Blasio in Interview," *New York Post*, October 2; see also Ian Schwartz. 2019. "Trump: 'Thrive' on Impeachment, Very Few People Could Handle It," *Real Clear Politics*, October 7.
50. Donald J. Trump. 2019. "Remarks by President Trump in Briefing with Military Leaders," The Cabinet Room, October 7.
51. Cf., "Don't Quit" by John Greenleaf Whittier. http://www.yourdaily poem.com/listpoem.jsp?poem_id=1820.
52. David Margolick. 2000. "The House That Fred Built, *New York Times*, December 3.
53. Philip Bump. 2016. "Donald Trump's Made-Up Coat-of-Arms Reveals His Electoral Strategy: Never Concede," *Washington Post*, October 24.
54. Trump quoted in Nancy Gibbs and Zeke Miller. 2015. "Donald Trump Explains All," *Time*. August 20, emphasis added.
55. Donald Trump (with Meredith McIver). 2008. *Trump: The Art of the Comeback*. New York: Times Books.
56. Michael Kranish. 2017. "A Fierce Will to Win Pushed Donald Trump to the Top," *Washington Post*, January 19.
57. Trump quoted in Pia Deshpande. 2019. "Trump on Impeachment and Nixon: 'He Left. I Don't Leave'," *Politico*, October 10.
58. Steve Benen. 2017. "Trump Is Convinced He's Always 'Ahead of Schedule'," *MSNBC*, October 16; Julian Z. Zelizer. 2017. "Grading President Trump," *Atlantic*, November 8.
59. Juan Williams. 2017. "Trump Is Becoming a Failed President," *The Hill*, October 16.
60. Peter Nicholas, Rebecca Ballhaus, and Siobhan Hughes. 2017. "Frustration with Republicans Drove Donald Trump to Deal with Democrats," *Wall Street Journal*, September 15.
61. Jim Tankersley and Thomas Kaplan. 2017. "House Passes Budget Blueprint, Clearing Path for Tax Overhaul," *New York Times*, October 26; see also Ben Casselman and Jim Tankersley. 2018. "Tax Overhaul Gains Public Support, Buoying Republicans," *New York Times*, February 19.
62. Maggie Haberman and Anni Karni. 2019. "Trump Celebrates Criminal Justice Overhaul Amid Doubts It Will Be Fully Funded," *New York Times*, April 1.

63. Alan Fram. 2018 "Congress' Immigration Push Sputters as Guns Grab Attention," *Real Clear Politics*, March 3.
64. Cf., Jeff Nesbit. 2016. "Donald Trump Is Failing His Crash Course in Leadership," *Time*, November 28; see also Jennifer Rubin Jennifer. 2017. "Trump Is Failing Faster Than Any President," *Washington Post*, July 17; Juan Williams. 2017. "Trump Is Becoming a Failed President," *The Hill*.
65. Stan Collander. 2017. "Last Week Was Trump's Worst Legislative Week Ever, and Congress Wasn't Even in Session," *Forbes*, September 4; see also Katie Reilly. 2017. "Here Are President Trump's 3 Biggest Setbacks in His First 100 Days," *Time*, April 25; Baker 2017.
66. Adam Entous, Devlin Barrett, and Rosalind S. Helderman. 2017. "Clinton Campaign, DNC Paid for Research That Led to Russia Dossier," *Washington Post*, October 24.
67. Catherine Lucey and Andrew Restuccia. 2020. "Trump Denounces Impeachment, Saying He 'Went Through Hell'," *Wall Street Journal*, February 6.
68. Office of the White House. 2017. "Presidential Executive Order on Reducing Regulation and Controlling Regulatory Costs," January 30; Clyde Jr. Crews. 2019. "Trump's Regulatory Reform Agenda by the Numbers (Summer 2019 Update)," *Forbes*, May 30.
69. Lisa Friedman and Brad Plumer. 2017. "P.A. Announces Repeal of Major Obama-Era Carbon Emissions Rule," *New York Times*, October 9.
70. Cf., Julie Hirschfeld and Miriam Jordan. 2017. "Trump Plans 45,000 Limit on Refugees Admitted to U.S," *New York Times*, September 26; see also Ron Nixon. 2017. "Trump Administration Punishes Countries That Refuse to Take Back Deported Citizens," *New York Times*, September 13; *Associated Press*. 2017. "U.S. to Arrest Parents, Sponsors Who Hire Smugglers to Bring Children Across Border," *Wall Street Journal*, June 30.
71. Michael D. Shear and Ron Nixon. 2017. "New Trump Deportation Rules Allow Far More Expulsions," *New York Times*, February 21.
72. Matt Zapotosky and Devlin Barrett. 2020. "Justice Dept. Sues 'Sanctuary' Jurisdictions in New Crackdown over Immigration Enforcement," *Washington Post*, February 10.
73. Peter Sullivan. 2018. "Trump Unveils Most Aggressive Action to Target Drug Prices," *The Hill*, October 25.
74. Brian Blase. 2019. "Trump's New Rule Will Give Businesses and Workers Better Health Care Options," *CNN*, June 14.
75. Amy Goldstein. 2018. "Trump Administration Takes Another Major Swipe at the Affordable Care Act," *Washington Post*, July 7.
76. Katie Rogers and Catie Edmondson. 2018. "Trump Administration Moves to Restrict Food Stamp Access the Farm Bill Protected," *New York Times*, December 20.

77. Stephanie Armour. 2019. "Government Watchdog Faults Trump Administration's Approval of Medicaid Work Requirements," *Wall Street Journal*, October 10.
78. Office of the White House. 2019. "Executive Order on Promoting the Rule of Law Through Transparency and Fairness in Civil Administrative Enforcement and Adjudication," October 9.
79. Lisa Rein and Andrew Tran. 2017. "How the Trump Era Is Changing the Federal Bureaucracy," *Washington Post*, December 30.
80. Eric Yoder. 2019. "Federal Employees Could Face More Discipline Under Proposed New Rules," *Washington Post*, September 17.
81. Andrew O'Reilly. 2019. "USDA Staffers Quit en masse as Trump Administration Eyes Moving Offices Out of DC," *Fox*, May 23.
82. Jessie Bur. 2019. "Senators Want to Move These Agency Headquarters Out of DC," *Federal Times*, October 24.
83. Robert Barnes. 2017. "Gorsuch Asserts Himself Early as Force on Supreme Court's Right," *Wall Street Journal*, June 27.
84. Madison Adler. 2020. "Blue States Create Hurdle for Trump's 2020 Judicial Appointments," *NPR*, February 11; see also John Wagner. 2020. "Senate confirms 200th judicial nominee from Trump, a legacy that will last well beyond November," *Washington Post*, June 24.
85. Kimberly Strassel. 2017. "Scalias All the Way Down," *Wall Street Journal*, October 12; see also Charles Savage. 2017. "Trump Is Rapidly Reshaping the Judiciary: Here's How," *New York Times*, November 11.
86. Jeremy W. Peters. 2018. "Trump's New Judicial Litmus Test: Shrinking 'the Administrative State'," *New York Times*, March 26.
87. Jonathan O'Connell. 2016. "How Is Trump Spending Thanksgiving? He Says He's Trying to Save an Indiana Factory," *Washington Post*, November 24.
88. Fred Imbert. 2019. "Dow Rallies 200 Points to Close Above 27,000 for the First Time Ever," *CNBC*, July 11.
89. Gregg Robb. 2019. "U.S. Adds 136,000 Jobs in September, Unemployment Rate Hits 50-Year Low," *Market Watch*, October 4.
90. https://tradingeconomics.com/united-states/gross-national-product. See also Natalie Kitroeff and Jim Tankersley. 2017. "U.S. Economy Grew at 3% Rate in 3rd Quarter, Despite Storms," *New York Times*, October 27.
91. Adam Taylor, Rick Noack, Miriam Berger, and Michael Brice-Saddler. 2020. "Fears Grow of a Coronavirus Pandemic as Markets Stumble Again; Japan Shuts Schools," *Washington Post*, February 22.
92. Mark Lander and David E. Sanger. 2017. "Trump to Force Congress to Act on Iran Nuclear Deal," *New York Times*, October 5.
93. Mark Lander. 2018. "On Foreign Policy, President Trump Reverts to Candidate Trump," *New York Times*, April 3.

94. Michael D. Shear, Julie Hirschfeld Davis, and Adam Liptak. 2019. "How the Trump Administration Eroded Its Own Legal Case on DACA," *New York Times*, November 12.
95. Donald J. Trump. 2017. "President Donald J. Trump's Letter to House and Senate Leaders & Immigration Principles and Policies," The White House: Office of the Press Secretary, October 8.
96. John Wagner and David Nakamura. 2017. "Trump Turns to Executive Powers in Bid to Force Congress into Action," *Washington Post*, October 14.
97. Sidney M. Milkis and Nicholas Jacobs. 2017. "'I Alone Can Fix It' Donald Trump, the Administrative Presidency, and Hazards of Executive-Centered Partisanship," *The Forum*, November 11.
98. Helen Cooper. 2019. "Trump Gives Military New Freedom: But with That Comes Danger," *New York Times*, April 5.
99. Karen DeYoung. 2017. "Under Trump, Gains Against ISIS Have 'Dramatically Accelerated'," *Washington Post*, August 4; see also Liz Sly and Aaso Ameen Schwan, "ISIS Is Near Defeat in Iraq: Now Comes the Hard Part," *Washington Post*, September 13.
100. Russell Walter Mead, Damir Marusic, and Andrew Bernard. 2017. "What the Syria Strikes Mean," *The National Interest*, March 7.
101. Choe Sang-Hun and Jane Perlez. 2017. "At U.N. and in the Air, North Korea and U.S. Trade Tough Messages," *New York Times*, September 23.
102. Simon Denyer. 2019. "North Korea and United States to Resume Nuclear Talks Saturday," *Washington Post*, October 1.
103. Chen Aizhu. 2017. "Exclusive: China's CNPC Suspends Fuel Sales to North Korea as Risks Mount—Sources," *Reuters*, June 27.
104. Travis J. Tritten. 2017. "Vinson and Reagan carrier Strike Groups Mass Near North Korea," *Washington Examiner*, June 1.
105. David Ignatius. 2017. "Here's What a Permanent Treaty with North Korea Might Look Like," *Washington Post*, August 15.
106. Eli Lake. 2019. "Yes, Iran Was Behind the Saudi Oil Attack: Now What?" *Bloomberg*, September 15.
107. Michael D. Shear, Eric Schmitt, Michael Crowley, and Maggie Haberman. 2019. "Strikes on Iran Approved by Trump, Then Abruptly Pulled Back," *New York Times*, June 20.
108. Julien Barnes and Thomas Gibblons-Neff. 2019. "U.S. Carried Out Cyberattacks on Iran," *New York Times*, June 22.
109. Lisa Friedman. 2017. "Trump Adviser Tells Ministers U.S. Will Leave Paris Climate Accord," *New York Times*, September 18; see also Donald J. Trump. 2017. " Statement by President Trump on the Paris Climate Accord," The White House, June 1.

110. Baker 2017; see also Yian Q. Mui. 2017. "President Trump Signs Order to Withdraw from Trans-Pacific Partnership," *Washington Post*, January 23.
111. Alexandra Stevenson. 2018. "Xi Jinping Urges Dialogue, Not Confrontation, After Trump Seeks Tariffs," *New York Times*, April 9.
112. Lingling Wei, Chao Deng, and Josh Zumbrun. 2019. "China Seeks to Narrow Trade Talks With U.S. in Bid to Break Deadlock?" *Wall Street Journal*, September 12.
113. Ana Swanson. 2019. "Trump Reaches Phase I Deal with China and Delays Planned Tariffs," *New York Times*, October 11.
114. Mark Lander. 2017. "White House Is Said to Draft Plan for U.S. Break From Nafta," *New York Times*, April 26; see also Kevin Liptak. 2017. "Trump Agrees 'Not to Terminate NAFTA at This *Time*'," *CNN*, April 26.
115. Jacob M. Schlesinger and Bob Davis. 2018. "U.S., Mexico and Canada Sign Pact to Replace Nafta," *Wall Street Journal*, November 30.
116. Andrea Shalal and David Lawder. 2020. "As Trump Takes Aim at EU Trade, European Officials Brace for Fight," *Reuters*, February 11.
117. Shawn Donnan 2019. Trump's Trade 'Bad Cop' Thinks He Has Found a Winning Formula," *Bloomberg*, December 2.
118. Peter Nicholas. 2017. "Trump's 'America First' Policy Proves to Be an Immovable Object at G-20," *Wall Street Journal*, July 9.
119. Steven Dinen. 2017. "Trump Moves to Restore Work Requirement for Welfare," *The Washington Time*s, August 30.
120. Harry Farley. 2017. "VP Mike Pence Says US Will Bypass UN and Give US Aid Directly to Christians in Iraq," *Christian Today*, October 26.
121. David A. Graham. 2017. "Trump Has Quietly Accomplished More Than It Appears," *The Atlantic*, August 2; see Delroy Murdock. 2017. "This Thanksgiving, Thank Donald J. Trump," *National Review*, November 23.
122. Matt Zapotosky and Sari Horwitz. 2017. "While Eyes Are on Russia, Sessions Dramatically Reshapes the Justice Department," *Washington Post*, November 24.
123. Skowronek 1977, p. 36. see also David A. Crockett. 2002. *The Opposition Presidency*. College Station, TX: Texas A&M Press; Julia Azari. 2020. "The Scrambled Cycle: Realignment, Political Time, and the Trump Presidency," in Zachary Callen and Philip Rocco (eds.), *American Political Development and the Trump Presidency*. Philadelphia, PA: University of Pennsylvania Press.
124. Ibid.
125. Ibid.
126. Skowronek 1977, p. 37.
127. Ibid.

5 LEADERSHIP STYLE, PRESIDENTIAL SUCCESS AND POLITICAL TIME 193

128. Ibid.
129. Karen Tumulty. 2017. "How Donald Trump Came Up with 'Make America Great Again'," *Washington Post*, January 18.
130. Mr. Skowronek went on to say about president Obama, "Trump won the 2016 election by talking up this fabricated image of the Obama presidency as a failure, but it had very little foundation in reality. One thing I can't understand is why the Democrats were so incompetent in conveying their accomplishments. But you have a fairly successful economy, a draw-down of unpopular wars, and high favorability ratings for the outgoing president." Skowronek quoted in Richard Kreitner. 2016. "What Time Is It? Heres What the 2016 Election Tells Us About Obama, Trump, and What Comes Next," *The Nation*, November 22.
131. Skowronek 1977, p. 39.
132. Skowronek 1977, p. 37, emphasis added.
133. Ibid. (emphasis added).
134. Anita Kumar and Andrew Desiderio. 2019. "Trump Showdown with House Democrats Ignites into All-Out War," *Politico*, March 23; see also "List of Republicans Who Opposed the Donald Trump Presidential Campaign, 2016." https://en.wikipedia.org/wiki/List_of_Republicans_who_opposed_the_Donald_Trump_presidential_campaign,_2016.
135. Michelle Goldberg. 2018. "The De-Trumpification Agenda," *The New York Times*, February 28.
136. Cf., "Democrats are eyeing an accelerated timetable for their impeachment inquiry that could mean the entire process—including a House vote to charge the president and a Senate trial—could be almost over by January." See Nicholas Fandos. 2019. "House Committee to Issue Blitz of Subpoenas, Raising Heat on Trump," *New York Times*, July 9.
137. Christine Marcos. 2019. "Trump Fires Back on Impeachment," *The Hill*, October 10.
138. Caitlin Opryskon. 2020. "It Was All Bulls—': Liberated Trump Lets Loose in Victory Speech After Acquittal," *Politico*, February 6.
139. Donald J. Trump. 2017. "The Inaugural Address," Capital Building, January 2.
140. Jessica Taylor. 2017. "Calling for 'Renewal of the American Spirit,' Trump Outlines His Vision," *NPR*, February 28.
141. Donald J. Trump. 2017. "Remarks by President Trump in Joint Address to Congress," U.S.
142. William K. Muir Jr. 1998. "Ronald Reagan: The Primacy of Rhetoric," in Fred I. Greenstein (ed.), *Leadership in the Modern Presidency*. Cambridge, MA: Harvard University Press, p. 288.
143. Shushannah Walshe. 2017. "ANALYSIS: Trump's Twitter Use Brings Risks and Rewards," *ABC News*, April 28.
144. Skowronek. 1977, p. 43.

194   S. RENSHON

145. Skowronek 1997, p. 449.
146. Julia Azari. 2020. "The Scrambled Cycle: Realignment, Political Time, and the Trump Presidency," in Zachary Callen and Philip Rocco (eds.), *American Political Development and the Trump Presidency*. Philadelphia, PA: University of Pennsylvania Press, p. 39.
147. Timothy Williams. 2019. "Murder Rate Drops Across U.S., But Not in All Large Cities," *New York Times*, September 30.
148. Michael D. Shear and Ron Nixon. 2017. "New Trump Deportation Rules Allow Far More Expulsions," *New York Times*, February 21.
149. Cf., "We have already shifted from attrition tactics where we shove them from one position to another in Iraq and Syria, to annihilation tactics where we surround them. Our intention is that the foreign fighters do not survive the fight to return home to North Africa, to Europe, to America, to Asia, to Africa." See Secretary James Mattis interviewed on *Face the Nation, CBS News*, May 28, 2017.
150. Baker 2017.
151. Louis Nelson. 2017. "Trump Predicts GOP Will Work with Dems 'for the Good of the Country'," *Politico*, December 22.
152. The Editors. 2016. "Against Trump," *National Review*, January 16.
153. David Frum. 2018. *Trumpocracy: The Corruption of the American Republic*. New York: Harper.
154. Janet Hook and Siobhan Hughes. 2017. "Republican Retirement Gives House Democrats Another Target," *Wall Street Journal*, September 8.
155. Skowronek 1977, p. 36.
156. Ibid.
157. Nina Agrawal. 2017. "President Trump Wants Other Members of NATO to Pay Their Fair Share: Here's What That Would Look Like," *Los Angeles Times*," February 6; see also Robert Barnes. 2017. "Gorsuch Asserts Himself Early as Force on Supreme Court's Right," *Wall Street Journal*, June 27.
158. Michael Birnbaum. 2019. "NATO Members Increase Defense Spending for Fourth Year in Row Following Trump Pressure," *Washington Post*, April 14.
159. Julian C. Barnes. 2016. "NATO Moving to Create New Intelligence Chief Post," *Wall Street Journal*, June 3; William James. 2017. "Trump Says NATO Is Obsolete But Still 'Very Important to Me'," *Reuters*, January 16.
160. Jeff D. Colgan and Robert O. Keohane. 2017. "The Liberal Order Is Rigged," *Foreign Affairs*, April 17.
161. Cf., "So it was a terrible deal. It was a terrible negotiation. It was negotiated by people that are poor negotiators against great negotiators. Persians being great negotiators, okay? It's one of those things. You might be Persian. But the Iranians, frankly, are great negotiators." See

Bob Woodward and Robert Costa. 2016. "Transcript: Donald Trump Interview with Bob Woodward and Robert Costa," *Washington Post*, April 2.
162. Bobby Jindal. 2018. "Trump Keeps His Predecessors' Promises," *Wall Street Journal*, April 3.
163. Lander 2018.
164. David A. Graham. 2018. "What's Behind Trump's Rising Popularity?" *The Atlantic*, February 14.
165. Carrie Johnson. 2017. "Robert Mueller May Not be the Savior the Anti-Trump Internet Is Hoping for," *NPR*, August 17.
166. Catherine Lucey. 2019. "Behind Trump's Syria Pullout Lies a Campaign Pledge," *Wall Street Journal*, October 8.

PART III

Psychiatry in the White House: Trump's Narcissism and "Fitness" for Office

CHAPTER 6

President Trump's Narcissism Reconsidered

One of the most unusual and unprecedented aspects of the Trump presidency is the degree to which anti-Trump "mental health professionals," office holders, news reporters, media pundits, celebrities, and ordinary people are willing to publicly share their psychiatric and psychological assessments of the president. They do so to buttress their view that he is a unique threat to this republic and the world, and therefore must be removed from office. Anti-Trump commenters treat that outpouring of psychological narrative diagnosis and characterization as synonymous with clinical truths. They are not.

The frequency and apparent acceptance of these commentaries lead this analysis into unusual territory for what is ordinarily an effort to develop valid explanatory theories of a president's psychology and their implications for his leadership and governing style. Any attempt to develop an accurate psychologically framed analysis of this president must, of necessity, address these issues. That is especially the case given the formal clinical and psychoanalytic training of the author.

These issues include but are not limited to the following kinds of questions: Is the president "mentally ill"?; Does he exhibit the characteristics of the severe psychopathology outlined in the DSM-5 (*Diagnostic and Statistical Manual of Mental Disorders*-V) manual?; If so, what are the diagnoses that best fit what "mental health practitioners," and others

© The Author(s) 2020
S. Renshon, *The Real Psychology of the Trump Presidency*,
The Evolving American Presidency,
https://doi.org/10.1007/978-3-030-45391-6_6

199

claim to see in Trump's psychology on the basis of their observations;? and is Trump therefore psychologically unfit to hold office?

It is essential to make absolutely clear at the outset that in addressing these and the related questions that follow, absolutely no Trump psychiatric or psychological "diagnosis" of any kind is being implied or will be offered. The Goldwater Rule takes the position that it is unethical to offer a "diagnosis," especially a public one, without having engaged with or treated the person involved. That makes good sense on ethical and assessment grounds for many reasons. Giving public "diagnoses" of any person, even a public figure, on the basis of news accounts—often inaccurate, limited, highly selected parts of a president's words, and not seriously coming to grips with ones' own strongly held political preferences—as most anti-Trump "mental health professional" do, is not only a severe lapse of professional ethics and personal integrity. It is a recipe for poor evaluation and analysis.

One central reason why this is the case is that what a patient thinks of what they do, and why they think that way, is a critical part of psychoanalytic and psychiatric evaluation and diagnosis in a clinical setting. One cannot simply infer that kind of foundational motivational information on the basis of what you observe casually at a distance by using the latest headline, relying on the latest narrative meme, or generalizing from your own self-confirming assumptions.

Consider for example one fairly common anti-Trump psychiatric meme, that Trump needs adoring crowds because of his narcissism. Why exactly does he need them? Is it to bolster grandiose or fragile levels of self-esteem? Or, is the first operating as a compensation for the second as Harold Lasswell's famous dictum that "political man" seeks power to "overcome low estimates of the self" suggests.[1] In theory, Trump's supposed need for adoring crowds either is to buttress or confirm his narcissism. Which is it though? Are his crowds meant to compensate for Trump's low self-esteem or confirm his sense of superiority?

That example makes the issue clear. One cannot simply attribute a motivation to Trump's "narcissism" without some attention to what that terms actually means beyond its ordinary, and even its basic clinical understanding. Moreover, the term itself provides no particular motivational diagnosis. A diagnostic category or term, by itself, is not synonymous with the motivation underlying it. Yet, the anti-Trump psychiatric narratives and memes often treat them as indistinguishable.

6 PRESIDENT TRUMP'S NARCISSISM RECONSIDERED   201

These questions point to more basic starting questions. Exactly what is meant by saying that Trump is "narcissistic," or has a "narcissistic personality" disorder? What does it mean to say that he suffers from "malignant narcissism"? If these characterizations are to be any more than psychiatric name calling, they must reflect real knowledge of, and grappling with the range of theory and analysis that underlies them. Most such characterizations of Trump do not.

A psychologically framed portrait of a president, such as this one, is very far from a "diagnosis," that seeks to place a president in a category that reflects his degree of functional capacity or impairment within the context of established psychiatric diagnostic categories. Our purpose here is to develop an understanding of this particular president and to use that knowledge to develop and refine a theory of presidential performance more generally. The basic question we ask is not how well the president functions according to psychiatric diagnostic criteria. It is rather whether our psychologically and political anchored portrait accurately describe the essential elements of this president's political leadership and governing choices.

PRESIDENT TRUMP'S PSYCHOLOGY AS A NATIONAL EMERGENCY

Many commentators are convinced they know the real Donald Trump. He is, they think, so obviously shallow, insecure, and garish that single clinical words or catch phrases are all that are needed to find a narrative that will psychologically tar and feather him. He is, take your pick: a "cruel sadist,"[2] a "sociopath,"[3] a "narcissistic sociopath,"[4] crazy,[5] a "raving lunatic,"[6] a monster,[7] shows a "degree of detachment from reality,"[8] or has "spiraled into an ideological psychosis."[9] These characterizations are little more than name-calling masquerading as analysis.

With sentiments like these voiced repeatedly by media commentators, carried by major news and media outlets and echoed by establishment power holders across the civic spectrum, it is small wonder that many alarmed Trump opponents feel that there is no line that shouldn't be crossed in their efforts to defeat him. That includes characterizing President Trump's psychology on the basis of speculations garnered from a single quote or the latest newspaper headlines and drawing the most radical, damaging, disparaging, and unsubstantiated conclusions.

One psychiatrist who has written an unrelievedly harsh partisan book on the president,[10] writes that Mr. Trump is such a clear and present danger to the county and the world that he should be immediately hospitalized against his will. The psychiatrist in question is Justin Frank MD who has written two highly partisan presidency books, one a psychology bashing exercise on George W. Bush and the other a fawning sycophantic adulatory book on Barack Obama.

In his personal blog entry entitled: "Now is the Time," posted March 5, 2017, he writes[11]:

> Donald Trump is unstable, and *there is no need to list the evidence here*. As President of the United States, his behavior presents a clear and present danger to an entire nation, if not the world. We cannot employ, as president, someone too impulsive to think, unable to reason, and unable to engage in complex discussions with the various government agencies from State to Defense to National Security to Justice. In fact, if he were my patient I would insist that he be hospitalized before attempting psychoanalytic treatment ... *the people I've treated who behave like President Trump require hospitalization—even if against their will.*

"No need to list the evidence here" is, of course, a way to avoid addressing and assessing it. This is the opposite of scholarship, whether psychoanalytically or otherwise based. It is, however, a recipe and detailed road map for blatant partisanship and shallow, fatuous analysis.

Dr. Frank is not alone in having been trained at one time on the necessity of careful professional analysis that is jettisoned when it comes to Donald Trump. John D. Gardner, PhD., an anti-Trump stalwart wrote a petition that read[12]:

> We, the undersigned mental health professionals (please state your degree), believe in our professional judgment that Donald Trump manifests a serious mental illness that renders him psychologically incapable of competently discharging the duties of President of the United States. And we respectfully request he be removed from office, according to article 4 of the 25th amendment to the Constitution, which states that the president will be replaced if he is "unable to discharge the powers and duties of his office."

This "mental health professional" recently claimed the following in his FaceBook page[13]:

PREPARE FOR THE APOCALYPSE I'm no Nostradamus, but as many of you know, from day one I have been uncannily prescient about one thing: Donald Trump. Here are my 15 predictions for 2020–2025:

1) Sanders will win the nomination 2) Trump will win re-election 3) Civil unrest will erupt with killings in the streets 4) The federal civil service will be purged of Democrats and others deemed not loyal starting at the top and working their way down the chain. 5) Millions of undocumented immigrants dragged from their homes and detained at the border will be held in the concentration camps in the desert 6) The Supreme Court will reverse Roe v. Wade by 7–2, and make a generation of partisan decisions. 7) Reporters and other political enemies and will be jailed by the state, or roughed up and killed by rogue MAGA-heads and shadowy paramilitaries 8) The pace of global warming will accelerate along with catastrophic weather events of Biblical proportions. 9) There will be more outbreaks of new diseases and our largely defunded public health system will be inadequate in response 10) The market and the economy will crash. 11) Israel will suffer a catastrophic attack. 12) The Western alliance will shatter, as Trump withdraws from NATO and our former friends realize we have switched sides. 13) Putin will dramatically escalate his cyberattacks and military aggression against Western democracies, while other strongmen also feel emboldened to commit atrocities. 14) No more free and fair elections. Through voter suppression, misinformation, foreign interference, and direct hacking of voting machines, Republicans will maintain one party minority rule no matter how small their base. 15) Trump will employ a "tactical" nuclear weapon—an unprovoked first strike—in an unnecessary war he precipitates without consulting Congress.

Dr. Frank's observation about there being "no need to list the evidence" seems to fit well with these observations by this self-described and self-congratulatory "uncannily prescient" pundit.

PRESIDENT TRUMP: NARCISSIST-IN-CHIEF?

If there is one term that is thought to define President Trump, it is narcissism.[14] At first glance the term seems to fit, at least in its common understanding. There is Mr. Trump's brash and indisputably ostentatious display of his wealth. That is frequently accompanied with a vocabulary of his self-proclaimed accomplishments that seems limited to superlatives. There are also his frequent public fights with those that oppose him. These, and similar items, have given rise to a cottage industry of pundits who define this president's more complex psychology with a single, overused, and misapplied clinical term.

Single Psychiatric Terms and Complex Psychological Realities

Every president comes into office with their own ambitions, their own strengths and limitations, and their own understandings of the circumstances they face and what to do about them. They also come into office with a distinctive set of psychological characteristics that either help or hinder their navigation of the presidency's complex demands. These basic considerations clearly apply to Mr. Trump as they do for every president.

Almost all modern presidents share some core psychological elements, like ambition, even though they can differ in the amounts they bring to the office.[15] Other traits like significant resilience, substantial reserves of personal energy, or overt public combativeness are less evenly distributed in the general or presidential population. A president's specific package of psychological traits—say *Reconstruction* level presidential ambitions, substantial amounts of energy, overt public combativeness and resilience may be very unique indeed. Donald Trump's constellation of core psychological elements is a case in point.

Consider in this regard just one of Trump's core traits—his energy levels and sleep patterns.

The following exchange with reporters took place following the president's physical[16]:

> *Q*: How much sleep does he get, on average?
> *DR. JACKSON*: He doesn't sleep much. I mean, I would say that—you know, this is just my guess based on being around him. I didn't ask him this question, so I could be wrong on this, but I would say he sleeps four to five hours a night. And I think he's probably been that way his whole life. That's probably one of the reasons why he's been successful, I don't know.

Trump has commented on his own sleeping habits as follows: "You know, I'm not a big sleeper. I like three hours, four hours, I toss, I turn, I beep-de-beep, I want to find out what's going on."[17] It's clear that Trump's unusual amount of sleep does not interfere with his energy levels.[18]

This is one of several clearly observable and consequential Trump psychological and leadership traits. It is the analyst's task to begin to

6 PRESIDENT TRUMP'S NARCISSISM RECONSIDERED   205

assemble the particular elements that comprise a president's psychology, ask how they are related, examine their origin and development, and examine how they affect the core elements of presidential performance—leadership and judgment reflected in choice.[19] A relentless focus on a single presidential trait is unlikely to provide an adequate account of a president's psychology or an explanation for his choices, especially if that trait—narcissism in the case of President Trump—is misapplied or poorly understood by those who reflexively reach for it as an explanation.

Trump's "Unfitness" for the Presidency

The issue of the use or misuse of a single psychological term to characterize a president who is clearly more complex than his caricatures is distinct from the question of what presidential characteristics, or lack therefore, constitute "unfitness" for the office.[20] In a previous publication I used the term "psychological suitability" to assess the character unfitness arguments on strictly psychological grounds.[21] As analyzed further in Chapter 7, Trump critics however use the term "unfit" to cover a vast range of psychological and political conceptual territory, and make a large number of unfitness claims. They offer numerous and varied reasons why Trump is "unfit," without much effort to describe or analyze the criteria they use. This does a disservice to an important set of issues for any president, not only for Mr. Trump.

Some criteria of Mr. Trump's unfitness, like his supposed "TV addiction,"[22] seem closer to hyperbole than analysis. Some others raise important questions that it would be useful to discuss, for example, what is adequate preparation for the presidency (see Chapter 9)? Other serious issues like the question of Trump's impulsiveness[23] would also benefit from analysis.

In Trump critics' view his impatience is a by-product of his narcissism because he needs instant gratification. The same holds true for his supposed impulsiveness. That too supposedly comes from a narcissistic inability to restrain himself. We argue below that there is a distinction between impatience and impulsiveness. They are not synonymous. Moreover, neither is necessarily linked to "narcissism." Other more fitting explanations are available.

President Trump's Narcissism, Impulsiveness, and Impatience

Among the many critical analyses of President Trump, concerns about his impulsiveness ranks high. Looking over the first 100 days of the Trump administration, the *Wall Street Journal* worried—"The most important issue is whether Mr. Trump can discipline his own pattern of setting policy by impulse."[24] Even before then, the ordinarily thoughtful[25] foreign policy analyst Robert Kagan worried that, "the thing that ought to keep you up nights as we head into the final 100 days of this campaign, is that the man cannot control himself. He cannot hold back even when it is manifestly in his interest to do so."[26] Impulsiveness is also a cornerstone of the argument that anti-Trump "mental health experts" make against allowing him to remain in office because (see Chapter 7), among other reasons, the "president lacked the ability to make rational decisions."[27]

It is true that Mr. Trump can be impulsive. However, part of his impulsiveness is due to his impatience. The two are not synonymous. Impulsiveness reflects an inability to restrain the discharge of impulses. Impatience is not so directly tied to failures of impulse control as it is to ambition's goals, wanting to accomplish them, and being frustrated by delays, whether intuitional or oppositional. Impatience reflects intelligence's assessment of what is standing in the way and making a judgment about what to do about that. It is therefore far from mindless instinctual discharge.

Impatience is then a reflection of wanting to do things quickly. That may be directly related to a deep personal need that requires immediate expression, but ordinarily isn't. Often impatience has more ordinary origins, like the desire to accomplish one's personal and professional ambitions, especially, as in Trump's case, when there are a lot of them. Given that fact, it is easy to draw the wrong conclusions about Trump's impulses and impatience, and many do.

Trump's Business World: Action, Patience, and Results

Mr. Trump's singular position at the top of the empire he created required the need for numerous fast paced decisions given the number and range of his projects. Trump is, and has been all his life, highly oriented toward getting results. However, as noted, and echoing a point made by Lincoln, Trump wrote in *The Art of the Deal*[28]:

6 PRESIDENT TRUMP'S NARCISSISM RECONSIDERED 207

you can't fool the people, at least not for long. You can create excitement, you can do wonderful promotions, and get all kinds of press and you can throw in a little hyperbole. *But if you don't deliver the goods, people will eventually catch on.*

Delivering the goods is of course the basis of Trump's promise keeper's strategy (Chapter 5). Delivering the goods is exactly what Trump kept his eye on doing, as a real estate developer and empire builder, even when it took decades for a deal to reach fruition. Examining Trump's business career, it is clear that he has been able to bide his time and control his impulses, and even his impatience.

In a detailed interview with the *Washington Post*, Trump recalled the property he owns in Aberdeen, Scotland that became one of his signature golf courses. He said: "Okay. I got it zoned. Nobody believed it. It took me four years, I got it zoned. I then built a golf course."[29] That interview then continued:

But I also got housing, and I have other things. It's a major development, but I haven't chosen to do the development because I don't have time to do it. But if I wanted to do it, or if I wanted to sell the land, or I wanted to do something I could. *I'm in no rush.* I don't need to do the housing because I don't need the money.

There are other examples. One of Trump's first big projects in Manhattan was a very large complex of apartment buildings and stores on the Upper West Side named Trump City. It was a 150-acre parcel of abandoned Penn Central rail yards, fourteen city blocks long, on which Trump wanted to build the world's tallest building and largest shopping center, plus 7600 luxury condos. That plan ran into intense opposition from city politicians, community leaders, and activists.[30] In a 1989 interview on his plans and the opposition, Trump had this to say[31]:

No problem. Believe me, if I don't get the zoning now, I'll sit back and wait until things get bad in the city, until construction stops and interest rates go up. And then I'll build it. But I will build it.

He did wait, decades in this case. Eventually, he did build it.[32] The final design for the project that was built differed substantially from the original design. However, in thirty years many battles had been fought, lost, and won. Zoning, economics, politics, and administrations had changed.

Of course, the design of the project developed and changed. The fact that this gigantic project was built at all remains an accomplishment. The fact that the project changed over thirty years it is not a reflection of what one serial critic alleged, that Trump had "failed."[33]

The Trump Presidency: Impatience, Action, Mistakes, Grudging Patience, and the Search for Results

The incremental nature of the American political system is ordinarily guaranteed to stymie exactly the kind of major changes that Mr. Trump envisions for his presidency. Recall the eight policy pillars of *American Restoration*, Trump's presidential ambitions: the courts, economic growth and opportunity (including jobs and energy development), deregulation, health care, immigration, foreign policy, trade, and lifting the fear of discussing many political debate topics (aka "political correctness"). Then further consider the very many policy initiatives that Trump has undertaken within each of those major areas, and one gains some perspective on the enormity of his presidential ambitions.

There is as well the issue of time, or more specifically the reality of the pace of policy change, the limits that imposes, and the lessons of Trump's experience with getting things done. Looking back on his life in another interview, he wistfully noted, "When I was 38, it was all going to last forever."[34] In the near collapse of his business empire, he apparently learned a basic but searing life lesson. That is one reason why time matters so much to him and he is so impatient.

One early analysis of his presidency noted, "An impatient New Yorker by nature, Mr. Trump has been unable in his first months in office to bend Washington to his 'you're fired!' ways."[35] He is well aware that he has limited time to move his vast agenda forward. As the *New York Times* headline correctly put it about just one of Mr. Trump's major areas of presidential initiatives: "Trade Deals Take Years. Trump Wants to Remake Them in Months."[36]

Trump is, and has been all his life highly oriented toward getting results and his presidency is no exception. It took time to plan and carry out the Syrian strike.[37] It will take months, if not years to work through the recently signed peace accord in Afghanistan.[38] The same is true for North Korea.[39] Adding to the passage of time is that Mr. Trump's eight policy pillars strike out in new directions and do not simply repeat what has been repeatedly tried many times in the past. In his view, NATO's mission does

6 PRESIDENT TRUMP'S NARCISSISM RECONSIDERED 209

need to evolve, the WTO does need to be reformed, a more skills based immigration policy does need to be enacted, and so on though that list.

There are a number of examples of Trump's political patience. Consider the president's attempt to revise or repeal "Obamacare." After the repeated failures of a Republican Congress to overturn it,[40] Trump has patiently and persistently chipped away at its underpinning.[41] He signaled his intent to revisit that issue in 2018,[42] and has done so,[43] but also showed some adjustment on his part to the varied rhythms of the presidency—an adjustment that other presidents have had to make as well.[44] When a lower federal court ruled that Obamacare might be wholly unconstitutional without its tax on non-compliance intact, Trump administration asked the Supreme Court to send the case back to the Texas court for further review, and they agreed,[45] thus avoiding a high stakes election year fight over the issue. Trump wants to repeal Obamacare, but is capable of biding his political time.

He did, as well, stop short several times of imposing sanctions on Iran to give them, and our allies time to move toward revising the nuclear agreement.[46] Regarding North Korea a *New York Times* analysis concluded that, "So far, Mr. Trump has played his hand militarily, at least as cautiously as his predecessors."[47] On the question of whether or not to declare Mexican drug cartels terrorist organizations (he decided to delay doing so[48]), Trump said[49]:

> I've been working on that for the last 90 days. You know, designation is not that easy. You have to go through a process and we're well into that process.

Observing Trump's approach to foreign policy more generally, one analysis was titled,[50] "Trump's 'no rush' foreign policy," and noted that "The president is affording himself ample room for protracted negotiations." And finally, given all the dire speculations about Trump's dangerousness as a reason for him to be removed from office (see Chapter 7) because he will get the country into a war to deflect attention from his own failings and political troubles, there is this analysis from the *Wall Street Journal*—"Trump Steers Clear of War Footing Toward Iran."[51]

Trump's strategy is clearly to set many policy initiatives into motion at one time and deal with each as they develop. Many, like his initiative to North Korea come to the fore, are addressed, and recede to make further progress, if possible later. Others, like the China trade deal continue on in dramatic form until they are at least partially resolved. Other initiatives like immigration policy are essentially holding actions, important as they are, in preparation for major legislative changes that may, or may not, happen.

Trump's presidential strategy is think big, act decisively across many of the domains of the eight policy pillars, continue to apply varying degrees of pressure to maintain some momentum, reach agreements where possible, and keep moving. It is a considered not an impulsive strategy since it recognizes the elements of policy progress unfolding, if and when they happen, over time.

Trump's expressed impatience in these circumstances may be strategic as well as real. Trump clearly feels the desire to get things done, but is restrained to some degree by the system he must work within. Trump has learned from his time as president, and it might be said of him that he has graduated from whatever impulsiveness he began his presidency with to impatience.

The Disrupter's Dilemma

There is no doubt that Mr. Trump's desire for results has caused problems for him, his presidency, and the public. Unexpected or rapidly made decisions, as a way of insuring that things get done, without preparing staff or the general public are a recipe for dysfunction and stress.[52] Trump's removal of many American troops from northern Syria is one example.[53] The botched roll out of the first travel ban is another.[54] Yet, he is patiently pursuing a determined legal strategy through the many twists and turns of the various courts to prevail,[55] as he must if he is to succeed, within the American constitutional system.

President Trump may wish to move at "Trump speed," but his government can't. So there is an inherent trade off, even in the best of political circumstances, which do not describe his realizing *reconstructive* policy ambitions in Skowronek's terms,[56] and the real time available to such presidential ambitions in one four-year term.

This might be called Trump's "*disruptor's dilemma*." Policy at Trump speed is necessary given the limited time of a four year term and the number and range of Trump's *restoration* ambitions. Yet, acceptance of change requires public explanation and understanding. *Restoration* at Trump speed attempts to simultaneously serve both those functions. Yet it is unclear it can do so successfully. Public understanding takes time.

Solidifying real policy support takes time as well. Yet time is no friend to ambitious presidents, especially those who wish to be "transformative."

Trump's presidency is a race against time. The inherently conservative nature of the American political system does not, in ordinary circumstances, lend itself to speed. In these circumstances, political patience is both a necessity and a luxury.

ON PRESIDENT TRUMP'S NARCISSISM

Trump critics treat the relationship between his narcissism and his psychological unfitness for office as essentially synonymous. They present their psychological/political diagnosis as a syllogism. Trump is narcissistic—therefore he is unfit. That is a logical *non sequitur*.

Is Donald Trump a "narcissist"? One report says he has been put forward as a "textbook case" since 1988.[57] More recently an article entitled "Therapists weigh in" agreed that he is.[58] Notice however the way the question is phrased and the way that critics answer. Those weighing in assume that the term accurately describes the whole of Mr. Trump's psychology, or all that it is necessary to know about it, rather than one element of it.

Moreover, for Trump critics that term is merely the starting point for more serious psychiatric characterizations. Does Trump suffer from a "narcissistic personality disorder"? Yes.[59] Worse, "President Trump exhibits classic signs of mental illness, including 'malignant narcissism,' shrinks say."[60]

Consider further this question and answer: "Is it wrong to say he's [Trump] mentally ill?" No, it is not because "from a psychiatric point of view the absolute worst-case scenario ... if I were to take the DSM (*Diagnostic and Statistical Manual of Mental Disorders*) and try to create a Frankenstein's monster of the most dangerous and destructive leader and had freedom to create any combination of diagnosis and symptoms," Trump would be the result.[61] That is not how diagnosis works. One does not simply search through the *DSM* and create a fictional diagnosis that fits your assumptions. This is not serious analysis, and the person who put it forward, trained in psychology, should know better.

The "Trump narcissism equals unfitness" syllogism falters on a number of grounds. There is the issue of conceptualizing his psychology as including only this one singular element. There is the issue of the range and weighing of the evidence used to support that single characterization of his psychology. And very importantly, there is the issue of considering alternative explanations and evidence.

Some time ago, Fred Greenstein cautioned political scientists reaching into other, less familiar disciplines, to resolve their own disciplinary conceptual and substantive puzzles. He said that rather than finding ready-made concepts and answers they would actually find unresolved debates about the nature and meaning of the terms they wish to borrow.[62] That is certainly true of psychiatric terms and syndromes.

On Clinical and Psychiatric Based Assessments of President Trump

Clinical and psychiatric assessments of individuals are enormously complicated. They involve much debated, highly complex clinical and definitional issues.[63] These complexities are not taken into account by those whose personal and political animus against the president has overwhelmed their professional training and judgment.[64] Nor are they taken into account by untrained pundits. For example, Richard Greene, a "communication specialist," writes, "Virtually every mental health professional I interviewed told me that they believed, with 100% certainty, that Mr. Trump satisfied the *DSM* criteria of this incurable illness and that, as a result, he is a serious danger to the country and the world." Thus, in the mind of the author and the selective unspecified sample he reports, the matter is settled.[65]

It would be fair to say that among Trump critics there is widespread agreement that he is a "narcissist." Yet it would be fair to ask: Just what does that term actually mean? There is no doubt that the trait of narcissism is an important part of Mr. Trump's psychology. However, that hardly controversial fact raises two more difficult issues.

First, what is the level and nature of Trump's narcissism? Is it so pervasive as to essentially define his psychology? Former acting CIA director Michael Morell, a Trump opponent and Hillary Clinton supporter put forward his own specific public measurement of Trump's level of narcissism in an interview. It is tied to no known clinical measure except his own subjective assertion[66]:

> *Morell*: What I would say is—you know, I worked for 33 years at CIA. I watched a lot of foreign leaders. There's a spectrum of narcissism among human beings. Right?
> *Glasser*: Foreign leaders often—leaders have a lot of it.

Morell: Leaders of any country, right? They have a lot of it. Right? *They are one or two standard deviations to the right of the mean. President Trump is no different from that, and in fact, he might be three or four standard deviations out. Right?*

Wrong. Or, at least unknowable without some more firmly grounded metric other than Mr. Morrell's blatant anti-Trump animus, and equally blatant public political support of his opponent. A second related question is this: what is the relationship between Trump's narcissism and his capacity for successful presidential performance? Does the existence or level of his narcissism preclude political success, or even disqualify him from continuing in office?

Varieties of Narcissism: Normal and Pathological

The answer to these questions turns on the difference that psychiatrists, psychoanalysts, and clinicians draw between "healthy"[67] and "pathological"[68] narcissism. As the Harvard historian of narcissism, Elizabeth Lunbeck, points out[69]:

> The fact is that narcissism is actually a remarkably protean concept. In clinicians' hands, *it refers to a broad range of behaviors and dispositions, encompassing traits both desirable and supportive of worldly success (ambition, self-confidence) on the one hand and despicable and undermining of that success (ruthlessness, a lack of empathy) on the other.*

Along similar lines, Elsa F. Ronningstam points out that[70]:

> the importance of normal narcissist functioning for individual mental health and capacity to live an optimal life has mostly been taken for granted. Healthy narcissism functions as the sense of the right to one's life, striving for the best in life, appreciation of health and beauty, *an ability to compete as well as to protect and defend oneself … to manage challenges, successes and changes; to overcome defeat, illness, trauma, and losses; to love and be productive and creative*; and to experience happiness, satisfaction and the course of one's life.

The psychiatrist Heinz Kohut summarizes the crux of this understanding as follows: "The establishment of the narcissistic self must be evaluated both as a maturationally pre-determined step *and as a developmental accomplishment*."[71] In his view, narcissism is a necessary ingredient for the capacity to live a well realized life of meaning and accomplishment.

It has its own developmental trajectory in each person's life history that helps to determine whether or not they are able to overcome obstacles on the way to achieving this "accomplishment."

The obvious question here is: how do you tell "ordinary"[72] "healthy"[73] narcissism, from its pathological counterpart? This is a difficult and complex question. Otto Kernberg, one of the most important psychiatric thinkers of his generation, writing on that differential diagnosis question points out that "within each culture there are norms for the degree to which the goals of beauty, power and wealth are legitimately and rightfully pursued."[74] He continues, "to exceed cultural limits is to enter the territory of Criterion 2 in the *DSM-IV* definition of NPD [narcissistic personality disorder] with fantasies of unlimited success, power, brilliance, beauty or ideal love."

Or consider Criterion1 of the NPD. That reads: "has a grandiose sense of self-importance (e.g., exaggerates achievements and talents, expects to be recognized as superior without commensurate achievement").[75] It does not seem to be particularly difficult in many cases to distinguish actual accomplishments from what might be called "pseudo-achievements." Would building, losing, and rebuilding a multi-billion dollar worldwide business empire or winning a literally astounding election to the presidency of the United States against monumental odds, qualify as real and not "pseudo" achievements. It would seem so.

Adding to the complexity of assessing the consequences of narcissism is the empirical evidence that even a substantial level of narcissism that might be considered "pathological," for example, so-called "grandiose narcissism" is <u>not</u> necessarily positively related to presidential unfitness. Watts et al. calculated objective measures of presidential success of forty-two presidents and the ratings of presidential experts using a clinically developed and empirically validated measure of narcissism. Among their major findings: "*grandiose* narcissism is tied to independently rated and objective indicators of presidential success."[76] Keep in mind that whatever else "grandiose narcissism," might mean it is ordinarily in the clinical range quite a degree higher than "ordinary narcissism."

Trump opponents have no interest in examining questions or research studies like the ones above. They simply add an adjective ("pathological"[77] or "malignant"[78]) before the noun narcissism to characterize Trump and presto, they believe they have an instant psychiatric diagnosis of "mental illness." No further analysis or evidence needed. Nor are they

6 PRESIDENT TRUMP'S NARCISSISM RECONSIDERED 215

at all interested in alternative explanations or evidence to the conclusions with which they begin.

Trump's Narcissism: Weighing the Evidence, Considering Alternative Formulations

The hallmark of someone with a "narcissistic personality disorder" is "an inflated sense of their own importance, a deep need for admiration and a lack of empathy for others."[79] Again, this seems on a first superficial glance, like a definition tailor made to fit Mr. Trump, and many, without much further reflection, have used it that way.

Don't Mr. Trump's repetitive superlatives—"huge," "great," "biggest," "wonderful," "historic," all reflect his inflated self-importance?[80] Doesn't his branding of everything from steaks to towers reflect his need, indeed his entitled demand for name recognition? Maybe. However, Ronningstam writes: "Due to its association with pathological narcissism, that is to, unrealistic and exaggerated overbearing interpersonal demandingness, entitlement as a fundamental healthy aspect of normal narcissism and normal life functioning tends to be easily disregarded." She continues, "normal entitlement refers to an inner experience of oneself as an agent of one's own intentions and actions and to expectations of predicable and reasonable responses."[81] In other words, at some basic level an ordinary sense of "entitlement," to be treated fairly for example, is not a reflection of pathology, but of (healthy) self-concern and self-respect.

Doesn't Trump's insistence on using his own family name for the branding of his buildings and products reflect a demand for recognition and admiration? One Trump critic notes[82]:

There's the compulsive promotion of the Trump name. Other giants of commerce and industry use their own names sparingly—even when they're businesspeople who have the opportunity to turn themselves from a person into a brand ... But the Trump name is everywhere in the Trump world, and there's a reason for that. You can look at something you've built with quiet pride and know it's yours, or you can look at it worriedly, insecurely, fretting that someone, somewhere may not know that you created it—diminishing you in the process. And so you stamp what you build with two-story letters identifying who you are—like a child writing his name on a baseball glove—just to make sure there's no misunderstanding.

This critic conflates a branding strategy with a pathological psychological trait suggesting that a very accomplished adult acts like a five year old child.

Don't Trump's repeated and often personal attacks on his rivals and opponents show a lack of empathy? Perhaps, to some degree, but one can also ask whether unrelenting attacks merit or sometimes require a response. There are as well the psychological issues of being attacked and not fighting back that we have already touched upon.

The general answers to all three of these questions is generally no. Many presidents have their own favorite superlatives.[83] Trump's branding is less a reflection of his narcissism than a business tool that he is able to discard when not needed.[84] Fighting back against those who attack you, sometimes savagely as in Trump's case, pits empathy for those who are doing it against your own self-respect and integrity.

Fighting back when you are repeatedly attacked, often on factually flimsy grounds, is a matter of self-preservation as well as self-respect.[85] The psychiatrist Michael Stone writes, "There will be occasions in the lives of most people when the ability to be assertive and if survival is seriously threatened aggressive are vital." Question: Does the all out, by any means necessary opposition-inspired war against Mr. Trump's candidacy and presidency,[86] including violent national anti-Trump protests after he won election[87] strenuous efforts to keep him from taking office,[88] efforts to then remove him from office,[89] and all those other efforts already detailed (see Chapter 3) constitute a serious survival threat to his presidency? Do they require, if Trump is to have any chance of achieving his *Restoration* purposes, an "assertive," even "aggressive" response?

The Trump Brand as Narcissism

It's understandable that many Trump opponents think they have found indisputable evidence of his narcissism in his superlative descriptions of his many business initiatives and successes. What they have done however is conflate the by-products of Mr. Trump's branding strategy with his character. That turns out to be an illustration not so much of rampant, out of control narcissism, but of Trump's capacity for innovation.

After running into severe liquidity troubles with some of his businesses, Mr. Trump engineered a successful repositioning of his highly leveraged building empire to one increasingly built primarily on his brand name.

It was an innovative corporate strategy at the time that Trump developed it. No one else had ever thought of marketing real estate that way. It was another career illustration of Trump's capacity for creativity and his resilience. Big, bold, brash, and successful were its sales themes. Mr. Trump's cascade of superlative descriptions is consistent with the strategy of building that brand's cachet. And he carried that strategy into the 2016 presidential campaign and on into the White House.

It is also understandable that Trump's psychology would be conflated with his persona. Several *Washington Post* reporters who spent over twenty hours interviewing Trump for their biography of him had this to say: "Even after all those hours of interviews, Trump seemed not quite real, a character he had built to enhance his business empire, a construct designed to be at once an everyman and an impossibly high-flying king of Manhattan, an avatar of American riches."[90]

CANDIDATE TRUMP: SEEKING ADULATION OR SOMETHING ELSE?

In a typical use of psychiatric jargon to attack Mr. Trump and his followers, one psychologist writes, "Demagogues and fascists require an admiring mob, and Trump thrives in co-dependence with an undereducated, aggrieved crowd who will never call him out."[91] There are many conceptual and logical problems with applying this idea to Mr. Trump. One immediate issue is that many presidents, Bill Clinton and Barack Obama being two among many, understandably drew emotional support when their efforts are favorably responded to in public or private settings. This is ordinarily a matter of validation, not a necessary reflection of "pathological narcissism." In any event, that dynamic is by no means President Trump's alone.

Moreover, the desire to be recognized for what you have accomplished, to "leave one's mark" is, according to the psychiatrist Michael Stone,[92] "an almost universal human desire, whether this takes the form of a graffiti's artist's wall signature or a mural by Diego Rivera." Karen Horney pointed out early in clinical discussions of narcissism that, "it is not narcissistic for a person to value a quality in himself which he actually possesses or to like to be valued by others."[93] The question that arises here is whether Trump has any actual accomplishments for which he might legitimately ask to be validated. The critics answer to this question is: few if any. A more reasoned and reasonable assessment is that Trump has many notable successes in his business and political ventures as well as some substantial setbacks.

It's possible of course that Mr. Trump's run for office was a reflection of the narcissist's need to find an admiring audience. During the presidential campaign, one observer building on this idea made the startling prediction that, "Given his personality type, I think he is exhibiting signs of intense frustration that comes from the diminishing amounts of undeserved adulation he received during his primary run. And that may very well lead him to simply take his ball and go home."[94] That obviously didn't happen, raising doubts regarding the premise responsible for the prediction.

The suggestion that Mr. Trump was so much in need of adoration that he was willing to leave a very comfortable and successful business and entertainment career has a number of conceptual and factual difficulties. It would have required Trump to take a gigantic risk with the odds substantially against him in order to win an election and have access to the cheering multitudes. This is the most basic flaw in this formulation— aside from the enormous risk of the very public failure of an unsuccessful presidential campaign.

There were more risks if he won. He would then immediately have to produce very real results to a highly expectant audience of supporters. Otherwise, he would alienate the very people who elected him. Support, much less adoration, would then be in short supply.

Why take the chance and leave a successful nation-wide television show that comes complete with celebrity status and its accompanying adulation and huge financial rewards, for the harsh uncertainties of political life for which you have no experience? This doesn't sound like a good percentage play. It wasn't unless something else besides Mr. Trump's supposed narcissism and need for adulation was in play. There was.

Considering Alternatives to "Pathological Narcissism": Respect and Validation

It is not love that President Trump wants, a common but mistaken assumption,[95] but respect. The "needy narcissist" formulation completely ignores an alternative formulation that fits the facts of Mr. Trump's developmental history and psychology much better. That alternative theory can be summed up in the title of Aretha Franklin's iconic song R-E-S-P-E-C-T.

Trump traces his childhood roots from the out-borough of Queens into the sophisticated heights of Manhattan. When Trump was trying to acquire the land on which he built Trump Tower,

> he first proposed buying the site, occupied by Bonwit Teller and owned by the Equitable Life Assurance Company, and found that there are 29 more years on the lease. He called Genesco Inc., owner of Bonwit's, for eight years, asking to buy the lease. *"They literally laughed at me,"* Mr. Trump recalls. Learning through a major stockholder that the conglomerate was cash-hungry, Mr. Trump called again and was sold the lease.

Mr. Trump proved his critics wrong. He relentlessly pursued the land on which Trump Tower now sits. He also went after and acquired the Plaza Hotel because it added tradition and class to his holdings, and to his efforts to be a major political player,[96] again a quest for respect.

Years later, President Obama mocked[97] Mr. Trump's political efforts and he wasn't the only one. Others like Mitt Romney, tried to gain Mr. Trump's financial support, but never took him seriously.[98] Others called Mr. Trump a "clown candidate."[99] As Mr. Trump noted before the New Hampshire primary, "A lot of people have laughed at me over the years. Now they're not laughing so much, I'll tell you."[100]

Mr. Trump, like many of us, has been seeking recognition, not admiration like the narcissist, for his accomplishments.

WHY TRUMP RAN FOR PRESIDENT: CONSIDERING SEVERAL EXPLANATIONS

Why did Trump run for president? Like almost all recent presidential candidates, Trump ran for a combination of reasons that included his views of the country's state and his own more personal motivations. The specifics of Mr. Trump's presidential motivations reveal some surprises.

Like many other aspects of the Trump presidency, his motives for wanting to be president are seen by his opponents as obviously base and suspect. Some said he really didn't want the role.[101] Some speculated he really wanted to build a media empire.[102] Others speculated that he didn't expect to get very far and was now stuck with the office.[103] Still others thought it was payback for a lifetime of being mocked from various establishment elites in the business and political world.[104] Many, as noted, saw it as a chance for him to gain public adulation.

For a number of major news commentators it was about making more money. According to Fareed Zakaria, "The Republican Party has given itself up to a single family and its business interests."[105] Asked about Trump's business interests while he's president, Trump biographer and critic Timothy O'Brien said, "Oh my god, it'll be the first thing on his mind when he wakes up in the morning."[106]

David Frum wrote[107]:

> Trump's goal is not to be a "successful president" in the usual sense of that term. It's obvious by now that he doesn't have much of a policy agenda. He has a personal agenda, and that agenda is going rather well. The Trump brand is thriving.

In short, Trump ran for the presidency for the most squalid reasons, either for the money or his own narcissism, and the country be dammed. Those characterizations, however, are inconsistent with Trump's decades of complaints about a number of American policies and his concern that they were hurting the country and many of its citizens.

Mr. Trump has said, "I don't need to do this, I have a wonderful life. I have a great, great company ... I wanted to do it, because somebody has to do it ... Our country is in trouble."[108] The first part of that statement seems objectively true from the outside. Yet, one can credit Trump's sincerity about love of country and wanting to help it in its time of trouble, without necessarily taking all his stated reasons fully at face value. Trump's motives are complex and not wholly devoid of self-interest, although that self- interest is not financial.

Trump's Presidential Motivations Reconsidered: Trump's Counter Narrative Policy Views

At a January 2016 political rally Trump admitted, "My whole life I've been greedy, greedy, greedy. I've grabbed all the money I could get. I'm so greedy."[109] That sounds like O'Brien, Frum, and Zakaria might be right.

Yet, in the very next sentence of that speech Mr. Trump said, "But now I want to be greedy for the United States. I want to grab all that money. I'm going to be greedy for the United States." That is certainly not the most uplifting or inspirational presidential rhetoric, but it makes the point about Mr. Trump that "he's in for you ... for us," as opposed to himself.

Mr. Trump "made his first political speech in New Hampshire in 1987. In Portsmouth he attacked American trading partners and allies in ways that sound familiar today."[110] In a 1988 interview with a Japanese TV anchor he said, "I'm not interested now in presidency but if I see the leaders still being stupid I might."[111] In a 1990 interview Mr. Trump said, "I don't want to be President. I'm 100 percent sure. I'd change my mind only if I saw this country continue to go down the tubes."[112]

That is apparently exactly what he saw. Interestingly, in early 1990 when he gave that interview, Gallup found that 55% of its survey respondents were "satisfied with the way things are going in this county at this time." By January 2015, when Mr. Trump announced his candidacy for the presidency,[113] that number stood at 32%.[114] Apparently by the time he had decided to run, Mr. Trump had concluded both that the country was headed in the wrong direction and was sinking, and many Americans agreed with him.

Never one to miss an opportunity to offer some hyperbole in order to inflate a basic insight, Mr. Trump put it this way in an early interview with Megyn Kelly before his official announcement: "I want to make this country great again. This country is a hellhole, and we're going down fast."[115] Donald Trump is not the first presidential candidate to believe the country is going in the wrong direction, needs help righting its course, while believing they would be the president who could accomplish that. That is a basic staple of almost every presidential candidacy. Still, Trump's skeptical views on American foreign and domestic policy have been a consistent, reoccurring theme over the last two decades. In reality, the political handwriting of his presidential run has been on the wall for many years.

A Shift in the Meaning of Trump's Life

It seems clear that on the personal motivation level, Mr. Trump was running partially for respect. It's also clear that his disagreements with long standing policy premises were also instrumental in fueling his run. Yet, in that 2016 speech admitting to greed, Mr. Trump also revealed something else that has escaped notice. The purpose of his life had changed.

In a very revealing interview with the *New York Times*, Mr. Trump was pressed about giving up his large empire so that he would be able to spend more time with his children[116]:

> *Unknown Times Reporter*: You could sell your company though, right? With all due respect, you could sell your company and then ...
>
> *Trump*: Well ...
>
> *Unknown Times Reporter*: And then you could see them [his children] all the time.
>
> *Trump*: That's a very hard thing to do, you know what, because I have real estate. I have real estate all over the world, which now people are understanding ... I'd say this, and I mean this and I said it on "60 Minutes" the other night: My company is so unimportant to me relative to what I'm doing, 'cause I don't need money, I don't need anything ...
>
> *Unknown Times Reporter*: Mr. President-elect ...
>
> *Trump*: Just a minute, because it's an important question ... *But I just want to say that I am given the right to do something so important in terms of so many of the issues we discussed, in terms of health care, in terms of so many different things. I don't care about my company. It doesn't matter. My kids run it ...*

And then this:

> *[Thomas] Friedman*: I came here thinking you'd be awed and over-whelmed by this job, but I feel like you are getting very comfortable with it.
>
> *Trump*: I feel comfortable. I feel comfortable. I am awed by the job, as anybody would be, but I honestly, Tom, I feel so comfortable and *you know it would be, to me, a great achievement if I could come back here in a year or two years and say — and have a lot of the folks here say, "You've done a great job." And I don't mean just a conservative job, 'cause I'm not talking conservative. I mean just, we've done a good job.*

To summarize: a man who has spent his life building a successful business empire and chasing financial success says in this *New York Times* interview (and previously in a *Sixty Minutes* interview[117]) that he no longer cares about his company or chasing financial success. Rather he cares about the issues he can have an impact on as president, and wants the *New York Times* to recognize that. Respect and validation indeed!

In many of his speeches and rallies Trump expresses the view that the country is going in the wrong direction with its basic policies and their assumptions, and that his new life's purpose is doing something about that. Mr. Trump comes across as an American nationalist with an observable, if bombastic, love of his country. *Obviously, a love of country is inconsistent with real "pathological narcissism," where there is no room for love of anybody or anything else but yourself*. Mr. Trump is unlikely to ever make the pivot to a quieter more conventional political persona. However, at the level of his life's fundamental purpose he had apparently changed, and very dramatically. There was, as well, something else.

Trump's Decision to Run for President: The Lure of a New Personal Challenge

Why did Mr. Trump seek the presidency? The most obvious answer is contained in his many critical commentaries and broadsides, made over decades, against the policies and political direction of the country. On trade, on immigration, on regulations and the economy, and on American foreign policies and our allies, Mr. Trump has been a consistent, though not deeply informed critic.

At the same time, looking back over two decades, it seems clear that Mr. Trump has been slowly but consistently testing the waters for a major political leadership role. His dissatisfaction with the way the country was being run is clearly one long-standing theme underlying that interest.

Yet there is more to Mr. Trump's motivation for seeking the presidency than his long-standing and apparently genuine distress at the direction of American politics and policies. There is even more to it than his desire to be respected and validated for what he sees as his skills and accomplishments. Mr. Trump has always liked, indeed needed, a large challenge to match his large ambitions and talents.

That manifested itself first in his move out of Queens into Manhattan and the building of the Trump real-estate empire there. It then extended outward to his numerous acquisitions—airlines, casinos, football teams, and so on. Building his business empire was his first greatest challenge and success.

He then almost totally destroyed that empire through a loss of focus and what he characterizes as his "complacency."[118] Yet he fought back and in so doing demonstrated the skill, perseverance, and resilience necessary to rebuild an even greater business empire. That was Mr. Trump's second, and to that point, greatest challenge and ultimate success.

Yet, for a restless, talented, ambitious man who had scaled, tumbled, and regained his footing at the Mt. Everest level of business success, one more hotel licensing agreement no longer held the satisfaction or the challenge that it had before. There was a hint of this restless ambition in an interview with Mr. Trump in 2004. Asked by Larry King why he had decided to do the TV show *The Apprentice*, this exchange took place[119]:

> *King*: Your reason for doing it was?
> *Trump*: Fun. Hey, I'm building buildings all over the place. *Let's do something different. It's fun. I'm having fun doing it.*

And what greater challenge could one imagine than putting oneself forward as a presidential candidate, with no political experience or standing? What greater challenge could there be than running against a crowded primary field containing many political heavyweights? What bigger personal and political challenge could there then be than to run against an enormously experienced, well connected Democratic candidate—potentially the first woman president—for the purpose of helping to restore a country being pulled apart by tendentious politics, failed policies and premises, and rampant public distrust of government and its leaders? It was a very high risk, high nerve, high courage move in which the chances of success were small and the likelihood of devastating public failure almost a certainty—a Trump-sized challenge, if you will.

Notes

1. Harold D. Lasswell. 1948. *Power and Personality*. New York: Norton.
2. Roger Cohen. 2017. "The Abnormal Presidency of Donald Trump," *New York Times*, January 31.
3. James Hamblin. 2016. "Donald Trump: Sociopath?" *Atlantic*, July 20.
4. Democratic Representative Steve Cohen quoted in Brandon Carter. 2018. "Dem: Trump 'Most Despicable Human Being' to Serve as President," *The Hill*, January 1.
5. Stephen F. Hayes. 2016. "Donald Trump Is Crazy, and So Is the GOP for Embracing Him," *Weekly Standard*, July 22.
6. Jennifer Rubin. 2016. "Trump Spews Crazy Talk—And He's Not Alone," *Washington Post*, October 14.

6 PRESIDENT TRUMP'S NARCISSISM RECONSIDERED 225

7. Erin C. Cassese. 2016. "Here Are 3 Insights into Why Some People Think Trump Is a 'Monster',", *Washington Post*, October 31.
8. Gabriel Schoenfeld. 2017. "What If Trump Loses His Mind?" *USA TODAY*, January 29.
9. Michael Gerson. 2016. "Trump Spirals into Ideological Psychosis," *Washington Post*, October 17.
10. Jerome A. Frank MD. 2018. *Trump on the Couch. Inside the Mind of the President* New York: Avery.
11. http://www.obamaonthecouch.com/blog. March 5, 2018.
12. https://www.change.org/p/trump-is-mentally-ill-and-must-be-rem oved.
13. https://www.facebook.com/aduty2warn/posts/147828915234 0448?__xts__[0]=68.ARBNJNhZdPq8h1Y-FEA9fdcYAVbqBdUs4L-ohhDJo09jd8Q_xTPNytLPtwD4we0dcOMVh5fygbvpuPMYnSSfaez gYme-3HH4lrwO0DSmaeRZ4mAxxUp1pUJspO-Z3RtTtF0HVi5DIP mb6PUEPMcKyB8yBhHRIcDz8aJCoKfcDhk31QWT6rvTBzuFZAhIQ lvuVQ41qAuq-43L0h46hOjhhKpwO4V2Bwp1qtMXIpR7cLBN50Fo kl3BL5oquCu39HgRSmFZPU3UMtyPN3NKUiTNfKfWVUDNrAQW OnU7DBksx1uJR5IapOzMsDIxmnp_fA9WEtV9X-jVXRpROnjLB9 Pdog&__tn__=-R.
14. Seth D. Norrholm. 2016. "Diagnosing the Trump Phenomenon," *USA TODAY*, March 23, November 24.
15. One clear distinction is between those presidents who wish to be "good" and those who aspire to be "great." See Stanley A. Renshon. 2017. "Doing Well vs. Being Great: Comparing the Bush and Obama Doctrines," in Meenekshi Bose (ed.), *The Constitution, Politics, and Policy Making in the George W. Bush Presidency*, Volume I, pp. 101–118. Washington, DC: Nova Press.
16. Press Briefing. 2018. "Press Briefing by Press Secretary Sarah Sanders and Dr. Ronny Jackson," The White House, January 16, p. 60.
17. Trump quoted in Abby Lange. 2016. "Donald Trump's 4-Hour Sleep Habit Could Explain His Personality," *The Daily Beast*, April 2.
18. David Jackson. 2016. "Trump Conducts Election Eve Campaign Marathon," *USA TODAY*, November 7.
19. Stanley Renshon. 1996a [1998]. *High Hopes: The Clinton Presidency and the Politics of Ambition.* New York: New York University Press [Routledge Press]; Stanley Renshon. 1996. *The Psychological Assessment of Presidential Candidates.* New York: New York University Press, Chapter 8.
20. An extensive conceptual and empirical analysis of the various psychological, political, and temperamental aspects of "fitness" is beyond the scope of this chapter.
21. Renshon 1996 [1998], chapters 1 and 2.

22. Emily Joffe. 2017. "Is Donald Trump a TV Addict?" *Politico*, July 7.
23. Ramesh Ponnuru. 2016. "How Clinton Can Demolish Trump," *Bloomberg*, May 26.
24. Editorial. 2017. "Trump's Next 200 Days," *Wall Street Journal*, April 27.
25. One recent Kagan op-ed though is titled: "Trump is the GOP's Frankenstein monster. Now he's strong enough to destroy the party." See Robert Kagan. 2016. "Trump Is the GOP's Frankenstein Monster: Now He's Strong Enough to Destroy the Party," *Washington Post*, February 25.
26. Robert Kagan. 2016. "There Is Something Very Wrong with Donald Trump," *Washington Post*, August 1.
27. World Mental Health Coalition. 2019. Petition to the Judiciary Committee of the U.S. House of Representatives," December 5.
28. Donald J. Trump [with Tony Schwartz]. 1987. *Trump: The Art of the Deal*. New York: Random House, p. 60.
29. *Washington Post*. 2016. "Interview with Donald Trump," *Washington Post*, May 13, emphasis added.
30. Eliot Brown. 2018. "Remember Trump City?" *New York Observer*, August 5.
31. Trump quoted in Glenn Plaskin. 1989. "Trump: 'The People's Billionaire'," *Chicago Tribune*, March 12.
32. C. J. Hughes. 2014. "Sewing Up a Loose End on West End," *New York Times*, November 14.
33. Michael Kruse. 2018. "The Lost City of Trump," *Politico*, July–August.
34. Trump quoted in Mark Bowden. 1977. "Trumpster Stages the Comeback of a Lifetime," *Playboy*, May.
35. Michael D. Shear, Charlie Savage, and Maggie Haberman. 2017. "Trump Attacks Rosenstein in Latest Rebuke of Justice Department," *New York Times*, June 16.
36. Keith Bradsher. 2018. "Trade Deals Take Years: Trump Wants to Remake Them in Months," *New York Times*, March 28.
37. Peter Nicholas, Gordon Lubold, and Dion Nissenbaum. 2018. "For Trump, a Hectic Week of Planning to Organize Syria Strike," *Wall Street Journal*, April 13.
38. Mujib Mashal. 2020. "Taliban and U.S. Strike Deal to Withdraw American Troops from Afghanistan," *New York Times*, February 29; see also Dan De Luce, Courtney Kube, and Mushtaq Yusufzai. 2018. "Impatient Trump Drives U.S. Push for Peace Talks in Afghanistan," *NBC News*, July 30.
39. John Hudson, Josh Dawsey, and Carol D. Leonnig. 2018. "In Private, Trump Vents Frustration over Lack of Progress on North Korea," *Washington Post*, July 22.

40. Rachael Roubein. 2017. "TIMELINE: The GOP's Failed Effort to Repeal ObamaCare," *The Hill*, September 26.
41. Robert Pear and Reed Abelson. 2017. "Foiled in Congress, Trump Moves on His Own to Undermine Obamacare," *New York Times*, October 11.
42. David Jackson and Deirdre Shesgreen. 2018. "President Trump's Ambitious Agenda: 7 Things to Watch in 2018," *USA TODAY*, January 1.
43. Tami Luhby. 2018. "Trump Officials Roll Out New Rule for Small Business Health Insurance Plans," *CNN*, June 19.
44. Gerald Seib. 2017. "What Trump's Early Days Tell Us About His Path Forward," *Wall Street Journal*, April 27.
45. Susannah Luthi. 2020. "Supreme Court Will Hear Major Challenge to Obamacare," Politico, March 2.
46. Mark Lander. 2018. "On Foreign Policy, President Trump Reverts to Candidate Trump," *New York Times*, April 3.
47. David E. Sanger and William J. Broad. 2017. "A Cuban Missile Crisis in Slow Motion in North Korea," *New York Times*, April 16.
48. Christopher Mele and Kirk Semple. 2019. "Trump Says He Will Delay Terrorist Designation for Mexican Cartels," *New York Times*, December 6.
49. Jessica Donati and José de Córdoba. 2019. "Trump Says U.S. to Designate Mexican Drug Cartels as Terrorists," *Wall Street Journal*, November 27.
50. Andrew Restuccia. 2019. "Trump's 'No Rush' Foreign Policy," *Politico*, June 22.
51. Michael C. Bender, Jessica Donati, and Lindsay Wise. 2019. "Trump Steers Clear of War Footing Toward Iran," *Wall Street Journal*, September 18.
52. Vivian Salama and Nancy A. Youssef. 2018. "Trump's Order on Migrant Families Sends Administration Scrambling," *Wall Street Journal*, June 22.
53. Thomas Gibbons-Neff and Eric Schmidt. 2018. "Pentagon Considers Using Special Operations Forces to Continue Mission in Syria," *New York Times*, December 21.
54. Aaron Blake. 2017. "Trump's Travel Ban Is Causing Chaos—And Putting His Unflinching Nationalism to the Test," *Washington Post*, January 29; see also Ron Nixon. 2018. "Travel Ban Caught Homeland Security by Surprise, Report Concludes," *New York Times*, January 19.
55. Adam Liptak. 2018. "Supreme Court to Consider Challenge to Trump's Latest Travel Ban," *New York Times*, January 19.
56. Stephen Skowronek. 1977. *The Politics that Presidents Make: Leadership from John Adams to Bill Clinton*, revised ed. Cambridge, MA: Belknap Press.

228   S. RENSHON

57. Jeva Lange. 2015. "Psychologists Having Been Using Donald Trump as an Example of Narcissism Since 1988," *This Week*, September 25.

58. Henry Alford. 2015. "Is Donald Trump Actually a Narcissist? Therapists Weigh in!" *Vanity Fair*, November 11.

59. Nigel Barber. 2016. "Does Trump Suffer from Narcissistic Personality Disorder?" *Psychology Today*, August 10, 2016.

60. Gersh Kuntzman. 2107. "President Trump Exhibits Classic Signs of Mental Illness, Including 'Malignant Narcissism,' Shrinks Say," *New York Daily News*, January 29. See also Jerrold M. Post and Stephanie Doucette. 2019. *Dangerous Charisma: The Political Psychology of Donald Trump and His Followers*. New York: Pegasus Books, p. 7.

61. John Gardner, a psychologist, and founder of "Duty to Warn" an organization dedicated to having President Trump removed from office because of his unfitness, quoted in Emily Willingham. 2107. "The Trump Psych Debate: Is It Wrong to Say He's Mentally Ill?" *Forbes*, February 19.

62. Fred I. Greenstein. 1969. *Personality and Politics: Problems of Evidence, Inference, and Conceptualization*. Chicago: Markham, 1969, pp. 12–13.

63. Two recent articles on the major issues surrounding the American Psychiatric Associations Revision (*DSM-5*) of its *Diagnostic and Statistical Manual* (*DSM-IV*) were recently published on line in which twenty-four psychiatrists with diverse views engaged each other in trying to answer the following six most essential questions in psychiatric diagnosis including the nature and definition of a mental disorder and the validation of evidence used to support these formulations. See James Phillips, Allen Frances, Michael A. Cerullo, John Chardavoyne, Hannah S. Decker, Michael B. First, Nassir Ghaemi, Gary Greenberg, Andrew C. Hinderlighter, Warren A. Kinghorn, Stephen G. LoBello, Elliot B. Martin, Aaron L. Mishara, Joel Paris, Joesph M. Pierre, Ronald W. Pies, Harold A. Pincus, Douglas Porter, Clair Pouncey, Michael A. Schwartz, Thomas Szasz, Jerome C. Wakefield, G. Scott Waterman, Owen Whooley, and Peter Zacher. 2012. "The Six Most Essential Questions in Psychiatric Diagnosis: A Pluralogue Part 2: Issues of Conservatism and Pragmatism in Psychiatric Diagnosis," *Philosophy, Ethics, and Humanities in Medicine: PEHM*, 7, 8.

64. Cf., Matthew Lee. 2017. "AP FACT CHECK: Overlooking Doubts on Syria Chemical Weapons," *ABC News*, April 10.

65. Richard Greene. 2017. "Is Donald Trump Mentally Ill? 3 Professors of Psychiatry Ask President Obama to Conduct 'a Full Medical and Neuropsychiatric Evaluation'," *Huffington Post*, December 18.

66. Morell quoted in Susan B. Glasser. 2017. "Ex-Spy Chief: Russia's election hacking was an 'intelligence failure'," *Politico*, September 11, emphasis added.

6 PRESIDENT TRUMP'S NARCISSISM RECONSIDERED   229

67. Heinz Kohut MD. 1971. *The Analysis of the Self: A Systematic Approach to the Psychoanalytic Treatment of Narcissistic Personality Disorders*. New York: International University Press; see also Heinz Kohut MD. 1977. *The Restoration of the Self*. New York: International University Press.
68. Otto Kernberg MD. 1975. *Borderline Conditions and Pathological Narcissism*. New York: Jason Aronson; see also Otto Kernberg MD. 1980. *Internal World and External Reality: Object Relations Theory Applied*. New York: Jason Aronson, p. 14.
69. Elizabeth Lunbeck. 2017. "The Allure of Trump's Narcissism," *Los Angeles Review of Books*, August 1, emphasis added; see also Elizabeth Lunbeck. 2014. *The Americanization of Narcissism*. Cambridge, MA: Harvard University Press.
70. Elsa F. Ronningstam. 2005. *Identifying and Understanding the Narcissistic Personality*. New York: Oxford University Press, p. 31, emphasis added.
71. Heinz Kohut MD. 1966. "Forms and Transformations of Narcissism," *Journal of the American Psychoanalytic Association*, Vol. 14, p. 249, emphasis added.
72. Otto Kernberg MD. 1975. *Borderline Conditions and Pathological Narcissism*. New York: Jason Aronson.
73. Kohut 1977.
74. Otto Kernberg MD. 1998. "Pathological Narcissism and Narcissistic Personality Disorder: Theoretical Background and Diagnostic Classification," in Elsa F. Ronningstam (ed.), *Disorders of Narcissism: Diagnostic, Clinical and Empirical Implications*, p. 24. New York: American Psychiatric Publishing.
75. Arnold M. Cooper MD. 1998. "Further Developments in the Clinical Diagnosis of NPD," in Elsa F. Ronningstam (ed.), *Disorders of Narcissism: Diagnostic, Clinical and Empirical Implications*, p. 67. New York: American Psychiatric Publishing.
76. Ashley Watts, Scott O. Lillenfield, Saerah Francis Smith, Joshua Miller, W. Keith Campbell, Irwin D. Waldman, Steven J. Rubenzer, and Thomas J. Faschingbauer. 2013. "The Double-Edged Sword of Grandiose Narcissism: Implications for Successful and Unsuccessful Leadership Among U.S. Presidents," *Psychological Science*, Vol. 24, No. 12 (December), pp. 2379–2389, 2386, emphasis added.
77. Alex Morris. 2017. "Trump's Mental Health: Is Pathological Narcissism the Key to Trump's Behavior?" *Rolling Stone*, April 5.
78. John Gardner. 2017. "Donald Trump's Malignant Narcissism Is Toxic: Psychologist," *USA TODAY*, May 4.
79. Mayo Clinic Staff. "Narcissistic Personality Disorder." Mayo Clinic. https://www.mayoclinic.org/diseases-conditions/narcissistic-person ality-disorder/symptoms-causes/syc-20366662.

80. Cf., "There is Trump's compulsive use of superlatives—especially when he's talking about his own accomplishments." See Jeffrey Kluger. 2015 "The Truth About Donald Trump's Narcissism," *Time Magazine*, August 11.
81. Elsa F. Ronningstam. 2005. *Identifying and Understanding the Narcissistic Personality.* New York: Oxford University Press, p. 33.
82. Kluger 2015.
83. Stephanie Schram and Joel Eastwood. 2018. "Trump's State of the Union: The 'Best Most Lowest Greatest' Words," *Wall Street Journal*, January 30.
84. Shivani Vora. 2016. "A New Trump Brand Not Named for Trump? Yes, Meet Scion," *New York Times*, October 25.
85. Michael Stone MD. 1988. "Normal Narcissism: An Etiological and Ethnological Perspective," in Elsa F. Ronningstam (ed.), *Disorders of Narcissism: Diagnostic, Clinical and Empirical Implications*, p. 11. New York: American Psychiatric Publishing.
86. Jonathan Martin and Alexander Burns. 2017. "Weakened Democrats Bow to Voters, Opting for Total War on Trump," *New York Times*, February 23.
87. Christopher Mele and Annie Correal. 2016. "Not Our President: Protests Spread After Donald Trump's Election," *New York Times*, November 9.
88. David Weigel. 2016. "Why Are People Giving Jill Stein Millions of Dollars for an Election Recount?" *Washington Post*, November 24; see also Kimberlee Kruesi and Bill Barrow. 2016. "Trump Opponents Try to Beat Him at the Electoral College," *Associated Press*, November 19.
89. Nicholas Fandos. 2019. "House Committee to Issue Blitz of Subpoenas, Raising Heat on Trump," *New York Times*, July 9.
90. Marc Fisher and Michael Kranish. 2016. "The Trump We Saw: Populist, Frustrating, Naive, Wise, Forever on the Make," *Washington Post*, August 12.
91. Ian Schwartz. 2016. "Hillary Confronted on 'Super Predator' Term on Black Radio Show; Calls Trump 'Dangerous,' 'Cancer'," *Real Clear Politics*, April 18.
92. Stone MD 1998, p. 26.
93. Karen Horney MD. 1939. *New Ways in Psychoanalysis*. London: Kegan, Paul, Trench, Trubner & Co., p. 90.
94. Ron Insana. 2016. "Trump's Going to Get Demolished by Clinton; Here's Why He Needs to Drop Out Now," *MSNBC*, June 8.
95. Cf. "Unlike the truly manly male, who hardly notices and cares little for how he is received by others, Trump demands universal love as the reward for his just denunciations and wise observations." See

Harvey Mansfield. 2017. "The Vulgar Manliness of Donald Trump," *Commentary*, August 14, 2017.
96. William Myers. 1988. "Stalking the Plaza," *New York Times*, September 25.
97. Office of the White House. 2011. "'The President's Speech' at the White House Correspondents' Dinner," May 1; see also https://www.youtube.com/watch?v=k8TwRmX6zs4&feature=youtu.be&t=2m51s.
98. Maggie Haberman and Alexander Burns. 2016. "Donald Trump's Presidential Run Began in an Effort to Gain Stature," *New York Times*, March 12.
99. Cohen 2017.
100. Candidate Trump quoted in Haberman and Burns 2016.
101. Michael Moore. 2016. "Trump Is Self-Sabotaging His Campaign Because He Never Really Wanted the Job in the First Place," *Huffington Post*, August 17.
102. Sarah Ellison. 2016. "Exclusive: Is Donald Trump's Endgame the Launch of Trump News?" *Vanity Fair*, June 16; see also Alex Griswold. 2106. "Report: Donald Trump Plans to Create Media Empire After Election," *Mediate*, June 16.
103. Mark Singer. 2016. "Trump, the Man and the Image," *New Yorker*, July 11–18; see also Michael Wolff. 2018. "Donald Trump Didn't Want to Be President," *New York Magazine*, January 3.
104. McKay Coppins. 2017. "How the Haters and Losers Lost,' *Buzzfeed*, July 17.
105. Fareed Zakaria. 2017. "America Would Be Trump's Banana Republic," *Washington Post*, July 21.
106. O'Brian quoted in Darren Samuelsohn and Josh Dawsey. 2016. "Trump Lays Out Limits of Business Involvement," *Politico*, December 16.
107. David Frum. 2017. "It's Not Over Yet for Donald Trump," *The Atlantic*, April 1.
108. Jake Tapper. 2017. "State of the Union: Interview with Presidential Candidate Donald Trump," *CNN*, March 13.
109. Trump quoted in Ezra Klein. 2106. "Trump: 'My Whole Life I've Been Greedy … Now I Want to Be Greedy for the United States'," *Vox*, January 26.
110. Trump quoted in Michael D'Antonio. 2015. "Donald Trump's Long Publicity Con," *Daily Beast*, November 28.
111. Japan TV. 1988. https://www.liveleak.com/view?i=dc1_1464663388#CIyk2eTbcLzDIM9s.99.
112. Michael Kruse. 2105. "The 199 Most Donald Trump Things Donald Trump Has Ever Said," *Politico* Magazine, August 14.
113. Reem Nasr. 2015. "Donald Trump Announces Candidacy for President,' *CNBC*, June 16.

114. Gallup. Satisfaction with the United States. http://www.gallup.com/poll/1669/general-mood-country.aspx.
115. Donald Trump quoted in Kaufman 2015. That interview may be found at: http://video.foxnews.com/v/4248222536001/?playlist_id=2694949842001#sp=show-clips.
116. "Donald Trump's *New York Times* Interview: Full Transcript," *New York Times*, November 23, emphasis added.
117. Leslie Stahl. 2016. "President-Elect Trump Speaks to a Divided Country," *CBS News*, November 13.
118. Donald Trump [with Meredith McIver]. 1997. *Trump: The Art of the Comeback*. New York: Times Books, p. 2.
119. *CNN*. 2004. "Larry King Interviews Donald Trump on Larry King Live," November 24, emphasis added.

CHAPTER 7

On President Trump's Psychological and Political Fitness for Office

The intense effort to make direct use of psychological and psychiatric theory for a clearly political purpose, to remove President Trump from office, is unprecedented. In response to what are seen as Mr. Trump's many personal, political, and policy provocations, his critics, including former President Obama,[1] have made a determined and persistent case that he is "unfit" to be president. Sometimes this argument is put forward in the form of a psychiatric based diagnosis regarding Mr. Trump's supposed severe psychopathology.[2] At other times it is framed as the damage his presidency will inflict on American politics and democratic institutions,[3] including their so-called "Guardrails of Democracy" (see Chapter 3). The term "unfit," as will be evident, covers a great deal of diverse territory.

Many of the accusations about Trump's unfitness muddle and inappropriately mix clinical and political domains. Politically, Trump has been repeatedly characterized as a Nazi,[4] a dictator,[5] a racist,[6] a traitor,[7] the greatest threat to our own country,[8] a threat to American democracy,[9,10] a threat to our world order[11] and worse.[12] Each of these diverse accusations are "political" in nature, but often they are ultimately based on some psychiatric or psychological theoretical foundation. The accusations vary widely in the nature of the behaviors that make Trump unfit. However rarely, if ever, are such characterizations accompanied by a careful analysis of evidence on their behalf.

© The Author(s) 2020
S. Renshon, *The Real Psychology of the Trump Presidency*,
The Evolving American Presidency,
https://doi.org/10.1007/978-3-030-45391-6_7

233

There are many ways of being "unfit" for the presidency—characterologically, psychologically, temperamentally, and politically. What is striking is that Trump has been accused of being unfit on the basis of all of those, and on several others as well. The result is a mélange of unfitness accusations that rely more on anti-Trump animus than they do on any fair-minded understanding of political or psychology theory. They are put forward by individuals with a wide diversity of backgrounds and training, often, but not always, irrelevant to the pronouncements they make.

Anyone can make a politically charged accusation of unfitness on the basis of no more evidence than their own opinions, and many anti-Trump critics do exactly that. However, accusations made by persons trained in psychology, whatever form that training takes, and it varies widely among anti-Trump critics, are in a different position. They often have some training in psychological theory and the basic elements of conducting research. They ought to be familiar with the standards of gathering evidence from a variety of sources and not only the ones that reflect their views. They should be familiar with the idea of weighing all the evidence fairly and considering alternative formulations. They should be very sensitive to being "objective," which, if that term means anything at all, requires them to take care and be scrupulous about not allowing their own views to weigh heavily in their analysis, especially of controversial presidents like Trump with whose views they clearly vehemently disagree.

Individuals who can professionally lay claim to the title "psychologist,"[13] and even those who can't do so legally as is the case with the vague title "mental health professional," have both increased professional status and responsibilities. Being trained and familiar with psychological theory gives you more standing to use psychology for analysis. Yet such individuals should be expected to be familiar with and to abide by the professional canons of research described above, as they relate specifically to the use and misuse of psychological theory. That would apply to all those with psychological training, even if it is not specifically medical, that is, acquired in conjunction with becoming a medical doctor (MD).

An additional and more forceful set of ethical constraints apply to those medically trained in psychiatry. The so-called Goldwater rule prohibits them from making diagnoses without having worked with the subject psychologically and without their permission. Anti-Trump psychiatrists have tried to counter this prohibition in two ways. First, they insist that they have a "duty to warn" and to keep the public from suffering the harm they feel is occurring because of Trump's presidency. Second, they say they have switched the rationale of their efforts from psychiatric and psychological diagnoses to the question of Trump's "dangerousness."

Psychiatrists in the forefront of the remove-Trump effort claim that they are not "diagnosing" Trump. Rather, they say, they are observing and analyzing his clear and immediately disqualifying level of "dangerousness." Their assessment of Trump's of dangerousness is, paradoxically, not based on any special political expertise they have beyond reading and interpreting the latest headline or Trump tweet, but on their training in psychology. So they are in fact making a clinical diagnostic judgment, but substituting the term dangerousness for diagnosis. Paraphrasing Shakespeare[14]: "A diagnosis by any other name," for example "dangerousness," is still a diagnosis.

In the sections that follow, we take up some of the most basic issues of assessing President Trump's psychological fitness for office at a distance whether in the form of a psychiatrically framed diagnosis or psychologically framed political diagnosis of dangerousness. We first take up the meaning and nature of the term "unfitness" for the presidency. We then analyze a startling and informative prologue to Trump unfitness arguments: The psychiatric assessment of Republican presidential candidate Senator Barry Goldwater in 1964.

Finally, we turn to a major effort by anti-Trump psychological professionals to assess Trump's dangerousness as a rational for opposing and removing him from office. That is the work of Bandy Lee MD, who has published a widely noted book whose title reflects its perspective: *The Dangerous Case of Donald Trump: 27 Psychiatrists and Mental Health Experts Assess a President*.[15] Many of the contributors to that book have some professional psychological background, though not necessary in the fields that would train someone to be knowledgable about the clinical or psychiatric assessments they freely make.

The contributors all clearly feel very strongly about their views The question to be addressed here is the extent to which their familiarity and training in psychological theory, however relevant, is put into the service of their views. Or, whether their views are a reasonable and legitimate set of inferences that can be drawn from their analyses. The analysis that follows is not focused on whether such efforts are or are not within APA Goldwater Rule guidelines. That topic has been and will continue to be debated.[16] We are interested here in the question of whether the "duty

236   S. RENSHON

to warn," or assessments of "dangerousness" void, or simply avoid that rule.

We also ask whether so-called "mental health experts," who conclude that President Trump is unfit for office and should be removed, adhere to basic procedures of psychological assessment and analysis. Those procedures would include, as noted, attention to the nature, extent, and adequacy of their evidence. Do those who make these accusations show any awareness or deal with the impact of their own clearly strong and deeply held political viewpoints? The failure to seriously engage these issues reflects a clear and avoidable substantive professional and ethical lapse.

On the Nature of Presidential Unfitness

One can think of any clinical "diagnosis" as a theoretical category with functional psychological consequences. Psychiatric diagnosis consists in placing individuals into established medical categories of psychological functioning and impairment. These categories can claim some behavioral, motivational, and predictive validity based on the continuing assessment of evidence from past and ongoing research. In the hands of skilled trained professionals making these placement judgements relies on extensive clinical training, personal knowledge of the person being assessed, and familiarity with the class of such people into which they diagnostically fit. The placement of a person in the American Psychiatric Association's *Diagnostic and Statistical Manual of Mental Disorders-V* points to varied levels of dysfunction and impairment in the numerous categories of "Disorders."[17]

Again, clinical and psychiatric assessments of individuals are enormously complicated. They involve much debated, highly complex clinical and definitional issues.[18] Among them is the issue of differential diagnosis in medicine and psychiatry because many diagnostic facts are compatible with more than one diagnostic category. For example, a cough can be part of disease syndromes as diverse as a cold or a lung tumor. In psychiatry, paranoid trends in the personality do not necessarily signal the presence of a paranoid character. The latter may or may not be accompanied by a flight of ideas, interior logic (meanings and connections which are not generally shared) or non-sequential reasoning, all of which may indicate a major thought disturbance.

Most clinical entities frequently present a mixed symptom picture. For example, in considering Trump's supposedly pathological narcissism one might first wish to consult this caution from the American Psychiatric Association, "It may take extended clinical observation, informant interview, or detailed history to distinguish impulsive, socially intrusive, or inappropriate behavior from narcissistic, aggressive, or domineering behavior to make this differential diagnosis."[19] Or, "Individuals with antisocial personality disorder also often have personality features that meet criteria for other personality disorders, particularly borderline, histrionic, and narcissistic personality disorders."[20] These complexities are rarely taken into account by those whose personal and political animus against the president have overwhelmed their professional training and judgment, and the ethical standards that frame them.[21]

Prologue to Trump Psychological Unfitness Claims: The Goldwater Assessment Fiasco[22]

The country has been down this road before. In the summer of 1964, a mass-circulation magazine sent a letter and a questionnaire to 12,356 psychiatrists, all members of the American Psychiatric Association, and asked them to provide their professional assessment of the mental health and psychological suitability of Barry Goldwater for president. Results of this survey were then published in two lengthy articles in the ironically named September/October issue of *FACT Magazine*, shortly before the election.

In 1964, the Republican Party nominated Barry Goldwater, United States Senator from Arizona, as its presidential candidate. Senator Goldwater had established himself as a leading spokesman for the conservative wing of his party. He espoused strong views on reducing government involvement in the lives of its citizens and equally strong views on the importance of a strong national defense and tough international stance vis-à-vis the Soviet Union. In part because of these views and in part because of some campaign statements, Senator Goldwater was viewed in some quarters as a political "extremist." During his nomination acceptance speech, he stated, "extremism in the pursuit of liberty is no vice," which became a frequently repeated quote to support that contention.

The *FACT* covering letter asking psychiatrists to evaluate the psychological fitness of Senator Goldwater began by stating that "Mr. Goldwater's illness is not just an emotional maladjustment, or a mild neurosis, or a queerness," but rather that he shows "unmistakable signs of paranoia."[23] Having already provided a preliminary diagnosis, the letter then asked whether it is possible "to determine conclusively, without a psychiatric interview, on the basis of what is known about him, whether Goldwater is a paranoid." And, in case the point was not getting through, the cover letter also asked whether, "he seem[s] callous to the downtrodden and needy." It also asked whether respondents could "offer any explanation of his public temper tantrums and his occasional outbursts of profanity."[24]

THE PSYCHIATRIC ASSESSMENT OF SENATOR GOLDWATER: PRELUDE TO THE TRUMP CLAIMED FITNESS ASSESSMENT MUDDLES

The effort to psychiatrically diagnosis Senator Goldwater made clear almost all of the methodological and political issues that have surfaced in connection with similar efforts to diagnose President Trump. What follows are a sampling of the responses to the assessment of Senator Goldwater that underline the same issues that appear in efforts to do so with President Trump, whether psychiatrically, psychologically, or politically.

General Diagnostic Dissensus: One psychiatrist wrote, "There is no doubt that Mr. Barry Goldwater is 'mentally deranged'."[25] Another felt he was, "intellectually honest, reliable, consistent and emotionally mature."[26] Another believed that he was "grossly psychotic,"[27] while another believed him to be "exceptionally well-adjusted."[28] The wide range of conclusions regarding the general level of Senator Goldwater's "mental health" is matched by the equally wide range of specific diagnostic assessments made at the level of clinical conceptualization.

Differential Diagnosis: One respondent characterized Goldwater as a "compensated schizophrenic,"[29] while another felt that he had "a narcissistic character disorder with not-too-latent paranoid elements."[30] Yet another mentioned the presence of a "severe obsessive-compulsive neurosis,"[31] while another wrote that, "My main concern regarding Goldwater is how suicidal is he?"[32]

Politically Biased Diagnosis: Political Scientist Arnold Rogow wrote that many who chose to answer the letter were "strong supporters of peace, integration and the welfare state," and concludes that it was, "inevitable that Goldwater ... would be disliked by a number of psychiatrists, some of whom were not hesitant to translate their [political] dislike into the language of the consulting room."[33]

One psychiatrist, for example, assessed the Senator as having a:

> brittle, rigid personality structure ... capable of either shattering like a crystal glass or bolstering itself by the assumption of a paranoid stance of more power over others. In his book *The Conscience of a Conservative*, his position is one of anachronistic authoritarianism, using the Constitution in a litigious way ... He seems unaware that modern nationwide transportation and communication have increased identification of the population with the nation as a whole—rather than the states ...[34]

Another respondent explicitly linked Goldwater's rejection of a major Federal government role in domestic policy to his sense of inferiority stating that[35]:

> Goldwater's insecurity and feelings of inadequacy cause him to reject all changes and to resent what he considers to be excessive power by the Federal government. His rejection, may in fact, reflect a threat by a father-image, namely someone [the Federal government] who is stronger than he, more masculine and more cultured.

Among the respondents who considered Goldwater psychologically fit to become president, almost a dozen linked psychiatric health with conservative politics. For example, one respondent wrote[36]:

> In my opinion Senator Goldwater is a highly-motivated patriotic American. I feel he is a mature, emotionally stable individual who is eminently qualified to hold the office of President ... and to lead the fight against socialism and the force of the far left, which seem so strongly entrenched in our present government.

Another respondent presents us with a mixed political/psychiatric syllogism of curious logic:

> We have long needed the opportunity for the public to choose between conservatism and modern socialism. Barry Goldwater's candidacy offers this choice. He is a sane man.[37]

Efforts to assess Donald Trump's fitness fair no better.

Varieties of Trump's Claimed Unfitness

The issue of the use or misuse of a single psychological term to characterize a president who is clearly more complex than his caricatures is distinct from the question of what presidential characteristics, or lack therefore, constitute "unfitness" for the office. One anti-Trump pundit with no relevant training of any kind, and no standing except as the husband of senior White House advisor Kellyanne Conway, writes that Trump is "unfit" for office because his, "narcissism makes it impossible for him to carry out the duties of the presidency in the way the Constitution requires."[38] How, exactly, does the Constitution prescribe how the president is to carry out his duties? This critic doesn't say except in a very general way noting that the Constitution requires that the president: "shall take care that the laws be faithfully executed" or "faithfully execute the Office of President of the United States."

In Mr. Conway's thinking, Mr. Trump's narcissism is a given, and its magnitude severely interferes with his ability to "faithfully" carry out his responsibilities. His 110,000 word article is a lawyer's brief for his viewpoint in which anonymous accusations and the citation of like-minded sources and views that support his position are the only evidence provided. Trump's clearly tongue -in- cheek remarks ("I'm a stable genius") are taken literally as dispositive clinical and diagnostic evidence. No information that runs counter to his views is presented and some material facts that he presents as true, are demonstrably false.[39]

Anti-Trump criticisms like George Conway's ultimately rest their claims of Trump's unfitness on the pathology of Trump's psychology[40]:

> The question of whether Trump can serve as a national fiduciary turns more on his narcissistic tendencies than his sociopathic ones, but Trump's sociopathic characteristics sufficiently intertwine with his narcissistic ones that they deserve mention here …
>
> But when you line up what the Framers expected of a president with all that we know about Donald Trump, his unfitness becomes obvious. The question is whether he can possibly act as a public fiduciary for the nation's highest public trust … *Given that Trump displays the extreme behavioral characteristics of a pathological narcissist, a sociopath, or a malignant narcissist—take your pick—it's clear that he can't.*

Mr. Conway has no training whatsoever in psychology. His conflation of three different clinical terms "pathological narcissist, a sociopath, or a malignant narcissist," and his advice to us to "take your pick," suggests he has little real knowledge about or interest in the underlying accuracy or substance of what he is writing.

VARIETIES OF TRUMP'S "UNFITNESS" REVISITED

Some argue that Trump should be removed from office, via impeachment[41] or the use of the 25th Amendment,[42] on the basis of his variously described "unfitness," often based on no more than a single tweet,[43] or the characterization of Mr. Trump as "tweeting hysterically at the media."[44] Or, it is said he is unfit because "he is an unstable conspiracy theorist with an authoritarian streak,"[45] or because "he is a TV addict,"[46] or because of his short attention span,[47] or because the Mueller Report provided ample evidence of Trump's "pervasive and profound pattern of lack of capacity,"[48] or because his behavior is simply not "normal."[49]

Trump is also believed to be "unfit" for the presidency because he "appeared to be disengaged" from the recovery of Puerto Rico from Hurricane Maria,[50] in spite of the enormous pre-storm efforts that the administration made.[51] He is said to be unfit because when publicly attacked during a major prime time speech at the Democratic national convention by the father of a marine killed in action, Trump responded.[52] He was said to be unfit because he did not stand up for President Obama when one of his (Trump's) supporters publicly raised the issue (in his, the supporter's mind) of President Obama's Muslim background.[53] He is said to be unfit because he lacks the "temperament or strength of character" to serve as president.[54] He is unfit because of "sleep deprivation,[which] we know, can make you cranky and temperamental, and throw off judgment."[55] He is unfit because he is "Not prepared to be President."[56]

He is unfit because his "lack of knowledge, seriousness and impulse control make him too dangerous to put in the presidency."[57] And he is unfit because, "Trump's Typos Reveal His Lack of Fitness for the Presidency."[58] If none of these many varied and sundry reasons suffice, one set of critics list 153 things that Trump has said or done that make him unfit.[59]

Trump's Presidential Demeanor as a Reflection of Unfitness

Mr. Trump's irreverent, iconoclastic style, his failure to act "presidential," and his "fight club" presidency are proof to his detractors that he is "unfit" to be president and, as a result, should be impeached and removed from office. That formulation is put forward very directly by the ordinarily moderate and sensible *Washington Post* columnist Robert Samuelson[60]:

> Imagine, if you will, the consequences if Trump had embraced this pivotal distinction [between campaigning and governing]. He need not have jettisoned many of his policy preferences. He could have still favored lower taxes, fewer regulations, tighter immigration controls, tougher trade policies against China and more pressure on our NATO allies to raise military spending. He might even have gently chided the Federal Reserve to loosen credit. Agree or disagree, these views are not wildly outside the political mainstream.
>
> *What mattered was tone*—the ability to debate issues without impugning the character of his opponents. To be sure, partisan debate is full of exaggerations and simplicities. Still, it usually respects some bounds of truth and civility. Following this traditional path, Trump might have boosted his popularity … Even fierce critics might have conceded that, in practice, the "boring" Trump wasn't so bad.

The last two sentences are highly dubious. Given the centrality and therefore the high stakes in involved revising the eight major pillars of policies that Trump has taken on, the fierce by any means necessary opposition to Trump's *Restoration* presidential purposes, the president's fight back response is understandable. It is not likely to be defused by more polite urging that for example, our NATO allies should contribute more to the costs of their defense, or of the other listed Trump policies that critics disdain.

Au contraire. These and other Trump policies are efforts to replace the now dominant paradigms, and it is this effort that has helped fuel the ferocious opposition to the president. As to Samuelson's ode to civility, very brutal and vicious personal attacks against Trump, his administration and his family have been plentiful since he won the Republican nomination (see Chapter 3). As noted, they include a Times Square billboard ad that depicts Trump being tied up and abused,[61] and a tweet made public by Barbara Streisand depicts Trump killed by being impaled on Nancy

Pelosi's high heels.[62] A picture depicting someone holding Trump's severed bloody head[63] shocks, but only briefly. Shortly thereafter, New York's Public Theater revival portraying Trump as Julius Caesar and being assassinated[64] entered the mainstream. Are these examples of "tone" just fine?

Samuelson supports his civility argument with a small list of Trump policies that "are collapsing." In his view, Trump has made no progress in limiting North Korea's nuclear arsenal. Leaving the Iran treaty has "emboldened" them. Trade negotiations with China have "fallen short."

Trump's policies "collapsing"? These are not serious criticisms, and they are surprising from someone of Samuelson's usual thoughtfulness. The North Korean nuclear issue has been an extremely difficult and complex one for over half a century. Iran was "emboldened" to test missile components and supported terrorism throughout the Middle East long before Trump came into office. And it's unclear what the ongoing, drawn out, complex and extremely difficult US–China trade negotiations have fallen short of at this point. A Phase I agreement has been signed. Isn't that a milestone that would require some analysis? Shouldn't an assertion that these efforts have "collapsed" be based on some idea of what is in the agreement and what remains to be done?

Diagnosing Trump's Dangerousness: Bandy Lee MD and the Dangerous Case of Donald Trump

Accusations that Trump is unfit because of one or more of his psychological traits is more than a collage industry, it is a major and thriving hub of the anti-Trump narrative. Rather than examine the literally thousands of such accusations, we proceed by examining in some detail a major effort to organize and publicly advance the psychologically framed and biased narrative that Trump is a clear and severe danger to the country and the world.

In focusing on Trump's "dangerousness" Dr. Lee and her contributors hope to bypass the ethical prohibitions against what they are doing. In fact, they still make the same extensive and questionable use of psychiatric and psychological terms and diagnoses, and run into the exact same problems. Simply putting the proscribed anti-Trump diagnosis into a new category, dangerousness, does not avoid the issues they try to finesse.

This effort was spearheaded by a psychiatrist, Dr. Bandy Lee and the contributors to a book she published entitled: *The Dangerous Case of*

Donald Trump: 27 Psychiatrists and Mental Health Experts Assess a President. The book's title is inaccurate in several respects. Several of the book's contributors are not "mental health experts," even by a loose understanding of that term. These include respectively a lawyer, a ghost writer for a major media personality, a "time perspective therapist"—whatever that is, a journalist, and a philosophy professor. Many of the other "mental health experts" have not earned the highest level degrees in the professions that would be most germane to providing the professional standing to make the kinds of psychological judgments they offer. What all the contributors do share is a clearly vehement aversion to all things Trump and a shared level of common assumptions and conclusions.

Twenty-Seven Psychiatrists and Mental Health Experts on Trump's Dangerousness

The Dangerous Case of Donald Trump tries to avoid the professional and ethical issues associated with violating the Goldwater rule by claiming that it is not interested in a psychiatric diagnosis of the president. Rather it is interested in assessing the degree of his "dangerousness." That assessment ultimately turns out to involve making a diagnosis, which they assert, in theory is not based on psychopathology using the *DSM-5* and related psychological categories. However their more political diagnosis of dangerousness relies on the very same *DSM-5* categories.

In the paradoxical words of Dr. Lee[65]:

> Dangerousness is about the situation not the individual; it is more about the effects and the degree of impairment than on the specific cause of illness, and it does not require a full examination but takes into account whatever information is available. Also, it requires qualified professional error on the side of safety, and may entail breaking other ordinary binding rules to favor urgent action.

This is a recipe for a slapdash analysis drawing on "whatever information" that can further the presumptions that frame the effort. Dr. Lee in effect creates her own definition of the term she intends to use and not surprisingly finds it perfectly acceptable, even praiseworthy given the need for "urgent action." It provides her and her contributors amply leeway, in theory, to bypass the ethical concerns that led to the Goldwater rule. In practice, the book stumbles over the very same ethical and assessment

7 ON PRESIDENT TRUMP'S PSYCHOLOGICAL AND POLITICAL ...

issues that Dr. Lee's definition seeks to reassure readers have been resolved through the power of her definition.

Given that almost every chapter in the book focuses directly on President Trump's dire and immediate psychological pathology and dangerousness, Dr. Lee adds this odd paradoxical disclaimer[66]:

> *In spite of its title, I would like to emphasize that this book is not about Mr. Trump.* It is about the larger context that has given rise to his presidency, and the greater population that he affects by virtue of his position.

Dr. Lee's own introduction to the book states,[67] "Some would argue that by paying attention to the president's mental state, we are colluding with him in deflecting attention from that by which he should be ultimately be judged: his actions ... *Certainly mental disturbance is not an excuse for tyrannical behavior; none the less, it cannot be ignored.*"

Translation: This book in which every chapter, but one,[68] takes up the specific issue of the level of President Trump's dire level of psychological dangerousness, based on assessments of his severe level of psychiatric disturbance, is not about President Trump. Moreover, by using the same essential psychological categories that one would use for psychiatric diagnosis, but calling the result "dangerousness," one can unconvincingly try to finesse and avoid the ethical responsibilities that accompany your professional training and title.

Given the book's disclaimer and reassurance that it is not attempting to provide a psychological or psychiatric diagnosis it is a bit of a surprise to find that the first and longest book chapter concludes by referring to: "*our case that Donald Trump is mentally unfit to be president of the United States.*" Readers will also be surprised to find another very early chapter devoted to Trump's "Delusional Disorder."[69] Perhaps by the fifth chapter, readers will not be surprised to find that the book's disclaimer and reassurances are not supported by its content—to wit, the following question asked and answered: "Could [the author's list of Trump behaviors] be expressions of significant mental derangement? The answer to that question is emphatically;Yes'."[70] And, of course, there are the *de rigueur* labelings of Trump's "malignant narcissism"[71] throughout the volume.

How Dangerous Is Donald Trump?

Leaving aside the large question of whether a diagnosis using psychiatric and psychological categories for analysis is still a diagnosis, one is left with the three questions. How dangerous is Donald Trump? Why is he dangerous? How do we know that he is dangerous?

The first question is easily answered. Every single author who addresses the issue of Trump's dangerousness expresses the view that Trump is an immediate and dire danger:

> Only in an emergency, should a physician breach the trust of confidentiality, and intervene without the consent, and only in an emergency should a physician breach the Goldwater rule. We believe that such an emergency now exists.[72]
>
> While there have surely been American presidents who could be said to be narcissistic, but none have shown sociopathic qualities to the degree seen in Mr. Trump. Correspondingly, none *have been so definitely and so obviously dangerous*.[73]
>
> [Trump] *evinces the most destructive and dangerous collection of psychiatric symptoms* possible for a leader. The worst case scenario is now our reality ... the election of Donald Trump is a true emergency, and the consequences are likely to be catastrophic ...[74]

Why Is Trump Dangerous?

That Trump is a very present, immediate, and dire danger is agreed to by almost every single one of the book's twenty-seven contributors. Why Trump's presidency is such a severe and present danger is not. Opinions vary, and the small sampling that follows cannot really do justice to the very large and diverse hypothetical calamities that a Trump presidency *could*, *might*, or *may* inflict on the country or the world—primarily war, nuclear or conventional. Other named consequences, like Trump's supposed lack of "flexibility to switch gears ... to deal with the functions of his job," is exactly the opposite of a trait for which he is often criticized:

> Fostered by the flattery of underlings and the chants of crowds, a political leader's [née Trump] grandiosity may morph into grotesque delusions of grandeur. Sociopathic traits may be amplified as the leader discovers he can violate the norms of civic society and even commit crime with impunity.[75]
>
> As is the case for extreme present hedonists, Trump is "chumming" for war, possibly for the most selfish of reasons: to deflect attention away from the Russian investigation.[76]

As pathological narcissists [née Trump] become increasing thought disordered their vision becomes clouded ... On a global scale, as it did with Nixon, that if it feeds your ego, step up military action.[77]

As President, Trump is systematically shredding trust in institutions he now commands. [examples given are the intelligence community, the judiciary, and the media].[78]

In only the first four months of his presidency, he teed up for starting wars in three places, Syria, Afghanistan and North Korea.[79]

The paranoia of severe sociopathy (referencing Trump) creates a profound risk of war, since the heads of other nations will inevitable disagree with or challenge the sociopathic leader, who will experience the disagreement as a personal attack, leading to rage reactions and impulsive action to destroy the "enemy."[80]

"See something, say nothing" seems to be the motto of the APA when it comes to national security. History will not be kind to a profession that aided the rise of an American Hitler through its silence.[81]

... surpassing the devastation of climate, health care education, diplomacy, social services, freedom of speech and liberty and justice for all [policies for which Trump is responsible for damaging] nothing is more incomprehensible than the now plausible prospect of all-out nuclear war ... because of this very real existential threat ...[82]

Trump anxiety disorder, albeit not a formal diagnosis ... Symptoms of Trump anxiety disorder include: feeling a loss of control; helplessness; rumination/worries, especially about the uncertain sociopolitical climate while Trump is in office; and a tendency toward excessive social media consumption.[83]

This is potentially tragic for those people and issues ignored as a result of the dysfunctional relationship with this president. I am experiencing personally, as I spend much more time reading news articles, organizing rallies, writing letters and making phone calls[rather than] working to improve the mental health system.[84]

He doesn't appear to have the flexibility to switch gears in order to deal with the functions of his job.[85]

How Do We Know That What Is Claimed About Mr. Trump's "Dangerousness" Is True?

It is one thing to use clinical labels, whatever they may be, and quite another to provide evidence that they fit and are appropriate. Almost all the entries in this book, with one exception, assign diagnostic labels to President Trump, without much evidence for their assertions beyond their having been made. Efforts from those authors who do try to provide evidence are instructive. "Reportedly" is a well-worn word in these entries, as in "reportedly" Trump did this, or "reportedly" Trump said that.[86] Efforts to follow through on and evaluate these "reportedly" reports are non-existent.

INCOMPLETE QUOTES, LAZY ANALYSIS, AND FACTUAL DISHONESTY

Interestingly, the use of the term "reportedly" refers to a number of reports that we now know are simply wrong. For example, the meme that Trump "demanded loyalty" from his then Attorney General is cited by several authors.[87] We now have available James Comey's memos of his conversations with President Trump and that part reads[88]:

> He [Trump] then returned to loyalty saying "I need loyalty." I replied that "he would always get honesty from me." He paused and said that's what he wants, "*Honest loyalty.*" I replied "you will get that from me."

Comey further writes that he understood that exchange to be consistent "with what I had said throughout the conversation. I will serve the president with loyalty to the office, the country, and the truth." However, almost all the reporting of that exchange, including those used to provide evidence in this book, say "Trump demanded loyalty," period. The further clarifying exchange about "honest loyalty," or Comey's written statements of what he took from the exchange were, and are, not reported leaving a damaging but factually false impression. Those errors are not corrected in a subsequent edition.

Another entry, written by two psychiatrists, fault Trump's presumed ignorance, and hence his unfitness, by directly relying on a reporter's assertion that Trump "could not answer the simple question of 'What are the top three functions of the American government?'"[89] At first, it seemed that the reporter and the authors were referring to the three basic branches of American government, but on further inspection that proved not to be the case. The article referred to in the two psychiatrist's bibliography, criticized Trump for not naming the top three functions that the author of the article thought *should* have been there. Trump named national security, health, and welfare—three key responsibilities as the government's top three functions. The authors criticized Trump

7 ON PRESIDENT TRUMP'S PSYCHOLOGICAL AND POLITICAL ... 249

for not saying "domestic tranquility," "conducting war, promoting peace and encouraging prosperity"[90] which were the three that the author of the quoted article thought were right.

It's hard to see how the two sets of answers—Trump's and the reporter who criticized him for giving essentially the same "right" answers that she provided, differ. It is even harder to understand after reading the article, why the two psychiatrists drew upon that article to make their Trump-ignorance claim. One wonders if they actually read or understood it.

Finally, along similar lines, several authors make reference to Trump's comment: "I alone can fix it,"[91] delivered at the Republican National Convention. One contributor uses this as evidence that Trump "finds himself to be uniquely superior."[92] Another chapter using this quote begins one section entitled "The Narcissistic Personality" with that quote and a framing for its elements: "Believing that you're better than others," "believing that you're special and acting accordingly," and so on.[93]

The reality is quite a bit more prosaic. Mr. Trump said[94]:

> I have joined the political arena so that the powerful can no longer beat up on people that cannot defend themselves. Nobody knows the system better than me, which is why I alone can fix it. I have seen firsthand how the system is rigged against our citizens, just like it was rigged against Bernie Sanders—he never had a chance.

Hyperbole? Clearly. Narcissistic? Not really. Trump has, in reality, spent an adulthood working the levers of the system as has almost every major business player seeking some favorable government ruling advantage. Does his familiarity with "the system" give him standing to say he knows the system? Yes, he has actually had an adulthood, starting with his apprenticeship with his father, of such familiarity.

Does his publicly stated promise to take this issue as a major focus of his presidency make him unusual, perhaps unique? Yes. As noted, Trump does see his *restoration* ambitions as including reforming a number of the country's basic institutions. Trump's convention assertion is also a strategically made election promise designed to reinforce his campaign stance as an outsider. He has followed through on efforts to reform some major domestic and international institutions including the FBI, DOJ, CDC,

250   S. RENSHON

NSC, VOA, WHO, WTO, and others. These are unusual presidential efforts in their seriousness and range.

THE POLITICS OF TRUMP PSYCHIATRIC ASSESSMENTS

In the chapters than make up Lee's book there are also many ordinary author appeals to authority/ies to buttress their claims. In almost all of these entries, the authorities cited are like minded progressives (liberals, Democrats—whatever one's preferred term). Among such cited authorities are vehemently anti-Trump individuals from the worlds of entertainment and politics: Eric Schneiderman (former New York State Attorney General), Morning Joe, Woody Guthrie, Adam Schiff, Rob Reiner, Rachel Maddow, Thomas Friedman, Lawrence O'Donnell, and Donny Deutsch.[95] *CNN*, *MSNBC*, the *New York Times*, and the *Washington Post*—reliable anti-Trump media outlets are credited by one contributor with helping to save the country and preventing Trump "from doing more harm, from going the really radical route of Hitler."[96]

The Goldwater diagnostic assessment was riddled with partisan political views, both liberal and conservative, undercutting any claim of professional objectivity. The same is true of Dr. Lee's Trump effort except that all the bias flows in one direction, consistent with liberal or progressive thinking. A few examples should suffice.

One psychiatrist clearly reflecting his idealization of previous Democratic presidents and their policies wrote: "That society [American society as a result for FDR's New Deal] reached the principle for its decency under the presidency of Barack Obama, who personified what it means to be a stable leader of a great and powerful nation."[97] Another, co-authoring his entry with Dr. Bandy Lee, who apparently approved of the sentiment, wrote[98]:

> About a week into Trump's term, the [Doomsday Clock] clock was moved again to two and one half minutes to midnight ... *I do not want to say that it is solely the impact of the Republican Party—obviously, that is false— but they are certainly in the lead openly advocating and working for the destruction of human species.*

One of the oddest moments among many in the book comes when one of the contributors, a clinical psychologist, reports on his reading of Trump's mind and dreams. He writes, "*There is considerable evidence to suggest that absolute tyranny is DT's wet dream.*"[99] The evidence?

Trump is noted to have said some very limited positive things about some very unsavory leaders with whom the United States has to deal. Trump pointed to the high odds against Kim Jong-un gaining power after his father died. He also noted Saddam Hussein's harsh and effective measures against terrorists trying to bring down his government. He further noted that Bashar Al-Assad was still in power in spite of US policy under President Obama to remove him. And he noted that President Putin had played a weak domestic and international hand very effectively.

It is true that Trump has expressed the wish to get along with Russia. Yet, he has also been extremely tough on them strategically, providing lethal arms to Ukraine and imposing tough economic sanctions. None of this supports the author's view that Trump "*has tried to become more of the tyrant he wants to be, not less.*"[100]

ON THINKING THAT WHAT YOU THINK YOU KNOW IS RIGHT

The various chapters in the Lee book provide very odd answers to the question of how do we know what we think we know and say in print about Trump? One contributor, a psychiatrist echoing Chief Justice Brennen on pornography, writes about Trump, "Sometimes a person's dangerousness is so obvious that one does not need professional training in either psychiatry or criminology to recognize it."[101] This article then simply applies a string of psychiatric labels to Mr. Trump. Apparently evidence is optional as well.

Finally, there is the very basic and unasked question of why so much of the behavior that has come to define Trump and his presidency is so obvious and public? His tweets and rallies give an immediate window into his thinking and concerns at any particular time. His fights are public, as are his unorthodox views on a variety of subjects like waterboarding (Trump uses these words "torture" or "waterboarding" interchangeably in his private conversations).[102]

Yet it is these very same public statements and views that form the basis of diagnoses of Trump as suffering severe psychological impairment. The dilemma is unwittingly spelled out in two contributions to Dr. Lee's book. In one, a psychiatrist who says that Trump has, "significant mental derangement" writes of him, "those who are good at manipulation, at appearing charming and caring, at concealing their immoral or illegal behavior and can bully their way to the top, do not end up as outcasts or in prison. There is a term for these people: successful sociopaths."[103]

The problem here is immediately clear. If there is one thing that Trump has not tried to do, it is to keep his psychology and his views under wraps. He has not tried to appear "charming and caring." Quite the contrary. Trump is clearly not afraid or inhibited to say what he thinks. Indeed, critics sometimes give the impression in talking about how Trump's presidential demeanor is part of the rationale for his unfitness that they would prefer he learn how to project and display more of the virtues they associate with their preferred presidents, whether they are real or contrived.

Nor has Trump taken pains to conceal what his detractors claim are his immoral or illegal behaviors. His conversation with the Ukraine president was in Trump's mind "perfect," and in his opponents' view grounds for impeachment. Trump did not need to make the transcript of that conversation public but did so in large part because he believed that he had done nothing wrong. Ditto for holding the next meeting of the G-7 at his MAR-a-LAGO golf club in Florida. That too was done publicly.

This dilemma was directly framed again, though not really addressed or resolved in another contribution to Dr. Lee's book, to wit[104]:

> Most abusers try to hide socially unacceptable actions; they are often polite to others, but abusive to a partner. Sadly, Trump makes no effort to mask his verbal abuse.

One could take the view that Trump's inability to hide or mask his psychology is one reflection of its unbridled and uncontrollable will to power. As such, it would then become an indicator of the degree of his severe pathology. Paradoxically, in this formulation, an ability to mask pathology and "act normally" indicates higher level functioning.

Or, one could take the also somewhat paradoxical position that Trump is, in many ways, the most transparent of presidents. He does not, for the most part, try to hide or sugarcoat his personal views of his enemies or their motivations to destroy him, his family, his administration, and his presidency's purposes. A number of his anti-critic salvos are startling for their bluntness, off-putting for the level of their personal nature, and unprecedented in their public nature. His policy views are also frequently bluntly stated, devoid of the usual hedging, and have not often been heard in the policy debates of the last four decades. That makes them startling and lightning rods for his critics.

A fair point would be that while Trump's honesty about what he thinks and says may reflect either transparency (Trump supporters' view) or pathology (Trump critics' views), they are data that must be taken into account. That would require drawing some analytical lines that so far have not been in evidence. It would require honesty in reporting more fully what Trump actually said rather than only a part of an exchange that supports a particular anti-Trump narrative, as with Mr. Comey. It would require distinguishing between understandable and even supportable responses to harsh and inaccurate anti-Trump claims and accusations, and responses that cross the line into regrettable and avoidable behavior like his comments on Senator McCain's military service or his unnecessary fight with the Democratic congresswoman riding in the car with a woman whose husband had just been killed in combat.

It would require honest acknowledgement that many disagreements with Trump are, basically, policy disagreements. They should be treated and debated as such. The assertions regarding Trump's presumed psychiatric mental health issues, using the same criteria to further the narrative of his "dangerousness" should not serve as proxy for policy debates.

Assessing the Twenty-Seven Mental Health Experts' Take on Donald Trump

Dr. Lee's book fails on two very basic grounds. First, the "mental health experts" reach very diverse and often incompatible conclusions about Trump's psychology. This is made very clear in an interview with Dr. Lee by a another, more professional and scholarly psychiatrist and published in *Psychodynamic Psychiatry*[105]:

> **Question**: One could argue that your edited volume supports the ongoing need for the Goldwater Rule. Experts offer various diagnoses where emphasis depends upon one's own perspective, and there is a risk of "throwing whatever you can at him to see what will stick." For example, he is an "extreme present hedonist" as well as narcissist and bully (Zimbardo and Sword), narcissistic personality disorder with psychopathy (Makin), paranoid (Friedman), sociopathic (Dudes), mistrusting (Sheehy), impaired relationship with reality (most contributors), delusional disorder (Tansey),

254   S. RENSHON

possible hypomanic temperament (Gartner), cognitive impairment. What do you make of the varied readings of Trump?

Dr. Lee: If you read them carefully, they are not actual diagnoses …The list was deliberately meant to be relatively "comprehensive" … *as an exhaustive list of potential differential diagnoses* that the public would benefit from knowing about, without our weighing in particularly on one diagnosis.

Here Dr. Lee acknowledges that she and her contributors are indeed making psychological and psychiatric diagnoses. She believes that her project is rescued by the making of "*an exhaustive list of potential differential diagnoses that the public would benefit from knowing about*, without our weighing in particularly on one diagnosis." The Goldwater prohibition is meant to caution regarding the making of public diagnosis. That issue is not avoided by making many diagnoses instead of one.

Moreover, each individual author did weigh in on one, or several, psychological and psychiatric diagnoses that they claimed characterized Trump. Collectively there were many, varied diagnoses, though most chapters focused in on one. In so doing, contributors were presented, and presented themselves, as qualified to do so. Their Trump observations, assertions really, were meant to be buttressed by what they doubtlessly felt was their professional authority. The fact that all these "mental health experts" reached very different conclusions echoes the diverse clinical and political views in the Goldwater assessment fiasco. This undercuts confidence both in their conclusions, the validity and legitimacy of their assessments, and their ethical lapses in providing them.

Second, and equally important, only one of the book's twenty-eight entries (see directly below), discussing cognitive assessments, raises an issue that permeates and undercuts the whole effort, namely whether the attempted diagnosis is psychiatric or political "dangerousness." This author writes[106]:

Based on the limited information available, persons with professional training could provide public opinions regarding a candidate's intellect [and by inference other traits], but the database that even professionals can use remains inadequate and incomplete, *and differentiation between objective and clinically "solid opinions versus political biased propaganda is an insurmountable problem. At the current time, I view this as a problem without any solution in the near future."*

Dr. Reiss concluded by worrying that, "pernicious manipulation by unscrupulous clinicians cannot be avoided."[107] He concludes thusly[108]: "applying clinical/ medical knowledge to a political process is practically complex and daunting with regard to the issues of objectivity, the setting of parameters (e.g., for qualification/disqualification) and the avoidance if ill-informed and /or malicious manipulation."

One wonders, reading through the rest of the entries in this book, how Dr. Reiss' paper highlighting a fundamental flaw in the whole effort, made it through the editor's review process.

"Mental Health Experts" Opine to Congress: Impeach Trump. We'll Testify

During the House impeachment hearings, Dr. Lee and her group of "mental health experts" petitioned Congress to immediately remove President Trump from office. They also offered to testify against him. A cornerstone of the argument that anti-Trump "mental health experts" made against allowing him to remain in office was because, among other things, the "president lacked the ability to make rational decisions."[109]

Their particular claims were a hodge-podge of political disagreements, dire and wholly speculative warnings of potential disaster ("We bear in mind that Donald Trump, as President, has the unfettered authority to launch nuclear weapons at any time for any reason"), and factual errors (the separation of families crossing the South border without permit was a policy initiated by President Obama).

The petition to Congress actually contains the following analysis (emphasis added):

> Without this external affirmation, President Trump has revealed that he feels, deep down, like a loser, a failure, weak, dumb, fat, ugly, fake, "crooked." We know this because these self-denigrating pictures of himself, President Trump *projects onto others*, whom he transforms into enemies, and compensates consciously by creating a grandiose image of himself as unique, a stable genius.

The organizers of this petition apparently feel that on the basis of their familiarity with Trump's tweets, that they have unique insight into the unconscious origins of his motivation. That astounding position in itself would qualify as "grandiose," aside from being wholly dependent on claimed "expertise," rather than real evidence. Their claim is fatally compromised by the level of unsubstantiated speculation, its public political nature, their reliance on presumed personal knowledge of Trump's unconscious motivations that they can't possibly intuit from his tweets, the lack of serious analysis that goes beyond quoting the latest headline, and their obvious and raw anti-Trump animus.

There is however one final element to consider in the analysis in the group Dr. Lee has assembled to diagnosis Trump and that is their dismissal of any views that differ with theirs. Dr. John Zimmer, one of the three major signers of the petition to Congress to impeach and remove Trump from office because of his dangerous mental impairments was asked about Republicans who defend Trump.

He[110] "dismissed Republicans who defend Mr. Trump by claiming that his style as that of a blunt-talking New York businessman as 'simply ignorant about the whole area of psychology that pertains to him.'" He continued, "These aren't alternative viewpoints," Dr. Zimmer explained, calling one "the product of very sound psychology … that comes from mainly from psychoanalytic theory, but is very established and sound and studied," and the other "*just ignorance and dismissiveness.*"

QED.

Notes

1. Issac Stanley-Becker and Sean Sullivan. 2016. "Obama: Trump Is 'Unfit to Serve as President'," *Washington Post*, August 2.
2. Greg Sargent. 2016. "Republicans Nominate Dangerously Insane Person to Lead America, Then Panic When He Proves He's Dangerously Insane," *Washington Post*, August 16; see also John Gardner and Steven Buser (eds.). 2018. *Rocket Man: Nuclear Madness and the Mind of Donald Trump.* New York: Chiron Books.
3. Michael D'Antonio. 2016. "Trump Never Wanted to be America's President; He Wants to be Its Czar," *CNN*, November 16; see Max Boot. 2016. "The Nazi Echoes in Trump's Tweets," *Los Angeles Times*, October 17; and Robert Kagan. 2016. "This Is How Fascism Comes to America," *Washington Post*, May 18. For a dissent of the Trump-as-Nazi view, see Rich Lowry. 2018. "The Tawdry and Dumb Nazi Charge," *Politico*, June 27.
4. Adil E. Shamoo and Bonnie Bricker. 2017. "It's Time to Take the Nazi-Trump Comparisons Seriously," *Foreign Policy in Focus*, August 23.
5. Brooke Singman. 2019. "Nadler Likens Trump to 'Dictator,' Threatens Barr with Contempt After Hearing Boycott," *Fox News*, May 2.

6. Michael Gerson. 2018. "Trump Has Revealed Who He Is. Now It's Our Turn," *Washington Post*, January 15.
7. James Risen. 2018. "Is Donald Trump a Traitor?" *The Intercept*, February 2; see also Max Boot. 2018. "We Just Watched a U.S. President Acting on Behalf of a Hostile Power," *Washington Post*, July 16.
8. David Rothkopf. 2017. "The Greatest Threat Facing the United States Is Its Own President," *Washington Post*, July 4. Rothkopf's indictment of President Trump's "fitness," employ the litany approach to supporting their assertions. Supposed examples supporting his view are asserted in a single sentence or as part of one. On occasion, "evidence" is presented in the form of links to others who have made the same accusations. Occasionally phrases like "tweeting hysterically at the media" or "his malignant and ever-visible narcissism" are made without further discussions or evidence—inviting the similarly inclined reader to share the author's assumptions. No actual evidence is considered. Assertions, not vetted and validated, are felt to suffice. And for many, they often do.
9. Steven Levitsky and Daniel Ziblatt. 2018. *How Democracies Die*. New York: Crown.
10. Yascha Mounk. 2018. *The People vs. Democracy: Why Our Freedom Is in Danger and How to Save It*. Cambridge, MA: Harvard University Press.
11. Anca Gurzu. 2019. "Labour's Thornberry: Trump Is a 'Threat to Our World Order'," *Politico*, April 27.
12. I have in my files a very large number of these kinds of guilty by conclusion, not by evidence assertions, already noted in endnote 8 above, that almost always rely on the author's conclusions regarding the latest Trump political tempest—without much effort to gather and weigh evidence beyond those that support their presumptions—usually quotes of liked minded people.
13. The term, and the training necessary to use it, may be specified in state law. In New York State, the term "psychologist" is so defined, but a term like "therapist" is not. Individuals with PhD's in Clinical or Counseling Psychology obviously have psychological training but may or may not be state licensed for a variety of reasons. The same is true of many persons who hold MSWs in Social Work.
14. Shakespeare 1600, Act-II, Scene-II.
15. Matthew Lee. 2017. "AP FACT CHECK: Overlooking Doubts on Syria Chemical Weapons," *ABC News*, April 10.
16. Richard C. Friedman MD and Jennifer Downey MD. 2018. "Editorial: Psychiatric Ethics and the Goldwater Rule," *Psychodynamic Psychiatry*, Vol. 46, No. 3 (Fall), pp. 323–333.
17. American Psychiatric Association. (2013). *Diagnostic and Statistical Manual of Mental Disorders* (Fifth ed.). Arlington, VA: American Psychiatric Publishing.

18. As noted in the last chapter, two recent articles on the major issues surrounding the American Psychiatric Associations Revision (*DSM-5*) of its *Diagnostic and Statistical Manual* (*DSM-IV*) were recently published online in which twenty-four psychiatrists with diverse views engaged each other in trying to answer the following six most essential questions in psychiatric diagnosis including the nature and definition of a mental disorder and the validation of evidence used to support these formulations. See James Phillips, Allen Frances, Michael A. Cerullo, John Chardavoyne, Hannah S. Decker, Michael B. First, Nassir Ghaemi, Gary Greenberg, Andrew C. Hinderliter, Warren A. Kinghorn, Steven G. LoBello, Elliot B. Martin, Aaron L. Mishara, Joel Paris, Joseph M. Pierre, Ronald W. Pies, Harold A. Pincus, Douglas Porter, Claire Pouncey, Michael A. Schwartz, Thomas Szasz, Jerome C. Wakefield, G. Scott Waterman, Owen Whooley and Peter Zacher. 2012. "The Six Most Essential Questions in Psychiatric Diagnosis: A Pluralogue Part 2: Issues of Conservatism and Pragmatism in Psychiatric Diagnosis," *Philosophy, Ethics, and Humanities in Medicine: PEHM*, Vol. 7, No. 8 (April).
19. American Psychiatric Association. (2013). *Diagnostic and Statistical Manual of Mental Disorders* (Fifth ed.). Arlington, VA: American Psychiatric Publishing, p. 103.
20. Ibid., p. 661.
21. Cf., Bandy Lee, MD et al. 2017. *The Dangerous Case of Donald Trump: 27 Psychiatrists and Mental Health Experts Assess a President*. New York: Thomas Dunne Books.
22. The section that follows draws on Stanley A. Renshon. 1996. *The Psychological Assessment of Presidential Candidates*. New York: New York University Press, chapter 5.
23. Ralph Ginzberg. 1964. "Goldwater: The Man and the Menace," *Fact*, Vol. 4, No. 2–4, p. 3.
24. Arnold Rogow. 1970. *The Psychiatrists*. New York: Putnam.
25. Ginzberg 1964, p. 54.
26. Ginzberg 1964, p. 62.
27. Ginzberg 1964, p. 63.
28. Ginzberg 1964, p. 54.
29. Ginzberg 1964, p. 3.
30. Ginzberg 1964, p. 3.
31. Ginzberg 1964, p. 37.
32. Ginzberg 1964, p. 40.
33. Rogow 1970, p. 129.
34. Ginzberg 1964, p. 24.
35. Ginzberg 1964, p. 30.
36. Ginzberg 1964, p. 63.
37. Ginzberg 1964, p. 42.

7 ON PRESIDENT TRUMP'S PSYCHOLOGICAL AND POLITICAL ... 259

38. George T. Conway III. 2019. "Unfit for Office," *The Atlantic*, October 3; see also Rothkopf 2017. Both Conway and Rothkopf's indictment of President Trump's "fitness," employ the litany approach to supporting their assertions in which single one-sided assessments of Trump's behavior or policies are aggregated to make the unfitness claim.
39. Cf., Conway writes that Trump "ordered the revocation of the security clearance of a former CIA director who had criticized him." He did not. See John Bennen. 2019. "Remember When Trump Said He'd Revoked Brennan's Security Clearance?" *NBC*, May 28.
40. Conway 2019, emphasis added.
41. Laurence H. Tribe. 2017. "Trump Must be Impeached. Here's Why," *Washington Post*, May 13; see also Allan J. Lichtman. 2017. *The Case for Impeachment*. New York: Dey St. Books; and Laurence Tribe and Joshua Matz. 2018. *To End a Presidency: The Power of Impeachment*. New York: Basic Books.
42. Ross Douthat. 2017. "The 25th Amendment Solution for Removing Trump," *New York Times*, May 16; Phil McCauslandl. 2017. "Democratic Bill Lays the Groundwork to Remove Trump from Office," *NBC* News, July 3; and Michael Isikoff. 2017. "Bill to Create Panel That Could Remove Trump from Office Quietly Picks up Democratic Support," *Yahoo News*, June 20.
43. Lauren Gill. 2018. "Trump 'Psychologically Unfit,' Nuclear Tweet Is Grounds for Removal, Former Bush Ethic Lawyer says," *Newsweek*, January 3.
44. Rothkopf 2017.
45. John McCormack. 2016. "Unfit to Serve," *The Weekly Standard*, May 16.
46. Emily Joffe. 2017. "Is Donald Trump a TV Addict?" *Politico*, July 7.
47. David Brooks. 2017. "When the World Is Led by a Child," *New York Times*, May 15.
48. Tana Ganeva. 2019. "Bandy X. Lee Discusses What Prompted Her to Speak Out About the President's Psychological Problems," *Salon*, May 7.
49. Megan McArdle. 2019. "When will Trump Supporters Finally Say, 'Okay, This Is Not Normal'?" *Washington Post*, August 23.
50. Michelle Goldberg. 2017. "An Unfit President Fails Puerto Rico," *New York Times*, October 3.
51. A comprehensive after report on the Federal government's efforts during the 2017 hurricane season including its preparation and response to Hurricane Maria that hit Puerto Rico can be found in FEMA 2018. https://www.fema.gov/media-library-data/1531743865541-d16 794d43d3082544435e1471da07880/2017FEMAHurricaneAAR.pdf.
52. Stanley-Becker and Sullivan 2016.

53. Jonathan Capehart. 2015. "Unfit for the Oval Office," *Washington Post*, September 21. Thomas Caplan. 2016. "John Kasich Calls Trump Unprepared to be President," *New York Times*, April 1; see also Chas Danner. 2015. "Donald Trump Responds to Muslim Question Controversy [Updated]," *New York Magazine*, September 20.
54. Alexander Burns. 2016. "Donald Trump Seeks Republican Unity But Finds Rejection," *New York Times*, May 6.
55. That quote continues, "The severely sleep-deprived are more impulsive, less adaptable and prone to snappish decisions, and they have trouble listening to others. They miss out on essential REM time, which allows people to process emotions and events in their lives. Smaller things set them off." See Timothy Eagan. 2016. "A Unified Theory of Trump," *New York Times*, February 26.
56. Caplan 2016.
57. Ramesh Ponnuru. 2016. "How Clinton Can Demolish Trump," *Bloomberg*, May 26.
58. John McWhorter. 2019. "Trump's Typos Reveal His Lack of Fitness for the Presidency," *The Atlantic*, January 11.
59. Chris Kirk, Ian Prasad Philbrick, and Gabriel Roth. 2016. "153 Things Donald Trump Has Said and Done That Make Him Unfit to Be President," *Slate*, November 7.
60. Robert J. Samuelson. 2019. "Why We Should Impeach and Remove President Trump," *Washington Post*, October 20, emphasis added.
61. Abha Bhattari. 2019. "Retailer Buys Controversial Trump-themed Billboard in Times Square," *Seattle Times*, October 18.
62. Leah Mcdonald and James Gordon. 2019. "Barbra Streisand Shares a Gruesome Cartoon of Nancy Pelosi Impaling and Killing Trump with a Giant Heel," *Daily Mail*, October 20.
63. Chancellor Agard. 2017. "Kathy Griffin Bloody Trump Pic Defended by Photographer," *Entertainment*, May 30.
64. Liam Stack. 2017. "Et Tu, Delta? Shakespeare in the Park Sponsors Withdraw from Trump-Like 'Julius Caesar'," *New York Times*, June 11.
65. Bandy Lee MD. 2017 "Introduction," in Bandy Lee (organizer), *The Dangerous Case of Donald Trump: 27 Psychiatrists and Mental Health Experts Assess a President*. New York: St. Martin's Press, pp. 11–22, p. 14.
66. Lee MD. 2017, p. 18, emphasis added.
67. Judith Lewis Hermann MD and Bandy Lee MD. 2017. "Prologue: Professions and Politics," in Bandy Lee (organizer), *The Dangerous Case of Donald Trump: 27 Psychiatrists and Mental Health Experts Assess a President*. New York: St. Martin's Press, pp. 1–10, p. 8, emphasis added.
68. David M. Reiss MD. 2017. "Cognitive Impairment. Dementia, and Potus," in Bandy Lee (organizer), *The Dangerous Case of Donald Trump:*

27 Psychiatrists and Mental Health Experts Assess a President. New York: St. Martin's Press, pp. 126–135.

69. Michael J. Tansey. 2017. "Why 'Crazy Like a Fox' Versus 'Crazy Like Crazy' Really Matters: Delusional Disorder, Admiration of Brutal Dictatorships, the Nuclear Code, and Trump," in Bandy Lee (organizer), *The Dangerous Case of Donald Trump: 27 Psychiatrists and Mental Health Experts Assess a President*. New York: St. Martin's Press, pp. 110–125.

70. Lance Dodes MD. 2017. "Sociopathy," in Bandy Lee (organizer), *The Dangerous Case of Donald Trump: 27 Psychiatrists and Mental Health Experts Assess a President*. New York: St. Martin's Press, pp. 83–92.

71. Lee MD. 2017, pp. 58, 84, 94, 98, passim.

72. Phillip Zimbardo and Rosemary Sword. 2017. "Unbridled and Extreme President Hedonism," in Bandy Lee (organizer), *The Dangerous Case of Donald Trump: 27 Psychiatrists and Mental Health Experts Assess a President*. New York: St. Martin's Press, p. 6.

73. Dodes MD. 2017, p. 91.

74. John D. Gardner. 2017. "Donald Trump Is (A) Bad, (B) Mad, (C) all of the Above," in Bandy Lee (organizer), *The Dangerous Case of Donald Trump: 27 Psychiatrists and Mental Health Experts Assess a President*. New York: St. Martin's Press, pp. 93–109, p. 107, emphasis added.

75. Hermann MD. and Lee MD. 2017, p. 7.

76. Zimbardo and Sword 2017, p. 47.

77. Craig Malkin. 2017. "Pathological Narcissism and Politics: A Lethal Mix," in Bandy Lee (organizer), *The Dangerous Case of Donald Trump: 27 Psychiatrists and Mental Health Experts Assess a President*. New York: St. Martin's Press, pp. 51–68, p. 62.

78. Gail Sheehy. 2017. "Trump's Trust Deficit Is the Core Problem," in Bandy Lee (organizer), *The Dangerous Case of Donald Trump: 27 Psychiatrists and Mental Health Experts Assess a President*. New York: St. Martin's Press, pp. 75–82, p. 76.

79. Sheehy 2017, p. 81.

80. Dodes MD. 2017, p. 91.

81. Gardner 2017, p. 107.

82. Tansey 2017, p. 121.

83. Jennifer Contarino Panning. 2017. "Trump Anxiety Disorder," in Bandy Lee (organizer), *The Dangerous Case of Donald Trump: 27 Psychiatrists and Mental Health Experts Assess a President*. New York: St. Martin's Press, pp. 235–243, p. 237.

84. Harper West. 2017. "In Relationship with an Abusive President," in Bandy Lee (organizer), *The Dangerous Case of Donald Trump: 27 Psychiatrists and Mental Health Experts Assess a President*. New York: St. Martin's Press, pp. 244–260, p. 258.

262   S. RENSHON

85. Steve Wruble MD. 2017. "Trump's Daddy Issues," in Bandy Lee (organizer), *The Dangerous Case of Donald Trump: 27 Psychiatrists and Mental Health Experts Assess a President*. New York: St. Martin's Press, pp. 268–280, p. 274.
86. Cf., Lee MD. 2017, pp. 63, 72, 120.
87. Ian Schwartz. 2018. "*CNN* Focus Group of Trump Voters: 'Exactly What I Voted for'," *Real Clear Politics*, February 13, p. 72.
88. James Comey. 2017. "My Notes from Private Session with PE 1/6/17," emphasis added. https://www.documentcloud.org/docume nts/4442900-Ex-FBI-Director-James-Comey-s-memos.html.
89. Nanette Gartrell MD. and Dee Mosbacher MD. 2017. "He's Got The World in His Hands and His Finger on the Trigger: The 25th Amendment Solution," in Bandy Lee (organizer), *The Dangerous Case of Donald Trump: 27 Psychiatrists and Mental Health Experts Assess a President*. New York: St. Martin's Press, pp. 319–342, p. 348.
90. Laura Brown. 2016. "Government Stumps Trump," *U.S. News and World Report*, March 31.
91. Lee MD. 2017, pp. 36, 95.
92. Dodes MD. 2017, p. 95.
93. Zimbardo and Sword 2017, pp. 36–37.
94. Politico Staff. 2016. "Donald Trump 2016 RNC Draft Speech Transcript," *Politico*, July 21.
95. Lee MD. 2017, pp. 96, 99, 100, 165, 255.
96. Henry J. Friedman MD. 2017. "On Seeing What You See and Saying What You Know: A Psychiatrist's Responsibility," in Bandy Lee (organizer), *The Dangerous Case of Donald Trump: 27 Psychiatrists and Mental Health Experts Assess a President*. New York: St. Martin's Press, pp. 160–169, p. 165.
97. Friedman MD. 2017, p. 166.
98. Noam Chomsky and Bandy Lee MD. 2017. "Epilogue," in Bandy Lee (organizer), *The Dangerous Case of Donald Trump: 27 Psychiatrists and Mental Health Experts Assess a President*. New York: St. Martin's Press, pp. 356–359, p. 358, emphasis added.
99. Tansey 2017, p. 115, emphasis in original.
100. Tansey 2017, p. 119, emphasis in original.
101. James Gilligan MD. 2017. "The Issue Is Dangerousness, Not Mental illness," in Bandy Lee (organizer), *The Dangerous Case of Donald Trump: 27 Psychiatrists and Mental Health Experts Assess a President*. New York: St. Martin's Press, pp. 170–180, p. 173.
102. Jonathan Swan. 2019. "Trump Said CIA Director Gina Haspel Agreed with Him '100%' on Torture," *Axios*, November 17.
103. Dodes MD. 2017, pp. 84–85.
104. West 2017, p. 254.

105. Larry Sandberg MD. 2018. "Interview with Bandy Lee," *Psychodynamic Psychiatry*, Vol. 46, No. 3, pp. 335–355, emphasis added.
106. Reiss MD. 2017, p. 128.
107. Reiss MD. 2017, p. 131.
108. Reiss MD. 2017, p. 134, emphasis added.
109. World Mental Health Coalition. 2019. "PETITION TO THE JUDICIARY COMMITTEE OF THE U.S. HOUSE OF REPRESENTATIVES," December 5.
110. Zimmer quoted in Andrew Fineberg. 2019. "Trump's Mental State Is deteriorating Dangerously Due to Impeachment with Potentially 'Catastrophic Outcomes,' Psychiatrists Urgently Warn Congress," *The Independent*, December 4.

CHAPTER 8

The Unexpected Trump

The opposition's assault on Mr. Trump is a defining characteristic of his presidency from which many consequences follow. One of the clearest is that there is little effort to analyze the president that goes beyond a narrow, shallow, one-dimensional view of him as either a pathological narcissist, a threat to the nation and the world, or a blundering buffoon whose every acted out policy impulse disrupts long established and preferable bi-partisan precedents. Lost in those battles are analyses of important parts of Mr. Trump himself—his psychology and leadership strategies.

Trump critics don't mind these omissions. They would argue that there is not much more to analyze once you have settled on one or more of the standard critiques noted above. The relatively few supportive Trump books don't add much depth to our overall psychological understanding of the president and his leadership beyond a defense of Trump policies, since that is not their primary purpose.[1] These few books do help provide some balance to the assessment of Trump's presidency. However they do not get us very deeply into the psychology that shapes his outlook and his actions. The same is true for the authentic, fair-minded behind the scenes narratives[2] that help to dispel the inaccurate, almost always anonymously sourced[3] narratives in which the most damaging, disparaging portrayals of that presidency are presented as authentic.[4]

Trump is a complex man and president. He does contain multitudes. Yet a fuller picture of him is largely terra incognita. In this chapter, as

© The Author(s) 2020
S. Renshon, *The Real Psychology of the Trump Presidency*,
The Evolving American Presidency,
https://doi.org/10.1007/978-3-030-45391-6_8

265

we have done to this point, we hope to continue widening the lens of our analysis to provide some evidence of Trump's psychological and leadership elements that have been neglected, overlooked, or that otherwise remain opaque. Here, as elsewhere in the book's analysis, there is the danger that some will confuse filling in a picture of Trump's psychology and leadership with efforts to "normalize" or support Trump. And again the answer to that concern is the same. The analysis is presented along with the supporting evidence for it in order to build a more comprehensive and accurate understanding of this unique president. As always, the chips are allowed to fall where they may.

The adjective, "unexpected" in the title of this chapter raises the question of why it was used. Its use reflects the fact that the analysis herein enters into new territory. That means not only territory that has not previously been part of the analysis of Trump, but territory that is seen as antithetical to analysis of Trump by critics and perhaps supporters as well. The "unexpected" Trump is part of the *Real Psychology of the Trump Presidency*.

DONALD TRUMP'S COMPASSION

Trump is a man and president who can be, and often is, difficult, demanding, tough, and sometimes hard. He is, on occasion, intentionally insulting, and those insults can sometimes be cruel. Yet, there is ample evidence that he also does have feelings of concern, caring, and contrary to conventional wisdom,[5] empathy.

The (retrospectively assembled, reconstructed account of a portion of one Trump day) story that follows appeared in a 1989 *Chicago Tribune* profile, and is worth quoting in full[6]:

> Now, silencing his intercom, he [Trump] slips out of his bullish boardroom skin. Something different. The blue eyes, typically hooded in skepticism, are tender. He is listening to Adam Orman, a 12-year-old whiz-kid visitor from Harrisburg, Pa., who suffers from a devastating muscle disorder called postviral neuromyasthenia. Adam has spent the last year in bed, managing a small stock portfolio and gobbling up every word he can find on his hero, Donald John Trump, businessman.
>
> His dream was to meet Trump. A single phone call did the job.
>
> "Your figures on the square footage of the Taj deal aren't quite accurate," Adam is challenging, the two of them squared off in Trump's glass-walled Trump Tower office overlooking New York's Central Park

South. The boy is dazzled by toy models of Trump's personal helicopter, proposed new high-rises and inscribed silver hard hats from past digs.

Trump tells Adam in an emotional farewell at the end of their hour-long visit that he has a very personal dream, too, and that is to see the boy next September, without walker, at the christening of the $750 million Taj Mahal casino. "I'll be there," Adam vows.

Another deal made.

It's possible to argue that Trump spent all that time with the sick boy because the boy idealized him. Yet there are many people who idealize Trump and would give anything to have the opportunity to say so in a personal meeting. Trump chose to spend his time with a very sick child with little time left to live to help him realize the dream of his life while he was alive.

There is a parallel involved in Mr. Trump taking time from a busy schedule to help a stricken child realize his dream and the bombing of Syria for crossing the red line against the use of chemical weapons that Trump had laid down. The bombing was certainly strategically meant to enforce American credibility (and Trump's), but there was another part to his decision. As noted in Chapter 4 the awful pictures of the effect of the gas attacks, especially on children, had a profound impact on Trump.[7]

Trump's Public and Private Charitable Giving: Empathy, Deductions, and Accusations

Charity reflects a measure of a person outside of their ambitions and careers. Being there for others financially, if you can afford that, or personally giving of yourself when others need comfort can be measures of essential humanness. Wealthy people like Mr. Trump are expected to give to charity and Trump does. Yet, like every other aspect of Trump's life, this one too is complex, and because it is about Trump it is also politically charged and controversial. Allegations, often ugly and frequently just accusatory, abound. The real facts are also sometimes difficult to establish because so much data is missing. As will become clear, this has not stopped the speculations, innuendo, and factually unanchored accusations.

Much has been said about the Trump family's charitable giving both by Mr. Trump and his critics. Mr. Trump has said repeatedly that, "I've given millions away ... I've given millions of dollars away to the vets and

I'm very honored by it."[8] Trump critics say that Trump has contributed very little of his personal money to the family charity that bears his name, especially given his wealth. That is true. Critics feel he should contribute more. Trump responds that this charitable trust is not his only charitable effort and is a rather minor one in his overall stream of giving. Critics want to see the evidence. Trump declines to provide it.

Critics also say that Trump has used his family charity to buy himself personal items, and that he has overcharged charities that use his facilities as a way to make money from his charity. Finally, they say that Trump pledges money but never follows through until asked by the media at which time he rushes to fulfill his pledge. The implication here is that if the media didn't ask, he would quietly renege.

Like many other aspects of Trump commentary there is much in this area that is inadequately reported. As a result, Trump's charitable giving, which could offer some real insights into his complex and often contradictory psychology are lost in the quest to raise ethical questions and come to conclusions about his character flaws and "illegal behavior." The analysis that follows is not Trump blemish-free, because Trump has acted inappropriately in at least one documented circumstance with his personal charity that involved using money from the charity to buy a picture of himself that he kept. That single documented transgression does not however, support the many narrow, harsh, unproven, and frequently disproved accusations that are publicly made about Trump's charity giving.

Trump Charitable Giving: The Question of Expectations and Reality

Trump's charitable giving represents an expected behavior on the part of the very wealthy. Any person worth many millions or even a billion that did not use some of his money to help others in some way would legitimately be considered selfish. Additionally, if such a man were to publicly tout his generosity, but in fact gave little or nothing, he would legitimately be considered a hypocrite. For all those reasons, a clearer more accurate accounting of Trump's charitable contributions is important.

Recalling growing up in the Trump household, his daughter Ivanka said[9]:

> "Over the years, on too many occasions to count, I saw my father tear stories out of the newspaper about people whom he had never met, who were facing some injustice or hardship," she said. "He'd write a note to

his assistant, in a signature black felt tip pen, and request that the person be found and invited to Trump Tower to meet with him. He would talk to them and then draw upon his extensive network to find them a job or get them a break."

Her remembrances can be discounted on the basis of a daughter's parental love. Yet, other independent observations add credibility to her memories. As noted in Chapter 1, there is substantial evidence that Mr. Trump can be very generous anonymously. We noted he once gave a dying child a check for $50,000.00 so that he could enjoy the last years of his life.[10] He also gave thousands of dollars to a family whose hardships he read about in the papers.[11] In another instance, he agreed to a dying child's wish to be "fired" from *The Apprentice*, but when it came time to say those words, Trump couldn't bring himself to say them to a dying child and gave him a check for several thousand dollars and told him "to go have the time of his life."[12]

He donated $10,000 to pay for chemotherapy for the father of one of his thousands of campaign volunteers.[13] The father of the volunteer was a member of the New York Vietnam Veterans Memorial Commission, Trump tapped his web of wealthy friends, and the then president himself to attend a fundraiser to help fund the NY State Vietnam memorial.[14]

There is as well this report among numerous other instances[15]:

ANNABEL HILL has coped with the suicide of her husband and a debt-laden farm that twice was put up on the auction block for nonpayment of loans. The insurance netted $175,000; the debts exceeded $300,000. Parts of the farm were sold, but even that wasn't enough. Last Sept. 2, the remaining 715 acres were up for auction again. This time Donald J. Trump, the New York real-estate developer, halted the sale. He phoned the auction block and assured the creditors that he would help Mrs. Hill.

"It's worked out real, real well," she says. "All 715 acres were saved."

Trump's documented charitable giving is less often noted than questioned about its reality and level. David Fahrenthold's examination of Trump's charitable giving established that his namesake charity was a relatively small foundation primarily but not exclusively funded by contributions to it that Mr. Trump solicited. The essence of Fahrenthold's report is that[16]:

For as long as he has been rich and famous, Donald Trump has also wanted people to believe he is generous. He spent years constructing an image as a philanthropist by appearing at charity events and by making very public—even nationally televised—promises to give his own money away. *It was, in large part, a facade*. A months-long investigation by *The Washington Post has not been able to verify many of Trump's boasts about his philanthropy*.

The two key phrases in that quote are the harsh conclusion that Trump's charitable work was a "façade" and that Fahrenthold has "not been able to verify many contributions." Notice that what is presented as a fact (Trump's charitable contributions are a "façade," is based on non-existent data). Why wasn't Fahrenthold able to verify his accusation? Fahrenthold writes, "It is impossible to know for certain what Trump has given to charity, because he has declined to release his tax returns." As a result, Fahrenthold's inability to document Trump's charitable giving because Trump would not make his detailed records available to him does not support Farhenthold's characterization that Trump's image as philanthropist is, "in large part, a facade." It simply means that Fahrenthold made the accusation without having real evidence to support it.

Trump has been very clear about why he has not provided this information. For critics, the suspicion is that he has something to hide. The reality is more prosaic. In the exchange below with the *Washington Post*, Trump was asked why he won't release a list of his charitable giving. He gives several reasons but the most honest answer is that he thought the *Washington Post* would search for and find a way to use it against him as they did with several other accusations about his charitable giving, also analyzed below.

In all, the *Post* was able to identify $7.8 million in charitable giving from Trump's own pocket since the early 1980s. The *Washington Post* asked Trump to provide detailed listings of the amounts of money he had contributed and to whom, and he declined to do so. Why? Consider the following exchanges:

> *Drew Harwell*: … you said you're an ardent philanthropist. You said you've given more than $100 million to charity over the last five years. But when you look into the money that was given to the Donald J. Trump Foundation, you haven't donated any actual money. It's all been the golf course and I'm sure—
> *Donald Trump*: *Well, you don't know that because I don't give most of the money to the foundation.*
> *Drew Harwell*: Where do you give it?

Donald Trump: Some people use the foundation. *The foundation is a very small part of what I give.*

Drew Harwell: How much of your personal money have you given to charity in the last five years?

Donald Trump: I think you wrote a story. I've given a lot.

Drew Harwell: How much of your personal money?

Donald Trump: If I give money through the foundation, then every charity looks at me and says, could you do this? Could you do that? Could you give me this? Because it's essentially public. I don't consider the foundation to be a major part of my giving.

The relationship of the somewhat small Trump Foundation to his overall charitable giving, then, and what would happen after he died, came up in a 2004 interview[17]:

Q: Now that you've achieved so much, why not give it all away, as Bill Gates and David Geffen have done?

DT: *I do give millions of dollars a year, but I do it personally. I just write checks and give it away.*

Q: But the Donald J. Trump Foundation contributed only $287,000, according to its most recent report.

DT: I'm surprised it's even that high, because it's not what you'd call a living foundation. It's set up for after I … when it's no longer my time. The foundation will become very active at that point.

Mr. Trump has not yet been asked to provide a copy of his will to verify this statement, but he has been asked to provide lists and details of the millions he says he gives away every year outside of his small foundation. He has declined to do so and said why in his *Washington Post* interview.

Drew Harwell: You won't give one charity that you've given it to.

Donald Trump: No. Why should I tell you? Why would I want to do that?

Drew Harwell: Well, because we want to share the word of your good giving.

Donald Trump: *Oh, you're not going to share it because you're going to put— anything I do, you'll put a negative spin. I've given millions of dollars away and you make it sound like it's a negative thing and not a positive thing.*

To summarize: Mr. Trump has been verified to have donated millions of dollars to individual and charitable causes and says he has donated millions more. Those additional millions cannot be verified because Mr. Trump has not released his tax returns which would presumably list his charitable contributions. He also wishes to keep his contributions less public so that he is not further inundated with contribution requests. He also very clearly views the *Washington Post*'s expressed motivation for extensive details of his charitable giving as an excuse to make further unproven accusations like the football helmet and family contributions to St. Jude's discussed below, provide print space for other's disappointments in the amount of Mr. Trump's contributions, devote space to Trump critics' evaluations of Mr. Trump's presumed nefarious motives, and uncover more possible instances of "self-dealing" (the Trump painted portrait) noted below.

Trump has ample experience along these lines with his illegally leaked tax returns.

Trump's tax returns are as, or more complicated than, Bloomberg's, Gates' or any other billionaire. Some of Trumps' tax returns were leaked to the *New York Times*,[18] and they had a group of accountants who raised questions. Some of them talked about Trump's tax return "bordering on fraud."[19] It's now two years later and nothing further has been heard from the New York State Attorney General's Office that sued Trump's charity foundation about this purported "fraud."

Trump most likely did what his accountant said he could and should do. Yet if the analysis of his leaked tax returns by the *New York Times* are any indication, it is certain that a detailed examination of very complex tax and charity calculations would likely result in "experts" who see some transaction that might break the law or skirt it, and say they needed more data, and perhaps suggest testimony in front of a Congressional oversight committee.

Trump's Personal Foundation: Portraits, Flag Fines, and Football Helmets

Mr. Trump did use his personally named, relatively small foundation, funded with donations from others, to inappropriately buy one item (a painting of himself found in one of his hotels).

David Fahrenthold was able to locate this portrait which was hanging in one of Trump's properties by crowdsourcing a request to his readers to help him check on Trump's charitable giving. Fahrenthold raised another possible instance of self-dealing, but was unable to provide or point to evidence that Trump violated any law or charitable disbursement requirement.

Mr. Fahrenthold asserted that, "Donald Trump used money donated for charity to buy himself a Tim Tebow-signed football helmet."[20] If true, that would have been a second documented instance of inappropriate self-dealing. However what Fahrenthold presented as proven fact turned out on closer inspection to be presumption. His article begins by asking "Did Donald Trump violate IRS rules, by using a charity's money to buy himself a signed football helmet?" The text of the article answers: "The answer may depend on what became of the helmet and jersey. If they are still in Trump's possession—perhaps on display at one of his homes or properties—that might be deemed improper, if the IRS ever looks."

That's a lot of "mays" and "ifs" for which no evidentiary answers are provided. Eric Trump said he wasn't sure what had become of the helmet, but he doubted his father kept it. He said "Knowing him, he probably gave that helmet to a child. Sometimes the only way to support [a cause] is by buying an item at this event. You don't want that item!" Mr. Fahrenthold never provided any further evidence on this matter.

Another Trump charity story long on the public record concerns Mr. Trump using proceeds from the foundation to pay a fine after having been found guilty for having flown a too large American flag from his South Florida property. In fact, the city levied fines of $1250.00 a day and Mr. Trump sued the town for Palm Beach in Federal Court for 25 million dollars. An agreement, reached through an initiative suggested and supervised by the court, settled the matter. The settlement agreement was that the fine would be $100,000 and that Trump would satisfy this fine by donating that amount to a veteran's group, which he did. The payment of that fine came from Mr. Trump's named charity. As part of the agreement Mr. Trump was allowed to fly a larger sized flag from his property.

The *Washington Post* reports of this incident did not report that the settlement arrangement was a result of the court's initiative, or that the court reviewed and supervised that settlement, including the payment from Trump's charity. Instead, the *Post* article used that unsubstantiated claim as an example for Trump using his foundation as his own piggy bank.[21] That was misleading, at best.

The New York State Attorney General took the view that the Florida court's sanctioned Trump veterans' contribution violated NY State charity laws. Trump signed a consent order to settle that NY State suit alleging improprieties while not admitting or denying any violations of law.[22] The most significant breach mentioned in the stipulation of the New York lawsuit concerned the donation of a million dollars to a veteran's organization. That donation was made, but announced at a campaign rally which violated the state's administrative distribution rules for charities.

St. Jude's Foundation Charitable Bequests: Accusations of Criminality and Their Reality

Fahrenthold also raised the possibility of clearly criminal violations regarding the Trump family's charitable giving. This example concerns Eric Trump's substantial support for the St. Jude's Foundation that helps young cancer victims. In an interview with the *Washington Post*'s David Fahrenthold, Eric Trump said that his foundation paid "zero" for the use of his father's golf course, where the fundraisers were held. The direct implication was all the money taken in was given to St. Jude's, a major beneficiary of the charity.

A supposed "exposé" raised questions about this after examining records and finding a line item ($87,655) for payment to Trump's property for the use of the golf facility. The article not too subtly hinted that both Trumps were profiting from money that should have gone to help the children.[23] The title of the article—"How Donald Trump Shifted Kids-Cancer Charity Money Into His Business"[24] implied unethical and possibly criminal behavior.

Washington Post reporter David Fahrenthold, who had published a series of stories on Trump family charity donations and called Trump's charity giving a "façade" without documenting evidence, then "asked Eric Trump if he lied to him in an interview about whether Trump used his father's golf course for free as the location of a fundraiser for the Eric Trump Foundation."[25] After expressing outrage at the accusation, Eric Trump responded as follows[26]:

> the payment was actually to cover the cost of outside vendors: to rent a stage, to rent extra golf carts and to hire extra golf caddies. In the past, his foundation had cut separate checks to all these outside parties. In 2014, he said, they decided to have the golf course handle the administrative burden of paying all the outside vendors. Then his foundation wrote one check to reimburse the golf course.

8 THE UNEXPECTED TRUMP 275

This is a reasonable and legitimate explanation, which presumably satisfied Mr. Trump's accusers since no more was heard of this set of accusations. What of the exposé of the Trumps' using their donations to make money on renting out their properties? After raising a long string of questions premised on the assumption of wrongdoing, that piece concluded (bold in original, emphasis added):

> **THE ULTIMATE TRAGEDY HERE** is that the Eric Trump Foundation has done so much good. Yes, Eric has indulged in the family trait of vainglory, from Eric Trump bobblehead dolls at the tournament to statements that leave the impression he's giving the money personally, even though tax records suggest he's donated six figures total, at most. (Trump wouldn't tell Forbes how much he's given to his own foundation. "I think it's totally irrelevant," he says, citing the fact that "'he never charge" for use of the courses.) *But in 2015, a new intensive-care unit at St. Jude opened with Eric Trump's name on it, and the foundation's money has funded research into a rare form of cancer.* It's hard to imagine how the early incarnation of the golf tournament—big hauls, understandable costs—would have any problem continuing to spew out millions for years to come. Last year, the Eric Trump Foundation donated $2.9 million, according to St. Jude.

It is unclear given the content of the above paragraph, what the "ultimate tragedy" is, but it certainly seems unrelated to the "understandable costs" that the article mentions or the substantial amount of money the charity received. The accusation that the Trumps "Shifted Kids-Cancer Charity Money Into His Business," proved both ugly and baseless.

For detailing the limited nature of Mr. Trump's personal foundation, for finding out that other people beside Trump had contributed to his foundation, for being unable to gain from Mr. Trump information about his other charitable giving, for locating a painted portrait for Mr. Trump in one of his hotels through crowdsourcing, for raising allegations of self-dealing with a football helmet for which he was unable to provide any evidence that it violated tax law, for raising allegations of self-dealing with respect to Trump's veteran's contribution to settle a Florida court case without noting that this settlement was supervised and vetted by a competent court, for implying that Mr. Trump did not follow through fast enough in vetting the recipients of promised donations—implying that if the point had not been publicly raised, Mr. Trump would have reneged on his commitment, and for documenting that Mr. Trump and his staff sometimes gave differing figures on the amounts of Trump' charitable contributions, Mr. Fahrenthold received a Pulitzer Prize.[27]

Charity and President Trump

Is Mr. Trump personally and anonymously generous with individuals who have fallen on hard times? Yes. Has the Trump foundation contributed many verified millions to major charities? Yes. Has Mr. Trump contributed millions more outside of his own small family foundation? He and his children say yes, however there is no direct evidence on that question one way or another for the reasons noted above.

Does Mr. Trump embellish his charity contributions? No doubt. Does Mr. Trump seek to get substantial tax benefits from his contributions from his land donations to the state? Yes. Has the Trump foundation made administrative errors in how it has dispensed money to charities? Yes. Did Mr. Trump inappropriately have his foundation buy a picture of himself that he then used in one of his properties without making the necessary adjustments to his tax filings? Yes. Does the Trump foundation operate to fraudulently mislead charities and funnel money into Trump family pockets. No. There is no evidence of this whatsoever.

In short, Mr. Trump's charitable giving reflects the same complicated mix that characterizes his presidential leadership. It is a complex amalgam of genuine caring encased in protective shell and leavened by an unknown amount of hyperbole. Here again, in his and his family's substantial charitable giving as elsewhere, there is more to Mr. Trump than the accusations of his critics allow.

BEING THERE FOR OTHERS

True narcissists expect others to be there for them as needed, but care little about being there for others. Their concerns start and end with themselves. That is why these two examples, among others, hold some interest and importance.

The first example reaches far back into Trump's developmental history and was related by a childhood acquaintance with a family connection to the Trumps for a *PBS* Frontline Program entitled *The Choice 2016*.[28] The interview is with Sandy McIntosh, now a progressive Hillary partisan. He got to know Donald Trump more than half a century ago, when the two were schoolmates at the New York Military Academy. In his interview he says:

Mr. McIntosh decided to send his son to New York Military Academy and he knew Donald's father Fred. So, "Fred Trump asked Donald, or told Donald, to take care of me." I think his father said: "Look, just take care of this kid. Show him the ropes, and keep him out of trouble." I went up there, and during that first year—and Donald, I did see him. He was up in the, I think, the middle school or already in the upper school. I was in the lower school building. But we would meet occasionally. He would always ask how I was doing. Sometimes he'd give me good advice. I think throughout the whole time that we knew each other at military school, he was kind to me and attentive when I needed it, got me out of some jams. . . .

What were those jams? In the interview he reports several, the most dire of which was disobeying a direct public order from his commander Major Dobias to box and not use judo in a sparring exercise. As a punishment:

Dobias put on the gloves, and he got in the ring and said [to me]: "I'm going to teach you how to do it. I'm going to teach you how to take it and how to give it." And he got in there, and he punched me around, not hard, but more like the humiliating kind of taps and so on. This went on for several days, I think. I can't remember how long—to me, it seems like it went on for years, but I know it didn't.

Then:

one day I met Donald as I was walking across the campus, and he asked me how I was doing. I told him what had been going on, and he said, "Well, you'd like this to stop, right?" And I said, "Yes, I would very much like this to stop." And he said, "Well, I'll have a word with Dobias." Then several days later, the boxing stopped, and I was actually transferred from that building to the upper school main barracks.

Summing up, Sandy McIntosh said:

To me, I saw him as a considerate, fairly soft-spoken person when he was with me. I have to say that I think he followed that promise that he made to his father. Even [though] I wasn't such a little kid when he was graduating, but still he followed that promise to sort of take care of me like that, or make sure that I was OK.

Much later in Trump's life there is also the case of Robert Kraft, a lifelong Democrat, Obama supporter, and owner of the New England Patriots.[29] He recalled[30]:

> "In the toughest time in my life, he [Trump] was there for me," Kraft told "Fox & Friends" host Brian Kilmeade. "He came to the funeral with Melania. He'd visit me at my home. ... He called me once a week for a year. 'How are you doing?' I was really depressed, and he invited me to things, and *he looked out after me*." Few other people were as devoted as Trump during that period, Kraft added.

There is a real, softer, caring, empathetic side to Donald Trump. It is obviously at variance with his brash tough persona, which are also real. Therein lies one of the many real paradoxes of the real psychology of Donald Trump. Neither the narrow anti-Trump narratives or Trump's frequently combative or brash expressions of his psychology capture the real and complex human being at their core.

President Trump's Vision and Creativity

It is an obvious and well-documented fact that Mr. Trump is very ambitious. Yet, along with his outsized ambitions, Trump is also very creative. It's worth pausing a moment to consider the nature of creativity and its relationship to vision. Creativity is not usefully thought of as a set of insights that revolutionizes how we see the world or ourselves, like Einstein's theory of relativity or Freud's charting of our emotional lives. Creativity can and often does come in smaller doses.

One thing that creativity does require is the ability to see things from a different, unconventional angle, and that is where vision enters the equation. Adding a caveat here or a slight refinement there to a long existing paradigm is ordinary incrementalism, not creativity. Creativity consists in part of having the vision to see the potential for a new departure, and being able to act on that vision and bring it to fruition. Both are necessary. Vision devoid of result is just a dream.

During his Manhattan building career, Trump proved to be not only creative, but for a very practical man, a visionary. How else can you look at the New York skyline in 1975 and imagine its Trump-shaped version decades later? As one profile noted[31]:

Trump used his early seed money to buy up Manhattan real estate that, at the time, was thought to be worthless. He then hired ground-breaking architects to construct palaces of glass and steel *that transformed the New York skyline.*

Trump's business (and political career) contain both elements—vision and creativity—combined with a one step at a time mentality, a necessity in both building and politics. In his building projects, he pursued the plodding, step by step process of accumulating land parcels, financing, government agency permissions, weathering economic downturns and civic opposition to complete projects that others had wanted but failed to gain development rights. As noted, Trump can be impatient for results, but he also knows how to bide his time.

In one of his earliest major interviews in the *New York Times*, he was asked what attracts him to the real estate business and he replied[32]: "I love the architectural creativeness ... for example the Commodore Hotel is one of the most important locations in the city and its reconstruction will lead to a rebirth in that area." Trump's creative vision for the neighborhood proved correct.

Certainly, there were elements of self-promotion and self-interest in gaining access to that land parcel to redevelop. It was, however, Trump's vision of a major and luxurious redesign of the old hotel's "old structure with 2000 tiny cubicles that felt more like closets than rooms,"[33] with a dramatic and sweeping redesign that included four exterior walls of mirrors as its façade that won him the rights to develop that site. Trump's determined and contagious commitment to the creatively redesigned hotel to help lift that area out of its descent also helped win Trump the opportunity to put his plan into action. That vision was just not hype, but a real set of innovative ideas. In biographer Gwenda Blair's words, "Donald's first opportunity to display his glittering vision was a grand slam,"[34] a "resounding success," and a "remarkable triumph."

Negotiating with the Penn Central Railroad for the property, finding a partner with experience in hotel management (Jay Pritzker of Hyatt Hotels), gaining the needed financing, and overcoming the opposition of his father (Trump quotes him as saying "buying the Commodore at a time when even the Chrysler Building is in bankruptcy is like fighting for a seat on the Titanic") were only a few of the roadblocks Trump needed to overcome. He did so over the course of several years.[35]

Not every Trump vision was successful. His grand plans for "Television City" on the site of the old Penn Central Railroad yards on New York's upper west side that he obtained an option to build on with the same combination of vision and can-do spirit never reached fruition. Over decades of controversy, civic and government opposition, economic upturns and downturns, Trump City, as it came to be called, was a vastly different project when it was built than the grand one Trump had envisioned. In those decades, Trump was forced to sell his interests in return for a management fee and the use of his name.[36]

On the other hand, his signature building, Trump Towers, is fairly considered a triumph of sweeping vision, meticulously carried through. As Trump biographer and critic Timothy O'Brien writes, "Trump Tower was Donald's deal in almost every aspect, and he set it in motion independently from his father."[37] Indeed, Trump Tower was another Trump project built over the initial objections of his father and others. Trump resisted "Efforts by his architects and others to get him to incorporate more traditional forms in his structures …"[38] Trump recalls that he attempted to explain

> my vision to my father. I described the bold beautiful innovative glass and bronze exterior that would distinguish Trump Tower … he couldn't understand. Brick had always worked for him, why not for me?[39]

Trump deeply loved, respected and admired his father. Yet he was determined to be, and did become, his own man. He learned to stand apart from his father's wishes for him, good practice for his go-it-alone, if necessary, stance as president. To this core trait he added his ambition, vision, creativity, and determination, all of which became vehicles for building his own unique adult identity.

Trump once told Wayne Barnett, a strong Trump critic who interviewed him for fifteen hours and went on to write a muckraking exposé of his business dealings that, "I won't make a deal just to make a profit. It has to have flair."[40] Trump Towers reflected that flair, its vision, and esthetic. Nothing like it had ever been built before in New York City and nothing like has been able to be built since.

There were many Trump innovations in the design and construction of that building. There were the usual complex issues of assembling parcels, getting city approvals, seeking and getting air-rights and financing. Yet there was also innovation. Trump cast the building using concrete rather

8 THE UNEXPECTED TRUMP   281

than the traditional steel framing. That allowed Trump to alter the design of the building as it was being built. It also allowed a new floor to be built every two days, warp speed for building construction.[41]

All of these completed elements and the voluminous decisions that accompanied them were the preliminaries to the main event which was the nature and style of the building itself. Trump did not want just another forty-floor boxy skyscraper,[42] "I wanted the most magnificent, dazzling, and admired showplace in the world. Since this building was going to bear my name, it would represent me, so I wanted it to be exceptional ..."

In that same interview Trump said, "For me, a major joy of my business is being able to exercise my own vision and creativity to express myself. I do it by developing bigger, bolder, more beautiful projects; ventures that have imagination, style, scope, depth and scale ..."

Narcissistic? One could say that, but only in the most ordinary understanding of that term's meaning (see Chapter 6). The capacity to have a vision, to envision a possible reality, and being able to successfully act on it is, for many who have that experience, deeply satisfying. Doing so takes courage; life never guarantees success. To borrow a favorite Trump word, his ambitions are "huge." Were they "Grandiose"? It certainly was a large vision. Yet it was one that Trump carried through to completion, just as he did in redesigning the Commodore and helping rescue that decaying neighborhood. Grandiose carries with it the implication that the person has taken on much more than they can possible accomplish. That would not seem to be the case here.

The design of the Trump Tower was highly unusual and dramatic, a twenty-eight sided saw-tooth fifty-eight story design.[43] *New York Times* architecture critic Ada Louise Huxtable called it "a dramatically handsome structure."[44] If anything the building's interior dazzled as much if not more than its exterior. Of that decision Trump notes:

> My advisors suggested beautiful paintings in the lobby of Trump tower ... the idea seemed old fashion and unoriginal to me. So I decided to install a waterfall instead. The waterfall is over eighty feet high and cost 2 million to build. It's absolutely spectacular and mesmerizing to watch.

One New York builder is quoted on the spectacular waterfall as follows: "He deserves full credit for his success. He spent $1 million on the waterfall in Trump Tower. No one else would have done that. If the building fails everyone will say: 'Well sure, what jackass spends a million bucks on a waterfall'?"

The multi-floor atrium for commercial space was also Trump's idea.[45] So was the *breccia pernice* pink marble stone personally selected from Italian quarries.[46] Paul Goldberger, then a *New York Times* critic called the Trump Tower interior "warm, luxurious and even exhilarating."[47] Taken as a whole, the glass and bronze saw-tooth exterior and multi-floor atrium for high-end shopping, complete with cascading eighty-foot waterfall were both unique and esthetically striking. It was, and remains, a unique accomplishment.

Trump had arrived at the fulfillment of his dream that he could hardly believe he had accomplished. He confided in one interview[48]:

> Even to this day If you ask me what's my favorite deal, it's always going to be Trump Tower. Because it was sort of like: *What am I doing here. I have an office in Brooklyn. I am from Queens.*

The reason for noting this is that the actual nature of Trump's accomplishments are not given much attention. They are worth noting because those accomplishments, and what it took to achieve them, are the template for the ambitions of his presidency. Lastly, they are worth noting on the matter for good taste. Those are words not ordinarily associated with Trump especially given the nature of some of his Twitter comments and his opulent, often over the top branding style. There is a Trump esthetic and it is not only to be found in opulently framed Trump branding.

Financial Creativeness in Times of Economic Success and Collapse

Ordinary creativeness poses its own set of challenges to most people. Creativity in times of dire duress poses an even larger set. In one interview Trump notes that[49]:

> And I like the financial creativeness too. There's a beauty in putting together a financial package that really works whether it be through tax credits, or a mortgage financing arrangement, or a leaseback arrangement.

Individuals coming from academic or policy backgrounds may find this statement puzzling. Isn't obtaining financing a rather cut and dried matter of assembling bank loans? No, that is not the case, especially at Trump's level of building and financing. That much might be acknowledged, but creative?

Consider these few examples. In order to make the Commodore project work, Trump needed a major hotel partner to help him build and run it because he had no "track record" at that time. Hyatt was interested, but dissuaded by the costs of building in New York. Trump's solution was a tax abatement program for the project. However, the city had never before given one for the development of commercial property. Was pushing the new abatement self-interest on Trump's part? Yes, of course.

However, no one had ever thought to propose one to the city for the purpose of revitalizing an area and Trump was the one who argued it through over several years. Faced with the prospect of seeing this vital anchoring New York neighborhood continue to decline or invest in a major effort with Trump's plan to revitalize it,[50] the city provided the first ever tax abatement for commercial property to this Trump project—The Business Investment Incentive Policy. That innovation is now used routinely to help the city foster development, jobs, and income for the city. Then only Trump thought of doing it and brought it to fruition.

A second example comes from the period of Trump's severe financial difficulties in the 1990s. He had taken on a great deal of debt, some of which he had uncharacteristically personally guaranteed. Unable to make some payments due on his debts and a severe economic downturn, Trump was forced to scramble to remain economically afloat. As Trump put it[51]:

> The problems at the [Trump] Castle [one of his Atlantic City Casinos] could have triggered a series of defaults, forcing me into personal bankruptcy. There was no way Donald Trump was going personally bankrupt! I would talk about bankruptcy and I would use that possibility as a tool to negotiate, but I would never do it. That would end the game.

What "game"? The long-running ever evolving mostly successful, to date, Trump Show. Trump did leverage his indebtedness to survive. He accomplished that in dozens of meetings with his creditors by convincing them that he was worth more to them semi-solvent than personally bankrupt. One Citibank Trump creditor, Harvey Miller, noted:

it was discovered that he had all of these different projects with different banks, and that each bank syndicate had different collateral. And basically that's what saved Donald. It was spread out.[52]

Trump's grave economic circumstances became the creative key to saving both his business and his reputation. Trump made a huge bet, arguing to his creditors, "I can tie you guys up for years—in court proceedings, bankruptcy filings and other legal maneuvers … but I'm willing to do something else," and laid out his deal.[53] O'Brien, a Trump critic, writes of this period that, "As negotiations progressed bankers looked for every alternative they could find to [Trump's personal] bankruptcy because none of the banks wanted to contend with the mess that would ensue if the talks collapsed."[54]

It seems paradoxical to credit creativity in the context of a business disaster brought on in part by Trump's own decisions. Yet the fact remains, that many were in Trump's dire circumstances and were in a position to make the same "worth more solvent than bankrupt" pitch to their creditors, but didn't. One of the major players during that period, Chase Manhattan's Sanford Morhouse who worked with a lot of real estate developers who had similar problems said, "almost all of them at one point or another, filed for bankruptcy protection. And Donald, to his credit did not."[55]

Trump suffered more potential missed debt payments and banks extended his loans for several more years. He was forced to give up some of his trophies and toys, and he lost control of several properties including the prized West Side Railroad yards that he had obtained options to develop years before, and the Plaza Hotel. A limit was placed on his personal spending.

Trump wrote that he hated having to go to his bankers "hat in hand" as he put it.[56] He further wrote that "I took tremendous punishment as I watched my empire collapse around me." That much certainly rings true. Fighting for your economic life while you watch the accomplishments you proudly built begin to slip away was profoundly sobering. President Trump has, in the last few months of his first presidential term has become reacquainted with catastrophic loss as the economic effect of the response to the Coronavirus pandemic has devastated the economic record that he had so assiduously built.

Recall that when Trump was thirty-eight he thought, "it was all going to last forever." Nothing does of course. Yet it was for Trump an unexpected and brutal lesson. He is now confronted with it again.

Trump was able to absorb and weather a tremendous amount of punishment. While doing so, he was able to persevere, fight back, and even rebuild what had been lost in a new and creative way (branding). In so doing, he was forced to both develop and rely on capacities that had not been evident in his prior more successful period. Those experiences and traits doubtless proved helpful in weathering the onslaughts of the Mueller investigation, the House impeachment inquiry, the opposition's offensive against his presidency, and monumental task of leading the country and his presidency back from the effects of the pandemic, the convulsive national demonstrations that followed the death of George Floyd, and the national demonstrations that followed that spilled into violence in a number of circumstances.

Writing before his fall, Trump wrote in *The Art of the Deal*[57]:

> I don't kid myself. Life is very fragile, and success doesn't change that. If anything success makes it more fragile. Anything can change without warning …

Trump had no idea when he wrote those words how right he was.

Trump also wrote, looking back on that period[58]:

> I consider the early part of the 1990s to be my most brilliant period. This is the time when my abilities showed the greatest in that I was under tremendous pressure to perform in an economy that had totally collapsed.

Much of that statement is pure Trump. Yet before dismissing its obvious hyperbole, it's useful to more closely examine the elements of truth it contains. Trump was in the process of going from "can do no wrong" to "can't do anything right." He was on his way to becoming a "has been" at the age of forty-four, right in the middle of his "mid-life." Had he gone personally bankrupt, he would have lost almost everything and never been able to create the circumstances that allowed him to rebuild his empire.

Trump's decision to place a bankruptcy bet with his creditors was an innovative foreshadowing insight. To step forward and do so quickly was also a decisive "look facts in the eye and do something about them" act.

It was an act in the service of endurance and resilience, pain now and pain later, for the chance to emerge to build again. Again, creativity would not have been successful without the ability to carry it through. The ability to doggedly carry on without much of a plan would have brought final failure. Trump's creative, painful strategy allowed him to accurately claim that he had fought back from dire economic circumstances, a story of grit and determination. That too became part of the Trump's oeuvre and persona.

Trump's successful strategy required him to continue "hat in hand" for many years. His determined effort to rebuild what he had lost in many small unheralded steps was a substantial economic accomplishment, but also a substantial personal and psychological one. Finding a way to successfully rebuild using the innovation of Trump branding was another creative accomplishment worth carefully considering when assessing Trump's approach to the presidency and his chances for success.

PRESIDENT TRUMP'S OPERATING METRIC IN LIFE, BUSINESS, AND POLITICS: THINK BIG

Trump's operative mantra for his ambition, whether a building project or a political initiative, is "think big." In an interview with Trump's daughter, Ivanka, there was the following exchange:

> *Q*: But what is the secret. What was the common denominator? What principle did he apply to all these ventures? To building, to television entertainment, to politics?
>
> *Ivanka Trump Kushner*: There is one principle going back to my childhood, something that he would always tell us … it's no secret really. He would say, "if you're going to be thinking anyway, think big." It was his approach in business, entertainment, and finally politics. He would swing for the fences. He wouldn't try for a single, He would try for a home run.

One might usefully add here not just any kind of home run. Trump was an excellent baseball player in high school and the *Washington Post* noted that, "By sixth grade, Donald's power as a right-handed hitter was enough that fielders shifted to left field when he batted. 'If he had hit the ball to right, he could've had a home run because no one was there,' said Nicholas Kass, a schoolmate. 'But he always wanted to hit the ball through people. He wanted to overpower them.'"

Translation: Trump could have notched up many more home runs and a better record if he had done the easier thing. Isn't that what a budding adolescent "malignant narcissist" would do to gain more bragging rights? Perhaps, but that's not what Trump did. He swung, directly, for the fences, a style much in evidence in his business and political life.

The evidence of the importance of these Trump statements and taking them seriously is not that Trump made them, that his daughter confirmed them, or that there is evidence of their existence early in his developmental history. The reality of all three certainly adds to our confidence in the observation. However, the clear fact is that Trump acted on those views in all his business efforts (the Commodore Hotel, Trump Tower, "Television City"), and in seeking the presidency as his first office, politics as well.

He is also acting on this presidential leadership premise in his presidency: revising trade deals, trying to renegotiate a new Iran agreement, bringing North Korea to the real negotiating table, trying to reach a real settlement of America's longest running war in Afghanistan,[59] and trying to forge a new Arab-Israeli agreement among other things. It is unlikely that all, or perhaps even most of these efforts will be successful. Yet, all are truly consistent with the go-big foundations of his ambitions, personal and presidential.

How Trump Approaches the Presidency: Innovation, Determination, and Ambition

It is now clear in retrospect that Trump won the Republican nomination and the general election by being both unconventional and creative. Yet, he also won both not only by *thinking differently* but also by *being different*. He has governed, much as he campaigned, by again doing both.

It is important therefore to clarify the differences between being unconventional and creative, being able to and acting differently as a president, and the implications of both for the *Politics of American Restoration*, Trump's policy ambitions.

The conventional understanding of Trump's victory was that he leveraged millions of dollars of free publicity to win. He was also credited with running a shoestring but nimble campaign. He is now also credited with successfully targeting key electoral college states.

The Real Nature of Trump's Political Creativity

Everything above is true. However, the nature of Trump's real innovations in his nomination campaign, general election victory, and chances for presidential success lie elsewhere. Among the most obvious non-traditional and creative parts of Trump's nomination strategy was to focus on the large gap between the establishment and ordinary Americans. He did this by leveraging the debates to highlight his policy differences with establishment narratives, a stance that also underlies the unconventional and creative dimensions of his presidential leadership.

Trump was also unconventional and creative in taking the fight directly to his opponents in a personal way, a stance that he also carried into his presidential leadership. In doing so, he underscored the fact through repeated demonstrations that he was and would be a different kind of Republican and president. He would not mince words. He would not allow attacks to go unanswered. He would not give voice to the usual policy platitudes. In doing all this he presented himself as a breath of fresh political air as well as a cleansing whirlwind. One by one his competitors faltered. However, his real audience was not the establishment but ordinary people, and they could not help but notice what was so entirely evident.

What was unconventional and creative about Trump's stance and leadership style? Certainly the fact that it was unprecedented made it unconventional. Yet, there was more to it than that. The creativity of Trump's candidacy was reflected in his recognition that a new kind of Republican and presidential leadership was not only needed but possible. Indeed it was longed for by substantial segments of the American public. They were amenable and responded to a candidacy that was more authentic, confrontational, and uninhibited, that was focused on getting things done, even if the style of doing so strayed very far from conventions of presidential propriety. In short, they were amenable to a man very much like Trump himself.

What was so creative about Trump's stances in his eight policy pillars? Others had criticized operating policies in one area or another, say the Iranian nuclear deal or immigration policy. What was unique about Trump was that he challenged the whole array of establishment policies, and did so not by offering incremental tweaks, but by challenging their basic premises. Trump did so by asking basic questions about the foundations of establishment assumptions.

8 THE UNEXPECTED TRUMP 289

Was it really possible to have a sovereign country without effective border and immigration controls? Was "free trade" mostly a "win-win" situation without substantial downside? Had the world, including the United States, substantially changed since the end of the Cold War, requiring a new look at old strategic assumptions and relationships with allies and competitors alike? Was low economic growth really the "new normal," and what if anything could be done about it? In these and every other area of the "eight policy pillars," Trump promised and provided fresh, if not always fully informed thinking.

Trump's Leadership Style: Meaning It

Trump said he would act on his campaign promises as president, and did. Recognize that Israel's capital was Jerusalem? Check. Focus on jobs (starting before he assumed office)? Check. Withdraw from the international climate accords? Check. Withdraw from the Iranian nuclear agreement? Check. Reduce regulations? Check? Enforce American immigration laws? Check. And so on.

No representation is being made here that all of these Trump initiatives (an additional list of items is found in Chapter 9), and his others will be successful or are preferable. Most Trump policies are not fully in place. Many of them are in transition from what they were pre-Trump to what they might become if Trump is successful in his presidential efforts and ambitions.

To note three examples among many: Acting Commissioner of US Customs and Border Protection Mark Morgan gave a lengthy press conference on the virtual end of catch and release at the Southern border, a success many months in the making.[60] It is still a large distance from that to the comprehensive skill based immigration program that Trump would like to put in place. So too, Trump has made substantial progress in getting NATO allies to shoulder more of their financial responsibility for the alliance, a success many years in the making.[61] Yet, the reorientation of NATO's core purposes in a post-Soviet Union world is still a work in progress. Finally, the long arduous road to a trade agreement and new economic relationship with China has successfully concluded Phase 1. Yet there is still substantial and hard bargaining ahead for both powers to further build on that accomplishment, which has been affected by questions regarding China's role in the Coronavirus pandemic.

The point of listing these efforts is to underscore both their range and uniqueness. Trump asks big, basic and long-unasked questions about a range of American policies. That is obviously "unconventional," but it is also creative. Why creative? Because in order to be authentically unconventional you have to be able to stand outside of and apart from conventional thinking. In Trump's particular case, this not only means doing so in one area but in the "eight policy pillars" we have noted.

It is central to his presidency is that Trump's creative rethinking of policy premises is accompanied by a determination to act on these understandings. That brings us back to Trump's leadership style. He has governed as he campaigned, giving substantial, but not absolute, free reign to his signature psychological and stylistic elements. Those include authenticity, being who he is and not being afraid to be seen that way. It also means being at ease with confrontation and standing apart, and a focus on "getting things done."

His supporters love this style. It is exactly what they had hoped for in giving Trump their votes. Those less fully in Trump's corner appreciate much of what he has done. They also recognize, if reluctantly, that Trump's unusual leadership style has something to do with that. They are torn between the wish that Trump would act more "normally" presidential, and the recognition that he would not be able to get as far as he's gotten had he done so.

A *Washington Post* reporter examining why Trump won wrote: "Trump, to his immense credit, understood that a) flouting the rules actually endeared him to a big swath of voters and b) there just might not be any real rules at all."[62] Matt Taibbi, no fan of Trump, notes, "Trump had said things that were true and that no other Republican would dare to say."[63] The opposition of course abhors all things Trump, including but certainly not limited to his presidential demeanor.

All three of these groups—supporters, latent supporters, and the opposition, make an understandable error. They do not err in taking Trump as he has repeatedly demonstrated himself to be as a candidate and president. That much is evident and true. Rather they err in assuming that what they see, as powerful as its impact is, is all there is to Trump's psychology. Trump is, surprisingly, given his well-deserved reputation for brashness, confrontation, and bull in the China shop presidential temperament, occasionally a thoughtful reflective man.

TRUMP REFLECTIVE?

Reflective is not a word typically associated with Trump. Quite the opposite. As noted, he is more often presumed to be impulsive, reflection's negation. Trump has said he was "not a believer" in therapy, whose purpose is (guided) reflection because in part he "Doesn't have time for it."[64] Elsewhere Trump is reported to have said he would be afraid of what he might find,[65] although as the examples below suggest he can be reflective.

The conventional wisdom is that Mr. Trump's capacity for thoughtful reflection is minimal. He is, among other ascribed failures, criticized for "having a achieved the ultimate luxury, an existence unmolested by the rumblings of a soul."[66] He is also routinely said to be thoughtless, cruel, and impulsive among many other traits that are antithetical to self-reflections on the meaning of (his) experience and life.

Even when Trump is clearly being reflective, that fact does not resister. One biographer and anti-Trump pundit[67] reports that Trump asked reflectively in an interview of his own life: "What does it mean?"[68] However, then according to the biographer "The reflection lasted but a moment and then Trump was on to another topic." The point was written to convey that Trump had a momentary flash of self-reflection, which he couldn't sustain because he's really uninterested or incapable.

The trouble with D'Angelo's characterization is evident when the article from which it is drawn is actually examined.[69] After Trump asked the question about his life's meaning, the article goes on to quote him for 260 more words and his concerns about a possible nuclear holocaust—an issue that his uncle, a MIT professor impressed upon him. That discussion clearly lasted more than "but a moment."

Ironically, this biographer exhibits the exact same behavior that he erroneously accuses Mr. Trump of exhibiting. He writes that Mr. Trump responds to questions about his life and what he has done by "invariably, he looks for ways to turn the conversation to the theme of his triumphs." D'Angelo then adds in a momentary flash of his own self-insight: "In fairness our conversation is about *him*."[70] However, the biographer then inserts a comma and continues on with his meme, "but it's hard to escape noticing that even as he notes a genuine success, he [Trump] can't resist exaggerating."

A closer examination of Trump's interviews over the years presents a decidedly different picture. Trump is not by nature introspective, but he has reflected on the meaning of his life, his accomplishments, and the inevitability of death. Asked about his death in a 1990 interview when he was forty-four, Trump responded: "No I'm fatalistic and I protect myself as well as anybody can prepare for things. But ultimately we all end up going to hopefully greener pastures."[71] In a 2004 interview at age fifty-eight, he reflected that, "I know life is fragile."[72] Recall that, as noted above, at thirty-eight Trump reflected that "I though it would last forever."

In another, 2010 interview at age sixty-four, he was asked whether he was still "driven." He replied, "I am highly driven and, at the same time, I sometimes wonder why. What's the purpose? You kick the bucket, your kids take over ... who knows what happens." Later in that interview he was asked whether he was afraid of anything and replied, "I guess you can always say yes but I like to think no. We are here, get a short period of time, a spec, and then we go."

Does Trump spend hours ruminating about the meaning of his life and its purpose? No, but it is on his mind, and he's clearly thought about it. Moreover, he's had close up experiences with death. There was his brother's death due to alcohol induced heart failure after a long decline (when Donald was thirty-five), the sudden death of his three closest business executives in a helicopter crash (when Trump was forty-three), and later in life his father (at age fifty-three) and mother (at age fifty-four).

There is as well his long experience with economic death—his own in the 1990s. In a 2004 interview he reflected back on his brush with bankruptcy and said,[73] "The hardest I've ever worked in my life was the period from 1990 to 1994 ... I wouldn't want to do it again, *but I learned that the world can change on the head of a dime*, and that keeps things in perspective."

In that same interview when he was asked about his wealth and its effect on his then young kids, he replied:

> My kids are extremely well adjusted. But I wonder what they think when they walk into Mar-a-Lago and see ceilings that rise to heights that nobody's ever seen before. And when my daughter's date picks her up at Trump Tower in a few years and sees the living room, how will he feel when he takes her out and tries to impress her with a studio apartment?

Asked in an interview that was part of a 2005 book (when Trump was fifty-nine) if, "Trump didn't exist, would we have to invent him," he replied, "No. The world would get along just fine ... you see people that are very important—they go and the world continues to get along."[74]

When asked whether he thought his buildings would still be there in a hundred years, he replied, "No, I don't think so."[75] He was right about his building not lasting a hundred years. The Grand Hyatt, one of Trump's original hotel creations when he first arrived in New York is scheduled to be torn down for a new mixed-use tower.[76]

These are hardly the thoughts of a supposed "malignant narcissist." There is clearly much more depth to Mr. Trump than the caricature his opponents present. Trump's temperament is geared toward accomplishment in the world. Yet, as the above quotes from many different periods of his life make clear, he does reflect on life's deeper meanings including that of his own life—and the circumstances he observes as he goes through it.

One of Trump's most interesting, nuanced, and reflective responses came when he was asked about the killing of a seventeen-year-old male gorilla that grabbed and dragged a three-year-old boy who fell into the moat in the gorilla enclosure at the Cincinnati Zoo. The gorilla, named Harambe, at times seemed to be protecting the boy and at other times dragged him around the enclosure. The zoo ultimately decided to shoot the gorilla to save the boy, a decision that has spurred a backlash from animal rights activists. Trump was asked whether the gorilla should have been killed, and replied[77]:

I think it's a very tough call. It was amazing because there were moments with the gorilla—the way he held that child—it was almost like a mother holding a baby—looked so beautiful and calm. And there were moments where it looked pretty dangerous. I don't think they had a choice. I mean, probably they didn't have a choice. You have a child—a young child who is at stake—and, you know—it's too bad there wasn't another way. I thought it was so beautiful to watch that you know powerful, almost 500-pound gorilla, the way he dealt with that little boy. But it just takes one second— one second.. It just takes one little flick of his finger. And I will tell you they probably had no choice.

There is clearly much more depth to Mr. Trump than the caricature his opponents present.

And finally there is the rather ordinary fluff interview of Mr. Trump showcased by *TMZ* and *Fox News*. Mr. Trump is being asked about his lavish style of living and how it was to grow up in Queens. He replies, speaking of his Queens childhood (emphasis added):

> *Trump*: I view it so differently. ... And now, when I go there it seems very quaint. ....
> *Harvey Levin, Interviewer*: You don't seem like a quaint guy.
> *Trump*: Well, you know, maybe I'm more quaint than you would think. *Sometimes when I'm on my way out to wherever I may be going, I'll stop because it's an exit, right?—Utopia Parkway. I'll get off the exit, and I'll stop and take a look at my house where I grew up with my parents and brothers and sisters. And you know, I had a good early life.*

This is a rosebud moment of reflective reverie. It seems that this world-famous, brash, rich, powerful business titan takes the time to physically return to his childhood home and no doubt allow the memories that are housed there to wash over him and be remembered. These are no doubt poignant moments for Mr. Trump as they would be for anyone who undertakes such an emotional and historical journey.

These are surprising and emotionally laden trips for a man who is said to be so "malignantly narcissistic" that he lacks the psychological depth to reflect.

NOTES

1. Cf., Newt Gingrich. 2020. *Trump and the American Future: Solving the Great Problems of Our Time.* New York: Center Street.
2. Doug Weed. 2019. *Inside the Trump White House: The Real Story of His Presidency.* New York: Center Street.
3. Anonymous. 2019. *A Warning.* New York: Twelve Books.
4. Michael Wolf. 2018. *Fire and Fury: Inside the Trump White House.* New York: Henry Holt.
5. Jerrold M. Post and Stephanie Doucette. 2019. *Dangerous Charisma: The Political Psychology of Trump and His Followers.* New York: Pegasus, pp. 3–7.
6. Glenn Plaskin. 1988. "Trump: 'The people's Billionaire'," *Chicago Tribune*, March 12.
7. The White House: Office of the Press Secretary. 2017. "Remarks by President Trump and His Majesty King Abdullah II of Jordan in Joint Press Conference," *Rose Garden*, April 5.
8. *Washington Post.* 2016. https://www.washingtonpost.com/wp-stat/graphics/politics/trump-archive/docs/donald-trump-interview-may-13-2016-with-oharrow-harwell-boburg.pdf.
9. Ivanka Trump quoted in Callum Borchers. 2017. "Patriots Owner on Trump: 'In the Toughest Time in My Life, He Was There for Me'," *Washington Post*, February 3.

8 THE UNEXPECTED TRUMP   295

10. Michael D'Antonio. 2015. "Donald Trump's Long Publicity Con," *Daily Beast*, November 28.
11. William E. Geist 1984. "The Expanding Empire of Donald Trump," *New York Times Magazine*, April 8.
12. Trump quoted in D'Antonio 2015, p. 264.
13. James Holcomb. 2017. "President Trump Gives $10,000 to Campaign Volunteer for His Father's Chemo," *Washington Post*, January 24; see also Justin Jouvenal. 2017. "In Donated Shoes and Suit, a Trump Supporter Comes to Washington," *Washington Post*, January 18.
14. William E. Geist 1984. "The Expanding Empire of Donald Trump," *New York Times Magazine*, April 8.
15. FOLLOW-UP ON THE NEWS 1987. "Surviving Tragedy on the Farm," *New York Times*, August 2.
16. David A. Fahrenthold. 2016. "Trump Boasts About His Philanthropy. But His Giving Falls Short of His Words," *Washington Post*, October 29.
17. David Hochman. 2015. "Playboy Interview: Donald Trump (2004)," *Playboy*, July 19, emphasis added.
18. David Barstow and Susanne Craig. 2019. "Decade in the Red: Trump Tax Figures Show Over $1 Billion in Business Losses," *New York Times*, May 8.
19. David Barstow, Susanne Craig, and Russ Buettner. 2018. "Trump Engaged in Suspect Tax Schemes as He Reaped Riches from His Father," *New York Times*, October 2.
20. David A. Fahrenhold. 2016. "Donald Trump Used Money Donated for Charity to Buy Himself a Tim Tebow-signed Football Helmet," *Washington Post*, July 1.
21. Frank Cerabino. 2015. "Trump's War with Palm Beach," *Politico*, September 5; see also Sally Apgar. 2007. "Trump Reaches Truce Over Flag at Huge Florida Home," *South Florida Sun-Sentinel*, April 27.
22. Supreme Court of the State of New York. 2018. "So Ordered Stipulation of Final Settlement." Index 451130/2018.
23. Dona Alexander. 2017. "How Donald Trump Shifted Kids-Cancer Charity Money Into His Business," *Forbes*, June 29.
24. The actual story opens a window into a complex number of issues including separating out the costs of different events held in the same venue, the actual legitimate costs associated with a venue's use, various quoted estimates of what they *should* cost, and the fact that Eric Trump's philanthropy branched out and contributed money to other legitimate charitable institutions. As seems obligatory in such stories a great deal of time is spent with various criticisms of Donald Trump's charitable giving.
25. Leagh DePiero. 2017. "*Washington Post* Journalist Asks Eric Trump If He Lied to Him in 2016 Interview," *Washington Examiner*, June 6.

26. Eric Trump quoted in David A. Fahrenthold. 2016. "Eric Trump: My Father Gives Millions to Charity But I won't Say More," *Washington Post*, July 6.
27. Paul Farhi. 2017. "*Washington Post*'s David Fahrenthold Wins Pulitzer Prize for Dogged Reporting of Trump's Philanthropy," *Washington Post*, April 10.
28. Jason M. Breslow. 2016. "The FRONTLINE Interview: Sandy McIntosh," *PBS*, September 27.
29. I am indebted to one of the three anonymous reviewers of this manuscript for bringing this example to my attention.
30. Robert Kraft quoted in Borchers 2017, emphasis added; see also Cork Gains. 2018. "After Robert Kraft's Wife Died, Trump Called Every Week for a Year to Console Him," *AOL*, February 1.
31. Tim Stanley. 2016. "Introducing the Real Donald Trump: A Careful Plotter and Media Master Who Is Far More Intelligent Than He Seems," *The Telegraph*, July 18, emphasis added.
32. Judy Klemesrud. 1996. "Donald Trump, Real Estate Promoter, Builds Image as He Builds Buildings," *New York Times*, November 1.
33. Gwenda Blair. 2000. *The Trumps: Three Generations That Built an Empire*. New York: Simon & Schuster, p. 63.
34. Blair 2000, pp. 74, 85.
35. Donald Trump [with Meredith McIver]. 2008. *Trump: The Art of the Comeback*. New York: Times Books, pp. 62–67.
36. Michael Kruse 2018. "The Lost City of Trump," Politico, July/August.
37. Timothy L. O'Brien. 2005. *TrumpNation: The Art of Being The Donald*. New York: Business Plus, p. 68.
38. Jerome Tuccille. 1985. *Trump: The Saga of America's Most Powerful Real Estate Baron*. New York: Donald I. Fine, p. 175.
39. Donald J. Trump [with Meredith McIver]. 2007. *Trump 101: The Way to Success*. New York: Wiley, p. 6.
40. Wayne Barnett. 1979. "Like Father, Like Son: Anatomy of a Young Power Broker," *Village Voice*, January 15.
41. O'Brien 2005, pp. 68–71.
42. Trump (with Meredith McIver) 2007. *Trump 101: The Way to Success*. New York: Wiley, p. 7.
43. Donald J. Trump (with Tony Schwartz). 1987. *Trump: The Art of the Deal*. New York: Random House, pp. 166–167.
44. Huxtable quoted in William E. Geist 1984. "The Expanding Empire of Donald Trump," *New York Times Magazine*, April 8.
45. Trump (with Schwartz) 2005, p. 165.
46. Jerome Tuccille 1985, p. 181.
47. Goldberger quoted in William E. Geist 1984. "The Expanding Empire of Donald Trump," *New York Times Magazine*, April 8.

48. Trump quoted in O'Brien 2005, pp. 73–74.
49. Judy Klemesrud. 1976. "Donald Trump, Real Estate Promoter, Builds Image as He Builds Buildings," *New York Times*, November 1.
50. A good overview of the deal Trump was able to achieve is found in Tuccille 1985, pp. 106–108.
51. Donald J. Trump [with Kate Bohner]. 1977. *The Art of the Comeback*. New York: Times Books, p. 12.
52. Miller quoted in O'Brien 2005, p. 162.
53. What Trump offered his creditors is detailed in Trump (with Bohner) 1977, pp. 16–17.
54. O'Brien 2005, p. 162.
55. O'Brien 2005, p. 164.
56. Trump (with Kate Bohner) 1997, *The Art of the Comeback*. New York: Times Books, p. 13.
57. Trump (with Schwartz) 2005, p. 63.
58. Trump [with Bohner] 1997, p. 198.
59. Jessica Donati and Catherine Lucey. 2020. "Trump Says 'Good Chance' of Deal with Taliban," *Wall Street Journal*, February 13.
60. Press Briefing. 2019. "Press Briefing by Acting CBP Commissioner Mark Morgan," The White House, November 14; see also Camilo Montoya-Galvez. 2019. "'Remain Home:' Trump Officials Say Policies Responsible for Sharp Drop in Border Apprehensions," *CBS News*, September 9.
61. Lorne Cook. 2019. "NATO Seeks to Head off Budget Dispute, Saying Spending Is Rising," *Associated Press*, November 29.
62. Chris Cillizza. 2016. "Trump Has Completely Upended the Political Game. We Need to Adjust Accordingly," *Washington Post*, December 11.
63. Matt Taibbi. 2016. "How America Made Donald Trump Unstoppable," *Rolling Stone*, February 24.
64. Trump quoted in O'Brien 2005, p. 191.
65. Trump quoted in Mark Singer. 2016. *Trump & Me*. New York: Penguin, p. 107.
66. Singer 2016, p. 86.
67. "I really think that he is this horrible creature, and he has no regard for anything but himself, and he's willing to go to lengths we've never seen before in order to satisfy his ego." D'Antonio quoted in Susan B. Glasser and Michael Kruse. 2016. "'I Think He's a Very Dangerous Man for the Next Three or Four Weeks'," *Politico*, October 12.
68. Michael D'Antonio 2019. *Never Enough: Donald Trump and the Pursuit of Success*. New York: Thomas Dunne/St. Martin's Press, pp. 151–152.
69. William E. Geist 1984. "The Expanding Empire of Donald Trump," *New York Times Magazine*, April 8.

70. D'Antonio 2019, p. 341, emphasis in original.
71. Trump quoted in Plaskin 1988.
72. David Hochman. 2015. "Playboy Interview: Donald Trump (2004)," *Playboy*, July 19.
73. Ibid., emphasis added.
74. Trump quoted in O'Brien 2005, p. 209.
75. Trump quoted in Hochman 2015.
76. Josh Barbanel. 2019. "New York's Grand Hyatt Hotel to Be Torn Down," *Wall Street Journal*, February 7.
77. Trump quoted in CBS. 2016. "Donald Trump Weighs in on Killing of Gorilla at Cincinnati Zoo," *CBS News*, June.

PART IV

The Trump Presidency in Practice

CHAPTER 9

Prelude to a Unique Presidency: Preparation, Expectations, and Judgment

The paradox and the challenge of analyzing President Trump is that he must do many of the things that every modern president must do. However, he does almost all of them in his own unique way. One consequence of this fact is that conventional models of presidential behavior, and the literature surrounding it, offer only limited insight into how Trump approaches his presidential responsibilities, and their resulting consequences. Analyses of Trump's presidency therefore would be advantaged by putting aside several major tradition-based expectations.

This is not a suggestion that Trump be excused from evaluations of his leadership. Mr. Trump, like any president, must be able to successfully carry out his responsibilities to "preserve and protect" and help Americans to prosper. He will obviously try to do so within the boundaries of his own vision of presidential leadership. That too will need to be assessed.

That said, analysts need to approach Trump's leadership style with an open mind. The real basic question of the Trump presidency is not how much it deviates from past practices, but what, exactly that entails, how well it accomplishes his purposes, and whether those purposes are in some very basic and accountable way, successful. Presidential leadership is an extremely robust activity. It is able to encompass presidents as diverse as George Washington, Abraham Lincoln, Rutherford B. Hayes, Warren G. Harding, Grover Cleveland, Lyndon Johnson, and others including now Donald J. Trump.

© The Author(s) 2020
S. Renshon, *The Real Psychology of the Trump Presidency*,
The Evolving American Presidency,
https://doi.org/10.1007/978-3-030-45391-6_9

American presidents and their circumstances have all of course, been more or less unique, and each presidency has reflected a particular mix. Donald Trump's does too. Yet he is also a truly unique president facing domestic and international circumstances whose nature has been in flux for several presidencies, and an unprecedented modern day pandemic. It is unclear whether the Trump presidency is helping to bring some of these circumstances to the fore, or whether they were reaching fruition as Trump assumed office. Either way, it is an extremely consequential period, domestically and internationally, in which to be president.

Trump's Unique CEO Experience: Prelude to an Unorthodox Presidency

It is true conventional wisdom that the presidency is a unique office. As a result, every president, including Trump, only begins to truly understand the nature of the office once he is in it. Still, presidential scholars continue to believe that certain kinds of prior experiences are helpful. Among them are past experience in formal political roles: Senator (Barack Obama), Governor (George W. Bush), Vice President (George H. W. Bush), Congressman (Andrew Jackson), or senior level military experience (Dwight D. Eisenhower). Many American presidents have had experience in both the private and public sectors over their careers. The common denominator here is political, business, and executive experience that results in familiarity with a wide swath of political, cultural, and economic life. These experiences allow potential presidents to gain some familiarity with balancing competing interests and views, and getting things done in a "political" setting.

Donald Trump represents a unique set of prior experiences for a president. He is not only a "businessman." He was the chief operating owner of a vast business empire that spanned the globe for over four decades. He has been at the center of every one of its thousands of ventures, at every stage of their development. The company under his direction has had many substantial successes, a number of projects that didn't reach fruition or live up to expectations, and in the 1990s a near business economic death that Trump eventually surmounted.

Trump's life is not a narrative of having advanced step by step through either a political or military hierarchy. Indeed his work history is more usefully seen as the free-wheeling, often creative, sometimes self-indulgent singular expressions of his ambition, drive, resilience, and unusual "out of the box" thinking. It is exactly that set of characteristics that makes Trump's transition from CEO to president worth examining in more than generic CEO terms.

Trump's experience as CEO of the Trump Organization has been viewed in part through his own highly varnished view of it in a series of Trump "How to" books,[1] myriad interviews in which he repeats his official version of his business history, and partisan attacks that he owes any success to his father's money, allegations of illegal and barely legal political ploys,[2] and shady if not shoddy personal behavior. As this analysis has attempted to make clear, there is both more and less than meets the eye to many observations about Trump, and in this area too, the need for fair factual analysis remains.

Trump's View of the Implications of His Business Experience for His Presidency

Mr. Trump's own view of how his business experience would be helpful in having a successful presidency is twofold. The first is that he is "not a politician [and] I have worked in business, creating jobs and rebuilding neighborhoods my entire adult life."[3] The implication is that the lack of a robust political resume may be a hindrance, but that he had the knowledge and experience to do that again as president. The evidence to date, before the pandemic, seemed to support that claim.[4]

The second premise had to do with Mr. Trump's branding of his own success and his assertion that the skills that led to it in business would carry over into his presidency. The question raised by this claim is: what are those skills? Mr. Trump's "successes" in business were real, but mixed,[5] as would be true for anyone building a vast empire. Some Trump initiatives didn't work out and his presidency would predictably be no different in that respect.

Mr. Trump's business successes reflected hard earned knowledge of the arenas in which he competed, for example, real estate and construction. He also had detailed knowledge of the specific circumstances, Clifford Gertz's "local knowledge,"[6] in which he operated. He knew the motivations and nature of the people he dealt with, what they wanted, what they needed, and what it would take to reach a deal.

As a political novice starting his learning curve in the presidency, he had little such knowledge either about national politics or governing. He didn't know the vast numbers of political players and stakeholders and their very specific legislative and political interests, with which he had to deal as president. He had no experience dealing with the slow incremental timing of the legislative process,[7] and even less experience with sustained, powerful, and united partisan opposition. He also had no real experience with the complex reality of trying to forge an effective set of domestic and foreign policies.

This experience and knowledge deficit understandably led Trump to make novice mistakes, the flawed roll out of travel restrictions on nationals of several counties with substantial terrorism problems being only the most visible. It is safe to say that Trump, like every president, has learned more of the office's powers and limitations as he has tried to both lead and govern.

Trump as CEO and President: Transferable Experience or Political Dead End?

Some think Trump's business career is irrelevant and even counter-productive to being an effective president. *Washington Post* pundit Daniel Drezner thinks so, writing[8]:

> The Trump administration has offered several object lessons in how not to govern. One of the most important is that success in the private sector means very little when it comes to managing the public sector.

Aiming for a tone of bemused condescension, he adds, "Maybe—and I'm just spitballing here—but maybe running the public sector well is different from running a for-profit organization."

One professor of business makes this point more explicitly writing that, "Trump wasn't a genuine CEO."[9] In his view a "genuine CEO" runs

> a public company [that] is subject to an array of constraints and a varying but always substantial degree of oversight. There are boards of directors, of course, that review all major strategic decisions, among other duties. And there are separate committees that assess CEO performance and deter-mine compensation, composed entirely of independent or outside directors without any ongoing involvement in running the business.

In other words, the CEO with experience in the large bureaucratic busi-ness organization will gain experience in managing those bureaucratic aspects of the presidency including dealing with other "outside" centers of power, oversight, and evaluation. The author's point is a fair one. Trump was not the CEO of a major public business and thus can't bring to the presidency those particular experiences. Yet, this leads to a rather strange criticism of Trump:

> His experience overseeing an interconnected tangle of LLCs and his one disastrous term as CEO of a public corporation suggest a poor background to be chief executive of the United States. As such, "nobody knows who's in charge" may be the mantra for years to come.

This is extremely odd since if there is one thing that Trump and anti-Trump supporters can easily agree with, it is that for better or worse Trump is the master of his own ship. The buck not only stops at his desk, it often and publicly doesn't travel very far from it.

Other Trump critics name several more issues. Princeton professor and former vice chairman of the Federal Reserve Alan Blinder writes,[10] "All the checks and balances that characterize American democracy would drive a hard-charging CEO, accustomed to getting his own way, crazy." That too is a fair point.

Blinder goes on to note that the generic CEO business type he discusses worships "efficiency," whereas "some notion of 'fairness' is typically paramount in government." He is absolutely right, again, except that given Trump's peripatetic decision-making style, he can never accurately be accused of being or aspiring to efficiency. There is, of course, a large irony in Trump's repeated support of the group he labels the "Forgotten Man" in support of fairness to overcome their having been left behind.[11] Blinder did not anticipate that Trump would add a new group to the American fairness debate.

Binder also points out that:

> Top business executives focus single-mindedly on "the bottom line," meaning profits. Among the reasons why so many smart business people fail in politics and government is that there is no bottom line—or perhaps I should say there are so many bottom lines that the search for a single one is futile.

Binder is absolutely right. We have noted that Trump is on record several times about his use of money as one measurement of success—"Money is

306 S. RENSHON

never a big motivator for me except as a way to keep score."[12] He does keep score.

However, there is also abundant evidence that creativity, bringing his vision to fruition, his palpable love of country, and doing what has not been done before are also a large part of Trump's motivation. As argued in Chapter 7, there is now more to Trump's ambition than applying those more personal wealth accumulation measurements to his business career. There is what he wants to accomplish as president.

While Trump honed the psychology that serves him in his presidency, for better or worse, one thing he did not bring to that office from his CEO experience was a deep knowledge of Washington, with all that term entails. He did not know the players, major or minor, or their histories. He did not know or understand their standard operating procedures, and the psychology and ideology of their foundations. He had few if any real relationships with them. And the same was true of Trump's knowledge in the foreign policy domain as well. Trump came to the presidency as an informational naïf.

Business Empire Building and Transformative Presidential Ambitions

Trump has said a number of times, in different ways[13] that there is much that he wants to do for the country. It could be argued that this is part of the "Trump con," and that in reality his presidency is an example of his efforts to increase the net worth of his business. To substantiate that claim, one would have to explain why the Trump presidency has had very mixed effects on his company's bottom line.[14] One would also have to explain why Trump, who has been single mindedly focused on publicly pointing to what he sees as his successes, would not be interested, for some reason, in being successful in his presidency. Finally one would need to explain the enormous amount of energy, resilience, and commitment, in the face of savage and unrelenting criticism, including impeachment, that he has invested to accomplish his presidential purposes. These are some of the traits a unique CEO like Trump brings to his presidency.

There are some other assets that Trump's CEO experience does allow him to bring to the presidency. One analysis asked whether good businessmen make bad presidents and concluded[15]:

a business background is not somehow uniquely qualifying. Presidents need to be smart, to have good judgment and good emotional IQ. They need wide experience of the world and people, and it probably matters little in what field that experience is gained, though knowledge of business certainly isn't a handicap.

Another observer pointed out that one of Trump's business assets is not having internalized a bureaucratic mindset as CEO. That analysis noted

> His lack of political nuance has resulted in taking on big issues, including an effort on significant deregulation and cutting back on bureaucratic red tape. It will take longer than just four weeks to see if Trump remains committed to those projects, but he didn't take long to at least get them started.[16]

In considering the impact of Trump's business career on his presidency it is impossible to ignore that his psychology has been instrumental to both. In business, Mr. Trump's ambitions (to "transform the New York skyline"), fierce will to win,[17] resilience,[18] creativity,[19] attention to detail (though one of the many psychological paradoxes about Mr. Trump is his enormous attention to detail in his work and the reverse in his many public pronouncements),[20] monumentally large work ethic,[21] and large big picture[22] and innovative[23] thinking were elements of his success when that happened. Those are obviously applicable psychological traits for a successful presidency in many, but not every political circumstance.

Large ambitious policy thinking, thinking big, for example can be a recipe for success, but only in a political context in which it is desired or needed. President Obama harbored large transformative ambitions for the country. However, he mostly kept them to himself and used his modulated tone to convey a moderate political persona that wasn't consistent with his ambitions. When his transformative ambitions and their progressive nature and direction became clear, strenuous grass-roots opposition arose (see Chapter 3).[24]

Mr. Trump also has transformative goals. His ambitions, *The Politics of American Restoration*, challenge the policy orthodoxies of the last several decades across a range of policy areas. Trump is quite direct and clear both in his repeated public rhetoric and the executive actions that he has taken to date.[25] There is no mistaking what he thinks or what he wants to do. He is unsettling, but he doesn't hide. As a result, his presidency is, paradoxically given his reputation, truthfully authentic and, as a result, a major motivator of his political opponents.

And lastly there is one more Trump asset that he brings to his presidency from his business career:

> Mr. Trump is not a child. He has been in negotiations all his life. It's the one skill he brought to office that can't be gainsaid.[26]

Mr. Trump's trade dispute with China for example, has been long, arduous, and complex. The issues that led to the dispute have been clear for years, decades in some cases. No other president has so directly confronted China over these difficult issues. No other president has seriously imposed sanctions and persevered through the many twists and turns of the negotiations to reach a solid preliminary agreement.[27] Trump's business experience and the psychology associated with it clearly was instrumental in his being able to successfully mount this effort.

TRUMP ENTERS THE OVAL OFFICE: EXPECTATIONS AND REALITY

At this point, almost four full years in the president's term of office, whatever errors and successes he has accumulated are a result of Trump's own leadership choices and governing style. They are much less the result of the preparation that his business career either did or did not provide him or the normal learning curve of first time presidents. Every president must, to some degree, learn on the job and Trump is no exception.[28]

Jenkins notes[29]:

> Serving as president has been an education for Mr. Trump as it would be for anybody. His rhetorical instincts may be unchanged but he can't help having picked up a degree of knowledge about public policy and how government functions. This unwonted expertise already has begun audibly leaking into his unscripted responses to press questions.

There are numerous small examples of Trump's learning curve in action. They are more important for demonstrating Trump's capacity to learn than for demonstrating any major changes in either his psychology and leadership style that are attributable to his becoming president. At many of his raucous nomination political rallies, his supports would yell "lock her up" referring to Hillary Clinton. By July before the election Trump would shake his head no, and say to his supporters "let's defeat her in November." *Washington Post* reporters, often critical of Trump pointed out,[30] "He's learned a lot, this first-time candidate. At the outset of his speech, the crowd was yelling 'Trump! Trump! Trump!'—until he told them to chant 'USA! USA!' instead." That is certainly an unexpected request for a purportedly "needy narcissist."

These are small changes to be sure, but others have been more substantial. For example in describing Trump's Asian trip in in early 2017, including his first post-inauguration phone call with China's Xi Jinping, a White House summit with Japan's Shinzo Abe, and twenty-seven holes of golf with Mr. Abe, a report noted, "Unlike some of his earlier encounters with foreign leaders, this round demonstrated sobriety, careful planning and respect for allies." In these and other cases Trump demonstrates a capacity for very basic and important diplomacy. Trump is clearly capable of ordinary presidential behavior.

Debates regarding Trump's presidential demeanor are a well-established motif of his presidency (see Chapter 4). Less examined and equally important are the assumptions with which Trump came into office. They can be divided into several categories: policy surprises; the nature of American political life; the scope and nature of government; on being adequately prepared to be president; and the real life consequences of command. Again, every new president, and Trump is no exception, has many things to learn about his new role, his political circumstances, and how his style will mesh or clash with these realities.

On Trump Being Adequately Prepared to Be President

When we say that no new president is ever fully prepared, that word, prepared, has a double meaning. It refers both to actual experience as would be the case for a second term president. Yet it also refers to feeling prepared in the sense of believing you can and actually have, the capacity to do the job well, even if you are not fully prepared for it in terms of actual experience.

No political party nominee or president elect has ever expressed public doubt about their ability to do the job, and Mr. Trump is, again, no exception. One report noted[31]:

Just a week ago, Mr. Trump was taking a breezy posture toward the job that awaits him. In an interview in his New York skyscraper on Friday, he halted the conversation when his cellphone rang. He was instantly absorbed by the call, broadly smiling and reveling in a brief chat about political strategy. "Oh, I can't believe I used to build buildings," Mr. Trump said as he turned his attention back to his guests. "Actually, truth, it's sort of the same thing."

Trump's not so "Easy" Presidential Promises

During the nomination process Trump expressed the view that several things would be "easy." The anti-Trump website *Huffington Post* collected a list of them in an article entitled "Donald Trump Thinks Being President Is So Easy, Even He Could Do It."[32] Those included expanding the American economy, building a barrier on the US–Mexican border, besting Hillary in the general election, lowering the deficit, and defeating ISIS.

Only in lowering the deficit has Trump made absolutely no progress and in fact has helped fuel its rise.[33] On all the other items, he has made substantial progress in the directions he promised. Although how "easily" he has done so is another matter.

A major element of Trump's nomination and general election pitch to the public was, "to jump-start America, and it can be done, and it won't even be that hard," Trump said in a speech to the Detroit Economic Club.[34] The *Huffington Post* quoted another one of its site's articles[35] warning Americans that "Trump's vaguely fleshed-out economic agenda could trigger the longest recession since the Great Depression." It has not. Quite the opposite. Trump's substantial reduction of regulations, the passage of a major tax cut and the resolution of two large trade disputes, NAFTA and China, have helped stabilize and expand the American economy. That has given the country an economic cushion from which to start recovering from the impact of the Coronavirus pandemic.

As to the barrier at the Southern Border, the *Huffington Post* articles quote Trump as saying, "It's not even a difficult project if you know what you're doing." In reality, there are a number of construction issues, all solvable, but not without their difficulties.[36] However, the most difficult part of building the barrier has clearly been political, not technical.

At a rally Trump said of his chances to become president: "Folks, I haven't even started yet," Trump told supporters of his presidential campaign in early May. "Now I'm going to start focusing on Hillary. It's going to be so easy."[37] Trump obviously won the presidential election and Hillary Clinton lost. Yet, it was a very close and difficult fight that Trump barely won. So it is hard to credit his boast that it would be easy, as more than campaign hyperbole.

As to defeating ISIS, before announcing his candidacy he told a radio interviewer: "There is a way of beating ISIS so easily, so quickly and so effectively, and it would be so nice," Trump told Iowa talk radio host Simon Conway last year before announcing his presidential candidacy. "I know a way that would absolutely give us absolute victory."

What was that way? In Trump's own words: "Bomb the sh-t out of them."[38] In more gentle language, Trump loosened the restraints on his military leaders,[39] and they in turn unleased a brutal bombing campaign against the caliphate. ISIS lost all its territory, its self-status as a state, and is now tarred with defeat. Trump announced that ISIS was 100% defeated, which was not 100% true, but close enough for government work as a wag would say. ISIS went underground and is trying to regroup. As result of Trump's engagement strategy, they had suffered a major incontestable defeat.

Trump's Optimism Sobered by Reality

Trump's optimism that he could do the job was tempered, as every president's is likely to be by the complex, difficult, even fraught realities of that office. Not surprisingly, Trump was soon admitting that "This is more work than in my previous life. I thought it would be easier."[40] When he met with an old friend Newt Gingrich he commented, "This is really a bigger job than I thought."

Trump's unexpected meeting with the realities of the presidency is not startling or novel, and his acknowledgement is a reassurance. He is, as is his style, more vocal about almost everything he is thinking and asked about, including what surprised him about the presidency. This is of keen interest to an analysis of the real psychology of the Trump presidency.

Trump Entering the White House: Policy Surprises

In transition talks with President Obama, the latter ran down a list of his views of the major problems facing the country and the new president. Asked about that, Trump discreetly kept his predecessor's advice confidential but said: "He told me what he thought his, what the biggest problems of the country were, which I don't think I should reveal, I don't mind if he reveals them. But I was actually surprised a little bit."[41] Speculation has centered on North Korea and perhaps Pakistan.

Trump also expressed surprise at General Mattis' response to a Trump question on waterboarding.[42] In an early interview with the *Wall Street Journal*, Trump also said that he had underestimated the complexities of the relationship between China and North Korea.[43]

Finally, at a meeting of the nation's governors at the White House discussing health care, Trump said:

> We have come up with a solution that's really, really I think very good. Now, I have to tell you, it's an unbelievably complex subject. Nobody knew health care could be so complicated.[44]

In reality, many people would be able to give detailed informed analyses of these and similar matters. They are most frequently found in the relevant bureaucracies (e.g., HEW [Department of Health, Education, and Welfare], the CIA, DOD [Department of Defense], State Department) or in the partisan think tanks that support one side or another in these and similar policy debates. The partisan talking points of presidential candidates count for much less as real knowledge since they often operate as ready-made responses to signal familiarity and depth, without however necessarily really being built on them in actuality.

It's not surprising that any president, including Trump, would have to be informed of the arcane intricacies of health care, Chinese-North Korean strategic considerations and history, or other complex policy matters. It is somewhat surprising, given that Trump rarely admits anything less than superlative about himself, that he would publicly admit a lack of knowledge. With waterboarding he did apparently change the policy, but not his mind. With North Korea he seems to have learned something that will help counter his impatience for results. He eventually did accept, as a fact of his political circumstances, as he must if his presidency is to survive, the vehement opposition to himself personally and his presidency's policies.

Trump Surprised by the Deep Conflictual Nature of American Political Life

Some of Mr. Trump's assumptions on entering office were surprisingly naive for a man touted by his followers, and himself, as suspicious, skeptical, and capable of being very tough when necessary. As a successful presidential candidate, Trump keenly grasped what many Americans wanted for their country and president. He was less able to fully grasp the degree of antipathy toward his presidential ambitions and himself personally.

In an interview for *Time Magazine* he said: "The détente with the press after the election that I had hoped for never came." In fact, "It's gotten worse. It's one of the things that surprises me."[45] Asked in that same interview if he feels his administration has been too combative, he makes a brief allowance. "It could be my fault," he says, "I don't want to necessarily blame, but there's a great meanness out there that I'm surprised at."[46]

Leaving aside the chicken or egg question, Trump clearly felt that things would change once he was elected. Perhaps the most startling example of this assumption was reported by Rush Limbaugh who said[47]:

> Trump, told me in February that he was surprised that the country had not unified around the presidency by that time. He was genuinely surprised at the continued opposition. Well, that told me that in his mind he expected after he won and was inaugurated that the country would come together. I couldn't believe he told me that when he told me.

Perhaps Mr. Trump's thinking reflected the assumption of a traditional "honeymoon period" for a new president. However, if Trump clearly grasped what some supporters wanted, he was much less in touch with what his opponents feared. They were alarmed that he would govern as he had promised, as a bold, brash, president used to doing what he wanted and getting his own way, who would follow through on his clearly stated intention to uproot four decades of traditional domestic and international policy premises.

Trump Surprised by the Real Scope of Government

"Huge" is a favorite word of Mr. Trump's, applied liberally to almost all of his undertakings. As big as his projects were, they did not seem to prepare him for the actual size of government. In one interview, he said he has been surprised by "the size, the magnitude of everything" and being president can be a "surreal experience in a certain way."[48]

In another interview, asked what surprised him, Trump replied[49]:

> I think the size, the magnitude of everything. So, I was a very big real estate person. I build a building for 500 million or $900 million. And here, you look at an airplane contract where you can save $600 million on 90 planes. I saved more than $600 million. I got involved in negotiation on a fighter jet, the F-35. And by the way, Lockheed Martin, a great company. But they weren't bringing their price up. I got involved, I saved more than $600 million as their (*inaudible*). But the magnitude of—you can do that at every level of government.

Later in his presidency, Mr. Trump personally become involved in negotiating the costs of two new Air Force One planes and was able to lower the initial costs to somewhere between one and three billion dollars.[50] Mr. Trump clearly does not share the depression mentality of his late father Fred who used to pick up and reuse nails lying on the ground of his construction projects. Yet, like his father, he does like to get good deals, and is proud of doing so.

Toward that end, he has repeatedly demonstrated in his business dealings the willingness and the stamina to engage in long term strenuous bargaining. This was an experience that was no doubt tested in his negotiations with China over trade. Indeed, one could usefully examine any presidency, but especially Trump's, though the perspective of policy bargaining. The essence of bargaining in business is appropriately getting as much of what you want as you can. The essential of presidential policy bargaining is the same thing.

There is nothing novel about this general observation. What is unique about Trump are the areas, range, and purpose of his many negotiations. In the eight policy pillar areas, and their numerous subsidiary elements, he is engaged in serious efforts to substantially revise existing establishment policies. In response, one of the major questions that must be addressed in this analysis is how entrenched conventional policy narratives change (see Chapter 12). Engaging in sometimes tense and difficult negotiations, and being able to keep pushing them in support of change is one part of Trump's answer to that question, and a strategy and associated set of skills that he has brought with him into the White House is another.

The Real Life Consequences of Command

The most powerful, most difficult, and most emotionally fraught decisions a president makes are those literally concerned with life or death. Every presidentially approved combat mission entails political risk. Yet, at their core they reflect the likelihood that as a direct result of the president's decision, people can and will die, even if the mission is successful. Every modern president confronts this reality for the first time in the presidency.

Asked how he has changed since taking office, the former businessman, who as a candidate touted his ability to cut deals, said: "The magnitude of everything is so big, and also the decisions are so big. You know, you're talking about life and death. You're not talking about 'you're going to make a good deal.'"[51]

A longtime friend of the president, Chris Ruddy at Mar-a-Lago at the time that the president authorized airstrikes on Syria[52] recalled the president emerging on the patio moments after the US began missile strikes against targets in Syria, which won praise even from some Democrats. "I congratulated him when it seemed to have gone well," and he said, "I had no choice," Mr. Ruddy recalled. "He was very sober. He wasn't gloating about it. I think he's coming to understand that these are life and death decisions he's making now."

As a result of the weight of such decisions, even the often emotionally voluble Mr. Trump will understandably be subdued.

The Scope of Trump's Decisions

Every president faces circumstances that require a response and those that are more discretionary. The 9/11 attacks and the Coronavirus pandemic are non-discretionary presidential problems. Nerve gas attacks against civilian populations in Syria during the Obama and Trump administrations were somewhat less non-discretionary circumstances. The far broader array of presidential policy interventions and decisions are "voluntary." They represent choices that the president makes to further the agenda he brought to his office, that need attention but are not pressing or in Trump's case items, like the color scheme of the New Air Force One jets or the architecture style of federal buildings,[53] that just interest him.

How a president is able to further that voluntary agenda depends on the distribution of party power within Congress. Obama came into office with a unified Democratic Party majority in both houses of Congress. As a result, he was able to pass a major health care plan before losing control of Congress to the Republicans. Thereafter, he had to operate domestically primarily via the administrative power of the presidency. He was also able to concentrate on foreign policy agreements that did not strictly speaking require Congressional approval, and were not formally submitted for approval (e.g., the Paris Climate Agreement, the Iranian nuclear agreement).

Trump faced a different and more difficult set of circumstances. He too started his term with a Republican Congress. However, they were far from unified behind him. Indeed one of his chief Senate Republican opponents, John McCain, was able to scuttle Trump's plan to repeal President Obama's health care plan. Thereafter, Trump was able to unite his party around a very traditional Republican preference for tax cuts, deregulation, and judicial appointments. Yet many in his party remained strongly opposed to him. In 2018 the Republican Party lost control of the House resulting in a literal barrage of investigations into the Trump administration.

Trump has also been slowed and in some cases stymied by his own lack of actual political and governing experience. It has taken Trump several years to learn how to more effectively manage his administration given his political circumstances. Those include the widespread and concerted opposition whose membership spans establishment institutions both inside and outside of government, and within his own White House as well. They also include a two year investigation of his administration by a Special Council, harsh preparation for governing in the midst of an impeachment inquiry, and afterwards, a Senate impeachment trial.

In considering the scope of Trump's presidential efforts it is also prudent to keep in mind one further distinction. Trump is aiming to reverse several decades of policies and policy narratives in the eight pillar policy areas already noted (see Chapters 1 and 3), and the numerous policy elements within them. Unlike President Obama, Trump is not seeking to add to the deepening or thickening of the liberal administrative state. He thus cannot count on the support that comes from those who benefit from and support the direction of those initiatives. Quite the contrary.

A President and Administration Interested in Many Things

It would be a mistake to conflate Trump's personal interest in any particular group of policy issues with his detailed knowledge of their substance and nuances. As the *Wall Street Journal* put it, when earlier in his term Trump was trying, and failing to repeal Obama's health care legislation, the "freedom caucus," has now been handed a final offer from a president who "can believably present himself as uninterested in the details of health care policy."[54] Trump has many more policies that he has an interest in changing than an in-depth knowledge regarding any one of them.

Given Trump's interests in a large number of policy areas several questions immediately arise. How is it possible for a president with a well-documented aversion to long-winded presentations or debates, and a relatively short attention span for those things that he's not interested in doing, to be in touch with the substance of so many policy areas? How is it possible for a president who is famously unschooled in the depth and nuances of many policy areas to have anything but a general interest in the policies he champions, if that?

Recall, that one of Trump's early traits as a builder and dealmaker was his extraordinary attention to detail.

Blanche Sprague, his vice president for condominium operations said of him[55]:

He'll show up at 6 to watch construction guys replace piece of cracked marble. Nothing escapes him and he drives me insane.

At the Trump Plaza, Trump's signature project[56]:

on a recent visit, Mr. Trump spotted a hairline crack that others could barely detect in a bathroom of one of the 140 cooperative apartments. He not only complained but stood there until a work crew came and replaced the marble.

At another major project, The Trump International Golf Club in Dubai, the *New York Times* reported[57]:

We walked through the golf course and he said: "You see that tree; move it 10 feet there. That tree is too small; make it bigger," recalled Niall

McLoughlin, a senior vice president at Damac Properties, which owns the project. "His attention to detail is tremendous."

A fair question is what happened to that Trump attention to detail in his presidency. One element of an answer is that his attention to detail in the building industry was a result of very early developmental experience. It was literally honed at his father's knee when, as a young child, he accompanied his father as he worked on his projects. Then, too, Trump came of age in that profession with enormous "local knowledge," an advantage he did not have in Washington. As Trump has remarked about what has surprised him, government is vast. That sounds like a truism and is, but it is one kind of knowledge in the abstract and quite another when you are in theory, and often literally, especially if there are any controversies, actually in charge of it all.

Given the scope of what Trump wishes to accomplish and the need to keep track of progress in his eight policy area pillars and their associated elements, one possibility is that his much commented upon attention to detail has developed into a capacity for keeping track and keeping up in a more general way in order to know when to provide added push. Yet Trump is perfectly capable of going into the weeds when it interests him as he did for the two new Air Force One planes, or the medals given to military personnel for an unsupported set of charges against Navy Seal Edward Gallagher. Trump is a man who likes to get things done. Sometimes that means keeping general track of a large list of ambitious initiatives, other times that requires of him a deeper more direct dive.

His is a restless and peripatetic ambition, not confined to discrete policy areas. Immigration is a case in point. Yes, Trump wants to build a "wall," or a barrier, but that is part of a much larger effort in immigration policy enforcement. And that larger effort is part of a still larger, as yet unrealized policy ambition, to reform the whole immigration system in favor of a skills/education emphasis.

We can see the same levels of policy change and Trump interest in other areas like health care. He has put forward policies to require transparency in medical costs[58] which sparked an industry furor,[59] to allow the importation of drugs from Canada,[60] and to expanded health care options for business[61] among other initiatives. At the same time, he has been actively and often intensely involved in other policy areas like developing and applying deterrence theory as the basis for his Iran policy, negotiating new trade deals with China, South Korea, and the NAFTA countries, pushing a "Space Force" initiative, and many others that could easily be listed.

At the same time, he has found the time and interest to negotiate a new less expensive deal with Boeing for the new models of Air Force One.[62] He suggested some new red, white, and blue paint design features for it as well[63] that one Democratic Congressman filed legislation to block.[64] His presidency is a combination of attention to necessary policy developments (e.g., what to do strategically about China, Iran, and North Korea), Trump signature issues (e.g., immigration, trade, domestic economic concerns), matters of public concern (health care, dealing with the Coronavirus pandemic), and issues that strike Trump's interest (the proposed new design elements of Air Force One and privatizing the United States Post Office[65]).

Again, this representative list does not imply that every Trump initiative will be successful according to his preferred outcomes. Nor does it imply that even if they are, they are necessarily desirable. It is meant only to call attention to a very basic and overlooked aspect of the Trump presidency. He is involved in a great many policy initiatives. Even considering his two to three year presidential learning curve, the initial disarray of his administration, the leaks, the internal efforts to sabotage his administration, lawsuits, and epic opposition, his presidency, like the man himself, is enormously energetic. Paying attention to all of this as Trump must, may be the presidential equivalent of moving golf course trees or seeing and fixing hairline cracks in one of his opulent apartments.

How Things Get Done: Trump's Work Ethic

No analysis of this president or his presidency would be accurate without noting Trump's work ethic, which is prodigious. Gwenda Blair who spent eleven years researching her Trump family biography said of that[66]:

> One of the things that perhaps surprised me most in working on this book was to grasp just how hard Donald, his father and his grandfather actually work ... the sheer effort involved is mind-boggling, as is true, I think, of almost everyone who achieves extraordinary success. It's easy to write him off as the son of a rich guy, but that kind of misses the point. These people never stop.

When Trump was on a Christmas Day video conference with troops serving abroad this exchange took place[67]:

> *GENERAL ODOM*: Sir, our real question for you, today, is: How are you going to spend your holiday here in the coming—today, tomorrow, and hopefully into the weekend, sir?
> *THE PRESIDENT*: Well, I'm at a place called "Mar-a-Lago." We call it the "Southern White House" *because I really, pretty much work—that's what I like to do is work.* And we've made a lot of progress.

For once, a simple statement sufficed, and it was accurate.

How does Trump spend his time? One reports says, "But most days and nights, if Trump is not on the campaign trail or a foreign trip, he happily stays inside his White House Bubble and the residence—*working late into the night and very early in the morning.*"[68] Another official quoted in that same story put the matter more succinctly:

> *He is a workaholic,* so he wakes up early and works out of the residence. It's just the way his internal work clock has been for decades.

Trump's work ethic has to be considered in the context of his rather unusual physiological temperament. Trump is a man who, from childhood on has been extremely physically active and according to the results of his annual presidential medical checkup, "he sleeps four to five hours a night. And I think he's probably been that way his whole life."[69] As a result, he has a lot of time, more than most people available to him to do what he likes. What he likes to do is work. That is as true of his presidency as it was of his business life.

How Trump Decides

Every president's primary task is making decisions. Yet obviously, presidents differ with regard to what they want to decide, what they have to decide, and how they go about deciding. One constant for almost every modern president, Trump included, is that they didn't go through the rigors of seeking the presidency to generally turn these responsibilities over to others. They—Obama, G. W. Bush, Clinton and those before them, are all "deciders."

This point arises because one of the narrative myths that follow some, especially Republican presidents, is that they are not the authors of their own decisions. Fred Greenstein's seminal analysis of Eisenhower's sharp intelligence surprised many.[70] Democratic "wise man" Clark Clifford referred to Ronald Reagan as an "amicable dunce,"[71] presumable incapable of mastering policy options and dependent on his advisors. Karl Rove was widely regarded as *Bush's Brain*,[72] the implication being that Bush didn't have one of his own. Trump too has been the subject of these kinds of observations with Steven Bannon ordinarily placed in the role of his Svengali,[73] and Stephen Miller the runner up for actually being in charge of Trump policy.[74]

Three-plus years into Trump's first term as president there is now enough data, from diverse sources, to draw a reasonably accurate picture of his decision making style. What follows are substantively based sketches of some of these major elements. They begin with the most elemental and obvious observation: There has never been a president who has more carefully and intensely guarded his own decision prerogatives. Trump has spent his whole adult life in singular charge of his vast empire and peripatetic tabloid-featured private life. After decades there, he is very much at home at center stage, savors that "Tiffany" location, and would no more cede it to others than he would immediately step down from his presidency and spend the rest of his life quietly living as a recluse in Mar-a-Lago.

Trump is a man and a president who truly likes, indeed relishes, being in charge.

He is also aware, even if he has not read Neustadt, that there is ample reason for him to be attentive to preserving his prerogatives. There are instances reported, and denied, of high level White House aides removing documents from his desk.[75] There are Anonymous White House policy saboteurs touting their opposition in the *New York Times*.[76] There are the fierce battles within the White House to modify or reverse some Trump policy views, domestically and in foreign policy (see Chapter 12 for a detailed example of this in foreign policy). In addition, there are for the Trump presidency, the normal ferocious political, legal and personal battles that every president faces.

Trump's Judgment: Essence of Understanding

Elsewhere I have taken up in some detail the nature of presidential judgment and what "good judgement" requires.[77] Here, for this section, I borrow a term that Graham Allison made famous in a book entitled *Essence of Decision*.[78] Somewhat modified, that title more closely reflects Trump's essential approach to judgment and decision making. He is, as noted, famously impatient with long winded presentations and meandering discussions.

In one pre-presidential interview Trump said he likes his briefings short, ideally one page if it's in writing[79]:

> I like bullets or I like as little as possible. I don't need, you know, 200-page reports on something that can be handled on a page. That I can tell you.

In a *Washington Post* interview Trump was discussing someone who wanted to send him a report on China trade practices[80]:

> But he said I'd love to be able to send you—oh, boy, he's got a lengthy report, hundreds of pages. I said no, no, give me three pages. I'm a very efficient guy. Now, I could also do it verbally, which is fine. I'd always rather have—but I want it short. There's no reason to do hundreds of pages because I know exactly what it is.

Trump is eager for results by nature but he is not always so. We noted that when Trump was in the building skyscraper phase of his career, he was able to bide his time when necessary because of economic or political circumstances. He was also able to move extremely quickly when windows of opportunity opened. Asked about his famously short attention span and its impact on his presidency, Trump responded[81]:

> Well I mean I have an attention span that's as long as it has to be. But I don't have to sit around with a group of generals to tell me about Iraq being a failure. Iraq was a total failure.

In that statement is an essence of Trump's view of his own decision making process. Trump, like every president, operates within multiple policy and political time frames. Some decisions require decisive action in

9 PRELUDE TO A UNIQUE PRESIDENCY ...   323

the political moment and others must be nurtured as they develop. Sometimes as in Trump's North Korean outreach, both kinds of time frames set the boundaries. Trump did startle conventional practice by initiating a meeting with Kim Jong-un. He did walk away from another meeting when it was not making progress. It's possible there will be another high level meeting at some point. The point here is not so much that Trump operates in multiple time frames as every president does, but that given the anti-Trump conventional narrative about his impulsivity that he can.

Instinct and Gut Feelings: A Partial Decision Metric for Trump

The president, as is widely reported, and as he acknowledges, has substantial confidence in his feelings in making his decision choices. Sometimes he frames these choice metrics with reference to his "gut." In an interview with the *Washington Post*, Trump said this[82]:

> I'm not happy with the Fed. They're making a mistake *because I have a gut, and my gut tells me more sometimes than anybody else's brain can ever tell me.*

Speaking of his decisions regarding Afghanistan policy, he used different phrasing:

> My original instinct was to pull out. And historically, I like following my instincts.[83]

It seems that Trump understands and uses both terms interchangeably, but what does he mean? It seems that both reflect back to Trump's feelings about a choice or set of them, most particularly whether one or another "seems right," or whether there is something clear or latent that gives him pause. Phrased in this way judgments seems almost mysterious and certainly not synonymous with the usual steps touted for models of "rational decision making."[84] Those have of course, long since been overtaken by understanding that "bounded rationality"[85] is much more prevalent.

The answer however is not particularly mysterious. When presidents like (G. W.) Bush or Trump say they rely on their "gut" or instincts, what they are really saying is that they rely on their experience, and their reflective judgment about it. Those experiences would most likely include circumstances when they choose wisely and those when they didn't. Their "instinct" then in any particular case would be a reflection of the degree of appropriate fit between their current circumstances and what they have taken from past ones.

The degree to which "instinct" fits is one question, but there are others. At what point does "instinct" decide? Does it close Trump off from fairly considering real options? Is it a deciding metric in all or only some cases, and which ones? Is it a metric used to decide among nuanced options, or is it also used to frame some very fundamental considerations? Very importantly, what is the relationship between relying to some degree on instinct and keeping an open mind?

Trump: Open Minded, to a Degree

No president comes into office fully aware of the many issues they will face, their history, and the various understandings of them that form the histories and narratives with which they are presented. Trump is not an exception to this rule. The questions then arise: what does he think he knows and how willing is he to change those views if and when he realizes he doesn't adequately understand?

Trump's Twitter troll that he is a "stable genius"[86] in response to accusations about his mental health notwithstanding, it is clear that he thinks very highly of his own intelligence. Asked about climate change in one interview, the president said[87]:

> One of the problems *that a lot of people like myself, we have very high levels of intelligence* but we're not necessarily such believers. You look at our air and our water, and it's right now at a record clean.

Trump's real intelligence (see Chapter 12 on whether Trump is best understood as a dunce, a hedgehog or a fox), clearly has an impact on his capacity to process policy information and make some accurate assessments regarding what he really does and doesn't know. A truly ignorant president would be overwhelmed by his responsibilities and presumably be highly dependent on others to help him through. A president who overvalued his own intelligence and knowledge would be too prone to depend on their own self-assessments of their capacities and be much less inclined to listen to other advisors or their debates.

In the minds of some critics, Trump represents the worst of both of these possibilities. George Will presents Trump as suffering from a "dangerous disability," characterized by "intellectual sloth but of an untrained mind bereft of information and married to stratospheric self-confidence."[88] Others, like pundit Daniel Drezner,[89] taking Trump literally for purposes of his criticism, focus on Trump's comment that:

> When I look at myself in the first grade and I look at myself now, I'm basically the same. The temperament is not that different.[90]

Did that mean that Trump had learned nothing in his six-plus decades building and heading a vast business empire? No, but Drezner presents Trump that way. Did it mean that Trump had not acquired views about adult subjects in his adulthood? No. He simply meant that in terms of energy levels, and an emphasis on getting things done, Trump could see the child in the adult.

One could have easily, if one were searching for a hook on which to hang another misreading of a Trump quote, have noted that Trump once said in response to fighting back against allegations regarding his pledged charitable giving to Veterans' Organizations, "You think I'm going to change? I'm not changing."[91] It's clear that in the context in which it was made that quote meant that Trump would not stop fighting back against allegations he thought unfair and unfounded. Did it mean Trump would never change his mind about any of his views regardless of advisors' advice or debates? No, as the evidence below makes clear.

There is now a substantial body of evidence, from different sources and from different policy debates that suggests that Trump is not only able to, but also has changed his thinking in response to new information. None of these data negates the fact that on large signature items that Trump feels strongly about, neither his advisors, critics, or experts can have much success in changing his mind or his determination. Examples of that include the Paris Climate Accords, the nuclear agreement with Iran, getting NATO to pay more of its fair share for defense, helping to develop a more modern mission for NATO, fairer trade agreements with China, NAFTA, and the EU, enforcing immigration laws, and a host of other matters. Here Trump has kept his word, his policies, and his views.

In several matters, however he has proven open-minded. Consider China's ability to press North Korea. This was an article of faith for

Trump until he discussed the matter at length with the Chinese premier. Trump reported on the conversation as follows[92]:

> And you know, you're talking about thousands of years ... and many wars. And Korea actually used to be a part of China. *And after listening for 10 minutes I realized that not—it's not so easy. You know I felt pretty strongly that they have—that they had a tremendous power over China. I actually do think they do have an economic power, and they have certainly a border power to an extent, but they also—a lot of goods come in. But it's not what you would think. It's not what you would think.*

On the efficacy of waterboarding,[93] that Trump supported, he had this to say:

> General Mattis is a strong, highly dignified man. I met with him at length and I asked him that question. I said, "what do you think of waterboarding?" He said—I was surprised—he said, "I've never found it to be useful." He said, "I've always found, give me a pack of cigarettes and a couple of beers and I do better with that than I do with torture." And I was very impressed by that answer. I was surprised, because he's known as being like the toughest guy. And when he said that, I'm not saying it changed my mind. Look, we have people that are chopping off heads and drowning people in steel cages and we're not allowed to waterboard. But I'll tell you what, I was impressed by that answer. It certainly does not—it's not going to make the kind of a difference that maybe a lot of people think. If it's so important to the American people, I would go for it. I would be guided by that.

On Trump's decision to support the continuation of the Export-Import Bank that he originally had not supported,[94] he had this to say.[95]

> I will tell you what, I was very much opposed to Ex-Im Bank, because I said what do we need that for IBM and for General Electric and all these—it turns out that, first of all lots of small companies will really be helped, the vendor companies, but also maybe more importantly, other countries give it. And when other countries give it, we lose a tremendous amount of business.

Finally, although it is not the only remaining example of this aspect of Trump's decision making, there was his reluctant decision to commit more American troops to Afghanistan. We noted above that Trump's *"original instinct was to pull out."*[96] Shortly after he came into office Trump initiated a major review of American options. In his speech to the nation, Trump said, "After many meetings, over many months, we held our final meeting last Friday at Camp David, with my Cabinet and generals, to complete our strategy." In fact, other reports indicate that Trump insisted that there be a detailed discussion of what "victory" would look like and also insisted on metrics to measure it.

The "what does victory look like" is the kind of basic question Trump is inclined to ask. It is not an "in the weeds" question that illuminates one or another detailed option being debated and which reflects the askers' detailed nuanced understanding. Rather it is a step back to consider a more basic primary question that can facilitate rethinking and reframing debates.

Mr. Trump finally put forward a broader strategy for Afghanistan, one that would require thousands more American troops but placed more conditions on the Afghan government. According to several officials it, "was less a change of heart than a weary acceptance of the case, made during three months of intense White House debate by the military leaders who dominate his war cabinet." So, contrary to the Trump is ignorant and impulsive narrative assumed by critics, there is evidence that the president's decision making is not limited to a narcissistically based repetition compulsion.

On some strongly felt matters, Trump won't budge. On a range of others, he can be convinced, even if reluctantly so. On some of his deeply held starting positions, like China's leverage with North Korea, his views can clearly be modified.

Trump Adopts a Public Version of Franklin D. Roosevelt's Competing Aides Strategy

The president has had an unusually high level of turnover among his aides. He has sought to find the right mix of views given his own anchoring positions on the policy spectrum. He has also been searching for individuals with whom he feels comfortable and who are, in turn, comfortable with his decision style.

Shortly before Gary Cohn resigned as Trump's senior economic advisor, "Trump dismissed talk of chaos in his White House while acknowledging that he deliberately fostered a fractious atmosphere."[97]

That "chaos" narrative is largely a by-product of the ordinary bureaucratic in-fighting conducted through leaks published in the nation's major media outlets, exacerbated by internal leaks designed to wound the administration by members of the opposition, and Trump's tendency to publicly test his own sometimes shifting thinking on some major policy issues. The net result is a narrative that emphasizes the Trump White House as a continuing seething caldron of chaos, conflict, carelessness, and confusion.

There was certainly a substantial amount of that in the formative period of Trump's first term. Yet, as this analysis has argued, there were from the, start two Trump presidencies. One was the public dire narrative of imminent collapse for one or another reason, including White House "chaos." The other the increasingly well-functioning administration effort to make progress on its agenda.

Interestingly, that bifurcated dual reality parallels what real insiders understood about Trump in his business empire building days. Norma Foerderer was Donald Trump's top aide for twenty-six years. When she joined the Trump Organization in 1981, he had only seven other employees and she knew Trump professionally and personally. In the only in-depth interview she ever gave, she said of Trump:

> there are two Donald Trumps: One is the Trump that appears to the public, making often outrageous comments on television to get attention for his brand and now his presidency; the other is the real Trump only insiders know. He listens without a touch of bravado. That private Trump is "the dearest, most thoughtful, most loyal, most caring man."

In the real world of Trump's presidential performance, he has clearly adapted a variant of FDR's strategy of setting various aides on the same information quests unbeknown to each other. That way, he receives a mix of different perspectives to consider. Unlike FDR though, Trump is willing to have his advisors scramble in public to keep up with his policy trial balloons. This often leads to stories regarding Trump "undercutting" his aides and there is some truth to that. Yet, much of Trump's supposed undercutting has less to do with reminding aides who is really in charge, although it certainly is a reminder, than in Trump's propensity to think aloud and publicly share his thoughts, whatever they may be at the moment.

Trump is a president who likes a wide variety of advice (see below), but he also learns from conflict and having his advisors debate the merits in front of him. In a Q & A, he had this is to say about that process[98]:

> I like conflict. I like having two people with different points of view, and I certainly have that. And then I make a decision. But I like watching it, I like seeing it, and I think it's the best way to go. I like different points of view.

As President Obama said of Trump,[99] "He's somebody who I think likes to mix it up and to have a vigorous debate."

Seeking a Wide and Eclectic Range of Advice

One question that arises with regard to Trump's decision style is whether and how he gets information relevant to the issues he faces. It's clear that Trump does not like or read long policy memos. It's also clear that brevity is a virtue to him in ordinary presentations, but that he is capable of and likes sitting through debates at which his advisors argue their positions and rationales (see above).

Trump was known to reach out to those he was working with when he was CEO of the Trump Organization during evenings, weekends, nights and whenever he wanted to discuss issues.

The evidence is that he hasn't changed that style. In an interview his former Secretary of State Rex Tillerson said[100]:

> I talk to him just about every day. I see him several times a week. *He calls me late at night, on the weekends, when something comes into his head and he wants to talk. He may call me at any moment, at any time.*

Another behind the scenes look at Trump's work style reported that, "the bulk of his work in the mornings, late afternoons, evenings and weekends happens in his private quarters where Trump can call staff and advisers as early as 6 a.m. and up to midnight."[101] And the *Washington Post* reports[102]:

> The chatterbox in chief has eschewed the traditional way that presidents communicate with members of Congress, calling lawmakers at all hours of the day without warning and sometimes with no real agenda. Congressional Republicans reciprocate, increasingly dialing up the president directly

to gauge his thinking after coming to terms with the fact that ultimately, no one speaks for Trump but Trump himself.

Trump is simply not, and never has been, a 9 to 5 worker. He spends a lot of his so called "Executive Time,"[103] for which some have criticized him,[104] seeking input, testing ideas, and building relationships.

The *New York Times* take on this aspect of Trump's style is that it reflects his insecurity. "Those who know him best say that his outer confidence has always belied an inner uncertainty, and that he needs to test ideas with a wide range of people."[105] The *Times* does not name "those who know him best" so there is no way to judge the accuracy of this statement. What is clear is that sounding out a wide eclectic variety of people has always been Trump's equivalent of reading long reports. As the evidence below suggests, he seems to learn from doing so.

Asked how he developed his heterodox views of the Republican Party he responded[106]:

> *I'm not sure I got there through deep analysis..* My views are what everybody else's views are. When I give speeches, sometimes I'll sign autographs and I'll get to talk to people and learn a lot about the party.

In response to the downing of an American drone by Iran, "President Trump bucked most of his top national-security advisers by abandoning retaliatory strikes in Iran on Thursday."[107] That report went on as follows:

> *The president is known for seeking a range of opinions*, and he did that again amid rising tensions with Iran, even reaching out to *Fox News* host Tucker Carlson, according to people familiar with those conversations. Mr. Carlson has opposed military intervention in Iran on his prime-time television show.

Yet more than conservative media celebrities, Trump is well known for reaching out to a very large group of unusual people for their views. The *New York Times* put it like this[108]:

> As Mr. Trump's White House advisers jostle for position, the president has turned to another group of advisers—*from family, real estate, media, finance and politics, and all outside the White House gates—many of whom he consults at least once a week.*

The list included in that article is an eclectic one including "moguls" (Rupert Murdoch); the media (Sean Hannity, Chris Ruddy); lawyers (Sheri A, Dillon); campaign advisors (Corey Lewandowski, Newt Gingrich); childhood friends (Richard LeFrak); peers (Thomas Barrack, Jr., Stephen Schwarzman, Steve Roth, Phil Ruffin, Carl Icahn), "Man of Mystery" (Roger J. Stone); Mar-a Lago members (Ike Permutter, Robert Kraft]; the (former) Speaker of the House (Paul D. Ryan); former NJ governor (Chris Christie); and Trump's wife and children (Melania Trump, Eric Trump, Donald Trump, Jr.).

Another report on the president's decision making regarding Afghanistan policy noted that the day before an important Principal's Meeting, Trump[109]:

> had invited four soldiers who had served in Afghanistan to the White House for lunch. His exchanges with these enlisted men, an official said, left him sober about the prospects for turning around a war that has dragged on for nearly 16 years. He showed up the next day determined to ask hard questions.

Those questions included the "what's victory look like" question noted above.

There is one other aspect of the above examples that may escape notice and that is that Trump listens. Whether it is while signing autographs, or discussing Afghanistan with four soldiers who fought there, Trump seems very interested in new, different views than the ones that any president ordinarily hears.

This does not seem to reflect a desperation to find "answers," so much as an effort to gain diverse perspectives as he moves toward initial decision or follow through. Many of these outreach efforts are not with people considered "expert" in the ordinary Washington use of that word. Trump has a deep set of mixed feelings about conventional experts. He learned early on in his presidency that sterling résumés are not synonymous with insight or perspective and, as a result, with good advice.

Trump retains a skepticism even towards experts whose knowledge and perspective he trusts. Here is Dr. Anthony Fauci on that distinction[110]:

> …because to his [Trump's] credit, even though we disagree on some things, he listens. He goes his own way. He has his own style. But on substantive issues, he does listen to what I say.

It seems clear that President Trump canvases a wide variety of people many of whom would be considered unorthodox presidential advisors. Yet, seeking and taking advice are not synonymous. That raises the question of whose advice does Trump trust?

Advising Trump: The Issue of Trust

Trump spent his adulthood in an extremely competitive, indeed fierce, business environment. Enormous amounts of money, power, and prestige went to those who succeeded. In the end for any project, ordinarily, only one business "won." Trump was willing to do what it took, but so were many others. It's not a set of circumstances that facilitates trust.

Asked about trust, Trump replied[111]:

> Do I feel I can trust anybody, OK? I'm a very suspicious person. I am not a person that goes around trusting lots of people.

Trump's adult long business experience is probably the source of the much repeated Trump quote[112]:

> Life is a series of battles that ultimately end in either victory or defeat. I enjoy combat. I enjoy fighting my enemies. I like beating people and winning, yes.

Trump's intense will to succeed in a fierce business environment is only part of the explanation of Trump's mistrustfulness. As the single owner of a vast business empire Trump was, and remains, a very powerful, very rich man. As a result, he is also to many people a possible exploitable mark and target.

There is no mistaking Trump's litigiousness. He has used lawsuits to obtain legitimate relief from individuals, governments, and businesses. He has used lawsuits to deter and punish those in business or in life who have, in his mind and in reality, tried to harm him. As president he has had to defend himself and his administration against myriad personal, political, and policy lawsuits meant to make life unbearable for him, his family and his supporters, and to impede his presidency.[113]

The number of these legal cases runs into the thousands.[114] They cover such expected areas as branding and trademark cases (85), casino related cases (1863), cases against his campaign (17), contract dispute cases (208), employment cases (130), golf club cases (63), government and tax cases (190), and media and defamation cases (14). Anti-Trump news stories highlight allegations meant to cast Trump in a bad light, without giving the countervailing claims or the disposition of the cases, which are often devised in Trump's favor.[115]

One anti-Trump legal author wrote[116]:

> I found myself deeply offended by his [Trump] anti-legal approach to the constitution, the courts and the rule of law ... "what to do about Trump?" I asked myself. "Write something" came the answer from my inner self ... Here I trust, I have "killed the monster."

These sentiments would seem to be an effective recipe for anti-Trump confirmation bias.

The *USA TODAY* listing of all the lawsuits share an anti-Trump perspective. One article from that series highlighted the claims of people who said they weren't paid by Trump for work they did. However, deep in the article this caveat appears,[117] "To be sure, Trump and his companies have prevailed in many legal disputes over missing payments, or reached settlements that cloud the terms reached by the parties." The same is true for legal claims of accidental falls on his properties, being passed over for advancement because of looks, and so on.

However, The *USA TODAY* disclaimer most relevant to Trump's trustfulness is this one[118]:

> As a public figure for decades, Trump has faced so many different kinds of lawsuits that not all can be easily categorized. These other suits involve everything from divorce-related cases with his ex-wives to *dozens of lawsuits from prisoners and other private citizens hoping to cash in on his enormous wealth or drag Trump into litigation. Many of those cases were dismissed before they could reach a courtroom.*

In an early interview there was the following exchange[119]:

> *Playboy*: You wrote in *The Art of the Comeback* that women are gold diggers. Do you still believe that?
>
> *DT*: *I think it's hard for women who go out with very wealthy guys not to get seduced by that lifestyle—the apartments at the top of Trump Tower, the helicopters and airplanes.* But I don't think all women are gold diggers..I've known a lot of really good women and have had amazing

relationships over the years. *But as with men, there are good ones and bad ones.*

In a business focused adulthood shaped by competitiveness, alliances of convenience, betrayal, false claims, and zero-sum circumstances, real trust is in short supply. And that was before Trump entered the White House. Yet, no president, even one who reaches out to many diverse people for their views, can avoid making judgments about which advisors and advice he trusts most.

The important answer to that question for Trump is family. Trump clearly develops confidence in some who work with him and advise him. He agreed, reluctantly, with General Mattis on waterboarding, but not on Afghanistan. For other advisors, it is the fit between their views and Trump's as it was on immigration with Jeff Sessions until as Attorney General he recused himself from the Russian probe and Trump forced him to resign.

Trump's confidence in his most trusted advisors seems to hinge on three general elements: that person's established independent stature in their field, the overlap of their general views with Trump's, and Trump's assessment that the person has his best personal and political interests at heart. Ordinary Trump advisors start out with a disadvantage if they can't established their bona fides in at least one of these three elements over time. Whom could you count on to hit the mark regularly on at least two of those three elements, especially the crucial one of having your best interests at heart? Family.

That is why among many people that Trump reaches out to for discussions and advice are his family, including his wife Melania, his daughter Ivanka, his son-in-law Jared Kushner, and his two sons Donald Trump, Jr. and Eric Trump.[120] Their concern with Trump's best interest does not necessarily mean that their advice will overlap with his views. Nor does it ensure that their views will be acted upon. However, one of the advantages that trusted family members bring to the president is that, as his son put it, "Ivanka, Eric and I have the ability to be very candid with our father." All have been given repeated high profile administration assignments,[121] a sign of the trust that Trump places in them.

Yet, in the end, Trump must turn to the only person who he can always count on to have all three of those important basic elements operating— himself.

NOTES

1. Cf., Donald J. Trump [with Meredith McIver]. 2004. *Trump: Think Like a Billionaire: Everything You Need to Know About Success, Real Estate, and Life*. New York: Random House; see also Donald J. Trump [with Meredith McIver]. 2004. *Trump: How to Get Rich*. New York: Ballantine Books.
2. David Kay Johnson. 2018. *It's Even Worse Than You Think: What the Trump Administration Is Doing to America*. New York: Simon & Schuster.
3. Aaron Blake. 2017. "Donald Trump's Best Speech of the 2016 Campaign, Annotated," *Washington Post*, August 19.
4. Neil Irwin. 2019. "How a Strong Job Market Has Proved the Experts Wrong," *New York Times*, December 6.
5. Steve Elder and Alicia Parlapiano. 2016. "Donald Trump's Ventures Began with a Lot of Hype: Here's How They Turned Out," *New York Times*, October 6.
6. Clifford Geertz. 1983. *Local Knowledge*. Basic Books.
7. Rebecca Shabad. 2017. "Mitch McConnell Grumbles: Trump Had 'Excessive Expectations' for How Quickly Congress Can Act," *CBS News*, August 8.
8. Daniel Drezner. 2017. "The One GOP Myth That the Trump Administration Has Managed to Discredit," *Washington Post*, August 16.
9. Bert Spector. 2017. "Trump Wasn't a Real CEO: No Wonder His White House Is Disorganized," *Washington Post*, February 21.
10. Alan Blinder. 2012. "The Case Against a CEO in the Oval Office," *Wall Street Journal*, October 1.
11. "Transcript: Donald Trump Interview with Bob Woodward and Robert Costa," 2016. *Washington Post*, April 2; see also Beverly Gage. 2016. "Who Is the Forgotten Man?" *New York Times*, November 9.
12. Donald J. Trump [with Tony Schwartz]. 1987. *Trump: The Art of the Deal*. New York: Random House.
13. Donald Trump's *New York Times* Interview: Full Transcript. 2016. *New York Times*, November 23.
14. Cf., Ana Swanson. 2016. "Donald Trump Isn't Going to Like This New Report About His Campaign's Impact on His Businesses," *Washington Post*, October 16.
15. Holman Jenkins, Jr. 2012. "Good Businessman, Bad President?," *Wall Street Journal*, October 23.
16. Edward Morrissey. 2017. "America Gets Its First Real Test of the CEO Presidency," *The Fiscal Times*, February 16.
17. Michael Kranish. 2017. "A Fierce Will to Win Pushed Donald Trump to the Top," *Washington Post*, January 19.

18. Cf., "Over the years, Mr. Trump has proved to be a resilient operator ..." See Glenn Thrush and Maggie Haberman. 2017. "Trump the Dealmaker Projects Bravado, but Behind the Scenes, Faces Rare Self-Doubt," *New York Times*, March 23.

19. Cf., "I like to create. I like to create great things. I don't go after money for money's sake. Money is an offshoot of what I do." Trump quoted in Robert H. Boyle. 1984. "The USFL's Trump Card," *Sports Illustrated*, February 13.

20. In a story about Mr. Trump's failed efforts in the airline industry, Henry Harteveldt, a former TWA and Continental executive who was the new airlines marketing director had this to say about Mr. Trump's efforts to make the new airline a success; "The attention to detail was incredible." See Barbara Peterson. 2015 "Noise Dive: The Crash of Trump Air," *Daily Beast*, October 14.

21. See Chat Transcript. 2016. "Gwenda Blair on the Trumps," *ABC News*, September 18.

22. Cf., "Keep the big picture in mind. There are always opportunities and possibilities, and thinking too small can negate a lot of them." See Trump Tweet. 2013. https://twitter.com/realDonaldTrump/status/389762002874150913.

23. Cf., "However, the notion that Donald is a spoilt brat bailed out by daddy is also untrue. He was a visionary. Trump hired ground-breaking architects to construct palaces of glass and steel that transformed the New York skyline. See Tim Stanley. 2016. "Introducing the Real Donald Trump: A Careful Plotter and Media Master Who Is Far More Intelligent Than He Seems," *The Telegraph*, July 18.

24. Parrik Jonsson. 2010. "Amid Harsh Criticisms, 'Tea Party' Slips into the Mainstream," *Christian Science Monitor*, April 3; see also "National Survey of Tea Party Supporters." 2010. *New York Times/CBS Poll*, April 5–12.

25. Cf., Michael D. Shear. 2017. "Trump Will Withdraw U.S. From Paris Climate Agreement," *New York Times*, June 1; see also Muzaffar Chishti and Jessica Bolter. 2017. "The Trump Administration at Six Months: A Sea Change in Immigration Enforcement," *Migration Policy Institute*, July 19.

26. Holman Jenkins. 2018. "Trump's Trade Tactic Might Just Work," *Wall Street Journal*, April 6.

27. Keith Bradsher, Alan Rappaport, Ana Swanson, and Chris Buckley. 2019. "U.S. and China Reach Initial Trade Deal," *New York Times*, December 13.

28. Chris Cillizza. 2017. "Being President Is Hard: The Education of Donald Trump," *CNN*, April 13.

29. Holman Jenkins, Jr. 2019. "How Bad Can a Trade War Get?" *Wall Street Journal*, September 3.
30. Carl M. Cannon and Emily Goodwin. 2016. "Trump to Disaffected Americans: 'I Am Your Voice'," *Washington Post*, July 22.
31. Michael C. Bender. 2017. "Donald Trump Seen Bringing 'Deliberate Chaos' to the White House," *Wall Street Journal*, January 20.
32. Nick Wing. 2016. "Donald Trump Thinks Being President Is So Easy, Even He Could Do It," *Huffington Post*, January 3.
33. Heather Long and Jeff Stein 2019. "The U.S. Deficit Hit $984 Billion in 2019, Soaring During Trump Era," *Washington Post*, October 25.
34. BBC. 2016. "Trump Aims to 'Jump Start' America with New Tax Plan," August 8.
35. Ben Walsh. 2016. "Trump Could Trigger the Longest Recession Since the Great Depression, Report Says," *Huffington Post*, June 27.
36. Kevin Schaul and Samuel Granados. 2017. "5 Challenges Trump May Face Building a Border Wall," *Washington Post*, January 25.
37. Trump quoted in Nick Wing. 2016. "Donald Trump Thinks Being President Is So Easy, Even He Could Do It," *Huffington Post*, January 3.
38. Tim Hains. 2015. "Trump's Updated ISIS Plan: 'Bomb the Shit Out of Them'," *Real Clear Politics*, November 13.
39. Dion Nissenbaum and Maria Abi-Habib. 2017. "Trump Gives Generals More Freedom on ISIS Fight," *Washington Post*, April 14.
40. Stephen J. Adler, Jeff Mason, and Steve Holland. 2017. "Exclusive: Trump Says He Thought Being President Would Be Easier Than His Old Life," *Reuters*, April 28.
41. "Transcript: Donald Trump Interview with Bob Woodward and Robert Costa," 2016. *Washington Post*, April 2.
42. Ibid.
43. Trump quoted in Gerardc Baker, Carole E. Lee, and Michael C. Binder. 2017. "Trump Says He Offered China Better Trade Terms in Exchange for Help on North Korea," *Wall Street Journal*, April 12.
44. Trump quoted in Kevin Liptak. 2017. "Trump Agrees 'Not to Terminate NAFTA at This Time'," *CNN*, April 26. Kevin Liptak. 2017. "Trump: 'Nobody Knew Health Care Could Be So Complicated'," *CNN*, February 28.
45. Trump quoted in Zeke J. Miller. 2017. "Read Donald Trump's Interview with *TIME* on Being President," *Time Magazine*, May 11.
46. Trump quoted in Michael Scherer and Zeke J. Miller. 2017. "Trump After Hours," *Time Magazine*, May 11.
47. Trump quoted in Rush Limbaugh. 2017. "Trump Must Not Play the Swamp's Game," June 16.
48. Trump quoted in Jon Sharman. 2017. "Donald Trump Says He Was Surprised Being US President Was Such a Big Job," *The Independent*, February 8.

49. Trump quoted in O'Reilly Factor. 2017. "Exclusive Interview with President Trump, Part 3," *Fox News*, March 20.
50. Doug Cameron. 2017. "U.S., Boeing Complete $3.9 Billion Air Force One Deal," *Wall Street Journal*, January 17; see also CBS. 2018. "Trump Reveals Details of Planned Air Force One Makeover," *CBS*, July 17.
51. Gerardc Baker, Carole E. Lee, and Michael C. Binder. 2017. "Trump Says He Offered China Better Trade Terms in Exchange for Help on North Korea," *Wall Street Journal*, April 12.
52. Eli Stokols. 2017. "Trump's Loyalists See Course Correction Amid the Tumult," *Wall Street Journal*, April 27.
53. Katie Rogers and Robin Pogrebin. 2020. "Draft Executive Order Would Give Trump a New Target: Modern Design," *New York Times*, February 5. The draft order "Making Federal Buildings Beautiful Again" can be found at: https://cdn.vox-cdn.com/uploads/chorus_asset/file/197 00169/Draft_of_Trump_White_House_Executive_Order_on_Federal_B uildings.pdf.
54. James Freeman. 2017. "Art of the Health-Care Deal," *Wall Street Journal*, March 24.
55. Sprague quoted in Glenn Plaskin. 1989. "Trump: 'The People's Billionaire'," *Chicago Tribune*, March 12.
56. William E. Geist. 1984. "The Expanding Empire of Donald Trump," *New York Times Magazine*, April 8.
57. Ben Hubbard, Eric Lipton, Dan Levin, and Richard. C. Paddock. 2017. "Trump's Dual Roles Collide with Openings in Dubai and Vancouver," *New York Times*, February 18.
58. Amy Goldstein. 2019. "New Trump Rule to Make More Health Care Rates Public," *Washington Post*, November 15.
59. Stephanie Armour. 2019. "Trump's Push for Health-Cost Transparency Sparks Furor," *Wall Street Journal*, September 27.
60. Berkeley Lovelace, Jr. 2019. "Trump Administration Is Drafting Plan to Allow US Consumers to Import Drugs from Canada," *Reuters*, July 30.
61. Brian Blase. 2019. "Trump's New Rule Will Give Businesses and Workers Better Health Care Options," *CNN*, June 14.
62. Michael D. Shear and Christopher Drew. 2016. "'Cancel Order!' Donald Trump Attacks Plans for Upgraded Air Force One," *New York Times*, December 6.
63. Mike Allen. 2018. "Donald Trump Wants to Get Rid of Air Force One's Legendary Paint Job," *Axios*, July 12.
64. Ana Radelat. 2019. "Courtney Foils Trump's Red, White, Blue Air Force One Plan," *The CT Mirror*, June 12.

9 PRELUDE TO A UNIQUE PRESIDENCY ...   339

65. Nicole Goodkind. 1999. "USPS Could Privatize as Early as Next Year," *Forbes*, December 27; see also Dave Jamieson. 2020. "Donald Trump Is About to Put His Stamp on the U.S. Postal Service," *Huffington Post*, January 11.
66. Blair quoted in *ABC News*. 2018. "Chat Transcript: Gwenda Blair on the Trumps," September 18.
67. Donald J. Trump, 2019. "Remarks by President Trump During Video Teleconference with Members of the Military," Palm Beach, FL, December 25.
68. Nancy Cook. 2019. "Forget the Oval: The Real Trump Action Is in the Residence," *Politico*, November 24, emphasis added.
69. Dr. Ronny Jackson quoted in Press Briefing. 2018. "Press Briefing by Press Secretary Sarah Sanders and Dr. Ronny Jackson," The White House, January 16.
70. Fred I. Greenstein. 1982. *The Hidden-Hand Presidency: Eisenhower as Leader*. New York: Basic Books.
71. Arnold Sawislak. 1981. "Reagan Called 'Amiable Dunce' on New Washington Tape," *UPI*, October 10.
72. Wayne Slater and James C. Moore. 2003. *Bush's Brain: How Karl Rove Made George W. Bush Presidential*. New York: Wiley.
73. Editorial. 2017. "President Bannon?" *New York Times*, January 30.
74. Joshua Green. 2017. "Does Stephen Miller Speak for Trump? Or Vice Versa?" *Bloomberg*, February 28.
75. Bob Woodward. 2018. *Fear: Trump in the White House*. New York: Simon and Schuster; see also Quint Forgey. 2018. "Former Trump Aides Break Their Silence on Woodward Book," *Politico*, September 11.
76. Anonymous. 2018. "I Am Part of the Resistance Inside the Trump Administration," *New York Times*, September 5.
77. Stanley A. Renshon. 1996. *The Psychological Assessment of Presidential Candidates*. New York: New York University Press [Routledge Press], chapter 8.
78. Graham Allison. 1971. *Essence of Decision: Explaining the Cuban Missile Crisis*. Boston: Little, Brown.
79. Mike Allen and Jim VandeHei. 2017. "Reality Bites: Trump's Wake-Up Call," *Axios*, January 18.
80. Marc Fisher and Michael Kranish. 2016. "Trump Interview," *Washington Post*, June 9.
81. Nancy Gibbs and Zeke Miller. 2015. "Donald Trump Explains All," *Time*, August 20, emphasis added.
82. Phillip Rucker, Josh Dawsey, and Damian Paletta. 2018. "Trump Slams Fed Chair, Questions Climate Change and Threatens to Cancel Putin Meeting in Wide-Ranging Interview with the Post," *Washington Post*, November 27, emphasis added.

83. Donald. J. Trump. 2017. "Remarks by President Trump on the Strategy in Afghanistan and South Asia," Ft. Meyer, VA, August 21.
84. Richard C. Snyder, H. W. Bruck, and Bert Sapin. 2002. "Decision-Making as an Approach to the Study of International Politics," in *Foreign Policy Decision-Making (Revisited)*. New York: Palgrave Macmillan.
85. Herbert A. Simon. 1990. "Bounded Rationality," in J. Eatwell, M. Milgate, and P. Newman (eds.), *Utility and Probability*. London: Palgrave Macmillan.
86. Quint Forgey and Daniel Lippman. 2019. "'Extremely Stable Genius': Trump Defends His Mental Fitness as He Tears into Pelosi," *Politico*, May 23.
87. Rucker et al. 2018.
88. George Will. 2017. "Trump Has a Dangerous Disability," *Washington Post*, May 17.
89. Daniel W. Drezner. 2015. "The Scariest Thing I Found Out About Donald Trump Yesterday," *Washington Post*, September 9.
90. Trump quoted in Michael Barbaro. 2015. "Donald Trump Likens His Schooling to Military Service in Book," *New York Times*, September 8.
91. Candidate Donald Trump quoted in Noah Bierman. 2016. "A Testy Donald Trump Lashes Out at News Media and Says, 'I'm Not Changing'," *Los Angeles Times*, May 31.
92. Trump quoted in *Wall Street Journal*. 2017. "WSJ Trump Interview Excerpts: China, North Korea, Ex-Im Bank, Obamacare, Bannon, More," *Wall Street Journal*, April 12, emphasis added.
93. *New York Times*. 2016. "Donald Trump's New York Times Interview: Full Transcript," *New York Times*, November 23. The president was clearly influence by Gen. Mattis' reputation: "you know he's known as Mad Dog Mattis, right? Mad Dog for a reason."
94. Andrew Ackerman. 2018. "White House, in Shift, Pushes to Revive U.S. Export-Import Bank," *Wall Street Journal*, June 14; see also Nick Timiraosk. 2017. "In Ending Ex-Im Bank Impasse, Trump Sides with Business Establishment," *Wall Street Journal*, April 13.
95. *Wall Street Journal*, 2017.
96. Trump 2017.
97. Kate Kelly and Maggie Haberman. 2018. "Gary Cohn Says He Will Resign as Trump's Top Economic Adviser," *New York Times*, March 6.
98. Donald J. Trump, 2018. "Remarks by President Trump and Prime Minister Löfven of Sweden in Joint Press Conference," The White House, March 6.
99. Barack Obama. 2016. "Press Conference by the President," James S. Brady Briefing Room, November 14.

100. Tillerson quoted in Abigail Williams. 2017. "Tillerson Faces Many Unfilled Top Spots at State Department," *NBC News*, August 27.
101. Nancy Cook. 2019. "Forget the Oval: The Real Trump Action Is in the Residence," *Politico*, November 24.
102. Seung Min Kim and Josh Dawsey 2019. "'He Just Picks Up': Trump and the Lawmakers He Loves to Talk to on the Phone," *Washington Post*, February 19.
103. Alexi McCammond and Jonathan Swan. 2019. "Scoop: Insider Leaks Trump's 'Executive Time'-Filled Private Schedules," *Axios*, February 3.
104. Jenna McGregor 2019. "Unlike Trump, Most CEOs Have Very Little 'Executive Time'," *Washington Post*, February 6.
105. Maggie Haberman and Glenn Thrush. 2017. "Trump Reaches Beyond West Wing for Counsel," *New York Times*, April 27.
106. Joshua Green. 2016. "How to Get Trump Elected When He's Wrecking Everything You Built," *Bloomberg*, May 26, emphasis added.
107. Michael C. Bender and Gordon Lubold. 2019. "Trump Bucked National-Security Aides on Proposed Iran Attack," *Wall Street Journal*, June 23, emphasis added.
108. Haberman and Thrush 2017, emphasis added.
109. Mark Lander and Maggie Haberman. 2017. "Angry Trump Grilled His Generals About Troop Increase, Then Gave In," *New York Times*, August 21.
110. Dr. Fauci quoted in Jon Cohen, 2020. "'I'm going to keep pushing.' Anthony Fauci tries to make the White House listen to facts of the pandemic," *Science*, March 22.
111. Trump quoted in Reuters. 2017. "Highlights of Reuters Interview with Trump," July 12.
112. Plaskin 1989.
113. Peter Baker. 2019. "Trump Makes Clear He's Ready for a Fight He Has Long Anticipated," *New York Times*, September 24.
114. Steve Reilly et al., 2016. "Donald Trump: Three Decades 4095 Lawsuits," *USA TODAY*, June 9.
115. Nick Penzenstadler and Susan Page. 2016. "Exclusive: Trump's 3500 Lawsuits Unprecedented for a Presidential Nominee," *USA TODAY*, June 1.
116. James D. Zirin. 2019, *Plaintiff in Chief: A Portrait of Donald Trump in 3500 Lawsuits*. New York: All Points Books, p. 237.
117. Steve Reilly. 2016. "USA Today Exclusive: Hundreds Allege Donald Trump Doesn't Pay His Bills," *USA TODAY*, June 9.
118. Reilly et al. 2016. "Donald Trump: Three Decades 4095 Lawsuits," *USA TODAY*, June 9 [other cases] emphasis added.
119. David Hochman. 2015. "Playboy Interview: Donald Trump (2004)," *Playboy*, July 19, emphasis added.

120. Monica Langley. 2016. "Campaign Influence of Donald Trump's Adult Children Grows," *Wall Street Journal*, June 21.
121. Jonathan Mahler. 2016. "In Campaign and Company, Ivanka Trump Has a Central Role," *New York Times*, April 16; see also Ashley Parker and John Wagner. 2017. "Kushner Has a Singular and Almost Untouchable Role in Trump's White House," *Washington Post*, April 3.

CHAPTER 10

Essentials of Leadership: The Core Sources of Trump's Presidency

Mr. Trump has now been president long enough for the patterns of his leadership style to have become crystal clear. He is a president of enormous physical energy and emotional stamina. At age seventy-four he is able to speak extemporaneously for more than two straight hours at campaign rallies.[1] He has proved able to continue making progress on his presidential ambitions in the face of unrelentingly fierce and determined resistance, and a worldwide pandemic.[2]

He has continued to redefine the roles of president and presidential leadership in unusual if not unprecedented ways.

However, one important question is how much of Trump's leadership style will survive his presidency, win or lose a second term. Trump is unique in terms of his adult career as CEO, his psychology, and the circumstances of this particular period of political time. Trump's most lasting contribution, should he achieve it, might be as a successful *Restoration* presidency rather than as an exemplar of the psychology behind his fight club presidency. That *Restoration* goal includes the herculean tasks of reforming the United States' major domestic (eg., DOJ CDC, the national media) and important international institutions (eg., WHO, WTO, NAFTA). In the history of the presidency, policy paradigms are more enduring than psychological leadership paradigms. The latter serve mostly as ideals and exemplars since every period of presidential political time requires its own attributes for success.

© The Author(s) 2020
S. Renshon, *The Real Psychology of the Trump Presidency,*
The Evolving American Presidency,
https://doi.org/10.1007/978-3-030-45391-6_10

343

Trump is a president of both determination and surprise in policy. Through political and legal setbacks and advances, he has relentlessly pursued building a border barrier, and has made progress.[3] In some areas like troop levels and strategy in Afghanistan,[4] and to a lesser extent in Syria, he has not acted on his "gut feeling," of total withdrawal for American troops, but has settled for a more gradual, circumstances-based strategy of winding down military commitments. He has pursued a policy of inexorable economic pressure on Iran and China, and to a lesser degree with Mexico on both trade and immigration policy.

In pursuing these goals, Trump has continued to be a master of controversy. He appears to value riling his allies and his enemies by refusing to conform to their expectations, criticisms, or hopes. Trump's fight club presidency shows no signs of winding down, in spite of the House voting to impeach him, his subsequent Senate acquittal, and facing a worldwide pandemic and a presidential election coming into clear view. It is unclear whether Trump could or would change during a second term, if he wins it. A major and at this point unresolved question is whether he will continue to govern primarily by presidential initiative and a working senate majority, whether a house Republican majority will be added to the equation, or whether he will govern alone without either.

In the meantime, basic questions about the Trump presidency remain to be addressed before we consider its future in Chapter 12. These include: the nature of his supporters and their relationship to Trump, how Trump thinks, and his equivocal relationship to various versions of "the truth."

TRUMP SUPPORTERS: REAL AND IMAGINED

The shock of Trump's election was exceeded only by the shock that so many people voted for him. Over 62 million people did so, and the question on many minds was—why? Many explanations of Trump voters were put forward (see Chapter 3).

Trump voters, it was suggested, were economically marginal[5] working-class people who had been steadily losing ground. However that proved to be inaccurate. In the words of political scientists Robert Griffin and John Sides[6]:

> The prevailing narrative of the 2016 presidential election and its aftermath focused heavily on the economic concerns of Americans, particularly

10 ESSENTIALS OF LEADERSHIP: THE CORE SOURCES OF TRUMP'S ...

among one key subset of the population—the "white working class," often defined as white people without a four-year college degree. These anxieties were said to be of unusual political salience, contributing to Donald Trump's success, especially with the white working class. Our research suggests that this storyline is flawed.

They found that "working-class white people were not distinctively distressed relative to other groups." Further, they found that "Trump voters in 2016 do not report more economic distress than do Clinton voters. If anything, the opposite is true."

Cultural Marginality, Status Threat, and "Racial Resentment"

Another study also found that among Trump supporters, "change in financial wellbeing had little impact on candidate preference."[7] What did? That study offered, "A possible explanation is dominant group status threat" that occurs when "When members of a dominant group feel threatened."

That study asserted that, "The 2016 election ... *was an effort by members of already dominant groups to assure their continued dominance and by those in an already powerful and wealthy country to assure its continued dominance.*" This raises the question of just which Trump supporters were members of the "dominant group"? When were working-class Americans without a college education the "dominant" group in the United States? What exactly does that word mean?

This study provides further puzzlement with the statement that, "The declining white share of the national population is unlikely to change white Americans' status as the most economically well-off racial group, but symbolically, it threatens some whites' sense of dominance over social and political priorities." Absolutely no data whatsoever is presented on anyone's views of that matter. The panel study "does not include repeated measures asking directly about racial status threat—[because] ... such measures might be susceptible to social desirability bias in any case." Even more to the point, the author concludes by saying, "Another limitation in the panel analyses is that I do not provide direct evidence that dominant groups feel threatened."

Translation: The purported sense of "some whites' sense of dominance over social and political priorities" is nowhere actually measured.

It is simply inferred and asserted. Nor as is usual in cases of such assertions, is the term "some whites" more clearly specified. Would that be a plurality? A majority? How do they compare with other whites who don't correspond to the characterization?

The author's second suggestion about group status threats is even farther afield, to wit: "Americans feel threatened by the increasing interdependence of the United States on other countries." More specifically:

> For white Americans, the political consequences of racial and global status threat seem to point in similar directions with respect to issue positions: opposition to immigration, rejection of international trade relationships, and perceptions of China as a threat to American wellbeing.

The phrase "for white Americans" seems to include all white Americans. Yet again, no data are presented. One other rather large problem with this analysis is that on immigration, the policy issue substantially associated with racial status concerns according to the authors, they report: "to the extent that immigration is perceived as threatening by Americans, scholars find that it is due to the increased economic burden Americans believe immigrants place on the social welfare system *rather than a threat to white status*." In other words, the "threat" from immigration was related to rising social welfare concerns, not "white status." Another problem is that some American workers might be angry at establishment trade policy for reasons having nothing to do with "racial and global status." They might well be upset about having their jobs exported to a foreign country.

There were, as noted, other explanations for Trump voters. They were said to be low information voters,[8] racist,[9] xenophobic and nativist,[10] worried about keeping their white privilege,[11] authoritarians looking for a Hitler-like leader who can make a complex world simple again,[12] or just too plain ignorant[13] or deplorable[14] to know that their real interests, economic and otherwise, were better served by Mrs. Clinton and the Democrats.[15] The general tenure of these explanations was well summed up in the title of an edited volume on Trump supporters entitled[16]: *Why Irrational Politics Appeals: Understanding the Allure of Trump.* **Translation**: Trump supporters embrace "irrational political appeals."

The most frequent explanation for Trump voters, however, is that they feel culturally marginalized and are, as a result, "racially resentful." One study reported that[17]:

> We find that racism and sexism attitudes were strongly associated with vote choice in 2016, even after accounting for partisanship, ideology, and

other standard factors. These factors were more important in 2016 than in 2012, suggesting that the explicitly racial and gendered rhetoric of the 2016 campaign served to activate these attitudes in the minds of many voters.

Michael Tesler, the author of *Post-Racial or Most-Racial? Race and Politics in the Obama Era*, is quoted as saying that the "evidence suggests that racial resentment is driving economic anxiety, not the other way around."[18] Philip Klinkner,[19] a political scientist at Hamilton College is quoted as saying "whether it's good politics to say so or not, the evidence from the 2016 election is very clear that attitudes about blacks, immigrants, and Muslims were a key component of Trump's appeal." For example, he says, "in 2016 Trump did worse than Mitt Romney among voters with low and moderate levels of racial resentment, but much better among those with high levels of resentment."

That leads directly to the following questions: What exactly is "racial resentment"? How is it measured? How does one know that it is an important, perhaps the most important, factor in motivating Trump voters?

"Racial Resentment" and Trump Voters

"Racial resentment" is to explanations of voters who support Trump, as narcissism is to explanations of Trump's psychology, the go-to explanation for their various deficiencies. Many studies use that term, and they almost all use the same four questionnaire items to measure it. As a result, it is easy to lose sight of the fact that *none* of the studies that use the term and those four questionnaire measures ever actually measure "racial resentment" directly. In reality, the term "racial resentment" is an exercise in concept-naming by inference—a form of racial tar and feathering by conceptual innuendo.

The *validity* of the measures that are used, that is, the extent to which they measure what they purport to measure is the issue here. A measure may be *reliable*, meaning you get comparable results each time it is used, but if the measures aren't *valid*, one is simply getting the same invalid and mistaken results repeatedly.

Sides et al., for example, use a four-item "racial resentment" scale, each answer to which is given a level of agreement number on a five-point scale. The questions are the following[20]:

1. Over the past few years, Blacks have gotten less than they deserve.
2. Irish, Italian, Jewish, and many other minorities overcame prejudice and worked their way up. Blacks should do the same without any special favors.
3. It's really a matter of some people not trying hard enough; if Blacks would only try harder they could be just as well off as Whites.
4. Generations of slavery and discrimination have created conditions that make it difficult for Blacks to work their way out of the lower class.

Are there any questions among these four "racial resentment" items that ask respondents directly about their level of anger, an elementary dimension of resentment? No. Anger is inferred and attributed on the basis of the use of scale's given name, "racial resentment," but not directly measured. That is circular science, not social science.

Are there any questions among these "racial resentment" items that ask respondents about the respondents' feelings regarding the unfairness of how they are being treated, another aspect of resentment? No. Are they asked if they are angry about that unfair treatment? No. Again, that respondents feel unfairly treated and angry about that, is inferred and attributed to them on the basis of the use of the term "racial resentment", but these key elements are not directly measured.

Finally on his point, Sides et al., write in their book: "Racial anxieties may not necessarily be about rank prejudice but about simple resentment: the belief that other racial groups are getting something they do not deserve—but that you do."[21] Are there any questions among these "racial resentment" items that ask respondents about the respondents' feelings regarding "racial groups are getting something they do not deserve—*but that you do* (emphasis added)"? No. Again, the observation that respondents' feel that they personally are not getting what they deserve to get is inferred and attributed to them on the basis of the use of the term "racial resentment," but not directly measured.

The problem with these questions, aside from their questionable validity, is that they are likely tapping something quite different than racial resentment, mostly likely political conservative policy views or ideology. For example, Feldman and Huddy found that[22]:

Among conservatives, racial resentment appears more ideological. It is closely tied to opposition to race-conscious programs regardless of recipient race and is only weakly tied to measures of overt prejudice. Racial resentment, therefore, is not a clear-cut measure of racial prejudice for all Americans.

One might well add that not only is "racial resentment," therefore, not a clear-cut measure of racial prejudice for all Americans, is it not a valid measure of what it purports to measure, because it doesn't really directly measure any of its claimed emotional elements.

There is substantial evidence of the decline of overt racism in the United States.[23] This is true even though wide disparities of outcome measures exist among some racial and ethnic groups, and deeply regrettable events like the death of George Floyd during a police stop can still occur. The data on views of interracial marriage, levels of interracial marriage, broad criticism of radical prejudice, and other factors all attest to this. Skeptics of these findings, whatever their reasons, are forced to conclude that, "outright stereotyping has declined, but in its place 'colorblind' racism has become the main way that racism is expressed."[24] In this view "colorblind racism" is "racism lite," in which "instead of proclaiming God placed minorities in the world in a servile position, it suggests they are behind because they do not work hard enough."[25]

The issue here is immediately apparent. This explanation eludes the important distinction between overt racism (minorities are inferior in some basic non-remedial way or God placed minorities in the world in a servile position), and the very widespread American cultural assumption that people who work hard get ahead; or that it takes hard work to succeed. Many conservative believe these cultural aphorism to be true, but so do many Americans who are not "conservatives."

Similar issues arise with the concept of "symbolic racism."[26] In the absence of much evidence of overt racism, the search for prejudice has focused on disguised ("color-blind") or analogous hidden forms (symbolic) of racism. Racial resentment is a term that does not directly measure or reflect over racism or feelings of resentment. As a result, its repeated application to Trump supporters is highly questionable.

Further Measurement Issues with Racial Resentment

Consider again the four questions used to measure racial resentment:

1. Over the past few years, Blacks have gotten less than they deserve.
2. Irish, Italian, Jewish, and many other minorities overcame prejudice and worked their way up. Blacks should do the same without any special favors.
3. It's really a matter of some people not trying hard enough; if Blacks would only try harder they could be just as well off as Whites.
4. Generations of slavery and discrimination have created conditions that make it difficult for Blacks to work their way out of the lower class.

One observer has written, "It's possible that agreement with a statement like 'Blacks should do the same without special favors' reflects a resentful spirit, but it could also reflect a respectful one—a confidence that blacks are as capable as anyone else."[27] It certainly might be expected to be associated with views on quota-based affirmative action policy, but not tellingly, with affirmative action policy designed to insure wide ranging outreach.

Again, the idea of groups "working their way up" is obviously a staple of American cultural assumptions. It is a reflection of experience with upward mobility opportunities in the country and an article of faith strong enough to be a cultural belief. Moreover, the idea that "over the last few years," "Blacks have gotten less than they deserve" might run headlong into the well- publicized efforts over the past four decades to overcome the barriers of past racial discrimination and its effects. The question would have been much better had it simply begun by saying, "In the past ...".

Considering those four questions, it seems likely that ideologically liberal respondents would strongly agree with the first and last of these four assertions and strongly disagree with the middle two. The opposite would be true of ideologically conservatives. True independents would probably range on the midpoint (3) of the 5-point scale.

Racial Resentment by Correlation

It is at this point that another measurement issue arises. Correlation analysis, which is the basis for all the "racial resentment" analyses takes a more (less) of this, the less (or more) of that approach. Scores on the 5-point scale for each question are aggregated to measure more, or less, "racial resentment."

On a 20-point scale, however, how many respondents actually score at the extreme range, say 17–20 (even assuming the questions validly measure what they purport to measure)? How many Trump supporters do? We don't know and the number is important, again assuming this scale measures something unique about them. Do 10% of Trump supporters score at the extreme? Is the figure 50, 60% or more? Reporting that Trump supporters are "more likely" to be racially resentful gives the impression that many or most are, without reporting the non-correlation data that would support that phrasing. If only 10% of Trump supporters score in the extreme range, are we justified in saying that "Trump supporters (notice the plural) evidence more racial resentment"? Perhaps not.

Are there overt racists that support Trump? No doubt there are. However it is certainly possible to hold conservative viewpoints without being racist.

Oddly, there is national data in data sets used by Sides et al. and others, who characterize Trump supporters as being suffused with "racial resentment" that would directly address the above questions. That is the ANES National Election Data set.[28] That study contains a number of relevant questions of racial identity (pp. 47–50) like the following:

How important is your race to you?
Does having white skin give whites more/less opportunities?
Does being White help/hurt you?

There are other, similar questions. However, the point here is that answers to these questions could shed direct light on the underlying feelings/dynamics that are an integral part of any real feelings associated with having "racial resentment" among respondents (including Trump followers). However, oddly, they are not reported in the many books and articles that purport to find Trump supporters marinated in "racial resentment."

About Those Obama Trump Voters

One other major problem with the racial resentment narrative concerning Trump voters is that a large number of Trump supporters voted for Obama in previous elections.[29] On election eve, Nate Cohen, the *New York Times* polling expert wrote that, "Clinton suffered her biggest losses in the places where Obama was strongest among white voters. It's not a simple racism story." Further, he wrote that "this election was decided by people who voted for Obama in 2012, and should figure into the analysis."[30]

Supporters of the "racial resentment" narrative of Trump voters have difficulty explaining how it was possible for racially resentful and racially prejudiced whites to vote once and even twice for President Obama and then support Trump.[31] What happened to their racial resentment when they voted for Obama? What happened to their racial prejudice?

Supporters of this narrative like Michael Tesler are forced to argue that, "*Barack Obama won lots of votes from racially prejudiced whites.*"[32] Perhaps, though he presents no evidence on this supposed link. Even if he did, it would still leave unanswered the two questions just raised. What happened to all that racial resentment and prejudice when white working-class voters pulled the lever for an African American instead of a white Republican candidate?

Other supporters of the racial resentment narrative have touted a massive study that studied vote switchers for both parties. It found that, "White voters with racially conservative or anti-immigrant attitudes switched votes to Trump at a higher rate than those with more liberal views on these issues."[33] Again, assume momentarily that the data and its analysis are correct. Those two nagging questions about what caused the unexpected change from voting Obama to voting Trump remain.

Note that the study finds that those with "racially conservative" or "anti-immigrant" attitudes were more likely to switch to Trump after Obama than whites with more "liberal" views, as characterized by the study. How were those views measured?

The racial attitudes scale was constructed of three items, each with a 5-point scale[34]:

1. "I am angry that racism exists."
2. "White people in the U.S. have certain advantages because of the color of their skin."
3. "Racial problems in the U.S. are rare, isolated situations."

It seems fairly clear what racially "liberal" or "conservative" means here, although it is unclear how requiring respondents to answer questions like No. 1 with a high degree of social desirability built into them (what kind of person are you that you aren't angry that racism exists!) gets the analysis very far. Still, the questions, their scale placement and their naming, and the data suggest that white working-class "conservatives" on racial attitudes did vote for Obama and then switched to Trump, leaving the question of "why" still unanswered. The "liberal" or "conservative" emphasis in this study suggests we are again dealing substantially with political views and ideology.

The immigration questions in the study are even more problematic. They are preceded by the question: "What do you think the US government should do about immigration? Select all that apply." [0 = selected, 1 = not selected]:

1. Grant legal status to all illegal immigrants who have held jobs and paid taxes for at least three years, and not been convicted of any felony crimes.
2. Increase the number of border patrols on the US–Mexican border.
3. Grant legal status to people who were brought to the US illegally as children, but who have graduated from a US high school.
4. Identify and deport illegal immigrants.

The study's hypotheses, supported by the data was (emphasis added):

H1b: *Anti-immigrant attitudes*: *White voters who express more punitive* views on immigration will be more likely to switch their vote to Trump than similarly situated White voters with less punitive views on immigration.

The authors, respectable academics with long research histories, make a basic, category placement mistake so often made in studies of these kinds. First, they characterize their questions and their scale as "anti-immigrant." That is their view, but it embodies a major conceptual and narrative error.

All four questions specifically reference those who have come into the United States without going through the necessary immigration procedures. As a result, they are here in violation of American immigration laws. Believing that immigration laws should be followed is not "anti-immigrant."

As the Mutz study noted above says, Americans are generally very pro-immigration even as they worry about the impact of undocumented aliens. It is possible for both to be true. To whatever degree Americans take different positions on the specifics of any of the four policy ideas given to respondents in this survey, calling a disagreement over a specific policy "punitive," as the authors do, is itself judgmental and ill-advised. Would "liberal" and "conservative" have done just as well here too?

Finally, one recent study goes even further in simply assigning racism on an a priori basis. In a recent issue of *Political Science* (*PS*) two researchers published an article with the title, "Explaining the Trump Vote: The Effect of *Racist* Resentment and Anti-Immigrant Sentiments."[35] They use those terms throughout and base their results on the very same troubled three-item index noted above (e.g., "I am angry that racism exists"). This study shares the conceptual and scale validity problems that the others examined in this section do. However, it does have the virtue of explicitly and directly making clear the working assumption contained in the naming of the term racial/racist resentment that supposedly characterize Trump voters. They are simply racist.

Respect and Standing: The Two Elements Linking Trump and His Supporters

Accusations of Trump supporters' racism and other pathological "irrationalities" are no truer for being serially repeated. Still, there is without doubt a strong emotional and political connection between Trump and his supporters. The question is: what is it?

In Chapter 3 we argued that many voters were disheartened and disappointed by the performance, competence, and integrity of establishment figures on both sides of the political aisle. Many establishment elites felt the same about a large number of Americans and voters and thought of themselves as more reliable guardians of the public's interests than the voters who put them into office.

We noted that Trump ran as the candidate and governed as a president who was serious about his intention to take on the problems he saw and act on them. For many Americans, this rekindled the hope that someone was really listening to their concerns. As a result, many millions of primary and general election voters were willing to take a chance on Trump, and did.

10 ESSENTIALS OF LEADERSHIP: THE CORE SOURCES OF TRUMP'S ...   355

Trump and His Supporters: A Powerful Emotional Connection

The analysis that follows allows a closer look at a truly remarkable and in some ways unprecedented emotional and political connection, both in level and intensity, between Trump and his supporters. The general markers of this relationship are fairly clear. They are found in substantial support among Republicans for the president, 89% according to Gallup.[36] That level of support has held even given some disapproval of Trump's presidential demeanor and having had two articles of impeachment voted against him in the House. It is also reflected in the overwhelming support for Trump in the Republican party apparatus,[37] something that did not exist when Trump won the Republican nomination in 2015.

Trump and his supporters obviously exist in relationship to each other. That statement means that each brings to the relationship their own histories, views, expectations, hopes, strengths, and needs. It is the degree of fit among these elements, the likelihood that the fit will be productive, and the alternatives that are available to both parties that determine whether the relationship prospers or withers.

For some anti-Trump pundits the relationship of Trump and his followers is easy and simple. One such shallow and reductionist analysis by a psychiatrist claims that[38]:

> The mirror-hungry personality, which is Donald Trump, needs the ego-gratifying applause and roars of approval from crowds. There is a natural psychological fit between Trump and his followers. Trump's core enthusiastic followers feel incomplete without a great inspirational leader to attach themselves to, someone to venerate.

We have already examined the gaping evidentiary and logical holes in the first part of this statement and speculative psychiatric narrative in Chapter 6. The second part of this assertion is no more substantive or useful. It envisions sixty million plus voters as being desperately incomplete people searching for a great inspirational leader to attach themselves to in order to feel complete. No evidence is presented for this psychiatric speculation beyond its assertion, which is as absurd on its face as well as fundamentally insulting to many millions of ordinary Americans.

Trump needed what every successful presidential candidate needs, a means to connect with and gain the support of enough voters to win the nomination and election. His standing as a true outsider without a long political history with either party was both an opportunity and a barrier.

He was free to construct his own candidacy from political policy elements that were not ordinarily associated with the past candidates or long-standing party narratives. He did that on trade, foreign policy, immigration, and what he saw as the generally ineffective and moribund thinking of establishment elites of both parties. In so doing, he was able to open up an important line of communication with voters who felt that many, if not all, of these elements were issues that a new nominee and president had to address.

These would be somewhat prosaic observations, and should be, were it not for the fact that they suggest that Trump's first major and serious connection with the voting public that eventually supported him was on policy grounds, an often overlooked basis of their relationship. Republicans and other supporters did not start out gravitating toward Trump because he demonstrated that he would be the bull in the country's policy china shop. They listened because he gave policy voice to what they thought.

Trump's demeanor including his willingness to do what is necessary to fight back effectively cemented that connection. Many Trump voters felt that leaders asked for their votes but weren't really interested in their views and either ignored or disparaged them after they got into office. They were suddenly faced with a nominee who had policy views similar to what they thought, and seemed willing to go the mat to defend them. You might, and many did, criticize how Trump thought, or what he said, but there was no doubt where he stood.

It was not only that Trump seemed "authentic." He was. It was also that his authenticity included having policy views that resonated with his potential supporters. He also signaled a style that promised that he wouldn't be bullied into submission, had the stamina and resilience to persist, and the determination to push forward on his policy goals come what may. He has kept those promises.

These twin core elements of Trump's relationship with his supporters are joined by a third and powerful emotional connective bridge. Both he and his supporters have been mocked and disparaged by establishment elites; Trump since the time he entered the Manhattan building industry, and his supporters in every possible way before and since Trump became a winning candidate and then president. A recent *Atlantic* profile captured their feelings: "Donald Trump's supporters would like to be clear: They are tired of being called racists."[39] That is not the only name they have been called or the only way in which they have been disparaged.

Many Trump supporters feel marginalized by establishment leaders and institutions. Yet feelings of not being listened to, heard, taken into real account, respected, and given the ordinary standing afforded Americans to give voice to their views long preceded Trump's arrival on the presidential stage. Trump too was mocked and never taken seriously. In fighting to be taken seriously, Trump is also at the same time fighting for their standing. It is a powerful emotional bond.

Trump's political brand is based in part on the insistence of standing and respect, for himself and those who support him. It is this sense in which Trump's supporters are the "forgotten man." Although in truth they have been less "forgotten" that disparaged and ignored.

Everything for His Base?

Those key elements define the relationship between Trump and his supporters. It began with an overlap of views. It was reinforced by a combative style of fighting for those views that gave supporters the feeling that Trump was listening to them, substantially agreed with them, cared what they thought, and would not forget or disparage them once he got into office.[40] He hasn't.

That is one reason why Trump has been able to retain support from some of the very groups that his policies, on trade for example, have harmed at least in the short term.[41] They trust he is acting in the country's best interests, and ultimately theirs. As a result, they are willing to experience some economic pain to allow him to do that.

Still the narrative persists that everything Trump does, he does is for his base. A fairly typical observation along these lines is the following[42]:

> President Trump pardoned a tough-on-immigration Arizona sheriff accused of racial profiling. He threatened a government shutdown if Congress won't deliver border wall funding. He banned transgender people from serving in the military. And he is openly contemplating ending a program that shields from deportation young undocumented immigrants who consider the United States home. These and other moves have helped cement an image of a president, seven months into his term, *who is playing only to his political base.*

Leave aside the tendentious framing of all these issues, some of which some of his supporters care about and many of which his supporters do not care about that much—what does only playing to his base mean? Does it mean that Trump has no personal position on these issues? Does it mean that he doesn't really care about them and is only using them to stimulate support for his presidency? Isn't it the case, that both Trump and his supporters both care about some of these issues (DACA [Deferred Action for Childhood Arrivals] security at the Southern border), but that there is a lot less overlap on other issues (pardoning the Arizona Sherriff, transgendered military service).

Trump's basic foreign policy is also supposedly all for his base. For example,

> Trump's moves against the Iran deal are chiefly motivated by his desire to unwind Obama's legacy and play to his political base at home.[43]

Again, does Trump really not have any real personal policy views on Iran independent of the fact that it is an Obama initiative? Does his "political base" care deeply about his issue, as opposed to other issues like jobs and the economy?

Who exactly are Trump's "political base?" That is an often-used term without any particular empirical anchor. Are they all 63 million-plus Trump election voters? Are they only the hundreds of thousands that have attended or watched one of his rallies, or the equally large number who have contributed to his presidential campaigns?

Every president considers his base, and Trump is no exception. Yet, as noted, this president is willing to pursue policies that cause some parts of his base economic pain in the short term. He has also determinedly pursued his economic program that has resulted in real economic gains for many, not only his base. He has pursued efforts to reform the criminal justice system[44] and signed that bill into law[45]—not a so-called base issue. Trump is making a bet that if he does enough of what he believes in and promised to do, his base (however defined) will give him some running room when he does things not on their list of preferences and concerns. Evidence suggests it was a prudent bet.

TRUMPTHINK/TRUMPTALK: HOW TRUMP UNDERSTANDS AND EXPLAINS HIS WORLD

The title of this section writes itself as an anti-Trump joke for those so inclined. Yet *how* Trump thinks and *how* he talks is at least important as *what* he thinks, for which by now we have plenty of data. It has long been known that the "rhetorical presidency"[46] has changed the nature of presidential leadership. Every president must now develop a strategy for mobilizing the public on behalf of his policies and informing the public of his views of the benefits and possible pitfalls of what he plans to do.

Given a divided and increasingly polarized political environment, any presidential initiative can expect intense opposition from those who oppose it. It will be well-organized, well-funded, opposition amplified by well-developed and refined media strategies. And, for any policies associated with President Trump there will be intense opposition. Small wonder that many modern presidents, including Trump[47] prefer emphasizing the positive rather than engaging the public with a frank public appraisal of possible risks and rewards.

Sometimes when presidents are honest and frank they are criticized. Speaking during a major press conference on the possible spread of the Coronavirus Trump said[48]:

> Now, it may get bigger, it may get a little bigger. It may not get bigger at all. We'll see what happens. But regardless of what happens, we are totally prepared. (February 27)

Speaking to a gathering of African American leaders, Trump said[49]:

> you know, it could get worse before it gets better. It could maybe go away. We'll see what happens. Nobody really knows. The fact is, the greatest experts—I've spoken to them all. Nobody really knows.

For these direct and honest appraisals, Trump was criticized in a *Washington Post* news report because he "only added to the uncertainty," and offered "a contradictory and ambiguous message about the virus."[50] Presumably, the reporters would have been preferred either a relentlessly upbeat or dire message, neither one of which was supported by the evidence.

Given this kind of tendentious response to frankness, it is not surprising that the public assessment of risks is now more substantially influenced vocal opposition that suggests dire consequences for a president's preferred policies. From the standpoint of effective public understanding and support that is not really a desirable alternative.

One consequence of these circumstances is that many presidents and presidential candidates have become increasing guarded and scripted. Talking points take the place of frank discussion. Spin insures that selected facts go in the right direction. Enormous effort is undertaken to present candidates and presidents as they wish to be seen, rather than who they are. One way to understand Trump's political persona and style is that he simply skips the ordinary pretenses. He does not hide who he is or what he thinks. There is a basic honest transparency in this leadership stance, for better or worse.[51]

TrumpTalk and the *TrumpThink* behind it is very unconventional. They reflect strong feelings rather than strong logic, and are often divorced from nuance. Yet they are also mostly devoid of scripted artifice, and startlingly original. Trump embellishes, presents the facts that he finds most congenial and omits others, is truly unversed in the nuances of most policy arguments, and is not overly impressed with expert views— although he does listens to some of them some of the time. No previous candidate or president had ever repeatedly talked in public like that.

TrumpThink

Entering into Trump's mind requires one to take a circuitous journey through uncommon assumptions, idiosyncratic associations, fragments of facts and analysis, and sometimes surprisingly acute insights. It's an unusual style, However, that doesn't negate the need to try and understand it and its implications, positive and negative, for his presidential leadership and prospects.

TrumpTalk places a burden on the public and on his presidency. A fair amount of effort is sometimes needed to understand the thinking beneath Trump's meandering and often somewhat opaque rhetorical style. This makes it difficult to fully immediately grasp his meaning.

When Trump was asked about what he would do in a second term, he replied[52]:

> We'll, one of the things that will be really great... You know, the word experience is still good. I always say talent is more important than experience. I've always said that, but the word experience is a very important word... I never did this before...I was from Manhattan from New York. Now I know everybody, and I have great people in the administration.

Critics and concerned supporters noted that there was no real listing or discussion of Trump's second-term policy plans,[53] and that was true. Trump was making a more basic argument in his own mind, namely, that he knew little of Washington and then all of a sudden he was actually president and had to learn a lot and did. Tested by experience, a very understated word for what his presidency has had to deal with, he was now a deeply seasoned president. His agenda? More restoration and more deeply honed skills to accomplish it. Of course, as reading the quote above makes clear, that is not how Trump put it.

To his critics, Trump's tweets and other off-script free associations reveal a mind riddled with an inchoate ménage of erroneous "alternative facts," prejudices against various groups, self-promotional puffery, and a lack of curiosity and knowledge, all of which mitigate against his being able to mount a real, factual, and logical argument. Moreover, his critics say, these traits are pathological because they reflect an incapacity for judgment and its foundation, clear thinking. In this view, Mr. Trump's free associations show he has no conscience able to contain his boisterous, uninhibited, and unrestrained Id.

To one well-known linguistics professor, "Trump's Typos Reveal His Lack of Fitness for the Presidency."[54] Perhaps. Yet, as one *New York Times* analysis noted, "in running his norm-breaking campaign, Donald J. *Trump shined a light on a larger truth*: Voters have had it with the artifice, emptiness and elements of corruption that pervade the country's politics."[55]

That analysis continued:

> In an era when so-called message discipline has been made into a cardinal virtue for candidates, draining much of the spontaneity out of campaigns but lessening the margin for error, Mr. Trump said out loud what was on his mind. He did not have the fear of gaffes that the members of the political-industrial complex often instill in candidates.
>
> *In this, he was more honest to the realm he had entered than most of the career politicians*: Like Mr. Trump, they too are consumed with their standing in polls, given to ridiculing their rivals and the news media and taken with their own talent and charm. They just do not say so in public.

There are, it seems, some larger Trump truths that exist side by side with his hyperbole, factual black holes, spelling and word usage errors, and his unusual and meandering thinking.

There is no doubt that Trump's tweets and off-script associations reflect a vast archipelago of lifetime experience, honed and refined in the world of business, not politics. He has had neither the inclination nor the necessity to develop and refine his views to ensure a lifetime career in political power. Moreover, as the single head of a vast worldwide business empire for many decades, he enjoyed, and that word is used deliberately, the ability to speak his mind freely.

The conclusions of Trump's thinking are not found on a yellow steno pad listing the pluses and minuses of an issue as were Richard Nixon's. Nor do they resemble the well-practiced smoothness of Barack Obama who was able to replay the talking points of both sides of an argument. That ability conveyed the illusion of his own moderation, while he was, in reality, tenaciously attached to his own progressive politically transformational views and ambitions.

Trump's meandering mind and thinking resembles neither of these presidents, nor any other president in our history. However, both those traits come with a political cost as well as advantages. They are disquieting even to those who support what he is attempting to do. That is one reason why so many Americans wish he would have tweet fights less often.[56]

Many Americans are uncomfortable with a president who insists on giving his unvarnished, sometimes harsh views. Longing for the end of partisan conflict, they are uncomfortable with a president who insists on repeatedly and publicly calling out his opponents and many enemies with little effort to hide his true feelings. This is a source of real discomfort to many Trump supporters even though they have felt ignored, managed, and insulted. One strong reason why they are willing to tolerate Trump's excesses, and their discomfort with them, is because they feel that Trump does really care about them and will successfully fight for them.

President Trump's serial brash, argumentative, and confrontation political style is unlikely to ever win majority, professional, or establishment praise. It is simply too jarring to deep public wishes for bi-partisan amity in spite of, or perhaps because of decades increasing harsh partisan political clashes that have been the rule. Yet, if Trump's style results in the successful accomplishment of the promises he made as candidate and president against the concerted opposition of establishment Democrats, Republicans, and conservatives alike, a two year long Special Council investigation of his presidency, acquittal on two articles of impeachment and a worldwide pandemic with catastrophic effect on American life, he will have carried off a truly remarkable example of modern presidential leadership.

TrumpTalk

Many Americans think that when their political leaders speak, they are literally, unbelievable. Into this minutely managed highly scripted political environment stepped Donald Trump. Rarely, if ever, in the history of presidential elections has a candidate said so much of what was on his mind. Moreover, he did so in a way that not only ignored well-established campaign decorum, but also violated the rules that govern ordinary conversation. Mr. Trump talked in public, as a candidate, like many people think in private—direct, earthy, and unvarnished by social convention.

Trump's tweets and frequent off-script riffs are the free associations of his presidency. They are his often spontaneous, certainly unrehearsed responses to the issues that grab Trump's attention, and his mind's association to them. As one observer notes, "Trump follows whatever train of thought is headed out of the station, letting his speeches spiral well out into the countryside before he brings them back in."[57]

Examples of Trump's meandering train of thought mixed with his stream of consciousness are legion. During Trump's presidential campaign a *Rolling Stone* reporter accompanied him to a rally and filed this report about their discussion[58]:

In those 26 minutes, he'll devote some 90 seconds to his typewritten notes, diverted instead by the mentions of him on *Fox* and the crowd of whims and tangents in his head. To sit alone with Trump is to be whipsawed and head-snapped by his sentences that start and stop, his thoughts that take hard detours or suddenly become questions in midstream.

And then there is his actual rally performance:

And for 58 minutes, he goes on like this, playing the crowd like a Telecaster. Mexico's taking your jobs. Ford and Nabisco are fleeing there. No more Oreos for Trump! *What's most striking is the ease with which Trump does it—no note cards, no teleprompter, no prep in the car. Running his first race for office at 69, an age when other men are seeking help for bladder conditions, he gives every impression of being born for this—and of having the time of his life.*

One need only watch any Trump rally replay like the two-hour Trump stemwinder in Battle Creek, Michigan.[59] That featured[60]: Trump talking about the 2016 election that no one thought he would win; the media's failure to refer to him as "President Trump" at the time, instead of Donald Trump; why the media got his election wrong; the country being in a battle of "survival of this nation"—as exemplified by the Green New Deal; his restraint in not attacking that idea more because when he attacked Senator Warren too early, she rebounded; then back to the Green New Deal which will severely curtail air travel.

From there he went on a riff about wind-based power:

> We'll have an economy based on wind. I never understood wind. You know, I know windmills very much. I've studied it better than anybody. I know it's very expensive. They're made in China and Germany mostly—very few made here, almost none. But they're manufactured tremendous—if you're into this—tremendous fumes. Gases are spewing into the atmosphere. You know we have a world, right? So the world is tiny compared to the universe. So tremendous, tremendous amount of fumes and everything. You talk about the carbon footprint—fumes are spewing into the air. Right? Spewing. Whether it's in China, Germany, it's going into the air. It's our air, their air, everything—right? So they make these things and then they put them up.

There is a certain amount of capacity and skill at work in these rally riffs. Speaking extemporaneously for one or two hours is no small feat, even for a much younger and presumably more energetic person. There is a degree of self-confidence in undertaking these performances, and a degree of intelligence at work as well. Trump has to reach into his mind and memory to summon his content, reprising old themes and weaving in new events. As noted, Trump does not possess the revolutionary cosmic brilliance of an Einstein or the deep pioneering analysis of a Freud. Yet it would be a large mistake not to recognize the keen intelligence at work.

Although Trump often speaks without any visible aides, he manages to make general associative sense in these riffs. They are not random unconnected thoughts. However, neither do they reflect the ordinary expectations of logic and sequential analysis that are associated with most politicians' practiced rhetoric. Trump has so far proved unable or unwilling to mount the seemingly wide-ranging and detailed factual arguments associated with highly traditional verbally facile presidents like Bill Clinton and Barack Obama. The word "seemingly" is used here because verbally facile presidents can often mount what appear to be convincing arguments, but they are based on facts selected and arranged for that purpose. Their delivery may be smooth and seamless, but their narrative is purposeful.

Rather than hiding what he really thinks behind a wall of political consultants and poll tested equivocation, Mr. Trump is confident enough in himself and in the public to let them know what he really thinks. This is a point worth emphasizing. The president is unafraid to let the public know what he thinks. Surprisingly that includes allowing public exposure of his generally poor spelling abilities. For a president who is widely considered to be incapable of acknowledging error, this is quite an anomaly.

Trump's tweets have been widely mocked by opponents for their many errors. A running count of these errors is available.[61] So is a detailed analysis of Trump's many language use eccentricities and errors that concludes[62]:

> The gaffes, lurches, rudenesses, and infelicities allow, it must be said, a certain transparency. No one could say that Trump uses language to dissimulate: The whole man is always blazingly on view.

That analysis ends: "That's just the problem: Trump speaks as an unmonitored self, making it up as he goes along, rather than in the monitored style of a nation outlining ideals."

TrumpTalk is often extremely provocative. Illustrative is the debate about whether Trump did really refer to some countries in scatological terms, if so which, and whether "dysfunctional" would have been a better word choice.[63] Many presidents privately say things behind closed doors that they wouldn't want revealed in public. Yet, Trump should be aware enough by this point in his presidency to know that nothing he says in a room full of people will not go unreported, and not always accurately. There is some truth in the dysfunctions he may have associated with some countries, yet sometimes diplomatic and empathetic discretion is preferable.

Some elements of *TrumpTalk* may be honest and heartfelt, but still better left as a private sentiment. Illustrative is a remark Trump made about how "incredible and so inspiring.." watching the Paralympics was to him, but that it was "a little tough to watch too much, but I watched as much as I could."[64] It's understandable how both could be true, the empathetic poignancy of athletes' circumstances and the admiration for what it takes to overcome that kind of adversity. Yet, it is likely that the participants would have preferred an emphasis on the latter. One is reminded of Trump's blunder across the line of a seven-year-old's belief in Santa Claus (see Chapter 1).[65] Stating the "total truth" as you know or feel it all the time no matter what, even if it could be known, is better left a conceit of fact-check enthusiasts, not presidents.

TrumpFacts

Trump's barrage of hyperbole and his use of a virtual catalogue listing of logical fallacies (of relevance,[66] ambiguity,[67] and presumption[68]) in his speeches and rhetoric have unleashed a torrent of "fact check" articles that now include his 140 character tweets.[69] They have documented the frequently loose factual foundation of a number of his assertions and assumptions. Many fact-checked Trump statements are assembled under the category of "false or misleading statements." That characterization is supplemented by the statement that Trump is "spouting exaggerated numbers, unwarranted boasts and outright falsehoods."[70] Of course the first two are very different than the third.

Mr. Trump often exaggerates, selects, and remembers the facts he likes best, ignores counter-evidence, is truly unversed in the nuances of many policy arguments, is not overly impressed with expert views— although he listens to some of them some of the time, as he did to former Secretary of Defense Mattis on waterboarding—[71] frequently changes his publicly stated understanding of policies or events, and has no hesitation in contradicting aides' publicly stated understandings.

Trump biographer Gwenda Blair recalls that she attended a Trump book signing event at which he spoke very briefly and then began signing books. She asked the clerk how many books had been sold and was told about two hundred, a respectable figure for those kinds of events. The next day she says[72]:

> I read Donald's account of this event. He said, "850 had been sold and signed in an hour and a half." Which would have been not just remarkable, but herculean. But this is who he is. He exaggerates everything, even when what he's starting with is pretty good.

One is reminded of one reporter's insight about Trump and his hyperbole, "When he makes claims like this, the press takes him literally, but not seriously; his supporters take him seriously, but not literally."[73] That reality has provided ample ammunition, though not necessarily uncontestable evidence, for his critics to contend that he is a con artist,[74] and a purveyor of "falsehoods."[75] More harshly and frequently, some like political scientist George Edward II, relying on the usual list of Trump "exaggerations' and distortions" categorically writes "To put it simply, the president is a brazen and incessant liar."[76]

It is worth pausing a moment to consider that last harsh word. Sissela Bok's definitive book on the subject makes clear that the central element of a lie is the conscious intent to deceive.[77] Yet most of the thousands of "lies" attributed to Trump include exaggerations, hyperbole, statements that "mislead" because they do not provide exhaustive background by which to judge a statement, statements that are at variance with the fact-check reviewer's own preferred view of the matters that Trump gives his views on, statements for which he personally does not provide evidence but around which debate has swirled, or just plain mistakes. As a result, many of Trump's assertions may well be mistaken, not fully accurate, in need of much more information to give a balanced view, or "misleading" as every utterance that doesn't contain the full, absolute and irrefutable "truth" can be said to be.

Yet calling each and every one of these kinds of omissions a "falsehood" or "lie" is an editorial and political decision. "Needs more context" is a very frequent fact-check characterization of many Trump statements. That simply means that Trump mentions his understanding and the fact check reminds readers that there are other facts and circumstances that might be relevant to consider. Not mentioning every fact that could be brought to bear on any long-standing complex political or political circumstances is de rigueur for almost all presidents. They are, after all, political leaders not doctoral students defending their Ph.D. dissertations. The lack of scrupulous adherence to factual balance and fairness is not a trait to be expected in any president trying to mobilize the public to support his preferred policies. It is a weak foundation on which to serve as a claim of a president's basic unfitness, or Edward's claim that Trump is a "brazen and incessant liar." That is one reason why *WSJ*'s editor-in-chief cautions that,[78] "editors should be careful about making selective moral judgments about false statements."

"Fact checks," of course, are not impartial arbiters of essential and incontestable "truths." They reflect limited, often narrowly framed and focused, but strongly held views of what should count as "true" or "false." They can be informative. Yet they can often be nitpicking, tendentious in style,[79] and not infrequently just plain wrong. For example, President Obama's promise that "if you like your health care you can keep it," was rated "Lie of the Year" by *Politifact*.[80] However in 2008, that same organization rated that same statement as "True."[81] President Obama's assertions on the status of Syria's chemical weapons system received a glowing factual endorsement,[82] only to be revised by another fact-check organization a few days later.[83]

Many of Trump's "misrepresentations" turn on different views of what the "facts" used mean. That is, they are interpretations using of particular facts and not others. Even a casual reading of the many fact checks that claim to uncover Trump's "false" or "misleading" claims,[84] would find ample reason to doubt that strong often unequivocal language.

A case in point are the payments made to Iran in connection with the nuclear deal. Trump has frequently made the point that money being fungible, Iran paid for its military initiatives with funds collected as part of the nuclear deal. On a recent *Face the Nation* interview,[85] Obama Secretary of State John Kerry agreed with that understanding. He and other supporters of the deal however argued that the money Iran received was owed to them from prior transactions[86]:

> There are nuances with the money Iran got. *The $150 billion is a false claim* Trump has repeatedly made; it refers to funds already belonging to Iran that were unfrozen as part of the nuclear deal signed in 2013, and it's on the very high end of estimates. Others suggest it's closer to $25 or $50 billion.

Given that money is fungible, Trump is likely correct that Iran did use money from the nuclear deal to fund its military initiatives. However, that money was already owed to Iran, and was unfrozen and given to them for their use. Trump simply noted that it was used for their military initiatives, which, according to Kerry, was accurate.

Trump used an estimate on the high side of ranges associated with that money. No suggestion is made that he made up the figure, just that he used one of many available. So the 150 billion is not a "false" claim in that it represents one of many efforts to estimate the amount of money

10 ESSENTIALS OF LEADERSHIP: THE CORE SOURCES OF TRUMP'S ... 369

Iran received. Nor is it a false claim that Iran used the money to finance its military efforts. Money can be owed and paid and still used exactly for the purposes Trump noted. From Trump's perspective the deal should never have been made and the money Iran gained as a result to fund its military activities should never have happened. This is a debatable policy position, and has been, but it is not a "false claim."

Descriptive Imprecision and "Larger Truths"

President Trump is often imprecise with his characterizations of his policies. Consider the "wall" at the Southern border, one of his signature domestic policies. In 2014, he tweeted: "SECURE THE BORDER! BUILD A WALL!"[87] In his June 2015 announcement of his candidacy he promised, "I would build a great wall, and no one builds walls better than me, believe me, and I'll build them very inexpensively. I will build a great wall and I'll have Mexico pay for that wall."[88] Throughout his campaign, Trump described his vision of a concrete wall, 30 to 50 feet (10–15 m) high and covering 1000 miles (1600 km) of the 1900 mile (3050 km) border, with the rest of the border being secured by natural barriers.

That vision changed substantially over time. As one useful overview noted: "'A WALL is a WALL!' Trump declares. But his definition has shifted a lot over time."[89] Sometimes he uses the words wall and fence interchangeably. Sometimes he said that a wall was better than fencing, because some existing border barriers are a "little fence" and can be scaled.[90] The wall would he noted, "be made of hardened concrete, and it's going to be made out of rebar and steel." Later, he tweeted that it would be a "Steel Slat Barrier" design.[91] He also said it would need to be "steel wall with openings," so that the border patrol could see what was happening on the other side. In January 9, 2019 he tweeted[92]:

> We are now planning a Steel Barrier rather than concrete. It is both stronger & less obtrusive. Good solution, and made in the USA.

Sometimes Trump used the term "great wall," conjuring up purposefully or inadvertently the "Great Wall of China." At other times he is much more explicit about the Great China Wall as in this speech:

They built the Great Wall of China. That's 13,000 miles. Here, we actually need 1,000 because we have natural barriers. So we need 1,000.

At one point Trump seemed to give up on characterizing whatever he was building in terms of stating basic and "larger" truths:

> I can't tell you when the government is going to reopen. I can tell you it's not going to be open *until we have a wall, a fence, whatever they'd like to call it. I'll call it whatever they want. But it's all the same thing. It's a barrier from people pouring into our country.*

It's easy enough to understand the general reasons for all these changes. Trump started out with an idea in his mind, a "wall" that evolved into a concept with increasingly refined elements. These were at least a partial by-product of responding, without necessarily publicly acknowledging, legitimate criticisms and also learning more about the nature of the project he wanted from experts, once Trump actually had to start bring the "wall" into policy existence.

The moving target of Trump's evolving understanding of what his wall or barrier idea would best entail in practice was one side of that truthfulness coin. The large, public debate about whether the barrier, however called, was actually being built was the other side of that coin. Trump, anxious to show progress on this campaign promise, touted wall construction at various points along the Southern border, though it was not strictly speaking "new" wall construction of which at first there wasn't much. Critics pointed out that this was not "new" wall construction, as Trump had promised, but the replacement of old border barriers and therefore didn't count as fulfilling his promise. That kind of criticism can provide an important deepening of the understanding of the large ambition of the project,[93] although that was not its purpose.

Ironically, both Trump and his critics are right about barrier construction. Trump was correct in pointing to substantial barrier construction. That was in the traditional, not the political understanding of that word, "new." It reflected the reality that the new barrier construction replaced old dilapidated fencing or four-foot high barriers that were designed to stop cars but not people. The new tall steel slat barrier designs represented a substantial improvement, but they were "replacements" for existing barriers not "new" wall construction where none had ever existed. So critics were also technically correct if you defined new as never before having existed.

This dispute was the focus of numerous "fact check" articles, almost all of which came to the conclusion that Trump was "misleading" the public if not worse. For example, the *Washington Post* wrote of Trump's 13,435 now estimated to be "more than 20,000" by the *Washington Post* "false or misleading claims[94]:"

> Almost one-fifth of these claims are about immigration, his signature issue—a percentage that has grown since the government shut down over funding for his promised wall along the U.S.–Mexico border. In fact, his most repeated claim—218 times—is that this border wall is being built. Congress balked at funding the concrete barrier he envisioned, so he has tried to pitch bollard fencing and repairs of existing barriers as "a wall."

Oddly, the *Washington Post* fact-check feature relies on the view that many Trump statements said to be part of his long list of "exaggerated numbers, unwarranted boasts and outright falsehoods" require "need more context" as the basis for awarding Pinocchio's. Yet more context is little in evidence in this and other fact-check analyses. It is not only that Trump has a point about how he sees those wholly new and more effective barriers as being part of building the wall. It is also that there are important reasons that they are relevant to the analysis as to why more of the wall has not been built.

The answer to why so little "new wall" and why so much "replacement wall" is clear. Opposition to Trump's wall has been furious, relentless, and to some degree effective. The House has stymied Trump's request for "new wall" construction funds. Court suits have been filed and been successful before reaching the Appellate level in limiting Trump's new wall construction. Building new wall construction takes longer as a process than replacements because of eminent domain and environmental issues that must be addressed or litigated.

Whether a very new kind of replacement barrier does or does not count as "new" is a very narrow conceptual and semantic issue. It is not a window into either Trump's veracity or the real motivations of his critics. That being the case, perhaps more "context" on the part of the fact check would have been informative and beneficial.

Policy Premises and "Larger Truths"

There is as well an interesting element of "larger truths" in assessing Trump. This seems, and is, paradoxical. It is also likely to be very controversial, but is no less real for that. One element of the "larger truth" argument is to point out that on a number of issues Trump does not have deep historical or factual understanding, but that doesn't mean he's not right. It is easiest to provide several general examples.

It is true that trade is generally a net advantage to countries that engage in it. However, the key word is "net." Trump is correct that there are downsides to trade that include, among other things, its effect on domestic industries and the jobs associated with them in a primarily trade induced service based economy. There are as well national security concerns when a country no longer is able to make the things it might need. This is aside from the fairness and reciprocity elements of trade agreements that Trump took on with NAFTA, China, and others, and reached fairer "free trade" agreements. There are also dangers in outsourcing key medical resources as supply chain problems during the pandemic revealed.

Trump also had a point as well about NATO's mission and purpose needing to evolve. He did not subscribe to the view that NATO was just fine as it was, still operating on the premises of its founding in 1949. Trump also had a point about enforcing existing country borders and immigration laws. He did not believe that there was no downside to failing to enforce immigration laws or agreeing to ever-higher levels of mass unskilled immigration. While there might be debate about the best policies to develop from these premises, the premises themselves were legitimate and sound.

These and other basic Trump policy premises were not buttressed by his assertion on their behalf with a large accumulation of analytical and historical facts. Trump simply does not possess them and is focused elsewhere. That does not mean his views were incorrect. Each of these policy premises has a large number of facts associated with them. A limited number were considered "conventional wisdom," and thus were made the basis for all "true" factual argumentation. Trump's facts might have truth value, but they were disparaged as partial truths at best, needing more "context," and falsehoods and lies at worse, given that other traditional and preferred facts contradicted those that Trump used.

10 ESSENTIALS OF LEADERSHIP: THE CORE SOURCES OF TRUMP'S ...   373

Facts contradicting other facts is not a sound basis for imputing that your sides' facts are true and the other sides' facts are lies.

Promise Keeping: An Essential "Truth"?

Trump does much better in keeping his promises than in speaking accurately about them.[95] His supporters are focused on the "essential" accuracies of Trump's positions that they support—(fairer trade agreements, enforcing immigration laws, creating more job for Americans). They are not focused on whether his facts need more context. Trump is betting that a number of Americans who don't support him now will do so for his reelection, and beyond, because of the weight of his accomplishments. He is betting that they too will be less concerned that his facts lack context, and more interested in their prospects because of a robust economy.

Trump's "promise keeper" approach to his presidency and reelection is another illustration of the "larger truth" element to Trump's presidency. As a candidate, Trump showed every indication that he intended to follow through on his campaign promises. As president, he did. We noted some follow throughs in Chapter 8. Here are some more.

Withdraw from the Pacific Trade Accords? Check. Start renegotiating NAFTA? Check. Bomb Syria for crossing the no use red line for chemical weapons? Check. Confront North Korea's decades long strategy of using threats to gain incentives? Check. Lay out a new foreign policy in which American national interests are essentially and explicitly part of its international leadership? Check?. Get laws passed that allow heads of agencies like Veterans Affairs to more easily fire those employees who are incompetent or uncaring about their responsibilities? Check. Pass a number of laws to help make health care more affordable and accessible. Check. Pass the largest overall tax cut in decades to help stimulate the economy? Check. Focus on the economy to stimulate job creation? Check. Dramatically cut back on federal regulations? Check. Renegotiate Chinese trade deals? Check. Sign a comprehensive Afghanistan withdrawal agreement. Check. Try to reopen parts of the country as quickly and safely as possible to help recovery from the pandemic? Check. Try to help development and pass a bill to reform some police practices like the use of "choke holds." Check. Take presidential action to try to prevent the destruction historic and some iconic statues that are part of America's heritage. Check. Send federal forces to cities, like Portland and Chicago, besieged by violence to augment local police efforts?[96] Check.

The above list is not meant to be definitive. Yet it does suggest why Trump supporters are keyed into a lager truth about his presidency. The border wall is Trump's new metaphor for taking immigration enforcement and reform seriously. It does not reflect the immigration enforcement and reform paradigms that have dominated the last three decades of immigration debate: more and more exceptions to the enforcement rules, major amnesties (DACA and DAPA [Deferred Action for Parents of Americans and Lawful Permanent Residents]) for undocumented aliens, and increasing unskilled legal immigration numbers. It is a new immigration paradigm that tightens enforcement and attempts to recalibrate the basis of new immigration from extended family reunification to education and skills.

Trump supporters clearly see in his response to the surge in undocumented aliens at the Southern border that Trump is serious about enforcement. He has tried in a number of ways, several very successful, to stem that surge.[97] They can see his efforts to overcome all the hurdles he must surmount to build "new" wall construction and give him credit for trying. He may call "replacement wall" building the wall, but they are attuned to a larger, and no less real, truth. The new barriers, "replacements," are more formidable and he is moving ahead.

Trump has followed through on his promises and views about immigration enforcement, of which the wall, new or "replacement:" is only one part. These efforts, both individually and in their entirety, are one large reason why Trump supporters don't care very much whether Trump receives several Pinocchio's for saying he is "building the wall," when "fact checkers" take him to task because it is not "new wall" as they define the term.

No claim is being made here that all or most of Trump's policies have already proved successful. One would have to more clearly define that metric. Yet, some Trump initiatives have been relatively successful by most metrics: a robust economy with very good job growth and wage increases before the pandemic and perhaps after it as well, reducing regulations, and enforcing immigration laws. Others like the withdrawal from the Iran nuclear and climate control agreements have been completed. NAFTA has been renegotiated (USMCA [United States–Mexico–Canada Agreement]) and at least phase one of the China trade agreements has been accomplished. Other issues like NATO, Iran, and North Korea remain very much works in progress.

Trump's efforts to keep his major campaign promises are more important to Trump's supporters than his numerous fact-check violations They concede that Trump embellishes and makes use of facts that others find questionable. They may even be aware that at least on one occasion Trump made up an impromptu trade deficit "fact" about the US having a trade deficit with Canada in a discussion with PM Justin Trudeau[98] that Trudeau insisted was not accurate. It turned out on checking, that Trump had stumbled on a factually accurate point, if you included energy and timber, which the Canadian PM had not. A more detailed analysis found that[99]: "In 2017, the United States had a 23.2 billion deficit with Canada in goods. However, the United States had a \$25.9 billion surplus, with Canada in services."

So in fact, both Trump and Trudeau were factually correct. They simply used different accurate facts, which itself reflected an even more basic truth. There is more than one correct fact associated with such issues. They are not "alternative" facts in the snarky use of that term by critics, but they are additional ones. That would argue for prudence and modesty in being too quick to label someone's fact "misrepresentations," "misleading," or "lies."

Trump supporters accept all this as Trump being Trump. They accept that Trump presents the facts as he sees and understands them. They understand that his critics respond with facts they consider truer and more compelling. They are not concerned with whether Trump's statements would benefit from adding more context. They are more interested in whether Trump's facts correctly speak to at least a portion of what they think is true. And ultimately, they care more about whether Trump is true to his presidential promises than whether he is judged truthful by the standards of his critics.

NOTES

1. Brett Samuels. 2019. "Trump Seeks to Make Impeachment a Campaign Asset," *The Hill*, December 22; see also Associated Press. 2019. "Trump Holds Record-Long Rally on Impeachment Day," *Washington Post*, December 18.

2. Michael D. Schear and Maggie Habberman. 2020. "Trump's Temporary Halt to Immigration Is Part of Broader Plan, Stephen Miller Says," *New York Times*, April 25.
3. Department of Homeland Security. 2019. "Press Release: CBP Completes Construction of 50 Miles of New Border Wall," July 11.
4. Michael Crowley. 2019. "Debate Flares over Afghanistan as Trump Considers Troop Withdrawal," *New York Times*, August 16.
5. William Galston. 2015. "The Bleak Reality Driving Trump's Rise," *Wall Street Journal*, December 15.
6. Robert Griffin and John Sides. 2018. "In the Red: Americans' Economic Woes are Hurting Trump," Democracy Fund-Voter's Study Group, September.
7. Diana C. Mutz. 2018. "Status Threat, Not Economic Hardship, Explains the 2016 Presidential Vote," *PNAS*, Vol. 115, No. 19 (April), pp. 330–339, emphasis added.
8. Richard Fording and Sanford Schram. 2016. "'Low Information Voters' Are a Crucial Part of Trump's Support," *Washington Post*, November 7.
9. Thomas Wood. 2016. "Racism Motivated Trump Voters More Than Authoritarianism," *Washington Post*, April 17.
10. Curtis Wilkie. 2014. "The South's Lesson for the Tea Party," *New York Times*, August 12.
11. Allison Skinner. 2017. "Trump Voters Were Scared: Increasing Diversity Might Make Americans More Xenophobic," *Salon*, January 10.
12. Matthew MacWilliams. 2016. *The Rise of Trump: America's Authoritarian Spring*. Amherst, MA: Amherst University Press.
13. Jason Brennan. 2016 "Trump Won Because Voters Are Ignorant, Literally," *Foreign Policy*, November 10.
14. Amy Chozick. 2016. "Hillary Clinton Calls Many Trump Backers 'Deplorables,' and G.O.P. Pounces," *New York Times*, September 2.
15. Amanda Taub. 2017. "Why Americans Vote 'Against Their Interest': Partisanship," *New York Times*, April 12; Catherine Rampell. 2016. "Why the White Working Class Votes Against Itself," *Washington Post*, December 22.
16. Mari Fitzduff. 2017. *Why Irrational Politics Appeals: Understanding the Allure of Trump*. Santa Barbara, CA: Preager.
17. Brian F. Schaffner, Matthew MacWilliams, and Tatishe Nteta. 2018. "Understanding White Polarization in the 2016 Vote for President: The Sobering Role of Racism and Sexism." *Political Science Quarterly*, Vol. 133, No. 1, pp. 9–34.
18. Tesler quoted in Mehdi Hasan. 2017. "Top Democrats Are Wrong: Trump Supporters Were More Motivated by Racism Than Economic Issues," *The Intercept*, April 6.
19. Klinkner quoted in Hasan 2017.

20. John Sides, Michael Tesler, and Lynn Vavreck. 2018. *Identity Crisis: The 2016 Election & the Battle for the Meaning of America.* Princeton, NJ: Princeton University Press, Appendix to chapter 8.
21. Sides, Tesler, and Vavreck 2018.
22. Stanley Feldman and Leonie Huddy. 2005. "Racial Resentment and White Opposition to Race-Conscious Programs: Principles or Prejudice?" *American Journal of Political Science*, Vol. 49, No. 1 (January), pp. 168–183; see also Edward G. Carmines, Paul M. Sniderman, and Beth C. Easter. 2011. "On the Meaning, Measurement, and Implications of Racial Resentment," *ANNALS, AAPSS*, Vol. 634 (March), pp. 98–116.
23. Howard Schuman, Charlotte Steeh, Lawrence Bobo, and Maria Krysan. 1997. *Racial Attitudes in America: Trends and Interpretations.* Cambridge, MA: Harvard University Press.
24. Susan McElwee and Jason McDaniel. 2016. "There's Powerful Evidence That Racial Attitudes Drive Tea Party Support," *Vox*, February 10.
25. Eduardo Bonilla-Silva. 2017. *Racism Without Racists: Color-Blind Racism and the Persistence of Racial Inequality in America*, 3rd ed. Lanham, MD: Rowman & Littlefield.
26. D. O. Sears and P. J. Henry. 2003. "The Origins of Symbolic Racism," *Journal of Personality and Social Psychology*, Vol. 85, No. 2, pp. 259–75.
27. James Taranto. 2010. "'Racially Resentful' Dissecting the Latest Bogus Tea-Party Poll," *Wall Street Journal*, April 29.
28. Codebook and User's Guide to the ANES 2016 Pilot Study. American National Election Studies, Stanford University & the University of Michigan February 23, 2016, https://electionstudies.org/project/anes-2016-pilot-study/.
29. Kevin Uhrmacher, Kevin Schaul, and Dan Keeting. 2016. "These Former Obama Strongholds Sealed the Election for Trump," *Washington Post*, November 9.
30. https://twitter.com/nate_cohn/status/796243185739632640?lang=en.
31. Zack Beauchamp. 2016. "A New Study Reveals the Real Reason Obama Voters Switched to Trump," *Vox*, October 16.
32. Michael Tesler. 2016. "Obama Won Lots of Votes from Racially Prejudiced Whites (and Some of Them Supported Trump)," *Washington Post*, December 7.
33. Tyler T. Reny, Loren Collingwood, and Ali Valenzuela. 2019. "Vote Switching in the 2016 Election: How Racial and Immigration Attitudes, Not Economics, Explain Shifts in White Voting," *Public Opinion Quarterly*, Vol. 83, No. 1 (Spring), pp. 91–113.
34. (5 = strongly disagree, 4 = somewhat disagree, 3 = neither agree nor disagree, 3 = somewhat agree, 1 = strongly agree). The responses were recoded to range between 0 (racially liberal) and 1 (racially conservative).

35. Marc Hooghe and Ruth Dassonneville. 2018. "Explaining the Trump Vote: The Effect of Racist Resentment and Anti-Immigrant Sentiments," *Political Science* (*PS*) (July), pp. 528–534, emphasis added.
36. Justin McCarthy. 2019. "Trump Approval Inches Up, While Support for Impeachment Dips," *Gallup*, December 18; see also Phillip Bump. 2018. "Why Is Trump So Much More Popular with Republicans Than Past Presidents?" *Washington Post*, July 24.
37. Alexander Burns and Jonathan Martin. 2019. "Trump's Takeover of the Republican Party Is Almost Complete," *New York Times*, April 3.
38. Post quoted in Chauncey DeVega. 2019. "Former CIA Profiler Jerrold Post on Donald Trump's 'Dangerous Charisma'," *Salon*, December 2.
39. Elaina Plott. 2019. "We're All Tired of Being Called 'Racists'," *The Atlantic*, August 2.
40. Julius Krein. 2015. "Traitor to His Class," *Weekly Standard*, September 7.
41. Carrie Johnson. 2017. "Robert Mueller May Not Be the Savior the Anti-Trump Internet Is Hoping For," *NPR*, August 17; James Hohmann. 2018. "Trump Supporters Suffer Unintended Consequences of His Policies," *Washington Post*, May 15; Patricia Cohen. 2019. "Pain of Tariffs Tests Farmers' Faith in Trump: 'How Long Is Short-Term?'," *New York Times*, May 24.
42. John Wagner. 2017. "In Action After Action, Trump Appeals Primarily to His Dwindling Base," *Washington Post*, September 3, emphasis added.
43. Ishaan Tharoor. 2018. "Is Regime Change in Iran Part of Trump's Agenda?" *Washington Post*, May 7.
44. Nicholas Fandos and Maggie Haberman. 2018. "Trump Embraces a Path to Revise U.S. Sentencing and Prison Laws," *New York Times*, November 14.
45. Matt Zapotosky. 2019. "3,100 Inmates to Be Released as Trump Administration Implements Criminal Justice Reform," *Washington Post*, June 19.
46. Jeffrey K. Tulis. 2018. *The Rhetorical Presidency*. Princeton, NJ: Princeton University Press.
47. Wesley Pruden. 2017. "Trumpspeak, a Language Rich in Adjectives," *Washington Times*, February 23; Kurt Anderson. 2018. "How to Talk Like Trump," *The Atlantic*, March.
48. Donald J. Trump. 2020. "Remarks by President Trump, Vice President Pence, and Members of the Coronavirus Task Force in Press Conference," The White House, February 2.
49. Donald J. Trump. 2020. "Remarks by President Trump in Meeting with African American Leaders," The White House, February 28.
50. Yasmeen Abutaleb, Ashley Parker, and Josh Dawsey. 2020. "Inside Trump's Frantic Attempts to Minimize the Coronavirus Crisis," *Washington Post*, February 29.

10 ESSENTIALS OF LEADERSHIP: THE CORE SOURCES OF TRUMP'S ...   379

51. One observer does note that Trump pays attention to the lines that get the best response, and he'll eventually narrow his rhetoric to highlight those zingers. See Phillip Bump. 2019. "What Trump Was Talking About in His Baffling Rant About wind Energy," *Washington Post*, December 23.
52. Donald Trump Town Hall Transcript with Sean Hannity June 25, 2020. https://www.rev.com/blog/transcript-category/donald-trump-transcripts.
53. W. James Antle III. 2020. "Republicans Wonder Where Trump Misplaced His Second-term Agenda," *Washington Examiner*, June 27.
54. John McWhorter. 2019. "Trump's Typos Reveal His Lack of Fitness for the Presidency," *The Atlantic*, January 11.
55. Jonathan Martin. 2016. "Donald Trump Was Essentially a Third-Party Candidate on a G.O.P. Ticket," *New York Times*, November 9, emphasis added.
56. Joe Concha. 2017. "Poll: Vast Majority Wants Trump to Tweet Less," *The Hill*, March 8.
57. Bump 2019.
58. Paul Solotaroff. 2015. "Trump Seriously: On the Trail with the GOP's Tough Guy," *Rolling Stone*, September 9, emphasis added.
59. https://www.youtube.com/watch?v=nMu9TmIGU3c.
60. Bump 2019.
61. Caitlin Gibson. 2017. "The Trump Administration Has a Spelling Problem: But How Bad Is It Really? We Investigate," *Washington Post*, February 15; see also Marina di Marzo. 2019. "How Often Does Trump Misspell Words on Twitter? These Researchers Have an Answer," *CNN Business*, November 3.
62. McWhorter 2018.
63. Maggie Habermane and Jonathan Martin. 2018. "Debate Continues over What Trump Said: But Does the Exact Word Matter?" *New York Times*, January 16.
64. Aaron Blake. 2018. "Trump Said It Was 'Tough to Watch Too Much' of the Paralympics: Was It Derogatory?" *Washington Post*, April 28.
65. Daniel Victor. 2018. "Kids, Please Don't Read This Article on What Trump Said About Santa Claus," *New York Times*, December 25.
66. http://www.logicalfallacies.info/relevance/.
67. http://www.logicalfallacies.info/ambiguity/.
68. http://www.logicalfallacies.info/presumption/.
69. Phillip Bump. 2016. "Now You Can Fact-Check Trump's Tweets—In the Tweets Themselves," *Washington Post*, December 19.
70. Glenn Kessler, Salvador Rizzo, and Meg Kelly. 2019. "President Trump Has Made 13,435 False or Misleading Claims over 993 Days," *Washington Post*, October 14.

71. Emily Stephenson. 2017. "Trump Says He Will Defer to Defense Secretary Mattis on Waterboarding," *Reuters*, January 27.
72. *ABC News*. 2018. "Chat Transcript: Gwenda Blair on the Trumps," September 18.
73. Salena Zito. 2016. "Taking Trump Seriously, Not Literally," *The Atlantic*, September 23.
74. Kathleen Parker. 2016. "Donald Trump: A Con Man Among Heroes," *Washington Post*, September 16.
75. Linda Qiu. 2017. "10 Falsehoods from Trump's Interview with the Times," *New York Times*, December 29.
76. George C. Edwards II. 2020. "The Bully in the Pulpit: The Impact of Donald Trump's Public Discourse," Paper Prepared for Delivery at the Annual Meeting of the American Political Science Association, Washington, DC, September 1, 2019; see also Aaron Blake. 2016. "President Trump Finally Went a Full 24 Hours Without a False or Misleading Claim," *Washington Post*, March 2.
77. Sissela Bok. 1978. *Lying: Moral Choice in Public Life*. New York: Random House.
78. Gerhard Baker. 2017. "Trump, 'Lies' and Honest Journalism," *Wall Street Journal*, January 4.
79. Nathan J. Robinson. 2016. "Why PolitiFact's 'True/False' Percentages Are Meaningless," *Current Affairs*, August 8; see also Doug Heye. 2017. "How Media Fact-Checking Can Stoke Voters' Cynicism," *Wall Street Journal*, August 17.
80. Angie Drobnic Holan. 2013. "Lie of the Year: 'If You Like Your Health Care Plan, You Can Keep It'," *Politifact*, December 12.
81. Angie Drobnic Holan. 2008. "Obama's Plan Expands Existing System," *Politifact*, December 9; see also Avik Roy. 2013. "Pants on Fire: *Politifact* Tries to Hide That It Rated 'True' in 2008 Obamacare's 'Keep Your Health Plan' Promise," *Forbes*, December 27.
82. John Greenberg. 2017. "Revisiting the Obama Track Record on Syria's Chemical Weapons," *Politifact*, April 5.
83. Matthew Lee. 2017. "AP FACT CHECK: Overlooking Doubts on Syria Chemical Weapons," *ABC News*, April 10.
84. Kessler, Rizzo, and Kelly 2019.
85. Kerry quoted in Transcript. 2020. "Face the Nation," *CBS*, January 12.
86. Aaron Blake. 2020. "As Trump Claims a Win on Iran, He Accuses Obama of Funding Its Attacks," *Washington Post*, January 8; emphasis added.
87. https://twitter.com/realdonaldtrump/status/496756082489171968?lang=en.
88. *Time*. 2015. "Here's Donald Trump's Presidential Announcement Speech," June 16.

89. William Cummings. 2019. "'A WALL Is a WALL!' Trump Declares: But His Definition Has Shifted a Lot Over Time," *USA TODAY*, January 8. The quotes that follow are drawn from that article unless otherwise noted.
90. Cf., On the difference between new replacement barriers and the old barriers they replace see: https://twitter.com/SpoxDHS/status/121576 1236903645184?ref_src=twsrc%5Etfw%7Ctwcamp%5Etweetembed%7Ct wterm%5E1215763660200718337&ref_url=https%3A%2F%2Fwww.wea selzippers.us%2F.
91. https://twitter.com/realdonaldtrump/status/1076239448461987841? lang=en.
92. https://twitter.com/realdonaldtrump/status/1082032550112047104? lang=en.
93. Nick Miroff and Adrian Blanco. 2020. "Trump Ramps Up Border-Wall Construction Ahead of 2020 Vote," *Washington Post*, February 6.
94. Kessler, Rizzo, and Kelly 2019 see also Glenn Kessler, Salvador Rizzo, and Meg Kelly. 2020. "President Trump has made more than 20,000 false or misleading claims," *Washington Post*, July 13.
95. Carrie Johnson. 2017. "Robert Mueller May Not Be the Savior the Anti-Trump Internet Is Hoping For," *NPR*, August 17.
96. Peter Baker, Zolan Kann-Youngs, and Monica Davey. 2020. "Trump Threatens to Send Federal Law Enforcement Forces to More Cities," *New York Times*, July 20; see also Zolan Kann-Youngs, Adam Goldman, and Mike Baker. 2020. "Feds Sending Tactical Team to Seattle, Expanding Presence Beyond Portland," *New York Times*, July 23.
97. Michelle Hackman and Alicia A. Caldwell. 2020. "U.S. Begins Returning Asylum Seekers at Arizona Border to Mexico," *Wall Street Journal*, January 2.
98. Josh Dawsey and Greg Barber. 2018. "Transcript of Trump's Remarks at Fundraiser in Missouri on March 14," *Washington Post*, March 15; see also Josh Dawsey, Damian Paletta, and Erica Werner. 2018. "In Fundraising Speech, Trump Says He Made Up Trade Claim in Meeting with Justin Trudeau," *Washington Post*, March 15.
99. Louis Jacobson. 2018. "Here's What's Wrong About Donald Trump's Attack on Canada Trade Deficit," *Politifact*, March 15.

CHAPTER 11

Conservative American Nationalism: The Trump Doctrine in Theory and Practice

Foreign policy is traditionally a setting in which the president is said to have more discretion because the checks and balances of domestic politics don't operate there. That has never been wholly true since the international system has its own version of restraining checks and balances—economic, political, and military consequences for serious miscalculations. Yet, that is true enough and is one major reason why presidential worldviews and foreign policy thinking weigh so heavily in assessing any president.

In my work on the G. W. Bush and Obama Doctrines,[1] I have pointed out the purposes that doctrines serve and why they matter. Often they are policy guideposts for a president's thinking that help allies and enemies alike to gauge their policies and thus further the benefits and opportunities of deterrence theories for the international community.

Doctrines often refer to specific geographical areas (e.g., The Monroe Doctrine for South America) or circumstances (e.g., the Truman Doctrine for the Cold war with the Soviet Union). The Trump Doctrine is

---

This chapter is a slightly revised version of: Stanley A. Renshon. 2020 (in press). "The Trump Doctrine and *Conservative American Nationalism*," in Stanley A. Renshon and Peter Suedfeld (eds.), *The Trump Doctrine and the Emerging International System*. New York: Palgrave Macmillan.

© The Author(s) 2020
S. Renshon, *The Real Psychology of the Trump Presidency*,
The Evolving American Presidency,
https://doi.org/10.1007/978-3-030-45391-6_11

different. It reflects a wide-ranging reassessment of *what* American policy will be worldwide, and *how* it will be carried out.

The most fitting conceptual name for the Trump Doctrine is *Conservative American Nationalism*. It is a framework that we argue is composed of six essential elements: (1) An America First premise in Trump policies; (2) An emphasis on American National Identity as a cornerstone of America's elemental and dual relationship with itself and the world; (3) Highly selective involvement, with a non-exclusive emphasis on its own terms and interests in defining America's role in the world; (4) An emphasis on American strength in all its forms, including resilience and resolve; (5) The use of maximum repeated pressure along a continuum of points in pursuit of key goals; and (6) Maximum tactical and strategic flexibility.

All of these elements are meant to further one basic core Trump presidential purpose that I've conceptualized as the *Politics of American Restoration*. That means reversing the policies and assumptions that have resulted in decades of many Americans feeling the country is moving in the wrong direction, in foreign as well as domestic policy. To do so, Trump has pivoted away from what he sees as the failed or outdated conventional policy premises of the last four decades.

That includes pivoting away from policies about which both political parties have inaccurately assured the American public, namely that: unlimited immigration and limited enforcement of immigration laws has no downside; that low economic growth is the new normal and Americans should get used to it; that free trade is always a "win-win" for everyone; and that it is better not to insist on greater reciprocity abroad with American allies, or take a strong stance against adversaries.

The Trump Doctrine is not only controversial, but also mysterious. What is it? One headline captures an essential puzzle and feature, "Depends who you ask."[2]

Not everyone believes there is a Trump Doctrine.[3] Among those who do, error is rampant. Some erroneously reduce the doctrine to the views of one now former foreign policy advisor John Bolton.[4] This neglects the fact that especially for this president his own views carry enormous weight,[5] as President Obama's did for him. Others erroneously see Trump as being concerned with one real foreign policy goal, one-upping President Obama.[6] That characterization of a single shallow motivation neglects Trump's decades-long publicly stated concerns with issues like trade and immigration that lie outside the conventional wisdom narratives.[7]

Along similar lines some NeverTrump pundits, again dismissing any policy thinking on Trump's part, argue that[8]:

Defining a foreign policy theory that might merit the title of "doctrine" is difficult in the Trump administration, which is dismissive of reflection, consistency and precedent. But in practice, it is the replacement of national pride with personal vanity.

Still others reduce the Trump Doctrine to one sound bite, "America First," which Larison notes amounts to a truism, if not an unstated premise,[9] for almost every American president. Finally, there has been the attempt to rush, erroneously and prematurely, to note that Trump embraces "key pillars" of President Obama's foreign policies.[10] As Trump's presidency has progressed, it is abundantly clear that he does not, as his withdrawal from the Paris climate accords and Iran nuclear deal demonstrate.

We argue that the Trump Doctrine is best understood as a doctrine of *Conservative American Nationalism*, as the president understands that phrase. The doctrine consists of a formulation of America's role in the world, as is generally the case for presidential doctrines. Yet, it also, unusually, makes a direct statement and envisions a direct relationship between America's role in the world and Trump's view that there is a core American national identity that helps define it. It is at its core, a traditionally conservative nationalist view that emphasizes American strength, patriotism, and sovereignty.

As with any presidential doctrine, these views are the president's, and in Trump's case particularly and idiosyncratically so. For example, Trump's emphasis on getting allies to pay their fair share is a direct by-product of Trump's business history as a CEO, and his focus on the "bottom line." However, unlike many other presidential foreign policy doctrines, the goals of Trump's *Conservative American Nationalism* doctrine are also partially defined by the psychological capacities needed to carry them out. These include the president's unusual, perhaps unique, leadership style. That combines bluster, unusual flexibility, determination, and equal amounts of pragmatism and hyperbole. It also includes core commitments to "strength" and persistence, and a willingness to stand apart from a conventional consensus and, if necessary, alone in pursuit of his view of American interests.

The Trump Doctrine owes as much to the president's psychology as it does to his policies. Indeed, it is difficult to imagine the later without the former. This holds implications for its historical half-life.

IMPATIENCE, ACTION, AND AMBITION: THREE PSYCHOLOGICAL SOURCES OF THE TRUMP DOCTRINE

Every president experiences the frustration of having his ambitions tempered by a constitutional system designed to stymie them. Trump also has to attempt to lead and govern in political circumstances that are unprecedented in the modern presidency. A powerful array of opposition forces have signed on the premise that Trump[11] "must be contained, neutralized, resisted, defeated and, if possible, humiliated. By any means necessary."

Those circumstances are particularly vexing for this peripatetic president. Mr. Trump is able to bide his time when necessary. As noted, some of his New York City projects played out over decades.[12] He has certainly been forced to adjust a number of his domestic policy initiatives to a court's schedule, not his. President Trump has adjusted, most likely begrudgingly to these facts of presidential life, even in foreign policy.

Trade talks with China? Trumps says, "there is no need to rush."[13] Talks with North Korea? Trump says, "I'm in no rush."[14] Talks with Iran? Trump says, "I'm ready when they are, but whenever they're ready, it's OK. And in the meantime, I'm in no rush. I'm in no rush."[15] We could add to these examples many of Trump's negotiations on trade with American allies. The message, and the reality is the same, what one analysis referred to as "Trump's 'no rush' foreign policy."[16]

Yet, it is also abundantly clear that Mr. Trump is a president who likes to get things done. Jeff Walker, a military school classmate who worked for the Trump Organization for more than a decade, had this to say about Trump's style[17]:

> He thought you could figure it out. That's what made him exciting to work for—no bureaucratic red tape. You got an assignment, you went off and did it, didn't let anything stand in your way. Move it, knock it down. He wouldn't tolerate it, neither should you.

Years later, his former Secretary of State, Rex Tillerson agreed[18]:

A lot of these—a lot of the early issues had to do with immigration policy, actions, implementation. And, you know, I shared the President's endpoint objective. *It was how do you want to get it done, you know. And he was— oftentimes wanted to do it: Boom, you know, this is it. Let's issue this.*

Mr. Trump's style is to not let problems continue without doing something about them. In an early *New York Times* interview, President Trump had this to say about North Korea[19]:

> *SCHMIDT*: So what are you going to do [about North Korea]?
> *TRUMP*: We'll see. That I can't tell you, Michael. But we'll see. I can tell you one thing: This is a problem that should have been handled for the last 25 years. This is a problem, North Korea. That should have been handled for 25, 30 years, not by me. This should have been handled long before me. Long before this guy has whatever he has.

Conservative American Nationalism: *Implementation at Trump Speed*

Trump's peripatetic leadership style has been most evident in his attempts to quickly change the direction for American foreign policy. He has done so not just in a limited range of areas, but in a substantial number of them. This is a joint function of his full speed ahead temperament, his liking to get things done, and his circumstances. He is unlikely, however, to accomplish his presidential purposes which are to change several long-standing narratives if he only serves one term. Opting for major changes across an array of foreign policy narratives is not the typical approach of conservative nationalists who tend to emphasize incrementalism. However, Trump clearly feels that reforming the entrenched narratives he wants to change will be more likely if he is able to establish another operating set of premises.

Not only does President Trump want to change and reform the dominant foreign policy narratives that have served as "conventional wisdom" for the past four decades, he also wants to change the actual policies and organizational assumptions of a number of major international institutions. Reforming the United Nations is a perennial international policy, but Trump wants to go much further. He wants to change the way that WHO, WTO, and NATO are organized, along with their actual policies. He wants to change and reform the international trading system. And he wants to, as President Obama did before him, albeit with a much more battle ready set of forces, recalibrate the use of American force abroad.

In the meantime, these efforts have another consequence as well, well captured by the *New York Times* columnist Thomas Friedman's complaints[20]: "It's Trump's willingness to unravel so many longstanding policies and institutions at once—from Nafta to Obamacare to the global climate accord to the domestic clean power initiative to the Pacific trade deal to the Iran nuclear deal—without any real preparation either on the day before or for the morning after."

Trump campaigned on exactly the policies that Friedman mentions. So, while Trump's follow through as president may have been a surprise to some, his intentions were clear. Moreover for each change, Trump has tried to provide explanations for why he has done so.[21] However, most people cannot absorb and make sense of all the changes Trump has set in motion. That probably includes the president himself.

He has put into motion so many whirling policy elements at any one time, that any president would find it difficult to explain them all. Trump's impressionistic and associative rhetorical style exacerbates this explanation gap. Yet it is also true that his critics make little if any effort to fairly address the president's goals or his diverse efforts to reach them.

Trump is no "hidden-hand" president, Greenstein's accurate and insightful characterization of Eisenhower.[22] Making substantial policy changes in a number of major areas, publicly and dramatically, within a short span of time can be politically, policy, and emotionally-disorienting for allies, enemies, and competitors. That is likely *one* strategic function of his style. Ordinary Americans are aware that the president is making a number of substantial changes to American foreign policy and that Trump opponents are upset to the point of repeated outrage about them. However, cutting though the many and varied accusations and counter-claims associated with the Trump presidency and its policies in any detail is not a primary motivation for most Americans.

It is unlikely that the president himself has been able, or interested in, absorbing all the implications of what he is doing. Trump seeks to reduce American commitments and responsibilities abroad in part by calling on allies to more fully share international leadership's burdens. That has been difficult to accomplish. His approach in this and other foreign policy areas is to set things in motion, push hard and often publicly, and see where they lead. He is much too occupied with implementing his doctrine and scrambling to deal with the fallout out that his new policies predictably cause, than to provide detailed public education before he tries to implement them. So many goals, so little time captures some of Trump's *restoration* dilemma. Trump's presidential goals cannot afford to patiently wait decades for implementation as he did with his plans for the old Penn Central Railroad properties that he bought and developed in New York. One four-year term and out, or two terms at the most are the Constitutional rules that limit any president's transformational ambitions.

The dilemma of the Trump presidency and doctrine is that he is really undertaking major policy reforms of long unchanged premises that are reflected in his many new policy initiatives. The composite scope and potential implications, both domestically and abroad, of Trump's *Conservative American Nationalism* doctrine are potentially enormous. Yet, they are unfolding in a Constitutional system designed to frustrate major changes. They are also unfolding in the face of determined opposition. These are element of the *Disrupter's Dilemma* (see Chapter 6).

One term as president is hardly sufficient time to implement Trump's doctrine much less gain public understanding and acceptance of it. Trump's first term is best understood then, as an audition for which he was barely selected, not a mandate of confidence that his plans would work or would be supported even if they did. In the meantime, as is Trump's style, and the necessity of his circumstances, it's full speed ahead.

Trump's full speed ahead leadership style has some obvious advantages when trying to make progress within what amounts to a Constitutional system of speed bumps. It is also a decided advantage by keeping Trump on the offensive against a determined opposition. Finally, it also conveys a willingness and determination to fight for his goals, an important consideration for his supporters but also those might become supportive in the future. If the president doesn't believe in his goals strongly enough to fight hard for them, why should anyone else take them seriously?

The Risks of Trump Speed

Trump wants to provide Americans with alternative domestic and foreign policy models based on reformulated basic premises to consider. Yet his time in office is (relatively) short and opposition to his presidency is fierce. In those circumstances full speed ahead is an understandable strategy.

Full speed ahead however is sometimes a recipe for mistakes, occasionally even substantial ones. This has been the case for some Trump initiatives as we have noted. That has raised the concern voiced by

Wright,[23] among others, as to whether the president is able to see beyond his latest frontline battle:

> Trump is no gardener. He can't look beyond the immediate. The very essence of America First is to say that the United States is like any other power and is essentially abandoning the long-term vision that diplomats like Acheson and Shultz believed in.

It is unclear that the president cannot "look beyond the immediate." His focus on "getting things done" has to be understood in a context of the substantial policy changes he is attempting, almost all of which are challenges to the dominant consensus premises of American foreign (and domestic) policy. As a result, he faces enormous opposition-generated headwinds. If anything is to be accomplished in those circumstances, a great deal of presidential attention to the here and now is required.

It is true that President Trump sometimes gives, for good reason, the impression of slapdash policy thinking and implementation. The most egregious example of the latter was the implementation, very early in his presidency, of requiring additional screening from those traveling from seven Muslim-majority countries that caught everyone, including those charged with carrying out the policy, by surprise. The new restrictions applied to countries that had already been excluded from programs allowing people to travel to the United States without a visa because of terrorism concerns by the Obama administration. There was however, little advanced preparation for the policy's roll out.

The result could fairly be described as chaotic[24] and it set the stage for years of litigation[25] in which Trump ultimately prevailed at the Supreme Court after numerous tweaks of that policy.[26]

That very flawed roll out helped establish an early narrative of the Trump presidency as "chaotic." That narrative was in some respects accurate. That narrative was legitimately reinforced by the unusual turbulence at the top tier of Trump administration officials[27] as Trump tried to find advisors who were a good fit for his style and views. Many, not always accurate anonymously sourced he said/they said "tell all" books and news reports filled with hyperbole, score settling, virtue signaling and NeverTrump invective added to the impression of a narrative of disarray.[28] He has slowly been trying to update and correct that first-impression narrative ever since.

Six Pillars of President Trump's *Conservative American Nationalism* Doctrine

We are now in a better position to make clearer the conceptual and strategic foundations of the Trump Doctrine noted at the start of this chapter. Recall that they consist of:

1. An America First premise in Trump policies;
2. An emphasis on American National Identity as a cornerstone of America's elemental and dual relationship with itself and the world;
3. Highly selective involvement, with a not exclusive emphasis on its own terms and interests in defining America's role in the world;
4. An emphasis on American strength in all its forms, including resilience and resolve;
5. The use of maximum repeated pressure along a continuum of points in pursuit of key goals; and
6. Maximum tactical and strategic flexibility.

Some of these elements, for example an emphasis on American national interests and selective international involvement are certainly not new, although their use in the Trump presidency does differ from past practices. Others, like the repeated use of maximum and often public pressure and the decided emphasis on American national identity are a new feature of the Trump presidency and doctrine. However, it is the *combination* of these elements into an overall working set of premises, not a single individual feature that defines the Trump Doctrine of *Conservative American Nationalism*.

1. America First

No single element of the Trump doctrine has generated more discussion, much of it mistaken, than Trump's emphasis on America First. There is first the muddled claim that "America First" really means Trump First because, "He's putting his own naked self-interest over what's good for America, and prioritizing the real-world policy realization of his own prejudices and hatreds over any good-faith, fact-based effort to determine, by any discernible standard, what might actually be in the country's interests."[29]

There is also the lazy claim that America First is a barely concealed endorsement of the term's association with, "the name of the isolationist, defeatist, anti-Semitic national organization that urged the United States to appease Adolf Hitler."[30] That racially charged accusation is inaccurate and unsustainable. It turns out that Mr. Trump was not familiar with the America First doctrine and was innocent of its historical meaning.

The term was suggested to Trump in an interview with David Sanger and Maggie Haberman of the *New York Times*, and it resonated with his policy instincts[31]:

> SANGER: What you are describing to us, I think is something of a third category, *but tell me if I have this right, which is much more of a, if not isolationist, then at least something of "America First" kind of approach,* a mistrust of many foreigners, both our adversaries and some of our allies, a sense that they've been freeloading off of us for many years.
>
> TRUMP: Correct. OK? That's fine.
>
> SANGER: OK? Am I describing this correctly here?
>
> TRUMP: I'll tell you—you're getting close. Not isolationist, *I'm not isolationist, but I am "America First." So I like the expression. I'm "America First."*

The more interesting questions about America First concern the issues of isolationism, national selfishness, and international leadership. Those issues are captured through a narrow frame in a *New York Times* headline, "In Donald Trump's Worldview, America Comes First, and Everybody Else Pays," that reports excerpts from two major foreign policy interviews.[32] According to critics,[33] "'America first' is becoming America alone."

That view is contradicted by the facts. Trump has repeatedly demonstrated that he, and the country are very involved in the world, as his efforts to revise and in his view, reform, a number of elements of American foreign policy suggest. These include the role of NATO, international trade (reforming NAFTA), or reaching out to old adversaries (North Korea, Russia, and Iran). In these, and in his efforts to reform specific international institution already noted, the United States remains very engaged in the world. There is of course another meaning to the "America alone " narrative that we will analyze shortly.

Trump's view of America's role in the world, going back almost forty years,[34] is that the United States has accomplished a lot, and could do more. Yet he also thinks that the United States has been taken advantage of by others, including its allies, and the incompetence of its own "elites." That's a broad indictment that contains enough truth to serve as a campaign platform. More importantly, it is what Trump believes, and he has acted on those beliefs as president.

International altruism is an illusion to true realists.[35] In their view, the liberal international order exists because it serves the purposes of the United States and its allies that created and make use of it. Allowing a certain degree of free riding by allies, as the United States has done over decades, is self-interested. It is the price that hegemons pay for burden sharing given the cost of international leadership. For America's allies such an informal agreement affords not only protection in a dangerous world, but also a discount for the costs of their safety.

Problems arise in this arrangement when the imbalances of trade, burden sharing, or the increasing reach of international institutions themselves (e.g., International Criminal Court, the World Trade Organization etc.) acting as if they have, or ought to have, real power begin to really encroach on America's power. Part of that power rests on the premises of American sovereignty. Those premises have begun to erode as some American leaders see themselves as international citizens as well as American nationals. That is precisely another major concern of President Trump and his doctrine.

2. Against Liberal Cosmopolitanism

President Trump is more than a conservative minded American nationalist. He is, at the core of his identity, an American from Queens coming of age in the 1950s. That is a more important and less obvious observation than it seems.

Although Trump grew up in a wealthy family, his father lived by a depression era mentality—always working hard to succeed and saving money—pinching pennies.[36] He tried to teach his children by example and instilled the expectation that you succeed by working hard and paying attention to details.

Donald Trump grew up in a wealthy household, but he was not pampered. As a child he had a paper route and made money by collecting empty soda bottles and returning them for the deposit. Most importantly, on weekends, as a younger child and on through his teenage years and into his early adulthood he would often go with his father to work-sites where he was expected to make himself useful. He therefore spent a lot of time around, and was comfortable with, ordinary working people. Trump's populism has authentic roots.

Along with wealth and hard work, the most basic foundation of his identity was as an American, a kid born and raised in Queens for whom the urbane sophistication of "Manhattan" was another world. Trump grew up in the 1950s when, "America was on a roll."[37] The American dream of mobility and success was a widely accepted part of the American dream (and was being lived out every day in Trump's own family life). The United States was the preeminent, even dominant power in world affairs. The many conflicts that began to seriously divide Americans in the decades after the 1960s, then lay beneath what seemed to be a broad, if ultimately illusionary, surface of consensus.

The assumption of an American national identity in the 1950s has dramatically changed. More recently Democratic presidential contenders speak Spanish during presidential debates to tout their bi-cultural identities. It is a political period in which Jeb Bush, a major Republican candidate for president, whose father and mother were decidedly from a WASP (White Anglo-Saxon Protestant) background, said of himself, "I'm bicultural—maybe that's more important than bilingual."[38] Bush also wrote on his voter registration card that he was "Hispanic."[39] That was meant to underscore his strong bi-cultural Spanish identity thought to be an important appeal as a modern presidential candidate in a political context in which some argued for the primacy of ethnic or racial identities.

Trump is the antithesis of an international cosmopolitan elite equally at home anywhere because of a fluid personal national identity. What distinguishes Trump is that, "The unifying thread running through his seemingly incoherent policies, what defines him as a candidate and forms the essence of his appeal, is that he seeks to speak for America."[40] The question is: what does he want to say when he speaks?

That sentiment is distilled and reflected in his CPAC (Conservative Political Action Conference) remarks[41]:

> Global cooperation—dealing with other countries, getting along with other countries—is good. It's very important. But there is no such thing as a global anthem, a global currency, or a global flag. *This is the United States of America that I'm representing. I'm not representing the globe. I'm representing your country.*

3. The Trump Doctrine and Isolationism: Standing Apart & If Necessary, Standing Alone

The president's foreign policy initiatives are not isolationist in any meaningful sense of that term. If they were, it would be hard to explain Trump's repeated outreach to China, North Korea, Russia, and most recently even Iran.[42] It would also be hard to reconcile with his numerous repeated efforts to revise and in his view reform some of the country's major alliance (NATO, South Korea, Mexico) relationships.

Being able when necessary to stand apart is not the same as the isolationist premise that "fortress America" must always stand alone. That basic element of Trump's leadership style is one area where an understanding of his doctrine and his view of America's place in the world, rests on understanding an important element of Trump's psychology. That ability is his capacity and comfort in being able to stand apart and alone, if necessary.

It takes a particular kind of psychology to develop and maintain such a stance. Such a person must be emotionally comfortable standing apart and be able to withstand some degree of emotional isolation. He must be able to withstand the disapproval that comes with standing against the crowd, especially if that crowd holds some degree of legitimacy and authority, as a number of Trump critics do.

It is also a highly unusual and odd set of psychological characteristics for a president to clearly have at the same time he is repeatedly accused of needing adulation for his supposedly narcissistic ego (see Chapter 6).

Recall (see Chapter 4) that at a presidential Town Hall on October 26, 2015 the following exchange took place[43]:

> *Q*: With the exception of your family, have you ever been told no?
> *Trump*: Oh, many times. ... *My whole life really has been a no and I've fought through it.* [Re: building in Manhattan] I was always told that would never work. Even my father [said] ... you don't want to go to Manhattan that's not our territory. 'Cause he was from Brooklyn and Queens where we did smaller things ... all my life I was told no, even for this [running for president] ... they said what do you want to do that for, don't do it, don't it ... you'll be up against professional politicians ... its always been you can't do this, you can't do that ...

In short, Mr. Trump has spent a lifetime not accepting what other people have told him he couldn't do, starting with his beloved father's response to his childhood dream of building skyscrapers in Manhattan. Early in his development he learned to stand up to his strong-willed father. That ability was further developed though an adulthood of experience forging his own way, often in the face of enormous odds against him, and a great deal of conventional wisdom that advised "that can't be done," or you can't do it.

Whether it is building skyscrapers in Manhattan, withdrawing from the Paris Climate Agreement, or continuing to press to add a citizenship question to the Census (see below), Trump the man and Trump the president are comfortable standing apart. That is a key to Trump's understanding of America's role in the world. He is not an isolationist operating with the premise that America must stand alone. He is an engaged internationalist who believes that sometimes the United States must be willing and able to stand apart, and sometimes that requires standing alone if necessary.

Early characterizations of Trump claimed he was a president whose policy views could be bought with flattery.[44] These claims were wrong.[45] Trump clearly has a capacity and a willingness to stand apart, and to take and keep unpopular positions, even (perhaps especially?) if those opinions are the ones uniformly held by elite international cosmopolitans.

It is very obvious that Trump is willing to fight for what he thinks is right and what he wants to accomplish. The primary purpose of his fight club presidency is not fighting for its own sake, or to avenge some insult. It is to accomplish his purposes. If he is not willing to fight back to achieve them, how much can they be worth to him and those who do and might in the future support him?

His basic stance is well captured in two interviews. In one, asked why he would want to antagonize the judge who was handling the Trump University lawsuit, by calling him unfair for allowing the lead plaintiff in the case to withdraw after a poor performance on her deposition. He responded: "because I don't care."[46]

There is a danger in antagonizing someone you want to help you. It might be a judge, a NATO ally, or a country (China) you've imposed tariffs on but want their help reining in their ally (North Korea). Yet, Trump seems disinclined to suppress his views or change his policies to curry favor for short term gains, as America's allies (Mexico, NATO) and competitors (China) have learned.

11 CONSERVATIVE AMERICAN NATIONALISM ...   397

In Osaka, Japan, where the president made some remarks and answered some question the following exchange took place[47]:

> Q (*Jim Acosta-CNN*): And what is it with your coziness with some of these dictators and autocrats at these summits? With Mohammad Bin Salman, the Crown Prince of Saudi Arabia, when you were asked about the case of Jamal Khashoggi, you did not respond to that question in front of the Saudi Crown Prince.
> *THE PRESIDENT*: I don't know that anybody asked me.
> Q: Were you afraid of offending him on that subject?
> *THE PRESIDENT*: No, not at all. I don't really care about offending people. I sort of thought you'd know that. (Audience Laughter)

There is understandable attention paid to Trump's public brusqueness, combativeness, and sometimes rudeness. They are real and very clearly antithetical to notions of traditional presidential demeanor. Given the all-out war declared by his opponents against the president, his policies, his administration, his supporters, and his family with few if any boundaries to what is alleged or how erroneously or vilely they are characterized, what is a president to do?

For Trump, as a matter of his psychology and history, the answer, as has been noted, is easy. You fight back hard with traditional rules of presidential decorum put aside. No modern president has ever adapted that strategy, and it is questionable whether it would be psychologically possible for them to do so.

However, unsettling as it is to many Americans, that willingness to fight sends an unmistakable signal to both Trump's allies and opponents domestically and abroad that you had better be ready for a real fight if you attack him. It takes a great deal of personal strength and resilience to withstand the enormous, unceasing, and personal and politically brutal criticism leveled against Trump and his presidency. He has done so and it is therefore no surprise that those traits play key roles in the Trump Doctrine.

4. Strength and Resilience: A Foundation of the Trump Doctrine

Every American president has emphasized "strength" as a foundation of American foreign policy and Mr. Trump is no exception. However, those elements have a strong personal foundation in Trump's life. They are also a reflection of one his most deeply held policy views, that the United States must be strong, tough, and resilient enough to survive and prosper in a dangerous world. Demonstrated strength and resilience is also a vehicle for gaining real respect. Adhering to a liberal international group consensus is a form of go along-get along respect that runs very counter to the president's psychology. Trump is aiming for the respect, even if it is given begrudgingly, that comes from independent thinking and action and that reflects the traditionally deeply held American values of freedom, opportunity, sovereignty, and democracy.

The gain from standing up for yourself, following your own path even when many others tell you it's not possible, and living a life in which freedom, opportunity, and a sense of personal autonomy are key, are exactly the formative experiences that defined Trump's childhood and later his adulthood. It is no surprise that they are a basic part of his essential foreign policy doctrine.

This amalgam of strength and respect is easily seen in several Trump's pre-presidential interviews:

> *Plaskin*: And how would President Trump handle it? [American foreign policy]
> *Trump*: He would believe very strongly in extreme military strength. He wouldn't trust anyone. He wouldn't trust the Russians; he wouldn't trust our allies; he'd have a huge military arsenal, perfect it, understand it. Part of the problem is that we're defending some of the wealthiest countries in the world for nothing. … We're being laughed at around the world, defending Japan.

And further:

> *Plaskin*: Do you think George [H. W] Bush is soft?
> *Trump*: I like George Bush very much and support him and always will. But I disagree with him when he talks of a kinder, gentler America. I think if this country gets any kinder or gentler, it's literally going to cease to exist. I think if we had people from the business community—the Carl Icahns, the Ross Perots—negotiating some of our foreign policy, we'd have respect around the world.

And finally[48]:

11 CONSERVATIVE AMERICAN NATIONALISM ... 399

Costa: Did you read Jeffrey Goldberg's article about Obama's foreign policy? In *the Atlantic* ... "Real power means you can get what you want without having to exert violence." That's Obama on global power. Do you agree?

DT: Well, I think there's a certaintruth to that. I think there's a certain truth to that. *Real power is through respect. Real power is, I don't even want to use the word, fear...*

There in premise form is Trump's theory of deterrence and international primacy. Power in all its dimensions, and the demonstrated willingness to use it leads to nations taking the United States seriously and acting accordingly. That includes an element of fear.

Instilling fear is considered by some to be an unmentionable aspect of American foreign policy. However, it has existed in the background of modern American policy since the 1950s. Opponents and enemies fearing what will happen if the United States is truly provoked is an indispensable element of deterrence. Yet for Trump, fear also plays a role with allies, not the fear of military action, but the fear of what will happen if the United States insists that its interests, as Trump understands them, be respected.

That formulation leads to the following question: If President Trump trusts no nation, ally, or opponent, how will they respond? One possibility is that for allies it might mean a more honest appraisal of the net value and real costs of their relationship. For opponents, it might lead to a more sober and realistic assessment of the risks and opportunity costs of provocative or reckless behavior. Is that not what deterrence seeks to further?

5. Maximum Repeated Pressure Along a Continuum of Points in Pursuit of Key Goals

Every president has available to them a variety of tools to advance their goals and counter resistance to them. These range from outright military and economic coercion to quieter more subtle political efforts to influence the behavior of others. What distinguishes President Trump's leadership style is that it is primarily, but not always, neither quiet nor subtle. It is weighted toward pushy, if not forceful coercion. The harsh, pejorative word used for this strategy is "bullying." The more traditional international relations word used for this thoroughly conventional strategy is "compellence."

The Trump doctrine is distinguished by its application of numerous tools to accomplish his purposes along a continuum of pressure points. It is the presidential leadership equivalent of a full-court press, on several policy basketball courts at once. Even though Trump is very results oriented, he views many of the major policy changes he wants to put in place as long-term projects. Trump also leads and governs by his long-standing personal premise: where there's a will there's a way. Trump has demonstrated what can best be described as fierce determination throughout his life and in his presidency.[49]

Trump is often criticized for governing by impulse, although impatience is a more accurate description (see Chapter 6). Yet, Trump has the ability to take the long view and bide his time, and find some firm policy footing from which to move forward. Recall that it took Trump more than twenty years to receive the government approvals, and be in the right economic circumstances he needed to develop the large former Penn Central railyards site on the upper west side of Manhattan.[50] Enforced patience is both a difficult but necessary strategy given Trump's *Restoration* ambitions and the opposition to them. However, necessary or not, Trump's ambitions still requires substantial political dexterity and cognitive flexibility.

Consider the president's immigration policies. He is on record as saying that American sovereignty requires enforcing immigration laws and that, "A country without borders is not a country at all."[51] It is quite clear that his effort to build a wall at the Southern border has been stymied in a variety of ways, but that he still presses on step by step and mile by mile.[52] It is also clear that Trump's long-term immigration goal is to move the United States to a more merit-based system and that he is very far away from achieving that goal.[53]

In 2019 a crisis developed at the Southern border that literally overwhelmed the immigration system's capacity to successfully address it. The reasons are legion and varied. There were court orders that limited government policy flexibility, and to which the Trump administration has adhered to while in force. There was a lack of House Congressional interest in fixing the legal issues. There were economic and political issues in a number of Central American countries. There were migration opportunities exploited worldwide by those who want to be in the United States and those who assist them either for political or economic reasons.

Limited by some courts, facing determined political and legal opposition from his opposition, and having little leverage with Democrats who control the House, Trump's options, in theory, seemed quite limited. In reality, they were as robust, within the existing law, as presidential and administrative creativity and determination could make them. In response to the crisis, Trump put into effect a host of new rules and backed them up with threats of an economic response. The new rules limited asylum claims from those "who did not apply for protection from persecution or torture where it was available in at least one third country outside the alien's country of citizenship, nationality, or last lawful habitual residence through which he or she transited in route to the United States."[54]

Trump also took a number of other initiatives including but not limited to the following: putting into place new more enforcement friendly guidelines for dealing with those not legally entitled to be in the county[55]; moving to expedite removals for those not legally entitled to be in the county[56]; revising and tightening bail requirements for asylum seekers[57]; cutting aid to several central American countries that he felt had not done enough to stem the tide of migrants (traveling through their countries to the United States),[58] and threatening to impose tariffs on Mexico which led them to make a serious effort to stem the flow of migrants coming through their country to the United States.[59] And under new Coronavirus pandemic immigration restrictions, undocumented aliens are being removed from the United States under very expedited rules.[60]

There have been other initiatives but these give a flavor of the range, but more importantly the seriousness of these efforts. All of these efforts have been effective in lowering the level of crisis at the Southern border. They also reflected the bedrock Trump Doctrine principles of maximum pressure along a series of policy lines to accomplish his purposes.

In all these ways and many others in his approach to migration problems at the Southern border Trump demonstrates his bedrock template to major national and international issues: (1) Take on the problem, and don't avoid it; (2) Keep the bottom line of your policy premises (in this case no border; no country) as your policy North Star; (3) Try every conceivable legal and legitimate solution and do not stop with what has been the norm or be deterred by what your opponents say you can't do; (4) be prepared for the strongest political and personal accusations to be made against you, the policy, and those who help carry it out and press on none the less; (5) be prepared for legal and political setbacks as opponents marshal their forces, but continue to press on legally through every legal avenue including court appeals and executive actions that can have an impact on other countries' behavior; and (6) use victories in any area where you've made an effort to gain further traction keeping in mind that large issues are rarely decided in one quick political stroke.

Repeat as necessary.

6. President Trump's Governing Strategy: Maximum Flexibility to Realize Core Goals

Consistency is important in a presidential doctrine's application. A publicly stated presidential doctrine backed up by related institutional and policy initiatives signals intent and seriousness, which are part of the underlying rationale for issuing such policy statements. Doctrines do change with time and circumstances to some degree. The Truman Doctrine and its key strategy of containment was applied across decades of diverse circumstances and developed and changed in response to them. Yet, the basic point remains: coherence and consistency are net advantages for a doctrine's clarity and impact.

Therein lies a large set of issues for the Trump Doctrine. As one somewhat generally overwrought critic wrote,[61] "the collection of impulses, deceptions, assertions, retractions, revisions and compromises that constitute President Trump's foreign policy record are difficult to gather into a consistent doctrine." Therein lies the issue of trying to understand the Trump Doctrine.

If you focus on his basic foreign policies and their premises, Trump has been consistent. He has slowed and tried to manage immigration. He has reframed America's commitment to globalization. He has resisted getting into wars and committing American troops. He has downsized America's commitment to ceding American sovereignty to international organizations.

President Trump prides himself on being unpredictable and he often is (but not with regard to his basic premises). That's generally a plus for negotiations. However, it presents difficulties for understanding his long-term strategies. His frequent hyperbole, combativeness, and unconventional beliefs are not "mainstream." So is his unusual way of thinking about political and policy matters. Trump firmly believes certain things are true, for example, no border-no country, and those basic understandings are the real starting point and North Stars for many of Trump's policies.

11 CONSERVATIVE AMERICAN NATIONALISM … 403

Critics often misunderstand and misinterpret Trump's decision-making and leadership style. Ivo Daalder, President Obama's ambassador to NATO, now president of the Chicago Council on Global Affairs writes[62]:

> I don't think he has a strategy. The reality is he shakes the tree, and then he walks away.

Daalder's first point is demonstrably true; his second demonstrably false. Trump certainly "shakes the tree," but he keeps at it trying to put his policies in place. Trump is a president who dislikes giving up, as his response to getting a citizenship question on the census and setbacks on immigration in some court jurisdictions and continuing efforts suggest.

Trump is not a president who feels the need for consistency. Indeed being "unpredictable" is one important tactic for trying to realize his goals. This tendency was clearly on display in his response to the Supreme Court's ruling against adding a question on citizenship for the 2020 Census. Trump's administration gave up; President Trump didn't, seeking to find a way to add the question.[63]

One report, worth quoting at some length, noted,[64] "The contentious issue of whether next year's all-important head count would include a citizenship question appeared to be settled. Or more accurately it was until the president began vowing on Twitter on Wednesday that the administration was 'absolutely moving forward' with plans, despite logistical and legal barriers." Mr. Trump's comments prompted a chaotic chain of events, with senior census planners closeted in emergency meetings and Justice Department representatives summoned to a phone conference with a federal judge in Maryland.

On Wednesday afternoon, Justice Department officials told the judge that their plan had changed in the span of twenty-four hours. They now believed there could be "a legally available path" to restore the question to the census, and they planned to ask the Supreme Court to help speed the resolution of lawsuits that were blocking their way. The reversal sent the future of the census, "which is used to determine the distribution of congressional seats and federal dollars, back into uncertain territory."

You could correctly place these efforts into Daalder's "shake the tree" observations of Trump's strategy, but not simultaneously to his supposed "walk away" proclivities. The Trump administration figured out another way to accomplish his census purposes and took it.[65] This seems like a clear example of Trump's pursuit of his goals, and the use of alternative innovative vehicles to accomplish them when necessary.[66]

Trump has many large presidential policy goals, and has made some progress in bringing a number of them to fruition. Yet in some cases, he is still at work on those efforts. Moving America's immigration system from a more family based to a more merit-based system was, and remains, one of Trump's most important domestic policy goals. It remains a very distant possibility, if it gets done at all.

Trump wants to move North Korea and Iran into serious new negotiations to accomplish his foreign policy goals. Yet, these two goals also remain at the level of distant aspirations and may never happen. Does this mean that he has no concrete specific strategy to reach these distant goals? That seems unlikely.

Trump's strategy of change is nicely captured in an interview with the *New York Times*[67]:

> *TRUMP*: But the Democrats should come to a bipartisan bill. And we can fix it. We can fix it. We can make a great health care plan. Not Obamacare, which was a bad plan. We can make a great health care plan through bipartisanship. We can do a great infrastructure plan through bipartisanship. And we can do on immigration, and DACA in particular, we can do something that's terrific through bipartisanship.
>
> *SCHMIDT*: It sounds like you're tacking to the center in a way you didn't before.
>
> *TRUMP*: No, I'm not being centered. I'm just being practical. No, I don't think I'm changing. Look, I wouldn't do a DACA plan without a wall. Because we need it.
>
> *SCHMIDT*: *So you're not moving. You're saying I'm more likely to do deals, but I'm not moving.*
>
> *TRUMP*: *I'm always moving. I'm moving in both directions.*

That movement in "both directions," which is to say several directions at once, can easily and for some people, be a reflection of a lack of core convictions. At the March 3, 2016 GOP Debate the following exchange took place[68]:

> *KELLY*: But the point I'm going for is you change your tune on so many things, and that has some people saying, what is his core?
>
> *TRUMP*: Megyn, I have a very strong core. *I have a very strong core. But I've never seen a successful person who wasn't flexible, who didn't have a certain degree of flexibility. You have to have a certain degree of flexibility.*

This is not a matter of simply accepting what the president says at face value. There are numerous examples in the public record making clear that Mr. Trump has stood very fast in his core convictions (the Iran nuclear deal, the China and Mexico tariffs, the effort to add a census question, and others) even as he searched for different and improved outcomes.

This is not solely a matter of "keeping them guessing," although there is some of that going on in Trump's personal leadership strategy. At a much more basic level, Trump is quite certain where he wants to go, but has no deeply thought through strategy of how to get there. Trump is an improvisational president who is not afraid to try many options, as was Franklin Roosevelt before him. Many will not work, but often one or more innovative efforts, as in the case of the crisis on the Southern border, will allow him to make progress.

In theory, one might argue that it would be better if the president had one specific announced and followed plan. Perhaps, but what, realistically is the proven and effective strategy to get your allies to shoulder more of the economic burden? Ask? That's been done for years. Remind them quietly behind the scenes and on occasion lightly and publicly? That too has been repeatedly tried. Forget about asking for more burden sharing? That is not a likely Trump approach. Publicly and privately demand a more forthcoming response? That's Trump's tack given the failures of other presidents to accomplish this purpose that they all thought legitimate.

What exactly is the proven long term-strategy to truly reform American immigration policy? Is it more grand bargains that wind up being repositories of every congressperson's wish list in which a little more enforcement capacity is traded for major expansions in admissions of all kinds? That has been the leitmotif of "comprehensive immigration reform," which is much more expansively comprehensive than it is about really reforming and reorienting American immigration policy.

This observation is simply a truism about how large congressional laws are put together. Trump appears to be serious about immigration reform. He wants to close a number of loopholes, bolster enforcement, and usher in bringing about a more merit-based system. Is he not better off starting out trying to put a wide range of his ideas into place until he's in a political position, if he ever is, to have a very different kind of grand bargain focused on his own policy premises?[69]

Impatience Revisited: The Trump Doctrine

Glasser writes[70]:

> Donald Trump is a really hard person to understand on foreign policy because I don't think he actually knows what he thinks. I think he acts on impulse.

The kind of cognitive flexibility necessary to search for improvised but possibly useful alternative foreign policy solutions in order to move further toward your goals are not necessarily synonymous with impulse. A *Washington Post* report on Trump's decision to target Qasem Soleimani said, "The upshot was that a president who has taken pride in rejecting collaboration and institutional processes in favor of unilateral action and impulsiveness is facing his most severe test of that approach at a crucial moment."[71] The view that the president takes pride in impulsiveness misunderstands both the president and the term.

Improvisation, one hallmark of Trump's presidential leadership, is by nature creative and dependent on circumstances. It is therefore hard to anticipate. It may superficially resemble impulse, but it is more tethered to reality than that, since it is purposely meant to advance a goal. Trump knows what he thinks about where he wants to go; the question for his political and policy improvisations is whether they will help him get there.

As noted, impatience is a reflection of annoyance at having to wait and knowing that there is only so much you can do to move things along and limited time to do so.[72] It also reflects an unwillingness, as Trumps sees it, to waste precious time, doing more of what hasn't worked before.[73] That is one reason that Trump reached out directly to Kim Jong-un.

The United States has spent fruitless decades trying for incremental progress with low level contacts. Why do more of the same? Trump tried to break the decades-long stalemate. That stalemate was definitely the status quo, but that doesn't mean it was stable or preferable. It was simply the way things had always been done.

Trump is, and has been all his life highly oriented toward getting results and as president this has both facilitated his success[74] and undermined it. In the North Korean case the two leaders are in direct contact, which represents a small improvement in the circumstances. Yet, there has as yet been no discernible movement toward a real agreement between the two countries. That by itself however is not legitimate policy reason for reverting back to an approach that hasn't produced much if any progress since the end of the Korean War.

THE TRUMP DOCTRINE AND THE USE OF FORCE

One of the many paradoxes of the Trump presidency is that critics repeatedly warn that he will either blunder or drag the country into war. Indeed, recall that in Chapter 7, one of the most often repeated claims concerning Trump's psychological fitness for office was exactly that concern. In reality, President Trump has been extremely cautious with actual military action and has used it judiciously and sparingly. Yet, he has used it.

There was the Seal Team Six counter terrorism operation in Yemen.[75] There were the air strikes against President Assad's suspected chemical warfare targets in Syria after he violated a US warning against using those weapons.[76] There was the lethal bombing campaign again ISIS. There was the strike on Iran that was approved because of Iran's role in the attacks on Saudi oil facilities, but called off at the last minute and a cyberattack ordered instead.[77] The cyberattacks on Iran in response to its actions again Saudi Arabia[78] reflected a series of steps away from being on a war footing with Iran.[79] There was the special operations raid that killed Abu Bakr al-Baghdadi, American-born leader and spokesperson for ISIS.[80] There was the US strike against the Iranian-backed militia in Iraq and Syria.[81] There was the drone strike that killed Gen. Qassim Soleimani, the head of Iran's elite Quds Force.[82]

The use of force by the Trump administration has several elements in common. They are all focused, limited, and not part of any major military deployments. Trump clearly prefers bluster and economic sanctions, whether he is dealing with allies to get a fairer trade or immigration deal (with Mexico), or doing the same with adversaries. A *Washington Post* headline and analysis captured this point well: "No president has used sanctions and tariffs quite like Trump."[83]

Yet, Trump is clearly comfortable with using military force when he feels it necessary. These facts undercut the narrative that Trump would involve the country in wars to satisfy his need for attention or to deflect attention away from his malfeasance. Far from the impulsive acting out, there is substantial evidence that when it comes to using military force Trump is very prudent.

Entrenched anti-Trump narratives however, die hard when they die at all. The *Washington Post* characterized the drone strike that killed Gen.

Qassim Soleimani as follows: "The moves also underscored how Trump's impulsive approach to the presidency can swiftly upend the status quo to produce a sense of disarray."[84] Actually, there was very little evidence that the administration or Trump's decision was "impulsive."

Detailed reconstructions of the decision by several news organizations described a process that took place over a number of days.[85] It involved widespread debate and analysis of various options by senior officials and the president.[86] It also involved presidential outreach to a number of his confidants to gauge their reactions.[87] It also involved a final decision that was itself dependent on another contingency, whether or not Soleimani was or was not met as he deboarded the plane, by Iraqi officials. Had he been the strike would have been canceled.[88]

In another similar situation, Trump's initial tentative decision to set airstrikes against Iran in motion in response to the Iranian downing of an American drone,[89] was followed by further thinking, reflecting, and information gathering. That eventually resulted in the United States stepping back from the original plan.[90] That doesn't seem to be very impulsive.

This was not really a surprise on two counts. First, Trump has said of himself that, "I have second thoughts about everything."[91] Aides scrambled to "explain" his comments which were in response to a question about Chinese tariffs.[92] Trump is extremely flexible in his approach to almost all his plans at the practical level. Trump may well be a "gut decider," but that doesn't forestall his revisiting his decisions.

Second, and again paradoxically if one believes the anti-Trump narratives, he apparently has deep feelings about the lethal consequences of the actions he must sometimes take. The *New York Times* headline captures this: "In Bracing Terms, Trump Invokes War's Human Toll to Defend His Policies."[93]

In an interview after one year in office Trump was asked about making decisions that ordered American forces into combat[94]:

D'Vorkin: Is it at times lonely?
Trump: It's a lonely position, because the decisions are so grave, so big.
D'Vorkin: Did business prepare you for that decision?
Trump: No, *nothing prepares you for that. Nothing prepares you for—when you send missiles, that means people are going to die. And nothing really prepares you for that.*

11 CONSERVATIVE AMERICAN NATIONALISM ... **409**

Contrary to the "Trump is a narcissist devoid of empathy" meme that critics claim (see Chapter 6), Trump is clearly a president who, along with his hyperbole, combativeness, and frequent lack of presidential demeanor, has some of those feelings when it counts, in considering literally life and death decisions. Recall, it was the harrowing pictures of the suffering caused by Assad's gas attack on Syrian villagers that Trump repeatedly cited as having moved him to use military force.[95] Recall [Chapter 8] Trump's thoughtful and empathetic response to the need to kill a 500 lb. gorilla to protect a small child that had fallen into the animal's enclosure.

The Future of the Trump Doctrine

The future of any presidential doctrine, after its originator leaves office depends on his successor and their circumstances. The Truman Doctrine and containment lived on because it continued to be an effective response to unfolding circumstances. The same is true of the Bush Doctrine, although it became a smaller overall part of a much differently focused Obama Doctrine.

Mr. Trump has, in almost all essential respects, reversed the premises and policies of his predecessor. It is obvious that most, if not all, of the premises that underlie the Trump Doctrine will be discarded if Senator Biden wins the presidency in 2020. In that case the narrative will quickly become established that the Trump Doctrine was an aberrant and abhorrent deviation from long established conventions and their consensus premises and policies.

If Trump wins reelection, he would have more of a chance to firmly establish his *Conservative American Nationalism* doctrine as a viable conceptual, strategic, and practical alternative to the policies he campaigned against and tried to change as president. The premises and policies that are the foundation of his doctrine would have eight years to work, or not, and the same number of years for the president to better learn how to convey his understanding and rationales for what he is doing.

That outcome is possible, even plausible, if he wins reelection. The one part of the Trump Doctrine that will have trouble surviving his presidency even if he wins a second term are those elements related to his own psychology. His ability to fight back, hard; his capacity to stand apart and even alone; and his unusual combination of a tough set of core beliefs coupled with the flexibility to be able to scramble in pursuit of his goals will be difficult to replicate.

410   S. RENSHON

Yet it can also be said with some degree of certainty that win or lose reelection, President Trump. "is raising questions about the foreign policy of the United States—about its external purposes, its internal cohesion, and its chances of success—that may not be fully answered for years."[96]

NOTES

1. Stanley A. Renshon. 2010. *National Security in the Obama Administration: Reassessing the Bush Doctrine.* New York: Routledge; Stanley A. Renshon. 2012. "Foreign Policy Legacies of American Presidents," in Timothy J. Lynch (ed.), *Oxford Encyclopedia of American Military and Diplomatic History.* Cambridge and New York: Oxford University Press; Stanley A. Renshon. 2013. "Understanding the Obama Doctrine," *White House Studies,* Vol. 12, No. 13, pp. 187–202; Stanley A. Renshon. 2017. "Doing Well vs. Being Great: Comparing the Bush and Obama Doctrines," in Meenekshi Bose (ed.), *The Constitution, Politics, and Policy Making in the George W. Bush Presidency,* Vol. 1, pp. 101–118. Washington, DC: Nova Press; see also Stanley A. Renshon and Peter Suedfeld (eds.). 2007. *Understanding the Bush Doctrine: Psychology and Strategy in an Age of Terrorism.* New York: Routledge.
2. Michael Warren, Zachary Cohen, and Michelle Kosinski. 2019. "What's the Trump Doctrine? Depends Who You Ask," *CNN,* February 22.
3. Rebecca Friedman Lissner. 2017. "There Is No Trump Doctrine, and There Will Never Be One," *Foreign Policy,* July 21; Daniel Larison. 2019. "There Is No 'Trump Doctrine'," *The American Conservative,* April 23.
4. Fareed Zakaria. 2019. "Does a Trump Doctrine on Foreign Policy Exist? Ask John Bolton," *Washington Post,* May 2.
5. Eliza Collins. 2016. "Trump: I Consult Myself on Foreign Policy," *Politico,* March 16.
6. Thomas L. Friedman. 2019. "Trump's Only Consistent Foreign Policy Goal Is to One-Up Obama," *New York Times,* June 18.
7. Charlie Laderman and Brendon Simms. 2017. *Donald Trump: The Making of a World View.* London: Endauvour Press.
8. Michael Gerson. 2018. "Trump Replaces National Pride with Personal Vanity," *Washington Post,* June 16.
9. Larison 2019.
10. Mark Lander, Peter Baker, and David E. Singer. 2017. "Trump Embraces Pillars of Obama's Foreign Policy," *New York Times,* February 2.
11. Andrew Ohehir. 2019. "Had Enough Debate About Donald Trump? Me Too: He's a Tyrant and a Killer: He Must Be Stopped," *Salon,* July 8.
12. Gwenda Blair. 2005. *Donald Trump: Master Apprentice.* New York: Simon & Schuster, pp. 59–93.

13. https://twitter.com/realdonaldtrump/status/1126815126584266753.
14. Trump quoted in Jeffrey Mason. 2019. "Trump Says He Is 'in No Rush' to Make a Nuclear Deal with North Korea," Reuters, June 12.
15. Trump quoted in Christina Wilkie. 2019. "Trump: If Iran Blocks the Strait of Hormuz, 'It's Not Going to Be Closed for Long'," CNBC, June 14.
16. Andrew Restuccia. 2019. "Trump's 'No Rush' Foreign Policy," *Politico*, June 22.
17. Walker quoted in Gwenda Blair. 2018. "Trump Has the White House He Always Wanted," *Politico*, April 5.
18. "Transcript of Interview with Former Secretary of State Rex Tillerson." 2019. House Committee on Foreign Affairs, June 27, p. 117, emphasis added.
19. *New York Times*. 2017. "Excerpts from Trump's Interview With *The Times*," December 28.
20. Friedman undercuts his observation by introducing it with an *ad hominem* attack, "... the most frightening thing about the Trump presidency. It's not the president's juvenile tweeting or all the aides who've been pushed out of his clown car at high speed or his industrial-strength lying." Lisa Friedman. 2017. "Trump Adviser Tells Ministers U.S. Will Leave Paris Climate Accord," *New York Times*, September 18, emphasis added.
21. Cf., Donald J. Trump. 2017. "Statement by President Trump on the Paris Climate Accord," The White House, June 1.
22. Fred I. Greenstein. 1994. *The Hidden Hand Presidency: Eisenhower as Leader.* Baltimore, MD: Johns Hopkins University Press.
23. Quoted in Henry Farrell. 2019. "Trump Has No Long-Term Foreign Policy Vision: Here's How That's Hurting America," *Washington Post*, June 17; see also Thomas J. Wright. 2017. *All Measures Short of War: The Contest for the Twenty-First Century and the Future of American Power.* New Haven: Yale University Press.
24. Aaron Blake. 2017. "Trump's Travel Ban Is Causing Chaos—And Putting His Unflinching Nationalism to the Test," *Washington Post*, January 29.
25. Wesley Lowry and Josh Dawsey. 2018. "Early Chaos of Trump's Travel Ban Set Stage for a Year of Immigration Policy Debates," *Washington Post*, February 6.
26. Adam Liptak and Michael D. Shear. 2018. "Trump's Travel Ban Is Upheld by Supreme Court," *New York Times*, June 26.
27. Kathryn Tenpas Tapas. 2019. *Tracking Turnover in the Trump Administration.* Washington DC: The Brookings Institution, July.
28. Michael Wolff. 2018. "Donald Trump Didn't Want to be President," *New York Magazine*, January 3; Cliff Simms. 2019. *Team of Vipers: My 500 Extraordinary Days in the Trump White House.* New York: Thomas Dunne Books.

29. Greg Sargent. 2018. "No, Trump Isn't Putting 'America First:' He's Putting Himself First," *Washington Post*, November 21.
30. Susan Dunn. 2016. "Trump's 'America First' Has Ugly Echoes from U.S. History," *CNN*, April 28.
31. David E. Sanger and Maggie Haberman. 2016. "Transcript: Donald Trump Expounds on His Foreign Policy Views," *New York Times*, March 26, emphasis added.
32. Sanger and Haberman 2016; see also "Transcript: Donald Trump Interview with Bob Woodward and Robert Costa," 2016. *Washington Post*, April 2.
33. Brian Klaas. 2017. "'America First' Is Becoming America Alone," *Washington Post*, June 28.
34. Reelin' in the Years Production. 1980. "Trump Interview with Rona Barrett," October 6.
35. Hans J. Morgenthau. 1948. *Politics Among Nations*. New York: McGraw Hill.
36. Blair 2005, p. 3.
37. Blair 2005, p. 2.
38. Quoted in David Frum. 2015. "Is Jeb Bush a Republican Obama?" *The Atlantic*, February 4.
39. David Rappaport. 2016. "I Feel a Deep Sense of Remorse, Donald Trump's Ghostwriter Says," *New York Times*, July 18.
40. Julius Krein. 2015. "Traitor to His Class," *Weekly Standard*, September 7.
41. Donald J. Trump. 2017. "Remarks by President Trump at the Conservative Political Action Conference," Gaylord National Resort & Convention Center, February 24.
42. Laura King. 2019. "Trump Says He's Open to Iran Talks Without Preconditions," *Los Angeles Times*, June 23.
43. Emphasis added https://www.youtube.com/watch?v=TXEOFHf1q9A.
44. Zeeshan Aleem. 2017. "China Isn't the First Country to Flatter Its Way to Trump's Heart: It Won't Be the Last," *Vox*, November 8; Evelyn Farkas. 2018. "Putin Has Already Won," *Politico*, July 11.
45. Peter Nicholas. 2017. "Trump's 'America First' Policy Proves to Be an Immovable Object at G-20," *Wall Street Journal*, July 9; Katie Rogers and Motoko Rich. 2019. "For Trump's Japan Trip, Abe Piles on the Flattery: But to What End?" *New York Times*, May 24.
46. Chris Cillizza. 2016. "Donald Trump Perfectly Summed Up His Life Philosophy in Just 6 Words," *Washington Post*, June 1, https://www.c-span.org/video/?410401-1/donald-trump-holds-news-conference-donations-veterans-groups&start=1868.
47. Donald J. Trump, 2019. "Trump in Press Conference Osaka, Japan," June 29, emphasis added.

48. Transcript 2016, emphasis added.
49. Michael Kranish. 2017. "A Fierce Will to Win Pushed Donald Trump to the Top," *Washington Post*, January 19.
50. Blair 2005, pp. 182–201.
51. Donald J. Trump. 2018. "Remarks by President Trump at a Meeting with the National Space Council and Signing of Space Policy Directive-3," The White House, June 18.
52. Department of Homeland Security. 2019. "Press Release: CBP Completes Construction of 50 Miles of New Border Wall," July 11.
53. Donald J. Trump. 2018. "Remarks by President Trump in Meeting with Bipartisan Members of Congress on Immigration," The White House, January 9; Jordyn Hermani. 2019. "Trump Pitches His 'Merit-Based' Immigration Proposal," *Politico*, May 16.
54. Department of Homeland Security. 2019. "DHS and DOJ Issue Third-Country Asylum Rule," July 15; Zolan Kanno-Youngs and Elisabeth Malkin. 2019. "Most Migrants at Border with Mexico Would Be Denied Asylum Protections Under New Trump Rule," *New York Times*, July 15.
55. Department of Homeland Security. 2019. "Enforcement of Immigration Laws to Serve the National Interests," February 17.
56. Department of Homeland Security. 2019. "Notice: Designating Aliens for Expedited Removal," July 23.
57. Michael D. Shear and Katie Benner. 2019. "In New Effort to Deter Migrants, Barr Withholds Bail to Asylum Seekers," *New York Times*, April 16.
58. Leslie Wroughton and Patricia Zengerle. 2019. "As Promised, Trump Slashes Aid to Central America over Migrants," *Reuters*, June 17.
59. Kirk Semple. 2019. "Mexico Cracks Down on Migrants, After Pressure from Trump to Act," *New York Times*, June 3; Peter Orsi. 2020. "Mexican Guardsmen Break Up Migrant Caravan Along Highway," *Associated Press*, January 23.
60. Nick Miroff. 2020. "Under Coronavirus Immigration Measures, U.S. Is Expelling Border-Crossers to Mexico in an Average of 96 Minutes," *Washington Post*, March 30.
61. Michael Gerson. 2018. "Trump Is Smashing the Hopes of Oppressed People Everywhere," *Washington Post*, July 19.
62. Quoted in Nahal Toosi. 2019. "Inside the Chaotic Early Days of Trump's Foreign Policy," *Politico*, March 1.
63. Michael Wines and Adam Liptak. 2019. "Trump Considering an Executive Order to Allow Citizenship Question on Census," *New York Times*, July 5.
64. Michael Wines, Maggie Haberman, and Robert Rappeport. 2019. "Justice Dept. Reverses Course on Citizenship Question on Census, Citing Trump's Orders," *New York Times*, July 3.

65. Katie Rogers, Adam Liptak, Michael Crowley, and Michael Wines. 2019. "Trump Says He Will Seek Citizenship Information from Existing Federal Records, Not the Census," *New York Times*, July 11.
66. Wang, Hansi Lo. 2020. "To Produce Citizenship Data, Homeland Security to Share Records with Census," *NPR*, January 4.
67. *New York Times* 2017, emphasis added.
68. Team Fix. 2016. "The Fox News GOP Debate Transcript, Annotated," *Washington Post*, March, 3, emphasis added.
69. Sarah Pierce. 2019. "Immigration-Related Policy Related Changes in the First Two Years of the Trump Administration," Migration Policy Institute, May.
70. Susan Glasser. 2019. "Just How Dangerous Is Donald Trump?" *Politico*, April 16.
71. David Nakamura and Josh Dawsey. 2020. "Amid Confusion and Contradictions, Trump White House Stumbles in Initial Public Response to Soleimani's Killing," *Washington Post*, January 7.
72. Keith Bradsher Keith. 2018. "Trade Deals Take Years: Trump Wants to Remake Them in Months," *New York Times*, March 28.
73. Dan De Luce, Courtney Kube, and Mushtaq Yusufzai. 2018. "Impatient Trump Drives U.S. Push for Peace Talks in Afghanistan," *NBC News*, July 30; see also John Hudson, Josh Dawsey, and Carol D. Leonnig. 2018. "In Private, Trump Vents Frustration over Lack of Progress on North Korea," *Washington Post*, July 22.
74. Peter Nicholas, Gordon Lubold, and Dion Nissenbaum. 2018. "For Trump, a Hectic Week of Planning to Organize Syria Strike," *Wall Street Journal*, April 13.
75. Eric Schmitt. 2017. "U.S. Commando Killed in Yemen in Trump's First Counterterrorism Operation," *New York Times*, January 29.
76. Daniel Arkin, F. Brinley Bruton, and Phil McCausland. 2018. "Trump Announces Strikes on Syria Following Suspected Chemical Weapons Attack by Assad Forces," NBC News, April 14.
77. Michael D. Shear, Eric Schmitt, Michael Crowley, and Maggie Haberman. 2019. "Strikes on Iran Approved by Trump, Then Abruptly Pulled Back," *New York Times*, June 20.
78. Julien Barnes and Thomas Gibblons-Neff. 2019. "U.S. Carried Out Cyberattacks on Iran," *New York Times*, June 22.
79. Michael C. Bender, Jessica Donati, and Lindsay Wise. 2019. "Trump Steers Clear of War Footing Toward Iran," *Wall Street Journal*, September 18.
80. Eric Schmidt, Maggie Haberman, and Rukmino Callimachi. 2019. "Special Operations Raid Said to Kill Senior Terrorist Leader in Syria," *New York Times*, October 27.

81. Barbara Starr, Kevin Bohn, and Ross Levitt. 2019. "US Strikes 5 Facilities in Iraq and Syria Linked to Iranian-Backed Militia," *CNN*, December 30.
82. Falih Hassan, Alissa J. Rubin, Michael Crowley, and Michael Schmitt. 2020. "Trump Orders Strike Killing Top Iranian General Qassim Suleimani in Baghdad," *New York Times*, January 2.
83. Adam Taylor. 2018. "No President Has Used Sanctions and Tariffs Quite Like Trump," *Washington Post*, August 29.
84. Toluse Olorunnipa, Robert Costa, and Anne Gearan. 2020. "Trump Plunges Toward the Kind of Middle Eastern Conflict He Pledged to Avoid," *Washington Post*, January 4.
85. Elaina Moore. 2019. "Timeline: How The U.S. Came to Strike and Kill a Top Iranian General," *NPR*, January 4.
86. Jennifer Jacobs and Jordan Fabian. 2019. "How Trump Planned the Drone Strike with a Tight Circle of Aides," *Bloomberg*, January 4; see also MIssy Ryan, John Dawsey, Dan Lamothe, and John Hudson. 2019. "How Trump Decided to Kill a Top Iranian General," *Washington Post*, January 3.
87. Daniel Lippman, Wesley Morgan, Meredith McGraw, and Nahal Toosi. 2019. "How Trump Decided to Kill Iran's Soleimani," *Politico*, January 3.
88. Eric Schmitt, Helene Cooper, Thomas Gibbons-Neff, Maggie Haberman, and Peter Baker. 2020. "For Trump, a Risky Decision on Suleimani Is One Other Presidents Had Avoided," *New York Times*, January 3.
89. Joshua Berlinger, Mohammed Tawfeed, Barbara Star, Shitzad Boxorgmehr, and Frederik Pleitgen. 2019. "Iran Shoots Down US Drone Aircraft, Raising Tensions Further in Strait of Hormuz," *CNN*, June 20.
90. Peter Baker, Eric Schmitt, and Michael Crowley. 2019. "An Abrupt Move That Stunned Aides: Inside Trump's Aborted Attack on Iran," *New York Times*, September 21.
91. Trump quoted in Anna Palmer and Jake Sherman. 2019. "*POLITICO* Playbook: Trump: 'I Have Second Thoughts About Everything'," *Politico*, August 25.
92. John Dawsey. 2019. "Trump Admits to Having 'Second Thoughts'—A Scramble Ensues to Explain What He Meant," *Washington Post*, August 25.
93. Michael Crowley. 2019. "In Bracing Terms, Trump Invokes War's Human Toll to Defend His Policies," *New York Times*, October 19.
94. Randell Lane. 2017. "Trump Unfiltered: The Full Transcript of the President's Interview with Forbes," *Forbes*, November 14, emphasis added.

95. Ashley Parker, David Nakamura, and Dan Lamothe. 2017. "'Horrible' Pictures of Suffering Moved Trump to Action on Syria," *Washington Post*, April 7.
96. Stephen Sestanovich. 2017. "The Brilliant Incoherence of Trump's Foreign Policy," *The Atlantic*, May.

PART V

Political Transformation in the Balance

CHAPTER 12

The Future of the Trump Presidency

Two major remaining questions about the Trump presidency are whether it has a future, especially given the Coronavirus' enormous and unprecedented challenge, and if so what kind? It is possible that the president will lose his reelection bid. In that case, Trump's reconstructive aspirations that we examined under the rubric of the *Politics of American Restoration* will die stillborn. Even if Trump wins reelection he likely to still face major opposition. As a result, a major question of a possible second term will be this: in a deeply and highly divided country, how will it be possible for President Trump to develop and sustain a new consensus around the eight policy pillars that have defined his presidential ambitions?

More generally and theoretically, the question arises: how do entrenched narratives change? Political Science and the "literature" provide little guidance. It's relatively easy enough to point to transformations when a country has suffered catastrophic military, economic, political, or cultural traumas. Yet, it is unclear just how much of an epoch-defining event the pandemic will be for the United States. At this point, the country has been through many months of economic and medical trauma, helped to some degree by pouring enormous government economic and administrative resources, at all levels, to try to mitigate the Coronavirus' effects. The fact that the country was doing economically well before the virus hit has provided a bit of a cushion.

© The Author(s) 2020
S. Renshon, *The Real Psychology of the Trump Presidency*,
The Evolving American Presidency,
https://doi.org/10.1007/978-3-030-45391-6_12

Trump did have a laundry list of plausible accomplishments to tout as he did during his 2020 State of the Union Address. One need not fully accept all of what he said to allow some substance to his claims. Yet, its fairly obvious that Trump's reelection will turn on the state of the country and its level of post-pandemic existence, and whether the President's overall response to the economic downtown, pandemic and racial equality crises are seen in a favorable way.

Trump's presidency was attempting some rare, substantial changes in arguably good circumstances before the pandemic. He was not a Lincoln facing the end of the Union. He was not an FDR facing economic catastrophe or a brutal World War, one following right after the other. The pandemic has been brutal, but a different kind of crisis than those just mentioned. As a result, Trump's presidency has entered into unchartered territory. We, analyzing his presidency, must follow.

America's Political Collision Course

The United States has been on the path to, and has arrived at, a dramatic fork in the road with the arrival of the Trump presidency. Donald Trump's presidency began and unfolded at the culmination of a long growing political and leadership crisis in the United States. That crisis is not of the type usually associated with that word, like major wars or economic dislocations, although those two have been part of this country's recent history. The crisis that Trump's election, and the response to it, has brought into much clearer focus is a surging disconnect between policy promises and performance and between what national leaders say and do and what growing segments of the population think. The pandemic has added its own unique impact to that already present and prevalent crisis as has the traumatic impact of George Floyd's death during a police stop and the peaceful demonstrations, riots, and assault on public statues of American history that followed.

The Trump presidency has clarified, exacerbated, and reflected these basic disconnections between promises, expectations, and performance. In the eight pillar policy areas and their many associated policies, President Trump literally has taken a rhetorical and policy sledgehammer to the narrative foundations that had been conventional wisdom for the last five decades. His goal is to encourage some alternative views to air and some alternative policies to audition.

Trump did not subscribe to the decades of soothing policy narratives favored by liberal, conservative, Democratic and Republican establishment leadership figures alike. As noted, he did not believe that there were no downsides to unlimited so-called "free trade." He did not believe that there was no downside to failing to enforce immigration laws already on the books. He did not subscribe to the view that NATO was just fine as it was, still operating on the premises of its founding in 1949, to name just three of many areas in which Trump took exception to the conventional wisdom policy narratives.

As a working shorthand, one can refer as a group to the narratives that have increasingly dominated American public life since Lyndon Johnson's Great Society, as the *establishment policy paradigm*. That concept reflects the liberal or progressive idea that more government programs designed to alleviate inequalities or difficulties wherever and however they appear are among the most important functions of government. Democratic and Republican leadership might disagree at the margins, but they have shared, to a large degree, these basic premises.

Over decades, that agreement was instrumental in developing two major contemporaneous political fault lines. These were a loss in confidence in policy promises and performance. Many major policies simply did not work as promised. The other fault line was the loss in confidence in political leaders who, with a few exceptions, recycled their parties' preferred policy talking points rather than having frank discussions about real policy options and their consequences (see Chapter 3).

A Nation and Its Institutions Take Sides

The direct manifestations of this policy and leadership gap were observable in one other basic contemporary political development, the sorting of the nation's political parties, individuals, and institutions along political lines. The political parties themselves began a process in which Republicans became more conservative and Democrats more liberal or progressive at the party leadership level. This was mirrored and reflected among ordinary party members.[1] The most obvious manifestation of this development was that on almost every single policy or political survey question asked one could find stark partisan differences.[2] As one review of a new book[3] on polarization points out: "Trump is more a vessel for our division than the cause, and [that is] why his departure will not provide any magical cure."[4]

422 S. RENSHON

At the same time, ordinary Americans increasingly got their news and views from starkly divergent sources that were more in accord with their starting premises or preferences. Major news outlets reflected these developments in their news departments. There had for some time been an undercurrent of partisan preference in the nation's major news and media outlets. That was essentially because they generally shared the same *establishment policy paradigm* about the necessity of the development and growth of the politically liberal administrative state.

With the arrival of the Trump presidency, several of the country's major national newspapers, the *Washington Post* and *New York Times*, publicly took the position that given Trump's unique danger to this country and its democracy, "neutrality" was not a viable option for reporting or commentary. The *Washington Post*'s new hyperbolic motto, "Democracy Dies in Darkness" would have been more accurate had it reflected the paper's real publishing premise, "Democracy Dies as a Result of Reporting Neutrality." They acted on this new anti-Trump principle and many other major news, media, and commentary organizations followed their lead.

However, what really changed in just the last decade was that the traditionally elite news and views organizations no longer sat alone atop the media hierarchy. The development of new social media, major alternative news sources such as *Fox*, a dramatic expansion of alternative non-traditional establishment news and views websites, and an explosion of bloggers and blogging aggregators all have rendered the traditional *establishment policy paradigm* monopoly on news and views no longer operative. One analysis pointed to these developments with the term the "era of historic media fragmentation,"[5] and it is a fitting term.

There is one more aspect of the *elemental polarization* that has recently emerged during the Trump presidency and thus has not, as yet, received sufficient attention or analysis. The occasion of its emergence into public clarity is a report by the GAO (Government Accountability Office) finding that the president's *delaying* of aid to the Ukraine "broke the law,"[6] as a number of news reports noted.[7] That finding was immediately pressed into the service of impeaching Trump.[8] The administration immediately responded that the GAO was mistaken as a matter of law and that the money was delayed for legitimate presidential review, and was released.

Deep in the *Washington Post* news report covering this event was the following:

Several administrations have been slapped by the GAO, including that of George Bush, Bill Clinton and George H. W. Bush. In general, the administrations were cited for freeing funds for spending, making lawsuits unnecessary.

Other reports soon brought to light other instances of the exact same presidential behavior resulting in a low-key GAO response. In one instance, the GAO found that the Bergdahl prisoner swap violated the law.[9] In another, the GAO report found that "Obama Administration Broke its Own Health Care Rule."[10] In all these cases, including the Trump Ukrainian case, the violations were contested by the administration involved, explained by other considerations, and were not considered serious enough by the GAO to sue the administrations involved, as they could have done.

In the Trump case, as expected, the GAO Ukrainian report led to a partisan public and political debate. Anti-Trump supporters insisted that the GAO report absolutely validated Trump's impeachment and removal from office. Another commentary took a contrary position, noting that that the GAO was an arm of Congress, and to that extent was not wholly "independent." In fact it said[11]:

GAO acknowledges in a footnote that its opinion was rendered at the request of Sen. Chris Van Hollen (D., Md.), who repeatedly prodded GAO staff to say whether they agreed with his claim of a Trump legal violation. But in the body of its opinion, GAO doesn't say it's acting to serve one of its legislative bosses but instead claims: "Pursuant to our role under the [Impoundment Control Act], we are issuing this decision."

That same report noted that the "'nonpartisan' GAO's personnel are represented by the AFL-CIO's International Federation of Professional and Technical Engineers whose PAC in 2016 gave 100% of its donations to Democrats and 0% to Republicans."

Why do these points matter? The answer is best captured in an analysis by Alan Dershowitz, that is worth quoting at some length[12]:

Whatever one may think about the substantive merits of what President Donald Trump did or did not do with regard to the Ukrainian money— which was eventually sent without strings—he certainly had the authority to delay sending the funds. The GAO was simply wrong in alleging that he violated the law, which includes the Constitution, by doing so.

To be sure, the statute requires notification to Congress, but if such notification significantly delays the president from implementing his foreign policy at a time of his choice, that too would raise serious constitutional issues.

Why then would a nonpartisan agency get it so wrong as a matter of constitutional law. There are two obvious answers: first, *in the age of Trump there is no such thing as nonpartisan*. The political world is largely divided into people who hate and people who love President Trump. *This is as true of long term civil servants as it is of partisan politicians. We have seen this with regard to the FBI, the CIA, the Fed and other government agencies that are supposed to be nonpartisan.* There are of course exceptions. *But most civil servants share the nationwide trend of picking sides.* The GAO does not seem immune to this divisiveness.

We can see this development of picking sides across America's major cultural, economic, and political institutions. It can be seen in the media, in education, in business, in civic, legal, and myriad professional organizations, and in federal, state, and local government bureaucracies. It would be a mistake to label all of this "picking sides" as *directly* politically partisan, although much of it is. Some of it can be traced back to the *establishment policy paradigm* discussed above. That is to say, some anti-Trump views and practices may originally stem not so much from direct political partisanship, but rather strong and fervent disagreement with Trump's efforts to revise and where necessary discard the *establishment policy paradigm* framed by the liberal or progressive premises of the last several decades. Admittedly, it is very difficult to find a clear bright line between the two. We can however see this distinction in operation in clearer form in the context of examining the concept of a so-called "national security interagency consensus." and how that somewhat elastic term was used to argue against the president's policy by a staffer at a Congressional hearing.

The National Security "Interagency Consensus"

Political and social scientists have long been familiar with the concept of "Regulatory Capture,"[13] the process by which those being regulated become part of their own regulation. This is a term ordinarily applied to the government regulation of non-governmental entities like banks or other businesses. However, there is another variant of that idea that is less

12 THE FUTURE OF THE TRUMP PRESIDENCY   425

often associated with that term. That occurs when supposedly independent non-partisan federal oversight agencies have a strong mission and rationale associated with their name and policy outlook, for example the Environmental Protection Agency or the Department of Education. In those circumstances, generations of its personnel move the agency as far as they can in the direction that they understand as the agency's mission. Many of the large federal bureaucracies—Health Education and Welfare, Education, Environmental Protection Agency, to name three, are almost synonymous with the Great Society premises of the *establishment policy paradigm*.

This is a familiar problem for Republican presidents, and Donald Trump is no exception. What Trump's presidency has added to our understanding is that the *establishment policy paradigm* is not only an ongoing issue for domestic policy executive agencies, but also for foreign policy. There it is not a case of the Department of Education being skeptical of "school choice," a liberal-conservative policy debate that is in some respects normalized by being played out recently across different presidencies and major city mayoralties.

Foreign policy obviously has its own ongoing debates. However, in this arena there is more of an expectation of independent minded analysis based on career long familiarity with the area or issues. Senior national security advisors to the president are expected to have views on the many issues that a president faces. North Korean experts are expected to be just that.

It is within that framework that the impeachment testimony of Lieutenant Colonel Alexander S. Vindman was given.[14] He testified that he *thought* the president was withholding foreign aid as a quid pro quo for the Ukrainians starting an investigation of corruption that would include Hunter Biden. He acknowledged that he had no first-hand evidence of his assumption, but that it is not the major point here.

In his prepared testimony, Vindman said:

> In the Spring of 2019, I became aware of outside influencers promoting a false narrative of Ukraine *inconsistent with the consensus views of the interagency.* This narrative was harmful to U.S. government policy. *While my interagency colleagues and I were becoming increasingly optimistic on Ukraine's prospects, this alternative narrative undermined U.S. government efforts to expand cooperation with Ukraine.*

There are many questions raised by this statement. What exactly is the "interagency consensus?" What was the process by which it was derived? How consensual was it? Were there any dissents? And if so, what were they? The most basic question that must be addressed here is where in the Constitution does it say that the "inner agency" consensus will have any, much less the deciding role, in making American foreign policy?

Lieutenant Colonel Vindman addressed none of these questions. However, what stands out about this statement is that the views of Lt. Colonel Vindman, a national security staffer, and the claimed consensus of presumably others just like him, should take precedence over that of a duly elected president. Lieutenant Colonel Vindman further said:

> I was concerned by the call. I did not think it was proper to demand that a foreign government investigate a U.S. citizen, and I was worried about the implications for the U.S. government's support of Ukraine. *I realized* that if Ukraine pursued an investigation into the Bidens and Burisma, it would likely be interpreted as a partisan play which would undoubtedly result in Ukraine losing the bipartisan support it has thus far maintained. This would all undermine U.S. national security. Following the call, I again reported my concerns to NSC's lead counsel.

As is clear from the transcript of the call, the president never "demanded" an investigation. He didn't demand anything. When Lieutenant Colonel Vindman said "I realized …" what he really meant is that "he thought …" or concluded or summarized what he thought was true. However, he presented no direct independent evidence of this before Congress except to say that was what he thought. His stated worry was that by asking for evidence that something was being done to address the very obvious and widely known corruption issue in Ukraine would "undermine bipartisan support it has thus far maintained."

This leads directly to two questions. First, did that bipartisan support include acceptance of widespread Ukraine corruption? If not, why would asking to do something about widespread corruption disrupt support for the country? Wouldn't it increase it?

The issue of inter-agency consensus makes another appearance in a *Washington Post* article about Trump's 2019 Syrian withdrawal:

> If members of the policy and defense community are experiencing whiplash from President Trump's latest Syria announcement, it is not because U.S.

intentions in Syria have changed. It is because, once again, key decisions—with massive political and security implications in the region—have been announced swiftly, *without warning, and in the absence of interagency consensus and planning.*

The phrase "absence of interagency consensus and planning" links to an article that carries that accusation, but also notes the following[15]:

> A senior administration official dismissed that characterization, insisting that senior national security officials were consulted. "That surprises me because this is something that was discussed among senior leadership here, at the State Department and the Pentagon, so I don't know how anybody could've been blindsided," the official told reporters on a conference call.

Trump himself took note in an interview of just how long, how many years, it took to get his Syrian policies followed. Asked about his Syrian reposition and drawdown the following exchange too place[16]:

> *Q*: Is it a firm decision, sir?
>
> *THE PRESIDENT*: It's always a firm decision. Last time I made a firm decision, but—and I said, "We'll do it over a period of time." *We've been doing this, actually, over a period of time—over a very long period of time.*

Another perspective on this debate comes from former Republican Senator Bob Corker, an establishment critic of Trump's foreign policies who, in speaking about Trump's tendency to reach out widely for advice, had this to say[17]:

> "I just have known through my years there that so many people have access to the president," Corker said, declining to name them. "Typically, you want the people who are giving input to have credentials and have knowledge of the area, but I know that's not the case necessarily today."

Translation: Trump asks for advice from many people, some or many of whom may be what Senator Corker believes to be the wrong kind of people.

The National Security Consensus and Trump's Syria Drawdown

There have been other examples of Trump deciding against an agency or even an interagency consensus, most notable recently in Syria which we noted briefly in Chapter 5. Trump's 2019 decision was to reposition, not remove,[18] fifty American military advisors from the path of an imminent Turkish incursion into Northern Syria. Again, as in 2018, Trump said he would leave some troops in Syria to protect the oil fields,[19] not necessarily the Kurds.[20]

In fact, there were two large and different groups of Kurds in Syria. The northern branch (YPP) had Marxist-Leninist origins, substantial ties to the Kurdistan Workers' Party (PPK), and is considered a terrorist group by the Turkish government and the US Department of State. The PKK "has been waging armed struggle against Turkey since 1984 at a cost of tens of thousands of lives."[21] More problematic still was that the PPK branch of Kurds, who, while allying themselves with the United States, used that opportunity to gain more territory on the Turkish border. As the *New York Times* put it[22]:

> Since 2012, Kurdish forces had harnessed the chaos of the Syrian civil war to carve out an autonomous region along the border with Turkey, free of Syrian government control. They greatly expanded their territory by partnering with American troops to force out Islamic State militants from the area.

This angered and concerned the Turkish government.

Those involved in developing and maintaining the policy that Trump decided against were also visibly upset.[23] Predictions of dire consequences immediately surfaced. Trump was "colluding with" and "selling out to" Turkey.[24] The United States, it was said, had "abandoned" our long-term allies, the (PPK) Kurds. They would be "at the mercy of the Turkish government" and slaughtered by Turkish soldiers.[25] ISIS would enter the vacuum caused by our withdrawal and in the words of one analyst: "there's a good chance ISIS could recoup its major losses."[26] Turkey would be emboldened and launch a full scale invasion of Northern Syria.

None of those dire predictions happened. The United States was soon partnering again with those same Kurdish allies against the individual remnants of ISIS.[27] They were not "abandoned." Nor were they slaughtered. Nor did the Turkish government launch a full scale invasion.

12 THE FUTURE OF THE TRUMP PRESIDENCY   429

The *New York Times* titled one of its major articles on Trump's decision[28]: "In Syria, Trump Distills a Foreign Policy of Impulse, and Faces the Fallout." Yet oddly, the very first paragraph of that report reads:

> No one should have been surprised, and yet it seems that everyone was. President Trump made clear long ago that he wanted to get out of the Middle East, but even some of his own supporters evidently assumed that he would not follow through or that someone would stop him.

How Trump's decision could be labeled as an impulse when he had "made it clear a long time ago", and discussed it numerous times on the campaign trail is unclear.[29] Presidential positions however deeply thought through or not, that are developed, discussed, and argued over time are more accurately considered policies, not impulses. Indeed, Trump had campaigned on this issue and has already announced his intention to begin withdrawing American troops from Northern Syria in 2018.[30] In trying to do so then, he had also invoked some of the same criticisms. As a result, he modified his orders increasing the drawdown period and leaving a 400-person residual force behind,[31] while still reducing their absolute numbers.

Policy and Political Opposition Within the Trump Administration

Syria was one of a number of policy arenas in which those responsible for and committed to past policy "slow-walked," tried to ignore or downplay the president's direct orders.[32] *The New York Times* noted in one of its reports that[33]: "The Pentagon had, for nine months, played down that presence, hoping Mr. Trump would not focus on the extent to which the American military was continuing to fight the Islamic State despite his order in December to pull out."

Another example concerned North Korea. The *New York Times* reported that when, "Mr. Trump decided to halt military exercises and informed the Pentagon afterward, Defense Department officials quietly continued the exercises but just did not refer to them as exercises."[34]

These incidents must have given the president a certain *déjà vu* feeling. Trump perhaps recalled reports that the head of his national economic council, Gary Cohn, had taken documents off his desk to keep him from signing them.[35] Or perhaps they recalled for him the *New York Times* op-ed by Anonymous,[36] who wrote that he or she was dedicated to staying

TRUMP SMARTS: DUNCE, HEDGEHOG, OR FOX?

in their White House job and sabotaging the Trump presidency for the good of the country.

Seeking advice is one thing; being smart enough to make use of it another. The prevailing wisdom about Trump's intelligence is that he is, in words attributed to former Secretary of State Tillerson, "a moron."[37] Trump replied to that report[38]: "I think it's fake news, but if he did that, I guess we'll have to compare IQ tests. And I can tell you who is going to win."

The certainty that Trump is both ignorant[39] and stupid[40] are staples of opposition characterizations. He "doesn't read",[41] and as a result likes to have oral intelligence briefings rather than written ones.[42] Plus, he speaks at a 3rd,[43] 4th,[44] or 6th grade level.[45] Take your pick, although "Presidential Speeches Were Once College-Level Rhetoric—Now They're for Sixth-Graders."[46] If Trump is ceded to have some modicum of intelligence, it is "a craven sort of cunning,"[47] or reptilian "Lizard wisdom,"[48] the kind that doesn't take any "real" intelligence to have. It's not worth wasting much time further detailing this serial name calling because it detracts from more interesting questions.

Trump has his own view of his intelligence.[49] He trolls opposition supporters by saying he is a "stable genius."[50] In Trump's view and words,[51] in response to allegations he is mentally ill:

> Now that Russian collusion, after one year of intense study, has proven to be a total hoax on the American public, the Democrats and their lapdogs, the Fake News Mainstream Media, are taking out the old Ronald Reagan playbook and screaming mental stability and intelligence. ... Actually, throughout my life, my two greatest assets have been mental stability and being, like, really smart. Crooked Hillary Clinton also played these cards very hard and, as everyone knows, went down in flames. I went from VERY successful businessman, to top T.V. Star ... to President of the United States (on my first try). I think that would qualify as not smart, but genius ... and a very stable genius at that!

Trump is certainly not a genius in any conventional understanding of that word, but there is some evidence he has a point. Richard Painter, a vociferous Trump critic, had this to say: "he would not have gotten this far as the first non-politician to be elected president since Dwight Eisenhower—if he were lacking in intelligence."[52] Susan Estrich, a longtime Democratic lawyer and operative had this to say[53]:

> I'm sorry, Donald Trump may be many things, but he is not stupid. He is not in over his head; he's been swimming along just fine. He is shrewd. You don't get to be president without being shrewd.

Shrewd is, of course a form of being smart. John Kelly, former White House Chief of Staff who thinks the president is[54]

> a super smart guy. He's very strong in terms of trade, taxes, business and he's a quick study on everything else. He's a pretty bright guy.

Trump may have his own more narrow element of "genius" (see below), but he is, as noted, no Freud or Einstein. He is however, clearly intelligent and has demonstrated that in a lifetime of business empire building. He has demonstrated it in his showmanship skills. He has displayed it in completely upending and dominating a very experienced field of seventeen Republican presidential candidates and winning the Republican nomination. He then won the general election against a very smart, very experienced, and very well connected Democratic nominee. Unless one seriously thinks that Trump is the political equivalent of Chauncey Gardner and that these accomplishments are the result of his being a moron or ignoramus, it is fair to credit his intelligence.

A more interesting question is what kind of intelligence Trump possesses. He is not an intellectual in the academic understanding of that term. He does not have the deep knowledge of a scholar about many, if not most things. His intelligence is of a different kind; the ability to see the essential nature of the circumstances that confront him or others, and move quickly to act on what he sees. The first is a by-product of intelligence, the second a by-product of his psychology.

This was the case when Trump first ventured into New York and saw the opportunity awaiting someone with the properties of the bankrupt Penn Central railroad yards on the upper west side of New York. It was true of his acquisition of the Commodore Hotel (Grand Hyatt) and the adjacent property. It was true of his decision to utilize bankruptcy to avoid the complete collapse of his business empire. It was the case for his decision to turn to branding real estate as an entrepreneurial vehicle, something that no one had ever thought to do before.

Trump's genius, if that's what it is, may be no more mysterious than being able to see the obvious, that is hidden in plain sight, while others are inhibited by their assumptions or lack of courage in seeing things as they are and yet not being able to act on that knowledge, if they do see it. One is reminded of the old saying: "In the land of the blind, the one eyed man is king"—or perhaps president.

Trump is not perfect. Neither are his abilities. His failure to see or stop himself from getting into his deep economic troubles in the 1990s attests to this fact. So does his inability, to date, to not respond to every provocation of which there are and will continue to be many.

It is true that Mr. Trump did not know much about the details of NATO, but he did know that Americans had been carrying a larger financial burden than their allies had promised, repeatedly, would be the case. He insisted NATO allies live up to their word. He also knew enough to know that NATO had been conceived in the Cold War and the world had changed. NATO therefore needed to think about its purpose. Stated directly, the insights sound commonplace, and they are, except for the fact that few others voiced them, if they saw them, and no establishment leaders were acting on them.

Or consider a domestic policy example. As president elect, Trump knew enough about business to insist that by leaning on the Carrier Corporation to keep jobs in America he was sending a signal about his focus on jobs as president. President Obama visited that exact same company with a very different message.

Obama mocked Trump's intentions to try to reverse the job losses saying[55]:

> When somebody says, like the person you just mentioned who I'm not going to advertise for, that he's going to bring all these jobs back, well how exactly are you going to do that? What are you going to do? There's—there's no answer to it. He just says, "Well, I'm going to negotiate a better deal." Well, how—what—how exactly are you going to negotiate that? What magic wand do you have? And usually, the answer is he doesn't have an answer.

Trump's intervention saved roughly a thousand of the jobs slated to be sent to Mexico.[56] In taking a different approach than President Obama,

Trump was signaling that he would be a different kind of president. In trying to help these thousand workers and their families and communities, he was also signaling that he was a different kind Republican president. In the past, "certainly for a Republican president-to-be the GOP is the party that is supposed to eschew the kind of government intervention in business decisions that Mr. Trump's actions represent."[57]

Trump was also sending a signal to other companies planning on moving out of the country.[58] Think twice. It won't be a free move. Trump promised tariffs on manufacturing items coming into the country from corporations that had once had their facilities in the United States but moved abroad for lower costs.

The same dynamic can be seen in Trump's views on immigration. Trump surprised one interviewer by saying quite directly and publicly that he had not followed immigration issues closely before descending the stairs at Trump Towers to make his candidacy announcement.[59] He said, "When I made my [announcement] speech at Trump Tower, the June 16 speech ... I didn't know about the Gang of Eight. ... *I just knew instinctively that our borders are a mess.*"

It is that last sentence that is a key to the nature of Trump's insights. According to one critic, "Donald Trump ran a brilliant Republican primary campaign."[60] Yet, it's wholly unsurprising that Trump could not place the Gang of Eight. Nor is it surprising that he could not expound on the details of American immigration policy. However, he did know one very large thing and was not afraid to say it loudly and publicly—"our borders are a mess."

Sir Isaiah Berlin distinguished between hedgehogs who view the world through the lens of a single defining idea, and foxes, who draw on a wide variety of experiences,[61] although his essay on Tolstoy suggests a person can be both. Trump appears to be such a hybrid. He is a business and political empire builder who relies on a variety of experiences.

Raising questions is one vital and another unusual aspect of Trump's presidential leadership style. Trump does not just take in and use various experiences. He asks about them.

Trump: A Man of Many Questions

We noted that Trump reaches out to a large diverse group of people for a sounding on his circumstances and to get advice. At one point, not uncommonly, "At a town hall meeting in Texas, Trump even polled audience members to get their input on the fate of the nation's undocumented immigrants."[62] However, Mr. Trump is more than an empty vessel waiting to be filled with information by others whose views he trusts. One aspect of Mr. Trump's active intelligence is that he is a president who asks many questions about a lot of things.

An opposition response to that fact would be: of course, he has to, he knows nothing. The opposition take on Trump is that he thinks he knows everything, but knows nothing. The fact that Trump asks lots of questions is inconsistent with that premise.

We have already covered one set of basic Trump questions consisting of various versions of: "Why can't I?" We noted that he asked Secretary of State Tillerson these questions about immigration policy because he really didn't have any governmental experience and really didn't know what specific laws and procedures were on the books. John Kelly's exit interview covered similar points.[63] Kelly said Trump did, however, often express frustration about the limits afforded by the law and frequently asked Kelly, "Why can't we do it this way?" Kelly explained why.

Trump's basic questions to his friends, family, and acquaintances about his circumstances are part of a larger more politically consequential set of Trump questions. As one analysis concluded[64]:

> No public official in modern times has challenged so many of the broad assumptions of American civic life, undermined so many of the canons of politics, recast so many of the conventions of public behavior. In a mere 18 months—to the consternation of establishment politicians, the news media and many of the special-interest groups that have controlled the conversation of the capital—he has upended the American political system. And while his rivals abhor him and scholars may condemn him, *history may well applaud him for raising vital questions about American political culture.*

The quote above noting Trump asking big basic questions of the American political system is echoed by those who have talked with him. Henry Kissinger had this to say about Mr. Trump and his questions[65]:

> *KISSINGER:* I believe he has the possibility of going down in history as a very considerable president ... *here is a new president who is asking a lot of unfamiliar questions.* And because of the combination of the partial [international power] vacuum *and the new questions,* one could imagine

12 THE FUTURE OF THE TRUMP PRESIDENCY   435

that something remarkable and new emerges out of it. I'm not saying
it will. I'm saying it's an extraordinary opportunity.

DICKERSON: Do you have a sense of what his emerging foreign policy
vision is?

*KISSINGER: I think he operates by a kind of instinct that is a different
form of analysis than my more academic one, that he's raised a number of
issues that I think are important, very important and, if they're addressed
properly, could lead to—could create results.*

We have already noted Trumps' seemingly naïve but very important
question "What is victory?" as a way of opening up debate on long
assumed and rarely discussed questions. Quite obviously that is not the
only unquestioned assumption that Trump has raised—on trade, on allies,
and on stationing and committing American troops. Indeed one *Foreign
Affairs* analysis has noted, "Trump's disruptions have forced foreign
policy analysts to question first principles for the first time in decades."[66]
It would seem prudent to reexamine operating assumptions at least every
few decades.

With the gradual loss of public confidence in the policies, leadership,
institutions, paradigms, and their associated narratives, the country does
indeed face large and important questions. It is part of Trump's "genius"
that he recognizes that and acts on the understanding. His questions are
not the final word on what questions must be asked and answered. He
is however raising new and needed questions for the country to consider
along with providing his rough version of some possible answers. That
is one reason why his presidency is so consequential and so politically
controversial.

ANNALS OF PRESUMPTION: TUTORING PRESIDENT TRUMP

From the start of his presidency, Mr. Trump has literally been viewed as
a misfit by the country's established leadership and their supporters in
all areas of American life. He has not said the right things. He has not
acted the way he should. He has not thought the right things. He has
not limited himself to talking with the right people or taking their correct
advice.

One major question that establishment figures faced is: what do you
do with such a president? The opposition had one answer: resist! The
country's political establishment had another: reeducate him.

Thanks to a new book by two *Washington Post* reporters with strong traditional credentials,[67] we now have a very detailed, behind the scenes, account of a truly extraordinary effort by establishment members of Trump's senior inner circle to tutor and reeducate him on the correct foreign policy understandings they thought he lacked. As a result of their carefully planned interventions, they thought, Trump would be less of a misfit and more of the kind of president whose actions and thinking they preferred.[68] They errored badly.

The reeducation effort took place six months into the administration (July 20, 2107) at "The Tank," one of a series of war rooms where high level strategic and military decisions are debated. The principle leaders of this effort were (then) Secretary of Defense Jim Mattis, Director of the National Economic Council Gary Cohn, and Secretary of State Rex Tillerson. Others included: the Chairman of the Joint Chiefs General Joseph F. Dunford Jr., newly confirmed Deputy Defense Secretary Patrick Shanahan, Vice President Pence, leaders of the military branches, Treasury Secretary Steven Mnuchin, White House chief strategist Stephen K. Bannon, and other staff.

In the words of Rucker and Leonnig, "Mattis invited Trump to the Tank for what he, Tillerson, and Cohn had carefully organized as *a tailored tutorial*." The reporters then write:

> What happened inside the Tank that day crystallized the commander in chief's berating, derisive and dismissive manner, foreshadowing decisions such as the one earlier this month that brought the United States to the brink of war with Iran. The Tank meeting was a turning point in Trump's presidency.

The two reporters, at least one of whom (Rucker) is no stranger to delivering anti-Trump slants in his writing, write with no apparent inkling as to why Trump had an adverse reaction to the effort to reeducate him. The reporters seem unaware, and do not mention, that the whole premise of the effort was condescending and infantilizing. It was of course not just a "*tailored tutorial*," but a remedial tutorial and another effort to "manage" Trump. That became clear to Trump almost immediately and he didn't like it.

Rucker and Leonnig write, "Trump appeared peeved by the schoolhouse vibe but also was allergic to the dynamic of his advisers *talking at him*." Yes, one would.

12 THE FUTURE OF THE TRUMP PRESIDENCY   437

However, it was more than that. The two reporters write:

> Rather than getting him to appreciate America's traditional role and alliances, Trump began to tune out and eventually push away the experts.

Rucker and Leonnig draw on extensive interviews of some of those who were in the room. However, they don't always specifically identify which people said what and whether those who did are accurately characterized as principals or staff. As is the case in many examples of this kind of inquiry, one gets many composite characterizations that force readers to rely on characterizations rather than verbatim evidence. For purposes of this section however, I will accept their characterizations of the sentiments they put forward.

What is the implication of Trump being in a room and "*talked at*" by his senior advisers and lower level staff who bring to their task the assumption, according to the reporters, that it was "*their duty was to protect the country by restraining his more dangerous impulses*"? Not only is that view smug and presumptuous, it's not the kind of condescending attitude that would be lost on Trump. He may not be deep, but he is very sensitive to how people treat him and whether they are being respectful. The operating premises and operating attitude behind the "tailored tutorial" with the premise of "protecting the country" from Trump's "dangerous impulses" and respect are antithetical.

What did the seminar try to teach Trump? Here is a sampling:

> Mattis then gave a 20-minute briefing on the power of the NATO alliance to stabilize Europe and keep the United States safe.
>
> Cohn spoke for about 20 minutes about the value of free trade with America's allies, emphasizing how he saw each trade agreement working together as part of an overall structure to solidify U.S. economic and national security.
>
> When Trump complained about the Iran nuclear agreement, saying "It's the worst deal in history!" Tillerson interjected. "Well, actually …" "I don't want to hear it," Trump said, cutting off the Secretary of State before he could explain some of the benefits of the agreement.

What unites these examples? They are all long held establishment narratives. Trump was very familiar with these arguments. He had been hearing them for years. It was not that he didn't want to hear what his seminar leaders wanted to say. He had already heard, repeatedly, the very same views and he didn't agree with them.

Interestingly, Rucker and Leonnig do not report anyone acknowledging or accepting even a small portion of any Trump point. For example when Trump complained about NATO being in arrears in its commitments:

> The general [Mattis] tried to calmly explain to the president that he was not quite right. The NATO allies didn't owe the United States back rent, he said. The truth was more complicated. NATO had a nonbinding goal that members should pay at least 2 percent of their gross domestic product on their defenses. Only five of the countries currently met that goal, but it wasn't as if they were shorting the United States on the bill.

Technically, that was accurate. However, there was also truth in the complaint that by repeatedly agreeing to that "goal" and never doing anything about it, American allies were signaling that they intended to remain "free riders," and the United States was signaling that it would continue to accept that. The ability of countries like Germany to pay more was not an issue. The goals of those NATO allies and their promises for the future, over the years became fig leaves for retaining their advantages. Mattis was well aware of this history and its meaning. Many prior administrations had made the same complaint, behind closed doors and with no results.

More importantly, Rucker and Leonnig did not note a single instance where anyone in that room calmly and respectfully asked Trump to explain and go into his thinking. They simply never thought to ask "what is your thinking about this," because they reasoned, they were right and Trump was wrong.

Could NATO stabilize Europe and still be improved? How? What about free trade? Could it be reformed? How would that be done, and what would it mean? What would a new Iranian deal look like and how would backing them into a military and economic corner achieve it? These are sample questions that could have been asked of Trump and might have led to some common ground and understanding.

Instead this reeducation debacle began and ended with its organizers' assumptions and the remedial efforts that flowed from it. As one staff member heavily involved in the planning of the seminar laid out the premises of the planned intervention:

12 THE FUTURE OF THE TRUMP PRESIDENCY   439

We were starting to get out on the wrong path, and we really needed to have a course correction and needed to educate, to teach, to help him understand the reason and basis for a lot of these things.. We needed to change how he thinks about this, to course correct. Everybody was on board, 100 percent agreed with that sentiment.

Translation: Everybody, 100 percent agreed that Trump had started his presidency by pursing erroneous and wrongheaded policies. These needed to be changed. Trump's views needed to be corrected. The only way to do so "was to teach him," to "help him understand" the basis for his errors and to change "how he thinks."

There is, of course, nothing less likely to change President Trump's (or any president's, one would think) mind than a grand reeducation seminar organized by some senior staff, and their aides, who believe the president's foreign policy thinking to be ill-informed (aka, ignorant, mistaken), and driven by "dangerous impulses."

In a master understatement Rucker and Leonnig write: "The plan by Mattis, Tillerson, and Cohn *to train the president to appreciate the internationalist* view had clearly backfired." The sentiment reflected in that last sentence, and the quote before it, clearly help explain Trump's angry response. The plan *"to train the president"* is more appropriate for a dog, or perhaps a parrot; but not for a president whom you hope will listen to what you have to say. Getting the president to "appreciate the internationalist view" was unlikely to happen by lecturing him yet again on views he had already heard many dozens of times. Had they asked the president more seriously about the basis of his thinking that might have started a real and useful dialogue.

This Trump reeducation seminar helps us to understand how difficult it was and will continue to be for him to succeed in his presidential purposes. The majority of the people gathered in that seminar room were smart, accomplished, and had strongly held views. They started from the assumption that they were right and Trump was wrong and proceeded accordingly. Imagine a country in which roughly half the people are exactly like that. Although they are not likely to be as smart and accomplished about the issues as Trump's educators thought they were, they would almost certainly be as strong in their views that Trump is wrong and they are right.

How then will it be possible, if it is, for Trump to successfully change that kind of country? How will it be possible for him to replace the long term *establishment policy paradigm* with the *Politics of American Restoration*? To state the obvious: The road to *Restoration* begins with reelection.

RESTORATION'S SECOND CHANCE?: TRUMP'S POSSIBLE REELECTION

There are many ways to view Trump's first term. One way is to understand it as a presidency elected as the country faced a profound political and policy fork in the road. As one retiring Republican put it[69]:

> There's a political realignment occurring in our country. The political ground is shifting right under our feet, and nobody knows how this is going to settle. It's going to affect both parties, and we'll see how it sorts itself out. It's going to take a few years.

The domestic realignment noted above coincides with another substantial change, in the international political system. Discussing the rise of nationalism worldwide and the emergence of new powerful, assertive, sometimes even militarily aggressive countries, like Russia, Iran, and China one analysis concluded[70]:

> The Cold War could have ended differently; largely, it ended peacefully. What you're now seeing, in my view, is across the board—*not just in the United States, not just with Donald Trump—a coming to an end of that order*.

Another lens through which to view Trump's election is as a political and policy audition. Trump's 2016 election victory was so narrow that it is impossible to completely rule out the impact of any single factor. Numerous efforts have been made to ascertain whether or not FBI Director Comey's off-again, on-again public statements about the Hillary Clinton investigation helped Trump or didn't matter. The same holds for reported Russian spending on *FaceBook* and its motivation, and a host of other factors that may, or may not have had an impact.

Trump has now been impeached according to the House's interpretation of the rules governing drawing up Articles of Impeachment. He has been acquitted on both impeachment charges by the Senate based on their governing rules. Trump's Constitutional legitimacy rests on more solid ground, even if the opposition continues to dispute his political legitimacy. His presidency thus carries with it the weight of core legitimacy, as well as the reality of it. As a result, if he wins reelection he will have another four years, and a more substantial opportunity to turn his first term audition into an historically rare, transformational presidency. That aspiration is unfolding now in the context of a pandemic of, at this point, uncertain consequences.

Trading Places: Narrative Negation and the 2020 Presidential Election

The fast approaching presidential election is already scrambling each candidate's best laid plans Neither is going be waging the kind of campaign they had planned for against the candidate that they had hoped to run against. Donald Trump was eagerly savoring a campaign against Bernie Sanders, the only Democrat who could make Trump look like a moderate centrist, while he ran on his real, and robust economic record.

The actual Democratic candidate Joe Biden envisioned a "return to normality" campaign. It would emphasize his steady, comparatively low wattage, and reliable political persona. That would present an obvious contrast to his opponent who would be portrayed as "President Bombast," who has riled America's traditional allies, refused to act as a normal president, and perhaps is incapable of doing so.

The Coronavirus pandemic upended both those narratives. President Trump cannot run on the economy he built. It no longer exists. And however leftward Mr. Biden inches forward, he is no Bernie Sanders. Mr. Biden's "return to normality" narrative has been compromised by events in which "normality" is in short supply. At some point he will have to convince the public that he is up to the task of leading the country and that he has the requisite amount of energy—both physical and cognitive, for being this country's chief executive. Trump's bull in the china shop persona—full steam ahead, explore any avenue, and get things done, is a possible advantage in the midst of this vast, enormously complex unprecedented pandemic challenge to the country, its leadership at all levels and its major institutions and agencies. Yet, there has been an erosion in the level of support in his handling of the pandemic and the demonstrations that followed.

In these new election defining circumstances, the likely campaign narratives are clear. Trump will lean heavily on James Madison who wrote that "energy in the executive" was "the leading character in the definition of good government," to which Trump will add, especially in times of crisis. A shattered economy? Trump will argue that during his first term his administration built "the greatest economy in the world," and will then promise, "we're going to do it again." He will compare himself, favorably of course, to "Slow Joe," the aged icon of the Democratic establishment whose level of real time alacrity is likely to be and remain an issue. He will support a number of useful policing practice reforms, while insisting that the country's basic premises of freedom and opportunity are worth preserving and building upon not "canceling" or tearing it down. Trump sending federal police resources to cities torn by violent demonstrations and spiking crime rates to help local police also sends a clear message of support for public order, as well as a signal of decisive resolve.

Mr. Biden does not have to do much to retain the support of Trump opponents. The question for his campaign is what real case can he make for his election? What will he promise? More solid, low key competence? More and better government programs defined by current progressive Democratic Party positions? A less combative presidential demeanor? The first of these is already being questioned. The second is likely to appeal to those government enthusiasts who have not yet lost their faith in those kinds of promises. And the last may prove preferable in theory, but not in practice given the many pandemic-caused crises that the country faces as the same time.

Still, Mr. Biden will present Trump as a president who had squandered valuable time responding to the pandemic by picking unnecessary fights with front-line governors desperate to get the resources they needed from an unresponsive administration. He will compare his "bipartisan" proposals to reforming policing practices in the wake of widespread public demonstrations with what he will characterize as Trump's heavy handed "law and order" response.

No firm prediction of the outcomes of those dueling narratives can be made at this point. Voters may well prefer a president who is seen as willing to go all out to fight for them, their livelihoods, and their country to one who promises a return to presidential decorum. Or, they may prefer a president who promises a return to normality, defined as status quo prior Trump. In the end, the 2020 president election may well come down to a contest between two leadership styles—full speed ahead v. the promise of a retro style of relative presidential public peacefulness.

12 THE FUTURE OF THE TRUMP PRESIDENCY   443

If Trump is not Reelected: What Then?

If Trump loses the 2020 election, the movement and the views that Trump represents and championed will die stillborn. Most of his executive actions will be rescinded. The pressure to rejoin the "international community" in "climate crisis" actions and to revive the Iranian nuclear agreement will intensify and probably be unavoidable. The new NAFTA treaty (USMCA) will be kept, but the political will to continue holding the Chinese accountable for their trade policies or to get NATO to spend more for their own defense will most likely dissipate. Here and there Trump policies will survive, but they will be dwarfed by the exploding cascade of the reestablishment of an even more progressive *establishment policy paradigm*. That holds as well for the one accomplishment that will be hard to rescind, but possible to negate—Trump's record of judicial appointments. Courts can be enlarged.

The above observations presuppose that a Trump reelection loss would be accompanied by a loss of Senate control as well, though that need not necessarily be the case. Still, a reduced Senate majority coupled with a major presidential loss are the ingredients of a long defensive crouch, not a burst of sustainable legislative Trumpism.

More consequential for the longer term would be that Trump's eight policy pillars and his approach to them would be ended for the most part, and the conventional *establishment policy paradigm* would be reinstated and extended. This would surely increase the disappointment, frustration, and anger, anxiety, and resentment of Trump supporters at what they lost. It would however turbocharge the opposition, making for a more volatile political climate. In terms of absolute raw political power there would be little Trump supporters could do with the levels of government power back in establishment hands. Nor is there much chance that a new Trump-like figure would rise out of the real Trump's political ashes.

Trump himself, as this analysis has argued, is truly *sui generis*, a unique political character and president. Who could possibly take his place? Mitt Romney? Ted Cruz? Jeb Bush? Nikki Haley? Listing the options answers the question. Moreover, after a Trump loss, NeverTrump Republicans and their establishment allies could legitimately argue: been there, done that.

If Trump Wins Reelection: Variations on a Theme

If Trump wins reelection his presidential legitimacy will be bolstered, even if his opponents attempt to diminish it, which they will. It's his actual reelection, not the popular vote margins that matter. You can't yield the powers of the presidency, which as both Trump and Obama among others have demonstrated are substantial, without being president.

That said, it does matter what the election means for the distribution of power in Congress. The most dire outcome for a Trump reelection would be the loss of a majority in both Houses of Congress. In that case, Trump's legislative agenda would essentially be comatose. His Senate judicial strategy would definitely be dead. He would be substantially defenseless against a continuing and heightened onslaught of investigations and lawsuits. They would be fueled by anger that he had somehow escaped electoral rejection. They would also be fueled by the still white-hot rage at his successful presidential accomplishments carried out in his first term, his leadership style in so doing, and ultimately his existence.

That would surely cripple Trump's second term presidency. It would put his *Restoration* ambitions on life support. He would still have, and doubtless would make use of, his executive presidential powers. However his accomplishments would be downsized and minimized, and his political troubles and setbacks would be the larger and more frequent narrative.

Keeping control of the Senate would be an essential element of a successful Trump second term. A Republican majority in the Senate after 2020 would look very different than the Republican majority there in 2016. That body is now much more closely aligned with Trump perspectives, and the "moderate" Republican senators up for reelection and somewhat vulnerable in 2020 (Senators Susan Collins of Maine, Joni Ernst of Iowa, Cory Gardner of Colorado, Martha McSally of Arizona, and Thom Tillis of North Carolina) if they won, would be past that kind of heightened reelection danger in seven years after Trump will have left office and could afford to be more supportive majority members.

A Trump aligned Republican Senate would act as a barrier to Democratic efforts to throw policy sand into the gears of Trump's *Restoration* presidential ambitions. It would as well forestall, maybe, efforts to mount a second round of Trump impeachment articles.[71] It would also allow Trump to continue his systematic and successful efforts to change the complexion of the federal judiciary and effectively respond to any Supreme Court openings that arise.

12 THE FUTURE OF THE TRUMP PRESIDENCY   445

A more difficult election likelihood is for Republicans to regain a House majority. Here too, were that to happen, the political stance of the Republicans would also be much more aligned with Trump perspectives than they were in the last Republican controlled House. If that happened, a major legislative immigration bill that closely resembles Trump's preferences[72] would be a very distinctive possibility, if not a likelihood. So would another round of tax cuts, geared to the middle and working classes, which Trump promised if he and a Republican Congress are elected.[73]

The implications of the Congressional election results for a second Trump term then are variable. It is not possible to say more about the future of the Trump presidency at this point without the election results. That leaves one more major theoretical question to again consider: How do entrenched narratives change?

CHANGING ENTRENCHED POLITICAL PARADIGMS

Truly transformational presidents are rare in American history. George Washington was one because his presidency was the first in post-revolutionary period when the country was a republic, in theory. Then it had no established and accepted operating ground rules to support that form of government in actual fact. Everything that Washington did, or didn't do was historic and transformational in establishing core foundation ways. Abraham Lincoln is part of the great presidents list because he fought a brutal Civil War to preserve the American union and succeeded. Franklin Delano Roosevelt is so considered because he guided the country though a catastrophic economic Depression and a savage worldwide war against Germany, Japan, and the Axis powers.

What makes these presidents "great" has been, is and will be debated. Some have made the case that Jefferson should be included because of his championing of the "Revolution of 1800" among other conservative political reforms. Others think that Andrew Jackson should be included in that list for restoring the power and the prestige of the presidency after years of decline.[74] Yet three striking and obvious similarities clearly stand out for all those presidents who are usually considered to belong in this category.

First, each "great," "transformational" president, after Washington encountered a set of circumstances that called into question the most basic assumptions of the country. Second, these presidents guided the country through a period of great dangers and perilous circumstances. As Crockett puts it about the importance of presidential leadership,[75] "It is during great crises, that energy in the government is most needed, and the president is best equipped to provide it." Third, in doing so, they also changed the way in which Americans thought about themselves and their country. Using those three elements as a metric we can say that many presidents may have been successful, but few have been transformational. Among those relatively few presidents considered "transformational," in the triple sense of that term noted above, all have also been considered "great."

In the American political circumstances that Trump faces, he more resembles Jefferson and Johnson than Lincoln and Roosevelt. President Trump and the country face no World War. However, he does face immediate catastrophic economic circumstances and increasingly widespread civic unrest and violence in across the country. These are in addition to the long simmering, ongoing and growing political malaise exacerbated by recent national racial and cultural/historical tensions have been decades in the making and reflect a lack of trust and confidence in the paradigms and narratives of establishment leadership and policies.

Trump's rational for a successful *Restoration* presidency is that the leadership and policy assumptions of the last four-plus decades have simply not worked as promised. They have, in his view, left many working- and middle-class Americans struggling economically, discouraged by the feeling that their own government doesn't listen to or care much about them, and worried and discouraged about the direction they see the country going. Those Americans are ready to reform or discard old paradigms and the narratives that support them, and demonstrated that fact in their votes for Trump.

However, many millions of Americans, and the leaders they support are not so inclined. This group is less economically vulnerable. They generally see the government as taking their claims and preferences seriously. They are satisfied for the most part with the perspectives, if not all of the results, of the dominant paradigms and narratives. In short, they do not support Trump's *Restoration* ambitions simply because they don't think very much needs restoring.

How then is it either possible or realistic for Trump to aspire to change the country's operative leadership and policy paradigms and the narratives that support them?

What Is a Dominant Paradigm?

Answering those questions requires us to first ask: what is a dominant paradigm? Answering that seemingly simple question allows us to understand what exactly, a dominant paradigm or narrative is, how it is sustained, and how and when it can be changed, if it can. It can also give us a model with which compare Trump's efforts along these lines.

The direct answer to that seemingly first simple question is that a dominant policy paradigm serves as an operating assumption for how the world works for people whose responsibilities include leadership and governance. Consequently, it substantially determines the nature, range, and scope of policies developed in the areas covered by the paradigm and its associated narratives.

That means that in economic and political organizations focused on international policy, the virtues of free trade, for example, will be considered an assumption, a given. Leaders speaking at or attending events associated with those organizations will speak on behalf of those assumptions and urge policies consistent with them. Those speeches will be reported and disseminated and form the basis of public understanding of the issue. Research supporting this position will be reported and highlighted. Professional thinking among economists and political leaders will reflect it.

When those national leaders return home that process will be repeated, National policies that enshrine them will be enacted. These too will be duly reported and praised by news organizations long accustomed to thinking of trade as an unalloyed virtue. Because paradigms need professional legitimacy to become and remain dominant, professional expertise will be tapped to provide it. The power of a dominant paradigm lies in its ability to command almost unquestioned legitimacy among numerous reinforcing institutional centers of power and standing, operating more frequently as assumption than the result of wide ranging analysis.

That trade is beneficial is a real fact and thus its use to buttress the economic paradigm and associated narratives that support it are honest, as far as they go. That however is never far enough to note and analyze its difficulties. It's only drawback, therefore, and it is a substantial one, is that it is not a wholly accurate accounting of trades' many consequences, some of which are undesirable.

"Free trade" does have some undesirable consequences. However, since they are rarely mentioned or discussed the experiences of millions of Americans (and others) were simply ignored or bypassed. Wide ranging research including the benefits and disadvantages "free trade" were not generally conducted or given much voice in public discussions. As a result, one major part of the effects of trade are simply lost from public view. In those circumstances how does a fuller, more complete, and more accurate understanding of free trade's benefits and liabilities get a public hearing?

Paradigm Change Without National Catastrophe: Presidential Megaphones and Determination

One answer to that question is having a president with a very different point of view. When that president has a loud, persistent voice amplified by the importance and connective reach of his office and its stature alternative views can at least be heard. In Trump's words: "I have the loudspeaker."[76]

That message is delivered personally and directly to Trump's multiple millions of supporters and amplified by national media on hair-trigger alert to respond to almost every Trump tweet and pronouncement. As a result, this president's views are not lost in the hundreds of ordinary speeches and interviews that every modern president makes. The novelty and controversial nature of Trump's views lift them out of relatively obscurity and operate as a form of ongoing public education.

One unique aspect of the Trump presidency is that this president has not been content to take the lead on one paradigm change issue, but a large number of them. In almost all the areas covered by the term used in this analysis, eight policy pillars, Trump has made his dissents against establishment paradigms and narratives clear. In the areas of economic growth (including jobs and energy development), immigration, trade, and foreign policy, Trump has consistently and forcefully laid out his counter paradigm positions in the face of loud and strenuous opposition.

Opposition to presidential political wishes is nothing new. What is new is that Trump's loud megaphone has forced those opposed to his counter paradigm and narrative to state their case publicly instead of being stealthy submerged within "conventional wisdom." As a result, often for the first time, a range of policy paradigms are subject to real public debate.

Is Trump changing many minds? Most likely not. If however, he can change enough minds, he won't have to change them all. What matters most now is that there are two sides debating. Trump is auditioning a

12 THE FUTURE OF THE TRUMP PRESIDENCY   449

new set of policy paradigms and narratives. He is giving loud voice to them, and in doing so is providing some education to the general public.

He is also educating himself at the same time. When Trump first raised the trade issue many decades ago his almost singular focus was on how badly America's leaders had failed the country on trade, how bad the trade deals were, and how other countries were taking advantage of the United States. That focus continued on though Trump's nomination and general election fight and into the first years of his presidency. Thereafter however, a needed subtlety entered Trump's trade diatribes, free vs fair trade.

The use of the term "fair trade" signaled Trump's acceptance of a major truth of the dominant "trade is good" paradigm. If handled correctly, trade *was* beneficial. Yet it also added the important qualifier "fair" that provided a route by which to reconcile the now two competing paradigms and narratives.

Narrative Wars: When Paradigms Collide

President Trump has taken a number of steps to provide the public with examples of *Restoration* paradigms and their associated narratives, to experience, and for their consideration. Trump's counter paradigm policies and narratives now have several exemplars in the area of trade, that can serve as case illustrations: the new USMCA (formerly NAFTA) China, South Korea, and Japan trade agreements. There are, of course, expected debates about how much these new agreements really accomplish. However, for each trade agreement, Trump can legitimately claim to have advanced American economic, and in the case of China, strategic interests. These cases in point transform Trump's *Restoration* ambitions from solely rhetorical to also directly experiential.

Moreover, trade is just one of the eight pillar areas in which Trump has begun to produce his own policies that are consistent with his *Restoration* ambitions. In his policies regarding the courts, economic growth and opportunity (including jobs and energy development), de-regulation, health care, immigration, and foreign policy Trump continues to replace the more liberal *establishment policy paradigm* with his own *Restoration* policies and narratives.

He has also taken steps, as president, to tilt the playing field in a more positive direction for him. Nearing the end of only his first year in office, the *Washington Post* reported that Trump has "undone" a substantial number of the *establishment policy paradigm*'s policies and procedural regulations[77] in a wide variety of areas.[78] These very early and preliminary lists (with additional lists within those lists) contain a number that are substantial (e.g, withdrawing from the Trans-Pacific Partnership; reversing an Obama ban on drilling for oil in the Arctic); others that are consequential (e.g., delayed and potentially rolling back automotive fuel efficiency standards); and others that are primarily symbolic (e.g., ending the declaration of June as Pride Month and the practice of recognizing the end of Ramadan with an iftar dinner). That list has only grown since Trump's first year in office and now includes such major "undoings" as the international climate accords and the Iran nuclear agreement, among many.

The anti-Trump take on his many initiatives is that they are primarily "anti-Obama." More accurately they are anti-Obama *establishment policy paradigm* initiatives. Trump's initiatives allow him to implement policies consistent with his own *Restoration* ambitions. You can't become an energy exporting powerhouse if you are barred from utilizing the shale drilling revolution. Removing policies and administrative procedures from a paradigm helps a president trying to substantially modify or replace old paradigms to showcase the new proposed paradigm exemplars with less competition.

Successful paradigmatic change elements reinforce each other. Successfully encouraging domestic shale oil production brings with it more energy jobs, helps the economy grow, helps trade balances, and makes the country less dependent on oil from elsewhere, which itself has national security and strategic benefits. The utility of Trump's counternarrative exemplars are not only to be found in their role as examples, but in their ability to generate actual public and political experiences that can then be taken into account.

Political War, Attrition, and the Death of Dominant Paradigms

After almost half the country, a large percentage of the country's establishment political leadership and their allies across many powerful institutions support the liberal *establishment policy paradigm*. As a result, they support neither the president or his *Restoration* ambitions. What then?

Trump's efforts at paradigmatic narrative replacement relies on top down, bottom up, and expansion outward strategies. The top down element is obviously Trump's attention, commanding presence, and clear

12 THE FUTURE OF THE TRUMP PRESIDENCY 451

leadership spearheading that fight. The bottom up element revolves around giving the public the opportunity to experience the virtues that Trump sees in the results of changing paradigms. And the building outward element rests on what is the second major Trump life motto beside Never Give Up: Never Stop, full speed ahead whenever possible.

Put in diagrammatic form, Trump's paradigmatic narrative replacement strategy would look like this: Establish accomplishment baseline →Initiate and sustain leadership opportunities →Build on success →hoped for outcome: cascading leadership accomplishments.

Keep in mind that in his business career Trump was a successful empire builder. That is a very unique kind of entrepreneur. He shows every sign of attempting to reprise that same role as president.

So, if you successfully complete trade deals with China and North America, try to leverage it to gain traction with North Korea[79] and also immediately begin publicly prepping for hard trade negotiations with the EU. In the president's words: "with the European Union—and, frankly, I'll be honest, I wanted to wait until I finished China before I went to work on, respectfully, Europe." Trump is more likely to move on to the next challenge than to savor the last.

If lower courts reject your travel restrictions on potential immigrants from some countries deemed dangerous, appeal. And when the Supreme Court rules in your favor, prepare to add more counties to that list.[80] Or in Trump's words in response to a question during a Davos Meeting Q & A[81]:

> I didn't lose the travel ban. The travel ban was lost in the lower courts and won in the Supreme Court, two years ago. No, we are—we're adding a couple of countries to it. We have to be safe.

And, if you believe that the United States had the "world's greatest economy," and know that it has been crippled by a world-wide pandemic, what do you do? You pledge to rebuild and do it again; "so I say I built the greatest economy—with all of the people that helped me and all of the people in this country, we built the greatest economy the world has ever seen. And we're going to do it again."[82]

Trump's Efforts at Narrative Change: Progress?

There is one more element that is relevant to Trump's effort to develop an alternative *Restoration* paradigm. That is the slow belated recognition that he may have a legitimate point in some of his complaints, even by supporters of the very paradigms that he is trying to replace. Again, using trade as an example, recently two well-credentialed academics wrote in a major establishment journal about "free trade[83]:"

> Those of us who have not only analyzed globalization and the liberal order but also celebrated them share some responsibility for the rise of populism. We did not pay enough attention as capitalism hijacked globalization. Economic elites designed international institutions to serve their own interests and to create firmer links between themselves and governments. *Ordinary people were left out.* The time has come to acknowledge this reality and push for policies that can save the liberal order before it is too late.

This is not the battle cry of someone vying for public office on a "populist" platform. It is part of a worried sober analysis by two mainstream, respected academics writing in *Foreign Affairs*, that most establishment-centered of major foreign policy journals.

Jared Bernstein, a top Obama economics advisor, wrote a *New York Times* op-ed entitled "The Era of Free Trade Might Be Over. That's a Good Thing."[84] More recently Federal Reserve Chairwoman Janet Yellen, in comments at the British Academy in London, speaking of globalization and technology and trade said that,[85] "Both of these things have been quite harmful to a very large share of the population." She continued, "Trade can be good, and it has been good. ... But there are losers, and it's challenging to design interventions that would help the losers."

And finally, at the 2020 Davos meeting press conference, Trump brought up his long-running dispute with the WTO about who was and who was not considered a "developing country" entitled to special treatment. Trump then invited the Director General of the World Trade Organization Roberto Azevêdo to speak, and he said[86]:

> And I think it's fair to say that we have been saying, for quite some time, that if the multilateral system, if the WTO is to deliver and perform its

12 THE FUTURE OF THE TRUMP PRESIDENCY   453

role in today's global economy, it has to be updated. It has to be changed. It has to be reformed.

Trump's effort to change the international trade paradigm had clearly found an ally in the very organization he was trying to change.

Paradigm Change: By Degree?

Therein lies an important point. In non-catastrophic circumstances, and short of using lethal force, paradigmatic and narrative change occurs by degree. That is why several recent solutions offered to the country's contentious political debates are not very likely. One solution can be summarily dismissed for the very reason that the author uses to describe it. It appeared in the *Washington Post*[87]:

> So how do we get the minority of haters to stop hating, if we ever want to get out of this quagmire and move forward as a country? It turns out that *as ridiculously naive as it may sound* Americans' support for political violence goes down when they are exposed to messages calling for peace.

At the other extreme is secession. In a provocative book that doesn't recommend it, the author writes that he sees "us on a train, bound for a break up."[88] And furthermore:

> In all the ways that matter, save for the naked force of the law, we are already divided into two nations. The contempt for opponents, the Twitter mobs, online shaming and no-platforming, the growing tolerance of violence—it all suggests we'd be happier in separate countries.

How that would actually work in practice? What would happen to Trump supporters, and everyone else if Blue States seceded, and vice versa, is very unclear. Would the secession be state by state, county by county, city by city, neighborhood by neighborhood, or person by person? The many difficulties are clear.

Still another idea suggests the conflict will be resolved by an as yet unknown and unlikely innovation. Henry Olsen writes[89]:

> American politics is currently akin to trench warfare with both sides exerting enormous amounts of energy, treasure, and manpower to gain very little ground. Victory will not come to the party who continues the

old tactics in the vain hope of new results. Breaking through the trenches *will ultimately require something entirely new that reshapes the battlefield itself. And that requires winning large majorities among people who don't fit neatly into either party's base.*

Who those people are and on what basis they might form a new operating majority or plurality is totally unclear and not easily envisioned. Mr. Olsen does not enlighten us on this basic question.

We are therefore still left with an unresolved earlier question. Will it be possible or realistic for Trump to aspire to change the country's major domestic and foreign policy paradigms and the narratives that support them, and if so how? In the above analysis, we have already given a provisional affirmative answer to the first question. It can be done, and Trump is assembling the basis for possibly doing so. But what of the "how question"?

A number of observers have summoned up the metaphor of a civil war to describe the country's circumstances and there is some truth in that. The country's level of *elemental polarization* is deep and wide. A relentless opposition war is being waged and defended against in every nook and cranny of the American political system and in the experience of ordinary Americans' daily lives.

The battles are being fought out within the confines of the country's legitimate and legal institutions, sometimes by finessing real constitutional guardrails.[90] Peter Baker captures the brutal nature of the Senate impeachment trial[91]: "With Mr. Trump's fate on the line, the trial, unfolding with just a few months before he faces re-election, has come to encapsulate the pitched three-year struggle that has consumed Washington since he took office, determined to disrupt the existing order, at times in ways that crossed longstanding lines."

In this civil warlike battle no lethal force is being used. There are no prisoner of war camps and no savage bombings or invasions. Moreover, a majority of the country are non-combatants. They have political views but are not ready to make their or the country's final stand for them. The country seems for all its conflict, diversity, and polarization more akin to a fractured mosaic than involved in a real civil war.

Yet, it is real war in many respects. It is being fought out hourly every day in biased news reports and their rebuttals, within institutions and recently again, as it was at the start of the Trump's presidency, in

12 THE FUTURE OF THE TRUMP PRESIDENCY 455

the streets. It is fought out in vicious and sometimes vile unsubstantiated accusations against the president and his family. It was, is and most likely will be again fought out in hostile interviews, in books and articles based primarily on leaks of dubiously sourced conversations or snippets of conversations whose accuracy is suspect. It was and will be again fought out in conversations across dinner tables, at offices, on billboard ads, at the theater, in the nation's educational system at all levels from kindergarten through professional credentialing schools, in public demonstrations, and in a variety of policy, political, and personal lawsuits against Trump, his supporters, and his families. This war is a form of civil war, but it also parallels World War II in its expansiveness, and resembles aspects of trench warfare during the First World War in its inch-by-inch battles to inflict as much harm to Trump and his presidency possible.

Sometimes ordinary all-out war can be clarifying. Edward Littwak's iconic article,[92] "Give War a Chance," captures this important possible essence:

> An unpleasant truth often overlooked is that although war is a great evil, it does have a great virtue: it can resolve political conflicts and lead to peace. This can happen when all belligerents become exhausted or when one wins decisively.

Neither President Trump or his opposition seems likely to become exhausted, exit the battlefield and give up on their preferred paradigms and narratives. Nor does a sweeping decisive political victory seem in sight where the successful Trump or opposition politically "occupy" the other's territory. It is at any rate, not clear how that could happen in our federal system of political and geographical checks and balances. As noted above, Trump may win reelection or not, but a veto proof majority in Congress by either Trump supporters or detractors, no matter which party wins the presidency, seems unlikely in 2020.

After November's election, there will be no surrender ceremonies on Pennsylvania Avenue, Main Street, Austin, or San Francisco. What then? Most likely there will be a continued *War of Political Attrition* until one paradigm and its associated narratives gains traction and possible supremacy, or until a quasi-truce emerges because the competing narratives have found an accommodation much like Trump's "free trade" vs "fair trade" dichotomy seems to have sparked some common ground.

American Restoration Amidst a War of Relentless Opposition: The Personal Psychological Challenge to Trump

Donald Trump's first term in office has been an enormous test of his presidency and himself. He has had to learn how to be president. He has had to assemble a working staff that he is comfortable with and vice versa. He has had to address the issue of his support in the Republican party. He has had to deal with a ferocious anti-Trump opposition. He has had to deal with a two year long Special Council investigation, being impeached and acquitted, an unprecedented number of Congressional investigations along with a virtual blizzard of political and personal lawsuits. He has had to respond to an unprecedented worldwide pandemic, and while that national trauma was unfolding numerous demonstrations across the country protesting claimed institutional police and American racism, which has led to widespread assaults on public monuments and widespread mass demonstrations, a number of which have become violent. He has, at very same time all of these elements were playing out, had to lead, govern, and protect the country, while trying to advance his own presidential goals.

This is not to lament Mr. Trump's circumstances. It is simply to acknowledge them. All of these circumstances test Trump politically but also in a directly personal way even more.

Trump faced several basic questions in his first years in office. First, would he be able to sufficiently, and even successfully, master the enormous powers and responsibilities of the modern presidency? Trump hinted at this key question several times. He was surprised, he said at, "the size, the magnitude of everything."[93] Yet, it's not only the government's magnitude and its consequences that are sobering. Recall that when asked how he has changed since taking office, the former businessman who, as a candidate, touted his ability to cut deals said:

> The magnitude of everything is so big, and also the decisions are so big. *You know, you're talking about life and death.* You're not talking about "you're going to make a good deal."

It was not only the scale and consequences of government that surprised Trump. It is also about the inherent paradox of successful presidential leadership. You often have to stumble, even fail in order to succeed. As Trump put it: "You make wrong calls, But they have to be wrong so that they don't have huge impact and they have to be wrong so that you can adjust."[94]

By any reasonable assessment Trump began his presidency facing a steep learning curve. It was steeper than any other modern president's because he had spent his adult life immersed in building, losing, and regaining a vast business empire. Trump is smart, cognitively nimble, and determined to succeed. Yet bringing those traits to the modern presidency do little more than give him the possibility of success or avoiding outright failure.

One of the great unacknowledged ironies of the Trump presidency is the core integrity that Mr. Trump brings to one part of his leadership role—expressing and acting on his views. There is the matter of his "truthful hyperbole," rhetorical imprecision, casual acquaintance with policy details, or nuance. These do accurately describe elements of Trump's leadership style. However, as noted in Chapter 9, Trump does not hide what he thinks, or what he would like to, will do, or does. There is a basic core personal integrity in that approach to his presidency.

Mr. Trump is serially accused of being willing to do anything to get reelected including putting his own reelection before the country's national interests according to John Bolton.[95]

Mr. Bolton and others who make the same claims do not explain the paradoxical fact that Mr. Trump insists on pursuing policies that will cause his election a great deal of difficulty because he believes they are correct right policies to pursue. Case in point, the Administration has asked the Supreme court, again, during this election season to negate "Obamacare."[96]

The administration's continued support for toppling the ACA is a political gamble as jobless claims stabilize around a historic high of about 20 million because of the pandemic. Democrats, including presumptive Democratic presidential nominee Joe Biden, are seeking to portray President Trump as endangering health coverage at a time when more than 150,000 deaths have been attributed to the coronavirus.

It would certainly have been more prudent to decouple the Administration from the group of seventeen states seeking to overturn that legislation, but Trump had the courage and the integrity to following through on what he thought was right. This is not an observation on the merits of that position, only on what Trump's choice suggests about the anything for reelection claim.

Every new role brings with it "can I successfully do this?" questions, and the Trump presidency is no exception. Yet Trump's reelection challenges raises more than the ordinary questions of can he succeed. He faces larger, more fundamental political and reelection questions.

Two are: Is it possible to be seen as having relatively successfully addressed the ordinary presidential vicissitudes of leading and governing this divided country while trying to bring it back from the ravages of the Coronavirus pandemic[97] and the claimed anti-police and American institutionalized racism and civil unrest that has convulsed the country? Second, is it possible to garner support for substantially modifying the country's domestic and international policy narratives and basic understandings while the country is going through this deeply unsettling and difficult period? To simply state both of these enormous hurdles to Trump's reelection so directly is to underscore their monumental nature.

Only once before in his life, when his business empire tottered on the brink of insolvency, has Trump ever faced such a potentially large gap between his circumstances and real questions about his capacity to surmount them. He has arrived the abyss again, this time its political. These enormous political reelection questions raise profound personal questions for President Trump. Among them are:

> Does he have the inner psychological resources and political insight to avoid electoral failure?
> Does he have the inner psychological resources to absorb all the emotional and political punishment that will substantially define his circumstances even if he is reelected, and to forge on, if he is not?

We have dealt with these questions in one form or another over the course of this book's analysis. If there is one thing about which one can be relatively certain about this president and his presidency, and their real psychology, it is this: Trump is a man of extraordinarily strong convictions and courage in seeing them through. He is a man of remarkable determination and resilience in the face of adversity. In his presidency, the last large act of his life, he is absolutely serious about putting into place the *Politics of American Restoration*. And, win or loose, he never gives up.

Wining reelection, and then successfully realizing his *Restoration* ambitions will be equivalent to scaling Mt. Annapurna. It will take skill, experience, determination, courage, resilience, luck, and a dedicated competence and effective group of support allies. Many imagine the climb. Few attempt it. Fewer succeed.

The risk are high, the chances of success low, but it would be unwise to place a large bet against President Trump.

NOTES

1. Doug Sosik. 2014. "Blue Crush: How the Left Took Over the Democratic Party," *Politico*, July 24; see also Alexander Burns and Jonathan Martin. 2019. "Trump's Takeover of the Republican Party Is Almost Complete," *New York Times*, April 3.
2. Jeffrey Jones. 2020. "Trump Third Year Sets New Standard for Party Polarization," *Gallup*, January 21.
3. Ezra Klein. 2020. *Why We're Polarized*. New York: Simon & Schuster.
4. Norm Ornstein. 2020. "Why America's Political Divisions Will Only Get Worse," *New York Times*, January 28.
5. Peter Hamby. 2018. "'That Is What Power Looks Like': As Trump Prepares for 2020, Democrats Are Losing the Only Fight That Matters," *Vanity Fair*, May 26.
6. https://www.gao.gov/assets/710/703909.pdf.
7. Jeff Stein and Ellen Nakashima. 2020. "White House hold on Ukraine Aid Violated Federal Law, Congressional Watchdog Says," *Washington Post*, January 16; see also Jeremy Herb. 2020. "Government Watchdog Concludes Trump Administration Broke Law by Withholding Ukraine Aid," *CNN*, January 16.
8. Chris Walker. 2020. "Pelosi: GAO Report Showing Trump Broke The Law Reinforces Need For Witnesses At Senate Impeachment Trial," *The Hill*, January 16.
9. https://www.gao.gov/assets/670/665390.pdf; see also Jeffrey Sparshott. 2014. "Bergdahl Swap Violated Law, GAO Says," *Wall Street Journal*, August 21.
10. Ricardo Alonso-Zaldivar. 2016. "Obama Administration Broke Its Own Health Care Rule, GAO Says," *Associated Press*, September 30.
11. James Freeman. 2020. "What Did GAO Staff Know and When Did They Know It?" *Wall Street Journal*, January 17.
12. Alan M. Dershowitz. 2020. "Trump Had Right to Withhold Ukraine Funds: GAO Is Wrong," Gatestone Institute, January 17, emphasis added.

13. Daniel Carpenter and David A. Ross. 2013. *Preventing Regulatory Capture: Special interest Influence and How to Limit It*. New York: Cambridge University Press.
14. Alexander S. Vindman. 2019. "Opening Statement of Lieutenant Colonel Alexander S. Vindman Before the House Permanent Select Committee on Intelligence, the House Committee on Foreign Affairs, and the House Committee on Oversight and Reform," October 29, emphasis added.
15. Wesley Morgan. 2019. "'POTUS Went Rogue': Trump's Syria Move Blindsides National Security Leaders," *Politico*, October 7.
16. Donald J. Trump. 2019. "Remarks by President Trump in Briefing with Military Leaders," The Cabinet Room, October 7, emphasis added.
17. Josh Dawsey. 2019. "Unswayed by Top Advisers, Trump Doubles Down on Decision to Withdraw Troops," *Washington Post*, October 13.
18. Paul D. Shinkman. 2019. "Trump Administration Appears to Reverse Syria Decision Following Backlash," *US News & World Report*, October 7.
19. One recent incident between Russian and US forces suggests this was a prudent consideration. See Ben Wolfgang. 2020. "Standoff: U.S. Troops Block Russian Forces from Capturing Syrian Oil Field," *Washington Times*, January 21.
20. Alex Johnson, Saphora Smith, and Shannon Pettypiece. 2019. "Trump Says He May Leave Some U.S. Forces in Syria to Protect Oil, But Not Kurds," *NBC*, October 21.
21. Michael Doran and Michael A. Reynolds. 2019. "Turkey Has Legitimate Grievances Against the U.S.," *Wall Street Journal*, October 8.
22. Annie Karni, Lara Jakes, and Patrick Kingsley. 2019. "Turkey Agrees to Pause Fighting, But Not to Withdraw Forces from Northern Syria," *New York Times*, October 17.
23. Morgan L. Kaplan. 2019. "Trump's Syria Announcement Is a Change of Speed—Not a Change of Direction," *Washington Post*, October 9.
24. William Saletan. 2019. "Guess Who Else Trump Is Colluding With," *Slate*, October 8.
25. Jen Kirby. 2019. "What Really Happened in Syria Over the Past 24 hours, Explained," *Vox*, October 23; see also Aaron Blake. 2019. "Trump's Former ISIS Envoy Offers Scathing Critique of His Syria Decision—And Entire Management Style," *Washington Post*, October 7.
26. Alex Ward. 2019. "Trump Just Reversed His Decision to Pull all US Troops Out of Syria," *Vox*, February 22.
27. Eric Schmitt. 2019. "U.S. Resumes Large-Scale Operations Against ISIS in Northern Syria," *New York Times*, November 25.
28. Peter Baker and Lara Jakes. 2019. "In Syria, Trump Distills a Foreign Policy of Impulse, and Faces the Fallout," *New York Times*, October 10, emphasis added.

12 THE FUTURE OF THE TRUMP PRESIDENCY 461

29. Catherine Lacy. 2019. "Behind Trump's Syria Pullout Lies a Campaign Pledge," *Wall Street Journal*, October 8.
30. Mark Lander, Helene Cooper, and Eric Schmitt. 2018. "Trump to Withdraw U.S. Forces from Syria, Declaring 'We Have Won Against ISIS'," *New York Times*, December 19.
31. Mark Lander and Helene Cooper. 2019. "In Latest Shift, Trump Agrees to Leave 400 Troops in Syria," *New York Times*, February 22.
32. Ben Wolfgang. 2019. "Military Slow-Walk or 'Deep State' Defiance?: Trump Sees Direct Orders Modified," *Washington Times*, December 1.
33. Eric Schmitt and Helene Cooper. 2019. "Hundreds of U.S. Troops Leaving, and Also Arriving in, Syria," *New York Times*, October 30.
34. Mark Lander and Helene Cooper. 2019. "In Latest Shift, Trump Agrees to Leave 400 Troops in Syria," *New York Times*, February 22.
35. Shawn Donnan. 2018. "Cohn Lifted Papers Off Trump's Desk to Stop Nafta Exit, Book Says," *Bloomberg*, September 4.
36. Anonymous. 2018. "I Am Part of the Resistance Inside the Trump Administration," *New York Times*, September 5.
37. Carol E. Lee, Kristen Welker, Stephanie Ruhle, and Dafna Linzer. 2017. "Tillerson's Fury at Trump Required an Intervention From Pence," *NBC News*, October 4.
38. Trump quoted in Randall Lane. 2017. "Inside Trump's Head: An Exclusive Interview with the President, and the Single Theory That Explains Everything," *Forbes*, October 10.
39. Daniel W. Drezner. 2017. "Why Did Trump Flip-Flop on Afghanistan? It's the Policy Ignorance, Stupid,' *Washington Post*, August 22.
40. Max Boot. 2017. "Is Donald Trump a Moron? Duh," *USA TODAY*, October 4.
41. Katie Rogers. 2018. "Trump's Book Club: A President Who Doesn't Read Promotes the Books That Promote Him," *New York Times*, November 30.
42. Carol D. Leonnig, Shane Harris, and Greg Jaffe. 2018. "Breaking with Tradition, Trump Skips President's Written Intelligence Report and Relies on Oral Briefings," *Washington Post*, February 9.
43. Jack Schaffer. 2018. "Drowning in News? Learn to Swim," *Politico*, March 12.
44. Cody Cain. 2018. "It Takes a Village Idiot: Thanks to Donald Trump, the President May Be Chosen by a Fourth-Grade Mentality If We Elect a Presidential Candidate Who Speaks and Thinks on a Fourth-Grade Level, What Does That Say About Us?" *Salon*, October 30.
45. Justin Moyer. 2016. "Trump's Grammar in Speeches 'Just Below 6th Grade Level,' Study Finds," *Washington Post*, March 18.
46. Derek Thompson. 2014. "Presidential Speeches Were Once College-Level Rhetoric—Now They're for Sixth-Graders," *The Atlantic*, October 14.

47. Kathleen Parker. 2017. "How Can You Still Doubt Trump's Intelligence?" *Washington Post*, June 23.
48. David Brooks. 2018. "Donald Trump's Lizard Wisdom," *New York Times*, May 10.
49. Meghan Keneally. 2018. "President Trump Has Called Himself Smart Six Times Before," *Washington Post*, January 9.
50. David Nakamura. 2016. "Trump Boasts That He's 'Like, Really Smart' and a 'Very Stable Genius' Amid Questions Over His Mental Fitness," *Washington Post*, January 6.
51. https://twitter.com/realDonaldTrump/status/949616329463615489?ref_src =twsrc%5Etfw%7Ctwcamp%5Etweetembed%7Ctwterm %5E949616329463615489&ref_url=https%3A%2F%2Fwww.washington post.com%2Fnews%2Fpost-politics%2Fwp%2F2018%2F01%2F06%2Ftrump-boasts-that-hes-like-really-smart-and-a-very-stable-genius-amid-questions-over-his-mental-fitness%2F.
52. Richard W. Painter. 2016. "It Is Possible for Trump to Be a Good President," *New York Times*, November 9.
53. Susan Estrich. 2018. "Donald Trump Numbers Not as Bad as Some Believe," *Boston Herald*, November 17.
54. Kelly quoted in Richard Gonzales and John Burnett. 2018. "John Kelly: Despite 'Times of Great Frustration,' No Regrets Taking White House Job," *NPR*, May 10.
55. Gwen Ifill. 2016. "Questions for President Obama: A Town Hall Special," *NPR*, June 1.
56. James Hill. 2016. "The Story Behind Donald Trump's Deal with Carrier to Keep 1,000 Jobs in the US," *ABC News*, November 30.
57. Gerald F. Seib. 2017. "Donald Trump Explains Why He Twists Businesses' Arms," *Wall Street Journal*, January 16.
58. Seib 2017.
59. Richard Greene. 2017. "Is Donald Trump Mentally Ill? 3 Professors of Psychiatry Ask President Obama to Conduct 'A Full Medical and Neuropsychiatric Evaluation'," *Huffington Post*, December 18, emphasis added.
60. Chris Cillizza. 2016. "Trump Is Running the Same Campaign That Won Him the GOP Nomination. There's a Big Problem with That," *Washington Post*, June 12.
61. Isaiah Berlin. 1953. *The Hedgehog and the Fox: An Essay on Tolstoy's View of History*. London: Weidenfeld & Nicolson.
62. Jenna Johnson, Robert Costa, and Philip Rucker. 2016. "How Trump Got from Point A to Point A on Immigration," *Washington Post*, September 1.
63. Michael Berke. 2018. "5 Revelations from John Kelly's *Los Angeles Times* Exit Interview," *The Hill*, December 30.

64. David M. Shribman. 2017. "Trump Mixes Up the Parties, Raises Questions," *Post-Gazette*, June 18.
65. Kissinger quoted in Transcript. 2016. "Face the Nation," *CBS*, December 18, emphasis added.
66. Daniel W. Drezner, Ronald R. Krebs, and Randall Schweller. 2020. "The End of Grand Strategy America Must Think Small," *Foreign Affairs*, May/June.
67. Philip Rucker and Carol Leonnig. 2020. "'You're a Bunch of Dopes and Babies': Inside Trump's Stunning Tirade Against Generals," *Washington Post*, January 17; Philip Rucker and Carol Leonnig. 2020. *A Very Stable Genius: Donald J. Trump's Testing of America*. New York: Penguin Press. The analysis and the quotes used in this section are drawn from these two sources (emphasis added unless otherwise noted).
68. Rucker and Leonnig 2020.
69. Dent quoted in Janet Hook and Siobhan Hughes. 2017. "Republican Retirement Gives House Democrats Another Target," *Wall Street Journal*, September 8.
70. Susan Glasser. 2018. "Just How Dangerous Is Donald Trump?" *Politico*, April 16, emphasis added.
71. Josh Gerstein and Kyle Cheney. 2019. "House Counsel Suggests Trump Could Be Impeached Again," *Politico*, December 23; see also Paul Waldman. 2019. "Could Democrats Impeach Trump Twice? They Might Have To," *Washington Post*, December 24. The idea is not as far-fetched as it sounds, especially if Trump wins reelection. Recently, having been tried and acquitted of two dubious Articles of Impeachment, Fred Hyatt the director of the Washington Post's editorial page, who previously proposed an update of four new possible impeachment articles, recently updated to six his examples of what he says are Trump's behavior that deserves impeachment consideration. These include: the accusation that "the president refused to acknowledge the danger [of the Coronavirus] because he did not want the stock market to tank"; that he abused law enforcement powers by exercising them to remove the U.S. attorneys of D.C. and the Southern District of New York, "who had been insufficiently attentive to his whims"; that he abused foreign policy power because one of his fired advisors claimed that Trump had told Xi Jinping that he was fine with concentration camps for Muslim Uyghurs. The reason according to this advisor is that Trump wanted China to buy farm products; and Trump's raising the concern of fraud when states send millions of mail ballots [not Absentee ballots]. As is typically the case in these kinds of claims of egregious criminal and Constitutional Trump presidential behavior, certain strategies are clear: never explore the full range of evidence and analysis relevant to the accusations; never analyze real policy debates as anything more than a claim that there is a gold standard

that Trump fails to measure up to; rely on anonymous sources; rely on sources that have an obvious and public grudge against the president; rely on highly partisan sources like Nancy Pelosi to buttress your claims; use high biased tendentious phrasing like "who had been insufficiently attentive to his whims" to insure like-minded readers get the point; and never ever assume better than the worst, most venal self-interested motivations on Mr. Trump's part. Almost four years into the Trump presidency, it is still surprising, and lamentable, to read such obvious and blatant diatribes by the editorial page director of what was once a major and fair-minded national newspaper. See Fred Hyatt. 2020. "Trump's articles of impeachment—updated," *Washington Post*, June 28; Fred Hyatt. 2020. "In just one month, Trump commits a whole new set of potentially impeachable offenses," *Washington Post*, July 26.

72. Donald J. Trump. 2019. "Remarks by President Trump on Modernizing Our Immigration System for a Stronger America," The White House, May 16.

73. Andrew Restuccia. 2020. "Trump Doubles Down on Threats to Impose Tariffs on European Cars," *Wall Street Journal*, January 21.

74. Mark Landy and Sidney M. Milkis. 2000. *Presidential Greatness*. Lawrence, KS: University Press of Kansas.

75. David Crockett. 2002. *The Opposition Presidency*. College Station, TX: Texas A&M Press, p. 45.

76. Trump quoted in Joshua Green. 2016. "How to Get Trump Elected When He's Wrecking Everything You Built," *Bloomberg*, May 26.

77. Juliet Ellperint and Damian Paletta. 2017. "Trump Administration Cancels Hundreds of Obama-Era Regulations," *Washington Post*, July 20.

78. Phillip Bump. 2017. "What Trump Has Undone," *Washington Post*, December 15.

79. Gerard Baker, Carole E. Lee, and Michael C. Bender, 2017. "Trump Says He Offered China Better Trade Terms in Exchange for Help on North Korea," *Wall Street Journal*, April 12.

80. Cf. "Mr. Trump Confirmed That He Is Planning to Add Additional Nations to an Updated Version of His Travel Ban That the Administration Is Expected to Release Later This Month." See Andrew Restuccia. 2020. "Trump Doubles Down on Threats to Impose Tariffs on European Cars," *Wall Street Journal*, January 21; see also Brett Samuels. 2020. "Trump Confirms Plans to Expand Travel Ban," *The Hill*, January 21.

81. Donald J. Trump. 2020. "Remarks by President Trump in Press Conference: Davos, Switzerland," January 22.

82. Donald J. Trump. 2020. "Remarks by President Trump, Vice President Pence, and Members of the Coronavirus Task Force in Press Briefing," *The Rose Garden*, April 27.

83. Jeff D. Colgan and Robert O. Keohane. 2017. "The Liberal Order Is Rigged," *Foreign Affairs*, April 17, emphasis added.
84. Jared Bernstein. 2016. "The Era of Free Trade Might Be Over: That's a Good Thing," *New York Times*, March 14.
85. Yellen quoted in Paul Hannon and David Harrison. 2017. "Yellen: Globalization, Technological Change Have Been Harmful to Many," *Wall Street Journal*, June 27.
86. Trump 2020.
87. Amanda Ripley. 2019. "Americans Are at Each Other's Throats. Here's One Way Out," *Washington Post*, December 20, emphasis added.
88. F. F. Buckley. 2020. *American Succession*. New York: Encounter Books.
89. Henry Olsen. 2018. "Blue Wave, Red Tide, or Something in Between?" *American Greatness*, October 16, emphasis added.
90. Ken Dilanian. 2020. "Two of 4 Warrants Letting FBI Spy on Ex-Trump Aide Carter Page Were Not Valid, Says DOJ," *NBC News*, January 23.
91. Peter Baker. 2020. "Trump Team, Opening Defense, Accuses Democrats of Plot to Subvert Election," *New York Times*, January, 25.
92. Edward N. Littwak. 1977. "Give War a Chance," *Foreign Affairs*, July/August.
93. Trump quoted in Factor O'Reilly. 2017. "Exclusive Interview with President Trump, Part 3," *Fox News*, March 20.
94. Trump quoted in Shane Savitsky. 2017. "What Trump Didn't Say," *Axios*, January 18.
95. Cf., "There really isn't any guiding principle—that I was able to discern other than—what's good for Donald Trump's reelection." See *ABC*. 2020. "TRANSCRIPT: John Bolton interview with ABC News' Martha Raddatz," June 21.
96. Stephanie Armour. 2020. "Trump Administration Asks Supreme Court to Invalidate Affordable Care Act," *Wall Street Journal*, June 26.
97. Kevin Liptak, Zachary Cohen, and Nicole Gaouuette. 2020. "Coronavirus Will Test the Trump Administration's Ability to Handle a Crisis," *CNN*, January 28.

Other Books by Stanley Renshon

The Trump Doctrine and the Emerging International System [with Peter Suedfeld].

Barack Obama and the Politics of Redemption.

National Security in the Obama Administration: Reassessing the Bush Doctrine.

Noncitizen Voting and American Democracy.

Understanding the Bush Doctrine: Psychology and Strategy in an Age of Terrorism [with Peter Suedfeld].

The 50% American: Immigration and National Identity in an Age of Terrorism.

In his Father's Shadow: The Transformations of George W. Bush.

Good Judgment in Foreign Policy: Theory and Application [with Deborah Larson].

America's Second Civil War: Dispatches From the Political Center.

One America?: Political Leadership, National Identity, and the Dilemmas of Diversity.

Political Psychology: Cultural and Cross Cultural Foundations [with John Duckitt].

© The Editor(s) (if applicable) and The Author(s), under exclusive license to Springer Nature Switzerland AG 2020
S. Renshon, *The Real Psychology of the Trump Presidency*,
The Evolving American Presidency,
https://doi.org/10.1007/978-3-030-45391-6

OTHER BOOKS BY STANLEY RENSHON

High Hopes: The Clinton Presidency and the Politics of Ambition.
Note: Winner of the American Political Science Association's Richard E. Neustadt Award for the Best Book Published on the Presidency-1977 and the National Association for the Advancement of Psychoanalysis' Gradiva Award for the best published work that advances psychoanalysis-category: biography-1998.

The Psychological Assessment of Presidential Candidates.

The Clinton Presidency: Campaigning, Governing, and the Psychology of Leadership.

The Political Psychology of the Gulf War: Leaders, Publics and the Process of Conflict.

Handbook of Political Socialization: Theory and Research.

Psychological Needs and Political Behavior.

References

ABC News. 2018. "Chat Transcript: Gwenda Blair on the Trumps." September 18.

ABC. 2020. "Transcript: John Bolton Interview with ABC News' Martha Raddatz." June 21.

Abrams, Rachel. 2017. "Nordstrom Drops Ivanka Trump Brand from Its Stores." *New York Times*, February 2.

Abutaleb, Yasmeen, Ashley Parker, and Josh Dawsey. 2020. "Inside Trump's Frantic Attempts to Minimize the Coronavirus Crisis." *Washington Post*, February 29.

Ackerman, Andrew. 2018. "White House, in Shift, Pushes to Revive U.S. Export-Import Bank." *Wall Street Journal*, June 14.

Adler, Madison. 2020. "Blue States Create Hurdle for Trump's 2020 Judicial Appointments." *NPR*, February 11.

Adler, Stephen J., Jeff Mason, and Steve Holland. 2017. "Exclusive: Trump Says He Thought Being President Would Be Easier Than His Old Life." *Reuters*, April 28.

Agard, Chancellor. 2017. "Kathy Griffin Bloody Trump Pic Defended by Photographer." *Entertainment*, May 30.

Agrawal, Nina. 2017. "President Trump Wants Other Members of NATO to Pay Their Fair Share. Here's What That Would Look Like." *Los Angeles Times*, February 6.

Ahlquist, John, and Scott Gehlbach. 2014. "What Can We Learn About The Electoral Behavior of Non-citizens from a Survey Designed to Learn About Citizens?" *Washington Post*, October 28.

© The Editor(s) (if applicable) and The Author(s), under exclusive license to Springer Nature Switzerland AG 2020
S. Renshon, *The Real Psychology of the Trump Presidency*,
The Evolving American Presidency,
https://doi.org/10.1007/978-3-030-45391-6

470 REFERENCES

Aizhu, Chen. 2018. "Exclusive: China's CNPC Suspends Fuel Sales to North Korea as Risks Mount—Sources." *Reuters*, June 27.

Aleem, Zeeshan. 2017. "China Isn't the First Country to Flatter Its Way to Trump's Heart. It Won't Be the Last." *Vox*, November 8.

Alexander, Dona. 2017. "How Donald Trump Shifted Kids-Cancer Charity Money into His Business." *Forbes*, June 29.

Alford, Henry. 2015. "IS DONALD TRUMP ACTUALLY A NARCISSIST? THERAPISTS WEIGH IN!" *Vanity Fair*, November 11.

Allen, Charlotte. 2017. "Trump Month One: Success for His Supporters." *USA Today*, February 17.

Allen, Jonathan. 2017. "Clinton Blames Herself, and Many Others." *Politico*, September 11.

Allen, Mike. 2018. "Donald Trump Wants to Get Rid of Air Force One's Legendary Paint Job." *Axios*, July 12.

Allen, Mike, and Jim VandeHei. 2017. "Reality Bites: Trump's Wake-Up Call." *Axios*, January 18.

Allen, Mike, and Jonathan Swan. 2017. "Exasperated Trump WH Staff Admit His Special Resilience." *Axios*, May 20.

Allison, Graham. 1971. *Essence of Decision: Explaining the Cuban Missile Crisis.* Boston: Little Brown.

Alonso-Zaldivar, Ricardo. 2016. "Obama Administration Broke Its Own Health Care Rule, GAO Says." *Associated Press*, September 30.

American Psychiatric Association. 2018. *Diagnostic and Statistical Manual of Mental Disorders (DSM–5)*, Washington, DC, October 1.

Anderson, Kurt. 2018. "How to Talk Like Trump." *The Atlantic*, March.

Andrews, Natalie. 2015. "House Judiciary Committee Subpoenas Corey Lewandowski and Rick Dearborn." *Wall Street Journal*, August 15.

Anonymous. 2018. "I Am Part of the Resistance Inside the Trump Administration." *New York Times*, September 5.

Anonymous. 2019. *A Warning.* New York: Twelve Books.

Antle, James W. III. 2020. "Republicans Wonder Where Trump Misplaced his Second-term Agenda." *Washington Examiner*, June 27.

Anton, Michael. 2019. "The Trump Doctrine." *Foreign Affairs*, April 20.

Apgar, Sally. 2007. "Trump Reaches Truce Over Flag at Huge Florida Home." *South Florida Sun-Sentinel*, April 27.

Armour, Stephanie. 2019a. "Trump's Push for Health-Cost Transparency Sparks Furor." *Wall Street Journal*, September 27.

Armour, Stephanie. 2019b. "Government Watchdog Faults Trump Administration's Approval of Medicaid Work Requirements." *Wall Street Journal*, October 10.

Armour, Stephanie. 2020. "Trump Administration Asks Supreme Court to Invalidate Affordable Care Act." *Wall Street Journal*, June 26.

Associated Press. 2017. "U.S. to Arrest Parents, Sponsors Who Hire Smugglers to Bring Children Across Border." *Wall Street Journal*, June 30.

Associated Press. 2019a. "Trump Holds Record-Long Rally on Impeachment Day." *Washington Post*, December 18.

Associated Press. 2019b. "Trump Asks Supreme Court to Unfreeze Border Wall Money." *Washington Post*, July 12.

Astor, Maggie. 2019. "Did Trump Cave on the Wall? Some Conservatives Say Yes." *New York Times*, January 25.

Avik, Roy, 2013. "Pants On Fire: PolitiFact Tries To Hide That It Rated 'True' in 2008 Obamacare's 'Keep Your Health Plan' Promise." *Forbes*, December 2.

Azari, Julie. 2020. "It's Time to Switch to Preference Preferences." *Washington Post*, February 18.

Azari, Julia. 2020. "The Scrambled Cycle: Realignment, Political Time, and the Trump Presidency." In *American Political Development and the Trump Presidency*, edited by Zachary Callen and Philip Rocco. Philadelphia, PA: University of Pennsylvania Press.

Bachner, Jennifer, and Benjamin Ginsberg. 2016. *What Washington Gets Wrong: The Unelected Officials Who Actually Run the Government and Their Misconceptions About the American People*. Amherst, NY: Prometheus Books.

Baker, Peter. 2017a. "Trump Abandons Trans-Pacific Partnership, Obama's Signature Trade Deal." *New York Times*, January 23.

Baker, Peter. 2017b. "The New Presidential Interview." *New York Times*, July 24.

Baker, Peter. 2017c. "Trump White House Tests a Nation's Capacity for Outrage." *New York Times*, July 24.

Baker, Peter. 2017d. "Trump Tries to Regroup as the West Wing Battles Itself." *New York Times*, July 29.

Baker, Peter. 2017e. "Trump: We'll Be There for Puerto Rico, a Day After Critical Messages." *New York Times*, October 13.

Baker, Peter. 2017f. "Pitched as Calming Force, John Kelly Instead Mirrors Boss's Priorities." *New York Times*, October 25.

Baker, Peter. 2018. "Trump's Meeting with Kim Jong-un Is Another Pledge to Do What Nobody Else Can." *New York Times*, March 8.

Baker, Peter. 2019a. "For a President Consumed with Winning, a Stinging Defeat." *New York Times*, January 25.

Baker, Peter. 2019b. "Trump Orders Navy to Strip Medals from Prosecutors in War Crimes Trial." *New York Times*, July 31.

Baker, Peter. 2019c. "As Trump Swerves on Trade War, It's Whiplash for the Rest of the World." *New York Times*, August 27.

Baker, Peter. 2019d. "Trump Fires John Bolton as National Security Adviser." *New York Times*, September 10.

Baker, Peter. 2019e. "Trump Makes Clear He's Ready for a Fight He Has Long Anticipated." *New York Times*, September 24.

Baker, Peter. 2019f. "On Day 1,001, Trump Made It Clear: Being 'Presidential' Is Boring." *New York Times*, October 18.

Baker, Peter. 2019g. "Trump Is Fighting So Many Legal Battles, It's Hard to Keep Track." *New York Times*, November 6.

Baker, Peter. 2020. "Trump Team, Opening Defense, Accuses Democrats of Plot to Subvert Election." *New York Times*, January 25.

Baker, Peter and Ana Swanson. 2018. "Trump Authorizes Tariffs, Defying Allies at Home and Abroad." *New York Times*, March 8.

Baker, Peter and Choe Sang-Hun. 2017. "Trump Threatens Fire and Fury Against North Korea if It Endangers U.S." *New York Times*, August 8.

Baker, Peter and Maggie Haberman. 2017. "Anthony Scaramucci's Uncensored Rant: Foul Words and Threats to Have Priebus Fired." *New York Times*, July 27.

Baker Peter and Sheryl Gay Stolberg. 2017. "Energized Trump Sees Bipartisan Path, at Least for Now." *New York Times*, September 7.

Baker, Peter, Eric Schmitt, and Michael Crowley 2019. "An Abrupt Move That Stunned Aides: Inside Trump's Aborted Attack on Iran." *New York Times*, September 21.

Baker, Peter, Zolan Kann-Youngs, and Monica Davey. 2020. "Trump Threatens to Send Federal Law Enforcement Forces to More Cities." *New York Times*, July 20.

Baker, Gerhard. 2017. "Trump, 'Lies' and Honest Journalism." *Wall Street Journal*, January 4.

Baker, Gerard, Carole E. Lee, and Michael C. Binder. 2017. "Trump Says He Offered China Better Trade Terms in Exchange for Help on North Korea." *Wall Street Journal*, April 12.

Baker, Peter, Michael S. Schmidt, and Maggie Haberman. 2017. "Citing Recusal, Trump Says He Wouldn't Have Hired Sessions." *New York Times*, July 19.

Balz, Dan. 2017a. "Amid Distractions of His Own Creation, Trump Moves Swiftly to Change the Country Dramatically." *Washington Post*, January 28.

Balz, Dan. 2017b. "With His Presidency Off Course, What Will Trump Learn from the Health-Care Debacle?" *Washington Post*, March 25.

Balz, Dan. 2017c. "Trump Governs as He Campaigned: Unconventionally and Unpredictably." *Washington Post*, April 28.

Balz Dan. 2018a. "The Opening Act Was Tumultuous. Phase Two of Trump's Presidency Could Be Even More So." *Washington Post*, March 24.

Balz, Dan. 2018b. "Trump's Bad Week: A Policy Rollback, a Political Setback and a Still-Defiant President." *Washington Post*, June 23.

Barbanel, Josh. 2019. "New York's Grand Hyatt Hotel to Be Torn Down." *Wall Street Journal*, February 7.

Barbaro, Michael. 2015. "Donald Trump Likens His Schooling to Military Service in Book." *New York Times*, September 8.

Barber, James David. 1992. *The Presidential Character: Predicting Performance in the White House.* 4th ed. Englewood Cliffs, NJ: Prentice Hall.

Barber, Nigel. 2015. "Does Trump Suffer from Narcissistic Personality Disorder?" *Psychology Today*, August 10, 2016.

Barnes, Julian C. 2016. "NATO Moving to Create New Intelligence Chief Post." *Wall Street Journal*, June 3.

Barnes, Julian C. 2017. "Tillerson Talks Tough With NATO Allies Over Military Spending." *Wall Street Journal*, March 31.

Barnes, Robert. 2017. "Gorsuch Asserts Himself Early as Force on Supreme Court's Right." *Wall Street Journal*, June 27.

Barnes, Julien, and Thomas Gibblons-Neff. 2019. "U.S. Carried Out Cyberattacks on Iran." *New York Times*, June 22.

Barnes, Julian E., Michael Schmidt, and Matthew Rosenberg. 2019. "Schiff Got Early Account of Accusations as Whistle-Blower's Concerns Grew." *New York Times*, October 2.

Barnett, Wayne. 1979. "Like Father, Like Son: Anatomy of a Young Power Broker." *Village Voice*, January 15.

Barnett, Wayne. 2015. "How a Young Donald Trump Forced His Way from Avenue Z to Manhattan." *Village Voice*, July 20.

Barrett, Ted. 2016. "Harry Reid Calls Donald Trump 'a racist'." *CNN*, September 26.

Barstow, David and Susanne Craig. 2019. "Decade in the Red: Trump Tax Figures Show Over $1 Billion in Business Losses." *New York Times*, May 8.

Barstow, David, Susanne Craig, and Russ Buettner. 2018. "Trump Engaged in Suspect Tax Schemes as He Reaped Riches from His Father." *New York Times*, October 2.

Barron, Anne Marie. 2014. "Opening Day for the Verrazano Bridge: Festivities, Fond Memories—And Then the Floodgates Open." Siliva.com, November 14.

Barton, Chris. 2018. "Revisiting Comedy Central's 'Roast of Donald Trump,' When 'President Trump' Was a Punchline and Trump Could Take a Joke." *Los Angeles Times*, April 27.

Bates, Daniel. 2020. "EXCLUSIVE: Donald Trump Was a Victim of 'Child Abuse' at the Hands of His Father, Who 'Caused Him Terror That Would Scar Him for Life', Claims President's Niece Who Believes He Could Be a 'Sociopath' in Explosive Memoir." *Daily Mail*, July 7.

BBC. 2016. "Trump Aims to 'Jump Start' America with New Tax Plan." August 8.

474 REFERENCES

Beauchamp, Zack. 2016. "A New Study Reveals the Real Reason Obama Voters Switched to Trump." *Vox*, October 16.

Beker, Bernie. 2010. "A Revised Contract for America, Minus 'With' and Newt," *New York Times*, April 14.

Belkin, Liksa. 2015. What's Up with Donald Trump and 'the Women'? Not What You Might Think." *Yahoo*, October 15.

Benak, Nancy. 2016. "For Trump, It's About America's Ego—And His Own." *Associated Press*, July 16.

Bender, Marilyn. 1983. "The Empire and Ego of Donald Trump." *New York Times*, August 7.

Bender, Michael C. 2017. "Donald Trump Seen Bringing 'Deliberate Chaos' to the White House." *Wall Street Journal*, January 20.

Bender, Michael C. and Gordon Lubold. 2019. "Trump Bucked National-Security Aides on Proposed Iran Attack." *Wall Street Journal*, June 23.

Bender, Michael C., Jessica Donati, and Lindsay Wise. 2019. "Trump Steers Clear of War Footing Toward Iran." *Wall Street Journal*, September 18.

Benen, Steve. 2017. "Trump Is Convinced He's Always 'Ahead of Schedule'." *MSNBC*, October 16.

Benitez, Jorge. 2016. "Why Trump Is Now the Most Dangerous Man in the World." *The Hill*, August 8.

Bennen, John. 2019. "Remember When Trump Said He'd Revoked Brennan's Security Clearance?" *NBC*, May 28.

Benner, Katie and Adam Goldman. 2019. "Justice Dept. Is Said to Open Criminal Inquiry into Its Own Russia Investigation." *New York Times*, October 24.

Berlin, Isaiah. 1953. *The Hedgehog and the Fox: An Essay on Tolstoy's View of History*. London, UK: Weidenfeld & Nicolson.

Berlinger, Joshua, Mohammed Tawfeed, Barbara Star, Shitzad Boxorgmehr, and Frederik Pleitgen. 2019. "Iran Shoots Down US Drone Aircraft, Raising Tensions Further in Strait of Hormuz." *CNN*, June 20.

Bernstein, Jared. 2016. "The Era of Free Trade Might Be Over. That's a Good Thing." *New York Times*, March 14.

Bhattari, Abha. 2019. "Retailer Buys Controversial Trump-Themed Billboard in Times Square." *Seattle Times*, October 18.

Bierman, Noah. 2016. "A Testy Donald Trump Lashes Out at News Media and Says, 'I'm Not Changing'." *Los Angeles Times*, May 31.

Bierman, Noah and Joseph Tanfani. 2016. "As a Young Donald Trump Began His Real Estate Career, He Fought Hard Against Allegations of Racial Bias." *Los Angeles Times*, August 15.

Birnbaum, Michael. 2019. "NATO Members Increase Defense Spending for Fourth Year in Row Following Trump Pressure." *Washington Post*, April 14.

Birnbaum, Michael and Toluse Olorunnipa. 2019. "Iran's Zarif Makes Surprise Trip to G-7, Catching Trump Off-Guard." *Washington Post*, August 25.

Biskupic, Joan. 2016. "Justice Ruth Bader Ginsburg Calls Trump a 'Faker,' He Says She Should Resign." *CNN*, July 13.

Black, Conrad. 2017. "Disgraceful Charade Unfolds in Battle Over Evidence Twixt Mueller and Congress." *New York Sun*, October 11.

Black, Conrad. 2018. "Trump and His Enemies." *National Review*, September 5.

Blade, Rachael. 2019. "'A Lack of Urgency': Democrats Frustrated as House Investigators Struggle to Unearth Major Revelations About Trump." *Washington Post*, July 23.

Blade, Rachael and Mike DeBonis. 2019. "Democrats Struggle to Figure Out Next Move Against Trump After Mueller Hearing Falls Flat." *Washington Post*, July 25.

Blair, Gwenda. 2000. *The Trumps: Three Generations That Built an Empire*. New York: Simon & Schuster.

Blair, Gwenda. 2005. *Donald Trump: Master Apprentice*. New York: Simon & Shuster.

Blair, Gwenda. 2018. "Trump Has the White House He Always Wanted." *Politico*, April 5.

Blake, Aaron. 2013. "Politifact Awards 'Lie of the Year' to Obama." *Washington Post*, December 12.

Blake, Aaron. 2016. "President Trump Finally Went a Full 24 Hours Without a False or Misleading Claim." *Washington Post*, March 2.

Blake, Aaron. 2017a. "Trump's Travel Ban Is Causing Chaos—And Putting His Unflinching Nationalism to the Test." *Washington Post*, January 29.

Blake, Aaron. 2017b. "Republicans Are Starting to Draw Red Lines on Trump Firing Sessions and Mueller." *Washington Post*, July 27.

Blake, Aaron. 2017c. "Donald Trump's Best Speech of the 2016 Campaign, Annotated." *Washington Post*, August 19.

Blake, Aaron. 2018. "Trump Said It Was 'Tough to Watch Too Much' of the Paralympics. Was It Derogatory?" *Washington Post*, April 28.

Blake, Aaron. 2019a. "Trump Finds Himself on His Heels and Fumbling at G-7." *Washington Post*, August 25.

Blake, Aaron. 2019b. "Trump's Former ISIS Envoy Offers Scathing Critique of His Syria Decision—And Entire Management Style." *Washington Post*, October 7.

Blake, Aaron. 2020. "As Trump Claims a Win on Iran, He Accuses Obama of Funding Its Attacks." *Washington Post*, January 8.

Blanton, Dana. 2017. "Fox News Poll: Voters Say Trump's Tweets Hurting Agenda." *Fox News*, June 28.

Blase, Brian. 2019. "Trump's New Rule Will Give Businesses and Workers Better Health Care Options." *CNN*, June 14.

Blinder, Alan. 2012. "The Case Against a CEO in the Oval Office." *Wall Street Journal*, October 1.

Blitzer, Ronn. 2019. "Whistleblower Attorney Defends 'Coup' Tweet, as Trump Calls for Impeachment Probe Shutdown." *Fox News*, November 7.

Blow, Charles. 2016. "Trump Is an Existential Threat." *New York Times*, November 3.

Blow, Charles. 2018. "Trump, Treasonous Traitor." *New York Times*, July 15.

Bohman, James and William Rehg (eds.). 1997. *Deliberative Democracy: Essays on Reason and Politics*. Cambridge, MA: MIT Press.

Bok, Sissela. 1978. *Lying: Moral Choice in Public Life*. New York: Random House.

Bonilla-Silva, Eduardo. 2017. *Racism Without Racists: Color-Blind Racism and the Persistence of Racial Inequality in America*. 3rd Edition. Lanthm, MD: Rowman & Littlefield Publishers.

Boot, Max. 2016. "The Nazi Echoes in Trump's Tweets." *Los Angeles Times*, October 17.

Boot, Max. 2017a. "Let's Count the Ways Donald Trump Has Gone Where No President Has Gone Before." *Los Angeles Times*, April 4.

Boot, Max. 2017b. "Is Donald Trump a Moron? Duh." *USA Today*, October 4.

Boot, Max. 2017c. "The First Victory Over ISIS." *Commentary*, November 13.

Boot, Max. 2017d. "Donald Trump Is Guilty. The Only Remaining Question Is What Exactly He's Guilty Of." *Washington Post*, December 5.

Boot, Max. 2018. "We Just Watched a U.S. President Acting on Behalf of a Hostile Power." *Washington Post*, July 16.

Boot, Max. 2019a. "Trump Is Trashing the Rule of Law to Stay in Power." *Washington Post*, April 9.

Boot, Max. 2019b. "Pence, Pompeo and Barr Deserve to Be Impeached, Too." *Washington Post*, October 9.

Borchers, Callum. 2017. "Patriots Owner on Trump: 'In the Toughest Time in My Life, He Was There for Me'." *Washington Post*, February 3.

Borja, Debbie. 1989. "3 Trump Execs, 2 Pilots Die as Helicopter Crashes in Parkway Median." *Atlantic City Press*, October 10.

Bowden, Mark. 1977. "Trumpster Stages the Comeback of a Lifetime." *Playboy*, May.

Boyle, Robert H. 1984. "The USFL's Trump Card." *Sports Illustrated*, February 13.

Bradsher, Keith. 2018. "Trade Deals Take Years. Trump Wants to Remake Them in Months." *New York Times*, March 28.

Bradsher, Keith, Alan Rappaport, Ana Swanson, and Chris Buckley. 2019. "U.S. and China Reach Initial Trade Deal." *New York Times*, December 13.

REFERENCES   477

Brady, Davis and Juliet Eilperin. 2018. "Scott Pruitt Steps Down as EPA Head After Ethics, Management Scandals." *Washington Post*, July 5.

Breeden, Aurelien. 2016. "France's President Says Trump's 'Excesses' Make People 'Want to Retch'." *New York Times*, August 3.

Brehm, Jack. 1996. *A Theory of Psychological Reactance*. New York: Academic Press.

Brennan, Jason. 2016 "Trump Won Because Voters Are Ignorant, Literally." *Foreign Policy*, November 10.

Brenner, Marie. 1980. "Trumping the Town," *New York Magazine*. November 17.

Brenner, Marie. 1990. "After the Gold Rush." *Vanity Fair*, September.

Breslow, Jason B. 2016a. "The FRONTLINE Interview: Sandy McIntosh." *PBS*, September 27.

Breslow, Jason M. 2016b. "The FRONTLINE Interview: Barbara Res." *PBS*, September 27.

Brinkley, Douglass. 1997. "Democratic Enlargement: The Clinton Doctrine Foreign Policy." *Wilson Quarterly* (Spring), pp. 534–551.

Brody, David. 2019. "New York Columnist David Brooks Admits to CBN News that Targeting Trump Is 'Good for Business'." *CBN*, June 17.

Brooks, David. 2017. "When the World Is Led by a Child." *New York Times*, May 15.

Brooks, David. 2018a. "The Decline of Anti-Trumpism." *New York Times*, January 8.

Brooks, David. 2018b. "Donald Trump's Lizard Wisdom." *New York Times*, May 10.

Brown, Eliot. 2018. "Remember Trump City?" *New York Observer*, August 5.

Brown, Laura. 2016. "Government Stumps Trump." *U.S. News and World Report*, March 31.

Bruni, Frank. 2017. "The Week When President Trump Resigned." *New York Times*, August 18.

Brunnstrom, David and Doina Chiacu. 2019. "North Korea Won't Give Up Nuclear Weapons: Ex-Trump Adviser Bolton." *Reuters*, September 30.

Bruni, Frank. 2016. "The Misery of the Mini-Trumps." *New York Times*, August 27.

Buckley, F. F. 2020. *American Succession*. New York: Encounter Books.

Bulman, Mary. 2017. "Donald Trump Has 'Dangerous Mental Illness', Say Psychiatry Experts at Yale Conference." *The Independent*, April 21.

Bump, Phillip. 2016a. "Now You Can Fact-Check Trump's Tweets—In the Tweets Themselves." *Washington Post*, December 19.

Bump, Phillip. 2016b. "Donald Trump's Made-Up Coat-of-Arms Reveals His Electoral Strategy: Never Concede." *Washington Post*, October 24.

478 REFERENCES

Bump, Phillip. 2017. "What Trump Has Undone." *Washington Post*, December 15.

Bump, Phillip. 2018. "Why Is Trump So Much More Popular with Republicans Than Past Presidents?" *Washington Post*, July 24.

Bump, Phillip. 2019a. "The White House Thinks the Post Ignored Trump's Summertime Successes. So, About That." *Washington Post*, September 6.

Bump, Phillip. 2019b. "What Trump Was Talking About in His Baffling Rant About Wind Energy." *Washington Post*, December 23.

Bur, Jessie. 2019. Senators Want to Move These Agency Headquarters Out of DC." *Federal Times*, October 24.

Burke, Michael. 2018. "5 Revelations from John Kelly's Los Angeles Times Exit Interview." *Los Angeles Times*, December 30.

Burnett, Erwin. 2015. "OUTFRONT: Interview with Donald Trump." *CNN*, September 28.

Burns, Alexander. 2016. "Donald Trump Seeks Republican Unity But Finds Rejection." *New York Times*, May 6.

Burns, Alexander and Jonathan Martin. 2019. "Trump's Takeover of the Republican Party Is Almost Complete." *New York Times*, April 3.

Burns, Max. 2019. "Donald Trump Isn't Julius Caesar. He's Republic-Killer Tiberius Gracchus." *Daily Beast*, October 13.

Burns, James MacGregor. 1973. *Presidential Government: The Crucible of Leadership*. Boston: Houghton Mifflin.

Byler, David. 2018. "Trump's Trump-iest Tweets Aren't Popular." *Weekly Standard*, July 19.

Cain, Cody. 2016a. "Marketer-in-Chief: Is Donald Trump Only Running for President to Exploit the Business Opportunities?" *Salon*, July 10.

Cain, Cody, 2016b. "It Takes a Village Idiot: Thanks to Donald Trump, the President May Be Chosen by a Fourth-Grade Mentality. If We Elect a Presidential Candidate Who Speaks and Thinks on a Fourth-Grade Level, What Does That Say About Us?" *Salon*, October 30.

Cameron, Doug. 2017. "U.S., Boeing Complete $3.9 Billion Air Force One Deal." *Wall Street Journal*, January 17.

Candidate Trump quoted in *New York Times* reporter Jose A. DelReal Tweet. https://twitter.com/jdelreal/status/693106681715281921.

Cannon, Carl M. and Emily Goodwin. 2016. "Trump to Disaffected Americans: 'I Am Your Voice'." *Washington Post*, July 22.

Capehart, Jonathan. 2015. "Unfit for the Oval Office." *Washington Post*, September 21.

Caplan, Thomas. 2016. "John Kasich Calls Trump Unprepared to be President." *New York Times*, April 1.

REFERENCES **479**

Carmines, Edward G., Paul M. Sniderman, and Beth C. Easter. 2011. "On the Meaning, Measurement, and Implications of Racial Resentment." *ANNALS, AAPSS*, 634, March, 98–116.

Carpenter, Daniel and David A. Moss. 2013. *Preventing Regulatory Capture: Special Interest Influence and How to Limit It*. New York: Cambridge University Press.

Carter, Brandon. 2017. "Missouri State Senator Posts, Deletes Comment 'Hoping' for Trump's Assassination." *The Hill*, September 18.

Carter, Brandon. 2018. "Dem: Trump 'Most Despicable Human Being' to Serve as President." *The Hill*, January 1.

Casselman, Ben and Jim Tankersley. 2018. "Tax Overhaul Gains Public Support, Buoying Republicans." *New York Times*, February 19.

Cassese, Erin C. 2016. "Here Are 3 Insights into Why Some People Think Trump Is a 'Monster'." *Washington Post*, October 31.

CBS. 2016. "Donald Trump Weighs in on Killing of Gorilla at Cincinnati Zoo." *CBS News*, June.

CBS. 2018. "Trump Reveals Details of Planned Air Force One Makeover." *CBS*, July 17.

Cerabino, Frank. 2015. "Trump's War with Palm Beach." *Politico*, September 5.

Chaitin, Daniel. 2019. "Coast Guard Rear Admiral Defends Trump from Storm of Backlash After Alabama Forecast." *Washington Examiner*, September 5.

Chat Transcript. 2016. "Gwenda Blair on the Trumps." ABC News, September 18.

Chinni, Danti. 2017. "Trump's Twitter Habit Gets Low Approval Rating from Both Parties." *WSJ*, September 26.

Chishti, Muzaffar and Jessica Bolter. 2017. "The Trump Administration at Six Months: A Sea Change in Immigration Enforcement," Migration Policy Institute, July 19.

Chomsky, Noam and Bandy M. D Lee. 2017. "Epilogue." In *The Dangerous Case of Donald Trump: 27 Psychiatrists and Mental Health Experts Assess a President*, edited by Bandy Lee. New York: St. Martin's Press, pp. 356–359.

Chozick, Amy. 2016. "Hillary Clinton Calls Many Trump Backers 'Deplorables,' and G.O.P. Pounces." *New York Times*, September 2.

Cillizza, Chris. 2016a. "Donald Trump Perfectly Summed Up His Life Philosophy in Just 6 Words." *Washington Post*, June 1.

Cillizza, Chris. 2016b. "Trump Is Running the Same Campaign That Won Him the GOP Nomination. There's a Big Problem with That." *Washington Post*, June 12.

Cillizza, Chris. 2016c. "President-Elect Donald Trump's Cataclysmic, History-Making Upset." *Washington Post*, November 9.

Cillizza, Chris. 2016d. "The 13 Most Amazing Findings in the 2016 Exit Poll." *Washington Post*, November 10.

480 REFERENCES

Cillizza, Chris. 2016e. "Trump Has Completely Upended the Political Game. We Need to Adjust Accordingly." *Washington Post*, December 11.

Cillizza, Chris. 2017. "Being President Is Hard: The Education of Donald Trump." *CNN*, April 13.

Clark, Leslie. 2016. "History of All Business and No Government Could Complicate a Trump Presidency." *McClatchy*, November 3.

Clark, Leslie. 2017 "Democrats Move to Formally Censure Trump Over Charlottesville." *McClatchy*, August 16.

Clifford, Geertz. 1983. *Local Knowledge: Further Essays In Interpretive Anthropology*. New York: Basic Books.

Clines, Frances X. 1993. "Death on the L.I.R.R.: The Rampage; Gunman in a Train Aisle Passes Out Death." *New York Times*, December 9.

Clinic, Staff. "Narcissistic Personality Disorder." Mayo Clinic.

Codebook and User's Guide to the ANES 2016 Pilot Study. 2016. American National Election Studies, Stanford University and The University of Michigan, February 23. https://electionstudies.org/project/anes-2016-pilot-study/.

Cohen, Jon. 2020. 'I'm Going to Keep Pushing.' Anthony Fauci Tries to Make the White House Listen to Facts of the Pandemic." *Science*, March 22.

Cohen, Patrica. 2019. "Pain of Tariffs Tests Farmers' Faith in Trump: 'How Long Is Short-Term?'." *New York Times*, May 24.

Cohen, Roger. 2017. "The Abnormal Presidency of Donald Trump." *New York Times*, January 31.

Colgan, Jeff D. and Robert O. Keohane. 2017. "The Liberal Order Is Rigged." *Foreign Affairs*, April 17.

Collander, Stan. "Last Week Was Trump's Worst Legislative Week Ever, and Congress wasn't Even in Session." *Forbes*, September 4.

Collins, Eliza. 2016. "Trump: I Consult Myself on Foreign Policy." *Politico*, March 16.

Collinson, Steve. 2016. "Donald Trump: Presumptive GOP Nominee; Sanders Takes Indiana." *CNN*, May 4.

Collinson, Stephen. 2019. "New Revelations Deepen Scandal Over Trump Whistleblower Complaint." *CNN*, September 20.

Comey, James. 2017. "My Notes from Private Session with PE 1/6/17." https://www.documentcloud.org/documents/4442900-Ex-FBI-Director-James-Comey-s-memos.html.

Committee on Foreign Affairs. 2019. "Foreign Affairs Committee Releases Transcript of Interview with Former Secretary of State Rex Tillerson." July 27.

Conant, Alex. 2017. "Why Trump's White House Won't Stop Leaking." *Politico*, July 27.

REFERENCES **481**

Concha, Joe. 2017a. "Poll: Vast Majority Wants Trump to Tweet Less." *The Hill*, March 8.

Concha, Joe. 2017b. "CNN Producer on New O'Keefe Video: Voters Are 'Stupid,' Trump Is 'crazy'." *The Hill*, June 30.

Continetti, Matthew. 2017. "Trump Goes Rogue." *New York Times*, July 31.

Conway, Madeline. 2017. "Schiff: There is now 'More Than Circumstantial Evidence' of Trump-Russia Collusion." *Politico*, March 22.

Conway, George T. III. 2019. "Unfit for Office." *The Atlantic*, October 3.

Conway, George T. III and Neal Katyal. 2019. "Trump Has Done Plenty to Warrant Impeachment. But the Ukraine Allegations Are Over the Top." *Washington Post*, September 20.

Cook, Lorne. 2019. "NATO Seeks to Head Off Budget Dispute, Saying Spending Is Rising," *Associated Press*, November 29.

Cook, Nancy. 2019. "Forget the Oval. The Real Trump Action Is in the Residence." *Politico*, November 24.

Cooper, Arnold M., MD. 1998. "Further Developments in the Clinical Diagnosis of NPD." In *Disorders of Narcissism: Diagnostic, Clinical and Empirical Implications*, edited by Elsa F. Ronningstam. New York: American Psychiatric Publishing.

Cooper, Helen. 2019. "Trump Gives Military New Freedom. But with That Comes Danger." *New York Times*, April 5.

Coppins, McKay. 2014. "36 Hours on the Fake Campaign Trail with Donald Trump." *Buzzfeed*, February 13.

Coppins, McKay. 2017. "How the Haters and Losers Lost." *Buzzfeed*, July 17.

Costa, Robert and Phillip Rucker. 2020. "'Tempted to Despair': Trump's Resilience Causes Democrats to Sound the Alarm." *Washington Post*, February 8.

Cramer, Katherine J. 2016. *The Politics of Resentment: Rural Consciousness in Wisconsin and the Rise of Scott Walker*. Chicago: University of Chicago Press.

Crews, Clyde Jr. 2019. "Trump's Regulatory Reform Agenda By The Numbers (Summer 2019 Update)." *Forbes*, May 30.

Crowley, Michael. 2017. "The Deep State Is Real." *Politico*, September/October.

Crowley, Michael. 2018. "Trump's Shock and Awe Foreign Policy." *Politico*, March 9.

Crowley, Michael. 2019a. "Debate Flares Over Afghanistan as Trump Considers Troop Withdrawal." *New York Times*, August 16.

Crowley, Michael. 2019b. "In Bracing Terms, Trump Invokes War's Human Toll to Defend His Policies." *New York Times*, October 19.

Cummings, William. 2019. "'A WALL Is a WALL!' Trump Declares. But His Definition Has Shifted a Lot Over Time." *USA Today*, January 8.

D'Antonio, Michael 2015. "Donald Trump's Long Publicity Con." *Daily Beast*, November 28.

482 REFERENCES

D'Antonio, Michael. 2016. "Trump Never Wanted to Be America's President; He Wants To Be Its Czar." *CNN*, November 16.

D'Antonio, Michael. 2019. *Never Enough: Donald Trump and the Pursuit of Success*. New York: Thomas Dunne/St. Martin's Press.

Dallek, Matthew. 2019. "Trump Is the Most Aggressive Micromanager in the History of the Oval Office." *Washington Post*, September 14.

Dann, Carrie. 2019. "'A Deep and Boiling Anger': NBC/WSJ Poll Finds a Pessimistic America Despite Current Economic Satisfaction." ABC, August 25.

Danner, Chas. 2015. "Donald Trump Responds to Muslim Question Controversy [Updated]." *New York Magazine*, September 20.

David, O. Sears and P. J. Henry. 2005. "Over Thirty Years Later: A Contemporary Look at Symbolic Racism and Its Critics." In *Advances in Experimental Social Psychology*, edited by Mark P. Zanna. New York, NY: Academic Press.

Davidson, Kate. 2016. "New Laws Haven't Made Big Banks Safer, Paper by Lawrence Summers Says." *Wall Street Journal*, September 15.

Davidson, Adam. 2012. "Do Good C.E.O.'s Make Good Presidents?" *New York Times*, December 16.

Davis, Julie Hirschfeld. 2017a. "Rumblings of a 'Deep State' Undermining Trump? It was Once a Foreign Concept." *New York Times*, March 6.

Davis, Julie Hirschfeld. 2017b. "Trump Calls Congressional Inquiry a 'Witch Hunt'." *New York Times*, March 31.

Davis, Julie Hirschfield. 2018. "Trump Appears to Endorse Path to Citizenship for Millions of Immigrants." *New York Times*, January 9.

Davis, Julie Hirshfeld and Maggie Haberman. 2018. "Trump, a Week After Porter Resigned, Says He's 'Totally Opposed' to Spousal Abuse." *New York Times*, February 14.

Davis, Hirschfeld Julie and Michael D. Shear. 2017. "An Over-the-Top New Yorker Will Run Trump's Communications Shop." *New York Times*, July 21.

Davis, Julie Hirschfeld and Miriam Jordan. 2017. "Trump Plans 45,000 Limit on Refugees Admitted to U.S." *New York Times*, September 26.

Dawsey, Josh. 2018. "Kelly Denies Calling Trump an 'Idiot,' Says News Report Is 'Pathetic Attempt to Smear People'." *Washington Post*, April 3.

Dawsey, Josh. 2019. "Unswayed by Top Advisers, Trump Doubles Down on Decision to Withdraw Troops." *Washington Post*, October 13.

Dawsey, John. 2019. "Trump Admits to Having 'Second Thoughts'—A Scramble Ensues to Explain What He Meant." *Washington Post*, August 25.

Dawsey, Josh and Greg Barber. 2018. "Transcript of Trump's Remarks at Fundraiser in Missouri on March 14." *Washington Post*, March 15.

Dawsey, Josh, Damian Paletta, and Erica Werner. 2018. "In Fundraising Speech, Trump Says He Made Up Trade Claim in Meeting with Justin Trudeau." *Washington Post*, March 15.

De Luce, Dan, Courtney Kube, and Mushtaq Yusufzai. 2018. "Impatient Trump Drives U.S. Push for Peace Talks in Afghanistan." *NBC News*, July 30.

De Pinto, Jennifer, Fred Backus, Kabir Khanna, and Anthony Salvanto. 2018. "Viewers Approve of Trump's First State of the Union Address." *CBS News*, January 30.

Deasvers, Oliva. 2020. "Democrats to Plow Ahead with Trump Probes Post-acquittal." *The Hill*, February 8.

DeBonis, Mike and Amber Phillips. 2019. "For House Democrats, Impeachment Probe Widens the Divide They Hoped to Bridge." *Washington Post*, October 5.

DeBonis, Mike and Karoun Demirjian. 2017. "House Passes Russia Sanctions Bill, Setting Up Veto Dilemma for Trump." *Washington Post*, July 25.

DeBonis, Mike, Kelsey Snell, Phillip Rucker, and Elise Viebeck. 2017. "Trump Sides with Democrats on Fiscal Issues, Throwing Republican Plans in to Chaos." *Washington Post*, September 7.

Denyer, Simon. 2019. "North Korea and United States to Resume Nuclear Talks Saturday." *Washington Post*, October 1.

Department of Homeland Security. 2019a. "Enforcement of Immigration Laws to Serve the National Interests." February 17.

Department of Homeland Security. 2019b. "Press Release: CBP Completes Construction of 50 Miles of New Border Wall." July 11.

Department of Homeland Security. 2019c. "DHS and DOJ Issue Third-Country Asylum Rule." July 15.

Department of Homeland Security. 2019d. "Notice: Designating Aliens for Expedited Removal." July 23.

DePiero. 2017 ."Washington Post Journalist Asks Eric Trump If He Lied to Him in 2016 Interview." *Washington Examiner*, June 6.

Dershowitz, Alan M. 2020. "Trump Had Right to Withhold Ukraine Funds: GAO Is Wrong." Gatestone Institute, January 17.

Deshpande, Pia. 2019. "Trump on Impeachment and Nixon: 'He Left. I Don't Leave'." *Politico*, October 10.

DeVega, Chauncey. 2019. "Former CIA Profiler Jerrold Post on Donald Trump's 'Dangerous Charisma'." *Salon*, December 2.

DeVega, Chauncey. 2020. "Biographer and Journalist David Maraniss on Trump, Obama and History Turned 'Upside Down'."*Salon*, January 30.

DeYoung, Karen. 2017. "Under Trump, Gains Against ISIS Have 'Dramatically Accelerated'." *Washington Post*, August 4.

di Marzo, Marina. 2019. "How Often Does Trump Misspell Words on Twitter? These Researchers Have an Answer." *CNN Business*, November 3.

Diamond, Jeremy. 2015 "Donald Trump Describes Father's 'Small Loan': $1 Million." *CNN*, October 27.

484 REFERENCES

Diaz, Daniella. 2019. "Warren: 'Congress Is Complicit' by Failing to Start Impeachment Proceedings Against Trump." *CNN*, September 21.

Dickerson, John. 2020. *The Hardest Job in the World: The American Presidency.* New York: Random House.

Dilanian, Ken. 2020. "Two of 4 Warrants Letting FBI Spy on Ex-Trump Aide Carter Page Were Not Valid, Says DOJ." *NBC News*, January 23.

Dimock, Carroll Doherty, Jocelyn Kiley, and Russ Oates. 2014. "Political Polarization in the American Public." *Pew*, June 12.

Dinen, Steven 2017. "Trump Moves to Restore Work Requirement for Welfare." *The Washington Times*, August 30.

Dodes, Lance. M. D. 2017. "Sociopathy." In *The Dangerous Case of Donald Trump: 27 Psychiatrists and Mental Health Experts Assess a President*, edited by Bandy Lee. New York: St. Martin's Press, pp. 83–92.

"Donald Trump Great Interview Answers—Over 30 Years!" YouTube. https://www.youtube.com/watch?v=rFMRjSE496c (at 2:26, emphasis mine).

Donald Trump's *New York Times* Interview: Full Transcript. 2016. *New York Times*, November 23.

Donald Trump Town Hall Transcript with Sean Hannity June 25, 2020. https://www.rev.com/blog/transcript-category/donald-trump-transcripts.

Donati, Jessica and Catherine Lucey. 2020. "Trump Says 'Good Chance' of Deal with Taliban." *Wall Street Journal*, February 13.

Donati, Jessica and José de Córdoba. 2019. "Trump Says U.S. to Designate Mexican Drug Cartels as Terrorists." *Wall Street Journal*, November 27.

Donnan, Shawn. 2018. "Cohn Lifted Papers Off Trump's Desk to Stop Nafta Exit, Book Says." *Bloomberg*, September 4.

Donnan, Shawn. 2019. "Trump's Trade 'Bad Cop' Thinks He Has Found a Winning Formula." *Bloomberg*, December 2.

Doran, Michael and Michael A. Reynolds. 2019. "Turkey Has Legitimate Grievances Against the U.S." *Wall Street Journal*, October 8.

Douthat, Ross. 2014. "The Tea Party Legacy." *New York Times*, May 24.

Douthat, Ross. 2017. "The 25th Amendment Solution for Removing Trump." *New York Times*, May 16.

Douthat, Ross. 2019. "The Nihilist in Chief." *New York Times*, August 6.

Dowd, Maureen. 2017. "Cruella de Trump." *New York Times*, July 1.

Drezner, Daniel W. 2015. "The Scariest Thing I Found Out About Donald Trump Yesterday." *Washington Post*, September 9.

Drezner, Daniel W. 2017a. "The One GOP Myth That the Trump Administration Has Managed to Discredit." *Washington Post*, August 16.

Drezner, Daniel W. 2017b. "Why Did Trump Flip-Flop on Afghanistan? It's the Policy Ignorance, Stupid.' *Washington Post*, August 22.

Drezner, Daniel W. 2019. "An Open Letter to Donald Trump from an Expert on Economic Coercion." *Washington Post*, June 11.

Drezner, Daniel W., Ronald R. Krebs, and Randall Schweller. 2020. "The End of Grand Strategy America Must Think Small." *Foreign Affairs*, May/June.

Duehren, Andrew. 2019. "Why Some Republicans May Be Choosing to Leave Congress." *Wall Street Journal*, October 29.

Dunn, Susan. 2016. Trump's 'America First' Has Ugly Echoes from U.S. History." *CNN*, April 28.

Duran, Michael and Michael A. Reynolds. 2019. "Turkey Has Legitimate Grievances Against the U.S." *Wall Street Journal*, October 9.

Dwyer, Colin. 2019. "'Go Back Where You Came From': The Long Rhetorical Roots of Trump's Racist Tweets." *NPR*, July 15.

Eagan, Timothy. 2016. "A Unified Theory of Trump." *New York Times*, February 26.

Eagan, Timothy. 2017. "One-Month Report Card." *New York Times*, February 17.

Eckstein, Harry. 2000. "Case Study and Theory in Political Science." In *Case Study Method: Key Issues, Key Texts*, edited by Roger Gomm, Martyn Hammersley, and Peter Foster. Newbury Park, CA: Sage.

Eder, Steve and Alica Parlapiano. 2016. "Donald Trump's Ventures Began with a Lot of Hype. Here's How They Turned Out." *New York Times*, October 6.

Editorial. 1993. "No Guardrails." *Wall Street Journal*, March 18.

Editorial. 2016. "Donald Trump Is a Unique Threat to American Democracy." *Washington Post*, July 22.

Editorial. 2017a. "President Bannon?" *New York Times*, January 30.

Editorial. 2017b. "Trump's Next 200 Days." *Wall Street Journal*, April 27.

Editorial. 2017c. "President Trump, Melting Under Criticism." *New York Times*, June 30.

Editorial. 2017d. "The Trump-McConnell Spat." *Wall Street Journal*, August 10.

Editorial. 2018. "Hillary Leans Out." *Wall Street Journal*, March 13.

Editorial. 2019a. "A Regulatory 'Guidance' Upgrade." *Wall Street Journal*, April 16.

Editorial. 2019b. "Undoing the Great Mistake of 2016." *Los Angeles Times*, October 20.

Editorial. 2019c. "The FISA Judge Strikes Back." *Wall Street Journal*, December 17.

Edwards II, George C. 2019. "The Bully in the Pulpit: The Impact of Donald Trump's Public Discourse." Paper Prepared for Delivery at the Annual Meeting of the American Political Science Association, Washington, DC, September 1.

Edwards, George W III. 2016. *Predicting the Presidency: The Potential of Persuasive Leadership*. Princeton, NJ: Princeton University Press.

486 REFERENCES

Egan, Matt. 2020. "Coronavirus Could Cost Trump the Election, Goldman Sachs Warns." *CNN Business*, February 27.

Eilperin, Juliet, Lisa Rein, and Marc Fisher. 2017. "Resistance from Within: Federal Workers Push Back Against Trump." *Washington Post*, January 31.

Elder, Steve and Alicia Parlapiano. 2016. "Donald Trump's Ventures Began with a Lot of Hype. Here's How They Turned Out." *New York Times*, October 6.

Ellison, Sarah. 2016. "Exclusive: Is Donald Trump's Endgame the Launch of Trump News?" *Vanity Fair*, June 16.

Ellperin, Jullet and Damian Paletta. 2017. "Trump Administration Cancels Hundreds of Obama-Era Regulations." *Washington Post*, July 20.

Elstein, Aaron. 2015. "The Charities Donald Trump Gave Money to and What It Says About His Candidacy." *Crain's New York Business*, July 31.

Entous, Adam, Devlin Barrett, and Rosalind S. Helderman. 2017. "Clinton Campaign, DNC Paid for Research That Led to Russia Dossier." *Washington Post*, October 24.

Epps, Garrett. 2019. "Can't Impeach Trump? Go After His Cabinet." *The Atlantic*, July 16.

Erikson. Erik. H. 1994. *Identity and the Life Cycle*. New York: Norton.

Estapa, Jessica. 2015. "Donald Trump on Carly Fiorina: 'Look at That Face!'." *USA Today*, September 10.

Estrich, Susan. 2018. "Donald Trump Numbers Not as Bad as Some Believe." *Boston Herald*, November 17.

Evans, Heidi 2000. "INSIDE TRUMPS' BITTER BATTLE Nephew's Ailing Baby Caught in the Middle." *Daily News*, December 19.

Face the Nation Transcript. 2016. "Conway, Kissinger, Donilon." *NBC*, December 18.

Fahrenthold, David A. 2016a. "Four Months After Fundraiser, Trump says He Gave $1 Million to Veterans Group." *Washington Post*, May 24.

Fahrenthold, David A. 2016b. "Trump Promised Millions to Charity. We Found Less Than $10,000 Over 7 Years." *Washington Post*, June 28.

Fahrenthold, David A. 2016c. "Donald Trump Used Money Donated for Charity to Buy Himself a Tim Tebow-Signed Football Helmet." *Washington Post*, July 1.

Fahrenthold, David A. 2016d. "Eric Trump: My Father Gives Millions to Charity But I Won't Say More." *Washington Post*, July 6.

Fahrenthold, David A. 2016e. "Trump Boasts About His Philanthropy. But His Giving Falls Short of His Words." *Washington Post*, October 29.

Fandos, Nicholas. 2019a. "House Committee to Issue Blitz of Subpoenas, Raising Heat on Trump." *New York Times*, July 9.

Fandos, Nicholas. 2019b. "Democrats Move Toward Bringing Impeachment Inquiry Public." *New York Times*, October 28.

Fandos, Nicholas and Maggie Haberman. 2018. "Trump Embraces a Path to Revise U.S. Sentencing and Prison Laws." *New York Times*, November 14.

Fandos, Nick, Peter Baker, Michael S. Schmidt, and Maggie Haberman. 2019. "White House Declares War on Impeachment Inquiry, Claiming Effort to Undo Trump's Election." *New York Times*, October 8.

Farhi, Paul. 2017. "Washington Post's David Fahrenthold Wins Pulitzer Prize for Dogged Reporting of Trump's Philanthropy." *Washington Post*, April 10.

Farkas, Evelyn. 2018. "Putin Has Already Won." *Politico*, July 11.

Farley, Harry. 2017. "VP Mike Pence Says US Will Bypass UN and Give US Aid Directly to Christians in Iraq." *Christianity Today*, October 26.

Farnsworth, Stephen J., S. Robert Lichter, and Roland Schatz. 2017. "News Coverage of Trump Is Really, Really Negative. Even on Fox News." *Washington Post*, February 28.

Farrell, Henry. 2017. "Trump Has no Long-Term Foreign Policy Vision. Here's How That's Hurting America." *Washington Post*, July 17.

Feldman, Stanley and Leonie Huddy. 2005. "Racial Resentment and White Opposition to Race-Conscious Programs: Principles or Prejudice?" *American Journal of Political Science*, Vol. 49, no. 1 (January), pp. 168–183.

FEMA. 2018. "2017 Hurricane Season FEMA After-Action Report." July 12. https://www.fema.gov/media-library-data/1531743865541-d16794d43 d3082544435e1471da07880/2017FEMAHurricaneAAR.pdf.

Ferris, Sarah. 2019. "Moderate Democrats Warn Pelosi of Impeachment Obsession." *Politico*, September 15.

Fesler, J. W. 1987. "The Brownlow Committee Fifty Years Later." *Public Administration Review*, Vol. 47, pp. 291–296.

Fisher, Marc. 2019. "Bluster, Bombast, Backing Down: What Happens When Someone Says No to Trump?" *Washington Post*, January 24.

Fisher Marc and Michael Kranish. 2016a. "Trump Interview." *Washington Post*, June 9.

Fisher, Marc and Michael Kranish. 2016b. "The Trump We Saw: Populist, Frustrating, Naive, Wise, Forever on the Make." *Washington Post*, August 12.

Fishkin, James S. 2009. *When the People Speak: Deliberative Democracy and Public Consultation*. Oxford: Oxford University Press.

Fitzduff, Mari. 2017. *Why Irrational Politics Appeals: Understanding the Allure of Trump*. Santa Barbara, CA: Preager.

Flegenheimer, Mat and Ashley Parker. 2016. "Heckled by New York Elite at Charity Dinner." *New York Times*, October 20.

Flegenheimer, Matt and Michael Barbaro, "Donald Trump Is Elected President in Stunning Repudiation of the Establishment." *New York Times*, November 9.

488 REFERENCES

Flower, Mayhill. 2011. "Obama: No Surprise That Hard-Pressed Pennsylvanians Turn Bitter." *Huffpost*, May 25.

FOLLOW-UP ON THE NEWS. 1987. "Surviving Tragedy On the Farm." *New York Times*, August 2.

Fording, Richard and Sanford Schram. 2016. "'Low Information Voters' Are a Crucial Part of Trump's Support." *Washington Post*, November 7.

Forgey, Quint. 2018. "Former Trump Aides Break Their Silence on Woodward Book." *Politico*, September 11.

Forgey, Quint and Daniel Lippman. 2019. "'Extremely Stable Genius': Trump Defends His Mental Fitness as He Tears into Pelosi." *Politico*, May 23.

Fram, Alan. 2018 "Congress' Immigration Push Sputters as Guns Grab Attention." Real Clear Politics, March 3.

Frances, Allen, MD. 2017. *Twilight of American Sanity: A Psychiatrist Analyzes the Age of Trump.* New York: HarperCollins.

Frank, Jerome A MD. 2019. *Trump on the Couch: Inside the Mind of the President.* New York: Avery.

Freeman, James. 2017. "Art of the Health-Care Deal." *Wall Street Journal*, March 24.

Freeman, James. 2020a. "Trump Receives Another Postcard from the Swamp." *Wall Street Journal*, January 16.

Freeman, James, 2020b. "What Did GAO Staff Know and When Did They Know It?" *Wall Street Journal*, January 17.

Freud, Sigmund. 1917. "On Narcissism." In *The Standard Edition of the Complete Psychological Works of Sigmund Freud: Volume 14.* London: Hogarth Press.

Freud, Sigmund. 1968. *The Standard Edition of the Complete Psychological Works of Sigmund Freud, 1968–1974.* London: Hogarth Press.

Friedman, Lisa. 2017. "Trump Adviser Tells Ministers U.S. Will Leave Paris Climate Accord." *New York Times*, September 18.

Friedman, Lisa. 2018a. "E.P.A. Chief's $43,000 Phone Booth Broke the Law, Congressional Auditors Say." *New York Times*, April 16.

Friedman, Lisa. 2018b. "The Investigations That Led to Scott Pruitt's Resignation." *New York Times*, April 18.

Friedman, Henry J. MD. 2017. "On Saying What You See and Saying What You Know." In *The Dangerous Case of Donald Trump: 27 Psychiatrists and Mental Health Experts Assess a President*, edited by Bandy Lee. New York: St. Martin's Press, pp. 160–169.

Friedman, Lisa and Brad Plumer. 2017. "P.A. Announces Repeal of Major Obama-Era Carbon Emissions Rule." *New York Times*, October 9.

Friedman, Richard C., MD and Jennifer Downey, MD. 2018. "Editorial: Psychiatric Ethics and the Goldwater Rule." *Psychodynamic Psychiatry*, Vol. 46, No. 3 (Fall): pp. 323–333.

Friedman, Thomas. 2018. "Time for G.O.P. to Threaten to Fire Trump." *New York Times*, December 24.

Friedman, Thomas L. 2019. "Trump's Only Consistent Foreign Policy Goal Is to One-Up Obama." *New York Times*, June 18.

Fromm, Eric. 1964. *The Heart of Man: Its Genius for Good and Evil*. New York Harper & Row.

Frum, David. 2015. "Is Jeb Bush a Republican Obama?" *The Atlantic*, February 4.

Frum, David. 2016. "The Seven Broken Guardrails of Democracy." *The Atlantic*, May 31.

Frum, David. 2017. "It's Not Over Yet for Donald Trump." *The Atlantic*, April 1.

Frum, David. 2018. *Trumpocracy: The Corruption of the American Republic*. New York: Harper.

Frum, David. 2019. "The Question Posed by Trump's Phone Call." *The Atlantic*, September 19.

Gains, Cork. 2018. "After Robert Kraft's Wife Died, Trump Called Every Week for a Year to Console Him." *AOL*, February 1.

Gallup. 2019. "Satisfaction with the United States." Gallup. http://www.gallup.com/poll/1669/general-mood-country.aspx.

Galston, William. 2015. "The Bleak Reality Driving Trump's Rise." *Wall Street Journal*, December 15.

Galvan, Astrid. 2020. "Trump to Celebrate Border Wall Milestone in Arizona." *Associated Press*, June 22.

Ganeva, Tana. 2019. "Bandy X. Lee Discusses What Prompted Her to Speak Out About the President's Psychological Problems." *Salon*, May 7.

Gardner, John. 2017a. "Donald Trump's Malignant Narcissism Is Toxic: Psychologist." *USA Today*, May 4.

Gardner, John. 2017b. "Trump Is '(A) Bad (B) Mad (C) All of the Above'." In *The Dangerous Case of Donald Trump: 27 Psychiatrists and Mental Health Experts Assess a President*, edited by Bandy Lee. New York: St. Martin's Press, pp. 93–109.

Gardner, John. 2019. "DEFCON 2? Nuclear Risk Is Rising as Donald Trump Goes Downhill." In *Rocket Man: Nuclear Madness and the Mind of Donald Trump*, edited by John Gardner, John and Steven Buser, 2018. New York: Chiron Books.

Gardner, John and Steven Buser (eds.). 2018. *Rocket Man: Nuclear Madness and the Mind of Donald Trump*. New York: Chiron Books.

Gearan, Anne. 2018. "Democrats Marshal Strike Force to Counter Trump on National Security in 2018, 2020 Elections." *Washington Post*, February 27.

490 REFERENCES

Gearon, Anne, Philip Rucker, and Simon Denyer. 2016. "Trump's Taiwan Phone Call Was Long Planned, Say People Who Were Involved." *Washington Post*, December 4.

Geist, William E. 1984. "The Expanding Empire of Donald Trump." *New York Times Magazine*, April 8.

George, Alexander L. 1974. "Review: Assessing Presidential Character." *World Politics*, Vol. 26, No. 2 (January), pp. 234–282.

George, Alexander L. and Andrew Bennett. 2015. *Case Studies and Theory Development in the Social Sciences*. Cambridge, MA: MIT Press.

Gerson, Michael. 2016a. "Trump Spirals into Ideological Psychosis." *Washington Post*, October 17.

Gerson, Michael. 2016b. "Dr. Jekyll and Mr. Hyde Are on Their Way to the White House." *Washington Post*, December 17.

Gerson, Michael. 2018a. "Trump Has Revealed Who He Is. Now It's Our Turn." *Washington Post*, January 15.

Gerson, Michael. 2018b. "Trump Replaces National Pride with Personal Vanity." *Washington Post*, July 16.

Gerson, Michael. 2018c. "Trump Is Smashing the Hopes of Oppressed People Everywhere." *Washington Post*, July 19.

Gerstein, Josh and Kyle Cheney. 2019. "House Counsel Suggests Trump Could Be Impeached Again." *Politico*, December 23.

Giartelli, Anna. 2019. "Trump Has Not Built a Single Mile of New Border Fence After 30 Months in Office." *Washington Examiner*, July 20.

Gibbons-Neff, Thomas and Eric Schmidt. 2018. "Pentagon Considers Using Special Operations Forces to Continue Mission in Syria." *New York Times*, December 21.

Gibbs, Nancy and Zeke Miller. 2015. "Donald Trump Explains All." *Time*. August 20.

Gibson, Caitlin. 2017. "The Trump Administration Has a Spelling Problem. But How Bad Is It Really? We Investigate." *Washington Post*, February 15.

Gill, Lauren. 2018. "Trump 'Psychologically Unfit.' Nuclear Tweet Is Grounds for Removal, Former Bush Ethic Lawyer Says." *Newsweek*, January 3.

Gilligan, James MD. 2017. "The Issue Is Dangerousness, Not Mental Illness." In *The Dangerous Case of Donald Trump: 27 Psychiatrists and Mental Health Experts Assess a President*, edited by Bandy Lee. New York: St. Martin's Press, pp. 170–180.

Ginzberg, Ralph. 1964. "Goldwater: The Man and the Menace." *Fact*, Vol. 4, No. (2–4).

Givhan, Robin. 2006. "Mussed for Success: Barack Obama's Smooth Wrinkles." *Washington Post*, August 11.

Glasser, Susan B. 2017. "Ex-Spy Chief: Russia's Election Hacking Was An 'Intelligence Failure'." *Politico*, September 11.

REFERENCES **491**

Glasser, Susan. 2018. "Just How Dangerous Is Donald Trump?" *Politico*, April 16.

Glassser, Susan B. and Michael Kruse. 2016a. "Trumpology: A Master Class." *Politico*, May/June 2016.

Glasser, Susan B. and Michael Kruse. 2016b. "I Think He's a Very Dangerous Man for the Next Three or Four Weeks." *Politico*, October 12.

Gold, Matea. 2017a. "The Campaign to Impeach President Trump Has Begun." *Washington Post*, January 20.

Gold, Matea. 2017b. "As Ivanka Trump's White House Role Expands, Her Company Is Sued for Unfair Competition." *Washington Post*, March 21.

Goldberg, Michelle. 2017. "An Unfit President Fails Puerto Rico." *New York Times*, October 3.

Goldberg, Michelle. 2018. "The De-Trumpification Agenda." *The New York Times*, February 28.

Goldman, Julianna. 2017. "Walter Shaub Says America Should Have Right to Know Motivations of Its Leaders." *CBS News*, July 6.

Goldstein, Amy. 2018. "Trump Administration Takes Another Major Swipe at the Affordable Care Act." *Washington Post*, July 7.

Goldstein, Amy. 2019. "New Trump Rule to Make More Health Care Rates Public." *Washington Post*, November 15.

Goldstein, Amy and John Wagner. 2017. "Health and Human Services Secretary Tom Price Resigns After Criticism for Taking Charter Flights at Taxpayer Expense." *Washington Post*, September 29.

Goldwag, Arthur. 2015. "Putting Donald Trump on the Couch." *New York Times*, September 1.

Gonzales, Richard and John Burnett. 2018. "John Kelly: Despite 'Times of Great Frustration,' No Regrets Taking White House Job." *NPR*, May 10.

Goodkind, Nicole. 2019. "USPS Could Privatize as Early as Next Year." *Fortune*, December 27.

Goodwin, Michael. 2017. "Trump Defied the Polls, Press, and Pundits to Win the White House." *New York Post*, January 22.

Goodwin, Michael. 2018. "Donald Trump Is Teaching Republicans How to Fight." *New York Post*, January 30.

Goodwin, Michael. 2019. "Trump Talks Impeachment, Dems and de Blasio in Interview." *New York Post*, October 2.

Gould, Roger MD. 1979. *Transformations: Growth and Change in Adult Life*. New York: Simon & Schuster.

Graham, David A. 2017. "Trump Has Quietly Accomplished More Than It Appears." *The Atlantic*, August 2.

Graham, David A. 2018a. "What's Behind Trump's Rising Popularity?" *The Atlantic*, February 14.

Graham, David A. 2018b. "The Tenacity of Trump." *The Atlantic*, April 6.

492 REFERENCES

Green, Joshua. 2008. "Penn Strategy Memo, March 19, 2007." *The Atlantic*, August 11.

Green, Joshua. 2016. "How to Get Trump Elected When He's Wrecking Everything You Built." *Bloomberg*, May 26.

Green, Joshua. 2017. "Does Stephen Miller Speak for Trump? Or Vice Versa?" *Bloomberg*, February 28.

Green, Jesse. 2017. "Review: Can Trump Survive in Caesar's Palace?" *New York Times*, June 9.

Greenberg, John. 2017. "Revisiting the Obama Track Record on Syria's Chemical Weapons." *Politifact*, April 5.

Greenfield, Jeff. 2017. "The Strange Authenticity of Hillary Clinton." *Politico*, September 20.

Greenstein, Fred I. 1967. "The Impact of Personality on Politics: An Attempt to Clear Away Underbrush." *American Political Science Review*, Vol. 61, No. 3, pp. 629–641.

Greenstein, Fred I. 1969. *Personality and Politics: Problems of Evidence, Inference, and Conceptualization*. Chicago: Markham.

Greenstein, Fred I. 1982. *The Hidden-Hand Presidency: Eisenhower as Leader*. New York: Basic Books.

Greenstein, Fred I. 2000. *The Presidential Difference: Leadership Style from FDR to Barack Obama*. New York: The Free Press.

Greenstein, Fred I. 2016. "Preface to the New Edition." In *Personality and Politics: Problems of Evidence, Inference, and Conceptualization*. Princeton, NJ: Princeton University Press.

Greenwald, Glenn. 2019. "Beyond BuzzFeed: The 10 Worst, Most Embarrassing U.S. Media Failures on the Trump-Russia Story." *The Intercept*, January 20.

Gregorian, Dareh. 2019. "Romney Blasts Trump Over 'wrong and Appalling' Call for China to Probe Bidens." *NBC News*, October 4.

Griffin, Robert and John Sides. 2018. "In the Red: Americans' Economic Woes are Hurting Trump." Democracy Fund-Voter's Study Group, September.

Grisham, Stephanie and Hogan Gidley. 2019. "The Washington Post's Lost Summer." *Washington Examiner*, September 5.

Griswold, Alex. 2016. "Report: Donald Trump Plans to Create Media Empire After Election." *Mediate*, June 16.

Gunther, Richard, Paul A. Beck, and Erik C. Nisbet. 2018. "Fake News May Have Contributed to Trump's 2016 Victory." Unpublished paper, March 8.

Guo, Jeff. 2016. "Washington's 'Governing Elite' Think Americans Are Morons." *Washington Post*, October 5.

Gurzu, Anca. 2019. "Labour's Thornberry: Trump Is a 'Threat to Our World Order'." *Politico*, April 27.

Gutmann, Amy. 2009. *Why Deliberative Democracy?* Princeton, NJ: Princeton Press.

Haberman, Maggie. 2017. "A Homebody Finds the Ultimate Home Office." *New York Times*, January 25.

Haberman, Maggie and Alexander Burns. 2016. "Donald Trump's Presidential Run Began in an Effort to Gain Stature." *New York Times*, March 12.

Haberman, Maggie and Anni Karni. 2019. "Trump Celebrates Criminal Justice Overhaul Amid Doubts It Will Be Fully Funded." *New York Times*, April 1.

Haberman, Maggie and Glenn Thrush. 2017. "Trump Reaches Beyond West Wing for Counsel." *New York Times*, April 27.

Haberman, Maggie and Jonathan Martin. 2018. "Debate Continues Over What Trump Said. But Does the Exact Word Matter?" *New York Times*, January 16.

Haberman, Maggie, Julie Hirschfeld, Michael S. Schmidt. 2018. "Kelly Says He's Willing to Resign as Abuse Scandal Roils White House." *New York Times*, February 9.

Haberman, Maggie and Katie Rogers. 2018. "'Drama, Action, Emotional Power': As Exhausted Aides Eye the Exits, Trump Is Re-energized." *New York Times*, June 10.

Haberman, Maggie and Mikayla Bouchard. 2017. "Tracking the Roller Coaster Relationship of Reince Priebus and Donald Trump." *New York Times*, July 29.

Haberman, Maggie, Nicholas Fandos, Michael Crowley, and Kenneth P. Vogel. 2019. "Trump Said to Have Frozen Aid to Ukraine Before Call with Its Leader." *New York Times*, September 24.

Hackman, Michelle and Alicia A. Caldwell. 2020. "U.S. Begins Returning Asylum Seekers at Arizona Border to Mexico." *Wall Street Journal*, January 2.

Hagen, Lisa. 2017. "Spicer: 'Negative' Trump Coverage Is 'Demoralizing'." *The Hill*, January 23.

Hains, Tim. 2015. "Trump's Updated ISIS Plan: "Bomb the Shit Out of Them," *Real Clear Politics*, November 13.

Hamberger, Tom and Rosaland S. Helderman. 2018. "Hero or Hired Gun? How a British Former Spy Became a Flash Point in the Russia Investigation." *Washington Post*, February 6.

Hamblin, James. 2016. "Donald Trump: Sociopath?" *Atlantic*, July 20.

Hamby, Peter. 2018. "That Is What Power Looks Like: As Trump Prepares for 2020, Democrats Are Losing the Only Fight That Matters." *Vanity Fair*, May 26.

Hamilton, Alexander. 1787. "The Insufficiency of the Present Confederation to Preserve the Union." Federalist No. 15, December 1.

Hamilton, Alexander. 1788. "The Executive Department Further Considered." Federalist No. 70, March 18.

494   REFERENCES

Hanley, Robert. 1989. "Copter Crash Kills 3 Aides of Trump." *New York Times*, October 11.

Hannon, Paul and David Harrison. 2017. "Yellen: Globalization, Technological Change Have Been Harmful to Many." *Wall Street Journal*, June 27.

Hargrove, Erwin C. 2013. *Effective Presidency: Lessons on Leadership from John F. Kennedy to Barack Obama*. New York: Routledge.

Harper, Jennifer. 2018. Unprecedented Hostility: Broadcast Coverage of President Trump Still 90% Negative, Says Study." *Washington Times*, March 6.

Harris, Shane and Michael Kranish. 2020. "Trump's Worldview Forged by Neglect and Trauma at Home, His Niece Says in New Book." *Washington Post*, July 7.

Hasan, Mehdi. 2017. "Top Democrats Are Wrong: Trump Supporters Were More Motivated by Racism Than Economic Issues." *The Intercept*, April 6.

Hassan, Falih, Alissa J. Rubin, Michael Crowley, and Michael Schmitt. 2020. "Trump Orders Strike Killing Top Iranian General Qassim Suleimani in Baghdad." *New York Times*, January 2.

Hayes, Stephen F. 2016. "Donald Trump Is Crazy, and So Is the GOP for Embracing Him." *Weekly Standard*, July 22.

Healy, Gene 2008. *The Cult of the Presidency: America's Dangerous Devotion to Executive Power*. Washington, DC: CATO Institute.

Heidi, Przybyla and Anna Schecter. "Donald Trump's Longtime Business Connections in Turkey Back in the Spotlight." *NBC News*, October 9.

Heil, Emily. 2016. "Is Obama's 2011 White House Correspondents' Dinner Burn to Blame for Trump's Campaign?" *Washington Post*, February 10.

Helderman, Rosalind S. and Tom Hamberger. 2016. "Who Is 'Source D'? The Man Said to Be Behind the Trump-Russia Dossier's Most Salacious Claim." *Washington Post*, March 29.

Heller, Karen. 2018. "A President Unlike Any Other." *Washington Post*, January 19.

Henninger, Daniel. 2016. "Trump's MAD." *Wall Street Journal*, June 1.

Herb, Jeremy. 2017. "Trump Hasn't Demonstrated the Stability or Competence to Be Successful." *CNN*, August 18.

Herb, Jeremy. 2020. "Government Watchdog Concludes Trump Administration Broke Law by Withholding Ukraine Aid." *CNN*, January 16.

Hermani, Jordyn. 2019. "Trump Pitches His 'Merit-Based' Immigration Proposal." *Politico*, May 16.

Hermann, Judith Lewis, MD and Bandy Lee MD. 2017. "Prologue: Professions and Politics." In *The Dangerous Case of Donald Trump: 27 Psychiatrists and Mental Health Experts Assess a President*, edited by Bandy Lee. New York: St. Martin's Press, pp. 1–10.

Hewitt, Hugh. 2019. "Why Do Conservatives Support Trump? Because He Implements Conservative Policies." *Washington Post*, October 12.

Heye, Doug. 2017. "How Media Fact-Checking Can Stoke Voters' Cynicism." *Wall Street Journal*, August 17.

Hicks, Josh. 2017. "Activists Disrupt Hearing to Demand That Hogan Oppose Trump." *Washington Post*, February 22.

Hill, James. 2016. "The Story Behind Donald Trump's Deal with Carrier to Keep 1,000 Jobs in the US." *ABC News*, November 30.

Hirschfeld, Julie and Michael D. Shear. 2017. "An Over-the-Top New Yorker Will Run Trump's Communications Shop." *New York Times*, July 21.

Hirschfeld, Julie and Miriam Jordan. 2017. "Trump Plans 45,000 Limit on Refugees Admitted to U.S." *New York Times*, September 26.

Hjelmgaard, Kim. 2016. "Total Global Disbelief as Trump Is Elected President." *USA Today*, November 9.

Hochman, David. 2015. "Playboy Interview: Donald Trump (2004)." *Playboy*, July 19.

Hohmann, James. 2018. "Trump Supporters Suffer Unintended Consequences of His Policies." *Washington Post*, May 15.

Holan, Angie Drobnic. 2013. "Lie of the Year: 'If You Like Your Health Care Plan, You Can Keep It'." *Politifact*, December 12.

Holan, Angie Drobnik. 2019. "In Context: Donald Trump's 'Very Fine People on Both Sides' Remarks (Transcript)." *Politifact*, April 20.

Holcomb, James. 2017. "President Trump Gives $10,000 to Campaign Volunteer for His Father's Chemo." *Washington Post*, January 24.

Hooghe, Marc and Ruth Dassonneville. 2018. "Explaining the Trump Vote: The Effect of Racist Resentment and Anti-immigrant Sentiments." *Political Science (PS)* (July), pp. 528–534.

Hook, Janet and Siobhan Hughes. 2017. "Republican Retirement Gives House Democrats Another Target." *Wall Street Journal*, September 8.

Horney, Karen, MD. 1939. *New Ways in Psychoanalysis*. London: Kegan, Paul, Trench, Trubner & Co.

Horowitz, Jason. 2017. "Back Channel to Trump: Loyal Aide in Trump Tower Acts as Gatekeeper." *New York Times*, March 27.

Howard, Blum. 1980. "Trump: The Development of a Manhattan Developer." *New York Times*, August. 26.

Hubbard, Ben, Eric Lipton, Dan Levin, and Richard C. Paddock. 2017. "Trump's Dual Roles Collide with Openings in Dubai and Vancouver." *New York Times*, February 18.

Hudson, John, Josh Dawsey, and Carol D. Leonnig. 2018. "In Private, Trump Vents Frustration Over Lack of Progress on North Korea." *Washington Post*, July 22.

Hughes, C. J. 2014. "Sewing Up a Loose End on West End." *New York Times*, November 14.

Hughes, Siobban and Andrew Duehren. 2019. "Democrats Set Rapid Timetable for Trump Impeachment Probe." *Wall Street Journal*, September 27.

Hulse, Carl. 2017. "Democrats Perfect Art of Delay While Republicans Fume Over Trump Nominees." *New York Times*, July 17.

Hunt, Cassie. 2017. "Trump Again Makes Debunked Claim: 'Illegals' Cost Me Popular Vote." *NBC News*, January 23.

Hurley, Lawrence and Andrew Chung. 2017. "In Victory for Trump, U.S. Supreme Court Revives His Travel Ban." *Reuters*, July 26.

Hurt III, Harry. 2016. *Lost Tycoon: The Many Lives of Donald Trump*. Brattleboro, VT: Echo Print Books & Media.

Hyatt, Fred. 2020a. "Trump's Articles of Impeachment—Updated." *Washington Post*, June 28.

Hyatt, Fred. 2020b. "In Just One Month, Trump Commits a Whole New Set of Potentially Impeachable Offenses." *Washington Post*, July 26.

Ifill, Gwen. 2016. "Questions for President Obama: A Town Hall Special." *NPR*, June 1.

Ignatius, David. 2017. "Here's What a Permanent Treaty with North Korea Might Look Like." *Washington Post*, August 15.

Imbert, Fred. 2019. "Dow Rallies 200 Points to Close Above 27,000 for the First Time Ever." *CNBC*, July 11.

Insana, Ron. 2016. "Trump's Going to Get Demolished by Clinton; Here's Why He Needs to Drop Out Now." *MSNBC*, June 8.

Ip, Greg. 2019. "Shutdown Shows American Institutions Are Alive and Kicking." *Wall Street Journal*, January 30.

Irwin, Neil. 2019. "How a Strong Job Market Has Proved the Experts Wrong." *New York Times*, December 6.

Isikoff, Michael. 2017. "Bill to Create Panel That Could Remove Trump from Office Quietly Picks Up Democratic Support." *Yahoo News*, June 20.

Isikoff, Michael. 2019. Maverick Republican William Weld Looks to Run Against Trump's 'Malignant Narcissism'." *Yahoo News*, March 8.

Jackson, David. 2016. "Trump Conducts Election Eve Campaign Marathon." *USA Today*, November 7.

Jackson, David and Deirdre Shesgreen. 2018. "President Trump's Ambitious Agenda: 7 Things to Watch in 2018." *USA Today*, January 1.

Jacobs, Jennifer and Jordan Fabian. 2019. "How Trump Planned the Drone Strike with a Tight Circle of Aides." *Bloomberg*, January 4.

Jacobson, Louis. 2018. "Here's What's Wrong About Donald Trump's Attack on Canada Trade Deficit." *Politifact*, March 15.

James, William. 2017. "Trump Says NATO Is Obsolete But Still 'Very Important to Me'." *Reuters*, January 16.

Jamieson, Dave. 2020. "Donald Trump Is About to Put His Stamp on the U.S. Postal Service." *Huffington Post*, January 11.

"Japan TV Shu Ueyama's Interview with Donald Trump," June 13, 1988. https://www.liveleak.com/view?i=dc1_1464663388#CIyk2eTbcLzD IM9s.99.

Jarrett, Laura. 2019. "Top Federal Prosecutor in Connecticut to Review Origins of Russia Probe." *CNN*, May 14.

Jenkins, Holman Jr. 2012. "Good Businessman, Bad President?" *Wall Street Journal*, October 23.

Jenkins, Holman Jr. 2016. "Trump's Market Mandate: Green Shoots Say the President-Elect Is the Real 'Hope and Change' Candidate." *Wall Street Journal*, December 20.

Jenkins, Holman Jr. 2019. "How Bad Can a Trade War Get?" *Wall Street Journal*, September 3.

Jennifer, Jacobs and Justin Sink. 2019. "Trump Orders Cut to National Security Staff After Whistle-Blower." *Bloomberg News*, October 5.

Jindal, Bobby. 2017. "Trump's Style Is His Substance." *Wall Street Journal*, February 14.

Jindal, Bobby. 2018. "A Look Ahead at the Post-Trump GOP." *Wall Street Journal*, July 31.

Jindal, Bobby. 2018. "Trump Keeps His Predecessors' Promises." *Wall Street Journal*, April 3.

Joan, Biskupic. 2016. "Justice Ruth Bader Ginsburg Calls Trump a 'faker,' He Says She Should Resign." *CNN*, July 13.

Joffe, Emily. 2017. "Is Donald Trump a TV Addict?" *Politico*, July 7.

Johnson, David Kay. 2018. *It's Even Worse Than You Think: What the Trump Administration Is Doing to America*. New York: Simon & Shuster.

Johnson, Alex, Saphora Smith, and Shannon Pettypiece. 2019. "Trump Says He May Leave Some U.S. Forces in Syria to Protect Oil, But Not Kurds." *NBC*, October 21.

Johnson, Carrie. 2017. "Robert Mueller May Not Be the Savior the Anti-Trump Internet Is Hoping For." *NPR*, August 17.

Johnson, Gene. 2019. "Judge Blocks Trump Policy Keeping Asylum-Seekers Locked Up." *Associated Press*, July 3.

Johnson, Jenna. 2017a. "Trump Brings Many Different Personas to Washington." *Washington Post*, January 20.

Johnson, Jenna. 2017b. "Whom to Trust When It Comes to Health-Care Reform? Trump Supporters Put Their Faith in him." *Washington Post*, March 16.

Johnson, Jenna. 2017c. "'I Will Give You Everything.' Here Are 282 of Donald Trump's Campaign Promises." *Washington Post*, November 7.

498 REFERENCES

Johnson, Jenna, Robert Costa, and Philip Rucker. 2016. "How Trump Got from Point A to Point A on Immigration." *Washington Post*, September 1.

Jones, Athena. 2008. "Obama: Change Comes from Me." *NBC-First Read*, November 26.

Jones, Jeffrey M. 2020a. "Trump Third Year Sets New Standard for Party Polarization." *Gallup*, January 21.

Jones, Jeffrey M. 2020b. "Trump Job Approval at Personal Best 49%." *Gallup*, February 4.

Jonsson, Parrik. 2010. "Amid Harsh Criticisms, 'tea party' Slips into the Mainstream." *Christian Science Monitor*, April 3.

Jouvenal, Justin. 2017. "In Donated Shoes and Suit, a Trump Supporter Comes to Washington." *Washington Post*, January 18.

Judis, John. 2010. "The Tea Party Movement Isn't Racist." *The New Republic*, June 2.

Kagan, Robert. 2016a. "Trump Is the GOP's Frankenstein Monster. Now He's Strong Enough to Destroy the Party." *Washington Post*, February 25.

Kagan, Robert. 2016b. "This Is How Fascism Comes to America." *Washington Post*, May 18.

Kagan, Robert. 2016c. "There Is Something Very Wrong with Donald Trump." *Washington Post*, August 1.

Kane, Paul. 2016. "One Reason the GOP Health Bill Is a Mess: No One Thought Trump Would Win." *Washington Post*, July 6.

Kanno-Youngs, Zolan and Elisabeth Malkin. 2019. "Most Migrants at Border with Mexico Would Be Denied Asylum Protections Under New Trump Rule." *New York Times*, July 15.

Kann-Youngs, Zolan, Adam Goldman, and Mike Baker. 2020. "Feds Sending Tactical Team to Seattle, Expanding Presence Beyond Portland." *New York Times*, July 23.

Kaplan, Morgan. L. 2019. "Trump's Syria Announcement Is a Change of Speed—Not a Change of Direction." *Washington Post*, October 9.

Karni Annie, Lara Jakes, and Patrick Kingsley. 2019. "Turkey Agrees to Pause Fighting, But Not to Withdraw Forces from Northern Syria." *New York Times*, October 17.

Karni, Annie and Maggie Haberman. 2019. "Trump's Personal Assistant, Madeleine Westerhout, Steps Down." *New York Times*, August 29.

Kelleher, Jennifer Sinco. 2017. "Judge in Hawaii Extends Order Blocking Trump's Travel Plan." *Associated Press*, March 30.

Keller, Megan. 2018. "Reporters Fire Back at Trump for Ripping 'Anonymous Sources'." *The Hill*, August 29.

Kelly, John. 2018 "Transcript: White House Chief of Staff John Kelly's Interview with NPR." *NPR*, May 11.

Kelly, Kate and Maggie Haberman. 2018. "Gary Cohn Says He Will Resign as Trump's Top Economic Adviser." *New York Times*, March 6.

Kendall, Bent and Jess Bravin, "Justice Neil Gorsuch Leans Conservative, Fulfilling Expectations," *Wall Street Journal*, June 27.

Kendall, Brent and Natalie Andrews. 2017. "Senate Fight Over Trump's Nominees Heats Up." *Wall Street Journal*, July 12.

Keneally, Meghan. 2018. "President Trump Has Called Himself Smart Six Times Before." *Washington Post*, January 9.

Kernberg, Otto, MD. 1975. *Borderline Conditions and Pathological Narcissism.* New York: Jason Aronson.

Kernberg, Otto, MD. 1980. *Internal World and External Reality: Object Relations Theory Applied.* New York: Jason Aronson.

Kernberg, Otto MD. 1998. "Pathological Narcissism and Narcissistic Personality Disorder: Theoretical Background and Diagnostic Classification." In *Disorders of Narcissism: Diagnostic, Clinical and Empirical Implications*, edited by Elsa F. Ronningstam. New York: American Psychiatric Publishing.

Kessler, Glenn. 2018. "President Trump's Repeated Claim: 'The Greatest Economy in the History of Our Country'." *Washington Post*, September 7.

Kessler, Glenn, Salvador Rizzo, and Meg Kelly. 2019. "President Trump Has Made 13,435 False or Misleading Claims Over 993 Days." *Washington Post*, October 14.

Kessler Glenn, Salvador Rizzo, and Meg Kelly. 2020. "President Trump has Made More than 20,000 False or Misleading Claims." *Washington Post*, July13.

Kessler, Glenn, Salvador Rizzo, and Sarah Cahlan. 2020. "Fact-Checking President Trump's 2020 State of the Union Address." *Washington Post*, February 4.

Kessler, Ronald. 2018. "The Real Donald Trump." *The Daily Caller*, April 23.

Kim, Seung Min and John Dawsey. 2018. "Chief of Staff John Kelly to Leave White House by End of Month, Trump Says." *Washington Post*, December 8.

Kim, Seung Min and Josh Dawsey. 2019. "'He Just Picks Up': Trump and the Lawmakers He Loves to Talk to on the Phone." *Washington Post*, February 19.

Kim, Seung Min. 2020. "In Historic Vote, Trump Acquitted of Impeachment Charges." *Washington Post*, February 5.

King, Laura. 2019. "Trump Says He's Open to Iran Talks Without Preconditions." *Los Angeles Times*, June 23.

Kirby, Jen. 2019. What Really Happened in Syria Over the Past 24 Hours, Explained." *Vox*, October 23.

Kirk, Chris, Ian Prasad Philbrick, and Gabriel Roth. 2016. "153 Things Donald Trump Has Said and Done That Make Him Unfit to Be President." *Slate*, November 7.

500 REFERENCES

Kirschbaum, Erik. 2017. "Protests Against Trump Are Unrolled Around the World Saturday." *Los Angeles Times*, February 4.

Kitroeff, Natalie and Jim Tankersley. 2017. "U.S. Economy Grew at 3% Rate in 3rd Quarter, Despite Storms." *New York Times*, October 27.

Klaas, Brian. 2017a. "America First' Is Becoming America Alone." *Washington Post*, June 28.

Klass, Brian. 2017b. *The Despot's Apprentice: Donald Trump's Attack on Democracy*. London, UK: C. Hurst & co.

Klein, Ezra. 2106. "Trump: 'My whole life I've been greedy … Now I want to be greedy for the United States'." *Vox*, January 26.

Klemesrud, Judy. 1996. "Donald Trump, Real Estate Promoter, Builds Image as He Builds Buildings." *New York Times*, November 1.

Kluger, Jeffrey. 2015 "The Truth About Donald Trump's Narcissism." *Time Magazine*, August 11.

Knight, Stef W. 2017. "The Insane News Cycle of Trump's Presidency in 1 Chart." *Axios*, September 28.

Kohut, Heinz MD. 1966. "Forms and Transformations of Narcissism." *Journal of the American Psychoanalytic Association*, Vol. 14, p. 249.

Kohut, Heinz MD. 1971. *The Analysis of the Self: A Systematic Approach to the Psychoanalytic Treatment of Narcissistic Personality Disorders*. New York: International University Press.

Kohut, Heinz MD. 1977. *The Restoration of the Self*. New York: International University Press.

Kirschbaum, Erik 2017. "Protests Against Trump Are Unrolled Around the World Saturday." *Los Angeles Times*, February 4.

Klein, Ezra. 2020. *Why We're Polarized*. New York: Simon & Shuster.

Kranish, Michael. 2017a. "A Fierce Will to Win Pushed Donald Trump to the Top." *Washington Post*, January 19.

Kranish, Michael. 2017b. "FBI Releases File on 1970s Trump Housing Discrimination Case." *Washington Post*, February 15.

Kranish, Michael. 2020. "Mary Trump Once Stood Up to Her Uncle Donald. Now Her Book Describes a 'Nightmare' of Family Dysfunction." *Washington Post*, July 2.

Kraz, Michal. 2017. "The Congresswoman Who Accused Trump of Upsetting a Dead Soldier's Widow Has a History of Antagonizing Trump." *Business Insider*, October 17.

Kranish, Michael and Marc Fisher. 2019. *Trump Revealed: The Definitive Biography of the 45th President of the United States*. New York: Scribner.

Krein, Julius. 2015. "Traitor to His Class." *Weekly Standard*, September 7.

Krieg, Gregory 2016. "Hillary Clinton's Would-Be Campaign Slogans, Ranked," *CNN*, October 19.

Krieg, Gregory. 2019. "Warren Backs Plan to Get Rid of the Electoral College." *CNN*, March 18.

Kristoff, Nicholas. 2017. "There's a Smell of Treason in the Air." *New York Times*, March 23.

Kristol, William. 2017. "The Election Came Down to 77,744 Votes in Pennsylvania, Wisconsin, and Michigan (Updated)." *Weekly Standard*, August 21.

Kruesi, Kimberlee and Bill Barrow. 2016. "Trump Opponents Try to Beat Him at the Electoral College." *Associated Press*, November 19.

Kruse, Michael. 2018. "The Lost City of Trump." *Politico*, July/August.

Kruse, Michael. 2015. "The 199 Most Donald Trump Things Donald Trump Has Ever Said." *Politico Magazine*, August 14.

Kumar, Anita and Andrew Restuccia. 2019. "Barrage of Setbacks Spoils Trump's Post-Mueller Reset." *Politico*, March 4.

Kumar, Anita, Gabby Orr, and Daniel Lippman. 2019. "Stephen Miller Pressuring Trump officials Amid Immigration Shakeups." *Politico*, April 8.

Kuntzman, Gersh. 2107. "President Trump Exhibits Classic Signs of Mental Illness, Including 'Malignant Narcissism,' Shrinks Say." *New York Daily News*, January 29.

Lacy, Catherine. 2019. "Behind Trump's Syria Pullout Lies a Campaign Pledge." *Wall Street Journal*, October 8.

Laderman, Charlie and Brendon Simms. 2017. *Donald Trump: The Making of a World View*. London: Endauvour Press.

Lake, Eli. 2019. "Yes, Iran Was Behind the Saudi Oil Attack. Now What?" *Bloomberg*, September 15.

Lander, Mark. 2017. "White House Is Said to Draft Plan for U.S. Break from Nafta." *New York Times*, April 26.

Lander, Mark. 2018a. "Trump Is Expected to Stop Short of Reimposing Strict Sanctions on Iran." *New York Times*, January 11.

Lander, Mark. 2018b. "Trump, Saying Mere Allegation Ruins Lives, Appears to Doubt #MeToo Movement." *New York Times*, February 10.

Lander, Mark. 2018c. "On Foreign Policy, President Trump Reverts to Candidate Trump." *New York Times*, April 3.

Lander, Mark. 2018d. "Trump Abandons Iran Nuclear Deal He Long Scorned." *New York Times*, May 8.

Lander, Mark and David E. Sanger. 2017. "Trump to Force Congress to Act on Iran Nuclear Deal." *New York Times*, October 5.

Lander, Marc and Helene Cooper. 2019a. "Bolton Walked Back Syria Statement. His Disdain for Debate Helped Produce It." *New York Times*, January 7.

Lander, Mark and Helene Cooper. 2019b. "In Latest Shift, Trump Agrees to Leave 400 Troops in Syria." *New York Times*, February 22.

502 REFERENCES

Lander, Mark, Helene Cooper, and Eric Schmitt. 2018. "Trump to Withdraw U.S. Forces from Syria, Declaring 'We Have Won Against ISIS'." *New York Times*, December 19.

Lander, Mark and Julie Hirschfield Davis. 2018. "After Another Week of Chaos, Trump Repairs to Palm Beach. No One Knows What Comes Next." *New York Times*, March 23.

Lander, Mark and Maggie Haberman. 2017a. "Dropping the Bluster, Trump Revives Banter with Reporters." *New York Times*, July 14.

Lander, Mark and Maggie Haberman. 2017b. "Angry Trump Grilled His Generals About Troop Increase, Then Gave In." *New York Times*, August 21.

Lander, Mark and Maggie Haberman. 2018. "Trump Chooses Bolton for 3rd Security Adviser as Shake-Up Continues." *New York Times*, March 22.

Lander, Mark, Peter Baker, and David Singer E. 2017. "Trump Embraces Pillars of Obama's Foreign Policy." *New York Times*, February 2.

Landy, Mark and Sidney M. Milkis. 2000. *Presidential Greatness*. Lawrence, LS: University Press of Kansas.

Lane, Randall. 2017a. "Inside Trump's Head: An Exclusive Interview with the President, and the Single Theory That Explains Everything." *Forbes*, October 10.

Lane, Randell. 2017b. "Trump Unfiltered: The Full Transcript of the President's Interview with Forbes." *Forbes*, November 14.

Lange, Abby. 2016. "Donald Trump's 4-Hour Sleep Habit Could Explain His Personality." *The Daily Beast*, April 2.

Lange, Jeva. 2015. "Psychologists Having Been Using Donald Trump as an Example of Narcissism Since 1988." *This Week*, September 25.

Langley, Monica. 2016. "Campaign Influence of Donald Trump's Adult Children Grows." *Wall Street Journal*, June 21.

Larison, Daniel. 2019. "There Is No 'Trump Doctrine." *The American Conservative*, April 23.

Larry King Live. 2004. "Interview With 'The Apprentice' Host Donald Trump." *CNN*, February 24.

Lasswell, Harold D. 1930. *Psychopathology and Politics*. Chicago: University of Chicago Press.

Lasswell, Harold D. 1948. *Power and Personality*. New York: Norton.

Lauter, David. 2016. "Trump's Victory Surprised Americans, Most Accept His Victory as Legitimate." *Los Angeles Times*, November 13.

Lee, Bandy X., MD and Tony Schwartz. 2018. "Inside the Mind of Donald Trump." *Politico*, July 27.

Lee, Bandy X., et. al. 2017. *The Dangerous Case of Donald Trump: 27 Psychiatrists and Mental Health Experts Assess a President*. New York: Thomas Dunne Books.

Lee, Carol E., Courtney Kube, Kristen Welker, and Stephanie Ruhle. 2018. "Kelly Thinks He's Saving U.S. from Disaster, Calls Trump 'Idiot,' Say White House Staffers." *NBC News*, April 30.

Lee, Carol E., Kristen Welker, Stephanie Ruhle, and Dafna Linzer. 2017. "Tillerson's Fury at Trump Required an Intervention from Pence." *NBC News*, October 4.

Lee, Jasmine C. and Kevin Quealy. 2017. "Trump Is on Track to Insult 650 People, Places and Things on Twitter by the End of His First Term." *New York Times*, July 26.

Lee, Jasmine C. and Kevin Quealy. 2018. "The 425 People, Places and Things Donald Trump Has Insulted on Twitter: A Complete List." *New York Times*, January 3.

Lee, Matthew. 2017. "AP FACT CHECK: Overlooking Doubts on Syria Chemical Weapons." *ABC News*, April 10.

Leibovich, Mark. 2017. "This Town Melts Down." *New York Times*, July 11.

Leonnig, Carol D., Shane Harris, and Greg Jaffe. 2018. "Breaking with Tradition, Trump Skips President's Written Intelligence Report and Relies on Oral Briefings." *Washington Post*, February 9.

Levinson, Daniel J. 1978. *The Seasons of a Man's Life*. New York: Knopf.

Levitsky, Steven and Daniel Ziblatt. 2018a. *How Democracies Die*. New York: Crown.

Levitsky, Steven and Daniel Ziblatt. 2018b. "This Is How Democracies Die?" *The Guardian*, January 21.

Lewis, Matt. 2015. "The Trump Gamble: Why Desperate People Make Dangerous Voters." *The Daily Caller*, June 19.

Lichtman, Allan J. 2017. *The Case for Impeachment*. New York: Dey St. Books.

Limbaugh, Rush. 2017. "Trump Must Not Play the Swamp's Game." June 16.

Lippman, Daniel, Wesley Morgan, Meredith McGraw, and Nahal Toosi. 2019. "How Trump Decided to Kill Iran's Soleimani." *Politico*, January 3.

Lipson, Charles. 2019. "What Pelosi Really Wants from Impeachment." *Real Clear Politics*, October 15.

Liptak, Adam. 2018. "Supreme Court to Consider Challenge to Trump's Latest Travel Ban." *New York Times*, January 19.

Liptak, Adam and Michael D. Shear. 2018. "Trump's Travel Ban Is Upheld by Supreme Court." *New York Times*, June 26.

Liptak, Kevin. 2017a. "Trump: 'Nobody Knew Health Care Could Be So Complicated'." *CNN*, February 28.

Liptak, Kevin. 2017b. "Trump Agrees 'Not to Terminate NAFTA at This Time'." *CNN*, April 26.

Liptak, Kevin, Zachary Cohen and Nicole Gaouuette. 2020. "Coronavirus Will Test the Trump Administration's Ability to Handle a Crisis." *CNN*, January 28.

504 REFERENCES

Lissner, Rebecca Friedman. 2017. "There Is No Trump Doctrine, and There Will Never Be One." *Foreign Policy*, July 21.

Lizza, Ryan. 2007. "Above the Fray." *GQ*, September.

Long, Heather and Jeff Stein. 2019. "The U.S. Deficit Hit $984 Billion in 2019, Soaring During Trump Era." *Washington Post*, October 25.

Lopez, German. 2020. "Trump Is Still Reportedly Pushing His Racist "Birther" Conspiracy Theory About Obama." *Vox*, November 29.

Lovelace, Berkeley Jr. 2019. "Trump Administration Is Drafting Plan to Allow US Consumers to Import Drugs from Canada." *Reuters*, July 30.

Lowi, Theodore. 1984. *The Personal Presidency: Power Invested, Promise Unfulfilled*. New York: Cornell University Press.

Lowry, Rich. 2018. "The Tawdry and Dumb Nazi Charge." *Politico*, June 27.

Lowry, Rich. 2019a. "There Are No Trump Mysteries." *Politico Magazine*, May 8.

Lowry, Rich. 2019b. "Trump Better Hope Voters Don't Tire of All the Drama." *New York Post*, August 22.

Lowry, Rich. 2017. "The Out That Trump Never Permits Himself." *National Review*, October 20.

Lowry, Wesley and Josh Dawsey. 2018. "Early Chaos of Trump's Travel Ban Set Stage for a Year of Immigration Policy Debates." *Washington Post*, February 6.

Lozada, Carlos. 2016. "A Biographer Sums Up Donald Trump in a Single, Devastating 210-Word Sentence," *Washington Post*, June 8.

Lu, Denise and Karen Yourish. 2019. "The Turnover at the Top of the Trump Administration." *New York Times*, September 5.

Lucey, Catherine. 2019. "Behind Trump's Syria Pullout Lies a Campaign Pledge." *Wall Street Journal*, October 8.

Lucey, Catherine and Andrew Restuccia. 2020. "Trump Denounces Impeachment, Saying He 'Went Through Hell'." *Wall Street Journal*, February 6.

Luhby, Tami. 2018. "Trump Officials Roll Out New Rule for Small Business Health Insurance Plans." *CNN*, June 19.

Lunbeck, Elizabeth. 2014. *The Americanization of Narcissism*. Cambridge, MA: Harvard University Press.

Lunbeck, Elizabeth. 2017. "The Allure of Trump's Narcissism." *Los Angeles Review of Books*, August 1.

Luttwak, Edward N. 1999. "Give War a Chance." *Foreign Affairs*, July/August, 78, 4.

Lyons, Gene. 2019. "Trump Displays Textbook 'Malignant Narcissism.' What's to Be Done?" *Chicago Sun Times*, August 29.

MacWilliams, Matthew. 2016a. *The Rise of Trump: America's Authoritarian Spring*. Amherst, MA: Amherst University Press.

MacWilliams, Matthew. 2016b. "The One Weird Trait That Predicts Whether You're a Trump Supporter." *Politico*, January 17.

Mahler, Jonathan. 2016. "In Campaign and Company, Ivanka Trump Has a Central Role." *New York Times*, April 16.

Mai-Duc, Christine. 2017. "Rep. Brad Sherman Introduces Articles of Impeachment Against Trump." *Los Angeles Times*, July 2.

Mansfield, Harvey. 2017. "The Vulgar Manliness of Donald Trump." *Commentary*, August 14.

Marcos, Cristina. 2017. "House Dems Push to Censure Trump Over Charlottesville Response." *The Hill*, August 16.

Marcus, Ruth. 2018. "If You Work for Trump, Quit Now." *Washington Post*, July 16.

Marcuse, Herbert. 1964. *One-dimensional Man: Studies in the Ideology of Advanced Industrial Society*. Boston: Beacon Press.

Markay, Lachian, Bruce Ackerman, and Erin Banco. 2018. "We See Ourselves as Rebels, Trump's Internal Resistance." *Daily Beast*, September 6.

Markon, Jerry. 2015. "Trump Says Building a U.S.-Mexico Wall Is 'Easy.' But Is It Really?" *Washington Post*, July 17.

Martin, Jonathan. 2016. "Donald Trump Was Essentially a Third-Party Candidate on a G.O.P. Ticket." *New York Times*, November 9.

Martin, Jonathan and Alexander Burns. 2017. "Weakened Democrats Bow to Voters, Opting for Total War on Trump." *New York Times*, February 23.

Martin, Jonathan, Alexander Burns, and Maggie Haberman. 2018. "Trump's Role in Midterm Elections Roils Republicans." *New York Times*, April 28.

Martin, Jonathan and Mark Lander. 2017. "Bob Corker Says Trump's Recklessness Threatens World War III." *New York Times*, October 8.

Martin, Jonathan, Sheryl Gay Stolberg, and Alexander Burns. 2018. "Trump Policy Gyrations Threaten Fragile Republican Coalition." *New York Times*, December 21.

Martin, Timothy W. 2019. "In Talks with North Korea, U.S. Faces New Chessboard." *Wall Street Journal*, September 10.

Mashal, Mujib. 2020. "Taliban and U.S. Strike Deal to Withdraw American Troops from Afghanistan." *New York Times*, February 29.

Mason, Jame and James Oliphant. 2018. "White House Shakeup Shows Trump Tired of Hearing 'no' for an Answer." *Reuters*, March 13.

McArdle, Megan. 2019. "When Will Trump Supporters Finally Say, 'Okay, This Is Not Normal'?" *Washington Post*, August 23.

McCain, John with Mark Salter. 2018. *The Restless Wave: Good Times, Just Causes, Great Fights, and Other Appreciations*. New York; Simon & Shuster.

McCammond, Alexi and Jonathan Swan. 2019. "Scoop: Insider Leaks Trump's "Executive Time"-Filled Private Schedules." *Axios*, February 3.

506 REFERENCES

McCarthy, Justin. 2014. "Americans Losing Confidence in All Branches of U.S. Gov't.' *Gallup*, June 30.

McCarthy, Justin. 2019. "Trump Approval Inches Up, While Support for Impeachment Dips." *Gallup*, December 18.

McCausland, Phil. 2017. "Democratic Bill Lays the Groundwork to Remove Trump from Office." *NBC News*, July 3.

McCormack, John. 2016. "Unfit to Serve." *The Weekly Standard*, May 16.

Mcdonald, Leah and James Gordon. 2019. "Barbra Streisand Shares a Gruesome Cartoon of Nancy Pelosi Impaling and Killing Trump with a Giant Heel." *Daily Mail*, October 20.

McElwee, Susan and Jason McDaniel. 2016. "There's Powerful Evidence That Racial Attitudes Drive Tea Party Support." *Vox*, February 10.

McGregor, Jenna. 2019. "Unlike Trump, Most CEOs Have Very Little 'Executive Time'." *Washington Post*, February 6.

McNeil, Stephanie. 2017. "Trump Supporters Love Everything He's Doing, But Some Think He Could Cool It on the Tweets." *Buzz Feed*, July 25.

McWhorter, John. 2018. "The Unmonitored President." *The Atlantic*, July 20.

McWhorter, John. 2019. "Trump's Typos Reveal His Lack of Fitness for the Presidency." *The Atlantic*, January 11.

Mead, Russell Walter, Damir Marusic, and Andrew Bernard. 2017 "What the Syria Strikes Mean." *The National Interest*, March 7.

Mele, Christopher and Annie Correal. 2016. "Not Our President: Protests Spread After Donald Trump's Election." *New York Times*, November 9.

Mele, Christopher and Kirk Semple. 2019. "Trump Says He Will Delay Terrorist Designation for Mexican Cartels." *New York Times*, December 6.

Miler, Zeke. 2017. "Trump Pays Holiday Visit to Wounded Troops at Walter Reed." *Associated Press*, December 21.

Milkis, Sidney M. and Nicholas Jacobs, "'I Alone Can Fix It' Donald Trump, the Administrative Presidency, and Hazards of Executive-Centered Partisanship." *The Forum*, November 11.

Miller, Greg, Ellen Nakashima, and Shane Harris. 2019. "Trump's Communications with Foreign Leader Are Part of Whistleblower Complaint That Spurred Standoff Between Spy Chief and Congress, Former Officials Say." *Washington Post*, September 18.

Miller, Jonathan and Steve Elder. 2016. "No Vacancies' for Blacks: How Donald Trump Got His Start, and Was First Accused of Bias." *New York Times*, August 27.

Miller, Sean J. 2010. "Survey: Four in 10 Tea Party members Aare Democrats or Independents." *The Hill*, April 4.

Miller, Zeke. J. 2017. "Read Donald Trump's Interview With TIME on Being President." *Time*, May 11.

Miroff, Nick and Adrian Blanco. 2020. "Trump Ramps Up Border-Wall Construction Ahead of 2020 Vote." *Washington Post*, February 6.

Miroff, Nick, Kevin Sieff, and John Wagner. 2019. "How Mexico Talked Trump Out of Tariff Threat with Immigration Crackdown Pact." *Washington Post*, June 10.

Mishara, Aaron L., Joel Paris, Joesph M. Pierre, Ronald W. Pies, Harold A. Pincus, Douglas Porter, Clair Pouncey, Michael A. Schwaetz, Thomas Szasz, Jerome C. Wakefield, G. Scott Waterman, Owen Whooley, and Peter Zachar. 2012. "The Six Most Essential Questions in Psychiatric Diagnosis: A Pluralogue Part 1: Conceptual and Definitional Issues in Psychiatric Diagnosis." *Philosophy, Ethics, and Humanities in Medicine*, Vol. 7, No. 1, p. 3.

Moe, Alex. 2019. "House Investigations of Trump and His Administration: The Full List." *NBC*, May 27.

Montes, Juan. 2019. "In Mexico's South, Police Check Buses, Trains in Migrant Crackdown." *Wall Street Journal*, June 10.

Montoya-Galvez, Camilo. 2019. "Remain Home:" Trump Officials Say Policies Responsible for Sharp Drop in Border Apprehensions." *CBS News*, September 9.

Moore, Elaina. 2019. "Timeline: How The U.S. Came to Strike and Kill a Top Iranian General." *NPR*, January 4.

Moore, Michael. 2016. "Trump Is Self-Sabotaging His Campaign Because He Never Really Wanted the Job in the First Place." *Huffington Post*, August 17.

Morgan, Wesley. 2019. "'POTUS Went Rogue': Trump's Syria Move Blindsides National Security Leaders." *Politico*, October 7.

Morgenthau, Hans J. 1948. *Politics Among Nations*. New York: McGraw-Hill.

Morris, Alex. 2017. "Trump's Mental Health: Is Pathological Narcissism the Key to Trump's Behavior?" *Rolling Stone*, April 5.

Morrissey, Edward. 2017. "America Gets Its First Real Test of the CEO Presidency." *The Fiscal Times*, February 16.

Mosconi, Angela. 1999. "Trump Patriarch Eulogized as Great Builder." *New York Post*, June 30.

Moser, Fredrick C. 1988. *The President Needs Help*. Lanham, MD: University Press of America.

Mounk, Yascha. 2018a. *The People vs. Democracy: Why Our Freedom Is in Danger and How to Save It*. Cambridge, MA: Harvard University Press.

Mounk, Yascha. 2018b. "Why Isn't Trump President for Life Yet?" *Slate*, March 18.

Moyer, Justin. 2016. "Trump's Grammar in Speeches 'Just Below 6th Grade Level,' Study Finds." *Washington Post*, March 18.

Moylan, Drian. 2016. "The Jerry Springer Show Turns 25: The 10 Most Outrageous Moments." *The Guardian*, September 29.

Mui, Yian Q. 2017. "President Trump Signs Order to Withdraw from Trans-Pacific Partnership." *Washington Post*, January 23.

Murdock, Delroy. 2017. "This Thanksgiving, Thank Donald J. Trump." *National Review*, November 23.

Mutz, Diana C. 2018, "Status Threat, Not Economic Hardship, Explains the 2016 Presidential Vote." *PNAS*, Vol. 115, No. 19 (April), pp. 330–339.

Myers, William. 1988. "Stalking the Plaza." *New York Times*, September 25.

Nakamura, David. 2016. "Trump Boasts That He's 'Like, Really Smart' and a 'Very Stable Genius' Amid Questions Over His Mental Fitness." *Washington Post*, January 6.

Nakamura, David and Josh Dawsey. 2020. "Amid Confusion and Contradictions, Trump White House Stumbles in Initial Public Response to Soleimani's Killing." *Washington Post*, January 7.

Nasr, Reem. 2015. "Donald Trump Announces Candidacy for President." *CNBC*, June 16.

"National Survey of Tea Party Supporters." 2010. *New York Times/CBS Poll*, April 5–12.

Nelson, Barbara. 2004. "Trump's Right Hand a Star in Own Right." *Real Estate Weekly*, August 4.

Nelson, Michael. 2018. *Trump's First Year*. Charlottesville, VA: University of Virginia Press.

Nelson, Michael. 2019. *Trump: The First Two Years*. Charlottesville, VA: University of Virginia Press.

Nesbit, Jeff. 2016. "Donald Trump Is Failing His Crash Course in Leadership." *Time*, November 28.

Neustadt, Richard. 1990. *Presidential Power and the Modern Presidents: The Politics of Leadership From Roosevelt to Reagan*. New York: Free Press.

New York Times. 2016. "Donald Trump's New York Times Interview: Full Transcript." *New York Times*, November 23.

New York Times. 2017a. "Partial Transcript: Trump's Interview with the Times." April 5.

New York Times. 2017b. "Excerpts from Trump's Interview with the Times." December 28.

Nguyen, Tina. 2016. "5 Signs Donald Trump Is Having a Full-Blown Identity Crisis." *Vanity Fair*, April 22.

Nicholas, Nassim. 2017. *The Black Swan: The Impact of the Highly Improbable*. New York: Random House.

Nicholas, Peter. 2017. "Trump's 'America First' Policy Proves to Be an Immovable Object at G-20." *Wall Street Journal*, July 9.

Nicholas, Peter and Michael C. Bender. 2017. "Trump Names Homeland Security Secretary John Kelly as New Chief of Staff." *Wall Street Journal*, July 28.

REFERENCES   509

Nicholas, Peter, Gordon Lubold, and Dion Nissenbaum. 2018. "For Trump, a Hectic Week of Planning to Organize Syria Strike." *Wall Street Journal*, April 13.

Nicholas, Peter, Michael C. Bender, and Rebecca Ballhaus. 2018. "Trump Relishes Off-Script Approach." *Wall Street Journal*, March 23.

Nicholas, Peter. 2019. "Trump Needs Conspiracy Theories." *The Atlantic*, November 29.

Nicholas, Peter, Rebecca Ballhaus, and Siobhan Hughes. 2017. "Frustration with Republicans Drove Donald Trump to Deal with Democrats." *Wall Street Journal*, September 15.

Nissenbaum, Dion and Maria Abi-Habib. 2017. "Trump Gives Generals More Freedom on ISIS Fight." *Washington Post*, April 14.

Nixon, Ron. 2017. "Trump Administration Punishes Countries That Refuse to Take Back Deported Citizens." *New York Times*, September 13.

Nixon, Ron. 2018. "Travel Ban Caught Homeland Security by Surprise, Report Concludes." *New York Times*, January 19.

Noonan, Peggy. 2017. "President Trump Declares Independence." *Wall Street Journal*, January 20.

Norman, Jim. 2016. "Americans' Confidence in Institutions Stays Low." *Gallup*, June 1–5.

Norman, Jim. 2017. "Trump Victory Surprises Americans; Four in 10 Afraid." *Gallup*, November 11.

Norman, Laurance and Michael R. Gordon. 2019. "European Leaders Join U.S. in Blaming Iran for Saudi Oil Attacks, Urge New Deal." *Wall Street Journal*, September 24.

Norrholm, Seth D. 2016. "Diagnosing the Trump phenomenon." *USA Today*, March 23, November 24.

O'Brien, Timothy L. 2015. *Trump Nation: The Art of Being the Donald*. New York: Grand Central Publishing,

O'Brien, Timothy L. 2016. "How Trump Bungled the Deal of a Lifetime." *Bloomberg*, January 27.

O'Brien, Timothy L. 2017. "Defining 'Presidential' Downward." *Bloomberg*, July 20.

O'Connell, Jonathan. 2016. "How Is Trump Spending Thanksgiving? He Says He's Trying to Save an Indiana Factory." *Washington Post*, November 24.

O'Connell, Jonathan. 2017. "Wine Bar Owners sue President Trump, Saying D.C. Hotel Unfairly Takes Away Business." *Washington Post*, March 9.

O'Reilly Factor. 2017. "Exclusive Interview with President Trump, Part 3." *Fox News*, March 20.

O'Reilly, Andrew. 2019. "USDA Staffers Quit en masse as Trump Administration Eyes Moving Offices Out of DC." *Fox*, May 23.

510 REFERENCES

Obama, Barack. 2016. "Press Conference by the President." James S. Brady Briefing Room, November 14.

Office of the Inspector General. 2019. "Report of Investigation of Former Federal Bureau of Investigation Director James Comey's Disclosure of Sensitive Investigative Information and Handling of Certain Memoranda." U.S. Department of Justice, August.

Office of the White House. 2011. "'The President's Speech" at the White House Correspondents' Dinner," May 1; see also https://www.youtube.com/watch?v=k8TwRmX6zs4&feature=youtu.be&t=2m51s.

Office of the White House. 2017. "Presidential Executive Order on Reducing Regulation and Controlling Regulatory Costs." January 30.

Office of the White House. 2019. "Executive Order on Promoting the Rule of Law Through Transparency and Fairness in Civil Administrative Enforcement and Adjudication." October 9.

Ohehir, Andrew. 2019. "Had Enough Debate About Donald Trump? Me Too. He's a Tyrant and a Killer: He Must Be Stopped." *Salon*, July 8.

Olorunnipa, Toluse and Josh Dawsay. 2019. "'What I Said Was Accurate!': Trump Stays Fixated on His Alabama Error as Hurricane Pounds the Carolinas." *Washington Post*, September 5.

Olorunnipa, Toluse, Josh Dawsey, and Yasmeen Abutaleb. 2020. "Pence Seizes Control of Coronavirus Response Amid Criticism of His Qualifications." *Washington Post*, February 27.

Olorunnipa, Toluse, Robert Costa, and Anne Gearan. 2020. "Trump Plunges Toward the Kind of Middle Eastern Conflict He Pledged to Avoid." *Washington Post*, January 4.

Olsen, Henry. 2018. "Blue Wave, Red Tide, or Something in Between?" *American Greatness*, October 16.

Olsen, Matthew and Benjamin Haas. 2017. "The Electoral College Is a National Security Threat." *Politico*, September 20.

Oprysko, Caitlin. 2020. "It Was All Bulls—': Liberated Trump Lets Loose in Victory Speech After Acquittal." *Politico*, February 6.

Ornstein, Norm. 2020. "Why America's Political Divisions Will Only Get Worse." *New York Times*, January 28.

Orsi, Peter. 2020. "Mexican Guardsmen Break Up Migrant Caravan Along Highway." *Associated Press*, January 23.

Osnos, Evan. 2016. "The Gathering Storm of Protest Against Trump." *New Yorker*, November 17.

Pach, Chester. 2006. "The Reagan Doctrine: Principle, Pragmatism, and Policy." *Presidential Studies Quarterly*, March 75–88.

Painter, Richard W. 2016. "It Is Possible for Trump to Be a Good President." *New York Times*, November 9.

Painter, Richard W. and Norman L. Eisen. 2017. "Who Hasn't Trump Banned? People from Places Where He's Done Business." *New York Times*, January 29.

Palmer, Anna and Jake Sherman. 2019. "POLITICO Playbook: Trump: 'I Have Second Thoughts About Everything'." *Politico*, August 25.

Panning, Jennifer Contarino. 2017. "Trump Anxiety Disorder." In *The Dangerous Case of Donald Trump: 27 Psychiatrists and Mental Health Experts Assess a President*, edited by Bandy Lee. New York: St. Martin's Press, pp. 235–243.

Parker, Ashley and John Wagner. 2017. "Kushner Has a Singular and Almost Untouchable Role in Trump's White House." *Washington Post*, April 3.

Parker, Ashley and Robert Costa. 2019. "The Narrator in Chief: Trump Opines on the 2020 Democrats—and So Much More." *Washington Post*, May 20.

Parker Ashley, David Nakamura, and Dan Lamothe. 2017. "'Horrible' Pictures of Suffering Moved Trump to Action on Syria." *Washington Post*, April 7.

Parker, Ashley, David Nakamura, and Dan Lamothe. 2019. "'Horrible' Pictures of Suffering Moved Trump to Action on Syria." *Washington Post*, April 7.

Parker, Ashley, Ellen Nakashima, Devlin Barrett, and Carol D. Leonnig. 2019. "Potentially Damaging Information in Mueller Report Ushers in New Political Fight." *Washington Post*, April 4.

Parker, Ashley, Philip Rucker, and Josh Dawsey. 2018. "'Not in a Punch-Back Mode': Why Trump Has Been Largely Silent on Stormy Daniels." *Washington Post*, March 26.

Parker, Ashley, Phillip Rucker, John Hudson, and Carol D. Leonnie. 2018. "Trump Ousts Tillerson, Will Replace Him as Secretary of State with CIA Chief Pompeo." *Washington Post*, March 13.

Parker, Kathleen. 2016. "Donald Trump: A Con Man Among Heroes." *Washington Post*, September 16.

Parker, Kathleen. 2017. "How Can You Still Doubt Trump's Intelligence?" *Washington Post*, June 23.

Parker, Kathleen. 2019. "Donald Trump's Rhetorical Race War." *Washington Post*, July 31.

Patterson, Thomas E. 2017. "News Coverage of Donald Trump's First 100 Days." John F. Kennedy School of Government, September 2017.

Paulson, Michael. 2016. "For a Young Donald J. Trump, Broadway Held Sway." *New York Times*, March 6.

Pear, Robert and Reed Abelson. 2017. "Foiled in Congress, Trump Moves on His Own to Undermine Obamacare." *New York Times*, October 11.

Peters, Jeremy W. 2009. "The 'Never Trump' Coalition That Decided Eh, Never Mind, He's Fine." *New York Times*, October 5.

Peters, Jeremy W. 2018. "Trump's New Judicial Litmus Test: Shrinking 'The Administrative State'." *New York Times*, March 26.

512 REFERENCES

Peterson, Barbara. 2015. "Noise Dive: The Crash of Trump Air." *Daily Beast*, October 14.

Peterson, Kristina, Michelle Hackman, and Siobhan Hughes. 2017. "Skinny' Repeal of Obamacare Fails in Senate." *Wall Street Journal*, July 28.

Pettigrew, Thomas F. 2017. "Social Psychological Perspectives on Trump Supporters." *Journal of Social and Political Psychology*, Vol. 5, No. 1, pp. 107–116.

Pew Issue Brief. 2002. "Inaccurate, Costly, and Inefficient." *The Pew Center for the States*, February.

Pew Research Center. 2017. "Public Trust in Government: 1958–2017," May 3.

Pew Research Center. 2019a. "Trust in Government: 1958–2019."

Pew Research Center. 2019b. "Trump's Staunch GOP Supporters Have Roots in the Tea Party." May.

Phillips, James, Allen Frances, Michael A. Cerullo, John Chardavoyne, Hannah S. Decker, Michael B. First, Nassir Ghaemi, Gary Greenberg, Andrew C. Hinderlighter, Warren A. Kinghorn, Stephen G. LoBello, Elliot B. Martin, Aaron L. Mishara, Joel Paris, Joesph M. Pierre, Ronald W. Pies, Harold A. Pincus, Douglas Porter, Clair Pouncey, Michael A. Schwartz, Thomas Szasz, Jerome C. Wakefield, G. Scott Waterman, Owen Whooley, and Peter Zacher. 2012. "The Six Most Essential Questions in Psychiatric Diagnosis: A Pluralogue Part 2: Issues of Conservatism and Pragmatism in Psychiatric Diagnosis." *Philosophy, Ethics, and Humanities in Medicine : PEHM*, 7, 8.

Pierce, Sarah. 2019. "Immigration-Related Policy Related Changes in the First Two Years of the Trump Administration." Migration Policy Institute, May.

Plaskin, Glenn. 1988. "Trump: 'The People's Billionaire'." *Chicago Tribune*, March 12.

Plaskin, Glenn. 1990. "The 1990 Playboy Interview with Donald Trump." *Playboy*, March 1.

Plott, Elaina. 2019. 'We're All Tired of Being Called Racists'." *The Atlantic*, August 2.

Plumer, Brad. A.J. Chavar, and Susan Joan Archer. 2017. " U.S. to Leave Paris Climate Accord. What Happens Now?" *New York Times*, June 1.

Politico Staff. 2016. "Donald Trump 2016 RNC Draft Speech Transcript." *Politico*, July 21.

Ponnuru, Ramesh. 2106. "How Clinton Can Demolish Trump." *Bloomberg*, May 26.

Porter, Tom. 2019. "MSNBC's O'Donnell Said He 'shouldn't Have Reported' His On-Air Claim That Trump Has Loans with Deutsche Bank Backed by 'Russian Billionaires Close to Vladimir Putin'." *Business Insider*, August 28.

Poulos, James. 2015. "Why Americans Secretly Love a Gladiatorial Blowhard Like Donald Trump." *The Week*, June 19.

REFERENCES   513

Pramuk, Joe. 2017. "Trump: Maybe 'Fire And Fury' Statement on North Korea Wasn't Tough Enough." *ABC News*, August 10.

Press Briefing. 2018. "Press Briefing by Press Secretary Sarah Sanders and Dr. Ronny Jackson." The White House, January 16.

Press Briefing. 2019. "Press Briefing by Acting CBP Commissioner Mark Morgan." The White House, November 14.

Press Conference. 2017. "NATO Secretary General Jens Stoltenberg Ahead of the Meeting of NATO Defence Ministers." June 28.

Prewitt, Scott. 2018. "Scott Pruitt's Resignation Letter." *Washington Post*, July 5.

PRRI Staff. 2019. "Fractured Nation: Widening Partisan Polarization and Key Issues in 2020 Presidential Elections." PRRI, October 20.

Pruden, Wesley. 2017. "Trumpspeak, a Language Rich in Adjectives." *Washington Times*, February 23.

Przybyla, Heidi and Anna Schecter. 2019. "Donald Trump's Longtime Business Connections in Turkey Back in the Spotlight." *NBC News*, October 9.

Public Policy Polling. 2017. "Americans Think Trump Will Be Worst President Since Nixon." January 26.

Publius Decius Mus [Michael Anton]. 2016. "The Flight 93 Election." *Claremont Review of Books*, September 5.

Qiu, Linda. 2017. "10 Falsehoods from Trump's Interview with the Times." *New York Times*, December 29.

Radelat, Ana. 2019. "Courtney Foils Trump's Red, White, Blue Air Force One Plan." *The CT Mirror*, June 12.

Radnofsky, Louise. 2017. "Trump Signs Sweeping Tax Overhaul into Law." *Wall Street Journal*, December 22.

Rampell, Catherine. 2016. "Why the White Working Class Votes Against Itself." *Washington Post*, December 22.

Rappaport, David. 2016. "I Feel a Deep Sense of Remorse, Donald Trump's Ghostwriter Says." *New York Times*, July 18.

Rappeport, Alan, Jeanna Smialek, and Nelson D. Schwartz. 2019. "Trump Plans More Tariffs for China. You'll Feel This Round." *New York Times*, August 2.

Rappeport, Alan. 2015. "Bush Listed Himself as "Hispanic" on Voter Form." *New York Times*, April 6.

Rappeport, Alan. 2016. "I Feel a Deep Sense of Remorse Donald Trump's Ghostwriter Says." *New York Times*, July 18.

Reelin' in the Years Production. 1980. "Trump Interview with Rona Barrett." October 6.

Reiley, Steve. 2016a. "Donald Trump: Three Decades." *USA Today*, June 9.

Reiley, Steve. 2016b. "USA TODAY Exclusive: Hundreds Allege Donald Trump Doesn't Pay His Bills." *USA Today*, June 9.

514 REFERENCES

Reilly, Katie. 2017. "Here Are President Trump's 3 Biggest Setbacks in His First 100 Days." *Time*, April 25.

Rein, Lisa and Andrew Tran. 2017. "How the Trump Era is Changing the Federal Bureaucracy." *Washington Post*, December 30.

Reinhard, Beth. 2019. "Alva Johnson, Former Campaign Staffer, Drops Lawsuit Accusing Trump of Kissing Her Without Her Consent." *Washington Post*, September 5.

Reiss, David M. MD. 2017. "Cognitive Impairment. Dementia, and Potus." In The *Dangerous Case of Donald Trump: 27 Psychiatrists and Mental Health Experts Assess a President*, edited by Bandy Lee. New York: St. Martin's Press, pp. 126–135.

Renshon, Jonathan, Allan Dafoe, and Paul Huth. 2018. "Leader Influence and Reputation Formation in World Politics." *American Journal of Political Science*, Vol. 62, No. 2, pp. 325–339.

Renshon, Stanley. 1996a [1998]. *High Hopes: The Clinton Presidency and the Politics of Ambition*. New York: New York University Press [Routledge Press].

Renshon, Stanley. 1996b [1998]. *The Psychological Assessment of Presidential Candidates*. New York: New York University Press [Routedge Press].

Renshon, Stanley A. 2004. *In his Father's Shadow: The Transformations of George W. Bush*. New York: Palgrave Macmillan.

Renshon, Stanley A. 2010. *National Security in the Obama Administration: Reassessing the Bush Doctrine*. New York: Routledge Press.

Renshon, Stanley A. 2011. *Barack Obama and the Politics of Redemption*. New York: Routledge.

Renshon, Stanley A. 2012. "Foreign Policy Legacies of American Presidents." In *Oxford Encyclopedia of American Military and Diplomatic History*, edited by Timothy J. Lynch. Cambridge and New York: Oxford University Press.

Renshon, Stanley A. 2013. "Understanding the Obama Doctrine." *White House Studies*, Vol. 12, No. 13, pp. 187–202.

Renshon, Stanley A. 2017. "Doing Well vs. Being Great: Comparing the Bush and Obama Doctrines." In *Volume I: The Constitution, Politics, and Policy Making in the George W. Bush Presidency*, edited by Meenekshi Bose. Washington, DC: Nova Press, pp. 101–118.

Renshon, Stanley A. 2020. "The Trump Doctrine and Conservative American Nationalism." In *The Trump Doctrine and the Emerging International System*, edited by Stanley A. Renshon and Peter Suedfeld. New York: Palgrave Macmillan.

Renshon, Stanley A. and Peter Suedfeld (eds.). 2007. *Understanding the Bush Doctrine: Psychology and Strategy in an Age of Terrorism*. New York: Routledge.

Reny, Tyler T., Loren Collingwood, and Ali Valenzuela. 2019. "Vote Switching in the 2016 Election: How Racial and Immigration Attitudes, Not

Economics, Explain Shifts in White Voting." *Public Opinion Quarterly*, Vol. 83, No. 1 (Spring), pp. 91–113.

Res, Barbara A. 2013. *All Alone on the 68th Floor: How One Woman Changed the Face of Construction*. 2nd Edition. New York: CreateSpace Independent Publishing Platform.

Restuccia, Andrew. 2019. "Trump's 'No Rush' Foreign Policy." *Politico*, June 22.

Restuccia, Andrew. 2020. "Trump Doubles Down on Threats to Impose Tariffs on European Cars." *Wall Street Journal*, January 21.

Restuccia, Andrew, Marianne Levine, and Nahal Toosi. 2017. "Federal Workers Turn to Encryption to Thwart Trump." *Politico*, February 2.

Reuters. 2017. "Highlights of Reuters Interview with Trump." July 12.

Reynolds, Glenn. 2017. "New Status Anxiety Fuels Trump Derangement.' *USA Today*, January 5.

Richard, Greene. 2017. "Is Donald Trump Mentally Ill? 3 Professors of Psychiatry Ask President Obama to Conduct 'A Full Medical and Neuropsychiatric Evaluation'." *Huffington Post*, December 18.

Richman, Jesse and David Earnest. 2014. "Could Non-citizens Decide the November Election?" *Washington Post*, October 24.

Riechmann, Deb. 2020. "Trump Says in His Mother's Eyes, He 'Could Do No Wrong'." *Associated Press*, May 8.

Ripley, Amanda. 2019. "Americans Are at Each Other's Throats. Here's One Way Out." *Washington Post*, December 20.

Risen, James. 2018. "Is Donald Trump a Traitor?" *The Intercept*, February 2.

Roarty, Alex. 2018. "Internal Dem Polling Shows Trump's Standing on the Rise.' *McClatchy*, February 13.

Robb, Greg. 2019. "U.S. Adds 136,000 Jobs in September, Unemployment Rate Hits 50-Year Low." *Market Watch*, October 4.

Roberts, Roxanne. 2016. "I Sat Next to Donald Trump at the Infamous 2011 White House Correspondents' Dinner." *Washington Post*, April 28.

Robinson, Eugene. 2017. "Abandoning Puerto Rico Would Be an Impeachable Offense." *Washington Post*, October 12.

Robinson, Julian. 2017. "NATO Allies—Excluding the US—Will Increase Defence Spending by 4.3% in Victory for Donald Trump After He Warned Member States 'Must Finally Contribute Their Fair Share'." *Daily Mail*, June 29.

Robertson, Michelle. 2018. "Sen. Kamala Harris Ruffles Feathers with 'Trump Death Joke' on 'Ellen' Show." *San Francisco Gate*, April 5.

Robinson, Nathan J. 2016. "Why PolitiFact's "True/False" Percentages Are Meaningless." *Current Affairs*, August 8.

Robles, Frances. 2017. "Emergency Manager Resigns in Puerto Rico; Army Ends Its Mission." *New York Times*, November 10.

516 REFERENCES

Rogers, Ed. 2017. "The 'Deep State' Is Real. The 'Alt Right' Is Fake." *Washington Post*, February 21.

Rogers, Katie. 2018a. "Trump Moves to Regulate Bump Stock Devices." *New York Times*, November 28.

Rogers, Katie. 2018b. "Trump's Book Club: A President Who Doesn't Read Promotes the Books That Promote Him." *New York Times*, November 30.

Rogers, Katie. 2019. "The Painful Roots of Trump's 'Go Back' Comment." *New York Times*, July 16.

Rogers, Katie and Motoko Rich. 2019. "For Trump's Japan Trip, Abe Piles on the Flattery. But to What End?" *New York Times*, May 24.

Rogers, Katie and Robin Pogrebin. 2020. "Draft Executive Order Would Give Trump a New Target: Modern Design." *New York Times*, February 5.

Rogers, Katie, Adam Liptak, Michael Crowley, and Michael Wines. 2019. "Trump Says He Will Seek Citizenship Information from Existing Federal Records, Not the Census." *New York Times*, July 11.

Rogers, Katie and Maggie Haberman. 2018. "Reliable Allies Refuse to Defend a President Content With Chaos." *New York Times*, December 21.

Rogow, Arnold. 1970. *The Psychiatrists*. New York: Putnam.

Romeroaug, Simon. 2015. "Trump Hotel Goes Up, and His Latino Views Barely Raise Eyebrows." *New York Times*, August 30.

Ronningstam, Elsa F. 2005. *Identifying and Understanding the Narcissistic Personality*. New York: Oxford University Press.

Ross, Brian and Matthew Mosk. 2017. "Source of Key Trump Dossier Claims." *ABC News*, January 30.

Rothkopf, David. 2017. "The Greatest Threat Facing the United States Is Its Own President." *Washington Post*, July 4.

Roubein, Rachel. 2017. "TIMELINE: The GOP's Failed Effort to Repeal ObamaCare." *The Hill*, September 26.

Rove, Karl. 2018. "Trump Wastes Another Weekend." *Wall Street Journal*, February 21.

Rubin, Jennifer. 2016. "Trump Spews Crazy Talk—And He's Not Alone." *Washington Post*, October 14.

Rubin, Jennifer. 2017a. "Trump Is Failing Faster Than Any President." *Washington Post*, July 17.

Rubin, Jennifer. 2017b. "Every Republican Must Sign a Censure of the President." *Washington Post*, August 16.

Rucker, Philip and Ashley Parker. 2019. "Trump's Lost Summer: Aides Claim Victory, But Others See Incompetence and Intolerance." *Washington Post*, September 1.

Rucker, Philip and Carol Leonnig. 2020. "'You're a Bunch of Dopes and Babies': Inside Trump's Stunning Tirade Against Generals." *Washington Post*, January 17.

Rucker, Philip and Carol Leonnig. 2020b. *A Very Stable Genius: Donald J. Trump's Testing of America*. New York: Penguin Press.

Rucker, Phillip and Robert Costa. 2018. "John Kelly Intends to Remain as Trump's Chief of Staff Through 2020 Reelection Bid." *Washington Post*, July 31.

Rucker, Philip, Ashley Parker, and Josh Dawsey. 2018. "'Pure Madness': Dark Days Inside the White House as Trump Shocks and Rages." *Washington Post*, March 3.

Rucker, Phillip and Michael Scherer. 2017. "In Sparring with a Grieving Widow, Trump Follows His No-Apology Playbook." *Washington Post*, October 23.

Rucker, Phillip, Josh Dawsey, and Damian Paletta. 2018. "Trump Slams Fed Chair, Questions Climate Change and Threatens to Cancel Putin Meeting in Wide-Ranging Interview with the Post." *Washington Post*, November 27.

Ruttenberg, Jim. 2016. "Trump Is Testing the Norms of Objectivity in Journalism." *New York Times*, August 7.

Ryan, Missy, John Dawsey, Dan Lamothe, and John Hudson. 2019. "How Trump Decided to Kill a Top Iranian General." *Washington Post*, January 3.

Saad, Lydia. 2010. "Tea Partiers Are Fairly Mainstream in Their Demographics." *Gallup*, April 5.

Sacchetti, Maria and Isaac Stanley-Becker. 2018. "In Blow to Trump's Immigration Agenda, Federal Judge Blocks Asylum Ban for Migrants Who Enter Illegally from Mexico." *Washington Post*, November 20.

Salama, Vivian. 2019. "Trump Sends Regards to Departed 'Mr. Tough Guy' Bolton." *Wall Street Journal*, September 11.

Salama, Vivian and Nancy A. Youssef. 2018. "Trump's Order on Migrant Families Sends Administration Scrambling." *Wall Street Journal*, June 22.

Saletan, William. 2019. "Guess Who Else Trump Is Colluding With." *Slate*, October 8.

Salvanto, Anthony, Sarah Dutton, Jennifer De Pinto, Fred Backus, and Kabir Khanna. 2017. "Viewers Strongly Approve of Trump's Speech to Congress." *CBS News*, March 1.

Samuels, Brett. 2019. "Trump Seeks to Make Impeachment a Campaign Asset." *The Hill*, December 22.

Samuels, Brett. 2020. "Trump Confirms Plans to Expand Travel Ban." *The Hill*, January 21.

Samuelsohn, Darren and Josh Dawsey. 2016. "Trump Lays Out Limits of Business Involvement." *Politico*, December 16.

Samuelson, Robert J. 2019. "Why We Should Impeach and Remove President Trump." *Washington Post*, October 20.

Sanderg, Larry S. MD. 2018. "Interview with Bandy Lee." *Psychodynamic Psychiatry*, Vol. 46, No. 3, pp. 335–355.

518 REFERENCES

Sang-Hun, Choe and Jane Perlez. 2017. "At U.N. and in the Air, North Korea and U.S. Trade Tough Messages." *New York Times*, September 23.

Sanger, David E. and Eric Schmitt. 2019. "In 'Cave-In,' Trump Cease-Fire Cements Turkey's Gains in Syria." *New York Times*, October 17.

Sanger, David E. and Maggie Haberman. 2016a. "In Donald Trump's Worldview, America Comes First, and Everybody Else Pays." *New York Times*, March 26.

Sanger, David E. and Maggie Haberman. 2016b. "Transcript: Donald Trump Expounds on His Foreign Policy Views." *New York Times*, March 26.

Sanger, David E. and William J. Broad. 2017. "A Cuban Missile Crisis in Slow Motion in North Korea." *New York Times*, April 16.

Saraiya, Sonia. 2016. "TV Review: 'OBJECTified: Donald Trump' on Fox News, Hosted by Harvey Levin." *Variety*, November 18.

Sargent, Greg. 2016. "Republicans Nominate Dangerously Insane Person to Lead America, Then Panic When He Proves He's Dangerously Insane." *Washington Post*, August 16.

Sargent, Greg. 2018. "No, Trump Isn't Putting 'America First.' He's Putting Himself First." *Washington Post*, November 21.

Savage, Charles. 2017a. "Liberal Lawyers Plan Wave of Resistance to Trump Policies." *New York Times*, January 30.

Savage, Charles. 2017b. "Trump Is Rapidly Reshaping the Judiciary. Here's How." *New York Times*, November 11.

Savage, Charles. 2019. "Court Orders F.B.I. to Fix National Security Wiretaps After Damning Report." *New York Times*, December 17.

Savitsky, Shane. 2017. "What Trump Didn't Say." *Axios*, January 18.

Sawislak, Arnold. 1981. "Reagan Called 'amiable Dunce' on New Washington Tape." *UPI*, October 10.

Sawyer, Dianne. 2009. "Interview with Donald Trump." *NBC* (Good Morning America), December 2.

Sayet, Evan. 2017. "He Fights." *Townhall*, July 13.

Schafer, Jack. 2015. "Donald Trump Talks Like a Third-Grader." *Politico*, August 13.

Schaffer, Jack. 2018. "Drowning in News? Learn to Swim." *Politico*, March 12.

Schaffner, Brian F., Matthew MacWilliams, and Tatishe Nteta. 2018. "Understanding White Polarization in the 2016 Vote for President: The Sobering Role of Racism and Sexism." *Political Science Quarterly*, Vol. 133, No. 1, pp. 9–34.

Scherer, Michael and Zeke J. Miller. 2017. "TIME Exclusive: Donald Trump After Hours." *Time*, May 12.

Schier, Steven J. and Todd Eberly. 2017. *The Trump Presidency: Outsider in the Oval Office*. East Lanham, MD: Rowman & Littlefield.

Schilling, Dave. 2016. "OBJECTified: Donald Trump Review—A Basket of Objectionables." *The Guardian*, November 19.

Schlesinger, Jacob M. and Bob Davis. 2018. "U.S., Mexico and Canada Sign Pact to Replace Nafta." *Wall Street Journal*, November 30.

Schlessinger, Arthur M. Jr. 1973. *The Imperial Presidency*. New York: Houghton Mifflin.

Schmidt, Eric Maggie Haberman and Rukmino Callimachi. 2019. "Special Operations Raid Said to Kill Senior Terrorist Leader in Syria." *New York Times*, October 27.

Schmitt, Eric. 2017. "U.S. Commando Killed in Yemen in Trump's First Counterterrorism Operation." *New York Times*, January 29.

Schmitt, Eric. 2019. "U.S. Resumes Large-Scale Operations Against ISIS in Northern Syria." *New York Times*, November 25.

Schmitt, Eric and Helene Cooper. 2019. "Hundreds of U.S. Troops Leaving, and Also Arriving in, Syria." *New York Times*, October 30.

Schmitt, Eric, Helene Cooper, Thomas Gibbons-Neff, Maggie Haberman, and Peter Baker. 2019. "For Trump, a Risky Decision on Suleimani Is One Other Presidents Had Avoided." *New York Times*, January 3.

Schoenfeld, Gabriel. 2017. "What If Trump Loses His Mind?" *USA Today*, January 29.

Schoenfeld, Gabriel. 2019. "'F: Demagogue Fail,' Grading President Donald Trump in His Second Year." *USA Today*, January 18.

Schram, Stephanie and Joel Eastwood. 2018. "Trump's State of the Union: The 'Best Most Lowest Greatest' Words." *Wall Street Journal*, January 30.

Schuessler, Jennifer. 2017. "'Charge the Cockpit or You Die': Behind an Incendiary Case for Trump." *New York Times*, February 20.

Schuman, Howard, Charlotte Steeh, Lawrence Bobo, and Maria Krysan. 1997. *Racial Attitudes in America: Trends and Interpretations*. Cambridge, MA: Harvard University Press.

Schwartz, Ian. 2016. Hillary Confronted on "Super Predator" Term on Black Radio Show; Calls Trump "Dangerous," "Cancer." *Real Clear Politics*, April 18.

Schwartz, Ian. 2018. "CNN Focus Group of Trump Voters: "Exactly What I Voted For." *Real Clear Politics*, February 13.

Schwartz, Ian. 2019. "Trump: 'Thrive' on Impeachment, Very Few People Could Handle It." *Real Clear Politics*, October 7.

Schwartz, Tony. 2017. "I Wrote the Art of the Deal with Donald Trump." In *The Dangerous Case of Donald Trump: 27 Psychiatrists and Mental Health Experts Assess a President*, edited by Bandy Lee. New York: St. Martin's Press, pp. 69–74.

Schwartz, Tony. 2019. "Why Trump Can't Change, No Matter What the Consequences Are." *Washington Post*, October 18.

520 REFERENCES

Schwartz, Wynn. 2016. "Trump Requires an Admiring Mirror: The Politics of Malignant Narcissism." December 21. http://freedomliberationreaction.blo gspot.com/2016/12/trump-requires-admiring-mirror.html.

Schwartzman, Paul and Michael E. Miller. 2016. "Confident. Incorrigible. Bully: Little Donny Was a Lot Like Candidate Donald Trump." *Washington Post*, June 27.

Scott, Eric Kaufman. 2015. "'America Is a Hellhole, and We're Going Down Fast': Donald Trump and Megyn Kelly Have a Testy Exchange About State of the Nation," *Salon*, May 21.

Sediqi, Abdul Qadir and Alexander Corwall. 2020. "U.S.-Taliban Sign Historic Troop Withdrawal Deal in Doha." *Reuters*, February 29.

Seib, Gerald F. 2009. "Obama Will Be Hands-on Chief." *Wall Street Journal*, January 13.

Seib, Gerld F. 2017a. "Donald Trump Explains Why He Twists Businesses' Arms." *Wall Street Journal*, January 16.

Seib, Gerald. 2017b. "What Trump's Early Days Tell Us About His Path Forward." *Wall Street Journal*, April 27.

Sellers, Francis Stead. 2015. "Donald Trump, a Champion of Women? His Female Employees Think So." *Washington Post*, November 24.

Semple, Kirk. 2019. "Mexico Cracks Down on Migrants, After Pressure from Trump to Act." *New York Times*, June 3.

Sestanovich, Stephen. 2017. "The Brilliant Incoherence of Trump's Foreign Policy." *The Atlantic*, May.

Shabad, Rebecca. 2017. "Mitch McConnell Grumbles: Trump Had 'Excessive Expectations' for How Quickly Congress Can Act." *CBS News*, August 8.

Shakespeare, William. 1600 [2018]. *Romeo and Juliet*. CreateSpace Independent Publishing Platform, September 15.

Shalal, Andrea and David Lawder. 2020. As Trump Takes Aim at EU Trade, European Officials Brace for Fight." *Reuters*, February 11.

Shalal, Andrea and Davikd Brjunnstrom. 2019. "Et tu, Mitt? Trump Blasts Republican Senator as Impeachment Battle Heats Up." *Reuters*, October 5.

Shamoo, Adil E. and Bonnie Bricker. 2017. "It's Time to Take the Nazi-Trump Comparisons Seriously." *Foreign Policy in Focus*, August 23.

Sharman, Jon. 2017. "Donald Trump Says He Was Surprised Being US President Was Such a Big Job." *The Independent*, February 8.

Sharp, Zoë. 2018. "HOW IT ENDS." *New York Times*, October 23.

Shear, Michael D. 2016. "Obama's Last Days: Aiding Trump Transition, But Erecting Policy Roadblocks." *New York Times*, December 31.

Shear, Michael D. 2017. "Trump Will Withdraw U.S. from Paris Climate Agreement." *New York Times*, June 1.

Shear, Michael D. and Christopher Drew. 2016. "'Cancel Order!' Donald Trump Attacks Plans for Upgraded Air Force One." *New York Times*, December 6.

Shear, Michael D. and Nick Coransaniti. 2016. "Obama Says Republicans Should Withdraw Support for Trump." *New York Times*, August 2.

Shear Michael D. and Ron Nixon. 2017. "New Trump Deportation Rules Allow Far More Expulsions." *New York Times*, February 21.

Shear, Michael D. and Julie Hirschfeld. 2017. "Trump Moves to End DACA and Calls on Congress to Act." *New York Times*, September 5.

Shear, Michael D. and Katie Benner. 2019. "In New Effort to Deter Migrants, Barr Withholds Bail to Asylum Seekers." *New York Times*, April 16.

Shear Michael D and Maggie Haberman. 2019. "Mexico Agreed to Take Border Actions Months Before Trump Announced Tariff Deal." *New York Times*, June 8.

Shear, Michael D., Charlie Savage, and Maggie Haberman. 2017. "Trump Attacks Rosenstein in Latest Rebuke of Justice Department." *New York Times*, June 16.

Shear, Michael D., Eric Schmitt, Michael Crowley, and Maggie Haberman. 2019. "Strikes on Iran Approved by Trump, Then Abruptly Pulled Back." *New York Times*, June 20.

Shear, Michael D., Glenn Thrush, and Maggie Haberman. 2017. "John Kelly, Asserting Authority, Fires Anthony Scaramucci." *New York Times*, July 31.

Sheehy, Gail. 2017. "Trump's Trust Deficit Is the Core Problem." In *The Dangerous Case of Donald Trump: 27 Psychiatrists and Mental Health Experts Assess a President*, edited by Bandy Lee. New York: St. Martin's Press, pp. 75–82.

Shinkman, Paul D. 2019. "Trump Administration Appears to Reverse Syria Decision Following Backlash." US News & World Report, October 7.

Shlaes, Amity. 2019. *Great Society: A New History*. New York: Harper.

Shribman David M. 2017a. "Trump Mixes Up the Parties, Raises Questions." *Post-Gazette*, June 18.

Shribman, David. 2017b. "Trump's Response to Las Vegas Shooting Is Significant in His Presidential Passage." *Globe and Mail*, October 3.

Sides, John, Michael Tesler, and Lynn Vavreck. 2018. *Identity Crisis: The 2016 Election & the Battle for the Meaning of America*. Princeton, NJ: Princeton University Press.

Siegel, Frederick F. 2014. *The Revolt Against the Masses: How Liberalism Has Undermined the Middle Class*. Washington, DC: Encounter Books.

Simms, Cliff. 2019. *Team of Vipers: My 500 Extraordinary Days in the Trump White House*. New York: Thomas Dunne Books.

Simon Herbert. A. 1990. "Bounded Rationality." In *Utility and Probability*, edited by J. Eatwell, M. Milgate, P. Newman. London: Palgrave Macmillan.

Singer, Mark. 2016a. *Trump & Me*. New York: Penguin.

Singer, Mark. 2016b. "Trump, The Man and The Image." *New Yorker*, July 11–18.

522 REFERENCES

Singh, Robert S. 2012. *Barack Obama's Post-American Foreign Policy: The Limits of Engagement*. London: Bloomsbury.

Singman, Brooke. 2019. "Nadler Likens Trump to 'Dictator,' Threatens Barr with Contempt After Hearing Boycott." *Fox News*, May 2.

Skinner, Allison. 2017. "Trump Voters Were Scared: Increasing Diversity Might Make Americans More Xenophobic." *Salon*, January 10.

Skowronek, Stephen. 1977. The Politics That Presidents Make. In *Leadership from John Adams to Bill Clinton*. Revised Edition. Cambridge, MA: Belknap Press.

Slater, Wayne and James C. Moore. 2003. *Bush's Brain: How Karl Rove Made George W. Bush Presidential*. New York: Wiley.

Sly, Liz and Aaso Ameen Schwan. "ISIS Is Near Defeat in Iraq. Now Comes the Hard Part." *Washington Post*, September 13.

Smith, Adam C. 2015. "Jeb Bush: 'I'm a Joyful Tortoise' in Long, Acrimonious Race." *Tampa Bay Times*, July 27.

Smith, Ben. 2015. "I Asked a Psychoanalyst To Explain Donald Trump." *BuzzFeed*, December 3.

Smith, Jasmil. 2015. "Yes, Donald Trump Is a Fascist." *The New Republic*, November 29.

Smith, Sebastian. 2019. "Trump's Immigration Crackdown Starts to Gain Traction." *Yahoo*, September 12.

Smith, Ben and Byron Tau. 2011. "Birtherism: Where It All Began." *Politico*, April 22.

Snyder, Richard C., H. W Bruck, and Bert Sapin. 2002. "Decision-Making as an Approach to the Study of International Politics." In *Foreign Policy Decision-Making* (Revisited). New York: Palgrave Macmillan.

Solotaroff, Paul. 2015. "Trump Seriously: On the Trail with the GOP's Tough Guy." *Rolling Stone*, September 9.

Sparshott, Jeffrey. 2014. "Bergdahl Swap Violated Law, GAO Says." *Wall Street Journal*, August 21.

Specia, Megan. 2019. "Why Is Turkey Fighting the Kurds in Syria?" *New York Times*, October 9.

Sperry, Paul. 2020. "Impeachment's Fail Was No Proof of Trump 2020 Motive." *Real Clear Investigations*, February 10.

Stack, Liam. 2017. "Et Tu, Delta? Shakespeare in the Park Sponsors Withdraw From Trump-Like 'Julius Caesar'." *New York Times*, June 11.

Stack, Liam. 2016. "Donald Trump Featured Paula Jones and 2 Other Women Who Accused Bill Clinton of Sexual Assault." *New York Times*, October 9.

Stahl, Leslie. 2106. "President-Elect Trump Speaks to a Divided Country." *CBS News*, November 13.

REFERENCES 523

Stanley, Tim. 2016. "Introducing the Real Donald Trump: A Careful Plotter and Media Master Who Is Far More Intelligent Than He Seems." *The Telegraph*, July 18.

Stanley, Tim. 2018. "Donald Trump's Winning Streak Is Transforming America." *CNN*, July 5.

Stanley-Becker, Issac and Sean Sullivan. 2016. "Obama: Trump Is 'Unfit to Serve as President'." *Washington Post*, August 2.

Starr, Barbara, Kevin Bohn, and Ross Levitt. 2019. "US Strikes 5 Facilities in Iraq and Syria Linked to Iranian-Backed Militia." *CNN*, December 30.

Stein, Jeff. 2019. "FBI Makes Arrests in Puerto Rico Corruption Scandal, Prompting Calls for Governor's Ouster and Concerns About Billions in Storm Aid." *Washington Post*, July 10.

Stein, Jeff and Ellen Nakashima. 2020. "White House Hold on Ukraine Aid Violated Federal Law, Congressional Watchdog Says." *Washington Post*, January 16.

Steinhauer, Jennife. 2017. "With Few Wins in Congress, Republicans Agree on Need to Agree." *New York Times*, August 4.

Stephens, Brett. 2017. "The 'No Guardrails' Presidency." *New York Times*, July 28.

Stephens, Brett. 2015. "The Donald and the Demagogues." *Wall Street Journal*, August 31.

Stephenson, Emily. 2017. "Trump Says He Will Defer to Defense Secretary Mattis on Waterboarding." *Reuters*, January 27.

Stevens, Brett. 2018a. "A Courageous Trump Call on a Lousy Iran Deal." *New York Times*, May 8.

Stevens, Brett. 2018b. "Resign, Mike Pompeo. Resign, John Bolton." *New York Times*, July 19.

Stevenson, Alxandra. 2019. "Xi Jinping Urges Dialogue, Not Confrontation, After Trump Seeks Tariffs." *New York Times*, April 9.

Stewart, James B. 2019. *Deep State: Trump, the FBI, and the Rule of Law*. New York: Penguin Press,

Stokols, Eli. 2017. "Trump's Loyalists See Course Correction Amid the Tumult." *Wall Street Journal*, April 27.

Stolberg, Sheryl Gay. 2017. "Jeff Flake, a Fierce Trump Critic, Will Not Seek Re-Election for Senate." *New York Times*, October 27.

Stolberg, Sheryl Gay. 2019. "Pelosi Pushes for Simple Message on Impeachment as Inquiry Barrels Ahead." *New York Times*, September 29.

Stone, Michael MD. 1988. "Normal Narcissism: an Etiological and Ethnological Perspective." In *Disorders of Narcissism: Diagnostic, Clinical and Empirical Implications*, edited by Elsa F. Ronningstam. New York: American Psychiatric Publishing.

Stoynoff, Natasha. 2005. "Donald Trump Weds Melania Knauss." *People*, January 23.

Strange, Niall. 2018. "The Memo: Dems Grapple with Trump's Resilience." *The Hill*, July 24.

Strassel, Kimberly. 2017. "Scalias All the Way Down." *Wall Street Journal*, October 12.

Sullivan, Margaret. 2017. "Is Media Coverage of Trump Too Negative? You're Asking the Wrong Question." *Washington Post*, June 11.

Sullivan, Margaret. 2020. "We Have Entered the Trump Unbound Era and Journalists Need to Step It Up." *Washington Post*, February 23.

Sullivan, Peter. 2018. "Trump Unveils Most Aggressive Action to Target Drug Prices." *The Hill*, October 25.

Superville, Darlene. 2019. "Trump Travels to Dover to Pay Respect to Soldiers Killed in Afghanistan Helicopter Crash." *Associated Press*, November 21.

Supreme Court of the State of New York. 2018. "So Ordered Stipulation of Final Settlement." Index 451130/2018.

Suri, Jeremi. 2017. *The Impossible Presidency: The Rise and Fall of America's Highest Office*. New York: Basic Books.

Sutton, Kelsey. 2017. "Maryland Blogger Settles Defamation Lawsuit Brought By Melania Trump." *Politico*, February 7.

Swan, Jonathan. 2016. "Government Workers Shun Trump, Give Big Money to Clinton." *The Hill*, October 26.

Swan, Jonathan. 2018. "John Kelly Blew Up at Trump in Oval Office Meeting, Threatened to Quit." *Axios*, April 7.

Swan, Jonathan. 2019. "Trump Said CIA Director Gina Haspel Agreed with Him "100%" on Torture." *Axios*, November 17.

Swanson, Ana. 2018. "Trump to Impose Sweeping Steel and Aluminum Tariffs." *New York Times*, March 1.

Swanson, Ana. 2016. "Donald Trump Isn't Going to Like This New Report About His Campaign's Impact on His Businesses." *Washington Post*, October 16.

Swanson, Ana. 2019. "Trump Reaches Phase I Deal with China and Delays Planned Tariffs." *New York Times*, October 11.

Taibbi, Matt. 2016. "How America Made Donald Trump Unstoppable." *Rolling Stone*, February 24.

Talese, Gay. 1964. "Verrazano Bridge Opened to Traffic." *New York Times*, November 22.

Talley, Ian. 2017. "Donald Trump's Campaign-Vow Reversal on Yuan Bets on the Long Game with China." *Wall Street Journal*, April 12.

Tankersley, Jim. "Trump's Tariffs Keep Allies, Markets and Industry Guessing." *New York Times*, March 24.

Tankersley, Jim and Thomas Kaplan. 2017. "House Passes Budget Blueprint, Clearing Path for Tax Overhaul." *New York Times*, October 26.

Tansey, Michael J. 2017. "'Why "Crazy Like a Fox" Versus Crazy Like Crazy' Really Matters: Delusional Disorder, Admiration of Brutal Dictatorships, the Nuclear Code, and Trump." In *The Dangerous Case of Donald Trump: 27 Psychiatrists and Mental Health Experts Assess a President*, edited by Bandy Lee. New York: St. Martin's Press, pp. 110–125.

Tapas, Kathryn Tenpas. 2019. "Tracking Turnover in the Trump Administration." Washington, DC: The Brookings Institution, July.

Tapper, Jake. 2017. "State of the Union-Interview with Presidential Candidate Donald Trump." *CNN*, March 13.

Tapper, Jake. 2019. "Trump Pushed to Close El Paso Border, Told Admin Officials to Resume Family Separations and Agents Not to Admit Migrants." *CNN*, April 9.

Taranto, James. 2010. "'Racially Resentful' Dissecting the Latest Bogus Tea-Party Poll." *Wall Street Journal*, April 29.

Taub, Amanda. 2017. "Why Americans Vote 'Against Their Interest': Partisanship." *New York Times*, April 12.

Taub, Amanda and Max Fisher. 2017. "As Leaks Multiply, Fears of a 'Deep State' in America." *New York Times*, February 16.

Taylor, Adam. 2018. "No President Has Used Sanctions and Tariffs Quite Like Trump." *Washington Post*, August 29.

Taylor, John. 2017. "Trump Princess: Inside Donald Trump's lavish 86m Superyacht." *Boat*, July 28.

Taylor, Adam, Rick Noack, Miriam Berger, and Michael Brice-Saddler. 2020. "Fears Grow of a Coronavirus Pandemic as Markets Stumble Again; Japan Shuts Schools." *Washington Post*, February 22.

Team Fix. 2016. "The Fox News GOP Debate Transcript, Annotated." *Washington Post*, March, 3.

Tesler, Michael. 2014. Methodological Challenges Affect Study of Non-Citizens' Voting." *Washington Post*, October 27.

Testler, Michael. 2016a. *Post-Racial or Most-Racial? Race and Politics in the Obama Era*. Chicago, Il: University of Chicago Press.

Tesler, Michael. 2016b. "Obama Won Lots of Votes from Racially Prejudiced Whites (and Some of Them Supported Trump)." *Washington Post*, December 7.

Tharoor, Ishaan. 2018. "Is Regime Change in Iran Part of Trump's Agenda?" *Washington Post*, May 7.

The White House: Office of the Press Secretary. 2017. "Remarks by President Trump and His Majesty King Abdullah II of Jordan in Joint Press Conference." Rose Garden, April 5.

Thompson, Derek. 2014. "Presidential Speeches Were Once College-Level Rhetoric—Now They're for Sixth-Graders." *The Atlantic*, October 14.

Thrush, Glenn. 2017a. "Sean Spicer Resigns as White House Press Secretary." *New York Times*, July 21.

Thrush, Glenn. 2017b. "New Outcry as Trump Rebukes Charlottesville Racists 2 Days Later." *New York Times*, August 14.

Thrush, Glenn. 2017c. "Trump, in Texas, Calls Harvey Recovery Response Effort a Real Team Effort." *New York Times*, August 29.

Thrush, Glenn and Maggie Haberman. 2017. "Trump the Dealmaker Projects Bravado, But Behind the Scenes, Faces Rare Self-Doubt." *New York Times*, March 23.

Tilman, Zoe. 2019. "The Court Fight Over Trump's Travel Ban Isn't Over." *Buzzfeed*, May 3.

Time. 2015. "Here's Donald Trump's Presidential Announcement Speech." June 16.

Timiraos, Nick. 2017. "In Ending Ex-Im Bank Impasse, Trump Sides with Business Establishment." *Wall Street Journal*, April 13.

Timiraos, Nick. 2018a. "While Trump Grumbles About Fed, His Picks Exude Pragmatism." *Wall Street Journal*, September 22.

Timiraos, Nick. 2018b. "Trump Criticizes Fed Rate Increases Again, But Says He Hasn't Spoken to Fed Chair Powell." *Wall Street Journal*, October 9.

Toosi, Nahal. 2019a. "Trump's Skeptics Pondering Whether He Deserves More Credit." *Politico*, February 5.

Toosi, Nahal. 2019b. "Inside the Chaotic Early Days of Trump's Foreign Policy." *Politico*, March 1.

Torbati, Yeganeh, Jeff Mason, and Mica Rosenberg. "Chaos, Anger as Trump Order Halts Some Muslim Immigrants." *Reuters*, January 29.

Transcript. 2006. "Meet the Press." *NBC*, October 22.

Transcript. 2020. "Face the Nation." *CBS*, January 12.

"Transcript of Interview with Former Secretary of State Rex Tillerson." 2019. House Committee on Foreign Affairs, June 27.

"Transcript: Acting Secretary Chad Wolf on 'Face the Nation'." *CBS*, June 21, 2020.

"Transcript: Donald Trump Interview with Bob Woodward and Robert Costa." 2016. *Washington Post*, April 2.

Traub, James. 2016. "It's Time for the Elites to Rise Up Against the Ignorant Masses." *Foreign Policy*, June 28.

Tribe, Laurence H. 2017. "Trump Must Be Impeached. Here's Why." *Washington Post*, May 13.

Tribe, Lawrence and Joshua Matz. 2018. *To End a Presidency: The Power of Impeachment.* New York: Basic Books,

REFERENCES 527

Tritten, Travis J. 2017. "Vinson and Reagan Carrier Strike Groups Mass Near North Korea." *Washington Examiner*, June 1.

Trump, Donald J. 2015. *Great Again: How to Fix Our Crippled America*. New York: Threshold Editions.

Trump, Donald J. 2017a. "Remarks by President Trump at the Conservative Political Action Conference." The White House, February 4.

Trump, Donald J. 2017b. "Statement by President Trump on the Paris Climate Accord." The White House, June 1.

Trump, Donald J. 2017c. "Trump's News Conference in New York: Video and Transcript." *New York Times*, August 15.

Trump, Donald J. 2017d. "Remarks by President Trump on the Strategy in Afghanistan and South Asia." Ft. Meyer, VA, August 21.

Trump, Donald J. 2017e. "President Donald J. Trump's Letter to House and Senate Leaders & Immigration Principles and Policies." The White House: Office of the Press Secretary, October 8.

Trump, Donald J. 2018a. "Remarks by President Trump in Meeting with Bipartisan Members of Congress on Immigration." The White House, January 9.

Trump, Donald J. 2018b. "Remarks by President Trump in State of the Union Address." The White House, January 30.

Trump, Donald J. 2018c. "Statement by President Trump on the Shooting in Parkland, Florida." The White House, February 15.

Trump, Donald J. 2018d. "Remarks by President Trump and Prime Minister Löfven of Sweden in Joint Press Conference." The White House, March 6.

Trump, Donald J. 2018e. "Executive Order Reducing Poverty in America by Promoting Opportunity and Economic Mobility." The White House April 10.

Trump, Donald J. 2018f. "Remarks by President Trump at a Meeting with the National Space Council and Signing of Space Policy Directive-3." The White House, June 18.

Trump, Donald J. 2019a. "Remarks by President Trump on Modernizing Our Immigration System for a Stronger America." The White House, May 16.

Trump, Donald J. 2019b. "Trump in Press Conference Osaka, Japan." June 29.

Trump, Donald J. 2019c. "Remarks by President Trump and President Macron of France in Joint Press Conference." Biarritz, France, August 26.

Trump, Donald J. 2019d. "Remarks by President Trump and President Niinistö of the Republic of Finland in Joint Press Conference." The White House, October 2.

Trump, Donald J. 2019e. "Remarks by President Trump in Briefing with Military Leaders." The Cabinet Room, October 7.

528 REFERENCES

Trump, Donald J. 2019f. "Remarks by President Trump During Video Teleconference with Members of the Military." Palm Beach, FL, December 25.

Trump, Donald J. 2020a. "Remarks by President Trump in Press Conference: Davos, Switzerland." January 22.

Trump, Donald J. 2020b. "Remarks by President Trump, Vice President Pence, and Members of the Coronavirus Task Force in Press Conference." James S. Brady Press Briefing Room, February 27.

Trump, Donald J. 2020c. "Remarks by President Trump in Meeting with African American Leaders." Cabinet Room, February 28.

Trump, Donald J. 2020d. "Remarks by President Trump at Signing of an Executive Order on Safe Policing for Safe Communities." The White House, June 16.

Trump, Donald J. 2020e. "Remarks by President Trump in State of the Union Address." U.S. Capital, November 4.

Trump, Donald J. and Bill Zanker. 2017. *Think Big and Kick ass in Business and Life*. New York: HarperCollins.

Trump, Donald J. [with Kate Bohner]. 1977. *The Art of the Comeback*. New York: Times Books.

Trump, Donald J. [with Meredith McIver]. 2004a. *Trump: Think Like a Billionaire-Everything you Need to Know About Success, Real Estate, and Life*. New York: Random House.

Trump, Donald J. [with Meredith McIver]. 2004b. *Trump: How to Get Rich*. New York: Ballantine Books.

Trump, Donald J. [with Meredith McIver]. 2007. *Trump 101: The Way to Success*. New York: Wiley.

Trump, Donald J. [with Meredith McIver]. 2008. *Trump: The Art of the Comeback*. New York: Times Books.

Trump, Donald J. [with Meredith McIver]. 2018. *Never Give Up: How I Turned my Biggest Challenges into Successes*. Hoboken, NJ: Wiley.

Trump, Donald J. [with Tony Schwartz]. 1987. *Trump: The Art of the Deal*. New York: Random House.

Trump, Mary L. 2020. *Too Much and Never Enough: How My Family Created the World's Most Dangerous Man*. New York: Simon & Shuster.

Trump Presidential Announcement Speech. 2015. *Time Magazine*, June 16.

Tuccille, Jerome. 1985. *Trump: The Saga of America's Most Powerful Real Estate Barron*. New York: Donald I. Fine.

Tuck, Lauren. 2016. "Donald Trump Reportedly Treated Miss USA Contestants Like 'Property'." *Yahoo*, June 17.

Tulis, Jefrey K. 2018. *The Rhetorical Presidency*. Princeton, NJ: Princeton University Press.

Tumulty, Karen. 2017. "How Donald Trump Came Up with 'Make America Great Again'." *Washington Post*, January 18.

Turley, Jonathan. 2020. "More Willful Blindness by the Media on Spying by Obama Administration." *The Hill*, July 25.

Twohey, Megan, Russ Buettner, and Steve Eder. 2016. "Inside the Trump Organization, the Company That Has Run Trump's Big World." *New York Times*, December 25.

Uhrmacher, Kevin, Kevin Schaul, and Dan Keeting. 2016. "These Former Obama Strongholds Sealed the Election for Trump." *Washington Post*, November 9.

United States Foreign Intelligence Surveillance Court. 2019. LeeAnn Flynn Hall, Clerk of Court. "IN RE ACCURACY CONCERNS REGARDING Docket No. Misc . 19-02 FBIMATTERS SUBMITTED TO THE FISC." Washington, DC, December 17. https://www.fisc.uscourts.gov/sites/default/files/MIsc%2019%2002%20191217.pdf.

Unger, Todd. 2016. "Local Electors Face Mounting Pressure to Not Vote for Trump." *WFAA 8 NBC*, November 17.

Victor, Daniel. 2018. "Kids, Please Don't Read This Article on What Trump Said About Santa Claus." *New York Times*, December 25.

Vindman, Alexander S. 2019. "Opening Statement of Lieutenant Colonel Alexander S. Vindman Before the House Permanent Select Committee on Intelligence, the House Committee on Foreign Affairs, and the House Committee on Oversight and Reform." October 29.

Viser, Matt. 2015. "Even in College, Donald Trump Was Brash." *Boston Globe*, August 28.

Vora, Shivani. 2016. "A New Trump Brand Not Named for Trump? Yes, Meet Scion." *New York Times*, October 25.

Wadhams, Nick and Glen Carey. 2019. "Trump's Confounding Syria Moves Again Spur Policy Confusion." *Bloomberg News*, October 8.

Wagner, John. 2017a. "In Action After Action, Trump Appeals Primarily to His Dwindling Base." *Washington Post*, September 3.

Wagner, John. 2017b. "Trump Signs Sweeping Tax Bill into Law." *Washington Post*, December 22.

Wagner, John. 2020. "Senate Confirms 200th Judicial Nominee from Trump, A Legacy that Will Last Well Beyond November." *Washington Post*, June 24.

Wagner, John and David Nakamura. 2017. "Trump Turns to Executive Powers in Bid to Force Congress into Action." *Washington Post*, October 14.

Wagner, John and Deanna Paul. 2019. "Trump Asks Lawyers If Census Can Be Delayed, Calls Supreme Court Decision 'Totally Ridiculous'." *Washington Post*, June 27.

530 REFERENCES

Wagner, John and Felicia Sonmez. 2019. "Trump Continues to Push Erroneous Claim About Alabama as Dorian Lashes Carolinas." *Washington Post*, September 5.

Waldman, Paul. 2016. "If You Voted for Trump Because He's 'Anti-establishment,' Guess What: You Got Conned." *Washington Post*, November 16.

Waldman, Paul. 2019. "Could Democrats Impeach Trump Twice? They Might Have To." *Washington Post*, December 24.

Walker, Chris. 2020. "Pelosi: GAO Report Showing Trump Broke the Law Reinforces Need for Witnesses at Senate Impeachment Trial." *The Hill*, January 16.

Wall Street Journal. 2017. "WSJ Trump Interview Excerpts: China, North Korea, Ex-Im Bank, Obamacare, Bannon, More." *Wall Street Journal*, April 12.

Walsh, Ben. 2016. "Trump Could Trigger the Longest Recession Since the Great Depression, Report Says." *Huffington Post*, June 27.

Walsh, Deirdre. 2019. "GOP Retirements Spike, Diminishing Hope of Retaking House Majority in 2020." *NPR*, September 6.

Wang, Hansi Lo. 2020. "To Produce Citizenship Data, Homeland Security to Share Records with Census." *NPR*, January 4.

Ward, Alex. 2019. "Trump Just Reversed His Decision to Pull all US Troops Out of Syria." *Vox*, February 22.

Ward, Emily. 2019. "Trump Has More Women as Top Advisers Than Obama, Bush, or Clinton." *Washington Times*, March 22.

Warren, Michael, Zachary Cohen, and Michelle Kosinski. 2019. "What's the Trump Doctrine? Depends Who You Ask." *CNN*, February 22.

Washington Post. 2016a. "Interview with Donald Trump." April 21.

Washington Post. 2016b. "Interview with Donald Trump." *Washington Post*, May 13.

Watson, Julie and Cedar Attanasio. 2019. "Trump Administration Puts Tough New Asylum Rule into Effect." *Washington Post*, September 12.

Watts, Ashley, Scott O. Lillenfield, Saerah Francis Smith, Joshua Miller, W. Keith Campbell, Irwin D. Waldman, Steven J. Rubenzer, and Thomas J. Faschingbauer. 2013. "The Double-Edged Sword of Grandiose Narcissism: Implications for Successful and Unsuccessful Leadership Among U.S. Presidents." *Psychological Science*, Vol. 24, No. 12 (December), pp. 2379–2389.

Weber, Sam and Laura Fong. 2016. "This System Calls for Popular Vote to Determine Winner." *PBS*, November 6.

Weed, Doug. 2019. *Inside the Trump White House: The Real Story of His Presidency*. New York: Center Street.

Wehner, Peter. 2017. "Seeing Trump Through the Glass Darkly." *New York Times*, October 7.

REFERENCES 531

Wei, Lingling, Chao Deng, and Josh Zumbrun 2019. "China Seeks to Narrow Trade Talks With U.S. in Bid to Break Deadlock?" *Wall Street Journal*, September 12.

Weigel, David. 2016. "Why Are People Giving Jill Stein Millions of Dollars for an Election Recount?" *Washington Post*, November 24.

West, Harper. 2017. "In Relationship with an Abusive President." In *The Dangerous Case of Donald Trump: 27 Psychiatrists and Mental Health Experts Assess a President*, edited by Bandy Lee. New York: St. Martin's Press, pp. 244–260.

Whipple, Chris. 2019. "Kennedy: The Day the Presidency Was Lost." *ABC News*, August 31.

Whitebook, Joel, 2017. "Trump's Method, Our Madness." *New York Times*, March 20.

Whitman Walt. 1892 Version. "Song of Myself".

Wiener, Jon. 2017. "Trump's Ghostwriter Says the President Is Now in Survival Mode." *The Nation*, November 3.

Wilentz, Sean. 2018. "They Were Bad. He May Be Worse." *New York Times*, January 20.

Wilkie, Curtis. 2014. "The South's Lesson for the Tea Party." *New York Times*, August 12.

Will, George. 2017. "Trump Has a Dangerous Disability." *Washington Post*, May 17.

Williams, Abigail. 2017. "Tillerson Faces Many Unfilled Top Spots at State Department," *NBC News*, August 27.

Williams, Juan. 2017. "Trump Is Becoming a Failed President." *The Hill*, October 16.

Williams, Pete. 2019. "Secret FISCA Court Issues a Highly Unusual Public Rebuke of the FBI for Mistakes." *NBC News*, December 17.

Willingham, Emily. 2017. "The Trump Psych Debate: Is It Wrong To Say He's Mentally Ill?" *Forbes*, February 19.

Willis, Jay. 2017. "Donald Trump's Thousands of Lawsuits Throughout the Years." *Esquire*, April 3.

Wilson, Scott. 2019. "Trump's Proposals to Tackle California Homelessness Face Local, Legal Obstacles." *Washington Post*, September 12.

Wines, Michael and Adam Liptak. 2019. "Trump Considering an Executive Order to Allow Citizenship Question on Census." *New York Times*, July 5.

Wines, Michael, Maggie Haberman, and Robert Rappeport. 2019. "Justice Dept. Reverses Course on Citizenship Question on Census, Citing Trump's Orders." *New York Times*, July 3.

Wing, Nick. 2017. "Donald Trump Thinks Being President Is So Easy, Even He Could Do It." *Huffington Post*, January 3.

Wiser, Callie. 2016a. "Interview: Louise Sunshine." *PBS*, September 27.

532 REFERENCES

Wiser, Callie. 2016b. "The FRONTLINE Interview: Louise Sunshine." *PBS FrontLine*, September 27.

Wolf, Michael. 2018a. *Fire and Fury: Inside the Trump White House*. New York: Henry Holt.

Wolff, Michael. 2018b. "Donald Trump Didn't Want to be President." *New York Magazine*, January 3.

Wolff, Richard. 2009. *Renegade: The Making of a President*. New York Crown.

Wolfgang, Ben. 2019. Military Slow-Walk or 'Deep State' Defiance? Trump Sees Direct Orders Modified." *Washington Times*, December 1.

Wolfgang, Ben. 2020. "Standoff: U.S. Troops Block Russian Forces from Capturing Syrian Oil Field." *Washington Times*, January 21.

Wood, Thomas. 2016. "Racism Motivated Trump Voters More Than Authoritarianism." *Washington Post*, April 17.

Woodward, Calvin. 2017. "Trump's Claim About Predecessors, Fallen Troops Disputed." *Associated Press*, October 17.

Woodward, Bob. 2018. *Fear: Trump in the White House*. New York: Simon & Shuster.

Woodward, Bob and Robert Costa. 2016. "Transcript: Donald Trump Interview with Bob Woodward and Robert Costa." *Washington Post*, April 2.

World Mental Health Coalition. 2019. "Petition to the Judiciary Committee of the U.S. House of Representatives." December 5.

Worley, Will. 2016. "Donald Trump Faces Impeachment If New Conflicts of Interest Bill Passed." *The Independent*, December 16.

Wright, Helana. 2017. "Donald Trump Is a Threat To Survival of Life on Earth: If Nuclear War Doesn't Get Us, Falling Oxygen Levels Will." *Newsweek*, September 24.

Wright, Thomas J. 2017. *All Measures Short of War: The Contest for the Twenty-First Century and the Future of American Power*. New Haven: Yale University Press.

Wroughton, Leslie and Patricia Zengerle. 2019. "As Promised, Trump Slashes Aid to Central America Over Migrants." *Reuters*, June 17.

Wruble, Steve. MD. 2017. "Trump's Daddy Issues." In *The Dangerous Case of Donald Trump: 27 Psychiatrists and Mental Health Experts Assess a President*, edited by Bandy Lee. New York: St. Martin's Press, pp. 268–280.

Yee, Vivian. 2017. "Judge Temporarily Halts New Version of Trump's Travel Ban." *New York Times*, October 17.

Yglesias, Matthew. 2019. "Trump's Racist Tirades Against 'the Squad,' Explained." *Vox*, July 18.

Yoder, Eric. 2019. "Federal Employees Could Face More Discipline Under Proposed New Rules." *Washington Post*, September 17.

York, Byron. 2019. "From Former Trump Lawyer, Candid Talk About Mueller, Manafort, Sessions, Rosenstein, Collusion, Tweets, Privilege, and the Press." *Washington Examiner*, April 3.

Zakaria, Fareed. 2017a. "Trump Is Putting on a Great Circus, But What About His Promises?" *Washington Post*, February 16.

Zakaria, Fareed. 2017b. "America Would Be Trump's Banana Republic." *Washington Post*, July 21.

Zakaria, Fareed. 2019. "Does a Trump Doctrine on Foreign Policy Exist? Ask John Bolton." *Washington Post*, May 2.

Zapotosky, Matt. 2019. "3,100 Inmates to Be Released as Trump Administration Implements Criminal Justice Reform." *Washington Post*, June 19.

Zapotosky, Matt and Devlin Barrett. 2020. "Justice Dept. sues 'Sanctuary' Jurisdictions in New Crackdown Over Immigration Enforcement." *Washington Post*, February 10.

Zapotosky, Matt and Sari Horwitz. 2017. "While Eyes Are on Russia, Sessions Dramatically Reshapes the Justice Department." *Washington Post*, November 24.

Zelizer, Julian Z. 2017. "Grading President Trump." *Atlantic*, November 8.

Zelizer, Julian Z. 2018. "Trump Just Put Himself in a Political Red Zone." *CNN*, April 5.

Zengerle, Jason. 2015. "Donald Trump Being a Clown Is Bad for Hillary." *GQ*, October 27.

Zernike, Kate and Megan Thee-Brenan. 2010. "Poll Finds Tea Party Backers Wealthier and More Educated." *New York Times*, April 14.

Zernike, Kate. 2010a. "Republicans Strain to Ride Tea Party Tiger." *New York Times*, January 23.

Zernike, Kate. 2010b. "Tea Party Looks to Move from Fringe to Force." *New York Times*, February 7.

Zimbardo, Phillip and Rosemary Sword. 2017. "Unbridled and Extreme President Hedonism." In *The Dangerous Case of Donald Trump: 27 Psychiatrists and Mental Health Experts Assess a President*, edited by Bandy Lee. New York: St. Martin's Press, pp. 26–50.

Zirin, James D. 2019. *Plaintiff in Chief: A Portrait of Donald Trump in 3,500 Lawsuits*. New York: All Points Books.

Zitner, Aaron. 2016. "U.S. Seen on Wrong Track by Nearly Three-Quarters of Voters." *Wall Street Journal*, July 17.

Zito, Salena. 2016. "Taking Trump Seriously, Not Literally." *The Atlantic*, September 23.

PROPER NAME INDEX

A
Abe, Shinzo, 309
Al-Asaad, Bashar, 251
al-Baghdadi, Abu Bakr (American-born leader and spokesperson for ISIS), 407
Allison, Graham, 322
Ammann, Othmar H., 126, 127

B
Balz, Dan, 8, 28–30
Bannon, Stephen K., 321, 436
Barber, James David, 28, 134, 153
Barnett, Wayne, 280
Barrack, Thomas, Jr., 331
Barr, William, 102
Beame, Abraham, 132
Bernstein, Jared, 452, 465
Biden, Joe, 145, 442
Blair, Gwenda, 53, 71, 126, 127, 151, 279, 296, 319, 366, 411
Blinder, Alan, 305

Boot, Max, 32, 72, 96, 102, 113, 115, 150, 256, 257, 461
Brennen, William J., 251
Brooks, David, 8, 30, 59, 72, 259
Bush, George H.W., 398
Bush, George W., 22, 31, 91, 202, 302, 320, 323, 383, 398, 423
Bush, Jeb, 123, 124, 394, 443

C
Carter, Jimmy, 26
Christie, Chris (former NJ Governor), 331
Cleveland, Grover, 301
Clifford, Clark, 321
Clinton, Bill, 89, 144, 170, 217, 365, 423
Clinton, Hillary, 15, 42, 79–81, 84, 86, 88, 89, 101, 123, 129, 144, 177, 185, 212, 276, 309–311, 430, 440

© The Editor(s) (if applicable) and The Author(s), under exclusive license to Springer Nature Switzerland AG 2020
S. Renshon, *The Real Psychology of the Trump Presidency*,
The Evolving American Presidency,
https://doi.org/10.1007/978-3-030-45391-6

535

536 PROPER NAME INDEX

Cohn, Gary (Director of National Economic Policy Council), 327, 436
Cohn, Roy, 134
Collins, Susan, 444
Comey, James, 248, 253, 262, 440
Conway III, George T., 73, 240, 241, 259
Conway, Kellyanne, 37, 240
Corker, Bob (former Senator), 27, 34, 427
Cruz, Ted, 91, 163, 443

D

Daalder, Ivo, 403
D'Antonio, Michael, 15, 32, 67, 71, 102, 115, 231, 256, 295, 297, 298
Dershowitz, Alan, 423, 459
Dobias, Theodore, 277
Douthat, Ross, 91, 110, 259
Dowd, Maureen, 140, 155
Dr. Jekyll and Mr. Hyde, 9, 163
Dunford Jr., Joseph F., 436
Durham, John, 43

E

Einstein, Albert, 278, 431
Eisenhower, Dwight D., 94, 148, 184, 302, 321, 388, 431
Ernst, Joni, 444
Estrich, Susan (longtime Democratic lawyer), 431

F

Fahrenthold, David, 31, 269, 270, 272–274, 276, 295, 296
Flake, Jeff (former Senator), 27
Floyd, George, 4, 166, 285, 349, 420
Foerderer, Norma, 14, 15, 328

Frank, Justin, 71, 74, 202, 203
Franklin, Aretha, 218
Freud, Sigmund, 17, 52, 70, 98, 104, 131, 147, 278, 364, 431
Friedman, Thomas, 250, 253, 388, 410
Frum, David, 93, 94, 112, 115, 150, 194, 220, 231, 412

G

Gallagher, Edward (Navy Seal), 318
Gardner, Cory, 444
Gardner, John D., 202, 228, 229, 256, 261
George, Alexander L., xi
Gertz, Clifford, 303
Gingrich, Newt, 294, 311, 331
Ginsburg, Ruth Bader, 79
Goldwater, Barry, 67, 235, 237–239, 254
Gorsuch, Neal, 174
Graff, Rhona, 14
Greenstein, Fred I., 45, 69, 212, 228, 321, 388, 411

H

Haley, Nikki, 443
Harding, Warren G., 301
Harris, Kamala, 101, 104
Hayes, Rutherford B., 301
Hitler, Adolf, 79, 84, 247, 250, 346, 392
Hollande, Francois, 79
Horney, Karen, 217, 230
Hussein, Saddam, 130, 251
Huxtable, Ada Louise (New York Times Architecture critic), 281

I

Icahn, Carl, 331, 398

PROPER NAME INDEX 537

J

Jackson, Andrew, 302, 445
Jefferson, Thomas, 445, 446
Jenkins Jr., Holman, 67, 308
Jinping, Xi, 309
Johnson, David Kay, 54, 71
Johnson, Lyndon, 301, 421, 446

K

Kagan, Robert, 206, 226, 256
Kavanaugh, Brett M., 174
Kelly, John F., 139, 140, 155, 431, 434
Kelly, Megyn, 221
Kennedy, Ted, 88
Kernberg, Otto, 17, 32, 214, 229
Kerry, John, 368
Khan, Khizr, 47
Kim Jong-un, 92, 156, 251, 323, 406
King George, 77
King, Larry, 224
Kissinger, Henry, 434, 463
Kohut, Heinz, 32, 213, 229
Kraft, Robert, 278, 296, 331
Kurosawa, Akira, 36
Kushner, Jared, 334

L

Lasswell, Harold D., xi, 64, 74, 200, 224
Lee, Bandy, 69, 235, 243–245, 250–256, 260–262
Lee, Robert E. (statue), 161
LeFrak, Sam, 129
Lewandowski, Corey, 331
Limbaugh, Rush, 313
Lincoln, Abraham, 78, 167, 206, 301, 420, 445, 446

M

Macron, Emmanuel, 50, 51, 70

Maddow, Rachel, 250
Madison, James, 441
Mattis, James, 194, 312, 326, 334, 366, 436–439
McCain, John, 47, 120, 150, 253, 316
McIntosh, Sandy, 276, 277
McSally, Martha, 444
Mnuchin, Steven, 436
Mohammad Javad Zarif, 51
Morell, Michael, 79, 212
Morgan, Mark, 289
Moses, Robert, 126, 127

N

Neustadt, Richard, 78, 98, 106, 113, 142, 155, 157, 168, 321
Nixon, Richard, 26, 170, 247, 362
Noonan, Peggy, 13, 26, 31, 33

O

Obama, Barack, 22, 25, 26, 31, 33, 38, 41, 42, 69, 79, 80, 83, 84, 86, 90, 94, 100, 107, 129, 172, 173, 175, 177, 193, 202, 217, 219, 241, 250, 251, 255, 278, 302, 307, 311, 315–317, 320, 329, 352, 353, 358, 362, 365, 368, 384, 385, 390, 399, 403, 423, 432, 443, 452
O'Brien, Timothy, 53, 71, 102, 115, 150, 220, 280, 284, 296–298
O'Donnell, Lawrence, 60, 250
Orman, Adam, 266

P

Parker, Kathleen, 94, 112
Pelosi, Nancy, 95, 243
Pence, Michael, 29, 63, 102, 111, 112, 156, 436, 464
Pompeo, Mike, 102

538 PROPER NAME INDEX

Pritzker, Jay (Hyatt Hotels), 279
Pruitt, Scott, 138, 139
Putin, Vladimir, 60, 181, 203, 251

R
Reade, Tara, 145
Reagan, Ronald, 61, 91, 94, 180,
    184, 321, 430
Reid, Harry, 79
Res, Barbara, 14
Rockefeller, Nelson, 126
Romney, Mitt, 120, 129, 130, 219,
    347, 443
Roosevelt, Franklin, 78, 327, 445,
    446
Roosevelt, Theodore, 78
Rove, Karl, 321
Ruddy, Chris, 315, 331
Ruttenberg, Jim, 55, 72
Ryan, Paul D., 331

S
Samuelson, Robert, 242, 243, 260
Sanders, Bernie, 86, 203, 249, 441
Schiff, Adam, 250
Schwarzman, Stephen, 331
Scutt, Derr, 128
Sessions, Jeff, 176, 334
Shanahan, Patrick, 436
Shaub, Walter, 58, 72
Skowronek, Stephen, 23, 25, 33,
    81–83, 105, 107, 135, 154, 162,
    176–180, 182, 185, 192–194,
    210, 227
Soleimani, Qasem, 406–408
Sondland, Gordon, 57
Spicer, Sean, 138, 139, 154
Stone, Michael, 216, 217, 230
Stone, Roger, 164, 331
Sullivan, Margaret, 56, 57, 72
Sunshine, Louise, 14

T
Taibbi, Matt, 290, 297
Tillerson, Rex, 139, 149, 329, 386,
    430, 434, 436, 437, 439
Tillis, Thom, 444
Traub, James, 85, 109
Trudeau, Justin, 375, 381
Trump, Donald, Jr., 331, 334
Trump, Eric, 273–275, 295, 296,
    331, 334
Trump, Fred C., 54, 55, 64, 71, 129,
    169
Trump, Fred, Jr., 131
Trump, Ivanka, 35, 67, 268, 286,
    294, 334
Trump, Mary (Mother), 65
Trump, Mary T. (Niece), 132
Trump, Melania, 70, 116, 278, 331,
    334
Tuccille, Jerome, 53, 71, 151, 296,
    297

V
Vindman, Alexander, 57, 425, 426,
    460

W
Wagner, Robert, 126
Warren, Elizabeth, 60, 101, 364
Washington, George, 445
Wehner, Peter, 59, 72
Woodward, Bob, 43

Y
Yellen, Janet, 452, 463

Z
Zakaria, Fareed, 32, 220, 231, 410

SUBJECT INDEX

A

Afghanistan, 141, 146, 247, 287, 326
Against liberal cosmopolitanism
growing up in Queens and, 294,
393–394
*"I'm not representing the globe. I'm
representing your country"*, 394.
*See also Conservative American
Nationalism*: six essential
elements, Maximum flexibility
to realize core Trump Doctrine
goals, Three Psychological
Sources of the Trump Doctrine,
Trump Doctrine, The Trump
Doctrine and the use of force
25th Amendment, 103, 202, 241
America First
erroneous association with Hitler
appeasement, 392
origins of Trump's use of the phrase
American alone and, 392. *See
also Conservative American
Nationalism*: six essential

elements, Maximum flexibility
to realize core Trump Doctrine
goals, Three Psychological
Sources of the Trump Doctrine,
Trump Doctrine, The Trump
Doctrine and the use of force
Trump's self-interest and?, 283, 391
American Restoration, 3, 92, 135,
138, 162, 173, 185, 208
amidst a "Resistance" War:
The personal psychological
challenge to, 456–459
includes trying to Trump of change
the premises and operation of a
number of major international
institutions (e.g., WHO, WTO,
and NATO), 387
includes wanting to reform the
primary premises and operation
of major domestic institutions
(e.g., the FBI, DOJ, and
CDC), 20

© The Editor(s) (if applicable) and The Author(s), under exclusive
license to Springer Nature Switzerland AG 2020
S. Renshon, *The Real Psychology of the Trump Presidency*,
The Evolving American Presidency,
https://doi.org/10.1007/978-3-030-45391-6

540 SUBJECT INDEX

transformative purposes of Trump presidency, 211, 307. *See also* Trump presidency

Trump's ambitions of, 170, 282, 306, 307, 400

America's Political Collision Course, 420

A Nation and Its Institutions Take Sides, 421

Annals of Presumption: Tutoring President Trump, 435

no-one in that room calmly and respectfully asked Trump to explain and go into his thinking, 438

trying to reeducate the president, 435

Anonymous Sources of Trump narratives

"according to a source familiar with their conversation", 62

"according to a White House official who spoke on the condition of anonymity to discuss internal deliberations", 62

"according to three people familiar with the situation", 62. *See also* Anti-Trump narratives

The Apprentice, 15, 224, 269

Anti-Trump narratives

abandon neutrality-at-all-costs journalism and Trump, 57

anonymous sources and anti-Trump news reports, 37, 43, 61–63, 73, 100, 164, 199, 240, 265, 276, 294, 296, 390

anti-Trump caricatures and, 9, 240

as "clown candidate", 219

assumption of guilt and, 57, 273

Bias by Omission, 63–64

changed reporting standards for Trump, 53, 253

"deep state" hypothesis and, 44, 101, 135

Incomplete Quotes, Lazy Analysis, and Factual Dishonesty, 248

"in the age of Trump there is no such thing as nonpartisan", 424

is the president "mentally ill", 199

narrative diagnosis and character-ization as synonymous with clinical truths., 199

"neutrality" not a viable option for reporting on Trump, 422

single trait Trump analysis, 17

taking Trump literally but not seriously, 125, 200, 367

Trump as "killer", 46, 54, 55

Trump repeatedly characterized as a Nazi, a dictator, a racist, a traitor, the greatest threat to our own country, a threat to American democracy, a threat to our world order and worse, 233

"Trump narcissism equals unfitness", 211

Trump needs adoring crowds because of his narcissism, 200

Trump's "Unfitness" for the Presidency, 205

Trump's "TV addiction", 205

Trump White House as a continuing seething caldron of chaos, conflict, carelessness, and confusion, 328

"very fine people" misquote, 161, 185. *See also* The "Resistance" against President Trump

SUBJECT INDEX   541

The Art of the Deal, 20, 31, 32, 70, 71, 131, 151, 159, 206, 226, 285, 296
As lone wolf in Manhattan, 146

B
Brownlow Committee, 78
Business Investment Incentive Policy, 283
Bush Doctrine, 409

C
Central Intelligence Agency (CIA), 312
Changing dominant entrenched political paradigms, 135, 145
  conflicting narratives: a nation and its institutions take sides, 413–421
  the example of free trade, 447
  Narrative Wars: When Paradigms Collide, 449–450
  paradigm change as civil war, 445, 454, 455
  Paradigm Change: By Degree?, 453–456
  Paradigm Change Without National Catastrophe, 448–449
  policy narratives, 176, 387
  Political War, Attrition, and the Death of Dominant Paradigms, 450–451
  Trump's Efforts at Narrative Change: Progress?, 452
  What Is a Dominant Paradigm?, 446–447
Charitable giving, 9
China, 19, 319, 396, 440, 449
China tariffs, 175
Conservative American Nationalism: six essential elements

an America First premise in Trump policies, 384, 391
an emphasis on American National Identity as a cornerstone of America's elemental and dual relationship with itself and the world, 384, 391
an emphasis on American strength in all its forms, resilience, and resolve, 384, 391
highly selective involvement, with a non-exclusive emphasis on its own terms and interests in defining America's role in the world, 384, 391
maximum tactical and strategic flexibility, 384, 391
the use of maximum repeated pressure along a continuum of points in pursuit of key goals, 384, 391. *See also* Against liberal cosmopolitanism, Trump Doctrine
The Claremont Review of Books, 80, 107
Conservative Political Action Conference (CPAC), 394
Core Set of Dualisms at the Heart of the Trump Presidency, 8
Mr. Trump's Two Presidencies, 163
Coronavirus, 4, 7, 19, 87, 144, 166, 171, 173, 174, 284, 319, 401, 441, 458

D
DACA, 374
Deferred Action for Parents of Americans and Lawful Permanent Residents (DAPA), 374
Department of Defense (DOD), 312
Department of Health, Education, and Welfare (HEW), 312

542   SUBJECT INDEX

DSM-5 (Diagnostic and Statistical Manual of Mental Disorders-V, 199

E

Eight pillars of policy initiative, 7, 136, 208, 210, 288–290, 314, 316, 419, 420, 443, 448, 449
  creativity of, 289–290
  listing of policy initiatives and, 45, 290
Elemental polarization political sorting, 422, 454
Energy in the executive, 77, 78, 442
Establishment policy paradigm, 421, 422, 424, 425, 440, 442, 443, 449, 450
Executive time and Trump, 58, 330

F

Fact-Checking, 36
Fact checks and "the truth", 37, 38, 124, 366–368, 371, 372
  Obama: "Lie of the Year" by Politifact, 368
  Policy Premises and "Larger Truths", 372
  Trump's Imprecision and "Larger Truths", 369
Fact Magazine and the Fiasco Analysis of Barry Goldwater, 237
  differential diagnosis and, 214, 236–238
  Goldwater Rule (American Psychiatric Association), 67, 200, 234, 235, 237, 244, 246
  politically biased diagnosis, 238
Fairer "free trade" agreements, 372
Fairer trade agreements with China, 325
Father and son, 128–130

love and idealization, 130, 132, 133. *See also* Trump, Mary (Mother)
Trump deeply loved, respected and admired his father, 280
Trump learned to stand apart from his father's wishes for him, good practice for his go-it-alone, if necessary, stance as president, 280
Trump's father lived by a Depression-era mentality, 393
FBI, 43
"Fight-club" presidency, 23, 99, 344
  downside of, 40, 146, 421
  "[I was] never intimidated by my father the way most people were. I stood up to him, and he respected that", 131. *See also* Father and son
  Origins and Motivations, 122–124
  The Psychological Foundations of Trump's Fighting Style, 124–126
  Trump's Fight for Recognition, 126–128
  Trump's Fight for Respect, 128–130
  Trump's First Real Political Fight, 133–134
  Trump's willingness and capacity, 51, 124, 138, 396. *See also* Trump, Mary (Mother)
Fighting back
  a Form of Self-Respect and Political Self-Validation, 138
  as a matter of self-preservation and self-respect, 216
  the biggest people are the people that never gave up, 169
  The Capacity to Fight Back and Presidential Resilience, 140

SUBJECT INDEX 543

freedom and creativity and, 141–146

The Hidden Dimension of Trump's Fighting Style: Freedom and Creativity, 142

"My whole life really has been a 'no' and I fought through it", 143. *See also* Trump core elements

not following Marquis of Queensbury rules, 162

presidential resilience and, 12, 142, 167, 204, 217, 302, 306, 307, 356, 397, 398, 458, 459

"self-help", 142, 168. *See also* "Fight-club" presidency

The Psychological and Political Functions of, 137

Trump as a Reflexive Counter Puncher, 146

Trump's first adult political fight: Housing discrimination charge, 134, 167

Why Trump Survives, 165

wistfulness and regret, 168, 169

Fighting for American restoration, 134–136

First travel ban, 210

FISA, 10, 30, 43

The Flight 93 Election, 80

Foreign policy doctrines, 385

as policy guideposts of a president's thinking, 383

geographical dimensions of, 383. *See also Conservative American Nationalism*: six essential elements, Maximum flexibility to realize core Trump Doctrine goals, Three Psychological Sources of the Trump Doctrine, Trump Doctrine, The Trump Doctrine and the use of force

The future of the Trump presidency, 419, 444

if Trump is not reelected: What then?, 442–443

G

G-7 Summit, 51, 252

Gang of Eight, 433

The Goldwater Assessment Fiasco, 237

Green New Deal, 364

Guardrails of Democracy, 93, 96, 97

argument of and Trump presidency, 4, 47, 94, 97–98, 233, 235, 243, 255, 360–362, 365, 372, 437

DACA court case setback, Trump complains, but complies, 99

international perspective, 96–97

travel ban court setback, Trump complains, but complies, 98

H

Hurricane Maria, 146

I

Immigration and Customs Enforcement (ICE), 173

impeachment, 316

Impeachment of Trump

articles of impeachment, 24, 61, 87, 92, 355, 363, 440

delaying aid to the Ukraine, 422

impeachment proceedings, 166

"Mental Health Experts" Opine to Congress: Impeach Trump. We'll Testify, 255

Mueller investigation, 9, 24, 96, 166, 285

Import-Export Bank, 326

544 SUBJECT INDEX

India, 19, 22
International Criminal Court (ICC), 393
Iran, 22, 319, 375, 407, 440
Iranian nuclear deal, 288, 316
Iraq, 407
ISIS, 22, 311, 407, 428
Israel, 22
Is Trump Smart?, 430
   Dunce? Hedgehog? or Fox?, 430
   Trump as the political equivalent of Chauncey Gardner, 431
   Trump's intelligence is the ability to see the essential nature of the circumstances that confront him or others, and move quickly to act on what he sees, 431

J
Japan, 19, 22, 449
Justice Department, 43

K
Kurdistan Workers' Party (PPK), 428

M
Manhattan real-estate empire (Trump's), 15, 223
Mar-a-Lago, 252, 292, 315, 320, 321
Maximum flexibility to realize core Trump Doctrine goals, 159, 405
   flexibility vs. consistency, 159, 171, 385, 400, 402, 403, 410
   unpredictability and, 6, 14, 160. *See also Conservative American Nationalism*: six essential elements, Three Psychological Sources of the Trump Doctrine,

Trump Doctrine, The Trump Doctrine and the use of force
Maximum repeated pressure along a continuum of points as core element of Trump Doctrine, 384, 391, 400
   as full-court press, on several policy basketball courts at once, 400
   "bullying" vs. "compellence", 399
   capacity for persistence and, 385. *See also Conservative American Nationalism*: six essential elements, Maximum flexibility to realize core Trump Doctrine goals, Three Psychological Sources of the Trump Doctrine, Trump Doctrine, The Trump Doctrine and the use of force
Mexico, 396, 432
Modern Presidential Leadership, 363
Monroe Doctrine, 383
Mueller Report, 241
Muller investigation, 10

N
NAFTA, 21, 325, 372. *See also* Trade and Trade Sanctions
Narcissism
   Alternatives to "Pathological Narcissism": Respect and Validation, 218
   as a developmental accomplishment, 213
   "healthy" narcissism, 17, 213–215
   "malignant narcissism", 46, 105, 201, 211, 228, 229, 245
   Trump as a "textbook case" since 1988, 211
   The Trump Brand as Narcissism, 216

Varieties of Narcissism: Normal and Pathological, 5, 213. *See also* Trump's narcissism

Narrative civil war, 58

The narrator in chief, 39

NATO, 22, 183, 325, 372, 375, 396, 403, 421, 432, 438

The National Inquirer, 164

The national security consensus and Trump's "tutorial", 437

The national security "interagency consensus", 424, 427

The National Security Consensus and Trump's Syria Drawdown, 427–429

"Regulatory Capture" and, 424

What exactly is the "interagency consensus?", 426

New Arab-Israeli agreement, 287

News at Trump speed, 7, 210

New York State Urban Development Corporation, 144

North Korea, 9, 22, 243, 247, 287, 312, 319, 325, 375, 387, 396, 406, 429

O

Obama Doctrine, 383, 409

P

Paris Climate accords, 19, 21, 145, 175, 191, 289, 385, 411

Pew Foundation, 41

Presidential demeanor, 121. *See also* Trump presidential leadership style

Being 'Presidential' Is Boring', 122

Demeanor is part of leadership style but they are not synonymous, 159

In the Eyes of the Beholder, 162

The Unexpected Becomes Expected, 161

Presidential Style, 130. *See also* Promise keeper strategy

The Disrupter's Dilemma, 210

The Early Family Origins of, 130. *See also* Presidential demeanor

Presidential success, 66, 142, 171–173, 214, 288

A Potentially Very Consequential Presidency: Slowly and Haltingly Gathers Momentum, 170

How Limited Are Trump's Restoration Prospects?, 136

The Major Legislation Success Metric, 172

Other Metrics, 173, 176

Promise Keepers: Trump's Strategy of Restoring Public Trust, 182. *See also* Prospects for a Successful Presidency

Success by Other Means?, 170

President Trump in Political Time: A Reconstructive or Preemptive President?, 21

A Nascent Reconstructive Presidency?, 179

A Preemptive Presidency?, 180

Promise keeper strategy, 125

"deliver the goods", 20, 125, 206

emphasis on getting results, 206, 406

reelection and, 373

restoring trust and, 95, 125, 185

Prospects for a Successful Presidency, 24

If Trump is not Reelected: What Then?, 443

Promise Keeping, 184

Psychological Reactance, 142

R

Racial Resentment, 35, 38, 347, 348, 351, 354
About Those Obama Trump Voters, 352
"anti-immigrant" questions are really anti-undocumented alien questions, 354, 374
correlation vs. absolute numbers and, 350–351
Cultural Marginality, Status Threat, and "Racial Resentment", 345
four question index of, 347, 350
Further Measurement Issues, 350
larger truth argument of and Trump's lack of deep historical understanding, 372
The "Resistance" against President Trump
Anonymous opposition and cloaking devices, 101
any means necessary, 104, 135, 137, 216, 242, 386
less legitimate tools of resistance, 104
never Trump opponents and, 24, 100, 162
The Personal Psychological Challenge to Trump, 456
policy as a source of, 106
Trump's Fault?, 106
using every tool available, 102. *See also* Anti-Trump narratives
Restoration's Second Chance: Trump's Possible Reelection, 440. *See also* The future of the Trump presidency
Narrative Negation and the 2020 Presidential Election, 441
Russia, 440

S

Saudi Arabia, 22, 407
Southern border, 21, 37, 173, 289, 310, 358, 369, 370, 374, 400, 401, 405
South Korea, 395, 449
"Space Force" initiative, 319
Steele Dossier, 120
Strategy of book's analysis
analyzing Trump while still in office and, 5–6
as still a mystery, 16, 35
"at a distance" presidential analysis, 35, 67
Beyond Psychological Caricature, 16
Correcting the Biographical Record, 53
Correcting the Reporting Record, 58
Defending Trump?, 45
Donald Trump Is Guilty (asumption that), 57
events data, 49–52
evidence for analysis, 66, 67, 266
the "literature" and, 5, 52
multiple vs. "alternative" facts, 37
News at Trump Speed, 7. *See also* Trump presidency
On the Nature of Trump Evidence, 48
Our purpose here is to develop an understanding of this particular president, 201
"presidential character" theory as a frame for analysis, 4
theoretical validity and reliability, 35
"Sources Say", 7. *See also* Anonymous Sources of Trump narratives
theoretical validity and reliability, 35
Trump Evidence-Events Data, 49

SUBJECT INDEX **547**

Trump's Q&A exchanges, 50
"what you see also is what you get"
perspective, 16
Strength and resilience as core element
of Trump Doctrine, 397–399
origins in Trump's life history,
397–399
role of fear and, 399. *See also
Conservative American Nationalism*: six essential elements,
Maximum flexibility to realize
core Trump Doctrine goals,
Three Psychological Sources of
the Trump Doctrine, Trump
Doctrine, The Trump Doctrine
and the use of force
Syria, 165, 184, 210, 247, 407, 426,
428, 429
Syrian drawdown as an "impulse",
427–429

T
Tea Party Movement, 89
Trade and Trade Sanctions
Mexico tariffs threat, 405
NAFTA (USMCA), 21, 175, 374,
443, 449
South Korean Trade Agreement, 21
Trans-pacific Trade Agreement,
175, 450
U.S.-China trade dispute, 51, 308
World Trade Organization (WTO),
xi, 176, 209, 250, 343, 387,
393, 452
Transpacific Partnership Trade, 21
Truman Doctrine, 383, 402, 409
Trump and the 2016 presidential
election
fight or die v. more of the same
election, 80–82
Hillary Clinton as a president of
articulation, 81

"Make America Great Again"
motto, 18, 88, 177
third party candidacy of Ross Perot
and, 89
Trump's hope and change
candidacy, 18–21, 86–87, 89
trust in government crisis and,
82–83
the 2009 Tea Party Movement and,
89–91
Trump CEO of Trump Organization
as sole decision maker of the Trump
Organization, 12, 148
becoming president as an
informational naïf, 306
Business Empire Building and
Transformative Presidential
Ambitions, 306–308, 328
one of Trump's business assets
is not having internalized a
bureaucratic mindset as CEO,
307
prelude to an unorthodox
presidency, 302–308
résumé (Trump's), 18, 88
Trump as CEO and President:
Transferable Experience or
Political Dead End?, 296–298,
304
Trump's Unique CEO Experience:
Prelude to an Unorthodox
Presidency, 302
Trump's View of the Implications
of His Business Experience for
His Presidency, 303
Trump City, 207, 280
150-acre parcel of abandoned Penn
Central rail yards, 207
Trump core elements, 5, 11, 20, 205,
356
impatience and

548 SUBJECT INDEX

I'm in no rush. I don't need
to do the housing because
I don't need the money,
207
Trump core psychological elements
coarseness of, 18, 87
complexity of, 212, 214
conspiracy theories and Trump,
41–44
desire to "leave one's mark", 217
energy levels, 204
ever been told no?, 143
highly oriented toward getting
results, 208
How Things Get Done: Trump's
Work Ethic, 319
impatience and, 205, 206, 210,
312, 323, 400
impatience and the Trump
Doctrine, 406
Impatience Revisited: The
Trump Doctrine, 406
political patience as both a
luxury and necessity, 211
Trump's 'no rush' foreign
policy, 209
Trump's business (and political
career) contains both
elements—vision and
creativity—combined with
a one step at a time
mentality, a necessity in
both building and politics,
279
"When I was 38, it was all
going to last forever", 208
impulsiveness and, 12, 205, 206,
406
Well I mean I have an attention
span that's as long as it has
to be, 322
relationships with women and, 10

resilience and, 141, 204, 398
rudeness of, 397
Trump is not by nature
introspective, but he
has reflected on the
meaning of his life, his
accomplishments, and the
inevitability of death, 292
Trump Reflective?, 291, 294
Trump's financial creativeness in
times of economic success and
collapse, 283–286
Trump's Vision and Creativity, 278,
286
Trump Towers, 280
wanting more out of his life than
money, 128
wilting under pressure?, 140. *See
also* Trump presidential leadership style, The Unexpected
Trump
Trump decision making
ability to stand apart, 145, 159, 396
Advising Trump: The Issue of
Trust, 332
a man of many questions, 433–435
annuals of presumption: Tutoring
President Trump, 435–440
a president interested in many
things, 317–319
asking seemingly naïve but
important questions, 435
avoidable mistakes of, 4
How Trump Decides, 320
I like having two people with
different points of view, .. And
then I make a decision. But I
like watching it, I like seeing
it, .. I like different points of
view, 329

SUBJECT INDEX **549**

Instinct and Gut Feelings: A Partial Decision Metric for Trump, 323

likes and learns from having his advisors debate the merits in front of him, 329

the issue of trust, advising Trump, 332–334

open minded, to a degree, 323–327

The Scope of Trump's Decisions, 314–315

Seeking a Wide and Eclectic Range of Advice, 329–332

sleep patterns and, 204

Tillerson: "I talk to him just about every day..He calls me late nat night, on weekends, when somnething comes into his head and he wants to talk. He may call mode at any moment, at any time", 329

to his [Trump's] credit, even though we disagree on some things, he listens. He goes his own way. He has his own style. But on substantive issues, he does listen, 332

Trump: A Man of Many Questions, 433

Trump: "Do I feel I can trust anybody, OK? I'm a very suspicious person. I am not a person that goes around trusting lots of people", 332

Trump: Open Minded, to a Degree, 324

Trump's confidence in his most trusted advisors seems to hinge on three general elements, 334

Trump's Judgment: Essence of Understanding, 322

Trump version of FDR's competing aides strategy, 328–329

The "what does victory look like" is the kind of basic question Trump is inclined to ask, 327

why can't I do that?, 149. *See also* Trump's judgment

Trump Doctrine

ability to stand apart and, 385, 395, 409

America First, 384, 385, 391, 392

and the disrupter's dilemma, 211, 389

and the *Politics of American Restoration*, 384

core American national identity that helps define it, 385

fight-club presidency and, 137, 159, 242, 343, 396

The Future of the, 409

if Trump wins reelection, 409

Impatience, Action, and Ambition: Three Psychological Sources of the Trump Doctrine, 386

impatience revisited, 406–407

Implementation at Trump Speed, 387

is there a Trump Doctrine?, 384

partially defined by the psychological capacities needed to carry its elements out future of the, 385

"Trump's 'no rush' foreign policy", 386

use of fear and, 399

the Use of Force and, 407. *See also* Conservative American Nationalism: six essential elements, Maximum flexibility to realize core Trump Doctrine goals, Three Psychological Sources of the Trump Doctrine, The

550 SUBJECT INDEX

Trump Doctrine and the use of force
The Trump Doctrine and the use of force, 407–409
Trump domestic policy
Deferred Action for Childhood Arrivals (DACA), 175, 358
economic growth, 7, 136, 208, 384, 448, 449
education and charter schools, 19, 21
energy production, 7, 19, 27, 136, 208, 448, 449
immigration, 7, 18, 19, 105, 136, 173, 208
immigration law enforcement, 21, 125, 181, 184, 325, 373, 374, 384, 400
jobs, 7, 18, 19, 21, 136, 208, 432, 448, 449
judicial appointments, 19, 21, 27, 443
tax reform, 19, 89. *See also* Eight pillars of policy initiative
Trump: dunce, hedgehog, fox?, 429–435
the nature of Trump's intelligence, 430
Trump's basic immigration insight, 433
Trump's genius: seeing the obvious, doing something about it, 432
TrumpFacts
NYT: "in running his norm-breaking campaign, Donald J. Trump shined a light on a larger truth", 361
policy premises and "larger truths", 372–373
Promise Keeping: An Essential "Truth"?, 373

TrumpFacts and fact checks, 37, 38, 366–368
TrumpFacts and lies, 367
TrumpFacts and logic, 366
TrumpFacts and Truthful hyperbole, 12, 36, 37, 50, 366, 367
TrumpFacts: building the wall, 371, 374
TrumpFacts: descriptive imprecision and "larger truths", 368–372
TrumpTalk and larger truths, 369, 372, 373
TrumpTalk: honesty and discretion, 365
Trump foreign policy: countries
Canada, 318
Europe (EU) (NATO), 325, 392, 395
Great Britain, 77
Guatemala, 51
Iran, 19, 51, 136, 175, 325, 392, 395, 404
Israel, 19
Mexico, 51, 395
North Korea, 19, 146, 175, 373, 386, 392, 395, 404, 425
Russia, 136, 392, 395
Saudi Arabia, 19
Syria (ISIS), 19, 136, 165, 175
Turkey, 165
Ukraine, 169, 251. *See also* Impeachment of Trump, Trump Doctrine
Trump, Fred/Trump, Donald
a father's life- long love of his son, 130
as his son's idol, 132
clashes over son's behavior, 130
father as one emotional anchor of the Trump family developmental continuum, 66
father's supposed "brutality", 131

SUBJECT INDEX 551

life lesson to his son: "love what you do", 54–55
personal motto: "Don't quit", 169
wanting his son Donald to stay in Queens, 128, 157. *See also* Trump, Mary (Mother)
Trump, Mary (Mother), 65
Anti-Trump psychiatric speculation: her "remoteness" and being "disengaged", 65
as one emotional anchor of the Trump family developmental continuum, 66
as "ordinary" mother, 65
developmental anchors (Mary Trump's "unconditional love"), 65
Nasty, biased psychiatric characterizations of, 66
unconditional love for her son, 65. *See also* Father and son
Trump presidency
and the media fragmentation, 422
as preemptive president, 82, 182
as reconstructive president, 25, 81, 82, 170, 177, 178, 182
from a preemptive to a reconstructive presidency?, 23, 182
in political time, 5, 21, 23, 176, 177, 179
on Trump being adequately prepared to be president, 309, 310
political persona and, 223, 307, 441
the real life consequences of command, 309, 315
the real nature of Trump's political creativity, 289
reinventing the presidency and, 160
restoration prospects for, 137
the "rhetorical presidency" and, 359

stuck in political time?, 182
transformational presidents in American history, 445
use of presidential time and, 52
Trump presidential leadership style
As a highschool baseball player, Trump always swung, directly, for the fences, 287
as authentic, 290
as "narrator-in-chief", 39
"chaos" and, 8, 328
core "dualisms" and, 8–11
disrupter's dilemma, 389
downsides of flexible style, 165
half-life of, 4, 386
"home-alone" presidency, 182
Improvisation, one hallmark of Trump's presidential leadership, 406
Innovation, Determination, and Ambition, 287
meaning it and, 288–290
never give up: Trump motto, 169, 451
news at Trump speed and, 7–8, 183
operating metric in business and politics: think big, 286–287
presidential demeanor and, 11, 104, 163, 164, 290
The Real Nature of Trump's Political Creativity, 288
Trump Adopts a Public Version of Franklin D. Roosevelt's Competing Aides Strategy, 327
Trump asks big, basic and long-unasked questions about a range of American policies, 290
Trump has put into motion so many whirling policy elements at any one time, that any president would find it difficult to explain them all, 388

552   SUBJECT INDEX

Trump is willing to have his advisors scramble in public to keep up with his policy trial balloons, 328

Trump's authenticity, 356

Trump seeks to speak for America, 394

Trump's Leadership Style: Meaning It, 289

Trump's Operating Metric in Life, Business, and Politics: Think Big, 286

Trump's style is to not let problems continue without doing something about them, 387

Trump's two presidencies, 163–165

Trump's work ethic, 307, 319, 320

unpredictability and, 6, 155. *See also* Trump core elements

Trump risk taking, 389

The Risks of Trump Speed, 389

Whatever Presidents do, or don't do, involves risk. trump is willing to take them, 389

Trump's bankruptcies, 53

Trump's charitable giving

The accusation that the Trumps "Shifted Kids-Cancer Charity Money Into His Business," proved both ugly and baseless, 275

Charity and President Trump, 276

Empathy, Deductions, and Accusations, 267, 272

"It is impossible to know for certain what Trump has given to charity, because he has declined to release his tax returns", 270

Palm Beach flag case, 273

The Question of Expectations and Reality, 268, 272

settlement with NYS Attorney General suit, 272, 273

St. Jude's, 272, 274

St. Jude's Foundation Charitable Bequests: Accusations of Criminality and their reality, 274

Trump's anonymous generosity, 269

Trump's charitable work was a "façade", 270

Trump's Personal Foundation: Portraits, Flag Fines, and Football Helmets, 272. *See also* The Unexpected Trump

Trump's Economic losses in the 1990's, 292

Financial Creativeness in Times of Economic Success and Collapse, 282

It was an act in the service of endurance and resilience, pain now and pain later, for the chance to emerge to build again, 286

Morhouse who worked with a lot of real estate developers who had similar problems said, "almost all of them at one point or another, filed for bankruptcy protection. And Donald, to his credit did not", 284

Trump's decision to place a bankruptcy bet with his creditors was an innovative foreshadowing insight, 285

Trump's strategy: As negotiations progressed bankers looked for every alternative they could find to [Trump's personal] bankruptcy because none of the banks wanted to contend with the mess that would ensue if the talks collapsed, 284. *See also* Against liberal cosmopolitanism, Trump Doctrine

Trump's emotional link with supporters
  defining Trump's political base, 358
  disparagement by "elites", 356
  everything for his base?, 357–358
  respect and standing, 355–375

Trump's empathy, 46, 147, 148, 215, 216, 266, 409
  Being There for Others, 276
  being there for others: Military academy family acquaintance, 276
  pictures of Syrian gassing pictures and, 148
  Trump reaches out to Robert Kraft a lifelong Democrat after his wife died, 278. *See also* The Unexpected Trump

Trump's judgment, 49, 59, 322, 361
  essence of understanding, 322–323. *See also* Trump decision making

Trump's litigiousness, 332

Trump's narcissism
  alternatives to "pathological narcissism": respect and validation, 218–219
  distinguishing actual accomplishments from "pseudo-achievements", 214
  Ego (Trump's), 17, 41, 395
  narcissist-in-chief?, 204–205
  "needy narcissist" trope, 218
  others laughing at Trump, 219
  search for respect, 17, 218
  seeking adulation or something else?, 217–219

Trump brand as narcissism, 217
Verrazano-Narrows Bridge designer neglect and claiming credit for accomplishments, 126. *See also* Narcissism, Trump's "unfitness" for the presidency

Trump's psychiatric "dangerousness"
  The Dangerous Case of Donald Trump: 27 Psychiatrists and Mental Health Experts Assess a President, 235, 244
  "dangerousness" as a stand-in for psychiatric diagnosis, 244, 245
  diagnosing Trump's dangerousness, 235, 243, 246
  Diagnostic and Statistical Manual of Mental Disorders-V, 199, 211, 236
  evidence regarding, 42
  How Dangerous Is Donald Trump?, 245
  The Politics of Trump Psychiatric Assessments, 213, 250
  thinking that what you think you know is right, 251–253
  Trump's "Delusional Disorder", 245
  why is Trump dangerous?, 246–247

Trump's "unfitness" for the presidency
  "applying clinical/ medical knowledge to a political process is practically complex and daunting with regard to the issues of objectivity, the setting of parameters (e.g., for qualification/disqualification) and the avoidance if ill-informed and /or malicious manipulation", 255
  "duty to warn" and Trump "unfitness", 228, 234, 235

554 SUBJECT INDEX

mélange of unfitness accusations, 234
"mental health experts": impeach Trump. we'll testify, 254–256
nature of, 236–237
Trump's Presidential Demeanor as a Reflection of Unfitness, 242, 243
Varieties of Trump's "Unfitness" Revisited, 241, 243. *See also* Trump's narcissism
Trump supporters: real and imagined
and racial resentment, 39, 80, 345, 349, 351, 352
as authoritarian, 84, 346
as economically marginal, 84, 344
as having low information, 84, 346
as ignorant, 84, 346
as racist, 84, 346, 351
looking for Hitler-like leader, 84, 346
some had supported Obama, 84, 90, 278, 352. *See also* Trump Voters
Trump surprised on entering the White House
expectations and reality, 301–312
On Trump Being Adequately Prepared to Be President, 309
policy surprises, 309, 311–312
The Real Life Consequences of Command, 315
Trump Enters the Oval Office: Expectations and Reality, 7. *See also* Trump CEO of Trump Organization
Trump Entering the White House: Policy Surprises, 311
Trump's not so "Easy" Presidential Promises, 310–311
Trump's Optimism Sobered by Reality, 311–320

Trump Surprised by the Deep Conflictual Nature of American Political Life, 313
Trump Surprised by the Real Scope of Government, 313–314
Trump surprised by the level of conflict after election, 142
TrumpTalk: How Trump explains his world
bold, 18, 38, 87, 144, 217, 313
brash, 18, 87, 144, 217, 313
conspiracy theories, 41
elements of TrumpTalk may be honest and heartfelt, but still better left as a private sentiment, 366
like many people think in private— direct, earthy, and unvarnished by social convention, 363
Speaking extemporaneously for one or two hours is no small feat, even for a much younger and presumably more energetic person, 364
Trump's bombastic, combative, and controversial leadership style, 11
Trump tweets, 40, 94, 164, 180, 183, 235, 361–363, 365
TrumpThink, 352–354
a meandering mind, 362
Entering into Trump's mind requires one to take a circuitous journey through uncommon assumptions, idiosyncratic associations, fragments of facts and analysis, and sometimes surprisingly acute insights, 360
How Trump Understands and Explains His World, 358–363
thinking patterns and, 3, 16

SUBJECT INDEX 555

Understanding Trump's thinking, 183

Trump Tower, 280, 281
"a dramatically handsome structure" (Ada Louise Huxtable), 281
highly unusual and dramatic, a twenty-eight sided saw-tooth fifty-eight story design, 281
Trump Tower interior "warm, luxurious and even exhilarating" (Paul Goldberger New York Times critic), 282
The waterfall is over eighty feet high and cost 2 million to build, 281

Trump: 2020 SOTU address, 37

Trump Voters, 346
Everything for His Base?, 357
"Racial Resentment" and Trump Voters, 347. See also Racial Resentment
Respect and Standing: The Two Elements Linking Trump and His Supporters, 354
Trump and His Supporters: A Powerful Emotional Connection, 355
Trump's first major and serious connection with the voting public that eventually supported him was on policy grounds, 356. See also Trump Supporters: real and imagined

Trust in Government Crisis, 82

Turkey, 165, 428

U

Ukraine, 426

The Unexpected Trump
architectural creativeness and vision, 279
charitable giving, 267–272, 274–276, 295, 325

compassion, 163, 266–267
failures Trump's vision, 43, 209, 291
meaning of "unexpected", 266
more to Trump than meets the eye, 303
nature of creativity in relation to vision, 278. See also Trump core psychological elements

US–China trade negotiations, 243

US Customs and Border Protection, 289

USMCA, United States–Mexico–Canada Agreement, 175

W

White Anglo-Saxon Protestant (WASP), 394

Why Trump ran for President
a reflection of the narcissist's need to find an admiring audience?, 218
A Shift in the Meaning of Trump's Life, 221, 223
The Lure of a New Personal Challenge, 223, 224
Seeking Adulation or Something Else?, 217
Trump's counter narrative policy views, 221
Trump's skeptical views on American foreign and domestic policy have been a consistent, reoccurring theme over the last two decades, 221

Why Trump survives, 161–166

Y

Yemen, 407

Printed in the United States
By Bookmasters